MW01088450

The Ancient Hebrew Lexicon of the Bible

~~~~~~~~~~~~~~~~~~~~~~~~~~~~~~~~~~

Hebrew Letters, Words and Roots Defined Within Their Ancient Cultural Context

Jeff A. Benner

Cover design by Jeff A. Benner. Ancient Inscription photo taken at the University of Pennsylvania, Museum of Archeology and Anthropology by the author. The inscription reads "Sh'ma" meaning hear (see Duet 6.4) and is inscribed on a piece of broken pottery dated 586 to 450 BCE.

"The Ancient Hebrew Lexicon of the Bible," by Jeff A. Benner. ISBN 1-58939-776-2.

Library of Congress Control Number: 2005932420

Acknowledgments

I would first like to thank my wife Denise for her patience and encouragement. I am extremely blessed to have been privileged with her as a gift from above and the one who has been my continual companion and confidant. She has always supported me in this endeavor and allowed me the space and time for research and writing. Without her devotion and inspiration this work would never have come to fruition.

I am also grateful to Dr. Larry S. Hirsch. Without his initial introduction into Hebrew thought and language and his instruction in Biblical studies I would never have started this journey into the Ancient Hebrew thought, culture and language.

Also my friend Michael Calpino who continually supported my studies in the Hebrew language, listened to my discoveries and assisted me by working out many word and root origins and meanings.

I would also like to thank the hundreds of people who have supported my work at the Ancient Hebrew Research Center Website with their suggestions, corrections and encouragement.

There are also many great Hebrew scholars who, with their research and work, have laid the foundations for me and others interested in the Hebrew culture and language who are much deserving of our thanks.

TABLE OF CONTENTS

The Ancient Hebrew Lexicon of the Bible

Introduction

Purpose of the Lexicon

In order to demonstrate the need for an Ancient Hebrew lexicon let us examine the word הלל (halel), how it is written and what it means.

The written word

The Hebrew word הלל, as it appears here, in Hebrew dictionaries and in Hebrew Bibles, is written with the Modern Hebrew script. But where did the Modern Hebrew script come from? Hebrew was originally written with a pictographic script similar to Egyptian Hieroglyphs but, when Israel was taken into captivity in Babylon they adopted the Aramaic script of the region and used it to write Hebrew. The Modern Hebrew script used today is in fact Aramaic in origin, not Hebrew.

The word meaning

According to Hebrew dictionaries and lexicons the word הלל is translated as "praise". The Ancient Hebrew language is a concrete oriented language meaning that the meaning of Hebrew words are rooted in something that can be sensed by the five senses such as a tree which can be seen, sweet which can be tasted and noise which can be heard. Abstract concepts such as "praise" have no foundation in the concrete and are a product of ancient Greek philosophy.

Where is the Hebrew?

If the word הלל is written with the Aramaic script and the definition "praise" is from the Greek, where is the Hebrew in this word? The purpose of the *"Ancient Hebrew Lexicon of the Bible"* is to restore the original Hebrew to the Hebrew language of the Bible.

The original Hebrew

The word הלל would have been written as ᴧᴧ𐤊 in the Early Hebrew script (over 3200 years ago) or as ᴧᴧ𐤋 in the Middle Hebrew script (between 3200 and 2500 years ago). The original pictographic letters of the parent root ᴧ𐤊 is a man with his arms raised "looking" at something spectacular and a shepherd staff that is used to move the flock

8

"toward" a place. When these are combined the idea of "looking toward" something is represented. The original meaning of $\mathcal{J}\maltese$ is the North Star, a bright light in the night sky that is "looked toward" to guide one on the journey.

If we are going to read the Bible correctly it must be through the perspective of the Ancient Hebrews who wrote it, not from a Modern Aramaic or Greek perspective. The word $\mathcal{J}\mathcal{J}\maltese$ in its original concrete meaning is a bright light that guides the journey and we "praise" Yah by looking at him to guide us on our journey through life.

Perspective of the Lexicon

The first and foremost concept that a reader of the Biblical text must learn is that the ancient Hebrews were products of an eastern culture while you as the reader are the product of a western culture. These two cultures are as different as oil and vinegar, they do not mix very well. What may seem rational in our western minds would be considered irrational to an easterner of an ancient Near East culture. The same is true in the reverse, what may be rational to an ancient Easterner would be completely irrational in our western mind.

The authors of the Biblical text are writing from within their culture to those of the same culture. In order to fully understand the text one needs to understand the culture and thought processes of the Hebrew people.

All existing Hebrew Lexicons of the Bible convert the vocabulary of the ancient Hebrews into a vocabulary compatible to our modern western language. The greatest problem with this is that it promotes western thought when reading the Biblical text. In this Lexicon the mind of the reader is transformed into an eastern one in order to understand the text through the eyes of the ancient Hebrews who penned the words of the Bible.

One of the greatest differences between this lexicon and others is the use of the ancient pictographic script which Hebrew was originally written in. Because the Ancient Hebrew language is based on these pictographs, they are used rather than the Modern Hebrew script.

Website

The *Ancient Hebrew Lexicon of the Bible* has its own website with additional material and information such as verb charts, listing of Biblical Hebrew words in order of their frequency, common Hebrew roots and updates to the lexicon and much more. The author is also available for questions, comments and requests.

Ancient Hebrew Lexicon of the Bible website
http://ahlb.ancient-hebrew.org

Ancient Hebrew Thought

The definition of a word is going to be directly related to the culture in which that word is being used. One word may have different meanings depending on the culture that is using it. In order to place the correct context to a Hebrew word from the Ancient Hebrew language one must first understand Ancient Hebrew thought.

Abstract and Concrete

Greek thought views the world through the mind (abstract thought). Ancient Hebrew thought views the world through the senses (concrete thought).

Concrete thought is the expression of concepts and ideas in ways that can be seen, touched, smelled, tasted or heard. All five of the senses are used when speaking, hearing, writing and reading the Hebrew language. An example of this can be found in Psalms 1:3; "He is like a *tree* planted by *streams of water*, which yields its *fruit* in season, and whose *leaf* does not *wither*". In this passage the author expresses his thoughts in concrete terms such as; tree, streams of water, fruit and leaf.

Abstract thought is the expression of concepts and ideas in ways that cannot be seen, touched, smelled, tasted or heard. Examples of Abstract thought can be found in Psalms 103:8; "The LORD is *compassionate* and *gracious*, Slow to *anger*, abounding in *love*". The words compassion, grace, anger and love are all abstract words, ideas that cannot be experienced by the senses. Why do we find these abstract words in a passage of concrete thinking Hebrews? Actually, these are abstract English words used to translate the original Hebrew concrete words. The translators often translate this way because the original Hebrew makes no sense when literally translated into English.

Let us take one of the above abstract words to demonstrate the translation from a concrete Hebrew word to an abstract English word. Anger, an abstract word, is actually the Hebrew word ⌐ᗷ (aph) which literally means "nose", a concrete word. When one is very angry, he begins to breathe hard and the nostrils begin to flare. A Hebrew sees anger as "the flaring of the nose (nostrils)". If the translator literally translated the above passage "slow to nose", the English reader would not understand.

11

Appearance and Functional Descriptions

Greek thought describes objects in relation to its appearance. Hebrew thought describes objects in relation to its function.

A Greek description of a common pencil would be; "it is yellow and about eight inches long". A Hebrew description of the pencil would be related to its function such as "I write words with it". Notice that the Hebrew description uses the verb "write" while the Greek description uses the adjectives "yellow" and "long". Because of Hebrew's form of functional descriptions, verbs are used much more frequently then adjectives.

To our Greek way of thinking a deer and an oak are two very different objects and we would never describe them in the same way. The Hebrew word for both of these objects is ᒐᒣᒍ (ayil) because the functional description of these two objects are identical to the Ancient Hebrews, therefore, the same Hebrew word is used for both.

The Hebraic definition of ᒐᒣᒍ is "a strong leader". A deer stag is one of the most powerful animals of the forest and is seen as "a strong leader" among the other animals of the forest. The wood of the oak tree is very hard compared to other trees and is seen as a "strong leader" among the trees of the forest.

Notice the two different translations of the Hebrew word ᒐᒣᒍ in Psalms 29:9. The NASB and KJV translates it as "*The voice of the LORD makes the deer to calve*" while the NIV translates it as "*The voice of the LORD twists the oaks*". The literal translation of this verse in Hebrew thought would be; "*The voice of the LORD makes the strong leaders turn*".

When translating the Hebrew into English, the Greek thinking translator will give a Greek description to this word for the Greek thinking reader, which is why we have two different ways of translating this verse. This same word "ayil" is also translated as a "ruler" (a strong leader of men) in 2 Kings 24.15.

Ancient Hebrew will use different Hebrew words for the same thing depending upon its function at the time. For example an ox may be identified as an ᐁᒍ (aluph) when referring to a lead ox, a ᒍᒪ (shor) when referring to a plow ox, ᒪ (baqar) when referring to an ox of the field or ᒪ (par) when referring to an ox of the threshing floor.

Static and Dynamic

In our Modern western language verbs express action (dynamic) while nouns express inanimate (static) objects. In Hebrew all things are in motion (dynamic) including verbs and nouns. In Hebrew sentences the verbs identify the action of an object while nouns identify an object of action. The verb ᴦᴗᴦ (malak) is "the reign of the king" while the noun ᴦᴗᴦ (melek) is the "the king who reigns". A mountain top is not a static object but the "head lifting up out of the hill". A good example of action in what appears to be a static passage is the command to "have no other gods before me" (Exodus 20:3). In Hebrew thought this passage is saying "not to bring another one of power in front of my face".

The Ancient Hebrew Alphabet

Evolution of the Hebrew Alphabet

The Hebrew alphabet was written with a script belonging to the Semitic family of languages. The Semitic script followed three basic stages of development, Early, Middle and Late.

The Early Semitic script was pictographic (fig. 1) where each letter represented an object. In figure 1, the top left corner letter is a picture of water representing the sound "M". The second letter from right at the bottom is a picture of a shepherd staff representing the sound "L".

The Middle Semitic script (fig. 2) is an evolved form of the original pictographic script into a simpler form and used by the different Semitic groups including the Hebrews (fig. 2), Moabites (fig. 3), Ammonites (fig. 4), Arameans (fig. 5) and others.

The Aramaic script of the Arameans in Babylon evolved into the Late Semitic script independently from other Semitic scripts (fig. 6). When the Hebrew people were taken into Babylonian captivity, they adopted the Aramaic script (fig. 7) and is still in use today (fig. 8).

While the majority of the Hebrew texts of the first century BCE and into the first century CE were written in the Late Semitic or Aramaic script, the Middle Semitic script was not lost. It was still used on occasion such as on many of the Jewish coins as well as some religious scrolls such as those found in the Dead Sea caves (fig. 9).

The Samaritans lived in the land of Samaria, a region of Israel, at the time of Israel's captivity; they were not taken into Babylon with Israel. As a result of their isolation they are the only culture to retain a script (fig. 13) similar to the Middle Semitic script and is still used to this day in the Samaritan community.

Around 1000 BCE, the Greeks adopted the Middle Semitic script (fig. 11) and began to evolve independently over the centuries to become the Greek script (fig. 12) used today.

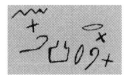

Figure-1 Ancient Semitic pictographic inscription on stone boulder c. 1500 BCE

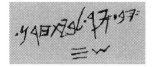

Figure-2 Ancient Hebrew inscription on potsherd c. 900 BCE

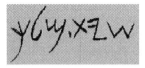

Figure-3 Moabite inscription on stone c. 900 BCE

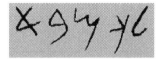

Figure-4 Ammonite inscription on stone c. 900 BCE

Figure-5 Aramaic inscription on stone incense altar c. 500 BCE

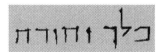

Figure-6 Aramaic inscription on stone plaque c. 20 CE.

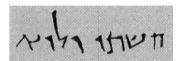

Figure-7 Hebrew writings from the Dead Sea Scrolls c. 200 BCE

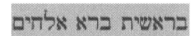

Figure-8 Modern Hebrew script from the Hebrew Bible.

Figure-9 Pictographic Hebrew writings from the Dead Sea Scrolls c. 100 BCE

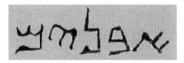

Figure-10 Samaritan scripts

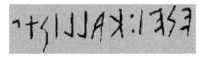

Figure-11 Greek inscription found on bowl c. 800 BCE

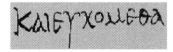

Figure-12 Greek writing on New Testament papyrus c. 200 CE

The Ayin and Ghah

While the Modern Hebrew alphabet consists of twenty-two letters, the evidence suggests that there were additional letters in the original Semitic and Hebrew alphabet. One of the ancient Semitic languages of Canaan was Ugarit. This ancient language is almost identical to the Hebrew language of the Bible but, instead of consisting of twenty-two letters it has twenty-eight letters. One of the major differences between Ugarit and Hebrew is the additional letter "ghah". Evidence, such as will be presented here, suggest that the letter "ghah" exists within the Hebrew text of the Bible.

One Word - Two Meanings

The strongest evidence of the missing ghah can be found in two different meanings of one Hebrew word. The Hebrew word ra' (רע in modern Hebrew) can mean "friend" or "bad". The examples in the table below (Table 1) list several of these double meaning words that contain the letter ע (ayin). The first column is the word as it appears in the modern Hebrew Bible. The second column is the word spelled with the ancient Hebrew letter ⊙ (ayin) and its meaning. The third column is the word spelled with the ancient Hebrew letter 𐤗 (ghah) and its meaning.

Table 1

Modern	Ancient with ayin		Ancient with ghah	
יעל	infant	ᴧᎿ⊙	wicked	ᴧᎿ𐤗
ענח	profit	ᴧ⊙ᴗ	goat	ᴧ𐤗ᴗ
עיף	heed	⚘ᴧ⊙	answer	⚘ᴧ𐤗
עור	weary	⊙ᴗᴧᴗ	darkness	ᴗᴧ𐤗
עיר	skin	ᴙᎿ⊙	blind	ᴙᎿ𐤗
רע	colt	ᴙᴗ⊙	city	ᴙᴗ𐤗
רעה	friend	⊙ᴙ	bad	𐤗ᴙ
שער	shepherd	⚘⊙ᴙ	break	⚘𐤗ᴙ
ערב	hair	ᴙ⊙⚡	storm	ᴙ𐤗⚡
ערם	weave	ᴘᴙ⊙	dark	ᴘᴙ𐤗
ערף	naked	ᴍᴙ⊙	crafty	ᴍᴙ𐤗
יעל	neck	⊙ᴙ⊙	rain	⊙ᴙ𐤗

Greek Transliterations of the Ghah

Additional evidence to the existence of the letter ghah is the Greek transliteration of Hebrew names. When the Hebrew Bible was translated into Greek about 2,000 years ago, the translator transliterated the Hebrew names into Greek.

When we examine Hebrew names that contain the Hebrew letter ayin (ע), we find two different methods of transliterating the letter. Table 2 below contains Hebrew names where the ayin is not transliterated because it is a silent letter, while Table 3 contains Hebrew names where the ayin is transliterated with the Greek letter "Gamma" (Γ or γ).

Table 2

Hebrew		Greek		English
Written	**Pronunciation**	**Written**	**Pronunciation**	
בּוּל	ba'al	Βααλ	Baal	Baal
בלעם	bilam	Βαλααμ	Balaam	Balaam
עשתרות	ashtarot	Ασταρωθ	Astaroth	Ashtaroth

Table 3

Hebrew		Greek		English
Written	**Pronunciation**	**Written**	**Pronunciation**	
עמרה	amorah	Γομορραφ	Gomorras	Gomorrah
עזה	azzah	Γαζαν	Gazan	Gaza
פעור	peor	Φογωρ	Pogor	Peor

Impact on Ancient Hebrew Studies

In the study of the ancient Hebrew language and alphabet we begin studying the language at its simplest roots, the letters. Each letter is a picture that represents a meaning. When the letters are combined to form roots, each letter supplies meaning to the root. By then studying the various words, which are derived out of any given root, we can begin to reconstruct the original root language of Hebrew. In order to be as accurate as possible, we need to be sure that we are using the correct words, roots and letters.

When we compare the meanings of the parent roots that were originally spelled with the letter ghah we notice the similarity in meaning with each of these words. The majority of these words are related to darkness (dark, storm, clouds, rain, blind) and wickedness (wicked, goat, city, bad, crafty).

The Samech, Shin and Sin

In the Modern Hebrew alphabet the letter shin (שׁ) represents two different sounds, an "sh" and an "s". To differentiate these two sounds a dot is placed above the shin in different locations. For the "sh" sound the dot is placed on the right (שׁ) and called a "shin" and for the "s" sound it is placed on the left (שׂ) and called a "sin".

In most cases words spelled with the sin are more closely related in meaning with words spelled with the samech (ס). In addition, Hebrew words spelled with the sin are written with the samech in other Semitic languages. In the Hebrew Bible several Hebrew words written with the שׂ are also written with a ס. Table 4 below are some examples.

Table 4

נשׂא	נסא	nasa	Lift up
שׂור	סור	sur	Remove
שׂכך	סכך	sakak	Cover
שׂוט	סוט	sut	Turn aside
שׂט	סט	set	Rebel
שׂשׂה	שסה	shasah	Plunder

Because the *Ancient Hebrew Lexicon of the Bible* is concerned with restoring Hebrew words to their original meaning and relationship with the ancient roots, words written with a שׂ in the Masoretic text will be written with the ancient pictograph ⋞ (sin/samech) in the Lexicon. For example, the word שׂשׂה appears as 𐤔𐤎𐤋𐤋 in the Lexicon with the spelling שׂשׂה noted under "defective spellings".

Reconstruction of the original Hebrew Alphabet

The Ancient Hebrew letters form the foundation to the Ancient Hebrew language and a thorough study of these letters is essential to understanding the cultural background to the words they form. The process of reconstructing the original Hebrew alphabet is similar to the field of archeology, which digs down to hidden depths to determine the origins, culture or way of life of Ancient civilizations. As artifacts are found, they are compared to artifacts of other cultures and other time periods to determine the distinctive characteristics of the culture and civilization. When studying Ancient alphabets, one digs down into the depths of time and compares the artifacts of pictographic and non-pictographic scripts to determine dates, meaning and sound.

Letter Characteristics

We usually associate two characteristics for each letter, a form and a sound, as in the first letter of our alphabet whose form is "A" and has the sound "a". The Ancient Hebrew alphabet has four characteristics: form, sound, name and meaning.

Form

The original letter is pictographic, meaning it represents a picture of something, such as the letter �>> representing a mouth. The original form is determined by examining the archeological record of ancient Semitic inscriptions and other related scripts such as the South Arabian and Punic. The name of the letter will help to determine the original pictograph.

Name

Each pictograph is associated with a single syllable of two consonants. This syllable is also the name of the letter. The name of the letter ⌐> is "peh" and is also the Hebrew word for "mouth". The name is determined by comparing the various names of this letter as used in Semitic languages as well as other non Semitic languages that have adopted the Semitic alphabet.

Meaning

The mnemonic meaning of a pictograph is the extended meanings related to the pictograph. These mnemonic meanings most often are related to the pictograph by their function rather than appearance. For example, the letter ⌐> has the extended mnemonic meanings, speak, blow and open, functions of the mouth.

Sound

The first letter of the syllabic name provides a singular sound for the purpose of forming words and sentences. The phonetic value of the letter ⌐> is therefore a "p". The original sound is determined by comparing the sound of the letter as used in other Semitic languages as well as non-Semitic languages that have adopted the Semitic alphabet.

The Reconstructed Alphabet

Al

The original pictograph for this letter is a picture of an ox head - 𐤀 representing strength and power from the work performed by the animal. This pictograph also represents a chief or other leader. When two oxen are yoked together for pulling a wagon or plow, one is the older and more experienced one who leads the other. Within the clan, tribe or family the chief or father is seen as the elder who is yoked to the others as the leader and teacher.

The Modern name for this letter is aleph (𐤀𐤋𐤐) and corresponds to the Greek name alpha and the Arabic name aleph. The various meanings of this root are oxen, yoke and learn. Each of these meanings is related to the meanings of the pictograph 𐤀. The root 𐤀𐤋𐤐 is an adopted root from the parent root 𐤀𐤋 (AL) meaning, strength, power and chief and is the probable original name of the pictograph 𐤀.

The 𐤋 is a shepherd staff and represents authority as well as a yoke (see Lam below). Combined these two pictographs mean "strong authority". The chief or father is the "strong authority". The 𐤀𐤋 can also be understood as the "ox in the yoke". Many Near Eastern cultures worshipped the god 𐤀𐤋 / AL, most commonly pronounced as "el" and depicted as a bull in carvings and statues. Israel chose the form of a calf (young bull) as an image of God at Mount Sinai showing their association between the word 𐤀𐤋 and the ox or bull. The word 𐤀𐤋 is also commonly used in the Hebrew Bible for God or any god.

The concept of the ox and the shepherd staff in the word 𐤀𐤋 has been carried over into modern times as the scepter and crown of a monarch, the leader of a nation. These modern items are representative of the shepherd staff, an ancient sign of authority, and the horns of the ox, an ancient sign of strength.

In Modern Hebrew this letter is silent but was originally used as the vowel "a" as well as a glottal stop. The Greek letter "alpha" derived from the "aleph" is also used for the "a" sound.

The Early Semitic pictograph 𐤀 was simplified to 𐤀 and 𐤀 in the Middle Hebrew script and continued to evolve into the א in the Late Hebrew script. The Modern

Hebrew letter א developed out of the Late Semitic. The Middle Semitic was adopted by the Greeks to be the letter "A" and carried over into the Roman "A". The Middle Semitic script 𐤀 became the number "1" we use today.

Bet

Several variations were used for the original pictograph including, ⊏, 凸, 冂 and ⊔. Each of these pictographs are representative of a house or tent. The pictograph ⊔ is chosen as it best represents the nomadic tents of the Hebrews. The tent was divided into two sections, men's and women's, with the entrance at the front of the tent in the men's section and an entrance from the men's to the women's section.

The Hebrew word (bet) means house or tent as well as family. A common designation for a family is to identify the "house" of the family patriarch such as in "The house of Jacob".

The meanings of this letter are house, tent, family as well as in, with, inside or within as the family resides within the house or tent.

The original name for this letter is bet, the parent root of the child root beyt (meaning house) and is equivalent to the Greek name beta and the Arabic name beyt. This letter is pronounced as a "b" when sounded as a stop such as in the word "beyt" or a "bh" (v) when sounded as a spirant as in the word "shubh" (shoov).

This letter is commonly used as a prefix to words to mean "in" or "with" as in "be'erets" meaning "in a land".

The Early Semitic letter ⊔ evolved into 𐤁 in the Middle Semitic script and into ⅃ in the Late Semitic script. The Modern Hebrew letter ב developed out of the Late Semitic. The Middle Semitic script was adopted by the Greeks to become the letter β (a reverse direction due to being written from right to left instead of left to right) and the Roman B and b. The Late Semitic script ⅃ became the number "2".

Gam

The earliest known pictograph for this letter is Ⴑ and is a picture of a foot. The Modern Hebrew name for this letter is "gimel", an adopted root. The original name to this letter is most likely "gam", the parent root of "gimel". This letter is the origin of the Arabic letter "Geem" and the Greek "gamma" supporting the theory that the original name for the letter did not include the "L".

The word "gam" means to gather together as a group of animals gathering at the water hole to drink. The pictographic script for the word "gam" is ᴧᴧႱ. The Ⴑ is the foot representing "walk" and the ᴧᴧ is "water" (See Mah below). Combined these mean "walk to the water".

The letter Ⴑ has the meanings of walk, carry or gather. The sound associated with this letter is a "g" as in "go".

The Early Semitic Ⴑ became Ⴑ and ⦧ (a turn of 180 degrees) in the Middle Semitic script. This letter further developed to λ in the Late Semitic script. The Late Semitic script further developed into the Modern Hebrew ג. The Middle Semitic script became the Greek Γ (a reversal of the letter due to direction of writing) as well as the Roman C and G. The Late Semitic λ became the number 3.

Dal

There are two possibilities for the original Early Semitic pictograph for this letter - ⤳, a picture of a fish and ⊓ a picture of a door. The modern Hebrew name for this letter is "dalet" and means "door". The word "dalet" is a derivative of the parent root "dal" also meaning "door". The Arabic name for this letter is "dal" giving support to the parent root as the original name. As the Hebrew word for a "fish" is dag, it is unlikely that the pictograph ⤳ is the pictograph for this letter but, rather the pictograph ⊓.

The basic meaning of the letter ⊓ is "door" but has several other meanings associated with it. It can mean "a back and forth movement" as one goes back and forth through the tent through the door. It can mean "dangle" as the tent door dangled down from a roof pole of the tent. It can also mean weak or poor as one who dangles the head down.

The sound for this letter is a "d" as in "door" as it is with the Greek and Arabic equivalents.

The Early Semitic pictograph ᚂ evolved into the Middle Semitic letter 𐤃. The Middle Semitic then evolved into the Late Semitic letter 𐡃, the early form of the Modern Hebrew ד. The Middle Semitic letter is the origin of the Greek letter Δ, The Roman D and the number 4.

Hey

The original pictograph for this letter is ᛘ or ᛉ, a man standing with his arms raised out. The Modern Hebrew and original name for this letter is "hey". The Hebrew word "hey" means "behold", as when looking at a great sight. This word can also mean "breath" or "sigh" as one does when looking at a great sight. The meaning of the letter ᛘ is behold, look, breath, sigh and reveal or revelation from the idea of revealing a great sight by pointing it out.

The Modern Hebrew sound for this letter is "h". Originally this letter doubled as a consonant, with an "h" sound, or as the vowel sound "eh". When the Greeks adopted this letter it became the "epsilon" with an "eh" sound.

This letter is commonly used as a prefix to words to mean "the" as in "ha'arets" meaning "the land". The use of this prefix is to reveal something of importance within the sentence.

The Early Semitic ᛘ evolved into the Middle Semitic 𐤄 by rotating the letter 90 degrees to the left. This letter then evolved into 𐡄 in the late Semitic script that developed into the Modern Hebrew ה. The Middle Semitic 𐤄 was adopted by the Greeks and the Romans to become the E (reversed due to the direction of writing). This Middle Semitic letter also became the number 5.

Waw

The original pictograph used in the Early Semitic script is a Y, a picture of a tent peg. The tent pegs were made of wood and may have been Y-shaped to prevent the rope from slipping off.

The Modern Hebrew name for this letter is "vav", a word meaning "peg" or "hook". This letter is used in Modern Hebrew as a consonant with a "v" sound and as a vowel.

If the Modern Hebrew letter appears as וֹ, it is the vowel sound "ow" and if it appears as וּ, it is the vowel sound "uw". When used as a vowel the ancient pronunciation was also an "ow" or "uw". In each of the consonant/vowel letters of the Ancient Hebrew language the pronunciation of the is closely related to the pronunciation of the vowel such as the letter "hey" (See above) is "h" and "eh" and the pronunciation of the letter "yud" (See below) is "y" and "iy". For this reason, it is probable that the original pronunciation of the letter Y was with a "w". In Modern Arabic language, this letter is also pronounced with a "w". Therefore, the original name of this letter would have been "waw" instead of "vav".

As the pictograph indicates, this letter represents a peg or hook, which are used for securing something. The meaning of this letter is to add or secure.

This letter is frequently used as a prefix to words to mean "and" in the sense of adding things together.

The Early Semitic Y evolved into the ϯ in the Middle Semitic script. This letter then became the 1 of the Late Semitic script and evolved into the Modern Hebrew ו. The Middle Semitic letter was adopted by the Greeks and the Romans to be the letter F but was dropped from the Greek alphabet later. The Late Semitic form of the letter became the number 9.

Zan

The ancient pictograph for this letter is ⟵⊏ and is some type of agricultural implement similar to a mattock or plow. The meanings of this letter are "harvest" or "crop" as this tool is used in the harvesting, "food" as from the harvest, "cut" from the function of the implement and "broad" from its shape.

The Modern Hebrew name for this letter is "zayin" but was originally the parent root "zan". When the Greeks adopted the letter its name was originally "zan" but later became "zeta", the modern name for this letter in the Greek alphabet.

The phonetic sound for this letter is a "z" as it is in Greek and Arabic.

The Early Semitic pictograph was simplified to ⊐⊏ and evolving into ᘔ in the Late Semitic script and evolved into the Modern Hebrew letter ז. The Greeks and Romans adopted this letter to become the letter "Z". The Late Semitic ᘔ became the number 7.

Hhets

The ancient pictograph ⲙ is a picture of a tent wall. The meanings of this letter are outside as the function of the wall is to protect the occupants from the elements, halp as the wall in the middle of the tent divides the tent into the male and female sections and secular as something that is outside.

The Modern Hebrew name for this letter is hhet meaning a string. A very similar word Hebrew word hhets is a wall and is most likely the original name for this letter. The sound of the letter, in ancient and modern times, is a guttural "hh" (as in the "ch" in the name Bach).

The early Semitic pictograph ⲙ evolved into Ⲏ in the Middle Semitic script by being rotated 90 degrees. This letter continued to evolve into Ⲡ in the Late Semitic script. The Middle Semitic script is the origin of the Greek and Roman H while the late Semitic script became the modern Hebrew ח. The Middle Semitic form of this letter became the number 8.

Thet

The original pictograph for this letter is ⊗, a container made of wicker or clay. Containers were a very important item among the nomadic Hebrews. They were used for storing grains and other items. Wicker baskets were used as nets for catching fish. The meanings of this letter are basket, contain, store and clay.

The twenty-second letter of the Hebrew alphabet is a tav with a "t" sound. It is unlikely that the original Hebrew had two letters with the same sound. When the Greeks adopted the Hebrew alphabet this letter the Greek theta. The original sound for this letter is was probably a "th".

The Modern Hebrew name for this letter is "tet" meaning mud or clay but would have been pronounced as "thet".

The Early Semitic letter ⊗ remained unchanged into the Middle Semitic script but was simplified to ⎔ in the Late Semitic script. The Late Semitic letter became the Θ, Theta, in the Greek alphabet, the Modern Hebrew ט and our number 6.

Yad

The Early Semitic pictograph of this letter is ⊢, an arm and hand. The meaning of this letter is work, make and throw, the functions of the hand. The Modern Hebrew name "yud" is a derivative of the two letter word "yad" meaning "hand", the original name for the letter.

The ancient and modern pronunciation of this letter is a "y". In Ancient Hebrew this letter also doubled as a vowel with an "i" sound. The Greek language adopted this letter as the "iota", carrying over the "i" sound.

The ancient pictograph ⊢, was turned 90 degrees to become the **ℤ** in the Middle Semitic script. The letter continued to evolve into the simpler form ⌐ in the Late Semitic script. The Middle Semitic form became the Greek and Roman I. The Late Semitic form became the Modern Hebrew י.

Kaph

The Ancient form of this letter is ש the open palm of a hand. The meanings of this letter are bend and curve from the shape of the palm as well as to tame or subdue as one who has been bent to another's will.

The Modern Hebrew name for this letter is kaph, a Hebrew word meaning "palm" and is the original name for the letter. This letter is pronounced as a "k", as in the word "kaph", when used as a stop or as a "kh" (pronounced hard like the German name Bach), as in the word "yalakh" (to walk) when used as a spirant.

The Early Semitic ש evolved into ℽ in the Middle Semitic script. This letter continued to evolve into ℽ in the Late Semitic script and becoming the Modern Hebrew כ and the ך (final kaph). The Middle Semitic ℽ became the Greek and Roman K (written in reverse direction).

Lam

The Early Hebrew pictograph is ✓, a shepherd's staff. The shepherd staff was used to direct sheep by pushing or pulling them. It was also used as a weapon against predators to defend and protect the sheep.

The meaning of this letter is toward as moving something in a different direction. This letter also means authority, as it is a sign of the shepherd, the leader of the flock. It also means yoke, a staff on the shoulders as well as tie or bind from the yoke that is bound to the animal.

This letter is used as a prefix to nouns meaning "to" or "toward".

The Modern Hebrew name of this letter is "lamed", similarly is the Greek name "lamda". The Arabic name however is "lam" retaining an older two letter root name for the letter and the probable original name. The phonetic sound for this letter is "l".

The original pictograph for this letter, ✓, has remained virtually unchanged through the ages. The Middle Semitic remained the same but changed slightly to ✔ in the Late Semitic script becoming the ל in the Modern Hebrew script. The Early Semitic ✓ is the origin of the Greek Λ (upside down) and the Roman L.

Mah

The Early Semitic pictograph for this letter is ᗰ a picture of waves of water. This pictograph has the meanings of liquid, water and sea, mighty and massive from the size of the sea and chaos from the storms of the sea. To the Hebrews the sea was a feared and unknown place, for this reason this letter is used as a question word, who, what, when, where, why and how, in the sense of searching for an unknown.

The modern Hebrew name for this letter is "mem" probably from the word "mayim" meaning "water". The word "mayim" is the plural form of "mah", probably the original name for this letter, meaning "what". The Greek name for this letter is "mu", a Hebrew word closely related to "mah". The sound for this letter is "m".

The Early Semitic ᗰ evolved into ᗰ in the Middle Semitic and continued to evolve into ל in the Late Semitic script. The Late Semitic script became the מ and ם (final mem) of the Modern Hebrew script. The Early and Middle Semitic script is the origin to the Greek and Roman M.

Nun

The ancient pictograph ⟨ is a picture of a seed sprout representing the idea of continuing to a new generation. This pictograph has the meanings of continue, perpetuation, offspring or heir.

The Modern Hebrew name is "nun", a Hebrew word meaning continue, offspring or heir. This two-letter word is the original name for the letter. The phonetic sound for this letter is "n".

The Early Semitic ⟨ evolved into ⟨ in the Middle Semitic script and continued to evolve into ⟨ in the Late Semitic script. The Late Semitic script became the Modern Hebrew נ and ן (final nun). The Middle Semitic script became the N (written in reverse direction) in both the Greek and Roman alphabets.

Sin

There are several possibilities for the original Semitic pictograph including ⟨ (a fish), ⟨ (possibly a thorn), ⟨ (a window?) and ⟨ (a thorn). The pictograph ⟨ is used almost exclusively through the history of this letter. This picture has the meanings of pierce and sharp. This letter also has the meaning of a shield as thorn bushes were used by the shepherd to build a wall or shield, made to enclose his flock during the night to protect them from predators. Another meaning is to grab hold as a thorn is a seed that clings to hair and clothing.

Of all the letters this is the most difficult to reconstruct due to the limited archeological and textual support. The Modern Hebrew name for this letter is samech (⟨⟨⟨⟨), which is a word that means support, with no apparent connection to a two letter parent root or to the meaning of the original picture of this letter. The Arabic alphabet does not have this letter and the Greek letter derived from this letter is called the ksi. The 21st letter of the Hebrew alphabet (ש) has two names and sounds, Shin (sh) and Sin (s). All the words using the sin are related in meaning to the words using a samech in the same place as the sin. It is possible that the original name for the samech was sin, meaning thorn, and later was divided into the samech and sin (which then became associated with the shin).

The original sound for this letter must be an "s" to which the samech and sin both agree. The Greek sound for the letter is "ks", similar to the "s".

The early Semitic ⪡ evolved into the ⪢ in the middle Semitic. This letter continued to evolve into ろ in the late Semitic. This letter became the ס in the modern Hebrew alphabet. The late Semitic is reversed in the Greek alphabet becoming the ξ and Ξ. The Greek letter Ξ became the Latin X.

Ayin

The Ancient picture for this letter is a picture of an eye ⌖. This letter represents the ideas of seeing and watching as well as knowledge as the eye is the window of knowledge.

The name of the letter is ayin, a Semitic word meaning eye. This letter is silent in modern Hebrew. There is no indication that the ancient Semitic had a sound for this letter as well and appears to have been silent in the past. The Greek language assigned the vowel sound "o" to the letter. As Hebrew did not have one letter for the "o" sound the Greeks took this silent letter and converted it into a vowel.

The early Semitic ⌖ evolved into the simpler O in the middle Semitic and remained the same into the late Semitic period. This letter evolved into the ע in the modern Hebrew script. The middle Semitic became the Greek O and the Latin O.

Pey

The Semitic word "pey" means a "mouth" and there are several ancient Semitic pictographs believed to be this letter, none of which resemble a mouth. The only exception is the South Arabian pictograph ⌒. This pictograph closely resembles a mouth and is similar to the later Semitic letters for the letter "pey".

This pictograph has the meanings of speak and blow from the functions of the mouth as well the edge of something from the lips at the edge of the mouth.

The modern Hebrew name for this letter is "pey" and as previously identified it is the Hebrew word for mouth. There are two sounds for this letter, the stop "P" and the spirant "Ph" or "f".

The early Semitic ⟳ evolved to the letter 𝟕 in the middle Semitic scripts. The letter continued to evolved into the Ɔ in the late Semitic script. This letter evolved into the Ɗ and ꓩ (final pey) in the modern Hebrew script. The middle Semitic 𝟕 became the Greek Π and the Latin P.

Tsad

The three Ancient pictograph possibilities for this letter are ⵉ, ⳺ and ⳾. The word "tsad" means "side" as a man lying on his side and may be the meaning of the last two pictographs. Most ancient Semitic alphabets used pictographs which closely resemble the last pictograph indicating that this was most likely the original form of the letter.

The meaning of this letter is the side of something as well as hunting and chasing through the idea of laying down in ambush. The modern name for this letter is tsade, a child root from the word tsad also meaning side. The phonetic sound of the letter is a "ts" in both ancient and modern Hebrew.

The early pictograph ⳾ evolved into ⵨ in the Middle Semitic script and continued to evolve into ⵕ in the Late Semitic Script. From the middle Semitic script comes the Modern Hebrew ץ and צ. Modern Greek and Latin has no letter derived from this Semitic letter.

Quph

Most of the pictographs used for this letter are ⵰ or ⵱. Ancient Semitic letter which were originally oriented in a horizontal plane were tilted to a vertical plane. More than likely this letter was originally written as ⊸.

The name of this letter is quph, a parent root. When all of the words derived from this parent root are compared the common theme of a circle or revolution are found. The pictograph of this letter is probably a picture of the sun at the horizon in the sense of a revolution of the sun.

The various meanings of this letter are sun, revolution, circle and horizon. This letter can also mean condense as the light gathers at the sun when it is at the horizon. It can also mean time as the revolution of the sun is used to calculate time. Hebrew, Greek and Arabic agree that the sound for this letter is "q". The Modern Hebrew and Arabic name for this letter is quph, a parent root.

The early pictograph -o- evolved into ϙ in the Middle Semitic script and continued to evolve into P in the Late Semitic Script. From the middle Semitic script comes the Modern Hebrew ק. The Middle Semitic script is the origin of the Latin letter Q.

Resh

The Ancient picture for this letter is ର, the head of a man. This letter has the meanings of head or man as well as chief, top, beginning or first.

The modern Hebrew name for this letter is resh, a Hebrew word meaning head. Hebrew, Aramaic and Greek agree that the sound for this letter is an "r".

The early pictograph ର evolved into 9 in the Middle Semitic script and continued to evolve into 7 in the Late Semitic Script. From the middle Semitic script comes the Modern Hebrew ר. The Middle Semitic script is also the origin of the Greek letter P and the Latin R.

Shin

The Ancient picture for this letter is ⊔⊔, a picture of the two front teeth. This letter has the meanings of teeth, sharp and press (from the function of the teeth when chewing). It also has the meaning of two, again, both or second from the two teeth.

The modern Hebrew name for this letter is shin, a Hebrew word meaning tooth. Hebrew and Arabic agree that the sound for this letter is "sh".

The early pictograph ⊔⊔ evolved into W in the Middle Semitic script and continued to evolve into ש in the Late Semitic Script. From the middle Semitic script comes the Modern Hebrew שׁ. The Middle Semitic script is also the origin of the Greek letter Σ and the Latin S.

Taw

The Ancient picture † is a type of "mark", probably of two sticks crossed to mark a place similar to the Egyptian hieroglyph of ⚲, a picture of two crossed sticks. This letter has the meanings of mark, sign or signature.

The Modern Hebrew, Arabic and Greek names for this letter is tav (or taw), a Hebrew word meaning, mark. Hebrew, Greek and Arabic agree that the sound for this letter is "t".

The early pictograph † evolved into ✗ in the Middle Semitic script and continued to evolve into ℏ in the Late Semitic Script. From the middle Semitic script comes the Modern Hebrew ת. The Early Semitic script is the origin of the Greek letter T and the Latin T.

Ghah

While this letter existed in ancient Semitic languages and some modern Semitic languages, it no longer exists in the modern Hebrew. Instead it has been absorbed into the letter ע (ayin). While the evidence exists showing that this is in fact a separate letter, there is very little evidence for reconstructing its original pictograph. The Ugarit and Arabic languages wrote this letter the same as the ayin but with an additional line or dot. The closest candidate for this letter is the ⸙, a twisted rope, as found in some ancient Semitic inscriptions.

In the Arabic language this letter is called the ghah but originally may have had the name ghah meaning "twisted". The meaning of the letter ghah is twisted from the twisting fibers of a rope and from this come the meaning of goats from their twisted horns. As goats are dark in color, this letter also carries the meaning of dark.

Because the Greek language transliterates this letter with a gamma (g sound) we know that this letter originally had a type of "g" sound such as in the word ring.

Hebrew Alphabet Chart

Table 5

Early				Middle	Late	Modern			
Script	**Picture**	**Name**	**Sound**	**Script**	**Script**	**Script**		**Name**	**Sound**
⅄	Head of an ox	al	a	⨉	Х	א		aleph	silent
⊔	Tent floorplan	bet	b,bh	9	ע	ב		beyt	b,bh
Ⅼ	Foot	gam	g	⅂	ג	ג		gimel	g
᠊ᠣ	Tent door	dal	d	Δ	⅂	ד		dalet	d
ⵍ	Arms raised	hey	h,e	ㅋ	ᴨ	ה		hey	h
Y	Tent peg	waw	w,o,u	↑	⅂	ו		vav	v,o,u
⌐	Mattock	zan	z	ᴢ	Ꝣ	ז		zayin	z
⊞	Tent wall	hhets	hh	ᴎ	ᴨ	ח		hhet	hh
⊗	Clay basket	thet	th	⊗	Ο	ט		tet	t
⅃	Closed hand	yad	y,i	ℨ	⅂	'		yad	y
⨆	Open palm	kaph	k,kh	⅁	⅂	ך ‎ כ		kaph	k,kh
⌣	Shepherd staff	lam	l	⌣	↳	ל		lamed	l
⌇	Water	mah	m	⌇	⅄	מ ‎ ם		Mem	m
⌐	Sprouting seed	nun	n	ᴴ	⅂	ן ‎ נ		nun	n
⩻	Thorn	sin	s	⩻	⅃	ס ‎ שׂ		samech, sin	s
⌀	Eye	ayin	'	ο	⅄	ע		ayin	silent
⌀	Open mouth	pey	p,ph	⅂	⅂	ף ‎ פ		pey	ph
⌒	Man on his side	tsad	ts	⩘	⅂	ץ ‎ צ		tsadey	ts
⌐	Horizon	quph	q	φ	Ρ	ק		quph	q
ᴖ	Head of a man	resh	r	⅂	⅂	ר		resh	r
⊔	Two front teeth	shin	sh	W	ⅴ	שׁ		shin	sh
†	Crossed sticks	taw	t	⤬	ℏ	ת		tav	t
⅄	Rope	ghah	gh	ο	⅄	ע		ayin	silent

The Hebrew Root System

Parent Roots

When two pictographs are put together, a Parent Root word is formed. When the ⊔ (B, a house) is combined with the ↖ (N, a seed which continues the next generation) the Parent Root ⊔↖ (pronounced ben) is formed. The two letters of this root have the combined meaning of "the house of seeds" or "the seeds that continue the house/family". This word is translated simply as "son".

These parent roots are often used in the Biblical text as words themselves. While these words are usually specific in nature, their original meaning was very broad. The Hebrew word ⊔↖ means "son", the more original broad meaning of the parent root ⊔↖ is to build (a house or family). This can be seen in the various other derivatives of the Parent Root having the meanings of build, house, bricks and children.

Child Roots

Formed out of the Parent Roots are thirteen different Child Roots. The first is formed by doubling the last letter of the Parent Root. Hebrew verbs require a three consonant root in order to be conjugated. Therefore, the second consonant in the Parent Root is duplicated to turn the two consonant Parent Root into a three consonant child root. The meaning of this derivative from the Parent Root is usually identical in meaning to the original Parent Root.

The other twelve Child roots are formed by placing a vowel within the Parent Root. Of the twenty-two letters of the Hebrew alphabet, four double as consonants and vowels. These are the ↙ (A), ⽊ (H, E), Y (W, O and U) and ↵ (Y, I).

A Child Root is formed by adding one of the consonant/vowels as a prefix (in front), a suffix (at the end) or an infix (in the middle) to the Parent Root. All of the Child Roots formed from the Parent Root are directly related in meaning to the Parent Root. Table 6 below are the Child Roots formed from the Parent Root ⌄⊔ (BL), which has the generic meaning of "flow", demonstrating the close relationship between the Parent and Child roots.

Table 6

Hebrew	Meaning	Connection to root
ꞁꞅꟻ	Wilt	Flowing away of life
ꞁꞅꟻ	Empty	Flowing out of contents
ꞁꞅꞅ	Panic	Flowing of the insides
ꞅꞁꞅ	Aged	Flowing away of youth
ꞁꞌꞅ	Flood	Heavy flowing of water
ꞁꞅꞁ	Steam	Flowing of water

Adopted Roots

An adopted root is a three letter root that is formed out of a parent root. These roots evolved over time out of the original parent roots. Adopted roots are formed by adding a third consonant to a Parent Root forming a new root that is more specific in meaning than the parent. In Table 7 adopted roots formed out of the parent root ꞁꞌ (with the generic meaning "to break") are listed. Each of the adopted roots have a more precise meaning of "to break".

Table 7

Hebrew	Meaning
ꞁꞌꞁꞌ	Break forth
ꞁꞌꞁꞌ	Break apart
ꞁꞌꞁꞌ	Break in pieces
ꞁꞌꞁꞌ	Break off
ꞁꞌꞁꞌ	Break open

There are also a few four letter adopted roots in the Biblical text, sixty-seven in all. Because of the scarcity of these roots it appears that these roots came into existence at an even later date than the three letter adopted roots of which there are hundreds.

Reconstruction of Roots

By comparing the various aspects of a parent root, the original meaning of the parent can be determined. For example, the two child roots ●─●─ᴧᴧ (MQQ) meaning "to rot" and ●─Yᴧᴧ (MQ) meaning "to stink" are formed out of the parent root ●─ᴧᴧ. These two ideas are connected in that something that rots begins to stink. When we examine the letters which form the parent root, ᴧᴧ and ●─, we find the original meaning. The ᴧᴧ is a picture of water and the ●─ is a picture of the sun at the horizon representing the gathering or condensing of light. When we combine the meaning of these two letters we have "water condensed". When the water of a pond condenses, such as dries up, the vegetation and fish that lived in that water die and begin to rot and stink. We know have a picture which will help us better understand the meaning of these words. One additional piece to the puzzle is the adopted root ●─ᴧᴧ◌ᴧ (TsMQ), an adopted root meaning "dry".

Many times the adopted roots alone can help to reconstruct the meaning of a Parent root. The original meaning of the parent root ᴚᴚᴏ (BHh) is very difficult to determine as the only word derived from it is the word ❦ᴚᴚᴏ◡ (av'hhah) from the child root ᴚᴚᴏ◡ (ABHh) meaning "sharp point". The adopted roots in Table 8 clearly show the original meaning of the parent root ᴚᴚᴏ as "slaughter" and the "point" is in reference to the knife that is used to slaughter.

Table 8

Hebrew	Meaning
ᴚᴚᴏ⊗	Slaughter
ᴚᴚᴏᴄ	Slaughter
ꝛᴚᴚᴏ	Choose (through the idea of choosing a sacrifice)
ꜱᴚᴚᴏ	Test (through the idea of testing for the choicest)
ꝛᴗᴏ*	Firstborn (the firstborn of the flock is chosen for sacrifice)

* - The letter ᴚᴚ has been exchanged for the similar sounding ᴗ

The Hebrew Language

Each root represents an action, an object that reflects the action and an abstract derived from the action of the object. The action is referred to as a verb while the object and abstract are referred to as nouns. The root ⱖⱓⱀⱄ (BRK) is the foundation to the verb ⱖⱓⱀⱄ (barak) meaning "to kneel" (action) and the noun ⱖⱓⱀⱄ (berek) meaning "knee" (object). The noun ⱖⱓⱀⱄⱦ (berakah) is derived from the root and can be a gift (object) or the abstract concept of a "blessing" in the sense of bringing a gift on bended knee.

Verbs

Hebrew verbs, like English verbs, describe action. Because the Hebrew language is an action oriented language rather than descriptive, it is prolific with verbs. When a Hebrew verb is conjugated in a sentence it identifies person, number, gender, tense, mood and voice. Understanding these different aspects of a verb is essential for proper interpretation of that verb.

Person
Each verb identifies the subject of the verb as first (I), second (you) or third (he) person.

Number
Each verb also indicates the subject of the verb as singular or plural (we, you or they).

Gender
Each verb also indicates the subject of the verb as masculine (he) or feminine (she).

Tense
There are four tenses in Hebrew verbs, perfect, imperfect, participle and imperative. In the English language the verb tenses are related to time; past, present and future, while the Hebrew verbs are all related to action. The perfect tense is a completed action and in most cases is related to the English past tense (he cut). The imperfect tense is an incomplete action and is closely related to the English present and future tenses (he cuts or he will cut). The participle can be a current action or one who performs the action (a cutting or cutter). The imperative identifies the action, similar to a command, with no reference to the subject (cut!). When the prefix ׳ (waw) meaning "and" is attached to

the verb, the verb tense (perfect or imperfect) reverses. For this reason this letter, when used in this context, is called the reversing or consecutive waw.

Voice

Each verb also includes voice of which there are three; active, passive or reflexive. The active voice identifies the action of the verb as coming from the subject (he cut). The passive voice does not identify the origin of action placed on the subject of the verb (he was cut). The reflexive voice places the action of the verb onto the subject (he cut himself).

Mood

Each verb also includes mood of which there are three; simple, intensive or causative. The simple mood is simple action of the verb (he cut). The intensive mood implies force or emphasis on the verb (he slashed or hacked). The causative mood expresses causation to the verb (he casued a cut).

The voice and mood of a verb is identified by seven different forms as shown in Table 9.

Table 9

Form	Mood	Voice	Example
Paal*	Simple	Active	He cut
Niphal	Simple	Passive	He was cut
Piel	Intensive	Active	He slashed
Pual	Intensive	Passive	He was slashed
Hiphil	Causative	Active	He made cut
Hophal	Causative	Passive	He was made cut
Hitpael	Intensive	Reflexive	He slashed himself

* Also called the "qal" form.

Verb Conjugations

While all of this appears complex and confusing at first it should be noted that the majority of the Hebrew verbs in the Bible are written in the paal form. It should also be noted that of these verbs most of them are written in the perfect tense, third person, masculine, singular, paal form.

Nouns

The most common noun form is the use of the two or three letter root. From the parent root אב (AB), meaning a tent pole, comes the noun אב (av) meaning "father". As was mentioned previously, all nouns are action oriented and the full understanding of the noun אב is "the one who holds up the tent/house". Just as the tent pole supports the tent, the father supports the family within the tent. The root פתח (PTHh) is the base for the verb פתח (patahh) meaning "to open" and the noun פתח (petahh) meaning a door.

Noun Derivatives

Additional nouns are also formed out of the base root by adding specific letters as prefixes, infixes and suffixes, in specific places within the root. The noun derivative מפתח (maph'teach) meaning a key is formed by adding the letter מ to the front of the noun פתח (petahh - a door). Some of the most common noun derivatives are formed by placing a מ(m) or ת(t) before the root or a י (i) or ו(o or u) within the root.

Feminine Derivatives

In Hebrew all nouns are either masculine or feminine. In most cases the nouns and noun derivatives are masculine and are converted into feminine nouns by adding one of four suffixes; ה (ah), ת (et), ות (owt), or ית (iyt). Generally, masculine nouns are concrete while feminine nouns are abstract.

Combination Derivatives

Additional noun derivatives are formed by combining different prefixes, infixes and suffixes. The four feminine suffixes can also be added to any of the other noun derivatives resulting in a wide variety of possible nouns.

Plural Nouns

Nouns are made plural by adding the suffix ים or ות. Generally the ים is used for masculine nouns and ות for feminine nouns. In some cases masculine words, usually very ancient words, will use the ות suffix. The Hebrew words אב (av - father) and אור (or - light) are masculine words but are written as אבות and אורות in the plural. In all modern languages the plural is always quantitative while in Ancient Hebrew a plural can be quantitative or qualitative. For instance the word "trees" refers to more than one tree (quantitative) while in Hebrew the plural word עצים (etsiym - trees) can mean more than one tree (quantitative) or one very large tree (qualitative). An example of this is the word בהמות (behemot or usually transliterated as behemoth in Job 40:15). This word is the plural form of the singular בהמה (behemah), meaning beast, but refers to a very large beast rather than more than one beast. One of the most common uses of the qualitative plural is the word ᴍᴫ>ᵗᵡᵞᶸᶀ (elohiym) which can be translated as "gods" (quantitative) or as "God" (qualitative).

Grammatical Tools

Hebrew uses nouns for other functions within the sentence. They can be used as adjectives, adverbs, prepositions, conjuctions, etc. The noun ⌂-•-◌ (eqev) can be the "heel" of the foot but, it can also mean "because" in the sense of being on the heel of the previous phrase. Because the Ancient Hebrew language does not make distinctions between these types of words the Lexicon lists them all as nouns and noun derivatives.

Determining the original meaning of Hebrew words

As it has been mentioned, Hebrew words are commonly defined from a western perspective. How is the original meaning of words from an Hebraic perspective determined? A Hebrew word that is often translated in an abstract manner will many times be used in a concrete manner somewhere in the text (most often in the book of Job, the oldest book of the Bible and therefore using the most ancient meanings of words). An example of this is the word ➤-ᴍᴫ (hhay). This word is usually translated as life but in one place, Job 38:39, this word is best translated as "stomach"; "Can you hunt the prey of the lion or fill the stomach of the young lion?". From this we see that life to the Ancient Hebrew is related to a full stomach.

By comparing the word in question with other words derived from the same or related roots the original meaning can be determined. The word ᴧᵡᵞᵁ (kohen) meaning "priest" is related to other words meaning base, foundation and level. From this we discover that the priests of the community are the foundation or the firm base of that community.

The pictographs also help to determine the original meaning of a word such as the Hebrew word for "mother", ᴍᴫᵞ (eym). The ᵞ is a picture of an ox representing strength and the ᴍᴫ is a picture of water. Combined these mean "strong water" or glue. The mother is understood by the ancient Hebrews as one who binds the family together.

Other devices used is to compare the use of this word with synonyms and antonyms in poetical passages, the context in which the word is used and the use of the word in other Semitic languages.

Letter Evolution

Over time words and their roots evolve. One of the most common evolutions of a word is an exchange for one sounding letter for another. All spoken sounds can be grouped into seven different categories. Table 10 below lists these categories and the letters that correspond to them.

Table 10

Category	Location	English	Hebrew
Labials	lip sounds	bfpvw	⌐Y<>
Dentals	tooth sounds	dt	+⊗⌐
Gutturals	throat sounds	ghjkqxy	⌐⌐⌐
Liquids	tounge sounds	lr	⌐ノ
Nasals	nose sounds	mn	⌐⌐
Fractives	whistle sounds	csz	⌐⌐
Vowels	breath sounds	aeiou	⌐Yⱷ⌐

This can be seen in many English words such as "vine" which is the origin of "wine" where the "w" is exchanged for the "v". The word "foot" comes from the ancient word "ped" meaning foot (as in pedal or pedestrian). This type of letter exchange occurs frequently in all languages including Hebrew.

Within the Biblical text we have the ancient parent root ⌐⌐ (zav) meaning "yellow". From this parent root two child roots are derived; ⌐⌐ (zahav) meaning "gold" and ⌐Y⌐ (zuv) meaning "puss", both being yellow in color. Another child root, ⌐⌐ (tsahav), also has the meaning "yellow" but, has no connection to the ancient parent root ⌐⌐ (tsav) meaning "wall". From this evidence we can conclude that ⌐⌐ is an evolved form of the root ⌐⌐. The letter ⌐ (ts) has replaced the ⌐ (z), both sounds being very similar.

Another common evolution is the replacement of letters. The Hebrew word ⌐ノ (lev) meaning heart has evolved into the Aramaic word ノ⌐ (bal), also meaning heart, by reversing the order of the letters.

In the *Ancient Hebrew Lexicon of the Bible* the original spelling of the words will be used. The spelling as found in the Biblical text will be listed under "defective spellings".

Ancient Hebrew Pronunciation

The following rules will assist the reader with pronouncing the Hebrew words without relying on the nikkud (vowel pointings) as used in most lexicons and dictionaries.

Spirants and Stops

A spirant is a letter whose sound can be prolonged. Some examples of this from the English language are the v, z, f, and sh. A stop is a letter whose sound ends abruptly such as the b, p, d and t. A few of the Hebrew letters will have a different pronunciation depending on their position within the word. The letter ⊔ will usually be pronounced as a stop (b) when at the beginning of the word and as a spirant (v) when it is anywhere else in the word. For example the word ꟼ⊔ is pronounced "bar" while the word ⊔ꟼ is pronounced "rav". Another letter that will change is the letter kaph - ⍗. When at the beginning of a word it will be pronounced as a stop (k), otherwise it will be pronounced as a spirant (kh – pronounced like the ch in the name Bach). The only other letter that will change is the letter pey - ⌒. When at the beginning of a word it will be a stop (p), otherwise it will be a spirant (ph).

Vowels

Four of the Hebrew letters double as consonants and vowels. These are the ⅄ (al), 𝚿 (hey), Ɣ (waw) and the ⊢ (yud). The al can be a glottal stop (silent pause) or the vowel sound "a". The hey is an "h" as a consonant or an "e" as a vowel. The waw is a "w" as a consonant or an "o" or "u" as a vowel. The yud is a "y" as a consonant or an "i' as a vowel. The waw and the yud are the two most commonly used as vowels in Hebrew words. When the waw appears at beginning of a syllable it will use the consonantal "w" sound. The same with the yud which will use the consonantal "y" when at beginning of a syllable.

Another type of vowel is the implied vowel sounds. This means that the vowel is not written but is necessary in order to pronounce the word. An example of this is the word ꟼ⊔ (grain) which consists of the two consonant B and R and cannot be pronounced without a vowel between them. In most cases the implied vowel will be an "a" or an "e". In this case the implied vowel is the "a" and the word ꟼ⊔ is pronounced "BaR".

Syllables

There are two types of syllables, open and closed. A closed syllable will include a consonant-vowel-consonant combination while an open syllable will have a vowel-consonant combination. The vowel may be one of the four consonant/vowel letters, usually the yud (I) or the waw (O or U) or an implied vowel. In most cases the final syllable will be a closed syllable. The word ⊢ꟼ⊔ (covenant) will have two syllables.

The first is ‎בֶ, an open syllable pronounced "be", and the second is ‎רִית, a closed syllable pronounced "riyt".

Generally a word with three consonants will be divided as Cv-CvC. A word with four consonants will be divided as Cv-Cv-CvC or CvC-CvC. When a word includes five consonants the breakdown is usually Cv-Cv-Cv-CvC or CvC-Cv-CvC.

If the word includes one of the four consonant/vowel letters, its position within the word will determine if it is used as a consonant or a vowel. Generally, when the consonant/vowel is placed at the beginning of a syllable or the end of a closed syllable it will take on the consonantal sound. When it is in the middle of a closed syllable or the end of an open syllable it will take on the vowel sound.

Masoretic Vowels

The Hebrew text of the Bible was originally written with only the twenty two letters of the Hebrew alphabet. About one thousand years ago a group called the Masorites created a system of dots and dashes called "nikkud" and placed them above and below the consonants to represent the vowels. It was discovered in the Dead Sea Scrolls that the four Hebrew letters, the al, hey, waw and yud, were used as vowels. The Masorites removed these vowels (usually the waw and yud) and replaced them with the nikkud. In Table 11 are some examples of Hebrew spellings of some Hebrew words in the Masoretic text and the Dead Sea Scrolls.

Table 11

Passage	Masoretic	Dead Sea Scroll	Translation
Isaiah 2:2	כֹּל	כול	All
Isaiah 2:3	אֱלֹהֵי יַעֲקֹב	אלוהי יעקוב	God of Jacob
Isaiah 2:4	וְלֹא	ולוא	And not

The Hebrew words in this lexicon have re-inserted the waw and yud wherever the nikkud pointings for the "o", "u" and "i" appear. This is to restore the spelling of Hebrew words based on the original vowels of Hebrew words rather than the nikkud.

Because the nikkud are of fairly recent origin and not part of the original Hebrew text they are not included in the *Ancient Hebrew Lexicon of the Bible*. In many cases the nikkud can be misleading causing one to rely more on them then on the consonants themselves for the meaning of the word.

Transliterations

Some words in the Lexicon are transliterated rather than translated such as the names of unknown minerals, plants and animals, instruments and all weights and measures. The method for transliterating Hebrew letters is defined in Table 12.

Table 12

Hebrew	English	Pronunciation
ⵏ	a e	father egg
⌶	b v	bat vine
⌶	g	good
⌐	d	dog
ⵌ	h	high
Y	w o u	water old tune
⌐	z	zebra
⌶	hh	Bach
⊗	th	bath
ⵏ	y i	yellow fly
�障	k kh	kite Bach
⌡	l	line
ⵥ	m	man
ⵝ	n	name
⵰	s	sign
ⵔ	ah	*silent*
ⵐ	p ph	pan phone
ⵀ	ts	pots
ⵐ	q	kite
ⵍ	r	rain
ⵖ	sh	shout
✝	t	time
ⵠ	gh	ring

Lexicon Format

Parent and Adopted Root Format

1345)   Each two letter Parent Root is identified by a four number digit ranging from 1001 to 1529. Each three letter Adopted root is identified by a four number digit ranging from 2001 to 2910. Each four letter Adopted root is identified by a four number digit ranging from 3001 to 3067. These numbers correspond to the alphabetical order of the root.

 עלם   Following the Parent or Adopted Root number is the Hebrew root written in the ancient pictographic script.

(אב AB)   The same root written in modern Hebrew script and transliterated into Roman characters using the following transliterations.

	א	A		ט	Th		ף	P
	ב	B		י	Y		ץ	Ts
	ג	G		כ	K		ק	Q
	ד	D		ל	L		ר	R
	ה	H		ם	M		ש	Sh
	ו	W		ן	N		ת	T
	ז	Z		ס	S		ע	Gh
	ח	Hh		ע	Ah			

ac: **Twist**   The action definition of the root.

co: **Root**   The concrete definition of the root.

ab: **Perverse**   The abstract definition of the root.

[from: ◯⊞]   The possible Parent root origin of the Adopted Root. (Used only with the Adopted Root entries)

(eng: ankle)   English words that are closely associated to a word or words derived from the parent root. These words may or may not actually be derived from the Hebrew but are added as familiar associations for Hebrew word recall.

Adopted Roots;   Following the Parent and Child Roots is a list of Adopted Roots derived out of the Parent Root. This list includes the Adopted Root number, the Adopted Root and the known action, concrete and abstract definitions of the Adopted Root.

Child Root Format

B)   Each child root is identified by a letter ranging from A to N. Child roots designated as "A" are words derived from the Parent root itself. Child roots designated as "B" are words derived by doubling the second letter of the Parent. Child roots with designations C thru N are derived by adding one of the four consonant/vowels within the root.

A-	GD	E-	AGD	I-	GDW	M-	GYD
B-	GDD	F-	GDH	J-	GWD	N-	YGD
C-	GDA	G-	GHD	K-	WGD		
D-	GAD	H-	HGD	L-	GDY		

𐤌𐤋𐤑   Following the Child Root designator is the Hebrew root in the ancient pictographic script.

(בזא BZA)   The same word written in modern Hebrew script and transliterated into Roman characters.

ac: **Twist**   The action definition of the root.

co: **Root**   The concrete definition of the root.

ab: **Perverse**   The abstract definition of the root.

Word Format

V, N or a	An upper case "V" represents a verb. An upper case "N" represents a base noun. Lower case letters "a" thru "t" represent a noun derivative. The letter "a" represents the most frequent noun derivative while the letter "t" represents the least frequent noun derivative.

a-	xxxמ[1]	f-	יxxx	k-	xxxמ[6]	p-	בxxx
b-	xיxx	g-	xxיx[4]	l-	XXxxx[7]	q-	יxxx[9]
c-	xיxx[2]	h-	xxxמ[5]	m-	ןxxx	r-	יxxx[10]
d-	xיxx[3]	i-	xxxה	n-	xxxא	s-	ןיxxx
e-	xxיx	j-	ןיxxx	o-	xxיx[8]	t-	xxxי

1- This prefix is pronounced mah.
2- This infix is pronounced o.
3- This infix is pronounced u.
4- This infix is pronounced o.
5- This prefix is pronounced miy.
6- This prefix is pronounced meh.

7- This deriviative is formed by doubling the last or last two letters of the root.
8- This infix is pronounced u.
9- This suffix is pronounced o.
10- This suffix is pronounced u.

ᵐ, ᶠ or ᵐ/ᶠ	The superscript "m" identifies the noun as masculine. The superscript "f" identifies the noun as feminine. A superscript "m/f" indicates the noun can be either masculine or feminine.
¹, ², ³ or ⁴	This superscript number following a superscript "f" identifies the feminine noun is written with one of the four feminine suffixes.

ᶠ¹-	הxxx	ᶠ²-	תxxx	ᶠ³-	תיxxx	ᶠ⁴-	תיxxx

ᵚᶥᶜᵗᵒᵍʳᵃᵖʰ	The word written in the ancient pictographic script.
(בריאה B-RY-AH)	The same word written in modern Hebrew script and transliterated into Roman characters with hyphens to divide the syllables.
— Fill:	A one or two word definition of the word. When necessary this definition is followed by a more specific definition.
I. II. III. IV.	Occasionally one Hebrew word may have more than one meaning. In this case each definition is preceded by a Roman Numeral.
[ms: אם]	Where the Masoretic text of the Bible has removed one of the consonant vowels and replaced it with one of the nikkud (vowel pointings), the Masoretic spelling of the word is written here.
[df: גן]	Defective spellings of this Hebrew word are written here.

47

[ar: אשׁא]   The Aramaic language occasionally spells the word differently than Hebrew. The Aramaic spellings are listed here.

[freq. 54]   The frequency that this Hebrew word is used in the Hebrew Bible.

(vf: Paal, Hiphil)   Verb forms used in the Hebrew Bible for this verb.

|kjv: grain, clean| The translations of this Hebrew word used in the King James Version.

{str: 1322}   The Strong's number/s corresponding to this Hebrew word.

The Lexicon

Parent and Child Roots

Al

1001) לל (אא AA) ac: ? co: ? ab: ?

~~~~~~~~~~

1002) לם (אב AB) ac: **Stand** co: **Pole** ab: ?: The pictograph ל represents strength, the ם represents the tent. Combined these mean "the strength of the house". This can be the tent poles which hold up the tent, the house, as well as the father who holds up the family, the household. (eng: pa - an exchange from a b and p and a reversal of the letters)

A) לם (אב AB) ac: ? co: **Pole** ab: ?: The support of the tent/house.

N^m) לם (אב AB) — **I. Fruit:** This word can also be fresh fruit, the father of the next generation of trees attached to the tree (pole). [Hebrew and Aramaic] **II. Father:** The father of the family provides the strength, support and structure to the household. The father fulfilled many functions for the family. He was the commander of the family army, provider of offspring to continue the family line, the priest and teacher. A father can be of the immediate family or a lineage such as Jacob who is the father of the

Israelites. A father can also be the patron of a profession or art. [Hebrew and Aramaic] [freq. 1229] |kjv: father, chief, families, desire, patrimony, prince, principle, greenness, fruit| {str: 1, 2, 3, 4}

N^{f1}) לםꚛ (אבה A-BH) — **Desire:** The desires of the father. [freq. 1] |kjv: desire| {str: 15}

B) לםם (אבב ABB) ac: ? co: **Grain** ab: ?

b^m) לםהם (אביב A-BYB) — **Green Grain:** The new green ears of growing grain as the parent seeds attached to the stalk (pole) of the next generation of crops. Also Abib, the name of a month in the Hebrew calendar. [freq. 8] |kjv: abib, corn| {str: 24}

J) לYם (אוב AWB) ac: ? co: **Wineskin** ab: ?: The wineskin hangs from the tent pole. A spiritist (possibly from their mumbling like the sound of wine poured out of the wineskin)

N^m) לYם (אוב AWB) — **I. Wineskin:** A leather bag that holds wine and is hung from the pole of the tent. **II. Medium:**

One who evokes the dead, a ghost, possibly from their mumbling like the sound of wine poured out of the wineskin. [freq. 17] |kjv: bottle, familiar spirit| {str: 178}

L) יאב (יאב YAB) ac: **Desire** co: ? ab: ?: The firm standing of the tent pole.

V) יאב (יאב Y-AB) — **Desire**: A standing firm for what is desired. [freq. 1] (vf: Paal) |kjv: long| {str: 2968}

M) איב (איב AYB) ac: **Hostile** co: **Spear** ab: **Enemy**: The tent pole is pointed at one end and doubles as a spear which can be used against an enemy to defend (also a support of) the family.

V) איב (איב AYB) — **Hostile**: To be hostile to another as an enemy. [freq. 1] (vf: Paal) |kjv: enemy| {str: 340}

N^(f1)) איבה (איבה AY-BH) — **Hostility**: [freq. 5] |kjv: enemy, hatred| {str: 342}

g^(m)) אויב (אויב AW-YB) — **Enemy**: [ms: איב] [freq. 282] |kjv: enemy, foe| {str: 341}

1003) לג (אג AG) ac: ? co: ? ab: ?

1004) לד (אד AD) ac: ? co: **Smoke** ab: ?: (eng: wood)

A) לד (אד AD) ac: ? co: **Mist** ab: ?: An overwhelming abundance of ash raked in the fire causing a cloud of dust.

N^(m)) לד (אד AD) — **Mist**: A misty vapor. [freq. 2] |kjv: mist, vapor| {str: 108}

J) אוד (אוד AWD) ac: ? co: **Charcoal** ab: ?: The abundant remnants of charred wood from a fire that is raked together causing a cloud of ash.

N^(m)) אוד (אוד AWD) — **Charcoal**: The wood remnants of a fire. [freq. 3] |kjv: firebrand, brand, because, cause, concerning| {str: 181}

N^(f3)) אודות (אודות AW-DWT) — **Because**: A turning over and bringing together of a thought. [ms: אדות] [freq. 11] |kjv: very, greatly, sore, exceedingly, great, much, diligently, good, might| {str: 182}

k^(m)) מאוד (מאוד M-AWD) — **Many**: An abundance of things (many, much, great), action (complete, wholly, strong, quick) or character (very). [ms: מאד] [freq. 299] |kjv: very, greatly, sore, exceedingly, great, much, diligently, good, might| {str: 3966}

M) איד (איד AYD) ac: ? co: **Heap** ab: ?: A pile of charred wood and ash as the remnants of a fire.

N^(m)) איד (איד AYD) — **Heap**: A pile of rubble from a fire or other calamity. [freq. 24] |kjv: calamity, destruction| {str: 343}

1005) לה (אה AH) ac: **Sigh** co: **Sigher** ab: **Where**: The pictograph ל represents strength of the ox. The 𐤀 is one looking at a great sight and sighing. Combined they mean "a strong sigh". This can be a sigh when searching as when the ox snorts when desiring food. This root is closely related to ל𐤀. (eng: ah; woe)

A) 𐤏 (אה AH) ac: **Sigh** co: ? ab:
?: The howling of one searching.

N^m) 𐤏 (אה AH) — **Ah:** The
sigh of one in exclamation out of
a desire. [df: אי אה] [freq. 4]
|kjv: ah, alas, woe| {str: 253,
337, 338}

B) 𐤏 (אהה AHH) ac: **Sigh** co:
? ab: ?: A screaming out of pain.

N^m) 𐤏 (אהה A-HH) — **Ah:**
[freq. 15] |kjv: ah, alas| {str:
162}

D) 𐤏 (יאה YAH) ac: **Desire** co:
? ab: ?: Rightful ownership of what
is desired.

V) 𐤏 (יאה Y-AH) —
Belong: [freq. 1] (vf: Paal) |kjv:
appertain| {str: 2969}

J) 𐤏 (אוה AWH) ac: **Sigh** co: ?
ab: **Desire:** A sigh out of a desire.

V) 𐤏 (אוה AWH) —
Desire: [freq. 26] (vf: Hitpael,
Piel) |kjv: desire, longing, covet,
lust, point out| {str: 183}

i^{f1}) 𐤏 (תאוה TA-WH) —
Desire: What is good or bad,
that is desired. [freq. 20] |kjv:
desire, lust, greedily| {str: 8378}

M) 𐤏 (איה AYH) ac: ? co:
Hawk ab: ?: A bird that flies high
searching for food and screeches as a
loud sigh.

N^f) 𐤏 (איה AYH) —
Hawk: [freq. 3] |kjv: kite,
vulture| {str: 344}

1006) 𐤏 (או AW) ac: ? co: ? ab:
Desire: The pictograph Y, replacing the
𐤀, is a peg representing the idea of
attaching something. This root has the
idea of adding something out of desire.

This root is closely related to the root
𐤏. (eng: or - with an added r)

A) 𐤏 (או AW) ac: **Desire** co: ? ab:
?

N^m) 𐤏 (או AW) — **Or:** An
alternative or optional desire.
[freq. 21] |kjv: also, and, desire,
either, least, nor, or, otherwise,
should, then, whether| {str: 176}

N^{f1}) 𐤏 (אוה A-WH) —
Desire: What is good or bad,
that is desired. [freq. 7] |kjv:
desire, lust after, pleasure| {str:
185}

f^m) 𐤏 (אוי A-WY) — **Oh:** A
passionate cry of desire. [freq.
24] |kjv: woe, alas| {str: 188}

f^{f1}) 𐤏 (אויה AW-YH) —
Woe: A passionate cry of desire.
[freq. 1] |kjv: woe| {str: 190}

af^m) 𐤏 (מאוי M-AWY)
— **Desire:** What is desired.
[freq. 1] |kjv: desires| {str: 3970}

H) 𐤏 (אוה AWH) ac: **Point** co:
? ab: ?

V) 𐤏 (אוה A-WH) —
Point: To point out what is
desired. [freq. 1] (vf: Hitpael)
|kjv: point| {str: 184}

1007) 𐤏 (אז AZ) ac: ? co: ? ab:
Time: The letter ᴢ represents an
agricultural implement of cutting used in
the harvest. The harvest is a very
prominent "time" to the early Hebrews.

A) 𐤏 (אז AZ) ac: ? co: ? ab: ?:
A specific time.

N^m) 𐤏 (אז AZ) — **At That
Time:** A point in time. [freq. 22]
|kjv: beginning, even, for, from,

hitherto, now, old, since, then, time, when, yet| {str: 227}

f^m) אזי (אזי A-ZY) — **At That Time:** A point in time. [freq. 3] |kjv: then| {str: 233}

~~~~~~~~

1008) אח (אח AHh) ac: **Protect** co: **Hearth** ab: **Brotherhood:** The pictograph אל represents strength. The חm is a wall. Combined these pictographs mean "strong wall". In Hebrew thought, a wall is more than a vertical barrier but anything that separates or divides. The hearth around the fire protected the house from the heat and embers of the fire.

A) אח (אח AHh) ac: **?** co: **Hearth** ab: **?**

    N^f) אח (אח AHh) — **I. Hearth:** A dividing wall that protects the family from the fire. **II. Brother:** One who stands between the enemy and the family, a protector. [Hebrew and Aramaic] [freq. 634] |kjv: brethren, brother, another, brotherly, kindred, hearth| {str: 251, 252, 254}

    N^f3) אחות (אחות A-HhWT) — **Sister:** [freq. 114] |kjv: sister, another| {str: 269}

    r^m) אחו (אחו A-HhW) — **Marsh Grass:** The tall grasses that line a marsh as a wall. [freq. 3] |kjv: meadow, flag| {str: 260}

J) אוח (אוח AWHh) ac: **?** co: **?** ab: **?**

    N^m) אוח (אוח AWHh) — **Oahh:** An unknown animal. [freq. 1] |kjv: creature| {str: 255}

K) אחו (אחו AHhW) ac: **?** co: **Hearth** ab: **?**

N^fl) אחוה (אחוה A-HhWH) — **Brotherhood:** A company of brothers. [freq. 1] |kjv: brotherhood| {str: 264}

~~~~~~~~

1009) אט (אט ATh) ac: **?** co: **Corral** ab: **Gentle:** The pictograph אל is an ox head. The ⊗ is a basket as used to contain something. Combined these mean "ox contained" in the sense of being tamed or gentle. The idea that one that can be rough and harsh but acts in a gentle manner.

A) אט (אט ATh) ac: **?** co: **?** ab: **Gentle**

    N^m) אט (אט ATh) — **I. Gentle:** To act gently or soft. **II. Charmer:** One who gentles a snake. [freq. 6] |kjv: softly, charmers, gently, secret| {str: 328}

~~~~~~~~

1010) אי (אי AY) ac: **?** co: **Place** ab: **Where:** The pictograph אל, replacing the 𐤉, is the hand and adds the idea of pointing to a place. This root is closely related to the root אי.

A) אי (אי AY) ac: **?** co: **?** ab: **Where:** A search for an unknown location.

    N^m) אי (אי AY) — **I. Where: II. Iy:** An unknown animal. [freq. 20] |kjv: where, what, whence, beast| {str: 335, 336, 338}

G) אהי (אהי AHY) ac: **?** co: **?** ab: **Where:** A search for an unknown location.

    N^m) אהי (אהי A-HY) — **Where:** [freq. 3] |kjv: will| {str: 165}

H) אֵיֹה (איה AYH) ac: ? co: ? ab: **Where:** A search for an unknown location.

N^m) אֵיֹה (איה A-YH) — **Where:** [df: איכוה איך הִיך] [freq. 15] |kjv: where, how, what| {str: 346, 349, 351, 1963}

~~~~~~~~

1011) עֵשׁ (אָך AK) ac: ? co: ? ab: ?

~~~~~~~~

1012) עֵל (אל AL) ac: **Yoke** co: **Ox** ab: **Strength:** The pictograph ע is a picture of an ox head and also represents its strength. The ל is a picture of a shepherd staff and also represents the authority of the shepherd. Combined these two pictographs mean "the strong authority" and can be anyone or thing of strong authority. The yoke is understood as a "staff on the shoulders" (see Isaiah 9:4) in order to harness their power for pulling loads such as a wagon or plow. Hence, the two pictographs can also represent "the ox in the yoke". Often two oxen were yoked together. An older, more experienced ox would be teamed up (yoked) with a younger, less experienced ox. The older ox in the yoke is the "strong authority" who, through the yoke, teaches the younger ox. (eng: all; elk; elephant)

A) עֵל (אל AL) ac: ? co: **Ox** ab: **Oath:** The power of the oxs muscles to perform work.

N^m) עֵל (אל AL) — **Power:** One who holds authority over others such as judges, chiefs and gods. In the sense of being yoked to one another. [freq. 245] |kjv: God, god, power, mighty, goodly, great, idols, strong, unto, with, against, at, into, in, before, to, of, upon, by, toward, hath,

for, on, beside, from, where, after, within| {str: 410}

N^{f1}) עֵלֹה (אלה A-LH) — **I. Oath:** A binding agreement including the curse for violating the oath. **II. Oak:** The strongest of the woods. [freq. 50] |kjv: oak, elm, teil tree, curse, oath, execration, swearing| {str: 423, 424, 427}

b^{f1}) אֵלִיֹה (אליה AL-YH) — **Fat-tail:** The fat part of a sheeps rump considered an Eastern delicacy. [freq. 5] |kjv: rump| {str: 451}

i^{f1}) תֵּאֵלֹה (תאלה TA-LH) — **Curse:** [freq. 1] |kjv: curse| {str: 8381}

j^m) אֵלֹוּן (אלון A-LWN) — **Oak:** The strongest of the woods. [freq. 17] |kjv: plain, oak| {str: 436, 437}

H) אֵלֹה (אלה ALH) ac: **Swear** co: **Yoke** ab: **?:** The yoking together of two parties. A treaty or covenant binds two parties together through an oath (yoke). The oath included blessings for abiding by the covenant and curses for breaking the covenant (see Deuteronomy 28). The God of the Hebrews was seen as the older ox that is yoked to his people in a covenant relationship.

V) אֵלֹה (אלה A-LH) — **I. Swear:** The placing of oneself in a binding agreement to a course of action including a curse for violating the oath. **II. Lament:** A wailing like the making of an oath. [freq. 7] (vf: Paal, Hiphil) |kjv: swear, curse, adjure, lament| {str: 421, 422}

N^m) אֵלֹה (אלה A-LH) — **Power:** The power or might of one who rules or teaches. One who yokes with another. Often applied to rulers or a god. [Aramaic only] [freq. 95] |kjv: god| {str: 426}

cᵐ) אלוה (אלוה A-LWH) — **Power:** The power or might of one who rules or teaches. One who yokes with another. Often applied to rulers or a god. [Hebrew and Aramaic] [df: אלה] [freq. 2663] |kjv: God, god, heathen deity| {str: 430, 433}

J) אול (אול AWL) ac: ? co: ? ab: **Strength:** The strength of the ox.

Nᵐ) אול (אול AWL) — **Strength:** [freq. 2] |kjv: mighty, strength| {str: 193}

L) יאל (יאל YAL) ac: ? co: **Yoke** ab: ?: The placing of the yoke upon the shoulders to perform a task.

V) יאל (יאל Y-AL) — **Yoke:** The placing of a yoke on the shoulders to perform work or undertake a task. [freq. 19] (vf: Hiphil) |kjv: content, please, would, taken upon me, began, assayed, willingly| {str: 2974}

M) איל (איל AYL) ac: ? co: **Ox** ab: **Strength:** Anyone or anything that functions as the "strong authority" is seen as the older ox. Such as a ram or stag deer (the strong leader of the flock or heard), chief (strong leader of the tribe), pillar (as the strong support of a building), oak tree (one of the strongest of the woods).

Nᵐ) איל (איל AYL) — **Strong One:** Anyone or thing that functions with strength like an ox. This can be a ram or stag (as strong leaders), chief, pillar

(as the strong support of a building), or oak tree (one of the strongest of the woods) [freq. 197] |kjv: ram, post, mighty, tree, lintel, oak, strength, hart| {str: 352, 353, 354}

Nᶠˡ) אילה (אילה AY-LH) — **Strong One:** The feminine form of anyone or thing that functions with strength. [freq. 8] |kjv: hind| {str: 355}

Nᶠ³) אילות (אילות AY-LWT) — **Strength:** [freq. 1] |kjv: strength| {str: 360}

mᵐ) אילן (אילן AY-LN) — **Tree:** [Aramaic only] [freq. 6] |kjv: tree| {str: 363}

pᵐ) אילם (אילם AY-LM) — **Arch:** The arch is the strongest architectural design for an entry through a building or wall. [ms: אלם] [freq. 15] |kjv: arch| {str: 361}

Adopted Roots;
2001 אול Guide, Yoke, Learn

1013) אם (אם AM) ac: **Bind** co: **Glue** ab: ?: The pictograph ל represents strength. The אם is water or any other liquid. Combined these pictographs mean "strong liquid". Glue was made by placing the hides and other animal parts of slaughtered animals in a pot of boiling water. As the hide boiled, a thick sticky substance formed at the surface of the water. This substance was removed and used as a binding agent. (eng: arm - with the addition of the r sound)

A) אם (אם AM) ac: ? co: **Arm** ab: ?: The arm that holds things together. The arm is seen as glue that encircles and holds together. A cubit was the length of the arm from elbow to fingertip. The mother of the family is the one who binds the family together by holding in her arms and by the work of her arms.

N^f) אמ (אם AM) — **Mother:** One whose arms hold the family together through her work and love. Also one who fulfills the role of a mother. [freq. 220] |kjv: mother, dam| {str: 517}

N^{f1}) אמה (אמה A-MH) — **I. Cubit:** A linear standard of measure equal to the length of the forearm. [Hebrew and Aramaic] **II. Bondwoman:** One who is bound to another. [freq. 304] |kjv: cubit, measure, post, handmaid, maidservant, maid, bondwoman, bondmaids| {str: 519, 520, 521}

j^m) אמון (אמון A-MWN) — **Craftsman:** An architect or artisan who uses the cubit for measuring. [freq. 3] |kjv: multitude, populace| {str: 527}

J) אום (אום AWM) ac: **Bind** co: **Tribe** ab: ?: A binding together.

N^{f1}) אומה (אומה AW-MH) — **Tribe:** A family lineage bound together. [Hebrew and Aramaic] [ms: אמה] [freq. 11] |kjv: people, nation| {str: 523, 524}

M) אים (אים AYM) ac: ? co: **Glue** ab: ?

N^m) אים (אים AYM) — **If:** A desire to bind two ideas together. [ms: אם] [freq. 43] |kjv: if, not, or, when, whether, doubtless, while, neither, saving| {str: 518}

~~~~~~~~~~

1014) אן (אן AN) ac: **Produce** co: **Produce** ab: ?: The pictograph ל represents the ox. The נ is a picture of a seed (plant, animal or man). The male searches out the female and approaches her for reproducing (see Jeremiah 2:24). This can also be a search for the purpose of producing something.

A) אן (אן AN) ac: ? co: **Ship** ab: **Where:** A ship searches through the sea for a distant coastline (of an island or mainland) in search of the produce for trade. The fig tree produces fruit that is desirable and prolific, since the fig is green and blends in with the leaves, the fruit must be searched out. The searching may result in success or failure.

N^m) אן (אן AN) — **Where:** A search for a place. [ms: אנה] [freq. 8] |kjv: whither, how, where, whithersoever, hither| {str: 575}

a^m) מהאן (מהאן MH-AN) — **Bowl:** As the shape of a ship. [Aramaic only] [freq. 7] |kjv: vessel| {str: 3984}

f^m) אני (אני A-NY) — **I. Ship:** A ship searches through the sea for a distant shore. **II. Island:** As the destination of a ship. [df: אי] [freq. 43] |kjv: ship, isle, island, country| {str: 339, 590}

f^{f1}) אניה (אניה AN-YH) — **Ship:** As searching through the sea for a distant shore. [freq. 32] |kjv: ship| {str: 591}

i^f) תאן (תאן T-AN) — **Fig:** The tree or fruit. A desirable and prolific fruit that must be searched for as the fruit is green, blending in with the leaves making it difficult to see. [freq. 39] |kjv: fig tree, fig| {str: 8384}

i^fl) 𐤚𐤍𐤀𐤕 (תאנה TA-NH) — **Occasion:** The time of sexual urges when the male searches out the female and approaches her for reproducing. This word can also be applied to any occasion as a result of searching. [df: תואנה] [freq. 2] |kjv: occasion| {str: 8385}

B) 𐤍𐤍𐤀 (אנן ANN) ac: ? co: ? ab: **Complain:** A complaining from a lack of production. (

V) 𐤍𐤍𐤀 (אנן A-NN) — **Complain:** [freq. 2] (vf: Hitpael) |kjv: complain| {str: 596}

H) 𐤚𐤍𐤀 (אנה ANH) ac: **Meet** co: ? ab: ?: The seeking out of another to meet with. A chance encounter or an arrival to another.

V) 𐤚𐤍𐤀 (אנה A-NH) — **Send:** The sending of one for an encounter. [freq. 4] (vf: Hitpael, Pual, Piel) |kjv: deliver| {str: 579}

i^fl) 𐤚𐤍𐤀𐤕 (תאנה TA-NH) — **Occasion:** The time of sexual urges when the male searches out the female and approaches her for reproducing. This word can also be applied to any occasion as a result of searching. [df: תואנה] [freq. 2] |kjv: occasion| {str: 8385}

J) 𐤍𐤅𐤀 (און AWN) ac: ? co: **Produce** ab: **Vigor**

N^m) 𐤍𐤅𐤀 (און AWN) — **I. Vigor:** The power within the belly, or loins, for reproduction or creative work. **II. Vanity:** The use of the power within the loins for vain or other improper

purposes. [freq. 90] |kjv: strength, might, force, goods, substance, iniquity, wicked, vanity, affliction, mischief, unrighteous| {str: 202, 205}

i^m) 𐤍𐤅𐤀𐤕 (תאון T-AWN) — **Toil:** An exhaustive work. [ms: תאן] [freq. 1] |kjv: lies| {str: 8383}

M) 𐤍𐤉𐤀 (אין AYN) ac: ? co: ? ab: **Nothing:** A search or work with no results.

N^m) 𐤍𐤉𐤀 (אין AYN) — **I. Without:** A lacking of something or the inability to do or have something. **II. Where:** The search for a place of unknown origin. [freq. 47] |kjv: except, fail, fatherless, incurable, infinite, innumerable, neither, never, no, none, not, nothing, nought, without, there not, where, whence| {str: 369, 370, 371}

~~~~~~~~~

1015) 𐤔𐤀 (אס AS) ac: ? co: ? ab: ?

~~~~~~~~~

1016) 𐤏𐤀 (אע AAh) ac: ? co: ? ab: ?

~~~~~~~~~

1017) 𐤐𐤀 (אף AP) ac: ? co: **Nose** ab: **Anger:** The pictograph 𐤏 represents strength. The ⌐ is a picture of the mouth and represents any type of hole. The nostrils (holes) are for breathing.

A) 𐤐𐤀 (אף AP) ac: ? co: **Nose** ab: ?: The nostrils of man flares when he breathes heavy in passion or anger.

N^m) 𐤐𐤀 (אף AP) — **I. Nose:** The nose and nostrils when written in the plural form. **II.**

Anger: The flaring of the nostrils in anger. **III. Moreover:** Greater in addition to something else in the sense of passion. [Aramaic only] [freq. 297] |kjv: anger, wrath, face, nostrils, nose, angry, before, also, even, yet, moreover, yea, with, low, therefore, much| {str: 637, 638, 639}

H) ✤⟩⟨ (אפה APH) ac: **Bake** co: **Oven** ab: ?: A heat for baking. The heat of anger.

V) ✤⟩⟨ (אפה A-PH) — **Bake:** The baking of something in an oven. [freq. 25] (vf: Paal, Niphal) |kjv: bake, baker| {str: 644}

aᵐ) ✤⟩⟨ᴍ (מאפה MA-PH) — **Baked:** What is baked. [freq. 1] |kjv: baken| {str: 3989}

J) ⟩Y⟨ (אוף AWP) ac: **Bake** co: **Hot** ab: ?: The heat of passion. The heating of foods.

isᵐ) ⟩⟨Y⟩⟨† (תאופין T-AW-PYN) — **Baked:** Something baked. [df: תפין] [freq. 1] |kjv: baken| {str: 8601}

M) ⟩⟨ (איף AYP) ac: ? co: ? ab: ?: [Unknown meaning;]

Nᶠˡ) ✤⟩⟨ (איפה AY-PH) — **Ephah:** A standard of measure. [ms: אפה] [freq. 40] |kjv: ephah, measure| {str: 374}

Adopted Roots;
2002 ⟩⟨ Snort, Breath
2377 ⟩⟨ Strike

1018) ⟨⟩⟨ (אץ ATs) ac: **Press** co: **Narrow** ab: ?: The letter ⟨ayin⟩ represents

the side as in the sides of a ravine. A narrow ravine where the walls press in.

J) ⟨Y⟩⟨ (אוץ AWTs) ac: ? co: **Press** ab: ?: The pressing into or on something causing it to move.

V) ⟨Y⟩⟨ (אוץ AWTs) — **Press:** A pressing into something. [freq. 10] (vf: Paal, Hiphil) |kjv: haste, narrow| {str: 213}

~~~~~~~~

1019) ⟨⟩⟨ (אק AQ) ac: ? co: ? ab: ?

A) ⟨⟩⟨ (אק AQ) ac: ? co: **Wild goat** ab: ?

qᵐ) Y⟨⟩⟨ (אקו A-QW) — **Wild goat:** [freq. 1] |kjv: wild goat| {str: 689}

~~~~~~~~

1020) ⟨⟩⟨ (אר AR) ac: **Order** co: **Box** ab: ?: Boxes are used to store items and keep them in order. Light is also necessary for order. (eng: order - with the addition of "der" also meaning order in Hebrew)

H) ✤⟨⟩⟨ (ארה ARH) ac: **Gather** co: **Box** ab: ?: A gathering of items or livestock to place in a box or pen.

V) ✤⟨⟩⟨ (ארה A-RH) — **Gather:** To gather up something to place in a box or other container. [freq. 2] (vf: Paal) |kjv: pluck, gather| {str: 717}

Nᶠˡ) ✤⟨Y⟩⟨ (אורה AW-RH) — **Stall:** A box for the livestock. [freq. 1] |kjv: cote| {str: 220}

fˡ) ✤⟩⟨⟩⟨ (אריה AR-YH) — **Stall:** A box for the livestock. [df: ארוה] [freq. 3] |kjv: stall| {str: 723}

jᵐ) ⟨Y⟩⟨ (ארון A-RWN) — **Box:** Any boxed shaped object.

[ms: ‎אָרָן‎] [freq. 202] |kjv: ark, chest, coffin| {str: 727}

J) ‎לאֵוֹ‎ (‎אוֹר‎ AWR) ac: ? co: **Light** ab: ?

V) ‎לאֵוֹ‎ (‎אוֹר‎ AWR) — **Light:** To be light or bright. [freq. 43] (vf: Paal, Niphal, Hiphil) |kjv: light, enlightened| {str: 215}

N^f) ‎לאֵוֹ‎ (‎אוֹר‎ AWR) — **Light:** The light from the sun, moon, stars, fire, candle or other giver of light [freq. 129] |kjv: light, fire, day, bright, clear, lightning, morning, sun {str: 216, 217}

N^{fl}) ‎לאֵוֹ‎פ‎ (‎אוֹרה‎ AW-RH) — **Light:** [freq. 4] |kjv: herbs, light| {str: 219}

a^m) ‎לאֵוֹ‎מ‎ (‎מאוֹר‎ M-AWR) — **Light:** What gives off light. [ms: ‎מאֹר‎] [freq. 19] |kjv: light, bright| {str: 3974}

k^{fl}) ‎לאֵוֹ‎פ‎מ‎ (‎מאוֹרה‎ M-AW-RH) — **Den:** The entrance has a lighted hole when viewed from inside. [freq. 1] |kjv: den| {str: 3975}

~~~~~~~~~~

1021) ‎לוּ‎ (‎אש‎ ASh) ac: **Press** co: **Fire** ab: **Despair:** The pictograph ‎לֹ‎ represents strength. The ‎וַ‎ is a picture of teeth and imply pressing as one does with the teeth to chew food. Combined these pictures mean "a strong pressing down". A fire is made by firmly pressing a wooden rod down onto a wooden board and spinning the rod with a bow drill. Wood dust is generated from the two woods rubbing together and is heated by the friction creating a small ember in the dust. Small tinder is then placed on the ember and is blown ignited the tinder. (eng: ash - as the product of fire)

A) ‎לוּ‎ (‎אש‎ ASh) ac: ? co: **Fire** ab: ?: The pressing of wood together with a fire drill to produce fire through friction.

N^f) ‎לוּ‎ (‎אש‎ ASh) — **Fire:** [Hebrew and Aramaic] [ar: ‎אשּׁא‎] [freq. 380] |kjv: fire, burning, fiery, flaming, hot| {str: 784, 785}

N^{fl}) ‎לוּ‎פ‎ (‎אשה‎ A-ShH) — **Fire:** A fire as well as an offering made by fire. [freq. 1] |kjv: fire| {str: 800}

j^m) ‎לוּ‎ל‎ (‎אשוׁן‎ A-ShWN) — **Furnace:** [Aramaic only] [ar: ‎אתּוׁן‎] [freq. 10] |kjv: furnace| {str: 861}

B) ‎לוּוּ‎ (‎אשש‎ AShSh) ac: **Press** co: **Foundation** ab: **Pressure:** The firm pressing down on something.

b^f) ‎לוּל-וּ‎ (‎אשיש‎ A-ShYSh) — **Foundation:** The pressing down of the soil to form a firm and flat surface. [freq. 1] |kjv: foundation| {str: 808}

b^{fl}) ‎לוּל-וּ‎פ‎ (‎אשישה‎ A-ShY-ShH) — **Raisin Cake:** Dried raisins, a food staple, were pressed into cakes. [freq. 4] |kjv: flagon| {str: 809}

E) ‎לוּ‎פ‎ (‎אשא‎ AShA) ac: **Press** co: **Foundation** ab: **Pressure:** The firm pressing down on something.

o^m) ‎לֹוּ‎פ‎ (‎אוּשא‎ AW-ShA) — **Foundation:** The pressing down of the soil to form a firm and flat surface. [Aramaic only] [ar: ‎אשּׁא‎] [freq. 3] |kjv: foundation| {str: 787}

H) ‎לוּ‎פ‎ (‎אשה‎ AShH) ac: ? co: **Fire** ab: ?

e^m) ‎לוּל‎פ‎ (‎אישה‎ AY-ShH) — **Fire:** A fire offering. [ar:

59

אשה] [freq. 65] |kjv: offering| {str: 801}

L) יאשׁ (יאש YASh) ac: **Press** co: ? ab: **Despair:** A strong pressing down on someone bringing despair or hopelessness.

V) יאשׁ (יאש Y-ASh) — **Despair:** A pressure of hopelessness. [freq. 6] (vf: Niphal, Piel) |kjv: despair, desperate, no hope| {str: 2976}

M) אישׁ (איש AYSh) ac: ? co: **Fire** ab: ?: The charred wood after being burned in the fire.

j^m) אישׁון (אישון AY-ShWN) — **Black:** The black of night or the pupil of the eye. In the sense of charring from a fire. [freq. 6] |kjv: apple, obscure, black| {str: 380}

N) אשי (אשי AShY) ac: ? co: **Pillar** ab: ?: A strong pressing down on something.

d^fl) אשויה (אשויה A-ShW-YH) — **Pillar:** A support for a roof where the roof presses down on the pillar. [ms: אשיה] [freq. 1] |kjv: foundation| {str: 803}

Adopted Roots;
2108 דעשׁ Extinguish
2584 סעשׁ Press, Oppression
2585 עשׁר Rich, Riches
2586 עשׁת Shine

1022) את (את AT) ac: **Plow** co: **Mark** ab: ?: The pictograph אל is a picture of an ox. The ת is a picture of two crossed sticks used to make a sign or mark. Combined these pictures represent "an ox moving toward a mark". When plowing a field with oxen, the plowman drives the oxen toward a distant mark in order to keep the furrow straight. A traveler arrives at his destination by following a mark. The traveling toward a mark, destination or person. The arrival of one to the mark. A "you" is an individual who has arrived to a "me". The coming toward a mark. A standard, or flag, with the family mark hangs as a sign. An agreement or covenant by two where a sign or mark of the agreement is made as a reminder to both parties. (eng: at - a moving at something)

A) את (את AT) ac: ? co: **Plow** ab: ?: The plowing of a field by driving the oxen to a distant mark.

N^f) את (את AT) — **I. Plow-point:** The plow-point is used to cut a deep furrow in the ground for planting seeds. [A common grammatical word that precedes the direct object of a verb] **II. Sign:** A sign, mark or wonder (as a sign). [Aramaic only] **III. At:** Something that moves near something to be with it. Also used as grammatical tool to mark the direct object of the verb. [df: ית] [freq. 7373] |kjv: plowshare, coulter, sign, against, with, in, upon| {str: 852, 853, 854, 855, 3487}

H) אתה (אתה ATH) ac: ? co: **Mark** ab: **Arrive:** The traveling toward a mark, destination or a person. The arrival of one to the mark.

V) אתה (אתה A-TH) — **Arrive:** To arrive at a destination. [Hebrew and Aramaic] [ar: אתא] [freq. 37] (vf: Paal, Hiphil, Hophal) |kjv: come, bring| {str: 857, 858}

60

N^m) ⅄+⅂ (אתה A-TH) —
You: As one who has arrived.
[Hebrew and Aramaic] [df: את]
[ar: אנת] [freq. 26] |kjv: thou,
thee, you, ye| {str: 607, 608,
859}

J) +⅄⅂ (אות AWT) ac: **?** co: **Mark**
ab: **Agree:** The coming toward a
mark. A standard, or flag, with the
family mark hangs as a sign. An
agreement or covenant by two where
a sign or mark of the agreement is
made as a reminder to both parties.

V) +⅄⅂ (אות AWT) — **Agree:**
Two parties to be in agreement.
[freq. 4] (vf: Niphal) |kjv:
consent| {str: 225}

N^f) +⅄⅂ (אות AWT) — **Mark:**
The sign of an agreement
between two parties. [freq. 79]

|kjv: sign, token, ensign, miracle,
mark| {str: 226}

M) +⅂⅄ (אית AYT) ac: **?** co:
Entrance ab: **?:** The entering into the
area of destination.

j^m) ⅂⅄+⅂⅄ (איתון AY-TWN)
— **Entrance:** [freq. 1] |kjv:
entrance| {str: 2978}

~~~~~~~

1023) 8⅄ (עא AGh) ac: **?** co: **?** ab: **?**

~~~~~~~

Bet

1024) ﬦﬧ (בא BA) ac: **Fill** co: **Void** ab: ?: The filling of an empty space. This root is closely related to ﬦ﬩ and ﬧﬦ.

A) ﬦﬧ (בא BA) ac: **Enter** co: **Entrance** ab: ?: To fill a space by entering it.

N[fl]) ﬦﬧﬨ (באה B-AH) — **Entrance:** [freq. 1] |kjv: entry| {str: 872}

J) ﬦﬨﬧ (בוא BWA) ac: **Fill** co: **Entrance** ab: ?: To come or go into a space is to fill it. A void within oneself that desires to be filled.

V) ﬦﬨﬧ (בוא BWA) — **Come:** To fill a void by entering it. This can be understood as to come or to go. [A generic verb with a wide application meaning to come or go as a filling of a void] [freq. 2577] (vf: Paal, Hiphil, Hophal) |kjv: come, enter, go| {str: 935}

a[m]) ﬦﬨﬧ﬩﬩ (מבוא M-BWA) — **I. Entrance:** A place of entering. **II. West:** The place where the sun enters the underworld. [df: מובא] [freq. 24] |kjv: going down, entry, come, entrance, enter, in, west| {str: 3996}

i[fl]) ﬨﬦﬨﬧﬨ (תבואה T-BW-AH) — **Filling:** An increase of produce, usually of fruit. [freq. 42] |kjv: increase, fruit, revenue, gain| {str: 8393}

k[fl]) ﬦﬨﬧ﬩﬩ (מבואה M-BW-AH) — **Entrance:** A place of entering. [freq. 1] |kjv: entry| {str: 3997}

1025) ﬧﬦ (בב BB) ac: ? co: ? ab: ?

A) ﬧﬦ (בב BB) ac: ? co: **Pupil** ab: ?: Pupil of the eye

N[fl]) ﬧﬦﬨ (בבה B-BH) — **Pupil:** [freq. 1] |kjv: apple| {str: 892}

1026) ﬦﬧ (בג BG) ac: ? co: ? ab: ?

1027) ﬦﬧ (בד BD) ac: **Separate** co: **Alone** ab: **Destruction:** The pictograph ﬦ is a representation of a tent. The ﬧ is a picture of the tent door. These two pictographs represent "the door of the tent". The father of the tent often sat alone at the door of the tent. Here he could receive shade from the sun, watch over his household and watch the road for approaching strangers. (see Genesis 18:1,2) (eng: bad - as being alone)

A) ﬦﬧ (בד BD) ac: **Separate** co: ? ab: ?: Anyone or anything that is alone, apart or separated from the whole or from something else.

N[m]) ﬦﬧ (בד BD) — **Separated:** Something that is separated from the whole. This can be a branch as separated from the tree (as well as a staff made from a branch). Linen cloth whose fibers are divided. A lie or liar as what causes a separation through careless words, lying, or bragging. [freq. 85] |kjv: linen, lie, liar, parts, stave, beside, branches, alone, only, strength| {str: 905, 906, 907}

B) ש־ד־ד (בדד BDD) ac: **?** co: **Alone** ab: **?:** Someone or something that is alone and separated from the whole.

V) ש־ד־ד (בדד B-DD) — **Alone:** [freq. 3] (vf: Paal) |kjv: alone| {str: 909}

N^m) ש־ד־ד (בדד B-DD) — **Alone:** [freq. 11] |kjv: alone, solitary, only, desolate| {str: 910}

C) ש־ד־ע (אבד ABD) ac: **Perish** co: **Lost** ab: **Destruction:** A wanderer is one alone or lost. A place separated from people is a place of ruin.

V) ש־ד־ע (אבד A-BD) — **Perish:** To be separated from the whole, life or functionality. [Hebrew and Aramaic] [freq. 191] (vf: Paal, Hiphil, Hophal, Piel) |kjv: lost thing, that which was lost| {str: 6, 7}

N^{f1}) ש־ד־ע (אבדה AB-DH) — **Lost Thing:** [freq. 4] |kjv: lost thing, that which was lost| {str: 9}

g^m) ש־ד־ע (אובד AW-BD) — **Perish:** [freq. 2] |kjv: perish| {str: 8}

j^f) ש־ד־ע (אבדון AB-DWN) — **Destruction:** A place of ruin. [df: אבדה] [freq. 7] |kjv: destruction| {str: 10, 11}

m^m) ש־ד־ע (אבדן AB-DN) — **Destruction:** A separation through extinction. [freq. 2] |kjv: destruction| {str: 12, 13}

E) ש־ד־ע (בדא BDA) ac: **Devise** co: **?** ab: **?:** A separation from truth.

V) ש־ד־ע (בדא B-DA) — **Devise:** To invent a false account or story. [freq. 2] (vf: Paal) |kjv: devise, feign| {str: 908}

M) ש־ד־ע (ביד BYD) ac: **?** co: **Ruin** ab: **?:** Something brought to ruin and left alone.

N^m) ש־ד־ע (ביד BYD) — **Ruin:** Someone or something brought to ruin. [df: פיד] [freq. 3] |kjv: destruction, ruin| {str: 6365}

Adopted Roots;

2005	✓־ד־ש	Separate, Piece
2006	־ד־ש	Repair, Breach
2007	־ד־ש	Scatter
2805	־ש־ש	Branch
3064	־ש־ש	Sceptor

1028) ש (בה BH) ac: **Need** co: **Box** ab: **?:** An empty space needing to be filled. This root is closely related to ש־ע and ש־ע. (eng: be - as something that exists filling a void)

A) ש (בה BH) ac: **?** co: **Box** ab: **?:** A void within oneself that desires to be filled.

i^f) ש (תבה T-BH) — **Box:** An empty container to be filled. [freq. 28] |kjv: ark| {str: 8392}

C) ש־ע (אבה ABH) ac: **Consent** co: **Box** ab: **?:** A void within oneself that desires to be filled.

V) ש־ע (אבה A-BH) — **Consent:** A filling of a void in space or action. To be willing to go somewhere or do something. [freq. 54] (vf: Paal) |kjv: would, will, willing, consent, rest, content| {str: 14}

N^m) ‏אבה‎ (אבה A-BH) —
Box: An empty container to be filled. [freq. 1] |kjv: swift| {str: 16}

J) ‏בוה‎ (בוה BWH) ac: ? co: **Empty** ab: ?: An empty space needing to be filled.

r^m) ‏בוהו‎ (בוהו BW-HW) — **Empty:** [ms: ‏בהו‎] [freq. 3] |kjv: void, emptiness| {str: 922}

~~~~~~~~

1029) ‏בו‎ (בו BW) ac: ? co: ? ab: ?

~~~~~~~~

1030) ‏בז‎ (בז BZ) ac: **Spoil** co: **Spoils** ab: **Despise:** The pictograph ﬦ represents a house. The ‏ﬤ‎ represents an agricultural implement or a weapon. Combined these pictographs have the meaning of "a house cut" or "attacked". An enemy would plunder a household for goods to supply themselves as a bird of prey attacks its prey. (eng: buzzard)

A) ‏בז‎ (בז BZ) ac: ? co: **Spoils** ab: ?: The removal of what is of value as when an attacking army takes from the defeated all that is of value or the loss of value of a food due to spoilage.

N^m) ‏בז‎ (בז BZ) — **Spoils:** [df: ‏בז‎] [freq. 26] |kjv: prey, spoil, booty| {str: 897, 957}

N^{f1}) ‏בזה‎ (בזה B-ZH) — **Spoils:** [freq. 10] |kjv: spoil, prey| {str: 961}

B) ‏בזז‎ (בזז BZZ) ac: ? co: **Spoil** ab: ?

V) ‏בזז‎ (בזז B-ZZ) — **Spoil:** [freq. 43] (vf: Paal, Niphal, Pual) |kjv: spoil, take away, prey, rob, take, caught, gathering. robber| {str: 962}

E) ‏בזא‎ (בזא BZA) ac: **Divide** co: ? ab: ?: A division of what is plundered.

V) ‏בזא‎ (בזא B-ZA) — **Divide:** A division made by cutting into pieces. [freq. 2] (vf: Paal) |kjv: spoiled| {str: 958}

H) ‏בזה‎ (בזה BZH) ac: **Despise** co: ? ab: ?: To treat something as spoiled, no longer of value.

V) ‏בזה‎ (בזה B-ZH) — **Despise:** [freq. 43] (vf: Paal, Niphal, Hiphil) |kjv: despise, disdain, scorn, contemned| {str: 959}

c^m) ‏בזוה‎ (בזוה B-ZWH) — **Despised:** Something that is considered vile. [ms: ‏בזה‎] [freq. 1] |kjv: despise| {str: 960}

fj^m) ‏בזיון‎ (בזיון BZ-YWN) — **Despised:** Something that is treated as spoiled, no longer of value. [freq. 1] |kjv: contempt| {str: 963}

J) ‏בוז‎ (בוז BWZ) ac: **Despise** co: ? ab: ?: To treat something as spoiled, no longer of value.

V) ‏בוז‎ (בוז BWZ) — **Despise:** [freq. 12] (vf: Paal) |kjv: despise, contemned| {str: 936}

N^m) ‏בוז‎ (בוז BWZ) — **Despised:** [freq. 11] |kjv: contempt, despise, shame| {str: 937}

N^{f1}) ‏בוזה‎ (בוזה BW-ZH) — **Despised:** [freq. 1] |kjv: despised| {str: 939}

Adopted Roots;
2008 ‏בזק‎ Lightning
2009 ‏בזר‎ Scatter
2031 ‏בצע‎ Cut, Profit

out of rashness. [freq. 2] |kjv: uttered| {str: 4008}

G) ⊗⅄ּ⅄ (בהט BHTh) ac: ? co: **Marble** ab: **?:** The intersecting lines of marble appear as broken pieces.

N^m) ⊗⅄ּ⅄ (בהט B-HTh) — **Red Marble**: [freq. 1] |kjv: red| {str: 923}

Adopted Roots;
2022 ⊗⅄ּ⅄ Waist
2015 ⅄⊗ּ⅄ Belly
2045 ⅃†ּ⅄ Virgin
2046 •-†ּ⅄ Cut
2047 ⅏†ּ⅄ Cut

1031) ּ⅄ (בה BHh) ac: **Slaughter** co: **Knife** ab: **?:** The killing of an animal for slaughter by inserting the point of the knife into throat to sever the artery.

C) ּ⅄⅄ (אבה ABHh) ac: **Slaughter** co: **Knife** ab: **?**

N^fl) ⅏ּ⅄⅄ (אבחה AB-HhH) — **Point**: The point of a sword or knife. [freq. 1] |kjv: point| {str: 19}

Adopted Roots;
2011 ⅄ּ⅄ Examine, Watchtower
2012 ⅏ּ⅄ Choose, Youth
2016 ⅏⅏ּ⅄ Firstfruit
2117 ּ⅄⅄ Sacrifice, Altar
2227 ּ⅄⊗ Slaughter, Flesh

1032) ⊗ּ⅄ (בט BTh) ac: ? co: **Cracks** ab: **?:** Something that is broken up into pieces.

A) ⊗ּ⅄ (בט BTh) ac: ? co: **Cracks** ab: **?:** The crevices, clefts and cracks in rock cliffs and outcroppings. Something that is broken into pieces. A place of desolation.

N^fl) ⅏⊗ּ⅄ (בטה B-ThH) — **Desolation**: [df: בתה] [freq. 2] |kjv: waste, desolate| {str: 1326, 1327}

E) ⅄⊗ּ⅄ (בטא BThA) ac: ? co: **Utter** ab: **?:** An incoherent, broken or rash utterance of words usually spoken as a vow.

V) ⅄⊗ּ⅄ (בטא B-ThA) — **Utter**: [df: בטה] [freq. 4] (vf: Paal, Piel) |kjv: pronounce, speak unadvisedly| {str: 981}

h^m) ⅄⊗ּ⅄ᴍ (מבטא MB-ThA) — **Utterance**: Words spoken

1033) ⅃ּ⅄ (בי BY) ac: **Need** co: **Empty** ab: **Sorrow:** The pictograph ּ⅄, a picture of the house represents what is inside. The ⅃ is the hand. When combined these mean "inside the hand". An empty hand desiring to be filled. This root is closely related to ⅄ּ⅄ and ⅏ּ⅄.

A) ⅃ּ⅄ (בי BY) ac: ? co: ? ab: ?

N^m) ⅃ּ⅄ (בי BY) — **Excuse Me**: Used as an introduction for an entreaty or request. [freq. 12] |kjv: O, oh, alas| {str: 994}

C) ⅃ּ⅄⅄ (אבי ABY) ac: ? co: ? ab: **Need:** A void within oneself that desires to be filled.

c^m) ⅃⅄ּ⅄⅄ (אבוי A-BWY) — **Sorrow**: A pain of desire. [freq. 1] |kjv: sorrow| {str: 17}

j^m) ⅄⅄⅃ּ⅄⅄ (אביון AB-YWN) — **Poor**: One who is in need. [freq. 61] |kjv: needy, poor, beggar| {str: 34}

j^fl) ⅏⅄⅃ּ⅄⅄ (אביונה AB-YW-NH) — **Desire**: Something looking to be filled. [freq. 1] |kjv: desire| {str: 35}

1034) מֻשׂ (בֻךְ BK) ac: **Weep** co: **Tears** ab: ?: The pictograph מ is a tent representing what is inside. The שׂ is the palms of the hand. Combined these mean the "inside the palms". The placing of one eyes in the palms when crying. A weeping from mourning or from the billowing of smoke in the eyes.

A) מֻשׂ (בֻךְ BK) ac: **Weep** co: ? ab: ?

N^f4) מֻשׂﬞﬞ+ (בכית B-KYT) — **Weeping**: [freq. 1] |kjv: mourning| {str: 1068}

f^m) מֻשׂﬞ (בכי B-KY) — **Weep**: [freq. 30] |kjv: weep, overflowing, sore| {str: 1065}

C) לﬞﬞﬞﬞﬞﬞﬞ (אבך ABK) ac: **Roll** co: ? ab: ?: The rolling of the tears down the cheek.

V) לﬞﬞﬞﬞﬞ (אבך A-BK) — **Roll**: The rolling of smoke. [freq. 1] (vf: Hitpael) |kjv: mount up| {str: 55}

E) מﬞﬞﬞﬞﬞﬞﬞﬞﬞﬞ (בכא BKA) ac: ? co: ? ab: ?

N^m) מﬞﬞﬞﬞﬞﬞﬞﬞﬞﬞ (בכא B-KA) — **Balsam**: A tree that weeps sap when cut. [freq. 4] |kjv: mulberry tree| {str: 1057}

H) מﬞﬞﬞﬞﬞﬞﬞﬞﬞﬞ (בכה BKH) ac: **Weep** co: ? ab: ?

V) מﬞﬞﬞﬞﬞﬞﬞﬞﬞﬞ (בכה B-KH) — **Weep**: [freq. 114] (vf: Paal, Piel) |kjv: weep, bewail, sore, mourned, wail| {str: 1058}

N^m) מﬞﬞﬞﬞﬞﬞﬞﬞﬞﬞ (בכה B-KH) — **Weep**: [freq. 1] |kjv: sore| {str: 1059}

J) מﬞﬞﬞﬞﬞﬞﬞﬞﬞﬞ (בוך BWK) ac: **Entangle** co: ? ab: **Confusion**: To be tangled, confused or lost in a place of uncertainty that can bring one to tears.

V) מﬞﬞﬞﬞﬞﬞﬞﬞﬞﬞ (בוך BWK) — **Entangled**: [freq. 3] (vf: Niphal) |kjv: perplexed, entangled| {str: 943}

k^f1) מﬞﬞﬞﬞﬞﬞﬞﬞﬞﬞ (מבוכה M-BW-KH) — **Confusion**: A state of entanglement. [freq. 2] |kjv: perplexity| {str: 3998}

Adopted Roots;
2368 מﬞﬞﬞﬞﬞﬞﬞﬞﬞﬞ Spring

1035) מﬞﬞﬞﬞﬞﬞﬞﬞﬞﬞ (בל BL) ac: **Flow** co: ? ab: **Nothing**: A flowing of any substance. (eng: ball; bowl; flow - with the exchange of the f for a b)

A) מﬞﬞﬞﬞﬞﬞﬞﬞﬞﬞ (בל BL) ac: ? co: ? ab: **Nothing**: To come to nothing when effort is given.

N^m) מﬞﬞﬞﬞﬞﬞﬞﬞﬞﬞ (בל BL) — **Nothing**: [freq. 9] |kjv: none, not, nor, lest, nothing, not, neither, no| {str: 1077}

e^f4) מﬞﬞﬞﬞﬞﬞﬞﬞﬞﬞ+ (בילית BY-LYT) — **Except**: A flowing away of all except one. Can also mean not or nothing in the sense of all things flowing away. [df: בלתי] [freq. 30] |kjv: but, except, save, nothing, lest, no, from, inasmuch| {str: 1115}

f^m) מﬞﬞﬞﬞﬞﬞﬞﬞﬞﬞ (בלי B-LY) — **Without**: [freq. 15] |kjv: not, without, lack, confusion| {str: 1097, 1099}

i^f) מﬞﬞﬞﬞﬞﬞﬞﬞﬞﬞ+ (תבל T-BL) — I. **Earth**: A land flowing with substance. II. **Confusion**: An action that lacks any results.

[Used in the sense of beastiality] [freq. 38] |kjv: world, habitable part, confusion| {str: 8397, 8398}

i^f4) תבלית (תבלית‎ TB-LYT) — **Ruin:** A complete flowing away of something by destruction. [freq. 1] |kjv: destruction| {str: 8399}

q^m) בלו (בלו‎ B-LW) — **Tribute:** [Unknown connection to root; Aramaic only] [freq. 3] |kjv: tribute| {str: 1093}

B) בלל (בלל‎ BLL) ac: **Mix** co: **Fodder** ab: **?:** A flowing or mixing of a liquid or solid.

V) בלל (בלל‎ B-LL) — **Mix:** [freq. 44] (vf: Paal, Hiphil) |kjv: mingle, confound, anoint, mix| {str: 1101}

b^m) בליל (בליל‎ B-LYL) — **Fodder:** A mixed feed for livestock. [freq. 3] |kjv: fodder, corn, provender| {str: 1098}

id^m) תבלול (תבלול‎ TB-LWL) — **Cataract:** The clouding color of the eyes that appear as a mixture. [freq. 1] |kjv: blemish| {str: 8400}

C) אבל (אבל‎ ABL) ac: **Flow** co: **Stream** ab: **?:** A flowing of tears.

V) אבל (אבל‎ A-BL) — **Mourn:** [freq. 39] (vf: Paal, Hiphil, Hitpael) |kjv: mourn, mourner, lament| {str: 56}

N^f) אבל (אבל‎ A-BL) — **I. Meadow:** A moist ground. **II. Mourning:** A flowing of tears. **III. Surely:** A flowing of certainty. [freq. 44] |kjv: mourning, plain, but, nevertheless| {str: 57, 58, 60, 61}

o^m) אובל (אובל‎ AW-BL) — **Stream:** A flowing of water. [ms: אבל‎] [freq. 3] |kjv: river| {str: 180}

E) בלא (בלא‎ BLA) ac: **?** co: **Old** ab: **?:** A flowing away life.

N^m) בלא (בלא‎ B-LA) — **Old:** [df: בלי] [freq. 3] |kjv: old| {str: 1094}

F) הבל (הבל‎ HBL) ac: **?** co: **Empty** ab: **?:** A flowing out or away of contents.

V) הבל (הבל‎ H-BL) — **Empty:** Void of usefulness, to be vain. [freq. 5] (vf: Paal, Hiphil) |kjv: become vain| {str: 1891}

N^m) הבל (הבל‎ H-BL) — **Emptyness:** The state of being empty of contents or usefulness. [freq. 73] |kjv: vanity| {str: 1892}

G) בהל (בהל‎ BHL) ac: **Stir** co: **?** ab: **Trouble:** The flowing of the insides through trouble, amazement, haste or anxiety.

V) בהל (בהל‎ B-HL) — **Stir:** [Hebrew and Aramaic] [freq. 50] (vf: Niphal, Hiphil, Pual, Piel) |kjv: haste, trouble, amaze, afraid, vex, rash, dismay, speedy, thrust out| {str: 926, 927}

N^f1) בהלה (בהלה‎ BH-LH) — **Trouble:** [freq. 4] |kjv: trouble, terror| {str: 928}

b^m) בהיל (בהיל‎ B-HYL) — **Haste:** [Aramaic only] [df: בהילו] [freq. 1] |kjv: haste| {str: 924}

H) בלה (בלה‎ BLH) ac: **Wear** co: **?** ab: **Terror:** A flowing away of function, life or strength.

V) ‮בלה‬ (בלה B-LH) — **Wear
Out:** [freq. 17] (vf: Paal, Piel)
|kjv: waxed old, old, consume,
waste, enjoy| {str: 1086, 1089}

N^m) ‮בלה‬ (בלה B-LH) —
Worn Out: [Hebrew and
Aramaic] [ar: בלא] [freq. 6]
|kjv: old, wear out| {str: 1080,
1087}

N^fl) ‮בלהה‬ (בלהה BL-HH) —
Terror: A flowing away of the
insides. [freq. 10] |kjv: terror|
{str: 1091}

J) ‮בול‬ (בול BWL) ac: ? co: **Flood**
ab: ?: A large flowing of water. As
the river rises and overflows its
banks, the surrounding lands are
flooded depositing the water for
growing the crops.

N^m) ‮בול‬ (בול BWL) — **Food:**
The crops grown in the flood
plains of rivers. [freq. 2] |kjv:
food, stock| {str: 944}

a^m) ‮מבול‬ (מבול M-BWL) —
Flood: [freq. 13] |kjv: flood|
{str: 3999}

L) ‮יבל‬ (יבל YBL) ac: **Flow** co:
Stream ab: ?: A flowing of wealth,
water or sound.

V) ‮יבל‬ (יבל Y-BL) — **Flow:**
[Hebrew and Aramaic] [freq. 21]
(vf: Hiphil, Hophal) |kjv: carry,
brought| {str: 2986, 2987}

N^m) ‮יבל‬ (יבל Y-BL) —
Stream: A flowing body of
water. [freq. 2] |kjv: stream,
course| {str: 2988}

N^f2) ‮יבלת‬ (יבלת YB-LT) —
Ulcer: A flowing lesion. [freq.
1] |kjv: wen| {str: 2990}

d^m) ‮יבול‬ (יבול Y-BWL) —
Produce: The growth of fruits
and crops from flooding waters.

[freq. 13] |kjv: increase, fruit|
{str: 2981}

g^m) ‮יובל‬ (יובל YW-BL) —
Trumpet: An instrument of
flowing air to make a sound, also
the horn of a ram used as a
trumpet. [ms: יבל] [freq. 27]
|kjv: jubilee, rams horn, trumpet|
{str: 3104}

o^m) ‮יובל‬ (יובל YW-BL) —
Stream: A flowing body of
water. [ms: יבל] [freq. 1] |kjv:
river| {str: 3105}

Adopted Roots;

2020	ܒܠܥ	Swallow
2021	ܒܠܛ	Empty
2228	ܛܒܠ	Dip
2369	ܢܒܠ	Flow
2806	ܫܒܠ	Flow, Flood

1036) ‮בם‬ (בם BM) ac: ? co: **High** ab:
?: Anything that is tall or high.

G) ‮בהם‬ (בהם BHM) ac: ? co:
Beast ab: ?: A tall creature.

N^fl) ‮בהמה‬ (בהמה BH-MH)
— **Beast:** [freq. 190] |kjv: beast,
cattle| {str: 929, 930}

H) ‮במה‬ (במה BMH) ac: ? co:
High ab: ?

N^f) ‮במה‬ (במה B-MH) —
High Place: [freq. 102] |kjv:
high place, heights, wave| {str:
1116}

L) ‮יבם‬ (יבם YBM) ac: **Marry**
co: **Brother-in-law** ab: ?: When a
husband dies his brother takes his
place as his sister-in-laws husband.
Any children born to him will be of
his brothers line in order to continue,
lift up, his family.

V) ישׁבם‎ (יבם Y-BM) —
Marry: The marrying of ones
sister-in-law as the next of kin.
[freq. 3] (vf: Piel) |kjv: marry|
{str: 2992}

N^m) ישׁבם‎ (יבם Y-BM) —
Brother-in-law: [freq. 2] |kjv:
husbands brother| {str: 2993}

N^f2) ישׁבמת‎ (יבמת YB-MT) —
Sister-in-law: [freq. 5] |kjv:
brothers wife, sister in law| {str:
2994}

~~~~~~~~~~

1037) שׁבן‎ (בן BN) ac: **Build** co: **Tent
panel** ab: **Intelligence:** The pictograph ב
is a picture of the tent. The שׁ is a picture
of a sprouting seed and represents
continuity as the seed continues the next
generation. The combined meaning of
these letters mean "the continuing of the
house". The tent was constructed of
woven goat hair. Over time the sun
bleaches and weakens the goat hair
necessitating their continual replacement.
Each year the women make a new panel,
approximately 3 feet wide and the length
of the tent. The old panel is removed
(being recycled into a wall or floor) and
the new strip is added to the tent. Since
the tent is only replaced one small piece
at a time the tent essentially lasts forever.
(eng: beam - a component of construction
with an exchange for the m and n;
between - with the t added)

A) שׁבן‎ (בן BN) ac: **?** co: **Tent Panel**
ab: **?:** There are many similarities
between building a tent out of goat
hair panels and the building of a
house out of sons (The idea of
building a house with sons can be
seen in Genesis 30.3). Just as the tent
panels are added to continue the tent,
sons are born to the family to

continue the family line. Just as the
tent is continually being renewed
with new panels, the family is
continually being renewed with new
sons.

N^m) שׁבן‎ (בן BN) — **Son:** One
who continues the family line.
[Hebrew and Aramaic;
Transforms to שׁבם‎ when used in
the possessive] [freq. 4925] |kjv:
son, children, old, first, man,
young, stranger, people| {str:
1121, 1123, 1247}

N^f2) תשׁבן‎ (בנת B-NT) —
Daughter: Also a village that
resides outside of the city walls
as the daughter of the city. [df:
בת] [freq. 588] |kjv: daughter,
town, village, first, apple,
branches, children, company,
eye, old| {str: 1323}

i^m) תשׁבן‎ (תבן T-BN) — **Straw:**
When more permanent structures
were built they were constructed
of stones and bricks made of
clay and straw, replacing the tent
panels as the main component of
construction for dwellings. [freq.
17] |kjv: straw, stubble, chaff|
{str: 8401}

ai^m) משׁבן‎ (מתבן MT-BN) —
Straw: When more permanent
structures were built they were
constructed of stones and bricks,
made of clay and straw,
replacing the tent panels as the
main component of construction
for dwellings. [freq. 1] |kjv:
straw| {str: 4963}

B) שׁבן‎ (בנן BNN) ac: **Build** co:
Building ab: **?:** The building of a
family or a structure for housing the
family.

b^m) ماحلحم (בנין B-NYN) —
Building: [Hebrew and
Aramaic] [freq. 8] |kjv: building|
{str: 1146, 1147}

C) محلل (אבן ABN) ac: **Build** co:
Stone ab: **?**

N^f) محلل (אבן A-BN) —
Stone: [Hebrew and Aramaic]
[freq. 282] |kjv: stone| {str: 68,
69, 70}

F) محلطم (הבן HBN) ac: **?** co: **Hard**
ab: **?**: The hardness of stone or brick.

N^m) محلطم (הבן H-BN) —
Ebony: A hard wood. [freq. 1]
|kjv: ebony| {str: 1894}

G) محطحلم (בהן BHN) ac: **Build** co:
Thumb ab: **?**: The part of the body
understood as the builder by the
Hebrews.

N^f) محطحلم (בהן B-HN) —
Thumb: Also the big toe by
extension. [freq. 16] |kjv: thumb,
great toe| {str: 931}

H) محطلم (בנה BNH) ac: **Build** co:
Building ab: **?**: A structure built for
occupation.

V) محطلم (בנה B-NH) — **Build:**
To build or construct a building,
home or family. [Hebrew and
Aramaic] [ar: בנא] [freq. 398]
(vf: Paal, Niphal) |kjv: build,
build up, builder, repair, set up,
building, make, children| {str:
1124, 1129}

b^{fl}) محطلحلم (בניה BN-YH) —
Building: [freq. 1] |kjv: building|
{str: 1140}

h^m) محطلمm (מבנה MB-NH) —
Structure: The framework of a
building. [freq. 1] |kjv: frame|
{str: 4011}

if^{f2}) محلحلمt (תבנית TB-NYT)
— **Pattern:** A model or pattern
for building something. [freq.
20] |kjv: pattern, likeness, form,
similtude, figure| {str: 8403}

J) محلهلم (בון BWN) ac: **Plan** co: **?**
ab: **Intelligence:** The skill of the
mind and hands to build. Before the
tent is constructed the location and
orientation must be carefully
considered according to weather,
view and size. The planning and
building of a house, structure or
family.

i^m) محلهلم (תבון T-BWN) —
Intelligence: One able to plan
and build. [freq. 43] |kjv:
understanding, discretion,
reasons, skillfulness, wisdom|
{str: 8394}

M) محطحلم (בין BYN) ac: **Plan** co: **?**
ab: **Understand:** The tent was
usually divided into two parts, one
for the females and the other for the
male. The wall makes a distinction
between the two sides.
Understanding as the ability to
discern between two or more things.

V) محطحلم (בין BYN) —
Understand: [freq. 170] (vf:
Paal, Niphal, Hiphil) |kjv:
understand, cunning, skilful,
teacher, taught, consider,
perceive, wise, viewed, discern,
prudent, consider| {str: 995}

N^m) محطحلم (בין BYN) —
Between: As the wall is between
the two sides of the tent.
[Hebrew and Aramaic] [freq. 36]
|kjv: between, among, asunder,
betwixt, within, out of, from|
{str: 996, 997, 1143}

N^{fl}) محطحلم (בינה BY-NH) —
Understanding: [Hebrew and

Aramaic] [freq. 39] |kjv: understanding, wisdom, knowledge, meaning, perfectly, understand| {str: 998, 999}

Adopted Roots;
2303 שׁבל White

1038) מב (בס BS) ac: **Trample** co: **Corral** ab: **?**: The corral or pen is used for storing livestock.

C) אבסל (אבס ABS) ac: **Feed** co: **Fat** ab: **?**: Livestock chosen for slaughter are placed in pens and fed to make them.

V) אבסל (אבס A-BS) — **Fat:** [freq. 2] (vf: Paal) |kjv: fatted, stalled| {str: 75}

d^m) אבוסל (אבוס A-BWS) — **Manger:** A feeding trough. [freq. 3] |kjv: crib| {str: 18}

ad^m) מאבוסלמ (מאבוס MA-BWS) — **Granary:** A place for storing feed. [freq. 1] |kjv: storehouse| {str: 3965}

J) בוסמ (בוס BWS) ac: **Trample** co: **?** ab: **?**: The ground inside the stall is heavily trampled by the livestock and made hard and compact.

V) בוסמ (בוס BWS) — **Tread:** [freq. 12] (vf: Paal, Hophal) |kjv: tread, loathe| {str: 947}

i^{fl}) תבוסהת (תבוסה T-BW-SH) — **Trampled:** To be destroyed by being tread upon. [freq. 1] |kjv: destruction| {str: 8395}

k^{fl}) מבוסהמ (מבוסה M-BW-SH) — **Trampled:** [freq. 3] |kjv: tread down, tread under foot| {str: 4001}

Adopted Roots;
2044 מלסש Trample
2249 שׁסמ Wash
2251 שׁמלס Subdue, Footstool

1039) מע (בע BAh) ac: **Swell** co: **Spring** ab: **?**: A gushing over or swelling up as an eruption or a fountain.

A) מע (בע BAh) ac: **Swell** co: **Heap** ab: **?**

f^m) מעי (בעי B-AhY) — **Heap:** A mound of dirt over a grave. [freq. 1] |kjv: grave| {str: 1164}

C) אבעל (אבע ABAh) ac: **Swell** co: **Boils** ab: **?**

ld^{fl}) אבעבועהל (אבעבעה AB-Ah-BW-AhH) — **Boils:** A swelling on the skin. [freq. 2] |kjv: blains| {str: 76}

H) מעה (בעה BAhH) ac: **Swell** co: **?** ab: **?**

V) מעה (בעה B-AhH) — I. **Swell:** II. **Request:** For a swelling desire. [Hebrew and Aramaic] [ar: בעא] [freq. 17] (vf: Paal, Niphal) |kjv: boil, swelling, seek, enquire, ask, desire, pray, request| {str: 1156, 1158}

J) בועמ (בוע BWAh) ac: **Swell** co: **Spring** ab: **?**: A swelling up of water from the ground.

a^m) מבועמ (מבוע M-BWAh) — **Spring:** [freq. 3] |kjv: fountain| {str: 4002}

Adopted Roots;
2370 לבע Belch

1040) מב (בף BP) ac: **?** co: **?** ab: **?**

~~~~~~~~~~~

1041) (בץ BTs) ac: **?** co: **Mud** ab: **?**

A) (בץ BTs) ac: **?** co: **Mud** ab: **?**

N^{m}) (בץ BTs) — **Mud:** [freq. 1] |kjv: mire| {str: 1206}

N^{f1}) (בצה B-TsH) — **Swamp:** [freq. 3] |kjv: mire, fens, miry place| {str: 1207}

J) (בוץ BWTs) ac: **?** co: **Linen** ab: **?:** [Unknown connection to root;]

N^{m}) (בוץ BWTs) — **Linen:** White and fine linen. [freq. 8] |kjv: linen| {str: 948}

M) (ביץ BYTs) ac: **?** co: **Egg** ab: **?:** The miry texture of egg whites.

N^{f1}) (ביצה BY-TsH) — **Egg:** [freq. 6] |kjv: egg| {str: 1000}

~~~~~~~~~~~

1042) (בק BQ) ac: **?** co: **Empty** ab: **?:** A thing or place empty of contents or inhabitants. (eng: vacuum - an exchange for the b and v; vacate)

A) (בק BQ) ac: **?** co: **?** ab: **?**

ld^{m}) (בקבוק BQ-BWQ) — **Bottle:** [ms: בקבק] [freq. 3] |kjv: bottle, cruse| {str: 1228}

B) (בקק BQQ) ac: **?** co: **Empty** ab: **?**

V) (בקק B-QQ) — **Empty:** [freq. 9] (vf: Paal, Niphal) |kjv: empty, make void, emptier, fail| {str: 1238}

C) (אבק ABQ) ac: **Wrestle** co: **Dust** ab: **?:** The arid landscape of an empty land.

V) (אבק A-BQ) — **Wrestle:** A rolling around in the dust. [freq. 2] (vf: Niphal) |kjv: wrestled| {str: 79}

N^{m}) (אבק A-BQ) — **Dust:** [freq. 6] |kjv: dust, powder| {str: 80}

N^{f1}) (אבקה AB-QH) — **Powder:** An aromatic dust. [freq. 1] |kjv: powders| {str: 81}

G) (בהק BHQ) ac: **?** co: **Rash** ab: **?:** A harmless skin rash or spot empty of fluid.

N^{m}) (בהק B-HQ) — **Rash:** [freq. 1] |kjv: freckled spot| {str: 933}

J) (בוק BWQ) ac: **?** co: **Empty** ab: **?**

N^{f1}) (בוקה BW-QH) — **Empty:** [freq. 1] |kjv: empty| {str: 950}

k^{f1}) (מבוקה M-BW-QH) — **Empty:** [freq. 1] |kjv: void| {str: 4003}

Adopted Roots;

2810 Leave

~~~~~~~~~~~

1043) (בר BR) ac: **Feed** co: **Grain** ab: **?:** The pictograph is a picture of a tent but also represents the family which resides inside the tent. The is a picture of a head. Combined these have the meaning of "family of heads". The plant families of grains such as wheat and barley have a cluster of seeds at the top of the stalk called "heads". These grains were used for food for both man and livestock. (eng: barley - a grain; beer -
~~~~~~~~~~~

made from grain; boar - as fat; barn - grain storage; pure - as clean with soap with an exchange for the p and b)

A) פֵּר (בר BR) ac: **?** co: **Grain** ab: **?:** Grains grown in fields were used for meal to make flour as well as feed for livestock. The stalks of the grains were burned to make potash for making soap. What is cleaned with soap becomes white or bright.

N[m]) פֵּר (בר BR) — **I. Grain:** Grain, and field, as a place for growing grain. **II. Soap:** Made from the ashes of the grain stalks. **III. Clean:** Cleanliness from soap. Also pure as a moral cleanliness. [freq. 33] |kjv: corn, wheat, son, about, clean, pur, choice, clear, purely, son| {str: 1248, 1249, 1250, 1251}

ld[m]) פֵּרבֵּור (ברבור BR-BWR) — **Fowl:** Birds fattened on the grains in the field. [freq. 1] |kjv: fowl| {str: 1257}

B) פֵּרֵר (ברר BRR) ac: **?** co: **Soap** ab: **?:** The stalks of the grains were burned to make potash for making soap.

V) פֵּרֵר (ברר B-RR) — **I. Clean:** The cleaning or polishing of something to make it bright or pure. **II. Choice:** Something that is clean or pure. [freq. 18] (vf: Paal, Niphal, Hiphil, Hitpael, Piel) |kjv: pure, choice, chosen, clean, clearly, manifest, bright, purge out, polished, purge, purified| {str: 1305}

C) פֵּרֵ֖ (אבר ABR) ac: **Fly** co: **Wing** ab: **?:** The fowl, fed on grain, becomes strong for the long flight.

V) פֵּרֵ֖ (אבר A-BR) — **Fly:** [freq. 1] (vf: Hiphil) |kjv: fly| {str: 82}

N[m]) פֵּרֵ֖ (אבר A-BR) — **Wing:** [freq. 3] |kjv: wing, winged| {str: 83}

N[fl]) פֵּרֵ֖ה (אברה AB-RH) — **Wing:** [freq. 4] |kjv: features, wing| {str: 84}

b[m]) פֵּירֵ֖ (אביר A-BYR) — **Strong:** The mighty power of a bird in flight. Anything or anyone of great strength, physical or mental. [freq. 23] |kjv: might, bulls, strong, mighty, stouthearted, valiant, angels, chiefest| {str: 46, 47}

E) פֵּרֵ֖א (ברא BRA) ac: **Fill** co: **Fat** ab: **?:** Grain is fed to the livestock making them fat or full.

V) פֵּרֵ֖א (ברא B-RA) — **Fill:** The fattening or filling up of something. The filling of the earth in Genesis 1 with sun, moon, plants, animals, etc. And the filling of man with life and the image of God. [freq. 54] (vf: Paal, Niphal, Hiphil, Piel) |kjv: create, creator, choose, make, cut down, dispatch, done, fat| {str: 1254}

b[m]) פֵּרֵ֖יא (בריא B-RYA) — **Fat:** [freq. 13] |kjv: fat, rank, firm, fatter, fed, plenteous| {str: 1277}

b[fl]) פֵּרֵ֖יאה (בריאה B-RY-AH) — **Fill:** [freq. 1] |kjv: new thing| {str: 1278}

F) פֵּהֵר (הבר HBR) ac: **Divide** co: **?** ab: **?:** [Unknown connection to root;]

V) אׁבֵּר (הבר H-BR) —
Divide: [freq. 1] (vf: Paal) |kjv:
astrologer| {str: 1895}

G) בַהׁר (בהר BHR) ac: **?** co: **Soap**
ab: **?:** What is cleaned with soap
becomes white or bright.

N[f2]**)** בַהֶרֶת (בהרת BH-RT) —
Blister: A white spot on the skin
and a possible sign of leprosy.
[freq. 13] |kjv: bright spot| {str:
934}

b[m]**)** בָהִיר (בהיר B-HYR) —
Bright: [freq. 1] |kjv: bright|
{str: 925}

H) בַרֵּה (ברה BRH) ac: **Eat** co:
Meat ab: **Covenant:** The grain is
used as food for man or livestock.
Livestock fed grains become fat and
are the choicest for slaughter.

V) בַרֵּה (ברה B-RH) — **Eat:**
[freq. 7] (vf: Paal, Hiphil, Piel)
|kjv: eat, choose, give| {str:
1262}

N[f3]**)** בָרוׁת (ברות B-RWT) —
Meat: The choicest meats are
those from fatted livestock.
[freq. 1] |kjv: meat| {str: 1267}

N[f4]**)** בַרִית (ברית B-RYT) —
Covenant: A covenant is
instituted through a sacrifice of a
choice, fatted, animal which is
cut into two and the parties of
the covenant pass through the
pieces. If one party fails to meet
the agreements of the covenant
then the other may do the same
to them. (see Genesis 15:10,17
and Jeremiah 34:18-20) [freq.
284] |kjv: covenant, league,
confederacy, confederate| {str:
1285}

f[m]**)** בָרִי (ברי B-RY) — **Fat:**
Livestock that are fed grains

become fat. [freq. 1] |kjv: fat|
{str: 1274}

ef[f1]**)** בִּירִיָה (ביריה BYR-YH)
— **Meat:** [ms: בריה] [freq. 3]
|kjv: meat| {str: 1279}

J) בוׁר (בור BWR) ac: **?** co: **Soap**
ab: **?**

N[m]**)** בוׁר (בור BWR) — **Clean:**
[ms: בר] [freq. 8] |kjv:
cleanness, pureness, never| {str:
1252, 1253}

N[f4]**)** בוׁרִית (בורית BW-RYT)
— **Soap:** [ms: ברית] [freq. 2]
|kjv: soap| {str: 1287}

M) בִיר (ביר BYR) ac: **?** co:
Palace ab: **?:** [Unknown connection
to root;]

N[f1]**)** בִירָה (בירה BY-RH) —
Palace: [Hebrew and Aramaic]
[freq. 17] |kjv: palace| {str: 1001,
1002}

m[f4]**)** בִירָנִית (בירנית BY-R-
NYT) — **Castle:** [freq. 2] |kjv:
castle| {str: 1003}

Adopted Roots;

2743	אבהש	Mix
2041	בדֶ	Thrust, Sword
2042	ברֶש	Cypress
2052	לבֶ	Prevail, Warrior
2520	סבֶ	Cross

1044) בש (בש BSh) ac: **Wither** co: **Dry**
ab: **Shame:** A drying up of a land,
stream, plant, etc. (eng: bashful)

A) בש (בש BSh) ac: **?** co: **?** ab:
Shame: When a wetland dries up the
fish and vegetation die and begin to
stink from the rotting matter.

m[f1]**)** בֻשׁנָה (בשנה BSh-NH) —
Shame: [freq. 1] |kjv: shame|
{str: 1317}

74

D) ‏באש‎ (באש BASh) ac: **Stink** co: **?** ab: **?**: The smell of a dried up marsh.

V) ‏באש‎ (באש B-ASh) — **Stink:** Something that gives off a bad odor or is loathsome. [Hebrew and Aramaic] [freq. 18] (vf: Paal, Niphal, Hiphil, Hitpael) |kjv: stink, abhor, abomination, loathsome, stinking, savour, displeased| {str: 887, 888}

N^m) ‏באש‎ (באש B-ASh) — **Stink:** A foul odor. [freq. 3] |kjv: stink| {str: 889}

N^fl) ‏באשה‎ (באשה BA-ShH) — **Stinkweed:** [freq. 1] |kjv: cockle| {str: 890}

d^f) ‏באוש‎ (באוש B-AWSh) — **Stink:** [Hebrew and Aramaic] [ms: ‏באש‎] [freq. 3] |kjv: stink, bad| {str: 873, 891}

J) ‏בוש‎ (בוש BWSh) ac: **?** co: **Genitals** ab: **Shame:** A dry and arid desert. Also Shame as one who is dried up.

V) ‏בוש‎ (בוש BWSh) — **Ashamed:** [freq. 109] (vf: Paal, Hiphil, Piel) |kjv: ashamed, confounded, shame, confusion, delayed, dry, long, shamed| {str: 954}

N^fl) ‏בושה‎ (בושה BW-ShH) — **Shame:** [freq. 4] |kjv: shame| {str: 955}

N^f2) ‏בושת‎ (בושת BW-ShT) — **Shame:** [ms: ‏בשת‎] [freq. 30] |kjv: shame, confusion, ashamed, greatly, shameful thing| {str: 1322}

a^m) ‏מבוש‎ (מבוש M-BWSh) — **Genitals:** The feeling of shame when exposed. [ms:

‏מבש‎] [freq. 1] |kjv: secrets| {str: 4016}

L) ‏יבש‎ (יבש YBSh) ac: **Dry** co: **?** ab: **?**: A dried up and withered land.

V) ‏יבש‎ (יבש Y-BSh) — **Dry:** To be dried up as well as withered, ashamed or confused. [freq. 78] (vf: Paal, Hiphil, Piel) |kjv: dry up, withered, confounded, ashamed, dry, wither away, clean, shamed, shamefully| {str: 3001}

N^m) ‏יבש‎ (יבש Y-BSh) — **Dry:** [freq. 9] |kjv: dry| {str: 3002}

N^fl) ‏יבשה‎ (יבשה YB-ShH) — **Dry:** A dry land. [freq. 14] |kjv: dry, dry land, dry ground, land| {str: 3004}

N^f2) ‏יבשת‎ (יבשת YB-ShT) — **Dry:** A dry land. [Hebrew and Aramaic] [freq. 3] |kjv: dry, land| {str: 3006, 3007}

Adopted Roots;
2521 ‏רסב‎ Rot

~~~~~~~~~~

1045) ‏בת‎ (בת BT) ac: **Lodge** co: **House** ab: **?**: The pictograph ‏ם‎ is the tent or house. The ‏ת‎ is two crossed sticks meaning a mark or sign. The family mark is the name of the patriarch of the family (such as "the house of Jacob"). The primary function of the tent is to provide a protection and a sleeping area at night. (eng: bed - for sleeping at night in the house; both - the letter beyt is the second letter of the Hebrew alphabet)

A) ‏בת‎ (בת BT) ac: **?** co: **?** ab: **?**: [Unknown meaning;]

N^m) ⅃ (⅃ BT) — **Bat:** A standard of measure. [freq. 15] |kjv: bath| {str: 1324, 1325}

J) ⅃Y⅃ (⅃⅃ BWT) ac: **?** co: **Lodge** ab: **?:** A place for spending the night.

V) ⅃Y⅃ (⅃⅃ BWT) — **Lodge:** To spend the night. [Aramaic only] [freq. 1] (vf: Paal) |kjv: passed the night| {str: 956}

M) ⅃⅃ (⅃⅃ BYT) ac: **?** co: **House** ab: **?:** The house or tent where the family spends the night.

N^m) ⅃⅃ (⅃⅃ BYT) — **I. House:** The structure or the family, as a household that resides within the house. **II. Within:** [Hebrew and Aramaic;

The short form "⅃" is used as a prefix meaning "in" or "with"] [freq. 2099] |kjv: house, household, home, within, family, temple, prison, place, dungeon| {str: 1004, 1005}

m^m) ⅃⅃ (⅃⅃⅃ BY-TN) — **Palace:** A large house. [freq. 3] |kjv: palace| {str: 1055}

1046) ⅃ (⅃⅃ BGh) ac: **?** co: **?** ab: **?**

Gam

1047) ᴅ⅃L (‫גא‬ GA) ac: ? co: **High** ab:
Pride: The pictograph **L**, a picture of the
foot representing the idea to carry or lift.
The ᴅ⅃ represents strength. Combined
these letters mean a "lifting strength". To
lift something up high. This root is related
to ⅍L and YL.

A) ᴅ⅃L (‫גא‬ GA) ac: ? co: **High** ab:
Pride

Nᵐ) ᴅ⅃L (‫גא‬ GA) — **Pride:**
Someone that is elevated to a
higher position. [freq. 1] |kjv:
pride| {str: 1341}

Nᶠ¹) ⅍ᴅ⅃L (‫גאה‬ G-AH) —
Pride: A lifting up of oneself.
[freq. 1] |kjv: pride| {str: 1344}

Nᶠ³) †Yᴅ⅃L (‫גאות‬ G-AWT) —
Pride: Someone that is elevated
to a higher position. Also the
idea of majestic. [freq. 8] |kjv:
pride, majesty, proudly, raging,
lift up, excellent things| {str:
1348}

jᵐ) ᐟYᴅ⅃L (‫גאון‬ G-AWN) —
Pride: Someone that is elevated
to a higher position. Also the
idea of majestic. [freq. 49] |kjv:
pride, excellency, majesty,
pomp, swelling, arrogancy,
excellent, proud| {str: 1347}

fjᵐ) ᐟY-ᴅ⅃L (‫גאיון‬ GA-YWN)
— **Pride:** Someone that is
elevated to a higher position.
[freq. 1] |kjv: proud| {str: 1349}

K) Yᴅ⅃L (‫גאו‬ GAW) ac: ? co: ? ab:
Pride

Nᶠ¹) ⅍Yᴅ⅃L (‫גאוה‬ GA-WH) —
Pride: A lifting up in a positive
or negative sense. [freq. 19] |kjv:

pride, excellency, haughtiness,
arrogance, highness, proud,
proudly, swelling| {str: 1346}

M) ᴅ-⅃L (‫גיא‬ GYA) ac: ? co:
Valley ab: ?: The high walls of a
valley, gorge or ravine.

Nᵐ/ᶠ) ᴅ-⅃L (‫גיא‬ GYA) —
Valley: [df: ‫גי‬] [freq. 60] |kjv:
valley| {str: 1516}

~~~~~~~~~

1048) ᴖL (‫גב‬ GB) ac: **Lift** co: **Back** ab:
?: The high arched curve of the back
when digging.

A) ᴖL (‫גב‬ GB) ac: ? co: **Arch** ab: ?

Nᵐ/ᶠ) ᴖL (‫גב‬ GB) — I. **Arch:**
The arch of the back when
digging. Also any high arched or
convex thing such as the
eyebrow, rim of a wheel, locust,
etc. [df: ‫גן‬] II. **Pit:** The work of
the back of digging a pit or
trench. [freq. 18] |kjv: back,
eminent place, rings, bodies,
bosses, eyebrows, naves, higher
place, pit, beam, ditch, locust,
den| {str: 1354, 1355, 1356,
1357, 1610}

E) ᴅᴖL (‫גבא‬ GBA) ac: **Dig** co:
Cistern ab: ?: The work of the back
of digging a pit for collecting water.

Nᵐ) ᴅᴖL (‫גבא‬ G-BA) —
Cistern: [freq. 3] |kjv: pit,
marshes| {str: 1360}

H) ⅍ᴖL (‫גבה‬ GBH) ac: **Lift** co:
High ab: ?: From the high arch of the
back when digging. Something that is
lifted up high. This can be something

physical or mental such as pride as the lifting up of the heart.

V) 𐤔ᏝᏝ (גבה G-BH) — **Lift:** To lift something up high. [freq. 34] (vf: Paal, Hiphil) |kjv: exalt, up, haughty, higher, high, above, height, proud, upward| {str: 1361}

N^m) 𐤔ᏝᏝ (גבה G-BH) — **High:** [freq. 4] |kjv: high, proud| {str: 1362}

N^{f3}) †Y𐤔ᏝᏝ (גבהות GB-HWT) — **Lofty:** [freq. 2] |kjv: lofty, loftiness| {str: 1365}

c^m) 𐤔YᏝᏝ (גבוה G-BWH) — **High:** [ms: גבה] [freq. 37] |kjv: high, higher, lofty, exceeding, haughty, height, highest, proud, proudly| {str: 1364}

g^m) 𐤔ᏝYᏝ (גובה GW-BH) — **High:** [freq. 17] |kjv: height, excellency, haughty, loftiness| {str: 1363}

J) ᏝYᏝ (גוב GWB) ac: **Dig** co: **Pit** ab: ?

V) ᏝYᏝ (גוב GWB) — **Dig:** [freq. 1] (vf: Paal, Participle) |kjv: husbandman| {str: 1461}

N^m) ᏝYᏝ (גוב GWB) — **I. Pit:** As dug out of the ground. [Aramaic only] [ms: גב] **II. Locust:** A digging insect. [freq. 12] |kjv: grasshopper, den| {str: 1358, 1462}

L) ᏝᏝᏝ (ינב YGB) ac: **Dig** co: **Field** ab: ?

V) ᏝᏝᏝ (ינב Y-GB) — **Dig:** [freq. 2] (vf: Paal) |kjv: husbandman| {str: 3009}

N^m) ᏝᏝᏝ (ינב Y-GB) — **Field:** A place plowed/dug for planting crops. [freq. 1] |kjv: field| {str: 3010}

Adopted Roots;

2048	ᏝᏝᏝᏝᏝ	Bald
2050	ᏝᏝᏝ	Lump
2051	ᏝᏝᏝ	Hill
2146	ᏝᏝᏝᏝ	Locust
2248	ᏝᏝᏝᏝᏝ	High, Helmet
2463	ᏝᏝᏝ	Lift, Tower
3006	ᏝᏝᏝᏝ	

~~~~~~~~~~~

1049) ᏝᏝ (גג GG) ac: **?** co: **Roof** ab: **?**

A) ᏝᏝ (גג GG) ac: **?** co: **Roof** ab: **?**

N^m) ᏝᏝ (גג GG) — **Roof:** [freq. 30] |kjv: roof, housetop, top, house| {str: 1406}

~~~~~~~~~~~

1050) ᏝᏝ (גד GD) ac: **Slice** co: **?** ab: **?:** (eng: gut - used to make cordage in the same sense as the tendon)

A) ᏝᏝ (גד GD) ac: **?** co: **Coriander** ab: **?:** A seed cut out of the plant. A prized spice.

N^m) ᏝᏝ (גד GD) — **I. Coriander: II. Fortune:** [freq. 4] |kjv: coriander, troop| {str: 1407, 1409}

B) ᏝᏝᏝ (גדד GDD) ac: **?** co: **Band** ab: **?**

V) ᏝᏝᏝ (גדד G-DD) — **I. Band:** To gather or assemble as a group for attacking or raiding. **II. Slice:** To cut something by slicing it. [Hebrew and Aramaic] [freq. 10] (vf: Paal) |kjv: cut, gather together, assemble by troop, gather, hew| {str: 1413, 1414}

d^{m/f}) ᏝᏝYᏝ (גדוד G-DWD) — **I. Band:** A gathering of men for attacking or raiding. **II. Slice:** [freq. 36] |kjv: band, troop, army, company, men, furrow, cutting| {str: 1416, 1417}

d^fl) 𐤔-ᴴᵧ-ᴸ (גדודה G-DW-DH) — **Slice:** [freq. 1] |kjv: furrow| {str: 1418}

H) 𐤔-ᴴ-ᴸ (גדה GDH) ac: **?** co: **Riverbank** ab: **?:** The water rushing by the bank undercuts a furrow inside the bank.

N^f) 𐤔-ᴴ-ᴸ (גדה G-DH) — **Riverbank:** [freq. 4] |kjv: bank| {str: 1415}

b^f) 𐤔-ᴶ-ᴴ-ᴸ (גדיה G-DYH) — **Riverbank:** [freq. 1] |kjv: bank| {str: 1428}

J) ᴴᵧᴸ (גוד GWD) ac: **Invade** co: **Band** ab: **?:** A group of men or things bound together.

V) ᴴᵧᴸ (גוד GWD) — **Invade:** The slicing through of a band of men. [freq. 3] (vf: Paal) |kjv: overcome, invade with troops| {str: 1464}

n^fl) 𐤔-ᴴᵧᴸ𐤷 (אגודה A-GW-DH) — **Band:** A group of men or things bound together. [freq. 4] |kjv: troop, bunch, burdens| {str: 92}

M) ᴴ-ᴶ-ᴸ (גיד GYD) ac: **?** co: **Sinew** ab: **?:** The animals tendon is used for making bowstrings and cords. The tendon is removed by making a slit in the flesh for its removal. The sinews are used for making cordage and bowstrings.

N^m) ᴴ-ᴶ-ᴸ (גיד GYD) — **Sinew:** [freq. 7] |kjv: sinew| {str: 1517}

Adopted Roots;
2054 ᴶ-ᴴ-ᴸ Magnify, Rope
2055 ⊙ᴴᴸ Cut
2056 ⊙ᴴᴸ Taunt

1051) 𐤔ᴸ (גה GH) ac: **Lift** co: **High** ab: **Pride:** A lifting high of something. This root is related to ᵧᴸ and ᴴᴸ.

D) 𐤔𐤷ᴸ (גאה GAH) ac: **Lift** co: **?** ab: **Pride:** The lifting up of something or oneself.

V) 𐤔𐤷ᴸ (גאה G-AH) — **Lift:** A lifting up high of something. [freq. 7] (vf: Paal) |kjv: triumph, risen, grow up, increase| {str: 1342}

N^m) 𐤔𐤷ᴸ (גאה G-AH) — **Proud:** One who lifts himself up. [freq. 9] |kjv: proud| {str: 1343}

F) 𐤔ᴸ𐤊 (הגה HGH) ac: **Lift** co: **?** ab: **?**

V) 𐤔ᴸ𐤊 (הגה H-GH) — **Lift out:** To lift something out of something else. [freq. 3] (vf: Paal) |kjv: take away, stayed| {str: 1898}

H) 𐤔𐤔ᴸ (גהה GHH) ac: **Heal** co: **Medicine** ab: **?:** The lifting of an illness.

V) 𐤔𐤔ᴸ (גהה G-HH) — **Heal:** [freq. 1] (vf: Paal) |kjv: cure| {str: 1455}

N^fl) 𐤔𐤔ᴸ (גהה G-HH) — **Medicine:** [freq. 1] |kjv: medicine| {str: 1456}

1052) ᵧᴸ (גו GW) ac: **?** co: **Back** ab: **?:** The back as the middle part of the body, used in lifting. This root is related to ᵧᴸ and 𐤔ᴸ.

A) ᵧᴸ (גו GW) ac: **?** co: **Back** ab: **?**

N^m) ᵧᴸ (גו GW) — **I. Back:** [Hebrew and Aramaic] **II.**

Middle: The middle or in the midst of anything as the back is in the middle. [Hebrew and Aramaic] [freq. 23] |kjv: back, midst, within the same, wherein, therein, among, body| {str: 1458, 1459, 1460}

N^(f1)) 𐤀YᴸL (גוה G-WH) — **I. Back: II. Pride:** A lifting up of something or oneself in a positive or negative sense. [Hebrew and Aramaic] [freq. 5] |kjv: body, pride, lifting up| {str: 1465, 1466, 1467}

f^(m)) ᴶYᴸL (גוי G-WY) — **Nation:** The people of a nation as the back, or body. [freq. 558] |kjv: nation, heathen, gentiles, people| {str: 1471}

f^(f1)) 𐤀ᴶYᴸL (גויה GW-YH) — **Back:** By extension, the body, either alive or dead, a corpse. [freq. 13] |kjv: body, corpse, carcass| {str: 1472}

~~~~~~~~~~

1053) ᴢᴸL (גז GZ) ac: **Shear** co: **Fleece** ab: **?:** The pictograph ᴸ is a picture of the foot and has a meaning of lifting. The ᴢᴄ is an agricultural implement for harvesting or cutting. The sheering and removal of the wool fleece from the sheep for clothing as well as the cutting of other materials with one stroke.

A) ᴢᴄᴸL (גז GZ) ac: **Shear** co: **Fleece** ab: **?**

N^(m)) ᴢᴄᴸL (גז GZ) — **Fleece:** The shearing of sheep for its fleece. Also the grasses that are sheared off with a sickle in harvest. [freq. 4] |kjv: fleece, mowings, mown grass| {str: 1488}

N^(f4)) +ᴶᴢᴄᴸL (גזית G-ZYT) — **Hewn Stone:** Stones that are sheered with one blow to form flat sides. [freq. 11] |kjv: hewn, wrought| {str: 1496}

B) ᴢᴢᴄᴸL (גזז GZZ) ac: **Shear** co: **?** ab: **?**

V) ᴢᴢᴄᴸL (גזז G-ZZ) — **Shear:** [freq. 15] (vf: Paal, Niphal, Participle) |kjv: shear, sheepshearer, shearers, cut off, poll, shave, cut down| {str: 1494}

C) ᴢᴸLᴵ (אגז AGZ) ac: **?** co: **Nut** ab: **?:** The sheering of a nut tree.

c^(m)) ᴢYᴸLᴵ (אגוז A-GWZ) — **Nut:** [freq. 1] |kjv: nuts| {str: 93}

E) ᴵᴢᴄᴸL (גזא GZA) ac: **?** co: **Stump** ab: **?:** A sheared off tree.

N^(m)) ᴵᴢᴄᴸL (גזא G-ZA) — **Stump:** [freq. 3] |kjv: stock, stem| {str: 1503}

H) 𐤀ᴢᴄᴸL (גזה GZH) ac: **Shear** co: **?** ab: **?**

V) 𐤀ᴢᴄᴸL (גזה G-ZH) — **Shear:** [freq. 1] (vf: Paal, Participle) |kjv: take| {str: 1491}

J) ᴢYᴸL (גוז GWZ) ac: **Sweep** co: **?** ab: **?:** The back and forth sweeping action of a sickle cutting grasses.

V) ᴢYᴸL (גוז GWZ) — **Sweep:** The sweeping away of something. [freq. 2] (vf: Paal) |kjv: cut off, brought| {str: 1468}

M) ᴢᴶᴄᴸL (גיז GYZ) ac: **Shear** co: **Fleece** ab: **?**

N^(f1)) 𐤀ᴢᴶᴄᴸL (גיזה GY-ZH) — **Fleece:** [ms: גזה] [freq. 7] |kjv: fleece| {str: 1492}

Adopted Roots;
2059 Pluck, Feather
2060 Devour, Caterpillar
2061 ut, Axe

~~~~~~~~~~~

1054) (גח GHh) ac: **?** co: **Belly** ab: **?**

A) (גח GHh) ac: **?** co: **Belly** ab: **?**

j^m) (גחון G-HhWN) — **Belly:** [freq. 2] |kjv: belly| {str: 1512}

M) (גיח GYHh) ac: **Burst** co: **?** ab: **?:** The bursting forth of an infant from the womb.

V) (גיח GYHh) — **Burst:** A forceful bursting forth from the womb (see Job 38:8), or other forceful bursting. [Hebrew and Aramaic] [df: גח גוח] [freq. 7] (vf: Paal, Hiphil) |kjv: come forth, take, bring forth, draw up| {str: 1518, 1519}

Adopted Roots;
2472 Laugh
2660 Laugh, Laugh

~~~~~~~~~~~

1055) (גט GTh) ac: **?** co: **?** ab: **?**

~~~~~~~~~~~

1056) (גי GY) ac: **?** co: **?** ab: **?**

~~~~~~~~~~~

1057) (גך GK) ac: **?** co: **?** ab: **?**

~~~~~~~~~~~

1058) (גל GL) ac: **Roll** co: **Round** ab: **?:** Something that is round or a second time around of a time or event. A dancing in a circle. (eng: skull - an added s and an exchange of the k and g, Greek golgotha)

A) (גל GL) ac: **?** co: **Round** ab: **?**

N^m) (גל GL) — **Mound:** A mound or pile of something such as rocks or a spring out of the ground. [freq. 36] |kjv: heap, wave, spring, billow, bowl| {str: 1530, 1531}

N^f1) (גלה G-LH) — **Mound:** A mound or pile of something such as a spring out of the ground or other rounded object. [freq. 14] |kjv: spring, bowl, pommel| {str: 1543}

l^m) (גלגל GL-GL) — **Wheel:** The wheel of a cart or a whirlwind. [Hebrew and Aramaic] [freq. 13] |kjv: wheel, heaven, rolling thing, whirlwind| {str: 1534, 1535, 1536}

l^f2) (גלגלת GL-G-LT) — **Skull:** The roundness of the head or skull. Also a census by the counting of heads. [freq. 12] |kjv: poll, skull, every, head| {str: 1538}

B) (גלל GLL) ac: **Roll** co: **Round** ab: **?**

V) (גלל G-LL) — **Roll:** [freq. 18] (vf: Paal, Niphal, Hiphil, Pilpel) |kjv: roll, seek occasion, wallow, trust, commit, remove, run down| {str: 1556}

N^m) (גלל G-LL) — **I. Round thing:** Something round such as stones or dung. [Hebrew and Aramaic] **II. For the Sake of:** As a rolling back around. [freq. 17] |kjv: dung, because, sake, because of thee, for, great|
~~~~~~~~~~~

{str: 1557, 1558, 1560, 1561, 5953}

b[m]) ᴸᏉᠴᏉᏉ (גליל G-LYL) — **I. Ring: II. Border:** As going around something. [freq. 4] |kjv: folding, ring| {str: 1550}

b[fl]) ᴸᏉᠴᏉᏉ☥ (גלילה G-LY-LH) — **Border:** As going around something. The border of a country is also representative of the country itself. [freq. 5] |kjv: border, coast, country| {str: 1552}

d[m]) ᴸᏉᏉᏉ (גלול G-LWL) — **Idol:** As made from a round log or stone. [ms: גלל] [freq. 48] |kjv: idol, image| {str: 1544}

g[fl]) ☥ᏉᏉᏉᏉ (גוללה GW-L-LH) — **Grape:** The harvested round grapes. [df: עוללה] [freq. 6] |kjv: gleaning grapes, grapegleanings, grapes| {str: 5955}

C) ᏉᏉᏔ (אגל AGL) ac: ? co: **Drop** ab: ?: A drop of dew as round.

N[m]) ᏉᏉᏔ (אגל A-GL) — **Drop:** [freq. 1] |kjv: drop| {str: 96}

D) ᏉᏔᏉ (גאל GAL) ac: ? co: ? ab: **Redeem:** The buying back, a bringing back around, of someone or something.

V) ᏉᏔᏉ (גאל G-AL) — **Redeem:** To restore one to his original position or avenge his death. In the participle form this verb means avenger as it is the role of the nearest relative to redeem one in slavery or avenge his murder. [freq. 104] (vf: Paal, Niphal) |kjv: redeem, redeemer, kinsman, revenger, avenger, ransom, deliver, kinsfolks,

kinsmans, part, purchase, stain, wise| {str: 1350}

d[fl]) ☥ᏉᏔᏉ (גאולה G-AW-LH) — **Redemption:** [ms: גאלה] [freq. 14] |kjv: redeem, redemption, again, kindred| {str: 1353}

J) ᏉᏌᏉ (גול GWL) ac: ? co: **Infant** ab: ?: A rejoicing at the birth of a child.

V) ᏉᏌᏉ (גול GWL) — **Milk:** To get milk. [df: עול] [freq. 5] (vf: Paal, Participle) |kjv: milch, young| {str: 5763}

N[m]) ᏉᏌᏉ (גול GWL) — **Infant:** One who takes milk. [df: עול] [freq. 2] |kjv: infant, child, babe, little one| {str: 5764}

b[m]) ᏉᏌᏉ (גויל G-WYL) — **Young:** [df: עויל] [freq. 2] |kjv: young, little one| {str: 5759}

l[m]) ᏉᏉᏌᏉ (גולל GW-LL) — **Infant:** One who takes milk. [df: עולל] [freq. 20] |kjv: suckling, infant| {str: 5768}

M) ᏉᏔᏉ (גיל GYL) ac: ? co: **Circle** ab: ?: A continual rolling or circling.

V) ᏉᏔᏉ (גיל GYL) — **Rejoice:** A rejoicing by dancing around in a circle. [df: גול] [freq. 44] (vf: Paal) |kjv: rejoice, glad, joyful, joy, delight| {str: 1523}

N[m]) ᏉᏔᏉ (גיל GYL) — **Circle:** A circle of rejoicing. [freq. 10] |kjv: rejoice, joy, gladness| {str: 1524}

N[fl]) ☥ᏉᏔᏉ (גילה GY-LH) — **Circle:** A circle of rejoicing. [df: גילת] [freq. 2] |kjv: rejoicing, joy| {str: 1525}

k[fl]) ☥ᏉᏔᏉᏜ (מגילה M-GY-LH) — **Scroll:** The leather or papyrus sheets of written text

that are rolled up. [Hebrew and
Aramaic] [ms: מגלה] [freq. 22]
|kjv: roll, volume| {str: 4039,
4040}

fj^m) ‎גליון‎ GY-L-
YWN) — **Scroll:** The leather or
papyrus sheets of written text
that are rolled up. [ms: גליון]
[freq. 2] |kjv: glasses, roll| {str:
1549}

Adopted Roots;
2049 Bound, Boundary
2063 Shave, Barber
2064 Skin
2065 Shave
2066 Wrap
2524 Round, Bullock

1059) (גמ GM) ac: **Gather** co: **Foot**
ab: **?:** The pictograph L is a picture of the
foot and means to walk. The water.
Combined these mean "walking to
water". The watering well or other place
of water is a gathering place for men,
animals and plants for drinking. Men and
animals may walk great distances for
these watering holes while plants grow in
abundance in them. (eng: game - from the
Latin word game meaning leg)

A) (גמ GM) ac: **Gather** co: **?**
ab: **?:** Any gathering of people,
things or ideas.

N^m) (גמ GM) — **Also:**
Through the idea of a gathering
of objects or ideas. [freq. 34]
|kjv: also, as, again, and| {str:
1571}

k^{fl}) (מגמה MG-MH)
— **Gather:** A horde or troop
gathered. [freq. 1] |kjv: sup up|
{str: 4041}

C) (אגמ AGM) ac: **?** co:
Pool ab: **?:** The place of gathering of
reeds. Ropes are made from the
fibers of the reeds.

N^m) (אגמ A-GM) — **I.**
Pool: A collection of water. **II.**
Reed: [freq. 10] |kjv: pools,
standing, reeds| {str: 98, 99}

j^m) (אגמון AG-MWN)
— **Reed:** As a large gathering in
a pond. Also a rope that is made
from reeds from reeds. [freq. 5]
|kjv: rush, bulrushes, caldron,
hook| {str: 100}

E) (גמא GMA) ac: **Drink**
co: **Reed** ab: **?:** A plant that grows
near the water.

V) (גמא G-MA) —
Drink: A drinking of water as
from a pond. [freq. 2] (vf:
Hiphil, Piel) |kjv: swallow,
drink| {str: 1572}

N^m) (גמא G-MA) —
Reed: As a large gathering in a
pond. [freq. 4] |kjv: rush,
bulrush| {str: 1573}

Adopted Roots;
2070 Yield

1060) (גן GN) ac: **?** co: **Garden** ab:
Protection: The pictograph L is a picture
of the foot and means to walk with an
extended meaning to gather. The is a
picture of a sprouting seed. Combined
these mean "a gathering of seeds". A
garden is a place for growing crops and is
often surrounded by a rock wall or hedge
to protect it from grazing animals. (eng:
genesis; beginning; genetics; genome)

A) (גן GN) ac: **?** co: **Garden** ab:
?: A garden enclosed by walls for

protection. A shield as a wall of protection.

N^{m/f}) ᴸ (גַן GN) — **Garden:** [freq. 42] |kjv: garden| {str: 1588}

N^{f1}) ᴸ (גַנָּה G-NH) — **Garden:** [freq. 12] |kjv: garden| {str: 1593}

a^m) ᴸ (מָגֵן MG-N) — **Shield:** A wall of protection. [freq. 63] |kjv: shield, buckler, armed, defense, ruler| {str: 4043}

e^{f1}) ᴸ (גִּנָּה GY-NH) — **Garden:** [ms: גנה] [freq. 4] |kjv: garden| {str: 1594}

B) ᴸ (גנן GNN) ac: ? co: **Shield** ab: ?: A wall of protection.

V) ᴸ (גנן G-NN) — **Shield:** A protection of an individual or community. [freq. 8] (vf: Paal, Hiphil) |kjv: defend| {str: 1598}

C) ᴸ (אגן AGN) ac: ? co: **Basin** ab: ?: A container enclosed by walls.

N^m) ᴸ (אַגָּן A-GN) — **Basin:** [freq. 3] |kjv: basons, cup, goblet| {str: 101}

Adopted Roots;
2073 ᴸ   Steal, Thief, Theft
2074 ᴸ   Store, Treasure
3010 ᴸ   Treasury

1061) ᴸ (גס GS) ac: ? co: ? ab: ?

1062) ᴸ (גע GAh) ac: Gasp co: ? ab: **Wear**

H) ᴸ (געה GAhH) ac: **Bellow** co: ? ab: ?

V) ᴸ (געה G-AhH) — **Bellow:** [freq. 2] (vf: Paal) |kjv: low| {str: 1600}

J) ᴸ (גוע GWAh) ac: **Gasp** co: ? ab: ?: A breathing out at the point of death.

V) ᴸ (גוע GWAh) — **Die:** To breath out the last breath of death. [freq. 24] (vf: Paal) |kjv: die, give up the ghost, dead, perish| {str: 1478}

L) ᴸ (יגע YGAh) ac: **Weary** co: **Labor** ab: ?: Work that brings about heavy breathing and weariness.

V) ᴸ (יגע Y-GAh) — **Weary:** [freq. 26] (vf: Paal, Hiphil, Piel) |kjv: weary, labour, fainted| {str: 3021}

N^m) ᴸ (יגע Y-GAh) — **Weary:** [freq. 4] |kjv: labour, weary| {str: 3022, 3023}

b^m) ᴸ (יגיע Y-GYAh) — **I. Labor: II. Weary:** [freq. 17] |kjv: labour, work, weary| {str: 3018, 3019}

b^{f1}) ᴸ (יגיעה Y-GY-AhH) — **Weariness:** [freq. 1] |kjv: weariness| {str: 3024}

1063) ᴸ (גף GP) ac: ? co: ? ab: ?

C) ᴸ (אגף AGP) ac: ? co: **Troop** ab: ?

N^m) ᴸ (אֲגַף A-GP) — **Troop:** An army or band of men. [freq. 7] |kjv: band| {str: 102}

J) ᴸ (גוף GWP) ac: ? co: **Shut** ab: ?

V) ᴸ (גוף GWP) — **Shut:** To close or shut something.

[freq. 1] (vf: Hiphil) |kjv: shut| {str: 1479}

N^(fl)) ‏גופה‏ (GW-PH) — **Corpse:** From the closed eyes. [freq. 2] |kjv: body| {str: 1480}

~~~~~~~~~

1064) ⊶ᒪ (‏גץ‏ GTs) ac: **?** co: **?** ab: **?**

~~~~~~~~~

1065) ⊶ᒪ (‏גק‏ GQ) ac: **?** co: **?** ab: **?**

~~~~~~~~~

1066) ᑫᒪ (‏גר‏ GR) ac: **Sojourn** co: **Traveler** ab: **Fear:** The pictograph ᒪ is a picture of the foot and means to walk. The ᑫ is a picture of a man. Combined these mean "a walking man". One traveling through a foreign land is a stranger to the people and culture. Fear is associated with strangers and seen as an enemy. This root also has the idea of laying out flat to sleep through the idea of spending the night. (eng: growl - a sound from the throat; grown)

A) ᑫᒪ (‏גר‏ GR) ac: **?** co: **Traveler** ab: **?:** One who travels in a strange land. Also the throat as the place where fear is felt.

N^(m)) ᑫᒪ (‏גר‏ GR) — **Stranger:** [df: ‏גיר‏] [freq. 92] |kjv: stranger, alien, sojourner, chalkstone| {str: 1616}

N^(fl)) ‏גרה‏ (G-RH) — **I. Cud:** The chewing of the cud by clean animals. **II. Gerah:** A standard of measure. [freq. 16] |kjv: cud, gerah| {str: 1625, 1626}

N^(f3)) ‏גרות‏ (G-RWT) — **Lodge:** A temporary residence.

[freq. 1] |kjv: habitation| {str: 1628}

i^(fl)) ‏תגרה‏ (TG-RH) — **Blow:** A striking of another out of anger. [freq. 1] |kjv: blow| {str: 8409}

j^(m)) ‏גרון‏ (G-RWN) — **Throat:** The throat is the place where fear is felt. [ms: ‏גרן‏] [freq. 8] |kjv: throat, neck, mouth| {str: 1627}

k^(fl)) ‏מגרה‏ (MG-RH) — **Saw:** Used in stone cutting (in the sense of chewing). [freq. 4] |kjv: saw, axe| {str: 4050}

l^(m)) ‏גרגר‏ (GR-GR) — **Berry:** A food harvested and consumed by travelers along the road. [freq. 1] |kjv: berry| {str: 1620}

l^(f2)) ‏גרגרת‏ (GR-G-RT) — **Neck:** [freq. 4] |kjv: neck| {str: 1621}

B) ᑫᑫᒪ (‏גרר‏ GRR) ac: **Chew** co: **Throat** ab: **?:** The throat is the place where fear is felt.

V) ᑫᑫᒪ (‏גרר‏ G-RR) — **Chew:** [freq. 5] (vf: Paal, Niphal, Participle) |kjv: catch, destroy, chew, saw, continuing| {str: 1641}

C) ᑫᒪ⅄ (‏אגר‏ AGR) ac: **Gather** co: **?** ab: **?:** A gathering together of small items for traveling such as grain, berries or coins.

V) ᑫᒪ⅄ (‏אגר‏ A-GR) — **Gather:** [freq. 3] (vf: Paal) |kjv: gather| {str: 103}

c^(fl)) ‏אגורה‏ (A-GW-RH) — **Coin:** Carried by travelers for the purchase of supplies. [freq. 1] |kjv: coin| {str: 95}

G) 𐤍𐤔𐤋 (גהר GHR) ac: **Prostrate** co: **?** ab: **?**: When a stranger meets another he lays prostrate in homage to the other.

V) 𐤍𐤔𐤋 (גהר G-HR) — **Prostrate:** [freq. 3] (vf: Paal) |kjv: stretch, cast down| {str: 1457}

H) 𐤔𐤍𐤋 (גרה GRH) ac: **Fight** co: **Throat** ab: **?**: The place of chewing and growling out of anger. Also scratching of the throat from fear or affliction.

V) 𐤔𐤍𐤋 (גרה G-RH) — **Fight:** A struggle or strife with another. [freq. 14] (vf: Hitpael, Piel) |kjv: stir up, meddle, contend, strive| {str: 1624}

J) 𐤍𐤅𐤋 (גור GWR) ac: **Sojourn** co: **Dwelling** ab: **Fear:** A temporary place of dwelling for the traveler.

V) 𐤍𐤅𐤋 (גור GWR) — **I. Sojourn:** To travel in a strange land. **II. Afraid:** Strangers bring fear to the inhabitants. [freq. 98] (vf: Paal) |kjv: sojourn, dwell, afraid, stranger, assemble| {str: 1481}

N^m) 𐤍𐤅𐤋 (גור GWR) — **Whelp:** Usually a young lion. [May be derived from the sound of the lion] [ms: גר] [freq. 7] |kjv: whelp, young one| {str: 1482, 1484}

N^fl) 𐤔𐤍𐤅𐤋 (גורה GW-RH) — **Whelp:** Usually a young female lion. [May be derived from the sound of the lion] [ms: גרה] [freq. 2] |kjv: whelp| {str: 1484}

a^m) 𐤍𐤅𐤋𐤌 (מגור M-GWR) — **Fear:** Strangers bring fear to the inhabitants. [ms: מגר] [freq. 8] |kjv: fear, terror| {str: 4032}

d^m) 𐤍𐤅𐤋𐤌 (מגור M-GWR) — **I. Stranger:** One who travels in a strange land. [ms: מגר] **II. Sojourn:** To travel a strange land. [freq. 11] |kjv: pilgrimage, stranger, dwelling, sojourn| {str: 4033}

kc^fl) 𐤔𐤍𐤅𐤋𐤌 (מגורה M-GW-RH) — **Fear:** A fear of an enemy. [freq. 1] |kjv: fear| {str: 4034}

kd^fl) 𐤔𐤍𐤅𐤋𐤌 (מגורה M-GW-RH) — **I. Fear:** A fear of an enemy. **II. Barn:** [Unknown connection to root] [freq. 3] |kjv: fear, barn| {str: 4035}

L) 𐤍𐤋𐤉 (יגר YGR) ac: **?** co: **?** ab: **Fear:** Fear of a stranger or enemy.

V) 𐤍𐤋𐤉 (יגר Y-GR) — **Afraid:** [freq. 5] (vf: Paal) |kjv: afraid, fear| {str: 3025}

c^m) 𐤍𐤅𐤋𐤉 (יגור Y-GWR) — **Afraid:** [freq. 2] |kjv: fear, afraid| {str: 3016}

M) 𐤍𐤋 (גיר GYR) ac: **?** co: **Limestone** ab: **?**: Used to make a plaster for making a flat level floor.

N^m) 𐤍𐤋 (גיר GYR) — **Plaster:** [Hebrew and Aramaic] [ms: גר] [freq. 2] |kjv: plaister| {str: 1528, 1615}

Adopted Roots;

2080	𐤌𐤍𐤋	Scratch, Itch
2081	𐤃𐤍𐤋	Scrape
2082	𐤆𐤍𐤋	Cut, Axe
2083	𐤋𐤍𐤋	Rough, Stone
2085	𐤏𐤍𐤋	Floor
2086	𐤑𐤍𐤋	Crush
2087	𐤎𐤍𐤋	Diminish, Ledge
2088	𐤓𐤍𐤋	Sweep away
2089	𐤔𐤔𐤍𐤋	Cast out, Pasture

1067) ᠘ᠤᠤ (גש GSh) ac: **?** co: **?** ab: **?**

B) ᠘ᠤᠤ (גשש GShSh) ac: **Grope** co: **?** ab: **?**

V) ᠘ᠤᠤ (גשש G-ShSh) — **Grope:** [freq. 2] (vf: Piel) |kjv: grope| {str: 1659}

M) ᠘ᠤ (גיש GYSh) ac: **?** co: **Clod** ab: **?**

N^m) ᠘ᠤ (גיש GYSh) — **Clod:** A dirt clod. [df: גוש] [freq. 1] |kjv: clod| {str: 1487}

1068) ᠘ (גת GT) ac: **?** co: **Winepress** ab: **?:** The pictograph ᠘ is a picture of the foot. The ┼ is a picture of a mark. Combined these mean "a foot marked".

After the graes are placed in the wine vat, treaders walk in the vat to crush the grapes freeing up the juices. The treaders feet and lower parts of their clothing are stained red, a sign of their occupation (see Isaiah 63:1-3).

A) ᠘ (גת GT) ac: **?** co: **Winepress** ab: **?**

N^f) ᠘ (גת GT) — **Winepress:** [freq. 5] |kjv: winepress, press, winefat| {str: 1660}

1069) ᠘ (גע GGh) ac: **?** co: **?** ab: **?**

Dal

1070) דﬡ (דא DA) ac: ? co: ? ab: ?

1071) ד﬒ (דב DB) ac: **Rest** co: ? ab: ?:
The pictograph דﬡ is a picture of the a
tent door. The ﬒ is a representation of a
tent. Combined these mean "the door of
the tent". The door of the tent was the
place of relaxation for the father. Here he
would watch his family, livestock and the
road for approaching visitors (see Genesis
18:1). This root is related to the root טד
(a reversal of the letters).

A) ד﬒ (דב DB) ac: ? co: **Slow** ab:
?: Something that is slow and quiet.
N^fl) ד﬒ﬨ (דבה D-BH) —
Slander: Speaking evil of
another (usually done quietly).
[freq. 9] |kjv: slander, evil report,
infamy| {str: 1681}

B) ד﬒﬒ (דבב DBB) ac: **Whisper**
co: ? ab: ?: A quiet speech.
V) ד﬒﬒ (דבב D-BB) —
Whisper: A quiet speaking as
when sleeping. [df: צפף] [freq.
5] (vf: Paal, Pilpel, Participle)
|kjv: speak, whisper| {str: 1680,
6850}

C) ד﬒ﬡ (אדב ADB) ac: **Grieve**
co: ? ab: ?: A quiet state.
V) ד﬒ﬡ (אדב A-DB) —
Grieve: [freq. 1] (vf: Hiphil)
|kjv: grieve| {str: 109}

D) דﬡ﬒ (דאב DAB) ac: ? co: ?
ab: **Sorrow:** A quiet state.
V) דﬡ﬒ (דאב D-AB) —
Mourn: [freq. 3] (vf: Paal) |kjv:

sorrow, sorrowful, mourn| {str:
1669}
N^fl) דﬡ﬒ﬨ (דאבה DA-BH)
— **Sorrow:** [freq. 1] |kjv:
sorrow| {str: 1670}
j^m) דﬡ﬒﬩ﬨ (דאבון DA-BWN)
— **Sorrow:** [freq. 1] |kjv:
sorrow| {str: 1671}

E) ד﬒ﬡ (דבא DBA) ac: ? co:
Rest ab: ?
N^m) ד﬒ﬡ (דבא D-BA) —
Rest: [freq. 1] |kjv: strength|
{str: 1679}

J) ד﬩﬒ (דוב DWB) ac: ? co: ? ab:
Sorrow
V) ד﬩﬒ (דוב DWB) —
Sorrow: One who moves
slowly. [freq. 1] (vf: Hiphil) |kjv:
sorrow| {str: 1727}
N^m/f) ד﬩﬒ (דוב DWB) —
Bear: A slow moving animal.
[Hebrew and Aramaic] [ms: דב]
[freq. 13] |kjv: bear| {str: 1677,
1678}

Adopted Roots;
2094 ד﬒אּאּ Honey

1072) ד﬙ (דג DG) ac: **Dart** co: **Fish** ab:
Anxiety: The pictograph דﬡ is a picture
of the a tent door which is a curtain hung
over the entrance of the tent. To gain
entrance to the tent or to leave, the curtain
moved back and forth. Also, the door is
used for moving back and forth from the
tent to the outside. The ﬙ is a
representation of a foot. The combined
meaning of these two letters is "the back

and forth moving of the foot (or tail)". The tail of a fish moves back and forth to propel itself through the water. The darting around of fish. (eng: dog - as a waging tail)

A) 𐤋𐤂 (דג DG) ac: **?** co: **Fish** ab: ?

N^(m)) 𐤋𐤂 (דג DG) — **Fish:** [df: דאג] [freq. 20] |kjv: fish| {str: 1709}

N^(fl)) 𐤀𐤋𐤂 (דגה D-GH) — **Fish:** [freq. 15] |kjv: fish| {str: 1710}

m^(m)) 𐤍𐤋𐤂 (דגן D-GN) — **Grain:** A plentiful crop. [freq. 40] |kjv: wheat, cereal, grain, corn| {str: 1715}

D) 𐤋𐤉𐤂 (דאג DAG) ac: **Dart** co: **?** ab: **Anxiety:** The back and forth darting of a fish in the water.

V) 𐤋𐤉𐤂 (דאג D-AG) — **Anxious:** An anxious behavior like a fish darting in the water. [freq. 7] (vf: Paal) |kjv: afraid, sorrow, sorry, careful, take thought| {str: 1672}

N^(fl)) 𐤀𐤋𐤉𐤂 (דאגה DA-GH) — **Anxiety:** An anxious behavior like a fish darting in the water. [freq. 6] |kjv: carefulness, fear, heaviness, sorrow, care| {str: 1674}

H) 𐤀𐤋𐤂 (דגה DGH) ac: **Increase** co: **?** ab: **?:** A net full of fish is an abundance or increase.

V) 𐤀𐤋𐤂 (דגה D-GH) — **Increase:** [freq. 1] (vf: Paal) |kjv: grow| {str: 1711}

J) 𐤋𐤉𐤂 (דוג DWG) ac: **Fish** co: **Fisherman** ab: **?:** One who catches fish and his equipment.

N^(m)) 𐤋𐤉𐤂 (דוג DWG) — **Fisherman:** [freq. 2] |kjv: fisher| {str: 1728}

N^(fl)) 𐤀𐤋𐤉𐤂 (דוגה DW-GH) — **Fishing:** [freq. 1] |kjv: fish| {str: 1729}

M) 𐤋𐤉𐤂 (דיג DYG) ac: **?** co: **Fish** ab: ?

N^(m)) 𐤋𐤉𐤂 (דיג DYG) — I. **Fish:** II. **Fisherman:** [freq. 3] |kjv: fish, fisher| {str: 1770, 1771}

1073) דד (דד DD) ac: **Move** co: **Breasts** ab: **Passion:** The pictograph דד is a picture of the a tent door which hangs down from the top of the tent entrance. The use of this letter twice indicates "two danglers" representing a womans breasts. The part of the female body invoking heat of passion and love. (eng: udder; dad - as beloved; teat - a double exchange for a t and d)

A) דד (דד DD) ac: **?** co: **Breasts** ab: ?

N^(m)) דד (דד DD) — **Breast:** [freq. 4] |kjv: breast, teat| {str: 1717}

H) 𐤀דד (דדה DDH) ac: **Move** co: **?** ab: **?:** The grace and beauty of the breast.

V) 𐤀דד (דדה D-DH) — **Move:** The graceful and soft movement of a woman. [freq. 2] (vf: Hitpael) |kjv: went, go slowly| {str: 1718}

J) דוד (דוד DWD) ac: **Boil** co: **Pot** ab: **Passion:** The boiling of a liquid in a pot or the passion of a person for another.

N^(m)) דוד (דוד DWD) — I. **Pot:** Pot A pot used for boiling liquids. [ms: דד] II. **Beloved:** One who is loved. Also the uncle as one who is loved by the nephew. [ms: דד] [freq. 68] |kjv: beloved, uncle, love, wellbeloved,. basket, pot, kettle, caldron| {str: 1730, 1731}

N^(fl)) דודה (DW-DH) — **Beloved:** One who is loved, the aunt. [freq. 3] |kjv: aunt| {str: 1733}

L) ידד (YDD) ac: **Boil** co: **?** ab: **Passion:** The passion of a person for another.

b^m) ידיד (Y-DYD) — **Beloved:** One who is loved. [freq. 9] |kjv: beloved, wellbeloved, loves, amiable| {str: 3039}

b^(f3)) ידידות (Y-DY-DWT) — **Passion:** [freq. 1] |kjv: dearly beloved| {str: 3033}

N) דדי (DDY) ac: **?** co: **?** ab: **Passion**

o^m) דודי (DW-DY) — **Mandrakes:** A plant boiled as an aphrodisiac. [freq. 7] |kjv: mandrake, basket| {str: 1736}

1074) דה (DH) ac: **Attack** co: **Bird of prey** ab: **?:** The pictograph דו is a picture of the a tent door with the extended meaning of moving back and forth. The ✲ represents one who is looking and pointing at a great sight. Combined these mean "a back and forth looking". Birds of prey fly around in a circle in search of their prey and dive down on it when seen.

D) דאה (DAH) ac: **Dive** co: **Eagle** ab: **?:** A bird of prey that dives down on its prey.

V) דאה (D-AH) — **Dive:** [freq. 4] (vf: Paal) |kjv: fly| {str: 1675}

N^(fl)) דאה (D-AH) — **Daah:** An unknown bird of prey. [freq. 1] |kjv: vulture| {str: 1676}

b^(fl)) דאיה (DA-YH) — **Dayyah:** An unknown bird of prey. [df: דיה] [freq. 2] |kjv: vulture| {str: 1772}

1075) דו (DW) ac: **Sick** co: **Sickness** ab: **Illness**

A) דו (DW) ac: **?** co: **Weak** ab: **?**

f^m) דוי (D-WY) — **Weak:** A weakness from illness or sorrow. [freq. 5] |kjv: sorrowful, languishing| {str: 1741, 1742}

H) דוה (DWH) ac: **Ill** co: **Disease** ab: **?**

V) דוה (D-WH) — **Ill:** [freq. 1] (vf: Paal) |kjv: infirmity| {str: 1738}

N^m) דוה (D-WH) — **Illness:** Also a womans cycle. [freq. 5] |kjv: faint, sick, sickness, menstruous cloth| {str: 1739}

a^m) מדוה (MD-WH) — **Disease:** What brings on an illness. [freq. 2] |kjv: disease| {str: 4064}

1076) דז (DZ) ac: **?** co: **?** ab: **?**

1077) דח (DHh) ac: **Push** co: **?** ab: **Worthless:** The pictograph דו is a door representing the idea of moving back and forth. The חח is a picture of a wall. Combined these pictures mean "the back and forth movement of a wall" (see Ps 62:3).

A) דחד (דח DHh) ac: **Throw down** co: **Ruin** ab: **?:** A continual pushing to cause a ruin or stumbling.

f[m]) דחדﾚ (דחי D-HhY) — **Stumble:** [freq. 2] |kjv: fall| {str: 1762}

h[f1]) ﾑדחדﾘ (מדחה MD-HhH) — **Ruin:** Something that is thrown down in ruin. [freq. 1] |kjv: ruin| {str: 4072}

j[f]) דחדﾚ (דחון D-HhWN) — **Instrument:** A musical instrument that is continually struck such as a harp. [Aramaic only] [freq. 1] |kjv: instrument, musick| {str: 1761}

H) דחדﾘ (דחה DHhH) ac: **Push** co: **?** ab: **?:** A continual pushing to throw down or out.

V) דחדﾘ (דחה D-HhH) — **Push:** To push something down or onward. [df: דחח] [freq. 11] (vf: Paal, Niphal, Pual) |kjv: outcast, thrust, sore, overthrow, chase, tottering, drive away, drive on, cast down| {str: 1760}

J) דﾥחד (דוח DWHh) ac: **?** co: **Clean** ab: **?**

V) דﾥחד (דוח DWHh) — **Clean:** Something that has been scrubbed clean. [freq. 4] (vf: Hiphil) |kjv: wash, purge, cast out| {str: 1740}

a[m]) דﾥחדﾑ (מדוח M-DWHh) — **Worthless:** What is cast away as worthless. [freq. 1] |kjv: causes of banishment| {str: 4065}

Adopted Roots;
2099 דחד•- Push

1078) דﾟד (דט DTh) ac: **?** co: **?** ab: **?**

1079) דﾚד (די DY) ac: **Saturate** co: **Ink** ab: **Sufficient:** Something that is completely filled.

A) דﾚד (די DY) ac: **Saturate** co: **Ink** ab: **?**

N[m]) דﾚד (די DY) — **Sufficient:** What is enough. [freq. 38] |kjv: enough, sufficient| {str: 1767}

a[m]) דﾚדﾑ (מדי MD-Y) — **Sufficient:** What is enough. [freq. 1] |kjv: sufficiently| {str: 4078}

q[m]) דﾚדﾥ (דיו D-YW) — **Ink:** Ink A liquid that saturates. [freq. 1] |kjv: ink| {str: 1773}

1080) דﾜﾘ (דך DK) ac: **Crush** co: **Mortar** ab: **?:** The pictograph ד is a door representing the idea of moving back and forth. The ﾜ is a picture of the palm of the hand representing a bowl from its shape. Combined these pictures mean "the moving back and forth in a cup". Seeds are placed in a stone mortar, a stone cup, the stone pestle is moved around the cup to crush the seeds into a powder.

A) דﾜﾘ (דך DK) ac: **Crush** co: **Mortar** ab: **?**

N[m]) דﾜﾘ (דך DK) — **I. Crush: II. Small:** Something that is crushed thin or into smaller pieces. [df: דק] [freq. 18] |kjv: oppressed, afflicted| {str: 1790, 1851}

f^m) דּ‑וּשׁ‑ـ (דכי D-KY) —
Wave: Wave A crushing of the
surf. [freq. 1] |kjv: wave| {str:
1796}

B) דּ‑וּשׁוּשׁ (דכך DKK) ac: ? co:
Powder ab: ?: The fine dust created
in the mortar by crushing something.

V) דּ‑וּשׁוּשׁ (דכך D-KK) —
Small: To crush or beat
something into small pieces.
[Hebrew and Aramaic] [df:
דקק] [freq. 23] (vf: Paal, Hiphil,
Hophal) |kjv: beat small,
powder, stamp, bruise, small,
dust, beat in pieces, break in
pieces| {str: 1854, 1855}

E) דּ‑וּשׁ‑ל (דכא DKA) ac: **Break**
co: ? ab: ?

V) דּ‑וּשׁ‑ל (דכא D-KA) —
Break: To break something by
beating it. [freq. 18] (vf: Niphal,
Hitpael, Pual, Piel) |kjv: break,
break in pieces, crush, bruise,
destroy| {str: 1792}

N^m) דּ‑וּשׁ‑ל (דכא D-KA) —
Broken: Something that is
broken into pieces. [freq. 3] |kjv:
contrite, destruction| {str: 1793}

F) דּ‑וּ‑שׁ‑צ (הדך HDK) ac: **Trample**
co: ? ab: ?: Walking over something
to trample on it as with a pestle in a
mortar.

V) דּ‑וּ‑שׁ‑צ (הדך H-DK) —
Trample: [freq. 1] (vf: Paal)
|kjv: tread down| {str: 1915}

H) דּ‑וּשׁ‑צ (דכה DKH) ac: ? co:
Bruise ab: ?: Something that is
bruised by beating it.

V) דּ‑וּשׁ‑צ (דכה D-KH) —
Bruise: [freq. 5] (vf: Paal,
Niphal, Piel) |kjv: break,
contrite, crouch| {str: 1794}

N^fl) דּ‑וּשׁ‑צ (דכה D-KH) —
Bruised: [freq. 1] |kjv: wounded|
{str: 1795}

J) דּ‑Y‑וּשׁ (דוך DWK) ac: **Beat** co:
Mortar ab: ?: A beating as with a
mortar in a pestle.

V) דּ‑Y‑וּשׁ (דוך DWK) — **Beat:**
[Hebrew and Aramaic] [df: דוק]
[freq. 2] (vf: Paal) |kjv: beat,
break into pieces| {str: 1743,
1751}

k^fl) דּ‑Y‑וּשׁ‑צ‑ₘₘ (מדוכה M-DW-
KH) — **Mortar:** [ms: מדכה]
[freq. 1] |kjv: mortar| {str: 4085}

M) דּ‑וּ‑שׁ (דיך DYK) ac: **Beat** co:
Siege works ab: ?

N^m) דּ‑וּ‑שׁ (דיך DYK) —
Siege works: Engines of war
constructed next to a city wall
for the purpose of battering it
into pieces to allow entry into
the city. [df: דיק] [freq. 6] |kjv:
fort| {str: 1785}

1081) דּ‑ U (דל DL) ac: **Back and Forth**
co: **Door** ab: ?: The pictograph דּ is a
door. The U is a picture of staff and
represents any rod. Combined these
pictures mean "the door on the rod". The
tent door was hung down as a curtain,
covering the entrance to the tent, from a
horizontal pole. The door was then moved
to the side for going in and out of the tent.
(eng: door - an exchange for the d and l)

A) דּ‑ U (דל DL) ac: ? co: **Door** ab:
Poor: Any object that dangles such
as a bucket that is hung from a rope
down a well to retrieve water. The
hair hangs from the head. A poor or
weak person hangs the head in
poverty.

N^m) ד־ל (דל DL) — **Weak:** One who dangles the head in poverty or hunger. [freq. 48] |kjv: poor, needy, weak, lean| {str: 1800}

N^{f1}) ד־ל🕮 (דלה D-LH) — **I. Poor:** One who hangs head low in weakness. **II. Hair:** What hangs from the head and is easily blown by the wind. [freq. 8] |kjv: poor, pinning, sickness, hair| {str: 1803}

N^{f2}) ד־לת (דלת D-LT) — **Door:** [freq. 88] |kjv: door, gate, leaves, lid| {str: 1817}

B) ד־לל (דלל DLL) ac: **Hang** co: ? ab: ?

V) ד־לל (דלל D-LL) — **Brought low:** To be brought down low such as the head in humility or a dried up river. [freq. 9] (vf: Paal, Niphal) |kjv: brought low, dried up, not equal, emptied, fail, impoverished, thin| {str: 1809}

H) ד־ל🕮 (דלה DLH) ac: **Lift** co: ? ab: ?: Anything that dangles down and swings back and forth, such as a branch, hair or door.

V) ד־ל🕮 (דלה D-LH) — **Lift:** The lifting of the bucket out of the well for drawing water. [freq. 5] (vf: Paal, Piel) |kjv: draw, enough, lifted| {str: 1802}

b^{f1}) ד־ל🕮 (דליה DL-YH) — **Branch:** Dangles from a tree blowing back and forth in the wind. [freq. 8] |kjv: branch| {str: 1808}

f^m) ד־ל (דלי D-LY) — **Bucket:** Dangles from a rope to draw water and lifted out of the well. [freq. 2] |kjv: bucket| {str: 1805}

Adopted Roos;
2101 ד־לב Leap

~~~~~~~~~~

1082) דם (דם DM) ac: ? co: **Blood** ab: **Likeness:** The pictograph דד is a door representing the idea of moving back and forth. The ממ is a picture of water and can represent any liquid especially blood. Combined these pictures mean "the moving back and forth of water" or the "flowing of blood". Similarly, the grape plant takes water from the ground and moves it to the fruit where the water becomes the blood of the grape. (eng: dumb)

A) דם (דם DM) ac: ? co: **Blood** ab: ?: The blood of man is also water, which moves through the body. When the blood is shed, the man or animal becomes silent. A son from the blood of his father resembles his father.

N^m) דם (דם DM) — **Blood:** [freq. 361] |kjv: blood, bloody, bloodguilt| {str: 1818}

B) דממ (דמם DMM) ac: **Silent** co: ? ab: ?: When the blood is shed, the man or animal becomes silent and still.

N^m) דממ (דמם D-MM) — **Silent:** [freq. 30] |kjv: silence, still, silent, cut off, cut down, rest, cease, forbear, peace, quieted, tarry, wait| {str: 1826}

N^{f1}) דממ🕮 (דממה DM-MH) — **Silent:** [freq. 3] |kjv: still, silence, calm| {str: 1827}

o^m) דוממ (דומם DW-MM) — **Silent:** [freq. 3] |kjv: silent, quietly wait, dumb| {str: 1748}

C) ᴀᴅᴍ (אדם ADM) ac: ? co: **Red** ab: ?: The color red, the color of blood, man and the earth.

V) ᴀᴅᴍ (אדם A-DM) — **Red:** To be red as a color or through the shedding of blood. [freq. 10] (vf: Paal, Hiphil, Hitpael, Pual) |kjv: dyed red, red, ruddy, man, Adam, person| {str: 119}

N^m) ᴀᴅᴍ (אדם A-DM) — **Man:** From the reddish skin. [freq. 552] |kjv: dyed red, red, ruddy, man, Adam, person| {str: 120}

N^fl) ᴀᴅ-ᴍʜ (אדמה AD-MH) — **Ground:** From its red color. [freq. 225] |kjv: land, earth, ground, country, husbandman| {str: 127}

c^m) ᴀ-ᴅᴡᴍ (אדום A-DWM) — **Red:** [ms: אדם] [freq. 9] |kjv: red, ruddy| {str: 122}

g^f) ᴀᴡ-ᴅᴍ (אודם AW-DM) — **Ruby:** A red precious stone. [ms: אדם] [freq. 3] |kjv: sardius| {str: 124}

I^m) ᴀ-ᴅᴍ-ᴅᴍ (אדמדם A-DM-DM) — **Reddish:** [freq. 6] |kjv: reddish| {str: 125}

jf^m) ᴀᴅ-ᴍᴡ-ɴʏ (אדמוני AD-MW-NY) — **Red:** [ms: אדמני] [freq. 3] |kjv: red, ruddy| {str: 132}

F) ʜᴅᴍ (הדם HDM) ac: ? co: **Pieces** ab: ?: [Unknown connection to root;]

N^m) ʜ-ᴅᴍ (הדם H-DM) — **Pieces:** Something cut into pieces. [Aramaic only] [freq. 2] |kjv: pieces| {str: 1917}

c^m) ʜ-ᴅᴡᴍ (הדום H-DWM) — **Stool:** [Unknown connection to root;] [ms: הדם] [freq. 6] |kjv: stool| {str: 1916}

G) ᴅʜᴍ (דהם DHM) ac: **Dumb** co: ? ab: ?: When excited or scared ones blood pressure increases and is unable to speak.

V) ᴅ-ʜᴍ (דהם D-HM) — **Dumb:** To be speechless. [freq. 1] (vf: Niphal, Participle) |kjv: astonied| {str: 1724}

H) ᴅᴍʜ (דמה DMH) ac: ? co: **Likeness** ab: **Compare:** A son from the blood of his father resembles his father.

V) ᴅ-ᴍʜ (דמה D-MH) — **I. Compare:** To perceive something like something else. [Hebrew and Aramaic] **II. Silence:** To become silent as one dead. [freq. 47] (vf: Paal, Niphal, Hitpael, Piel) |kjv: like, liken, thought, compared, devised, mean, similitude| {str: 1819, 1820, 1821}

N^f3) ᴅ-ᴍᴡᴛ (דמות D-MWT) — **Likeness:** Likeness A son from the blood of his father resembles his father. [freq. 25] |kjv: likeness, similitude, like, manner, fashion| {str: 1823}

f^m) ᴅ-ᴍʏ (דמי D-MY) — **Silent:** When the blood is shed, the man or animal becomes silent. [freq. 4] |kjv: silence, cut off, rest| {str: 1824}

fj^m) ᴅᴍ-ʏᴡɴ (דמיון DM-YWN) — **Likeness:** A son from the blood of his father resembles his father. [freq. 1] |kjv: like| {str: 1825}

J) ᴅᴡᴍ (דום DWM) ac: **Silent** co: ? ab: ?: When the blood is shed, the man or animal becomes silent.

N^{f1}) (דומה DW-MH) — **Silent:** [ms: דמה] [freq. 3] |kjv: silence, destroyed| {str: 1745, 1822}

N) (דמי DMY) ac: **Silent** co: **?** ab: **?:** When the blood is shed, the man or animal becomes silent.

g^{f1}) (דומיה DW-M-YH) — **Silence:** [freq. 4] |kjv: wait, silent, silence| {str: 1747}

Adopted Roots;
2698 Face, East, Before
2754 Sleep

~~~~~~~~~~~

1083) (דן DN) ac: **Rule** co: **Ruler** ab: **Quarrel:** The pictograph is a picture of a door. The is a picture of a seed representing the idea of life. Combined these pictures mean "the door of life". The ancient Hebrew concept of a "judge" is one who restores life. The goal of one that rules or judges is to bring a pleasant and righteous life to the people. This can also mean a deliverer as one whom restores life to his people. (eng: damn - with an added m; dean - as a judge)

A) (דן DN) ac: **Quarrel** co: **?** ab: **?:** A quarrel requiring the need of a ruler or judge to mediate the incident.

k^{m}) (מדן M-DN) — **Quarrel:** [freq. 3] |kjv: discord, strife| {str: 4090}

ac^{m}) (מדון M-DWN) — **Quarrel:** [freq. 18] |kjv: strife, contention, discord| {str: 4066}

hb^{m}) (מדין MD-YN) — **Quarrel:** [freq. 9] |kjv: contention, brawling| {str: 4079}

C) (אדן ADN) ac: **?** co: **Base** ab: **Lord:** The foundation of a column or pillar as the support of the structure.

N^{m}) (אדן A-DN) — **Base:** [freq. 56] |kjv: socket, foundation| {str: 134}

c^{m}) (אדון A-DWN) — **Lord:** The ruler as the foundation to the community. [ms: אדן] [freq. 335] |kjv: lord, owner, master, sir| {str: 113}

cf^{m}) (אדוני A-DW-NY) — **Lord:** The ruler as the foundation to the community. [ms: אדני] [freq. 434] |kjv: lord, god| {str: 136}

M) (דין DYN) ac: **Judge** co: **?** ab: **Judge**

V) (דין DYN) — **Judge:** [Hebrew and Aramaic] [df: דון] [freq. 26] (vf: Paal, Niphal) |kjv: judge, plead the cause, contend, execute, strife| {str: 1777, 1778}

N^{m}) (דין DYN) — **I. Judge:** [df: דון] **II. Judgment:** [Hebrew and Aramaic] [freq. 28] |kjv: judge, judgment, cause, plea, strife, tread, out| {str: 1779, 1780, 1781, 1782}

k^{f1}) (מדינה M-DY-NH) — **Province:** The jurisdiction of responsibility of a judge or lord. [Hebrew and Aramaic] [freq. 55] |kjv: province| {str: 4082, 4083}

~~~~~~~~~~~

1084) (דס DS) ac: **?** co: **?** ab: **?**

F) (הדס HDS) ac: **?** co: **Myrtle** ab: **?:** The tree or its wood.

N^m) 𐤀𐤃𐤎 (הדס H-DS) —
Myrtle: [freq. 6] |kjv: myrtle,
myrtle tree| {str: 1918}

~~~~~~~~

1085) עד (דע DAh) ac: **See** co: **?** ab:
Knowledge: The pictograph דּ is a
picture of a door. The עֵ is a picture of
the eye. Through the eyes one
experiences his world and learns from it.
Combined these pictures mean "the door
of the eye". The eye is the window into
the mans very being. Experience is gained
through visual observation. Knowledge is
achieved through these experiences.

A) עד (דע DAh) ac: **?** co: **?** ab:
Knowledge: To have an intimate
relationship with another person, an
idea or an experience.

N^m) עד (דע DAh) —
Knowledge: [freq. 5] |kjv:
opinion, knowledge| {str: 1843}

N^{f1}) 𐤀עד (דעה D-AhH) —
Knowledge: [freq. 6] |kjv:
knowledge| {str: 1844}

N^{f2}) 𐤕עד (דעת D-AhT) —
Knowledge: [freq. 93] |kjv:
knowledge, know| {str: 1847}

a^m) עדᴍ (מדע MD-Ah) —
Knowledge: [freq. 6] |kjv:
knowledge, thought, science|
{str: 4093}

J) עYד (דוע DWAh) ac: **?** co: **?**
ab: **Why:** A desire to know
something.

a^m) עYדᴍ (מדוע M-DWAh)
— **Why:** [ms: מדע] [freq. 6]
|kjv: wherefore, why, how| {str:
4069}

L) עדﾋ (ידע YDAh) ac: **See** co:
? ab: **Knowledge:** To have an
intimate relationship with another
person, an idea or an experience.

V) עدﾋ (ידע Y-DAh) —
Know: [Hebrew and Aramaic]
[freq. 994] (vf: Paal, Niphal,
Hiphil, Hitpael, Hophal, Pual,
Piel, Participle) |kjv: know,
known, knowledge, perceive,
shew, tell, wist, understand,
certainly, acknowledge,
acquaintance, consider, declare,
teach| {str: 3045, 3046}

k^m) עדYᴍ (מודע MW-DAh)
— **Kinsman:** A relative who is
known. [ms: מדע] [freq. 2] |kjv:
kinsman, kinswoman| {str:
4129}

k^{f2}) 𐤕עדYᴍ (מודעת MW-D-
AhT) — **Kindred:** The
community of relatives. [freq. 1]
|kjv: kindred| {str: 4130}

mf^m) ﾋﾢעدﾋ (ידעני YD-
Ah-NY) — **Wizard:** One with
special knowledge. [freq. 11]
|kjv: wizard| {str: 3049}

Adopted Roots;
2383 עدﾋ Knowledge

~~~~~~~~

1086) עד (דף DP) ac: **Push** co: **?** ab:
Slander

F) עدﾢ (הדף HDP) ac: **Thrust**
co: **?** ab: **?:** To push, shove or thrust
another away.

V) עدﾢ (הדף H-DP) —
Thrust: [freq. 11] (vf: Paal) |kjv:
thrust, drive, cast out, expel| {str:
1920}

J) עYد (דוף DWP) ac: **Slander**
co: **?** ab: **?**

f^m) ﾋעYد (דופי DW-PY) —
Slander: [ms: דפי] [freq. 1]
|kjv: slander| {str: 1848}

~~~~~~~~

1087) ᴅᴧᴛ (דץ DTs) ac: **Leap** co: ? ab: ?

J) ᴅᴧYᴛ (דוץ DWTs) ac: **Leap** co: ? ab: ?: A leaping of joy.

V) ᴅᴧYᴛ (דוץ DWTs) — **Leap:** [freq. 1] (vf: Paal) |kjv: turn into joy| {str: 1750}

1088) ᴅ•ᴛ (דק DQ) ac: ? co: **Curtain** ab: ?

A) ᴅ•ᴛ (דק DQ) ac: ? co: **Curtain** ab: ?

N^m) ᴅ•ᴛ (דק DQ) — **Curtain:** [freq. 1] |kjv: curtain| {str: 1852}

1089) ᴅᴙ (דר DR) ac: ? co: **Circle** ab: ?: The pictograph ᴛ is a door representing a moving back and forth. The ᴙ is the head of a man. Combined these mean "the back and forth movement of man". A generation is one revolution of the family line. The Hebraic understanding of order is the continual cyclical process of life and death or renewal and destruction. This root can also have the meanings of circling around of something in a wide area or to cover a large area. (eng: adore - as honor)

A) ᴅᴙ (דר DR) ac: ? co: **Circle** ab: ?: A circling around as the flight of a bird or a dance.

N^m) ᴅᴙ (דר DR) — **I. Generation:** As a circle of the family. **II. White:** From the whiteness of the pearl. [freq. 5] |kjv: white, generation| {str: 1858, 1859}

I^m) ᴅᴙᴅᴙ (דרדר DR-DR) — **Thistle:** Used by the shepherd to build a corral around the flock at night [freq. 2] |kjv: thistle| {str: 1863}

B) ᴅᴙᴙ (דרר DRR) ac: ? co: **Circle** ab: ?: A circling around as the flight of a bird or a dance.

c^f) ᴅᴙYᴙ (דרור D-RWR) — **I. Swallow:** A bird that flies in a circle. **II. Free Flowing:** A flowing liquid. [freq. 10] |kjv: pure, swallow| {str: 1865, 1866}

C) ᴙᴛ𝔶 (אדר ADR) ac: **Wide** co: **Robe** ab: ?: What covers a large area.

V) ᴙᴛ𝔶 (אדר A-DR) — **Wide:** [freq. 3] (vf: Niphal, Hiphil, Participle) |kjv: glorious, honourable| {str: 142}

N^m) ᴙᴛ𝔶 (אדר A-DR) — **I. Wide: II. Robe:** A wide garment. [freq. 2] |kjv: goodly, mantle, threshing floor| {str: 145}

N^f²) †ᴙᴛ𝔶 (אדרת AD-RT) — **I. Robe:** A wide garment. **II. Noble:** Something that is wide in majesty. [freq. 12] |kjv: mantle, garment, glory, goodly, robe| {str: 155}

b^m) ᴙᴌᴛ𝔶 (אדיר A-DYR) — **Noble:** Someone or something that is wide in authority or majesty. [freq. 27] |kjv: noble, excellent, mighty, principle, famous, gallant, glorious, goodly, lordly, worthies| {str: 117}

e^m) ᴙᴛᴌ𝔶 (אידר AY-DR) — **Threshing floor:** A wide area. [Aramaic only] [freq. 1] |kjv: threshingfloor| {str: 147}

E) 𝔶ᴙᴛ (אדרא DRA) ac: ? co: ? ab: ?: [Unknown meaning]

97

j^m) דראון (דראון DR-AWN)
— **Abhor:** [freq. 2] |kjv: abhorring, contempt| {str: 1860}

F) הדר (הדר HDR) ac: **Swell** co: ? ab: **Honor:** To swell in an outward direction. To make another swell through honor or pride (as in a swelling up of the chest).

V) הדר (הדר H-DR) — **Swell:** Someone or something that is wide in size or majesty. To honor. [Hebrew and Aramaic] [freq. 10] (vf: Paal, Niphal, Hitpael) |kjv: honour, countenance, crooked places, glorious, glorified, put forth| {str: 1921, 1922}

N^m) הדר (הדר H-DR) — **Honor:** Someone or something that is swollen in size, pride or majesty. [freq. 34] |kjv: honour, majesty, glory, beauty, comeliness, excellency, glorious, goodly| {str: 1923, 1925, 1926}

N^{fl}) הדרה (הדרה HD-RH) — **Swelling:** [freq. 5] |kjv: beauty, honour| {str: 1927}

G) דהר (דהר DHR) ac: **Gallop** co: ? ab: ?: The repetitious rhythmic running of a horse in a circular direction.

V) דהר (דהר D-HR) — **Gallop:** [freq. 1] (vf: Paal) |kjv: prancing| {str: 1725}

N^m) דהר (דהר D-HR) — **Gallop:** [df: דרהה] [freq. 2] |kjv: prancing| {str: 1726}

i^m) תדהר (תדהר TD-HR) — **Tidhar:** The wood or the tree of an unknown species. Probably from its wide or circular growth. [freq. 2] |kjv: pine, pine tree| {str: 8410}

J) דור (דור DWR) ac: **Dwell** co: **Dwelling** ab: ?: The nomadic camp was set up in a circle with the tents set up outside of the circle.

V) דור (דור DWR) — **Dwell:** [Hebrew and Aramaic] [freq. 8] (vf: Paal) |kjv: dwell| {str: 1752, 1753}

N^m) דור (דור DWR) — **I. Circle:** [ms: דר] **II. Ball: III. Generation:** The circle of life from generation to generation. [freq. 170] |kjv: generation, all, many| {str: 1754, 1755}

k^m) מדור (מדור M-DWR) — **Dwelling:** [Aramaic only] [ms: מדר] [freq. 4] |kjv: dwelling| {str: 4070}

k^{fl}) מדורה (מדורה M-DW-RH) — **Pile:** A round pile of wood for fires. [ms: מדרה] [freq. 2] |kjv: pile| {str: 4071}

ib^{fl}) תדירה (תדירה T-DY-RH) — **Continue:** As a swelling. [Aramaic only] [ar: תדירא] [freq. 2] |kjv: continually| {str: 8411}

Adopted Roots;

2057	בדר	Enclose, Wall
2093	סדר	Order, Word
2468	עדר	Order, Row
2530	קדר	Miss, Rake, Order
2576	שׂדק	Arrange, Plan

1090) דש (דש DSh) ac: **Thresh** co: **Grass** ab: ?: The pictograph דר is a door representing the idea of moving back and forth. The שׁ is a picture of teeth meaning to press. Combined these pictures mean "the back and forth movement of pressure". The grains were placed on the threshing floor where they were trampled on and beaten in order to separate the hulls from the grain. (eng: dash - as tread on and broken)

C) ⨀⊔⊓⌀ (אדש ADSh) ac: **Thresh** co: ? ab: ?

V) ⨀⊔⊓⌀ (אדש A-DSh) — **Thresh:** [freq. 1] (vf: Paal) |kjv: threshing| {str: 156}

E) ⌀⊔⊓⌀ (דשא DShA) ac: **Sprout** co: **Grass** ab: ?: What comes from the grains.

V) ⌀⊔⊓⊓ (דשא D-ShA) — **Sprout:** To sprout green sprouts. [freq. 2] (vf: Paal, Hiphil) |kjv: spring, bring forth| {str: 1876}

N^m) ⌀⊔⊓⊓ (דשא D-ShA) — **Grass:** Young green sprouts. [Hebrew and Aramaic] [ar: דתאא] [freq. 17] |kjv: grass, herb, green| {str: 1877, 1883}

J) ⊔⊔Y⊓ (דוש DWSh) ac: **Thresh** co: ? ab: ?

V) ⊔⊔Y⊓ (דוש DWSh) — **Thresh:** [Hebrew and Aramaic] [df: דיש] [freq. 15] (vf: Paal, Niphal, Hophal) |kjv: thresh, tread, tear, tread it down| {str: 1758, 1759}

k^{f1}) ⌀⊔⊔Y⊓〰 (מדושה M-DW-ShH) — **Threshing:** [freq. 1] |kjv: threshing| {str: 4098}

M) ⊔⊔⊳⊓ (דיש DYSh) ac: **Thresh** co: ? ab: ?

N^m) ⊔⊔⊳⊓ (דיש DYSh) — **Threshing:** [freq. 1] |kjv: threshing| {str: 1786}

j^m) ⅃Y⊔⊔⊳⊓ (דישון DY-ShWN) — **Dishon:** Unknown clean animal. [Unknown connection to root;] [ms: דיש] [freq. 1] |kjv: pygarg| {str: 1788}

~~~~~~~~~

1091) ✝⊓ (דת DT) ac: ? co: ? ab: **Law:** The pictograph דר is a picture of a door meaning enter or entrance. The ✝ is a mark. Combined these pictures mean "entering with a mark". When two parties agree to follow the laws of a covenant, a mark is given as a sign of continued allegiance.

A) ✝⊓ (דת DT) ac: ? co: ? ab: **Law**

N^f) ✝⊓ (דת DT) — **Law:** A law, decree or edict. [Hebrew and Aramaic] [freq. 36] |kjv: law| {str: 1881, 1882}

~~~~~~~~~

1092) ⵐ⊓ (דע DGh) ac: ? co: ? ab: ?

~~~~~~~~~

Hey

1093) 𐤅𐤀𐤉 (הא HA) ac: **Look** co: ? ab: **Behold:** The pictograph 𐤀 represents one who is looking at a great sight with his hands raised as when saying behold. A looking toward someone or something. This root is closely related to 𐤀𐤀, 𐤉𐤀, and 𐤀𐤉. (eng: he)

A) 𐤅𐤀𐤉 (הא HA) ac: **Look** co: ? ab: ?

N^m) 𐤅𐤀𐤉 (הא HA) — **Behold:** To draw attention to something important. [Hebrew and Aramaic] [df: האה] [freq. 17] |kjv: lo, behold, even| {str: 1887, 1888, 1889}

J) 𐤅𐤉𐤀 (הוא HWA) ac: **Look** co: ? ab: ?

N^m) 𐤅𐤉𐤀 (הוא HWA) — **He:** A looking toward another. [Hebrew and Aramaic; Also the feminine she, sometimes written as 𐤀𐤉𐤅] [df: היא] [freq. 45] |kjv: that, him, same, this, he, which, who, such, wherein, be, it, one| {str: 1931, 1932}

~~~~~~~~~~~

1094) 𐤁𐤀 (הב HB) ac: **Give** co: **Gift** ab: **Love:** The pictograph 𐤀 represents one who is looking at a great sight with his hands raised as when saying behold. The 𐤁 is a representation of the tent or house. Combined these pictures mean "look toward the house" or "provide for the family". One does not choose the household which one is born into, including tribe, parents, children and wife (as marriages were often arranged by the father), it is a gift from God. These gifts are seen as a privilege and are to be cherished and protected. (eng: have - as given)

A) 𐤁𐤀 (הב HB) ac: **?** co: **Gift** ab: **?**

I^m) 𐤁𐤀𐤁𐤀 (הבהב HB-HB) — **Gift:** [freq. 1] |kjv: offering| {str: 1890}

C) 𐤀𐤀𐤁𐤉 (אהב AHB) ac: **?** co: **?** ab: **Love:** The expressions and actions toward the family, which one was privileged with.

V) 𐤀𐤀𐤁𐤉 (אהב A-HB) — **Love:** [freq. 208] (vf: Paal, Niphal, Piel, Participle) |kjv: love, lover, friend, beloved, like, lovely, loving| {str: 157}

N^m) 𐤀𐤀𐤁𐤉 (אהב A-HB) — **Beloved:** One who is loved. [freq. 2] |kjv: lover, loving| {str: 158}

N^fl) 𐤀𐤀𐤁𐤉 (אהבה AH-BH) — **Love:** [freq. 40] |kjv: love| {str: 160}

g^m) 𐤀𐤀𐤉𐤁𐤉 (אוהב AW-HB) — **Love:** [ms: אהב] [freq. 1] |kjv: loves| {str: 159}

L) 𐤁𐤀𐤉 (יהב YHB) ac: **Give** co: **Gift** ab: **?:** A giving of someone or something to one who is deserving or to be privileged.

V) 𐤁𐤀𐤉 (יהב Y-HB) — **Give:** [Hebrew and Aramaic] [freq. 62] (vf: Paal) |kjv: give, go, bring, ascribe, come, set, take, delivered, laid, paid, prolonged, yielded| {str: 3051, 3052}

N^m) 𐤁𐤀𐤉 (יהב Y-HB) — **Burden:** A heavy gift that is

difficult to bear. [freq. 1] |kjv: burden| {str: 3053}

~~~~~~~~~~

1095) 𐤄𓀀 (הג HG) ac: **?** co: **?** ab: **Ponder:** A murmuring or soft speech while in a continual contemplation over something.

A) 𐤄𓀀 (הג HG) ac: **Ponder** co: ? ab: ?

N^{f3}) †Yᒪ𓀀 (הגות H-GWT) — **Pondering:** [freq. 1] |kjv: meditation| {str: 1900}

s^{f1}) 𓀀◣ᒪ𓀀 (הגינה H-GY-NH) — **Ahead:** Something that is in front as something that is contemplated. [freq. 1] |kjv: directly| {str: 1903}

fj^{m}) ↶Y◣ᒪ𓀀 (הגיון HG-YWN) — **Melody:** [freq. 4] |kjv: higgaion, meditation, solemn sound, device| {str: 1902}

B) ᒪᒪ𓀀 (הגג HGG) ac: **Ponder** co: ? ab: ?

b^{m}) ᒪ◣ᒪ𓀀 (הגיג H-GYG) — **Pondering:** [freq. 2] |kjv: meditation, musing| {str: 1901}

H) 𓀀ᒪ𓀀 (הגה HGH) ac: **Ponder** co: ? ab: ?

V) 𓀀ᒪ𓀀 (הגה H-GH) — **Ponder:** To be in continual contemplation over a matter. [freq. 25] (vf: Paal, Hiphil) |kjv: meditate, mourn, speak, imagine, study, mutter, utter, roaring, sore, talk| {str: 1897}

N^{m}) 𓀀ᒪ𓀀 (הגה H-GH) — **Pondering:** The outward sounds of contemplation. [freq. 3] |kjv: sound, tale, mourning| {str: 1899}

~~~~~~~~~~

1096) 𐤃𓀀 (הד HD) ac: **Shout** co: ? ab: ?: (eng: hoot)

A) 𐤃𓀀 (הד HD) ac: **Shout** co: ? ab: ?

N^{m}) 𐤃𓀀 (הד HD) — **Shout:** [freq. 1] |kjv: sounding| {str: 1906}

B) 𐤃𐤃𓀀 (הדד HDD) ac: **Shout** co: ? ab: ?

e^{m}) 𐤃𐤃◣𓀀 (הידד HY-DD) — **Shout:** [freq. 7] |kjv: shout| {str: 1959}

J) 𐤃Y𓀀 (הוד HWD) ac: **Shout** co: ? ab: **Splendor**

N^{m}) 𐤃Y𓀀 (הוד HWD) — **Splendor:** A prominent beauty or work as shouting out. [freq. 24] |kjv: glory, honour, majesty, beauty, comeliness, goodly| {str: 1935}

b^{f1}) 𓀀𐤃◣Y𓀀 (הוידה H-WY-DH) — **Shout:** [ms: הידה] [freq. 1] |kjv: song of thanksgiving| {str: 1960}

~~~~~~~~~~

1097) 𓀀𓀀 (הה HH) ac: **Breathe** co: **Breath** ab: **Exist:** The pictograph 𓀀 represents one who is looking at a great sight with his hands raised and taking a long breath. The pictograph 𓀀 represents one who is looking at a great sight with his hands raised and taking a long breath.

A) 𓀀𓀀 (הה HH) ac: **?** co: **Breath** ab: ?

N^{m}) 𓀀𓀀 (הה HH) — **Woe:** A heavy breath. [freq. 1] |kjv: woe| {str: 1929}

J) 𓀀Y𓀀 (הוה HWH) ac: **Exist** co: **Breath** ab: ?

V) 𐤉𐤅𐤉 (הוה HWH) — **Exist:** To exist or have breath. That which exists has breath. In Hebrew thought the breath is the character of someone or something. Just as a man has character, so do objects. [Hebrew and Aramaic] [ar: הוא] [freq. 75] (vf: Paal) |kjv: be, hath, was| {str: 1933, 1934}

M) 𐤉𐤉𐤉 (היה HYH) ac: **Exist** co: **Breath** ab: **?**

V) 𐤉𐤉𐤉 (היה HYH) — **Exist:** To exist or have breath. That which exists has breath. In Hebrew thought the breath is the character of someone or something. Just as a man has character, so do objects. [A generic verb with a wide application meaning to exist or be] [freq. 74] (vf: Paal, Niphal) |kjv: was, come to pass, came, been, happened, become, pertained, better for thee| {str: 1961}

~~~~~~~~~~

1098) 𐤉𐤏 (הו HW) ac: **?** co: **Sigh** ab: **Disaster:** The pictograph 𐤉 represents one who is looking at a great sight with his hands raised as when saying behold. This root is closely related to 𐤉𐤋, 𐤉𐤉 and 𐤉. (eng: ho)

A) 𐤉𐤏 (הו HW) ac: **?** co: **Sigh** ab: **Disaster:** A moaning sigh from a disaster or evil.

N^m) 𐤉𐤏 (הו HW) — **Woe:** [freq. 2] |kjv: alas| {str: 1930}

N^fl) 𐤉𐤏𐤉 (הוה H-WH) — **Disaster:** A wicked or disastrous event. [Hebrew and Aramaic] [df: היה] [freq. 21] |kjv: calamity, wickedness, perverse,

mischief| {str: 1942, 1943, 1962}

~~~~~~~~~~

1099) 𐤉𐤆 (הז HZ) ac: **?** co: **?** ab: **?**

~~~~~~~~~~

1100) 𐤉𐤄𐤄 (הח HHh) ac: **?** co: **?** ab: **?**

~~~~~~~~~~

1101) 𐤉𐤈 (הט HTh) ac: **?** co: **?** ab: **?**

~~~~~~~~~~

1102) 𐤉𐤉 (הי HY) ac: **Sigh** co: **?** ab: **Disaster:** The pictograph 𐤉 represents one who is looking at a great sight with his hands raised as when saying behold. This root is closely related to 𐤉𐤋, 𐤉𐤉 and 𐤉.

A) 𐤉𐤉 (הי HY) ac: **?** co: **Sigh** ab: **?**: A sigh out of lamentation.

N^m) 𐤉𐤉 (הי HY) — **Woe:** [freq. 1] |kjv: woe| {str: 1958}

J) 𐤉𐤏𐤉 (הוי HWY) ac: **?** co: **Sigh** ab: **?**: A sigh out of joy or lamentation.

N^m) 𐤉𐤏𐤉 (הוי HWY) — **Ah:** [freq. 52] |kjv: ah, alas, ha, ho, o, woe| {str: 1945}

~~~~~~~~~~

1103) 𐤉𐤔 (הך HK) ac: **?** co: **?** ab: **?**

~~~~~~~~~~

1104) 𐤉𐤋 (הל HL) ac: **Shine** co: **Star** ab: **Distant:** The pictograph 𐤉 is a picture of a man with his arms raised looking at a great sight. The 𐤋 is a shepherd staff representing the idea of "toward" as the staff is used to move a sheep toward a direction. Combined these letters mean "a looking toward something" such as the looking toward a light in the distance.

The stars have always been used to guide the traveler or shepherd to find his home or destination.

A) (הל HL) ac: **Look** co: **?** ab: **?:** To look toward a sight.

N^m) (הל HL) — **I. These:** Designating a group that is with the speaker. In the sense of looking toward a sight. [Hebrew and Aramaic; The short form "" is used as a prefix meaning "look" and translated as "the".] [df: אלה אל] **II. Toward:** A moving to or toward something to be with it as the ox moves toward a destination. [df: אל] [freq. 69] |kjv: these, those, this, thus, who, so, such, some, same, other, which, another, whom, they, them| {str: 411, 412, 413, 428, 429,}

e^m) (היל HYL) — **These:** Designating a group that is with the speaker. In the sense of looking toward a sight. [Aramaic only] [df: אלך] [freq. 14] |kjv: these, those| {str: 479}

i^f1) (תהלה TH-LH) — **Folly:** In the sense of shining. [freq. 1] |kjv: folly| {str: 8417}

r^m) (הלו H-LW) — **Behold:** As to look at a sight. [Aramaic only] [df: אלו] [ar: ארו] [freq. 10] |kjv: behold, lo| {str: 431, 718}

s^m) (הלין H-LYN) — **These:** Designating a group that is with the speaker. In the sense of looking toward a sight. [Aramaic only] [df: אלן] [freq. 5] |kjv: these, the| {str: 459}

ie^f1) (תהילה T-HY-LH) — **Shining:** A shining through ones actions or words. May be in a positive (praise) or negative (folly) sense. [freq. 57] |kjv: praise| {str: 8416}

B) (הלל HLL) ac: **Shine** co: **?** ab: **?:** To cause a shining of one by praising or giving thanks to another or to ones self.

V) (הלל H-LL) — **Shine:** To shine through ones actions or words. [freq. 165] (vf: Paal, Hiphil, Hitpael, Pual, Piel, Participle) |kjv: praise, glory, boast, mad, shine, foolish, commended, rage, celebrate| {str: 1984}

a^m) (מהלל MH-LL) — **Shine:** [freq. 1] |kjv: praise| {str: 4110}

e^m) (הילל HY-LL) — **Star:** [freq. 1] |kjv: Lucifer| {str: 1966}

g^f1) (הוללה HW-L-LH) — **Madness:** As one shining in a negative sense. [freq. 4] |kjv: madness| {str: 1947}

o^f3) (הוללות HW-L-LWT) — **Madness:** As one shining in a negative sense. [freq. 1] |kjv: madness| {str: 1948}

bd^m) (הילול HY-LWL) — **Shine:** [ms: הלול] [freq. 2] |kjv: praise, merry| {str: 1974}

C) (אהל AHL) ac: **Shine** co: **Tent** ab: **?**

V) (אהל A-HL) — **I. Shine: II. Pitch tent:** [denominative of] [freq. 4] (vf: Hiphil, Paal, Piel) |kjv: shine, tent| {str: 166, 167}

N^m) (אהל A-HL) — **Aloe:** The glistening oils of the plant. The oils or the tree. [freq.

4] |kjv: aloes, trees of aloes| {str: 174}

g^m) ꝇ☥Υꝇ (אוהל AW-HL) — **Tent:** The shining light of the campfire next to the tent in the distance is a guide for those returning home late just as a star is used as a guide. [ms: אהל] [freq. 345] |kjv: tabernacle, tent, dwelling| {str: 168}

E) ꝇꝇ☥ (הלא HLA) ac: **Distant** co: **?** ab: **?:** A distant sight that is looked toward.

V) ꝇꝇ☥ (הלא H-LA) — **Distant:** To be far off. [freq. 1] (vf: Niphal) |kjv: cast far off| {str: 1972}

N^{fl}) ☥ꝇꝇ☥ (הלאה HL-AH) — **Distant:** Something far off in the distance. [freq. 16] |kjv: beyond, forward, hitherto, back, thenceforth, henceforth, yonder| {str: 1973}

K) Υꝇ☥ (הלו HLW) ac: **?** co: **Here** ab: **?:** An arrival to the distant place.

p^m) ᄴΥꝇ☥ (הלום H-LWM) — **Here:** [freq. 11] |kjv: hither, here, thither| {str: 1988}

L) ꝇ☥ᒣ (יהל YHL) ac: **?** co: **Bright** ab: **?**

qp^m) ᄴΥꝇ☥ᒣ (יהלום YH-LWM) — **Diamond:** A hard and precious stone that glitters. [ms: יהלם] [freq. 3] |kjv: diamond| {str: 3095}

~~~~~~~~~

1105) ᄴ☥ (הם HM) ac: **Roar** co: **Sea** ab: **Tumult:** The pictograph ☥ represents a looking toward. The ᄴ is a picture of water. Combined these pictures mean "a looking toward the water". A large body of water seen as a place of chaos because of its storms, turbulent surf and the commotion of the waves.

A) ᄴ☥ (הם HM) ac: **Roar** co: **Multitude** ab: **?**

j^m) ꝇΥᄴ☥ (המון H-MWN) — **Multitude:** A loud group. [ms: המן] [freq. 83] |kjv: multitude, noise, tumult, abundance, many, store, company| {str: 1995}

B) ᄴᄴ☥ (המם HMM) ac: **Destroy** co: **Destruction** ab: **Destruction:** An uproar.

V) ᄴᄴ☥ (המם H-MM) — **Destroy:** A loud commotion. [freq. 13] (vf: Paal) |kjv: discomfit, destroy, vex, crush, break, consume, trouble| {str: 2000}

H) ☥ᄴ☥ (המה HMH) ac: **Roar** co: **Abundant** ab: **?**

V) ☥ᄴ☥ (המה H-MH) — **Roar:** A loud speaking or wailing. [freq. 34] (vf: Paal) |kjv: roar, noise, disquieted, sound, troubled, aloud, loud| {str: 1993}

N^m) ☥ᄴ☥ (המה H-MH) — **Abundant:** [freq. 1] |kjv: any| {str: 1991}

f^{fl}) ☥ᒣ ᄴ☥ (המיה HM-YH) — **Roar:** A loud noise [freq. 1] |kjv: noise| {str: 1998}

J) ᄴΥ☥ (הום HWM) ac: **Roar** co: **Sea** ab: **?**

V) ᄴΥ☥ (הום HWM) — **Roar:** To make a loud noise. [freq. 6] (vf: Paal, Niphal, Hiphil) |kjv: rang, noise, move, destroy| {str: 1949}

i^f) ᄴΥ☥+ (תהום T-HWM) — **Sea:** A deep and tumultuous water. [ms: תהם] [freq. 36] |kjv: deep, depth| {str: 8415}

k^{fl}) 𐤑ᗯ𐤉𐤑ᗯ (מהומה M-HW-MH) — **Tumult:** [freq. 12] |kjv: destruction, trouble, vex, tumult, discomfiture| {str: 4103}

1106) 𐤍𐤑 (הן HN) ac: Look co: ? ab: Here: The pictograph 𐤑 represents the idea of looking toward something of interest. The 𐤍 is a seed representing continuation. Combined these pictures mean "a looking toward something continually".

A) 𐤍𐤑 (הן HN) ac: ? co: There ab: ?: A person, place or thing that is somewhere else. A desired place or outcome.

N^m) 𐤍𐤑 (הן HN) — **I. There:** A possible or desired location. [df: המון המו המה המ] [ar: אן] **II. They:** A people or things over there. [Hebrew and Aramaic] [df: המה הם] [ar: הסו אנון המון] **III. If:** A possible or desired outcome. [Hebrew and Aramaic] [freq. 110] |kjv: lo, behold, if, though, or, whether, therein, whithal, which, they, them, these, those| {str: 581, 1992, 1994, 2004, 2005, 2006, 3860, 3861}

N^{fl}) 𐤑𐤍𐤑 (הנה H-NH) — **They:** A people or things over there. [freq. 26] |kjv: they, their, those, them| {str: 2007}

H) 𐤑𐤍𐤑 (הנה HNH) ac: ? co: Here ab: ?: To draw attention to a place or event.

N^m) 𐤑𐤍𐤑 (הנה H-NH) — **Here:** [freq. 14] |kjv: hither, here, now, way, since| {str: 2008}

e^m) 𐤑𐤉𐤍𐤑 (הינה HY-NH) — **Behold:** A looking at what is here. [ms: הנה] [freq. 17] |kjv: behold, see, lo| {str: 2009}

J) 𐤍𐤅𐤑 (הון HWN) ac: ? co: Substance ab: ?: An abundance of something that fills what is desired.

V) 𐤍𐤅𐤑 (הון HWN) — **Sufficient:** [freq. 1] (vf: Hiphil) |kjv: ready| {str: 1951}

N^m) 𐤍𐤅𐤑 (הון HWN) — **Substance:** [freq. 26] |kjv: rich, substance, wealth, enough, nought| {str: 1952}

M) 𐤍𐤉𐤑 (הין HYN) ac: ? co: Wealth ab: ?

N^m) 𐤍𐤉𐤑 (הין HYN) — **Hiyn:** A standard of measure. [freq. 22] |kjv: hin| {str: 1969}

1107) 𐤎𐤑 (הס HS) ac: ? co: ? ab: ?

H) 𐤑𐤎𐤑 (הסה HSH) ac: ? co: Quiet ab: ?

V) 𐤑𐤎𐤑 (הסה H-SH) — **Silence:** To keep silent by holding the tongue, silent and still. [freq. 8] (vf: Hiphil, Piel) |kjv: silent, hold peace, hold tongue, still| {str: 2013}

1108) 𐤏𐤑 (הע HAh) ac: ? co: ? ab: ?

1109) 𐤐𐤑 (הף HP) ac: ? co: ? ab: ?

1110) 𐤑𐤑 (הץ HTs) ac: ? co: ? ab: ?

1111) 𐤒𐤑 (הק HQ) ac: ? co: ? ab: ?

1112) 𐤀𐤓𐤑 (הר HR) ac: **High** co: **Hill** ab:
?: The pictograph 𐤓 is a representation of
a head. In Hebrew thought all things are
in motion. A mountain or hill is not
inanimate but the head of the landscape
rising up out of the ground. (eng: hill - an
exchange for the l and r)

A) 𐤀𐤓𐤑 (הר HR) ac: **?** co: **Hill** ab: **?**

N^m) 𐤀𐤓𐤑 (הר HR) — **Hill:** [freq.
546] |kjv: mountain, mount, hill|
{str: 2022}

Ic^m) 𐤀𐤅𐤄𐤓𐤑 (הרהור HR-HWR)
— **Thought:** As a mental
pregnancy. [Aramaic only] [ms:
הרהר] [freq. 1] |kjv: thought|
{str: 2031}

B) 𐤀𐤓𐤓𐤑 (הרר HRR) ac: **?** co: **Hill**
ab: **?**

N^m) 𐤀𐤓𐤓𐤑 (הרר H-RR) — **Hill:**
[freq. 13] |kjv: mountain, hill,
mount| {str: 2042}

H) 𐤄𐤓𐤑 (הרה HRH) ac: **Pregnant**
co: **?** ab: **?**

V) 𐤄𐤓𐤑 (הרה H-RH) —
Pregnant: [freq. 43] (vf: Paal,
Pual) |kjv: conceive, with child,
bare, progenitor| {str: 2029}

N^{f1}) 𐤄𐤓𐤑 (הרה H-RH) —
Pregnant: [df: הרי] [freq. 16]
|kjv: with child, conceive| {str:
2030}

j^m) 𐤍𐤅𐤓𐤑 (הרון H-RWN) —
Pregnancy: From the mound of
the belly. [df: הריון] [freq. 3]
|kjv: conception| {str: 2032}

L) 𐤀𐤓𐤄𐤉 (יהר YHR) ac: **?** co: **?** ab: **?**
Pride

b^m) 𐤀𐤓𐤉𐤄𐤉 (יהיר Y-HYR) —
Proud: One who has made
himself high. [freq. 2] |kjv:
proud, haughty| {str: 3093}

1113) 𐤔𐤄𐤑 (הש HSh) ac: **?** co: **?** ab: **?**

1114) 𐤕𐤑 (הת HT) ac: **Assail** co: **?** ab: **?**

B) 𐤕𐤕𐤑 (התת HTT) ac: **Assail** co: **?**
ab: **?**

V) 𐤕𐤕𐤑 (התת H-TT) — **Assail:**
[freq. 1] (vf: Piel) |kjv: imagine
mischief| {str: 2050}

1115) 𐤏𐤄𐤑 (הע HGh) ac: **?** co: **?** ab: **?**

Waw

1116) ᒡΥ (וא WA) ac: ? co: ? ab: ?

1117) ᒪΥ (וב WB) ac: ? co: ? ab: ?

1118) ᒪΥ (וג WG) ac: ? co: ? ab: ?

1119) ᖶΥ (וד WD) ac: ? co: ? ab: ?

1120) ᖷΥ (וה WH) ac: ? co: ? ab: ?

1121) ΥΥ (וו WW) ac: **Add** co: **Peg** ab: ?:
The pictograph Υ represents a tent peg with the idea of joining or attaching things together. The tent peg is a "Y" shaped wooden peg, which is driven into firm soil. The tent ropes were attached to these pegs. The "Y" shape prevents the rope from slipping off the peg.
   A) ΥΥ (וו WW) ac: ? co: **Peg** ab: ?
      N^m) ΥΥ (וו WW) — **Peg:** A peg, nail or hook as used for attaching one thing to another. [The short form "Y" is used as a prefix meaning "add" or "and".] [freq. 13] |kjv: hook| {str: 2053}

1122) ᔍΥ (וז WZ) ac: ? co: ? ab: ?

1123) ᙁΥ (וח WHh) ac: ? co: ? ab: ?

1124) ᙚΥ (וט WTh) ac: ? co: ? ab: ?

1125) ᔌΥ (וי WY) ac: ? co: ? ab: ?

1126) ᙎΥ (וך WK) ac: ? co: ? ab: ?

1127) ᒑΥ (ול WL) ac: ? co: ? ab: ?

1128) ᙏΥ (ום WM) ac: ? co: ? ab: ?

1129) ᒐΥ (וך WN) ac: ? co: ? ab: ?

1130) ᔎΥ (וס WS) ac: ? co: ? ab: ?

1131) ᙇΥ (וע WAh) ac: ? co: ? ab: ?

1132) ᙈΥ (וף WP) ac: ? co: ? ab: ?

1133) ᙊΥ (וץ WTs) ac: ? co: ? ab: ?

1134) ᙐΥ (וק WQ) ac: ? co: ? ab: ?

1135) ᙉΥ (ור WR) ac: ? co: ? ab: ?

1136) ᒧᒧΥ (וש WSh) ac: ? co: ? ab: ?

1137) ⸸Y (ות WT) ac: ? co: ? ab: ?

1138) ⸙Y (וע WGh) ac: ? co: ? ab: ?

Zan

1139) ᴠ⅄ᴐ (אֹז ZA) ac: ? co: ? ab: ?

1140) ᴨ⅄ᴐ (בֹז ZB) ac: **Issue** co: **Yellow** ab: ?: The pictograph ᴐ is an agricultural implement representing the idea of harvest or food. The ᴨ is a representation of the house. Combined these pictures mean "the food of the house". The main staple of the Hebrews was grain and is yellow in color. This grain was usually ground into a meal for making breads.

C) ᴨᴐ⅄ (אֹזב AZB) ac: ? co: **Hyssop** ab: ?

c^m) ᴨ⅄ᴐ⅄ (אֹזוב A-ZWB) — **Hyssop:** From its yellowish color. [freq. 10] |kjv: hyssop| {str: 231}

D) ᴨ⅄ᴐ (בֹאז ZAB) ac: ? co: **Wolf** ab: ?

N^m) ᴨ⅄ᴐ (בֹאז Z-AB) — **Wolf:** A yellowish colored animal. [freq. 7] |kjv: wolf| {str: 2061}

G) ᴨ⚹ᴐ (בֹהז ZHB) ac: **Gleam** co: **Gold** ab: ?

V) ᴨ⚹ᴐ (בֹהז Z-HB) — **Gleam:** The shine of gold. [df: בֹהצ] [freq. 1] (vf: Hophal) |kjv: fine| {str: 6668}

N^m) ᴨ⚹ᴐ (בֹהז Z-HB) — **Gold:** [Hebrew and Aramaic] [df: בֹהד] [freq. 412] |kjv: gold, golden| {str: 1722, 2091}

a^fl) ⚹ᴨ⚹ᴐᴧ (בֹהזמ MZ-H-BH) — **Gold:** [df: הבֹהדמ]

[freq. 1] |kjv: golden city| {str: 4062}

c^m) ᴨ⅄⚹ᴐ (בֹהוז Z-HWB) — **Yellow:** [df: בֹהצ] [freq. 3] |kjv: yellow| {str: 6669}

J) ᴨ⅄ᴐ (בֹוז ZWB) ac: **Issue** co: **Puss** ab: ?: A yellow discharge.

V) ᴨ⅄ᴐ (בֹוז ZWB) — **Issue:** A flowing out of something. [freq. 42] (vf: Paal, Participle) |kjv: flow, issue, gush| {str: 2100}

N^m) ᴨ⅄ᴐ (בֹוז ZWB) — **Issue:** [freq. 13] |kjv: issue| {str: 2101}

Adopted Roots;

2116	ᴨᴨᴨᴐ	Endow, Dowry
2118	ᴠᴨᴐ	Dwell, Dwelling
2119	⅃ᴨᴐ	Purchase
2532	ᴨᴐᴐ⊙	Leave
3007	ᴨᴨᴐᴫ	Treasurer
3031	ᴨᴐᴨ⅃	

1141) ᴫᴐ (גֹז ZG) ac: ? co: **Grape-skin** ab: ?: The pictograph ᴐ is a picture of an agricultural implement implying harvest. The ᴫ is a picture of the foot. The combined meaning of these pictures is "the harvesting by the feet". The juice of the grape is removed, or harvested, by treading on them in a vat leaving the grape-skins behind.

A) ᴫᴐ (גֹז ZG) ac: ? co: **Grape-skin** ab: ?

N^m) ᴫᴐ (גֹז ZG) — **Grape-skin:** [freq. 1] |kjv: husk| {str: 2085}

1142) בזד (זד ZD) ac: **Boil** co: ? ab: **Pride:** The boiling of a soup or pride. (eng: sod - past tense of seethe)

  A) בזד (זד ZD) ac: ? co: ? ab: **Pride**

    N^m) בזד (זד ZD) — **Proud:** [freq. 13] |kjv: proud, presumptuous| {str: 2086}

    j^m) בזדון (זדון Z-DWN) — **Proud:** [freq. 11] |kjv: pride, presumptuously, proud| {str: 2087}

  C) בזדא (אזד AZD) ac: **Depart** co: ? ab: ?: [Unknown connection to root;]

    N^m) בזדא (אזד A-ZD) — **Depart:** [Aramaic only] [freq. 2] |kjv: gone| {str: 230}

  J) בזוד (זוד ZWD) ac: **Boil** co: ? ab: ?

    V) בזוד (זוד ZWD) — **Boil:** To boil a soup or boil with pride. [Hebrew and Aramaic] [df: זור] [freq. 11] (vf: Paal, Hiphil) |kjv: proudly, presumptuously, presume, sod| {str: 2102, 2103}

  M) בזיד (זיד ZYD) ac: **Boil** co: ? ab: ?

    j^m) בזידון (זידון ZY-DWN) — **Boiling:** [freq. 1] |kjv: proud| {str: 2121}

Adopted Roots;
2386 לבזד Stew

1143) בזה (זה ZH) ac: **Stand-out** co: ? ab: **This:** Something that stands out, is prominent or is pointed out. This root is related in meaning to בזו. (eng: this; that; the; they)

A) בזה (זה ZH) ac: ? co: **This** ab: ?: Someone or something that is prominent.

  N^m) בזה (זה ZH) — **This:** [Hebrew and Aramaic] [df: גה] [ar: דא די דכ דכן דן] [freq. 191] |kjv: this, as, but, now, then| {str: 1454, 1668, 1768, 1791, 1797, 1836, 2063, 2088, 2090}

C) לבזה (אזה AZH) ac: **Kindle** co: **Hot** ab: ?: [Unknown connection to root;]

  N^m) לבזה (אזה A-ZH) — **Hot:** [Aramaic only] [ar: אזא] [freq. 3] |kjv: headed, hot| {str: 228}

1144) בזו (זו ZW) ac: **Stand-out** co: ? ab: **This:** Something that stands out, is prominent or is pointed out. This root is related in meaning to בזה.

A) בזו (זו ZW) ac: ? co: **This** ab: ?: Someone or something that is prominent.

  N^m) בזו (זו ZW) — **This:** [freq. 17] |kjv: that, this, which, wherein| {str: 2097, 2098}

  N^f4) תבזוית (זוית Z-WYT) — **Corner:** The prominent part of a building which provides structure. [freq. 2] |kjv: corner, corner stone| {str: 2106}

M) בזיו (זיו ZYW) ac: ? co: **Bright** ab: ?

  N^m) בזיו (זיו ZYW) — **Bright:** [Aramaic only] [freq. 6] |kjv: countenance, brightness| {str: 2122}

1145) בזז (זז ZZ) ac: ? co: ? ab: ?

J) רזוZ (זוז ZWZ) ac: ? co: **Post** ab: ?

k^fl) מזוזה (מזוזה M-ZW-ZH) — **Post:** [ms: מזוזה] [freq. 19] |kjv: post| {str: 4201}

M) רזיZ (זיז ZYZ) ac: ? co: **Creature** ab: ?

N^m) רזיZ (זיז ZYZ) — **Creature:** [freq. 3] |kjv: wild beast, abundance| {str: 2123}

~~~~~~~~~~~~

1146) רזHh (זח ZHh) ac: ? co: **Belt** ab: ?

A) רזHh (זח ZHh) ac: ? co: **Belt** ab: ?

k^m) רזHh (מזח M-ZHh) — **Belt:** [ms: מזח] [freq. 3] |kjv: strength, girdle| {str: 4206}

B) רzHhHh (זחח ZHhHh) ac: **Remove** co: ? ab: ?

V) רzHhHh (זחח Z-HhHh) — **Remove:** [freq. 2] (vf: Niphal) |kjv: loose| {str: 2118}

M) רzYHh (זיח ZYHh) ac: ? co: **Belt** ab: ?

a^m) רzYHh (מזיח M-ZYHh) — **Belt:** [ms: מזח] [freq. 3] |kjv: strength| {str: 4206}

~~~~~~~~~~~~

1147) ⊗ר (זט ZTh) ac: ? co: ? ab: ?

~~~~~~~~~~~~

1148) רZY (זי ZY) ac: ? co: ? ab: ?

~~~~~~~~~~~~

1149) רZK (זך ZK) ac: **Refine** co: ? ab: **Pure:** An oil or other substance that is clear and free of impurities.

A) רZK (זך ZK) ac: ? co: ? ab: **Pure**

N^m) רZK (זך ZK) — **Pure:** An oil or other substance that is free of impurities. Also a person without impurities. [freq. 11] |kjv: pure, clean| {str: 2134}

r^f) רZKW (זכו Z-KW) — **Innocence:** One without impurities. [Aramaic only] [freq. 1] |kjv: innocency| {str: 2136}

B) רZKK (זכך ZKK) ac: **Refine** co: **Crystal** ab: ?

V) רZKK (זכך Z-KK) — **Refine:** To remove the impurities by washing or refining to make pure. [df: זקק] [freq. 11] (vf: Paal, Hiphil, Pual, Piel) |kjv: clean, pure, refine, fine, purge| {str: 2141, 2212}

c^f4) רZKWKYT (זכוכית Z-KW-KYT) — **Crystal:** A mineral without impurities. [freq. 1] |kjv: cyrstal| {str: 2137}

H) רZKH (זכה ZKH) ac: ? co: ? ab: **Pure**

V) רZKH (זכה Z-KH) — **Pure:** To be without impurities. [freq. 8] (vf: Paal, Hitpael, Piel) |kjv: clean, clear, pure| {str: 2135}

~~~~~~~~~~~~

1150) רZL (זל ZL) ac: **Shake** co: **Branch** ab: ?: The pictograph ר is a picture of n agricultural cutting implement. The J represents a staff. Combined these mean "cut the staff". A staff is made by cutting a branch from the tree, this green branch shakes and bends easily until it has hardened. (see Isaiah 18.5)

A) רZL (זל ZL) ac: ? co: **Cymbal** ab: ?: What is shaken easily.

111

k^f2) +ᒍ/ᕫᨇ (מזלת MZ-LT) —
Cymbal: An instrument that
vibrates when shaken. [df:
מצלת] [freq. 13] |kjv: cymbal|
{str: 4700}

l^f) ᒍᕫᒍᕫ (זלזל ZL-ZL) —
Twig: A small branch that
shakes easily. [df: תלתל] [freq.
2] |kjv: sprigs, bushy| {str: 2150,
8534}

el^m) ᒍᕫᒍᐥᕫ (זילזל ZY-L-
ZL) — **Cymbal:** An instrument
that vibrates when shaken. [df:
צלצל] [freq. 6] |kjv: cymbal|
{str: 6767}

B) ᒍᒍᕫ (זלל ZLL) ac: **Shake** co:
? ab: ?

V) ᒍᒍᕫ (זלל Z-LL) —
Shake: A shaking from fear or
overeating. [df: צלל] [freq. 12]
(vf: Paal, Niphal) |kjv: flow
down, vile, glutton, riotous,
tingle, quiver| {str: 2151, 6750}

C) ᒍᕫᐣ (אזל AZL) ac: **Waver**
co: ? ab: ?: An unsteady, shaking or
to and fro motion.

V) ᒍᕫᐣ (אזל A-ZL) —
Waver: To go about in a
shaking motion. [Hebrew and
Aramaic] [freq. 13] (vf: Paal,
Pual) |kjv: gone, fail, gaddest
about, to and fro, spent, went|
{str: 235, 236}

J) ᒍΥᕫ (זול ZWL) ac: **Shake** co: ?
ab: **Vile:** A shaking out of
something.

V) ᒍΥᕫ (זול ZWL) — **Shake:**
To shake out. [freq. 2] (vf: Paal,
Hiphil) |kjv: lavish, despise| {str:
2107}

N^fl) ⚤ᒍΥᕫ (זולה ZW-LH) —
Except: An exception in the
sense of shaking everything out

except one. [freq. 16] |kjv:
beside, save, only, but| {str:
2108}

N^f3) +ΥᒍΥᕫ (זולות ZW-LWT)
— **Vile:** One who shakes easily.
[ms: זלות] [freq. 1] |kjv: vilest|
{str: 2149}

M) ᒍᐥᕫ (זיל ZYL) ac: **Shake** co:
Bell ab: ?

k^fl) ⚤ᒍᐥᕫᨇ (מזילה M-ZY-
LH) — **Bell:** [ms: מצלה] [freq.
1] |kjv: bell| {str: 4698}

Adopted Roots;
2030 ᒍᓂᨆ Peel, Onion
2626 ᒍᓂᔲ Peel, Strip
2387 ᒍᕫᐣ Flow, Stream

~~~~~~~~~~

1151) ᨇᕫ (זם ZM) ac: **Plot** co: **Plan**
ab: **Mischief:** The devising of a plan of
action.

A) ᨇᕫ (זם ZM) ac: ? co: ? ab:
Mischief: An action or plan to do
wickedness or a sexual perversion.

N^fl) ⚤ᨇᕫ (זמה Z-MH) —
Mischief: [freq. 29] |kjv:
lewdness, wickedness, mischief,
heinous crime| {str: 2154}

k^fl) ⚤ᨇᕫᨇ (מזמה MZ-MH)
— **Mischief:** [freq. 19] |kjv:
discretion, device, thought,
wickedly, inventions, lewdness,
mischievous| {str: 4209}

B) ᨇᨇᕫ (זמם ZMM) ac: **Plot** co:
Plan ab: ?

V) ᨇᨇᕫ (זמם Z-MM) —
Plot: To device a plan of action,
usually with evil intent. [freq.
13] (vf: Paal) |kjv: thought,
devise, consider, purpose,
imagine, plot| {str: 2161}

Nᵐ) ᴧᴧᴧᴧᴄᴃ (זמם Z-MM) —
Plan: [freq. 1] |kjv: wicked
device| {str: 2162}

G) ᴧᴧᴘᴄᴃ (זהם ZHM) ac: Loathe
co: ? ab: ?

V) ᴧᴧᴘᴄᴃ (זהם Z-HM) —
Loathe: [freq. 1] (vf: Piel) |kjv:
abhorreth| {str: 2092}

~~~~~~~~~

1152) ᴧᴃ (זן ZN) ac: Harvest co:
Mattock ab: ?: The pictograph ᴄᴃ is a
picture of an agricultural cutting
implement such as the mattock or hoe.
The ᴧ is a picture of a seed. Combined
these mean "mattock of the seed". One of
the many agricultural tools was a hoe or
mattock. This implement had a wide
blade for cutting a plant stalks at the
roots. The crops were harvested for a
supply of foods, which were stored in
jars.

A) ᴧᴃ (זן ZN) ac: ? co: Harvest
ab: ?

Nᵐ) ᴧᴃ (זן ZN) — Kind: A
species of plant or animal.
[Hebrew and Aramaic] [freq. 7]
|kjv: kind, diverse kinds, all
manners of store| {str: 2177,
2178}

B) ᴧᴧᴃ (זנן ZNN) ac: ? co: ? ab:
Whoredom: In the sense of being
spread broad.

dᵐ) ᴧᴦᴧᴃ (זנון Z-NWN) —
Whoredom: [freq. 12] |kjv:
whoredom| {str: 2183}

C) ᴧᴃᴘ (אזן AZN) ac: Hear co:
Ear ab: Balance: The broad ear for
picking up sounds.

V) ᴧᴃᴘ (אזן A-ZN) — Hear:
To listen or pay attention. [freq.
42] (vf: Hiphil, Piel) |kjv: give

ear, hearken, hear, gave good
heed| {str: 238, 239}

Nᵐ) ᴧᴃᴘ (אזן A-ZN) —
Weapon: A broad sharp blade
like a mattock. [freq. 1] |kjv:
weapon| {str: 240}

gᶠ) ᴧᴃᴘ (אוזן AW-ZN) —
Ear: The ear as broad. [ms: אזן]
[freq. 187] |kjv: ear, audience,
hearing| {str: 241}

agᵐ) ᴧᴃᴘᴦᴧᴧ (מואזן MWA-
ZN) — Balance: A pair of scales
used for weighing. From the ear
as the place where balance is
determined. [Hebrew and
Aramaic] [ms: מאזן] [freq. 16]
|kjv: balances| {str: 3976, 3977}

H) ᴘᴧᴄᴃ (זנה ZNH) ac: ? co:
Whore ab: Whoredom: In the sense
of being spread broad.

V) ᴘᴧᴄᴃ (זנה Z-NH) —
Whore: [freq. 93] (vf: Paal,
Hiphil, Pual) |kjv: harlot, go
whoring, whoredom, whore,
commit fornication, whorish|
{str: 2181}

Nᶠ³) ᴛᴦᴧᴄᴃ (זנות Z-NWT) —
Whoredom: [freq. 9] |kjv:
whoredom| {str: 2184}

iᶠ³) ᴛᴦᴧᴄᴃᴛ (תזנות TZ-NWT) —
Whoredom: [ms: תזנת] [freq.
20] |kjv: whoredom, fornication|
{str: 8457}

J) ᴧᴦᴄᴃ (זון ZWN) ac: Feed co:
Food ab: ?: Food harvested from the
crops or flock.

V) ᴧᴦᴄᴃ (זון ZWN) — Feed:
[Hebrew and Aramaic] [freq. 2]
(vf: Hophal) |kjv: fed| {str: 2109,
2110}

Nᶠ) ᴧᴦᴄᴃ (זון ZWN) — Flesh:
[ms: זן] [freq. 1] |kjv: armour|
{str: 2185}

a^m) ᴸY𐤀ᴍᴍ (מזון M-ZWN) — **Meat:** [Hebrew and Aramaic] [freq. 4] |kjv: meat, victuals| {str: 4202, 4203}

1153) 𐤀ᴢ (זס ZS) ac: **?** co: **?** ab: **?**

1154) 𐤏ᴢ (זע ZAh) ac: **Tremble** co: **Sweat** ab: **?**: The pictograph ᴢ is a picture of an agricultural cutting implement such as the mattock or hoe and associated with weapons. The 𐤏 is a picture of the eye and meaning experience or knowledge. Combined these mean "weapon seen". Fear or an enemy.

A) 𐤏ᴢ (זע ZAh) ac: **?** co: **Sweat** ab: **?**: A sweating from fear.

N^{f1}) 𐤑𐤏ᴢ (זעה Z-AhH) — **Sweat:** [freq. 1] |kjv: sweat| {str: 2188}

J) 𐤏Yᴢ (זוע ZWAh) ac: **Tremble** co: **?** ab: **Terror**: A trembling from fear.

V) 𐤏Yᴢ (זוע ZWAh) — **Tremble:** [Hebrew and Aramaic] [freq. 5] (vf: Paal, Pilpel) |kjv: moved, tremble, vex| {str: 2111, 2112}

N^{f1}) 𐤑𐤏Yᴢ (זועה ZW-AhH) — **Terror:** An object of terror that causes trembling. [df: זעוה] [freq. 13] |kjv: remove, trouble, vexation| {str: 2113, 2189}

L) 𐤏ᴢᴸ (יזע YZAh) ac: **?** co: **Sweat** ab: **?**

N^m) 𐤏ᴢᴸ (יזע Y-ZAh) — **Sweat:** [freq. 1] |kjv: sweat| {str: 3154}

Adopted Roots;
2129 ᴍ𐤏ᴢ Enrage
2130 ᴏ𐤏ᴢ Sad, Sadness
2131 𐤏ᴢ Call out, Outcry
3012 𐤏Uᴢ Horror

1155) 𐤐ᴢ (זף ZP) ac: **Cover** co: **Pitch** ab: **?**: A thick tarry liquid used for covering the joints of boats to keep them afloat.

A) 𐤐ᴢ (זף ZP) ac: **Float** co: **Pitch** ab: **?**

N^{f1}) 𐤑𐤐ᴏᴧ (צפה Ts-PH) — **Float:** [df: צפה] [freq. 1] |kjv: swim| {str: 6824}

N^{f2}) †𐤐ᴢ (זפת Z-PT) — **Pitch:** [freq. 3] |kjv: pitch| {str: 2203}

I^{f1}) 𐤑𐤐ᴢ𐤐ᴢ (זפזפה ZP-Z-PH) — **Willow:** A tree that covers over a stream. [df: צפצפה] [freq. 1] |kjv: willow| {str: 6851}

rf^m) ᴸY𐤐ᴢ (זפוי Z-PWY) — **Overlay:** A hammered out sheet of gold used to overlay something. [df: צפוי] [freq. 5] |kjv: overlay, covering| {str: 6826}

J) 𐤐Yᴢ (זוף ZWP) ac: **Float** co: **Pitch** ab: **?**

V) 𐤐Yᴢ (זוף ZWP) — **Float:** [df: צוף] [freq. 3] (vf: Paal, Hiphil) |kjv: flow, overflow, swim| {str: 6687}

N^m) 𐤐Yᴢ (זוף ZWP) — **Honey:** A thick sticky mass like pitch. [df: צוף] [freq. 2] |kjv: honeycomb| {str: 6688}

Adopted Roots;
2673 𐤐ᴸᴧ Wrap, Turban

2683 ‌‌‍ Hide, Treasure

1156) ‌‌‍ (‌‌‍ ZTs) ac: ? co: ? ab: ?

1157) ‌‌‍ (‌‌‍ ZQ) ac: **Bind** co: **Shackle** ab: ?: The arms or feet are bound with chains. The binding of different metals to form alloys. (eng: shackle - an exchange for the sh and z and the addition of the l)

A) ‌‌‍ (‌‌‍ ZQ) ac: ? co: **Shackle** ab: ?

N‌‌‍) ‌‌‍ (‌‌‍ ZQ) — I. **Shackle: II. Spark:** [Unknown connection to root] [freq. 7] |kjv: chain, spark, firebrand, fetter| {str: 2131}

C) ‌‌‍ (‌‌‍ AZQ) ac: ? co: **Shackle** ab: ?

N‌‌‍) ‌‌‍ (‌‌‍ A-ZQ) — **Chain:** Used for binding prisoners. [freq. 2] |kjv: chains| {str: 246}

1158) ‌‌‍ (‌‌‍ ZR) ac: **Spread** co: ? ab: ?: The pictograph ⌐ represents the harvest. The ‌‌‍ is the picture of the head of a man. Combined these mean "harvest of heads". After the grain has been harvested and the heads of grain have been broken open, the heads are thrown into the wind where the chaff is blown away and the seed falls to the ground where they can be gathered.

A) ‌‌‍ (‌‌‍ ZR) ac: **Spread out** co: **Span** ab: ?: Something that is spread or scattered over a large area.

N‌‌‍) ‌‌‍ (‌‌‍ ZR) — **Spread out:** Something that is spread or scattered over a large area. [freq. 10] |kjv: crown| {str: 2213}

N‌‌‍) ‌‌‍ (‌‌‍ Z-RT) — **Span:** The span of the fingers, often used as a measurement. [freq. 7] |kjv: span| {str: 2239}

lb‌‌‍) ‌‌‍ (‌‌‍ ZR-ZYR) — **Zarziyr:** An unknown animal. [freq. 1] |kjv: greyhound| {str: 2223}

B) ‌‌‍ (‌‌‍ ZRR) ac: **Sneeze** co: ? ab: ?: The spreading out of the breath.

V) ‌‌‍ (‌‌‍ Z-RR) — **Sneeze:** [freq. 1] (vf: Piel) |kjv: sneeze| {str: 2237}

G) ‌‌‍ (‌‌‍ ZHR) ac: **Warn** co: ? ab: ?

V) ‌‌‍ (‌‌‍ Z-HR) — **Warn:** [Unknown connection to root; Hebrew and Aramaic] [freq. 23] (vf: Niphal, Hiphil) |kjv: warn, admonish, teach, shine, heed| {str: 2094, 2095}

E) ‌‌‍ (‌‌‍ ZRA) ac: ? co: **Vomit** ab: ?: Something spread out.

V) ‌‌‍ (‌‌‍ Z-RA) — **Vomit:** [freq. 1] (vf: Paal) |kjv: loathsome| {str: 2214}

H) ‌‌‍ (‌‌‍ ZRH) ac: **Scatter** co: **Pitchfork** ab: ?

V) ‌‌‍ (‌‌‍ Z-RH) — **Scatter:** [freq. 39] (vf: Paal, Niphal, Pual, Piel) |kjv: scatter, disperse, fan, spread, winnow, cast away, compass, strawed| {str: 2219}

h‌‌‍) ‌‌‍ (‌‌‍ MZ-RH) — **Pitchfork:** Used to scatter the grain in the wind. [freq. 2] |kjv: fan| {str: 4214}

k^m) 𐤑𐤄ᴄᴧᴧ (מזרה MZ-RH) —
Wind: A strong scattering wind.
[freq. 1] |kjv: north| {str: 4215}

I) 𐤄ᴄY (וזר WZR) ac: **Scatter** co: ?
ab: ?

N^m) 𐤄ᴄY (וזר W-ZR) —
Scatter: [freq. 1] |kjv: strange|
{str: 2054}

J) 𐤄Yᴄ (זור ZWR) ac: **Squeeze** co:
? ab: ?: When the grain is squeezed
the seed inside comes out.

V) 𐤄Yᴄ (זור ZWR) —
Strange: To be strange. One
who is scattered abroad. [freq.
77] (vf: Paal, Niphal, Hophal,
Participle) |kjv: stranger, strange,
estranged, gone, fanner, another|
{str: 2114}

a^m) 𐤄Yᴄᴧᴧ (מזור M-ZWR) —
Snare: [Unknown connection to
root;] [freq. 1] |kjv: wound| {str:
4204}

Adopted Roots;
2134 ᴌ𐤄ᴄ Heat
2136 ᴧᴧ𐤄ᴄ Gush, Semen
2137 ᴏ𐤄ᴄ Sow, Seed
2293 ᴏᴌᴌᴟ Sorcery
2138 ᴏ𐤄ᴄ Sprinkle, Bason

1159) ᴌᴌ/ᴄ (זש ZSh) ac: ? co: ? ab: ?

1160) ✝ᴄ (זת ZT) ac: ? co: **Olive** ab: ?:
The pictograph ᴄ represents the harvest.
The ✝ represents a mark or sign.
Combined these mean "harvest of the
sign". The oil from the olive fruit was
used as an anointing oil, as a sign, for
those to hold a kingly or priestly office.
The oil is also used as a medicinal
ointment.

M) ✝ᴑ/ᴄ (זית ZYT) ac: ? co: **Olive**
ab: ?

N^m) ✝ᴑ/ᴄ (זית ZYT) — **Olive:**
The fruit or the tree. [freq. 38]
|kjv: olive, olive tree, oliveyard,
olivet| {str: 2132}

1161) 𐤋ᴄ (זע ZGh) ac: ? co: ? ab: ?

Hhets

1162) 𐤋𐤄 (חא HhA) ac: ? co: ? ab: ?

1163) 𐤄𐤁 (חב HhB) ac: **Hide** co: **Bosom** ab: **Refuge:** The pictograph חב is a picture of a wall. The ם is a picture of a tent or house. Combined these mean "wall of the house". The walls of the house enclose the home as refuge for the family. A refuge functions as a place of hiding from any undesirable person or situation.

A) 𐤄𐤁 (חב HhB) ac: ? co: **Bosom** ab: ?: A place where one is hidden in the arms and cherished.

N^m) 𐤄𐤁 (חב HhB) — **Bosom:** [freq. 1] |kjv: bosom| {str: 2243}

B) 𐤄𐤁𐤁 (חבב HhBB) ac: **Cherish** co: ? ab: ?: One that is cherished is held close to the bosom.

V) 𐤄𐤁𐤁 (חבב Hh-BB) — **Cherish:** [freq. 1] (vf: Paal) |kjv: love| {str: 2245}

E) 𐤋𐤄𐤁 (חבא HhBA) ac: **Hide** co: **Refuge** ab: ?: Any place where one hides in secret or for lurking.

V) 𐤋𐤄𐤁 (חבא Hh-BA) — **Hide:** [freq. 33] (vf: Niphal, Hiphil, Hitpael, Hophal, Pual) |kjv: hide, held, secretly| {str: 2244}

a^m) 𐤋𐤄𐤁𐤌 (מחבא MHh-BA) — **Refuge:** A place of hiding. [df: מחבוא] [freq. 2] |kjv: hiding place, lurking place| {str: 4224}

H) 𐤄𐤁𐤄 (חבה HhBH) ac: **Hide** co: ? ab: ?: A refuge functions as a place of hiding from any undesirable person or situation.

V) 𐤄𐤁𐤄 (חבה Hh-BH) — **Hide:** [freq. 5] (vf: Paal, Niphal) |kjv: hide| {str: 2247}

fj^m) 𐤋𐤄𐤁𐤉𐤍 (חביון HhB-YWN) — **Hiding:** [freq. 1] |kjv: hiding| {str: 2253}

J) 𐤄𐤅𐤁 (חוב HhWB) ac: **Endanger** co: ? ab: ?: [Unknown connection to root;]

V) 𐤄𐤅𐤁 (חוב HhWB) — **Endanger:** [freq. 1] (vf: Piel) |kjv: endanger| {str: 2325}

N^m) 𐤄𐤅𐤁 (חוב HhWB) — **Debtor:** [freq. 1] |kjv: debtor| {str: 2326}

M) 𐤄𐤉𐤁 (חיב HhYB) ac: ? co: **Bosom** ab: ?: A place of refuge.

N^m) 𐤄𐤉𐤁 (חיב HhYB) — **Bosom:** [df: חק חוק חיק] [freq. 39] |kjv: bosom, bottom, lap| {str: 2436}

Adopted Roots;

1164) 𐤄𐤂 (חג HhG) ac: **Feast** co: **Circle** ab: **Terror:** The pictograph חם is a picture of a wall representing outside. The 𐤋 is a picture of a foot and represents a gathering. Combined these mean "outside gathering". The gathering together for a festival, usually in the form of a circle for dancing and feasting. (eng: hug - as an encircling; circ - an exchange of the h and c and the g and c; cog - an exchange of the h and c)

A) Lᴍ (חג HhG) ac: ? co: **Feast** ab: **?:** The participants of a festival would gather together and dance in a circle.

Nᵐ) Lᴍ (חג HhG) — **Feast:** [freq. 62] |kjv: feast, sacrifice| {str: 2282}

B) LLᴍ (חגג HhGG) ac: ? co: **Feast** ab: **?:** The participants of a festival would gather together and dance in a circle.

V) LLᴍ (חגג Hh-GG) — **Feast:** [freq. 16] (vf: Paal) |kjv: keep, feast, celebrate, dance, holyday, reel to and fro| {str: 2287}

E) ϒLᴍ (חגא HhGA) ac: ? co: ? ab: **Terror:** A spinning around in fear.

Nᶠ) ϒLᴍ (חגא Hh-GA) — **Terror:** [freq. 1] |kjv: terror| {str: 2283}

J) LΥᴍ (חוג HhWG) ac: ? co: **Circle** ab: ?

V) LΥᴍ (חוג HhWG) — **Circle:** [freq. 1] (vf: Paal) |kjv: compassed| {str: 2328}

Nᵐ) LΥᴍ (חוג HhWG) — **Circle:** [freq. 3] |kjv: circle, circuit, compass| {str: 2329}

kᶠˡ) ϠLΥᴍ⋀⋀ (מחוגה M-HhW-GH) — **Compass:** An instrument for making a circle. [freq. 1] |kjv: compass| {str: 4230}

K) ϒLᴍ (חגו HhGW) ac: ? co: **Refuge** ab: **?:** A place where one is encircled by a wall.

Nᵐ) ϒLᴍ (חגו Hh-GW) — **Cleft:** A refuge in the rock. [freq. 3] |kjv: cleft| {str: 2288}

Adopted Roots;
2147 **ϡLᴍ** Bind, Belt

~~~~~~~~~~~~

1165) ᴛᴍ (חד HhD) ac: **Unite** co: **Unit** ab: **Unity:** The pictograph ᴍ is a picture of a wall. The ᴛ is a picture of a door. Combined these mean "wall door". A wall separates the inside from the outside. Only through the door can one enter or exit uniting the inside with the outside.

A) ᴛᴍ (חד HhD) ac: ? co: **Unite** ab: **?:** Two or more coming together as a unity. The sharp edge of a blade is the coming together of the two to one point.

Nᵐ) ᴛᴍ (חד HhD) — **I. Unit:** A singular of a larger group. **II. Sharp:** The two edges of a sword that meet to form one point. [Hebrew and Aramaic] [freq. 19] |kjv: one, first, together, sharp| {str: 2297, 2298, 2299}

B) ᴛᴛᴍ (חדד HhDD) ac: **Sharp** co: ? ab: **?:** The two edges of a sword that meet to form one point.

V) ᴛᴛᴍ (חדד Hh-DD) — **Sharp:** [freq. 6] (vf: Paal, Hiphil, Hophal) |kjv: sharpen, fierce| {str: 2300}

dᵐ) ᴛΥᴛᴍ (חדוד Hh-DWD) — **Sharp:** [freq. 1] |kjv: sharp| {str: 2303}

C) ᴛᴍϤ (אחד AHhD) ac: **Unite** co: ? ab: **Unity:** A uniting together. All things are a unity with something else (one man is a unity of body, breath and mind, one family is a unity of father, mother and children, one tree is a unity of trunk, branches and leaves, one forest is a unity of trees).

V) אחד (אחד A-HhD) —
Unite: [freq. 1] (vf: Hitpael)
|kjv: go one way or other| {str: 258}

N^m) אחד (אחד A-HhD) —
Unity: A group united are one of a group. [freq. 951] |kjv: one, first, another, other, any, once, every, certain, an, some| {str: 259}

H) חדה (חדה HhDH) ac: **Join** co: ? ab: ?: A uniting together in joy.

V) חדה (חדה Hh-DH) —
Join: [freq. 3] (vf: Paal, Piel) |kjv: rejoice, join, glad| {str: 2302}

J) חוד (חוד HhWD) ac: ? co: **Riddle** ab: ?: The riddle begins by dividing the hearer from the listener by creating the riddle. The riddle ends with the answer uniting the two.

V) חוד (חוד HhWD) —
Propose: To give a riddle. [freq. 4] (vf: Paal) |kjv: put forth| {str: 2330}

L) יחד (יחד YHhD) ac: **Unite** co: ? ab: **Unity:** A uniting together. All things are a unity with something else (one man is a unity of body, breath and mind, one family is a unity of father, mother and children, one tree is a unity of trunk, branches and leaves, one forest is a unity of trees).

V) יחד (יחד Y-HhD) —
Unite: [freq. 3] (vf: Paal, Piel) |kjv: unite, join| {str: 3161}

N^m) יחד (יחד Y-HhD) —
Together: [freq. 142] |kjv: together, alike, likewise, withal| {str: 3162}

b^m) יחיד (יחיד Y-HhYD) — **Unity:** A child as the product

of a union. The soul as a unity of body, soul and breath. [freq. 12] |kjv: only, darling, desolate, solitary| {str: 3173}

M) חיד (חיד HhYD) ac: ? co: **Riddle** ab: ?: The riddle begins by dividing the hearer from the listener by creating the riddle. The riddle ends with the answer uniting the two.

N^{fl}) חידה (חידה HhY-DH) — **Riddle:** [freq. 17] |kjv: riddle, dark saying, hard question, dark sentence, proverb, dark speech| {str: 2420}

n^{fl}) אחידה (אחידה A-HhY-DH) — **Riddle:** [Aramaic only] [freq. 1] |kjv: hard sentence| {str: 280}

Adopted Roots;

2149	חדק	Thorn
2150	חדר	Surround, Chamber
2151	חדש	Renew, New moon, New
2255	שחד	Hide
2700	רחד	Set apart, Special
2822	שחד	Bribe

1166) חה (חה HhH) ac: ? co: ? ab: ?

1167) חו (חו HhW) ac: **Declare** co: ? ab: **Declaration**

A) חו (חו HhW) ac: **Declare** co: **Town** ab: ?

N^{fl}) חוה (חוה Hh-WH) — **Town:** As a place where one declares the words of another. [freq. 4] |kjv: town| {str: 2333}

H) חוה (חוה HhWH) ac: **Declare** co: ? ab: ?

V) חוה (חוה Hh-WH) — **Declare:** [Hebrew and Aramaic]

[ar: חוא] [freq. 20] (vf: Piel) |kjv: shew| {str: 2324, 2331}

K) אחו (אחו AHhW) ac: **Declare** co: ? ab: **Declaration**

N^fl) אחוה (אחוה AHh-WH) — **Declaration:** [freq. 1] |kjv: declaration, shewing| {str: 262}

f^fl) אחויה (אחויה A-HhW-YH) — **Declaring:** [Aramaic only] [freq. 1] |kjv: declaration, shewing| {str: 263}

~~~~~~~~~~~~~~~

1168) חז (חז HhZ) ac: **See** co: ? ab: **Perceive:** The ability to see beyond what is seen in the physical present as a light piercing through the darkness. (eng: haze; gaze - an exchange for the h and g)

A) חז (חז HhZ) ac: ? co: **Vision** ab: ?: A perception beyond the normal experiences.

N^f) חז (חז HhZ) — **Vision:** [Hebrew and Aramaic] [freq. 3] |kjv: vision| {str: 2378, 2379}

N^f3) חזות (חזות Hh-ZWT) — **Vision:** [freq. 5] |kjv: vision| {str: 2380}

j^m) חזון (חזון Hh-ZWN) — **Vision:** [freq. 35] |kjv: vision| {str: 2377}

fj^m) חזיון (חזיון HhZ-YWN) — **Vision:** [freq. 9] |kjv: vision| {str: 2384}

B) חזז (חזז HhZZ) ac: ? co: **Light** ab: ?

b^m) חזיז (חזיז Hh-ZYZ) — **Lighting:** A moment of vision in the dark of night. [freq. 3] |kjv: lightning, bright clouds| {str: 2385}

C) אחז (אחז AHhZ) ac: **Hold** co: ? ab: ?: [Unknown connection to root;]

V) אחז (אחז A-HhZ) — **Hold:** To grab something and keep hold of it. Also ones holdings. [freq. 67] (vf: Paal, Niphal, Hophal, Piel) |kjv: hold, take, possess, caught, fastened| {str: 270}

N^fl) אחזה (אחזה AHh-ZH) — **Holdings:** [freq. 66] |kjv: possession| {str: 272}

H) חזה (חזה HhZH) ac: **Perceive** co: **Light** ab: ?

V) חזה (חזה Hh-ZH) — **Perceive:** To see something that is not physically present. [Hebrew and Aramaic] [df: הזה] [ar: חזא] [freq. 83] (vf: Paal) |kjv: see, behold, look, prophecy, provide, dream| {str: 1957, 2370, 2372}

N^m) חזה (חזה Hh-ZH) — **Chest:** The breast of a sacrificed animal (possibly as a sacrifice for a vision). [freq. 13] |kjv: breast| {str: 2373}

a^fl) מחזה (מחזה MHh-ZH) — **Vision:** [freq. 4] |kjv: vision| {str: 4236}

f^m) חזי (חזי Hh-ZY) — **Chest:** [Aramaic only] [ar: חדי] [freq. 1] |kjv: breast| {str: 2306}

g^m) חוזה (חוזה HhW-ZH) — **Seer:** [ms: חזה] [freq. 22] |kjv: seer, see, agreement, prophet, stargazer| {str: 2374}

k^fl) מחזה (מחזה MHh-ZH) — **Light:** [freq. 4] |kjv: light| {str: 4237}

r^m) Y⸱⸱⸱ (חזו Hh-ZW) —
Vision: [Aramaic only] [freq. 12] |kjv: vision, look| {str: 2376}

J) ⸱⸱Y⸱⸱ (חוז HhWZ) ac: **Look** co: **Haven** ab: **?**

a^m) ⸱⸱Y⸱⸱⸱⸱ (מחוז M-HhWZ) — **Haven:** A placed looked for. [freq. 1] |kjv: haven| {str: 4231}

~~~~~~~~~~~~~~~

1169) ⸱⸱⸱⸱ (חח HhHh) ac: **?** co: **Thicket** ab: **?**: The pictograph ⸱⸱ is a picture of a wall. The wall around crops or livestock was constructed of thistles or rocks with thistles laid on top. The thorns prevented intruders from entering. (eng: hook - an exchange for the k and h)

A) ⸱⸱⸱⸱ (חח HhHh) ac: **?** co: **Thorn** ab: **?**: A sharp object that penetrates the flesh.

N^m) ⸱⸱⸱⸱ (חח HhHh) — **Ring:** As pierced through the nose or lip. [freq. 8] |kjv: hook, chain, bracelet| {str: 2397}

J) ⸱⸱Y⸱⸱ (חוח HhWHh) ac: **?** co: **Thorn** ab: **?**: A sharp point

N^m) ⸱⸱Y⸱⸱ (חוח HhWHh) — **Thorn:** [freq. 12] |kjv: thistle, thorn, brambles| {str: 2336, 2337}

~~~~~~~~~~~~~~~

1170) ⊗⸱⸱ (חט HhTh) ac: **Measure** co: **Cord** ab: **Miss:** Cords are used for binding as well as measuring. A cord is also used as measuring device by placing knots incrementally. The cord is stretched between the two points to measure and the knots are counted.

A) ⊗⸱⸱ (חט HhTh) ac: **Measure** co: **?** ab: **Sin:** When shooting an arrow or other object to a target, the distance that one misses is measured

with a cord. The wrong actions of one are also measured against the correct action.

f^m) ⸱⊗⸱⸱ (חטי Hh-ThY) — **Sin:** [Aramaic only] [freq. 1] |kjv: sin| {str: 2408}

E) ⸱⊗⸱⸱ (חטא HhThA) ac: **Measure** co: **?** ab: **Sin:** When shooting an arrow or other object to a target, the distance that one misses is measured with a cord. The wrong actions of one are also measured against the correct action.

V) ⸱⊗⸱⸱ (חטא Hh-ThA) — **Miss:** To miss the target, whether a literal target or a goal that is aimed for. [freq. 238] (vf: Paal, Hiphil, Hitpael, Piel) |kjv: sin, purify, cleanse, sinner, committed, offended, blame, done| {str: 2398}

N^m) ⸱⊗⸱⸱ (חטא Hh-ThA) — **Sin:** A missing of the target. Also a sinner as one who misses the mark. [freq. 51] |kjv: sinner, sinful, offender, sin, faults, grievously, offences| {str: 2399, 2400}

N^{f1}) ⸱⸱⸱⊗⸱⸱ (חטאה HhTh-AH) — **Sin:** A missing of the target. Also the sin offering which by transference becomes the sin. [Hebrew and Aramaic] [df: חטאת] [freq. 305] |kjv: sin, sin offering, punishment, purifying| {str: 2401, 2402, 2403}

b^f) ⸱⸱⊗⸱⸱ (חטיא Hh-ThYA) — **Sin:** The sin offering which by transference becomes the sin. [Aramaic only] [freq. 1] |kjv: sin offering| {str: 2409}

J) ⊗Y⸱⸱ (חוט HhWTh) ac: **Join** co: **Cord** ab: **?**

V) ⊗Υחח (חוט HhWTh) — **Join:**
A tying with a cord. [Aramaic only] [freq. 1] (vf: Participle) |kjv: join| {str: 2338}

N^m) ⊗Υחח (חוט HhWTh) —
Cord: [freq. 7] |kjv: thread, line, cord, fillet| {str: 2339}

Adopted Roots;
2155 ᴹ⊗חח Refrain
2156 ⇐⊗חח Catch
2162 ⊗Jחח Catch

~~~~~~~~~~

1171) חי⊐ (חי HhY) ac: **Live** co:
Stomach ab: **Life:** When the stomach is empty one is famished and week and when it is filled one is revived. This organ is seen as the life as an empty stomach is like death but a revived stomach is life.

A) ⊥חח (חי HhY) ac: ? co:
Stomach ab: **Life**

N^f) ⊥חח (חי HhY) —
Stomach: Literally the organ that holds food (see Job 38:39) but figurative of life. [Hebrew and Aramaic] [freq. 508] |kjv: live, life, beast, alive, creature, running, living thing, raw, springing, appetite, quick| {str: 2416, 2417}

N^f3) ⊥Υחח (חיות Hh-YWT) —
Living: [freq. 1] |kjv: living| {str: 2424}

H) ✡⊥חח (חיה HhYH) ac: ? co:
Sustenance ab: **Life**

V) ✡⊥חח (חיה Hh-YH) —
Live: The revival of life from food or other necessity. [Hebrew and Aramaic] [ar: חיא] [freq. 268] (vf: Paal, Hiphil, Piel) |kjv: live, alive, save, quicken, revive, life, recover| {str: 2418, 2421}

N^m) ✡⊥חח (חיה Hh-YH) —
Lively: Having the vigor of life. [freq. 1] |kjv: lively| {str: 2422}

h^fl) ✡⊥ חחᴹ (מחיה MHh-YH) —
— **Sustenance:** A food that revives life. [freq. 8] |kjv: revive, quick, preserve life, sustenance, victuals, recover| {str: 4241}

K) Υ⊥חח (חיו HhYW) ac: ? co:
Beast ab: ?

N^fl) ✡Υ⊥חח (חיוה HhY-WH) —
Beast: A living creature. [Aramaic only] [ar: חיוא] [freq. 20] |kjv: beast| {str: 2423}

M) ⊥⊥חח (חיי HhYY) ac: ? co: ?
ab: **Life**

V) ⊥⊥חח (חיי HhYY) — **Live:**
[freq. 23] (vf: Paal, Piel) |kjv: live, life| {str: 2425}

~~~~~~~~~~

1172) Ⴞחח (חך HhK) ac: **Stick** co:
Palate ab: **Tarry:** The חח represents a wall such as the ridge in the middle of the palate. The Ⴞ represents the palm, a curved surface such as found on the roof of the mouth. The roof of the mouth.

A) Ⴞחח (חך HhK) ac: ? co: **Palate**
ab: ?

N^m) Ⴞחח (חך HhK) — **Palate:**
[freq. 18] |kjv: mouth, roof of the mouth, taste| {str: 2441}

N^fl) ✡Ⴞחח (חכה Hh-KH) —
Hook: As fastened to the roof of a fishes mouth. [freq. 3] |kjv: angle, hook| {str: 2443}

H) ✡Ⴞחח (חכה HhKH) ac: **Stick**
co: ? ab: ?: When the mouth is dry the tongue sticks to the roof of the mouth causing the speaker to wait to speak.

V) חכוש‎ (חכה Hh-KH) — **Tarry:** [freq. 14] (vf: Paal, Piel) |kjv: tarry, wait, long| {str: 2442}

Adopted Roots;
2178 חנוש‎ Dedicate, Dedication

~~~~~~~~~~~

1173) חל‎ (חל HhL) ac: **Bore** co: **Hole** ab: **Pain:** A hole is drilled with a tool called a bow drill. The string of the bow is wrapped around the drill. By moving the bow back and forth, and firmly pressing down, the drill spins around drilling the hole. (eng: hole; hollow)

A) חל‎ (חל HhL) ac: **Bore** co: **Hole** ab: **Pain:** Anything that is bored through, perforated or drilled.

N[m]**)** חל‎ (חל HhL) — **Common:** A place, person or thing that is not set apart for a specific function. [Unknown connection to root;] [freq. 7] |kjv: profane, common, unholy| {str: 2455}

N[fl]**)** חלה‎ (חלה Hh-LH) — **Cake:** As perforated. [freq. 14] |kjv: cake| {str: 2471}

f[m]**)** חלי‎ (חלי Hh-LY) — **Earring:** An ornament that is put through a hole. [freq. 24] |kjv: ornament, jewel| {str: 2483}

f[fl]**)** חליה‎ (חליה HhL-YH) — **Earring:** An ornament that is put through a hole. [freq. 1] |kjv: jewel| {str: 2484}

i[fl]**)** תחלה†‎ (תחלה THh-LH) — **Begin:** The spot to be drilled is first scored to make an indentation to accept the drill and the beginning of the drilling

is the most difficult as the drill can easily slip out. [freq. 22] |kjv: beginning, first, begin| {str: 8462}

j[m/f]**)** חלון‎ (חלון Hh-LWN) — **Window:** A hole in the wall. [freq. 31] |kjv: window| {str: 2474}

k[fl]**)** מחלה‎ (מחלה MHh-LH) — **Cave:** A place with a hole in the ground or rock. [freq. 1] |kjv: cave| {str: 4247}

l[fl]**)** חלחלה‎ (חלחלה HhL-Hh-LH) — **Pain:** As from a piercing sword. [freq. 4] |kjv: pain| {str: 2479}

af[m]**)** מחלי‎ (מחלי MHh-LY) — **Pain:** As from a piercing sword. [freq. 1] |kjv: disease| {str: 4251}

B) חלל‎ (חלל HhLL) ac: **Bore** co: **Flue** ab: **?:** Anything that is bored through, perforated or drilled.

V) חלל‎ (חלל Hh-LL) — **I. Pierce: II. Begin:** The spot to be drilled is first scored to make an indentation to accept the drill and the beginning of the drilling is the most difficult as the drill can easily slip out. **III. Common:** To make something common that is meant to be set apart for a special function. [Unknown connection to root;] [freq. 141] (vf: Paal, Niphal, Hiphil, Hophal, Pual, Piel) |kjv: begin, profane, pollute, defile, break, wound, eat, slay| {str: 2490}

N[m]**)** חלל‎ (חלל Hh-LL) — **Pierced:** [freq. 94] |kjv: slay, wound, profane, kill| {str: 2491}

b^m) ⟨חליל Hh-LYL⟩ —
Flute: An instrument with
drilled holes. [freq. 6] |kjv: pipe|
{str: 2485}

b^{fl}) ⟨חלילה Hh-LY-
LH⟩ — **Far be it:** [Unknown
connection to root;] [ms: חללה]
[freq. 21] |kjv: god forbid, far be
it, lord forbid| {str: 2486}

E) ⟨חלא HhLA⟩ ac: **Sick** co:
Disease ab: **?:** A spinning or piercing
pain.

V) ⟨חלא Hh-LA⟩ —
Diseased: [freq. 1] (vf: Paal)
|kjv: diseased| {str: 2456}

N^{fl}) ⟨חלאה HhL-AH⟩
— **Rust:** A metal pitted from
oxidation. [freq. 5] |kjv: scum|
{str: 2457}

id^m) ⟨תחלוא THh-
LWA⟩ — **Sick:** [ms: תחלא]
[freq. 5] |kjv: disease, sick,
sickness, grievous| {str: 8463}

H) ⟨חלה HhLH⟩ ac: **Sick** co:
Disease ab: **?:** A spinning or piercing
pain.

V) ⟨חלה Hh-LH⟩ — **I.
Sick: II. Beseech:** To request
intervention from a sickness or
other trouble. [freq. 75] (vf:
Paal, Niphal, Hiphil, Hitpael,
Hophal, Pual, Piel) |kjv: sick,
beseech, weak, grievous,
diseased, wounded, pray, intreat,
grief, grieved, sore, pain,
infirmity| {str: 2470}

a^m) ⟨מחלה MHh-LH⟩
— **Disease:** [freq. 6] |kjv:
sickness, disease, infirmity| {str:
4245}

f^m) ⟨חלי Hh-LY⟩ —
Sickness: A piercing pain. [freq.

2] |kjv: sickness, disease, grief,
sick| {str: 2481}

J) ⟨חול HhWL⟩ ac: **Twist** co:
Dance ab: **?:** To twist and spin
around from joy or pain as the drill.

V) ⟨חול HhWL⟩ —
Twist: A twisting in pain or joy.
[df: חיל] [freq. 62] (vf: Paal,
Hophal, Participle) |kjv: pain,
formed, bring forth, tremble,
travail, dance, calve, grieve,
wound, shake| {str: 2342}

N^m) ⟨חול HhWL⟩ —
Sand: Sand is used as an
abrasive ingredient for drilling
by placing it in the hole being
drilled. [freq. 23] |kjv: sand| {str:
2344}

a^m) ⟨מחול M-HhWL⟩
— **Dance:** [freq. 6] |kjv: dance|
{str: 4234}

k^{fl}) ⟨מחולה M-HhW-
LH⟩ — **Dance:** [freq. 8] |kjv:
dance, company| {str: 4246}

M) ⟨חיל HhYL⟩ ac: **?** co:
Wall ab: **?:** Bores through the enemy
by strongly pressing in.

N^m) ⟨חיל HhYL⟩ — **I.
Wall:** What is bored through by
the enemy to enter a city. [ms:
חל] **II. Army:** What bores
through the wall. [Hebrew and
Aramaic] **III. Pain:** A spinning
or piercing pain. **IV. Power:** The
strength and wealth of a person
or army. [freq. 267] |kjv: wall,
rampart, host, trench, poor,
bulwark, army, pain, pang,
sorrow, man of valour, host,
force, valiant, strength, wealth,
power, substance, might, strong|
{str: 2426, 2427, 2428, 2429}

N^{fl}) 𝍠✓⌐ꟼꟼ (חילה HhY-LH)
— **Wall:** What is bored through by the enemy to enter a city. [freq. 1] |kjv: bulwark| {str: 2430}

Adopted Roots;
2062 ✓⌐🜄 Ember
2161 ᴛᴜ✓ꟼꟼ Age
2164 ᴀᴀᴀ✓ꟼꟼ Dream, Dream
2165 ◠✓ꟼꟼ Pass
2168 ᴜᴜ✓ꟼꟼ Weaken, Weak
2203 ⊗🜚ꟼꟼ Engrave, Pen
2208 ◠🜚ꟼꟼ Pierce, Winter
2209 ᴀᴧ🜚ꟼꟼ Sharp, Hoe
2210 ●🜚ꟼꟼ Gnash
2211 ᴜᴜ🜚ꟼꟼ Scratch, Craftsman
2212 ᵗ🜚ꟼꟼ Engrave

~~~~~~~~~~

1174) ᴀᴀᴀꟼꟼ (חם HhM) ac: **Heat** co: **Cheese** ab: ?: The pictograph ꟼꟼ is a picture of a wall meaning "to separate". The ᴀᴀ is a picture of water. Combined these mean "separate water". Cheese was made by placing milk in a bag made out of an animal skin. The bag was hung out in the sun and pushed back and forth. The skin of the bag contained an enzyme that when heated and shaken caused the milk to sour and separate into its two parts, fat (curds or cheese) and water (whey). The whey could be drunk and the curds eaten or stored for future consumption.

A) ᴀᴀᴀꟼꟼ (חם HhM) ac: **Heat** co: **Sun** ab: ?: The heat from the sun heats the contents of the bag.

N^m) ᴀᴀᴀꟼꟼ (חם HhM) — **I. Hot: II. Father-In-Law:** One who is hot. [freq. 20] |kjv: hot, warm, heat, father-in-law, husbands father| {str: 2524, 2525, 2527}

N^{fl}) 𝍠ᴀᴀᴀꟼꟼ (חמה Hh-MH) — **I. Sun:** The source of heat. [ar:

חמא] **II. Fury:** An intense heat from anger. [ar: חמא] [freq. 132] |kjv: sun, heat, fury, wrath, poison, displeasure, rage, anger, bottle| {str: 2528, 2534, 2535}

N^{f2}) ᵗᴀᴀᴀꟼꟼ (חמת Hh-MT) — **Skin bag:** Used for holding the cheese. Also used for water or any other liquid. [freq. 4] |kjv: bottle| {str: 2573}

N^{f3}) ᵗᵧᴀᴀᴀꟼꟼ (חמות Hh-MWT) — **Mother-In-Law:** [ms: חמת] [freq. 11] |kjv: mother-in-law| {str: 2545}

m^m) ⸜ᴀᴀᴀꟼꟼ (חמן Hh-MN) — **Sun idol:** An object of worship representing the sun god. [freq. 8] |kjv: image, idol| {str: 2553}

B) ᴀᴀᴀᴀᴀꟼꟼ (חמם HhMM) ac: **Warm** co: ? ab: ?: The heat from the sun warms the contents of the bag.

V) ᴀᴀᴀᴀᴀꟼꟼ (חמם Hh-MM) — **Warm:** The warmth of the sun or from passion. [freq. 13] (vf: Paal, Niphal, Hitpael, Piel) |kjv: hot, heat, warm, enflame| {str: 2552}

E) ◿ᴀᴀᴀꟼꟼ (חמא HhMA) ac: ? co: **Cheese** ab: ?: The curds produced from the skin bottle. This cheese has a buttery texture and flavor.

N^{fl}) 𝍠◿ᴀᴀᴀꟼꟼ (חמאה HhM-AH) — **Cheese:** [df: חמה] [freq. 10] |kjv: butter| {str: 2529}

a^{fl}) 𝍠◿ᴀᴀᴀꟼꟼᴀᴀᴀ (מחמאה MHh-M-AH) — **Cheese:** [freq. 1] |kjv: butter| {str: 4260}

J) ᴀᴀᴀᵧꟼꟼ (חום HhWM) ac: ? co: **Black** ab: ?: The color of wood when burned.

N^m) ᴀᴀᴀᵧꟼꟼ (חום HhWM) — **Black:** [freq. 4] |kjv: brown| {str: 2345}

N^{f1}) 𒐫ꭥꭥ𒐫 (חומה HhW-MH)
— **Wall:** [Unknown connection to root;] [freq. 133] |kjv: wall, walled| {str: 2346}

L) ꭥꭥꭥ (יחם YHhM) ac: **Heat** co: ? ab: ?: The heat from the sun warms the contents of the bag.

V) ꭥꭥꭥ (יחם Y-HhM) — **Heat:** Natural body heat as well as the time of heat when animals mate. Conception from an animals heat or through the heat of passion. [freq. 10] (vf: Paal, Piel) |kjv: conceive, warm, hot, heat| {str: 3179}

Adopted Roots;

2169 חꭥꭥ , Desire
2172 חꭥꭥ Shake, Violence
2173 חꭥꭥ Sour
2491 ꭥꭥ Bristle, Hair
2305 חꭥꭥ Fight, Bread
2600 חꭥꭥ Burn, Charcoal

~~~~~~~~~~

1175) ꭥꭥ (חן HhN) ac: **Camp** co: Camp ab: **Beauty:** The pictograph חח is a picture of a wall. The ꭥ is a picture of a seed meaning "to continue". Combined these mean "wall continues". A nomads camp consisted of many family tents, which make up the clan camp. The camp can have as many as fifty tents or more in it. The tents are placed in a circular configuration, forming one continuous wall surrounding the camp. (eng: home - an exchange for the m and n)

A) ꭥꭥ (חן HhN) ac: ? co: **Camp** ab: **Beauty:** Within this wall is the family clan, a place of freedom, compassion and beauty. An encampment of tents. The tent is supported by the poles.

N^m) ꭥꭥ (חן HhN) — **Beauty:** As the beauty of the camp. To give or show beauty, grace or mercy to another. [freq. 69] |kjv: grace, favour, gracious, pleasant, precious| {str: 2580}

N^{f3}) חꭥꭥ (חנות Hh-NWT) — **Room:** As surrounded by walls. [freq. 1] |kjv: cabin| {str: 2588}

N^{f4}) חꭥꭥ (חנית Hh-NYT) — **Spear:** Made from tent poles which support the tent. [freq. 47] |kjv: spear, javelin| {str: 2595}

i^{f1}) חꭥꭥ (תחנה THh-NH) — **I. Beauty:** As the beauty of the camp. To give or show beauty, grace or mercy to another. **II. Supplication:** [freq. 25] |kjv: supplication, favour, grace| {str: 8467}

i^{f1}) חꭥꭥ (תחנה THh-NH) — **Camp:** [freq. 1] |kjv: camp| {str: 8466}

p^m) חꭥꭥ (חנם Hh-NM) — **Freely:** To work or do an action without wages or without cause. [Unknown connection to root;] [freq. 32] |kjv: without cause, for nought, causeless, in vain, free, without cost, freely, innocent, cost me nothing, for nothing, without wages| {str: 2600}

B) ꭥꭥ (חנן HhNN) ac: ? co: ? ab: **Compassion:** Within this wall is the family clan, a place of freedom, compassion and beauty. An encampment of tents.

V) ꭥꭥ (חנן Hh-NN) — **Beauty:** As the beauty of the camp. To give or show beauty, grace or mercy to another. [freq. 82] (vf: Paal, Niphal, Hitpael, Hophal, Piel) |kjv: mercy,

126

gracious, merciful, supplication, favour, besought, pity| {str: 2589, 2603, 2604}

b^f) חח–נ‏ (חנין Hh-NYN) — **Compassion:** [freq. 1] |kjv: favour| {str: 2594}

d^m) חח–נו‏ (חנון Hh-NWN) — **Compassion:** [freq. 13] |kjv: gracious| {str: 2587}

id^m) +חח–נו‏ (תחנון THh-NWN) — **Supplication:** [freq. 18] |kjv: supplications, intreaties| {str: 8469}

H) חח–‏ (חנה HhNH) ac: **?** co: **Camp** ab: **?:** The first step to setting up the tent is to arrange the poles. The tent poles were sharpened at one end (and could be used as a weapon) and were driven into the ground. An encampment of tents.

V) חח–‏ (חנה Hh-NH) — **Camp:** To stop for the night and pitch the tents. [freq. 143] (vf: Paal) |kjv: pitch, encamp, camp, abide, dwelt, lie, rest| {str: 2583}

a^m) חח–‏מ‏ (מחנה MHh-NH) — **Camp:** The inhabitants of a camp. [freq. 216] |kjv: camp, host, company, tent, army, band, battle, drove| {str: 4264}

M) חח–‏ (חין HhYN) ac: **?** co: **?** ab: **Beauty:** As the beauty of the camp. To give or show beauty, grace or mercy to another.

N^m) חח–‏ (חין HhYN) — **Beauty:** [freq. 1] |kjv: comely| {str: 2433}

Adopted Roots;
2231 חח–⊗ Grind, Mill
~~~~~~~~~~~~~~

1176) חח‏ (חס HhS) ac: **Support** co: **Refuge** ab: **?:** A place of support and trust. (eng: house - as the place of refuge)

A) חח‏ (חס HhS) ac: **?** co: **Refuge** ab: **?**

N^f3) +Yחח‏ (חסות Hh-SWT) — **Refuge:** [freq. 1] |kjv: trust| {str: 2622}

H) חח‏ (חסה HhSH) ac: **?** co: **Refuge** ab: **?**

V) חח‏ (חסה Hh-SH) — **Refuge:** To take refuge or place ones trust in one or thing of support. [freq. 37] (vf: Paal) |kjv: trust, refuge, hope| {str: 2620}

a^m) חח‏מ‏ (מחסה MHh-SH) — **Refuge:** Refuge, shelter, hope, trust. [freq. 20] |kjv: refuge, shelter, hope, trust| {str: 4268}

J) חח‏Y‏ (חוס HhWS) ac: **?** co: **Spare** ab: **?:** One who has been given refuge.

V) חח‏Y‏ (חוס HhWS) — **Spare:** To give refuge to another. [freq. 24] (vf: Paal) |kjv: spare, pity, regard| {str: 2347}

L) חח‏ל (יחס YHhS) ac: **?** co: **Lineage** ab: **?:** One is supported by his family line.

V) חח‏ל (יחס Y-HhS) — **Lineage:** Ones history within the family. [df: יחש] [freq. 20] (vf: Hitpael) |kjv: genealogy| {str: 3187}

N^m) חח‏ל (יחס Y-HhS) — **Lineage:** Ones history within the family. [df: יחש] [freq. 1] |kjv: genealogy| {str: 3188}

Adopted Roots;
2181 חח‏ד Bow, Kindness

2187 חֽ⟨?⟩ Diminish, Lacking

~~~~~~~~~~

1177) חַע (עח HhAh) ac: ? co: ? ab: ?

~~~~~~~~~~

1178) חפ (חף HhP) ac: **Cover** co: **Cover** ab: **Innocent:** The pictograph חפ is a picture of a wall. The ⟨ is a mouth meaning "open". Combined these mean "wall opened". The tent is opened to allow one into its covering for protection. Anyone entering a tent will be protected at all costs by the owner. A secret is something that is covered and hidden. A haven as a place covered over for protection.

A) חפ (חף HhP) ac: **Cover** co: ? ab: **Innocent**

N^m) חפ (חף HhP) — **Innocent:** One whose actions are covered. [freq. 1] |kjv: innocent| {str: 2643}

B) חפפ (חפף HhPP) ac: **Cover** co: ? ab: ?: A cover of protection.

V) חפפ (חפף Hh-PP) — **Cover:** [freq. 1] (vf: Paal) |kjv: cover| {str: 2653}

E) חפא (חפא HhPA) ac: **Cover** co: ? ab: ?: Something that is covered and hidden.

V) חפא (חפא Hh-PA) — **Cover:** [freq. 1] (vf: Piel) |kjv: secretly| {str: 2644}

H) חפה (חפה HhPH) ac: **Cover** co: ? ab: ?

V) חפה (חפה Hh-PH) — **Cover:** [freq. 12] (vf: Paal, Niphal, Piel) |kjv: cover, overlay, cieled| {str: 2645}

J) חופ (חוף HhWP) ac: **Cover** co: ? ab: ?: A covered or hidden place for protection.

N^m) חופ (חוף HhWP) — **Shore:** A place covered. [freq. 7] |kjv: haven, shore, coast, side| {str: 2348}

N^fl) חופה (חופה HhW-PH) — **Canopy:** A covering. [ms: חפה] [freq. 3] |kjv: chamber, closet, defence| {str: 2646}

L) יחפ (יחף YHhP) ac: **Uncover** co: ? ab: ?

N^m) יחפ (יחף Y-HhP) — **Barefoot:** An uncovered foot. [freq. 5] |kjv: barefoot, unshod| {str: 3182}

Adopted Roots;
2098 חפט Push
2188 רחפ Haste
2189 חפש Search
2191 חפמ Delight
2283 שׁפ Cover, Lid, Atonement
2284 שׁחפ Cover
2763 אפחפ Flutter

~~~~~~~~~~

1179) חמץ (חץ HhTs) ac: **Divide** co: **Tent Wall** ab: ?: The pictograph חפ is a picture of a wall. The ⟨ is a picture of a man laying on his side. Combined these mean "wall of sides". The tent wall divides or separates the inside from the outside. The wall inside the tent divides the tent into two sections.

A) חמץ (חץ HhTs) ac: ? co: **Arrow** ab: ?

N^m) חמץ (חץ HhTs) — **Arrow:** As dividing flesh. [freq. 53] |kjv: arrow, dart, shaft, wound| {str: 2671}

N^{f3}) †Ⴀ⌐⌐ (חצות Hh-TsWT)
— **Middle:** [freq. 3] |kjv: mid|
{str: 2676}

a^{f4}) †⌐⌐⌐⌐⌐ (מחצית MHh-
TsYT) — **Half:** As dividing flesh.
[freq. 17] |kjv: half, much| {str:
4276}

f^m) ⌐⌐⌐⌐ (חצי Hh-TsY) —
Arrow: As dividing flesh. [freq.
3] |kjv: arrow| {str: 2686}

B) ⌐⌐⌐⌐ (חצץ HhTsTs) ac:
Divide co: **Arrow** ab: **?**

V) ⌐⌐⌐⌐ (חצץ Hh-TsTs) —
Divide: A division of something
or a band as a division. [freq. 3]
(vf: Paal, Pual, Piel, Participle)
|kjv: band, archer, midst| {str:
2686}

N^m) ⌐⌐⌐⌐ (חצץ Hh-TsTs) —
Arrow: As dividing flesh. [freq.
3] |kjv: gravel, arrow| {str:
2687}

H) ⌐⌐⌐⌐ (חצה HhTsH) ac: **Divide**
co: **?** ab: **?**

V) ⌐⌐⌐⌐ (חצה Hh-TsH) —
Divide: To divide into half.
[freq. 15] (vf: Paal, Niphal) |kjv:
divide, part, half, midst| {str:
2673}

J) ⌐⌐Y⌐ (חוץ HhWTs) ac: **?** co:
Outside ab: **?:** To be outside of the
tent walls.

N^m) ⌐⌐Y⌐ (חוץ HhWTs) —
Outside: [ms: חץ] [freq. 164]
|kjv: without, street, abroad, out,
outside, fields, forth, highway|
{str: 2351}

M) ⌐⌐⌐⌐ (חיץ HhYTs) ac: **?** co:
Tent Wall ab: **?**

N^m) ⌐⌐⌐⌐ (חיץ HhYTs) —
Wall: [freq. 1] |kjv: wall| {str:
2434}

j^m) ⌐⌐⌐⌐ (חיצון HhY-
TsWN) — **Outside:** Also the idea
of secular as being outside. [freq.
25] |kjv: utter, outward, without,
outer| {str: 2435}

Adopted Roots;

2154 ⌐⊗⌐   Carve, Carving
2194 ⌐⌐⌐   Hew
2195 ⌐⌐⌐   Bosom
2196 ⌐⌐⌐ Urge
2197 ⌐⌐⌐   Blow, Yard

~~~~~~~~~

1180) ⌐⌐ (חק HhQ) ac: **Inscribe** co: **?**
ab: **Custom:** The pictograph חק is a
picture of a wall representing a
separation. The ⌐ is a picture of the sun
at the horizon representing the idea of
"coming together". Combined these mean
"separation and coming together". A
custom brings a people separated
together.

B) ⌐⌐⌐ (חקק HhQQ) ac:
Inscribe co: **?** ab: **Custom:** The
appointment of a specific time,
function or duty. A custom as
something that is appointed.

V) ⌐⌐⌐ (חקק Hh-QQ) —
Inscribe: To write a decree or
custom. [freq. 19] (vf: Paal,
Hophal, Pual, Participle) |kjv:
lawgiver, governor, decree,
grave, portray, law, printed, set,
note, appoint| {str: 2710}

N^m) ⌐⌐⌐ (חקק Hh-QQ) —
Custom: [freq. 2] |kjv: thought,
decree| {str: 2711}

H) ⌐⌐⌐ (חקה HhQH) ac:
Inscribe co: **?** ab: **?:** To write a
decree or custom.

V) ⌐⌐⌐ (חקה Hh-QH) —
Inscribe: [freq. 4] (vf: Hitpael,

Pual, Participle) |kjv: portray, carve, print| {str: 2707}

J) ◦-Yחק (חוק HhWQ) ac: ? co: ? ab: **Custom:** The appointment of a specific time, function or duty. A custom as something that is appointed.

N^(m)) ◦-Yחק (חוק HhWQ) — **Custom:** [ms: חק] [freq. 127] |kjv: statute, ordinance, decree, due, law, portion, bounds, custom, appointed, commandment| {str: 2706}

N^(f1)) ♀-◦-Yחק (חוקה HhW-QH) — **Custom:** [ms: חקה] [freq. 104] |kjv: statute, ordinance, custom, appointed, manners, rites| {str: 2708}

~~~~~~~~~~~

1181) חר (חר HhR) ac: **Burn** co: ? ab: ?: The pictograph חר is a picture of a wall representing the outside. The ח is a picture of a man. Combined these mean "outside man". A man outside in the desert sun becomes pale and hot.

A) חר (חר HhR) ac: **Burn** co: ? ab: ?: The heat from the sun. Heat of anger. Also tomorrow or later time as a delay.

a^(f)) חרMWW (מחר MHh-R) — **Later:** [freq. 52] |kjv: tomorrow, time to come| {str: 4279}

a^(f2)) †חרMWW (מחרת MHh-RT) — **Tomorrow:** [df: מחרתם] [freq. 32] |kjv: morrow, next day, next| {str: 4283}

f^(m)) ﹏חר (חרי Hh-RY) — **Burning:** [freq. 6] |kjv: fierce, heat| {str: 2750}

j^(m)) ﹏Yחר (חרון Hh-RWN) — **Burning:** [ms: חרן] [freq. 41] |kjv: fierce, wrath, fury,

wrathful, displeasure| {str: 2740}

l^(m)) חרחר (חרחר HhR-HhR) — **Burning:** [freq. 1] |kjv: burning| {str: 2746}

B) חרר (חרר HhRR) ac: **Burn** co: ? ab: ?: The heat from the sun. Also anger as a hot emotion.

V) חרר (חרר Hh-RR) — **Burn:** [freq. 11] (vf: Paal, Niphal, Pilpel) |kjv: burn, dried, angry, kindle| {str: 2787}

N^(m)) חרר (חרר Hh-RR) — **Burn:** [freq. 1] |kjv: parched place| {str: 2788}

C) אחר (אחר AHhR) ac: **Delay** co: **Back** ab: ?: Rather than work in the heat of the sun, one waits until the breeze of the day.

V) אחר (אחר A-HhR) — **Delay:** [freq. 17] (vf: Paal, Piel) |kjv: tarry, defer, slack, continue, delay, hinder, stay, late| {str: 309}

N^(m)) אחר (אחר A-HhR) — **I. After:** A time to come beyond another event. [Hebrew and Aramaic] **II. Other:** A time, person or thing that follows after. [freq. 878] |kjv: after, follow, afterward, behind, other, another, next, following| {str: 310, 311, 312}

N^(f4)) †אחרית (אחרית AHh-RYT) — **End:** The latter time as coming after everything else. [Hebrew and Aramaic] [freq. 62] |kjv: end, latter, last, posterity, reward, hindermost| {str: 319, 320}

c^(m)) אחור (אחור A-HhWR) — **Back:** The part of the body that is behind. To be in the back of or behind something. [ms: אחר] [freq. 41] |kjv: back, backward, behind, next, delay, hinder part| {str: 268}

f^m) אחרי (AHh-RY) — **Other:** A time, person or thing that follows after. [Aramaic only] [freq. 6] |kjv: another, other| {str: 317}

j^m) אחרון (AHh-RWN) — **After:** To be behind or following after something. [ms: אחרן] [freq. 51] |kjv: last, after, latter, end, utmost, following, hinder| {str: 314}

m^m) אחרן (AHh-RN) — **Other:** A time, person or thing that follows after. [Aramaic only] [freq. 5] |kjv: another, other| {str: 321}

s^m) אחרין (AHh-RYN) — **End:** The latter time as coming after everything else. [Aramaic only] [freq. 1] |kjv: last| {str: 318}

cm^f4) אחורנית (A-HhW-R-NYT) — **Backward:** [freq. 7] |kjv: backward, again| {str: 322}

E) חרא (HhRA) ac: ? co: **Dung** ab: ?: What comes from the backside (as behind).

N^m) חרא (Hh-RA) — **Dung:** [freq. 1] |kjv: dung| {str: 2716}

a^fl) מחראה (MHh-R-AH) — **Privy:** [freq. 1] |kjv: draught house| {str: 4280}

i^m) תחרא (THh-RA) — **Collar:** The hole in the middle of a rectangular garment for the head to pass through. [Unknown connection to root] [freq. 2] |kjv: habergeon| {str: 8473}

H) חרה (HhRH) ac: **Burn** co: ? ab: **Anger:** One who is hot.

V) חרה (Hh-RH) — **Burn:** [freq. 90] (vf: Paal, Niphal, Hiphil, Hitpael) |kjv: kindle, wroth, hot, angry, displease, fret, incense burn, earnest, grieve| {str: 2734}

i^m) תחרה (THh-RH) — **Compete:** From the heat of passion. [freq. 2] |kjv: closest, contend| {str: 8474}

J) חור (HhWR) ac: ? co: **White** ab: ?: A bleaching by the sun.

V) חור (HhWR) — **White:** To become white. [freq. 1] (vf: Paal) |kjv: wax pale| {str: 2357}

N^m) חור (HhWR) — **I. White:** [Hebrew and Aramaic] [ms: חר] **II. Noble:** [Unknown connection to root] [ms: חר] [freq. 16] |kjv: white| {str: 2353, 2358, 2715}

f^m) חורי (HhW-RY) — **White:** [freq. 2] |kjv: network| {str: 2355, 2751}

L) יחר (YHhR) ac: **Delay** co: ? ab: ?: Rather than work in the heat of the sun, one waits until the breeze of the day.

V) יחר (Y-HhR) — **Delay:** [df: יחל] [freq. 43] (vf: Paal, Niphal, Hiphil, Piel) |kjv: hope, wait, tarry, trust, stay| {str: 3176, 3186}

b^m) יחיר (Y-HhYR) — **Delay:** [freq. 1] |kjv: hope| {str: 3175}

i^f2) תוחרת (TW-Hh-RT) — **Hope:** An expectation for

what will come. [df: תוחלת]
[freq. 6] |kjv: hope| {str: 8431}

Adopted Roots;

2199	ⲟⲟ⌐ⲗⲟⲟ	Waste, Sword
2200	ⳑ⌐ⲗⲟⲟ	Tremble
2201	ⲧ⌐ⲗⲟⲟ	Tremble
2204	ⲱ⌐ⲗⲟⲟ	Roast, Grill
2205	ⳑ⌐ⲗⲟⲟ	Nettle
2232	⌐ⲗⲟⲟ⊗	Burn, Hemorrhoids

1182) ⳑⳑⲟⲟ (חש HhSh) ac: **Bind** co: ?
ab: ?: Something that is bound. (eng:
hush)

H) ⲟⲥⳑⳑⲟⲟ (חשה HhShH) ac: ? co:
Silence ab: ?: A mouth that is bound.

V) ⲟⲥⳑⳑⲟⲟ (חשה Hh-ShH) —
Silence: [freq. 16] (vf: Paal,
Hiphil) |kjv: hold, still, silence,
silent| {str: 2814}

J) ⳑⳑⲨⲟⲟ (חוש HhWSh) ac: ? co: ?
ab: ?

m^m) ⳑⳑⳑⲨⲟⲟ (חושן HhW-ShN)
— Breastplate: As bound to the
chest. [freq. 25] |kjv: breastplate|
{str: 2833}

Adopted Roots;

2218	ⳑⳑⳑⲟⲟ	
2219	ⲟⳑⳑⳑⳐⲟⲟ	Attach, Desire
2220	⌐ⳑⳑⳑⲟⲟ	Gather
2308	ⳑⳑⲟⲟⳑ	Whisper, Whisper

1183) ⳑⲟⲟ (חת HhT) ac: **Break** co: ? ab:
Fear: An action or person that is broken
in terror, fear or dismay. (eng: hate)

A) ⳑⲟⲟ (חת HhT) ac: **Break** co: ?
ab: **Fear**

N^m) ⳑⲟⲟ (חת HhT) — **Break:**
Also to be in fear as if broken.

[freq. 4] |kjv: dread, broken,
fear, dismayed| {str: 2844}

N^{fl}) ⲟⲥⳑⲟⲟ (חתה Hh-TH) —
Fear: [freq. 1] |kjv: terror| {str:
2847}

a^{fl}) ⲟⲥⳑⲟⲟ⳰⳰ (מחתה MHh-TH)
— **Firepan:** [Unknown
connection to root] [freq. 22]
|kjv: censer, firepan, snuffdish|
{str: 4289}

l^m) ⲟⲟⳑⲟⲟ (חתחת HhT-HhT) —
Fear: [freq. 1] |kjv: fear| {str:
2849}

B) ⳑⳑⲟⲟ (חתת HhTT) ac: **Break** co:
? ab: **Fear**

V) ⳑⳑⲟⲟ (חתת Hh-TT) —
Break: To broken in fear or
terror. [freq. 54] (vf: Paal,
Niphal, Hiphil, Piel) |kjv:
dismayed, afraid, break in
pieces, broken, break down,
abolish, amazed, confound,
discouraged, beat down, scarest,
terrify| {str: 2865}

N^m) ⳑⳑⲟⲟ (חתת Hh-TT) —
Breaking: [freq. 1] |kjv: cast
down| {str: 2866}

b^f) ⳑ⳾ⳑⲟⲟ (חתית Hh-TYT) —
Fear: [freq. 8] |kjv: terror| {str:
2851}

H) ⲟⲥⳑⲟⲟ (חתה HhTH) ac: **Seize** co:
? ab: ?: To break down causing a
great fear.

V) ⲟⲥⳑⲟⲟ (חתה Hh-TH) —
Seize: [freq. 4] (vf: Paal) |kjv:
take, heap| {str: 2846}

M) ⳑ⳾ⳑⲟⲟ (חית HhYT) ac: ? co:
Ruin ab: ?: Something that is broken
into pieces.

k^{fl}) ⲟⲥⳑ⳾ⳑⲟⲟ⳰⳰ (מחיתה M-HhY-
TH) — **Ruin:** [ms: מחתה] [freq.
11] |kjv: destruction, terror, ruin,
dismay| {str: 4288}

Adopted Roots;

2224 ⅃†⊓⊏   Relate, Wedding, In-law

2225 ⊂†⊓⊏   Snatch, Prey

1184) 𐤀⊓⊏ (חע HhGh) ac: ? co: ? ab: ?

Thet

1185) 𐤋⊗ (טאל ThA) ac: **Sweep** co: **Broom** ab: **?:** The pictograph ⊗ is a basket which were made from fibers. The fibers were woven and spun into products such as baskets and other products such as brooms.

A) 𐤋⊗ (טאל ThA) ac: ? co: **Broom** ab: ?

al^m) 𐤋⊗𐤋⊗ᴧ (מטאטא M-ThA-ThA) — **Broom:** [freq. 1] |kjv: besom| {str: 4292}

J) 𐤋Y⊗ (טוא ThWA) ac: **Sweep** co: ? ab: ?

V) 𐤋Y⊗ (טוא ThWA) — **Sweep:** [freq. 1] (vf: Pilpel) |kjv: sweep| {str: 2894}

~~~~~~~~

1186) ⊡⊗ (טב ThB) ac: ? co: ? ab: **Good:** The pictograph ⊗ is a picture of a basket, used to contain or surround something. The ⊡ is a picture of a tent or house. Combined these mean "surround the house". The house is surrounded by grace, beauty, love, health and prosperity, something that is functional.

A) ⊡⊗ (טב ThB) ac: ? co: ? ab: **Good:** Something that functions properly.

N^m) ⊡⊗ (טב ThB) — **Good:** [Aramaic only] [freq. 2] |kjv: good, fine| {str: 2869}

D) ⊡𐤋⊗ (טאב ThAB) ac: ? co: ? ab: **Glad:** One is glad when all is good.

V) ⊡𐤋⊗ (טאב Th-AB) — **Glad:** To be glad. [Aramaic

only] [freq. 1] (vf: Paal) |kjv: glad| {str: 2868}

J) ⊡Y⊗ (טוב ThWB) ac: ? co: ? ab: **Good**

V) ⊡Y⊗ (טוב ThWB) — **Good:** To be good such as in being functional. [freq. 33] (vf: Paal, Hiphil) |kjv: well, good, please, goodly, better, cheer, comely| {str: 2895}

N^f) ⊡Y⊗ (טוב ThWB) — **Good:** Something that functions properly. [freq. 591] |kjv: good, better, well, goodness, goodly, best, merry, fair, prosperity, precious, fine, wealth, beautiful, fairer, favour, glad| {str: 2896, 2898}

L) ⊡⊗𐤉 (יטב YThB) ac: ? co: ? ab: **Good**

V) ⊡⊗𐤉 (יטב Y-ThB) — **Good:** To be good such as in being functional. [Hebrew and Aramaic] [freq. 108] (vf: Paal, Hiphil) |kjv: well, good, please, merry, amend, better, accepted, diligently| {str: 3190, 3191}

k^m) ⊡⊗𐤉ᴧ (מיטב MY-ThB) — **Best:** [freq. 6] |kjv: best| {str: 4315}

Adopted Roots;
2767 ⊡⊗ᴴ   Moist, Fresh
3058 ⊔⬡⊗ᴴ

~~~~~~~~

1187) 𐤋⊗ (טג ThG) ac: ? co: ? ab: ?

~~~~~~~~

1188) ד⊗ (טד ThD) ac: ? co: ? ab: ?

C) ד⊗ל (אטד AThD) ac: ? co: **Thorn** ab: ?

    N^m) ד⊗ל (אטד A-ThD) — **Thorn:** [freq. 6] |kjv: bramble, thorn| {str: 329}

1189) ⊗ (טה ThH) ac: **Spin** co: **Yarn** ab: ?: The pictograph ⊗ is a basket used for storing various tools and materials including yarn.

J) Y⊗ (טוה ThWH) ac: **Spin** co: **Yarn** ab: ?: The spinning of fibers into a strong yarn.

    V) Y⊗ (טוה ThWH) — **Spin:** [freq. 2] (vf: Paal) |kjv: spin| {str: 2901}

    a^m) Y⊗ᴍ (מטוה M-ThWH) — **Yarn:** A spun fiber. [freq. 1] |kjv: spun| {str: 4299}

1190) Y⊗ (טו ThW) ac: ? co: ? ab: ?

1191) ⊗ (טז ThZ) ac: ? co: ? ab: ?

1192) ⊞⊗ (טח ThHh) ac: **Grind** co: **Plaster** ab: ?: The pictograph ⊗ is a picture of a basket, the ⊞ is a picture of a wall. Combined these mean "contain the wall". Limestone was ground into a powder and mixed with water. This plaster is used as a strong and durable coating on floors and walls. Limestone was ingested to calm an upset stomach.

A) ⊞⊗ (טח ThHh) ac: ? co: **Hand Mill** ab: ?

    N^{fl}) ⊞⊗ (טחה Th-HhH) — **Stomach:** In the sense of digesting medicinal herbs. [freq. 2] |kjv: inward parts| {str: 2910}

    j^m) Y⊞⊗ (טחון Th-HhWN) — **Mill:** A hand mill for grinding medicinal herbs into a powder. [freq. 1] |kjv: grind| {str: 2911}

H) ⊞⊗ (טחה ThHhH) ac: **Spread** co: ? ab: ?

    V) ⊞⊗ (טחה Th-HhH) — **Spread:** The area which a bow can be shot from a central point. [freq. 1] (vf: Piel, Participle) |kjv: shot| {str: 2909}

J) Y⊞⊗ (טוח ThWHh) ac: ? co: **Plaster** ab: ?

    V) Y⊞⊗ (טוח ThWHh) — **Plaster:** To spread plaster out on a surface. [freq. 12] (vf: Paal, Niphal) |kjv: daub, shut, overlay, plaister| {str: 2902}

M) ⊞⊗ (טיח ThYHh) ac: ? co: **Plaster** ab: ?

    N^m) ⊞⊗ (טיח ThYHh) — **Plaster:** A plaster that is spread out on a surface. [freq. 1] |kjv: daubing| {str: 2915}

Adopted Roots;
2831 ⊞⊗ᴜᴜ Spread

1193) ⊗⊗ (טט ThTh) ac: ? co: **Basket** ab: ?: The pictograph ⊗ is a picture of a basket. The basket or bowl, made of clay or wicker, was used for storing foods and other supplies in the nomadic tent. Clay as a common material for constructing baskets, pots and bowls is clay. (eng: tote)

M) ⊗⊗ (טיט ThYTh) ac: ? co: **Clay** ab: ?: A common material for constructing baskets, pots and bowls is clay.

N^m) ⊗⤙⊗ (טיט ThYTh) —
Mud: [Hebrew and Aramaic]
[ar: טין] [freq. 15] |kjv: mire,
clay, dirt, miry| {str: 2916,
2917}

~~~~~~~~~

1194) ⤙⊗ (טי ThY) ac: ? co: ? ab: ?

~~~~~~~~~

1195) ⊠⊗ (טך ThK) ac: ? co: ? ab: ?

~~~~~~~~~

1196) ✔⊗ (טל ThL) ac: **Scatter** co: **Dew**
ab: ?: A covering over of a large area.

A) ✔⊗ (טל ThL) ac: **Scatter** co:
Dew ab: ?

N^m) ✔⊗ (טל ThL) — **I. Dew:**
[Hebrew and Aramaic] **II. Ruin:**
A city that is covered over and
made into a mound. [df: תל]
[freq. 41] |kjv: dew, heap,
strength| {str: 2919, 2920, 8510}

l^fl) ✿✔⊗✔⊗ (טלטלה ThL-Th-LH) — **Scattering:** As covering
a large area. [freq. 1] |kjv:
captivity| {str: 2925}

B) ✔✔⊗ (טלל ThLL) ac: **Cover** co:
? ab: ?

V) ✔✔⊗ (טלל Th-LL) — **I.
Cover:** [Hebrew and Aramaic]
II. Sadow: [Aramaic only] **III.
Lofty:** [df: תלל] [freq. 3] (vf:
Paal, Piel, Participle) |kjv: cover,
shadow, eminent| {str: 2926,
2927, 8524}

E) ✘✔⊗ (טלא ThLA) ac: ? co:
Spots ab: ?: A covering of color or
spots.

V) ✘✔⊗ (טלא Th-LA) —
Spot: To be covered with spots.
[freq. 8] (vf: Paal, Pual,

Participle) |kjv: spotted, diverse
colours, clout| {str: 2921}

N^m) ✘✔⊗ (טלא Th-LA) —
Lamb: As covered with spots.
[freq. 1] |kjv: lamb| {str: 2922}

H) ✿✔⊗ (טלה ThLH) ac: ? co:
Spots ab: ?: A covering of color or
spots.

N^m) ✿✔⊗ (טלה Th-LH) —
Lamb: As covered with spots.
[freq. 2] |kjv: lamb| {str: 2924}

J) ✔⟊⊗ (טול ThWL) ac: **Cast** co: ?
ab: ?

V) ✔⟊⊗ (טול ThWL) — **Cast:**
To throw something in the sense
of spreading it out. [freq. 14] (vf:
Hiphil, Hophal, Pilpel) |kjv: cast,
carry away, send out| {str: 2904}

M) ✔⤙⊗ (טיל ThYL) ac: **Spread**
co: **Hammered** ab: ?: The
hammering of a metal into a sheet.

k^m) ✔⤙⊗⋀⋀ (מטיל M-ThYL)
— **Hammered:** A metal that has
been hammered out. [freq. 1]
|kjv: bars| {str: 4300}

~~~~~~~~~

1197) ⋀⋀⊗ (טם ThM) ac: ? co: **Unclean**
ab: ?: The pictograph ⊗ is a picture of a
basket or container, the ⋀⋀ is a picture of
water. Combined these mean "container
of water". A bowl of water is used to
wash dirt off.

C) ⋀⋀⊗✔ (אטם AThM) ac: **Shut**
co: **Shut** ab: ?: [Unknown
connection to root]

V) ⋀⋀⊗✔ (אטם A-ThM) —
Shut: The closing of the eyes,
ears or a window. [freq. 8] (vf:
Paal, Hiphil) |kjv: narrow, stop,
shut| {str: 331}

136

E) ⤷ⵡⴳ⊗ (טמא ThMA) ac: ? co: **Unclean** ab: ?

V) ⤷ⵡⴳ⊗ (טמא Th-MA) — **Unclean:** [freq. 161] (vf: Paal, Niphal, Hitpael, Pual, Piel) |kjv: unclean, defile, pollute| {str: 2930}

N^m) ⤷ⵡⴳ⊗ (טמא Th-MA) — **Unclean:** [freq. 87] |kjv: unclean, defiled, infamous, polluted, pollution| {str: 2931}

o^fl) 𐤔⤷ⵡⴳⵛ⊗ (טומאה ThWM-AH) — **Unclean:** [ms: טמאה] [freq. 37] |kjv: uncleanness, filthiness, unclean| {str: 2932}

H) 𐤔ⵡⴳ⊗ (טמה ThMH) ac: ? co: **Unclean** ab: ?

V) 𐤔ⵡⴳ⊗ (טמה Th-MH) — **Unclean:** [freq. 2] (vf: Niphal) |kjv: defile, vile| {str: 2933}

1198) ⵡ⊗ (טן ThN) ac: **Weave** co: **Basket** ab: ?: The pictograph ⊗ is a picture of a basket, the ⵡ is a picture of a seed that represents continuance. Combined these mean "basket continues". A tapestry or basket as woven items.

A) ⵡ⊗ (טן ThN) ac: ? co: **Basket** ab: ?

I^m) ⵡ⊗ⵡ⊗ (טנטן ThN-ThN) — **Palm leaf:** Used for making baskets. [df: סנסן] [freq. 1] |kjv: bough| {str: 5577}

el^f2) ⵜⵡ⊗ⵡⵍⵛ⊗ (טינטנת ThY-NTh-NT) — **Basket:** [df: צנצנת] [freq. 1] |kjv: pot| {str: 6803}

C) ⵡ⊗⤷ (אטן AThN) ac: ? co: **Tapestry** ab: ?: A covering woven from cloth.

N^m) ⵡ⊗⤷ (אטן A-ThN) — **Tapestry:** [freq. 1] |kjv: fine linen| {str: 330}

E) ⤷ⵡ⊗ (טנא ThNA) ac: ? co: **Basket** ab: ?

N^m) ⤷ⵡ⊗ (טנא Th-NA) — **Basket:** [freq. 4] |kjv: basket| {str: 2935}

F) ⵡ⊗𐤔 (הטן HThN) ac: ? co: **Chariot** ab: ?

g^m) ⵡ⊗ⵛ𐤔 (הוטן HW-ThN) — **Chariot:** As a basket. [df: הצן] [freq. 1] |kjv: chariot| {str: 2021}

1199) ⵗ⊗ (טס ThS) ac: ? co: ? ab: ?

1200) ◠⊗ (טע ThAh) ac: ? co: ? ab: ?

H) 𐤔◠⊗ (טעה ThAhH) ac: **Stray** co: ? ab: ?

V) 𐤔◠⊗ (טעה Th-AhH) — **Stray:** [freq. 1] (vf: Hiphil) |kjv: seduce| {str: 2937}

1201) ◠⊗ (טף ThP) ac: ? co: **Round** ab: ?: (eng: trip - with the addition of the r)

A) ◠⊗ (טף ThP) ac: ? co: **Children** ab: ?: The tripping around of children.

N^m) ◠⊗ (טף ThP) — **Children:** [freq. 42] |kjv: little ones, children, family| {str: 2945}

B) ◠◠⊗ (טפף ThPP) ac: **Skip** co: ? ab: ?: The skipping around of children.

V) ◠◠⊗ (טפף Th-PP) — **Skip:** [freq. 1] (vf: Paal) |kjv: mince| {str: 2952}

Adopted Roots;
2537 Cover

~~~~~~~~~~~

1202) (טץ ThTs) ac: **?** co: **?** ab: **?**

~~~~~~~~~~~

1203) (טק ThQ) ac: **?** co: **?** ab: **?**

~~~~~~~~~~~

1204) (טר ThR) ac: **Contain** co: **Wall** ab: **?:** The pictograph is a picture of a basket or other container, the is a picture of a man. Combined these mean "contain man". A wall that contains one for protection or as a jail.

A) (טר ThR) ac: **?** co: **Watch** ab: **?**

a^fl) (מטרה MTh-RH) — **I. Target:** As aimed at. [df: מטרא] **II. Prison:** A place watched and surrounded by walls. [df: מטרא] [freq. 16] |kjv: mark, prison| {str: 4307}

f^m) (טרי Th-RY) — **Fresh:** Something that is moist. [Unknown connection to root] [freq. 2] |kjv: new, putrify| {str: 2961}

C) (אטר AThR) ac: **Shut** co: **?** ab: **?:** The closing of the doors to the wall.

V) (אטר A-ThR) — **Shut:** [freq. 1] (vf: Paal) |kjv: shut| {str: 332}

N^m) (אטר A-ThR) — **Shut:** Something that is not used such as the left hand. [freq. 2] |kjv: left| {str: 334}

G) (טהר ThHR) ac: **?** co: **Clean** ab: **?:** [Unknown connection to root]

V) (טהר Th-HR) — **Clean:** [freq. 94] (vf: Paal, Hitpael, Pual, Piel) |kjv: clean, purify, purge, purifier| {str: 2891}

N^fl) (טהרה ThH-RH) — **Cleansing:** [freq. 13] |kjv: cleansing, purifying, purification, cleansed| {str: 2893}

c^m) (טהור Th-HWR) — **Clean:** [ms: טהר] [freq. 96] |kjv: clean, pure, fair| {str: 2889, 2890}

g^m) (טוהר ThW-HR) — **Cleanness:** [ms: טהר] [freq. 4] |kjv: purify, clearness,| {str: 2892}

J) (טור ThWR) ac: **?** co: **Row** ab: **?:** As the wall as a row.

N^m) (טור ThWR) — **I. Row: II. Range:** A row of mountains. [Aramaic only] [freq. 28] |kjv: row, mountain| {str: 2905, 2906}

M) (טיר ThYR) ac: **?** co: **Village** ab: **?:** A place carefully watched over.

N^fl) (טירה ThY-RH) — **Village:** [freq. 7] |kjv: castle, palace, row, habitation| {str: 2918}

Adopted Roots;
2245 Tear, Prey
2400 Guard

~~~~~~~~~~~

1205) (טש ThSh) ac: **Pounce** co: **?** ab: **?:** (eng: toss)

J) (טוש ThWSh) ac: **?** co: **Pounce** ab: **?:** The swooping down of a bird onto its prey.

V) ⊔⊔Y⊗ (שוט ThWSh) —
Pounce: [df: שוט] [freq. 1] (vf:
Paal) |kjv: haste| {str: 2907}

Adopted Roots;
2309 ⊔⊔⊗∫ Sharp
2401 ⊔⊔⊗ˤ Spread, Branch
2539 ⊔⊔⊗⌐ Sneeze
2605 ⊔⊔⊗⌐ Spread, Hammer
2768 ⊔⊔⊗ᴙ Hack

~~~~~~~~~~

1206) ✝⊗ (טת ThT) ac: **Fast** co: ? ab: ?

J) ✝Y⊗ (טות ThWT) ac: **Fast** co: ?
ab: ?

N^m) ✝Y⊗ (טות ThWT) —
Fasting: [Aramaic only] [freq.
1] |kjv: fasting| {str: 2908}

~~~~~~~~~~

1207) 8⊗ (טע ThGh) ac: ? co: ? ab: ?

~~~~~~~~~~

139

Yad

1208) יאל (יא YA) ac: ? co: ? ab: ?

1209) יבל (יב YB) ac: **Cry** co: ? ab: ?

B) יבבל (יבב YBB) ac: **Cry** co: ? ab: ?

V) יבבל (יבב Y-BB) — **Cry:** [freq. 1] (vf: Piel) |kjv: cry| {str: 2980}

1210) יגל (יג YG) ac: **Afflict** co: ? ab: **Sorrow**

A) יגל (יג YG) ac: ? co: ? ab: **Sorrow**

i[fl]) תוגה+ (תוגה TW-GH) — **Sorrow:** [freq. 4] |kjv: heaviness, sorrow| {str: 8424}

j[m]) יגון (יגון Y-GWN) — **Sorrow:** [freq. 14] |kjv: sorrow, grief| {str: 3015}

H) יגה (יגה YGH) ac: ? co: ? ab: **Affliction**

V) יגה (יגה Y-GH) — **I. Afflict: II. Remove:** [Unknown connection to root] [freq. 9] (vf: Niphal, Hiphil, Piel, Participle) |kjv: afflict, grief, sorrow, vex| {str: 3013, 3014}

1211) ידל (יד YD) ac: **Throw** co: **Hand** ab: **Thanks:** The pictograph ל is a picture of a hand, the ד is a picture of door that allows movement in and out of the tent. Combined these mean "hand moves". The hand is the part of the body that enables man to perform many works.

(eng: yard - with the addition of the r, a measurement equal to the length of the arm)

A) ידל (יד YD) ac: ? co: **Hand** ab: ?: With the hand one can throw away or grab hold, kill or heal, make or destroy.

N[f]) ידל (יד YD) — **Hand:** [Hebrew and Aramaic] [df: יד] [freq. 1632] |kjv: hand, by, him, power, tenons, thee, coast, side| {str: 3027, 3028, 3197}

i[fl]) תודה+ (תודה TW-DH) — **I. Thanks: II. Confession:** In the sense of raising up the hands. [freq. 32] |kjv: thanksgiving, praise, thanks, confession| {str: 8426}

B) ידדל (ידד YDD) ac: **Throw** co: ? ab: ?: The work of the hand.

V) ידדל (ידד Y-DD) — **Throw:** [freq. 3] (vf: Paal) |kjv: cast| {str: 3032}

G) יהדל (יהד YHD) ac: ? co: **Hand** ab: ?: The throwing out of the hand for throwing, praising, or confessing.

V) יהדל (יהד Y-HD) — **Jew:** To be from the tribe of Judah. [A denominative verb from the name Yehudah (Judah)] [freq. 1] (vf: Hitpael) |kjv: Jew| {str: 3054}

H) ידהל (ידה YDH) ac: **Throw** co: **Hand** ab: ?: The throwing out of the hand for throwing, praising, or confessing.

V) ידהל (ידה Y-DH) — **I. Throw:** [df: הדה] **II. Praise:**

[Hebrew and Aramaic] [ar: יד‏א]
III. Confess: In the sense of
raising up the hands. [freq. 117]
(vf: Paal, Hiphil, Hitpael, Piel)
|kjv: praise, thank, confess,
thanksgiving, cast, shoot, put|
{str: 1911, 3029, 3034}

1212) ﬥﭏ (יה YH) ac: ? co: ? ab: ?

1213) ﬥY (יו YW) ac: ? co: ? ab: ?

1214) ﬥﬡ (יז YZ) ac: ? co: ? ab: ?

1215) ﬥ▥ (יח YHh) ac: ? co: ? ab: ?

1216) ﬥ⊗ (יט YTh) ac: ? co: ? ab: ?

1217) ﬥﬥ (יי YY) ac: ? co: ? ab: ?

1218) ﬥ▥ (יך YK) ac: ? co: ? ab: ?

1219) ﬥﬗ (יל YL) ac: ? co: ? ab: ?

1220) ﬥﬃ (ים YM) ac: ? co: **Sea** ab:
Terror: The pictograph ﬥ is a picture of
a hand representing work, the ﬃ is a
picture of water. Combined these mean
"working water". The sea or other large
body of water is the place of storms and
heavy surf. This parent root is closely
related to ﬃﭏ.

A) ﬥﬃ (ים YM) ac: ? co: **Sea** ab: ?

N^m) ﬥﬃ (ים YM) — **Sea:**
Also the direction of the sea, the
west. [Hebrew and Aramaic]
[freq. 398] |kjv: sea, west,
westward, seafaring men| {str:
3220, 3221}

B) ﬥﬃﬃ (ימם YMM) ac: ? co: ?
Spring ab: ?: A spring of water in
the wilderness.

N^m) ﬥﬃﬃ (ימם Y-MM) —
Spring: [freq. 1] |kjv: mule| {str:
3222}

C) ﬥﬃﬗ (אים AYM) ac: ? co: ?
ab: **Terror:** The sea is considered a
place of chaos and terror because the
depth, storms and heavy surf.

N^fl) ﬥﬃﬗﭏ (אימה AY-MH)
— **Terror:** [ms: אמה] [freq. 17]
|kjv: terror, fear, terrible, dread,
horror, idols| {str: 367}

c^m) ﬥﬃYﬗ (איום A-YWM) —
Terrible: [ms: אים] [freq. 3]
|kjv: terrible| {str: 366}

J) ﬥﬃY (יום YWM) ac: ? co: **Day**
ab: ?: The day ends and the new day
begins when the sun sets in the west,
over the Mediterranean sea.

N^m) ﬥﬃY (יום YWM) — **Day:**
[Hebrew and Aramaic] [freq.
2290] |kjv: day, time, daily,
every, year, continually, when,
as, while, full, alway, whole|
{str: 3117, 3118}

p^m) ﬥﬃﬃY (יומם YW-MM)
— **Day:** [freq. 51] |kjv: day,
daytime, daily, time| {str: 3119}

1221) ﬥﬗ (ין YN) ac: ? co: **Wine** ab: ?
J) ﬥYﬗ (יון YWN) ac: ? co: **Mire**
ab: ?

N^m) ﹃ﻱ﹄ (יון YWN) — **Mire:** [freq. 2] |kjv: miry, mire| {str: 3121}

N^{fl}) ﻥﻱ﹄ (יונה YW-NH) — **Dove:** [Unknown connection to root] [freq. 32] |kjv: dove, pigeon| {str: 3123}

M) ﹄ﻱ﹄ (יין YYN) ac: ? co: **Wine** ab: ?

N^m) ﹄ﻱ﹄ (יין YYN) — **Wine:** From the mire in the wine. [freq. 140] |kjv: wine, banqueting| {str: 3196}

1222) ﻱ﹄ (יס YS) ac: ? co: ? ab: ?

1223) ﻱ﹄ (יע YAh) ac: **Sweep** co: **Shovel** ab: ?

A) ﻱ﹄ (יע YAh) ac: ? co: **Shovel** ab: ?

N^m) ﻱ﹄ (יע YAh) — **Shovel:** [freq. 4] |kjv: shovel| {str: 3257}

H) ﻥﻱ﹄ (יעה YAhH) ac: **Sweep** co: ? ab: ?

V) ﻥﻱ﹄ (יעה Y-AhH) — **Sweep:** [freq. 1] (vf: Paal) |kjv: sweep away| {str: 3261}

1224) ﻱ﹄ (יף YP) ac: ? co: ? ab: **Beauty**

A) ﻱ﹄ (יף YP) ac: ? co: ? ab: **Beauty:** A place, thing or event that goes beyond the normal such as a miracle, sign, wonder or beauty.

f^m) ﻱ﹄﹄ (יפי Y-PY) — **Beauty:** [freq. 19] |kjv: beauty| {str: 3308}

H) ﻥﻱ﹄ (יפה YPH) ac: ? co: ? ab: **Beauty:** A place, thing or event that goes beyond the normal such as a miracle, sign, wonder or beauty.

V) ﻥﻱ﹄ (יפה Y-PH) — **Beautiful:** To be beautiful. [freq. 8] (vf: Paal, Hitpael, Pual, Piel) |kjv: fair, beautiful| {str: 3302}

N^m) ﻥﻱ﹄ (יפה Y-PH) — **Beauty:** [freq. 42] |kjv: fair, beautiful, well, beauty| {str: 3303, 3304}

1225) ﻱ﹄ (יץ YTs) ac: ? co: ? ab: ?

1226) ﻱ﹄ (יק YQ) ac: ? co: ? ab: ?

1227) ﻱ﹄ (יר YR) ac: **Throw** co: ? ab: **Fear:** The pictograph ﹄ is a picture of a hand, the ﻥ is a picture of a man. Combined these mean "hand of man". The hand of man is used for the throwing. A flowing of water in a river. A throwing of the finger to show a direction to walk or live. The throwing of an arrow. The throwing down of water in rain. Awe or fear where one throws self to the foot of one in authority. Related to ﻥﻥ and ﹄ﻥ.

D) ﻥﻱ﹄ (יאר YAR) ac: ? co: **River** ab: ?: A flowing of water in a river.

N^m) ﻥﻱ﹄ (יאר Y-AR) — **River:** [freq. 64] |kjv: river, brook, flood, stream| {str: 2975}

E) ﻥﻱ﹄ (ירא YRA) ac: ? co: ? ab: **Fear:** A flowing of the insides.

V) ﻥﻱ﹄ (ירא Y-RA) — **Fear:** [freq. 314] (vf: Paal, Niphal, Piel) |kjv: fear, afraid, terrible, dreadful, reverence, fearful| {str: 3372}

142

Nᵐ) יֵרָא (ירא Y-RA) — **Fear:** [freq. 64] |kjv: fear, afraid, fearful| {str: 3373}

Nᶠˡ) יִרְאָה (יראה YR-AH) — **Fear:** [freq. 45] |kjv: fear, dreadful, fearfulness| {str: 3374}

kᵐ) מוֹרָא (מורא MW-RA) — **Fear:** [ms: מרא] [df: מרה] [freq. 13] |kjv: fear, terror, dread, terribleness| {str: 4172}

H) יָרֹה (ירה YRH) ac: **Throw** co: **Rain** ab: **?:** A throwing of the finger to show a direction to walk or live. The throwing of an arrow. The throwing down of water in rain.

V) יָרֹה (ירה Y-RH) — **I. Throw:** [df: ירא] **II. Rain: III. Teach:** To point the way one is to walk in life. [freq. 84] (vf: Paal, Niphal, Hiphil) |kjv: teach, shoot, archer, cast, teacher, rain, laid, direct, inform, instruct, show, shooter, through watered| {str: 3384}

gᵐ) יוֹרֶה (יורה YW-RH) — **First rain:** [freq. 2] |kjv: first rain, former| {str: 3138}

iᶠˡ) תּוֹרָה (תורה TW-RH) — **Teaching:** The direction one is to take in life. [ms: תרה] [freq. 219] |kjv: law| {str: 8451}

kᵐ) מוֹרֶה (מורה MW-RH) — **I. Rain: II. Archer:** One who throws an arrow. **III. Razor:** [Unknown connection to root] [freq. 3] |kjv: former rain, rain| {str: 4175}

—————

1228) יֵשׁ (יש YSh) ac: **Exist** co: **?** ab: **?:** (eng: yes; is)

A) יֵשׁ (יש YSh) ac: **Exist** co: **?** ab: **?**

Nᵐ) יֵשׁ (יש YSh) — **There is:** Something that exists. [df: אש] [freq. 135] |kjv: is, be, have, can, there| {str: 786, 3426}

nfᵐ) יֶשׁיּ (אישי AY-ShY) — **There is:** Something that exists. [Aramaic only] [ar: איתי] [freq. 17] |kjv: be| {str: 383}

—————

1229) יֵת (ית YT) ac: **?** co: **?** ab: **?**

—————

1230) יֵע (יע YGh) ac: **?** co: **?** ab: **?**

—————

Kaph

1231) שׁﬡ (כﬡ KA) ac: ? co: ? ab: ?

1232) שׁﬞﬗ (כﬗ KB) ac: ? co: **Star** ab: ?: The pictograph שׁ is a picture of the palm of the hand and represents a covering, the ﬗ is a picture of a tent. Combined these mean "covering of the tent". The black goat hair fabric used for the roof of the tent allows some light through giving the appearance of stars overhead. When it rains the hair fibers swell sealing all of these holes.

B) שׁﬗﬗ (כﬗﬗ KBB) ac: ? co: **Star** ab: ?

g^m) שׁﬠﬗﬗ (כﬗﬗﬗ KW-BB) — **Star:** [df: כﬞﬗﬗ] [freq. 37] |kjv: star| {str: 3556}

D) שׁﬡﬗ (כﬡﬗ KAB) ac: ? co: ? ab: **Sorrow:** [Unknown connection to root]

V) שׁﬡﬗ (כﬡﬗ K-AB) — **Sorrow:** [freq. 8] (vf: Paal, Hiphil, Participle) |kjv: sorrowful, sore, pain, sad, mar, grieve| {str: 3510}

N^m) שׁﬡﬗ (כﬡﬗ K-AB) — **Sorrow:** [freq. 6] |kjv: sorrow, grief, pain| {str: 3511}

ac^m) שׁﬡﬠﬗﬦ (מﬗﬡﬗ MK-AWB) — **Sorrow:** [ms: מﬗﬡﬗ] [freq. 16] |kjv: sorrow, pain, grief| {str: 4341}

H) שׁﬗﬤ (כﬗﬤ KBH) ac: **Quench** co: ? ab: ?: [Unknown connection to root]

V) שׁﬗﬤ (כﬗﬤ K-BH) — **Quench:** [freq. 24] (vf: Paal,

Piel) |kjv: quench, out| {str: 3518}

Adopted Roots;
2246 שׁﬗﬤﬦ Heavy, Liver, Honor
2250 שׁﬗﬦ Multiply, Net, Abundance

1233) שׁﬤ (כﬕ KG) ac: ? co: ? ab: ?

1234) שׁﬤﬦ (כﬕ KD) ac: **Strike** co: **Flint** ab: **Destruction:** A fire is started by striking an iron implement on a piece of flint rock that creates a spark.

A) שׁﬤﬦ (כﬕ KD) ac: ? co: **Flint** ab: ?

N^m) שׁﬤﬦ (כﬕ KD) — **Jar:** [Unknown connection to root] [freq. 18] |kjv: pitcher, barrel| {str: 3537}

I^m) שׁﬤﬦשׁﬤﬦ (כﬕﬕ KD-KD) — **Flint:** [freq. 2] |kjv: agate| {str: 3539}

B) שׁﬤﬤﬦ (כﬕﬕ KDD) ac: ? co: **Spark** ab: ?: Formed by striking iron on flint.

ec^m) שׁﬦﬤﬠﬦ (כﬕﬠﬦ KY-DWD) — **Spark:** [freq. 1] |kjv: spark| {str: 3590}

M) שׁﬦﬤﬦ (כﬦﬕ KYD) ac: **Strike** co: **Spear** ab: ?

N^m) שׁﬦﬤﬦ (כﬦﬕ KYD) — **Destruction:** [freq. 1] |kjv: destruction| {str: 3589}

j^m) שׁﬦﬤﬠﬦﬠ (כﬦﬕﬠﬠ KY-DWN) — **I. Spear:** Used to strike at the enemy. **II. Shield:** Takes the

blow of the spear. [freq. 9] |kjv:
spear, shield, lance, target| {str:
3591}

1235) שׁהּ (כה KH) ac: **Burn** co: **Brand**
ab: **?**: The burning of the skin. Related to
שׁל.

A) שׁהּ (כה KH) ac: **?** co: **Brand**
ab: **?**

N^m) שׁהּ (כה KH) — **So:** To do
something in a certain manner, a
reference to the previous or
following context. [Hebrew and
Aramaic] [df: ככה] [freq. 35]
|kjv: thus, so, after, like, hitherto,
while, manner| {str: 3541, 3542,
3602}

N^f1) שׁההּ (כהה K-HH) —
Darkening: [freq. 1] |kjv:
healing| {str: 3545}

B) שׁההּ (כהה KHH) ac: **?** co:
Dark ab: **?**: The charred color of
wood that has been burned.

V) שׁההּ (כהה K-HH) —
Dark: To be dark in the eyes or
knowledge. [freq. 8] (vf: Paal,
Piel) |kjv: dim, fail, faint,
darken, utterly, restrain| {str:
3543}

N^m) שׁההּ (כהה K-HH) —
Dark: [freq. 9] |kjv: dark,
darkish, dim, smoking,
heaviness| {str: 3544}

D) שׁאהּ (כאה KAH) ac: **Sad** co: **?**
ab: **?**: A darkening of the soul.

V) שׁאהּ (כאה K-AH) — **Sad:**
[freq. 3] (vf: Niphal, Hiphil)
|kjv: sad, broken, grieve| {str:
3512}

J) שׁוהּ (כוה KWH) ac: **Burn** co: **?**
ab: **?**

V) שׁוהּ (כוה KWH) — **Burn:**
[freq. 2] (vf: Niphal) |kjv: burn|
{str: 3554}

f^f1) שׁויהּ (כויה KW-YH) —
Burn: [freq. 2] |kjv: burn| {str:
3555}

h^f1) שׁוהּמ (מכוה MK-WH) —
Burning: [freq. 5] |kjv: burn|
{str: 4348}

1236) שׁו (כו KW) ac: **?** co: **Window** ab:
?

A) שׁו (כו KW) ac: **?** co: **Window**
ab: **?**

N^f) שׁו (כו KW) — **Window:**
[Aramaic only] [freq. 1] |kjv:
window| {str: 3551}

1237) שׁז (כז KZ) ac: **?** co: **?** ab: **?**

1238) שׁח (כח KHh) ac: **Chastise** co:
Firm ab: **?**: The pictograph ש is a picture
of the palm of the hand, the ח is a
picture of a wall. Combined these mean
"palm wall". To correct or chastise with a
firm hand.

J) שׁוח (כוח KWHh) ac: **?** co:
Firm ab: **?**

N^m) שׁוח (כוח KWHh) —
Strength: [ms: כח] [freq. 126]
|kjv: strength, power, might,
force, ability, able, chameleon,
substance, wealth| {str: 3581}

L) שׁחי (יכח YKHh) ac: **Chastise**
co: **?** ab: **?**

V) שׁחי (יכח Y-KHh) —
Chastise: [freq. 59] (vf: Niphal,
Hiphil, Hophal) |kjv: reprove,
rebuke, correct, plead, reason,

chasten, appoint, argue| {str: 3198}

i^{f1}) ✚**m**שׁYt (תוכחה TW-KHhH) — **Chastise:** [freq. 28] |kjv: reproof, rebuke, reprove, argument| {str: 8433}

~~~~~~~~

1239) ⊗שׁ (כט KTh) ac: ? co: ? ab: ?

~~~~~~~~

1240) ל—ﬥﬡשׁ (כי KY) ac: **Burn** co: ? ab: ?: Related to ✚שׁ.

A) ל—ﬥﬡשׁ (כי KY) ac: **Burn** co: ? ab: ?

N^m) ל—ﬥﬡשׁ (כי KY) — **I. Burning: II. Because:** A reference to the previous or following context. [freq. 47] |kjv: burning| {str: 3587, 3588}

~~~~~~~~

1241) שׁשׁ (כך KK) ac: ? co: ? ab: ?

~~~~~~~~

1242) Jﬥﬡשׁ (כל KL) ac: **Complete** co: **Vessel** ab: **Whole:** The pictograph שׁ is a picture of the bent palm representing the bending or subduing of the will, the J is a picture of a shepherd staff or yoke. Combined these mean "tame for the yoke". An animal or land that is tamed has been worked and is complete and ready for use. Taming include; construction of holding pens, putting the soil to the plow, harvesting of crops, milk or meat. One eats once the harvest is complete. (eng: whole; cell; cellar)

A) Jﬥﬡשׁ (כל KL) ac: **Complete** co: **Vessel** ab: **Whole:** A container for holding contents. Something that is full or whole.

N^{f1}) ✚Jﬥﬡשׁ (כלה K-LH) — **Completion:** Something that has been completed or made whole. This can be in a positive sense or negative such as in a failure. [freq. 22] |kjv: end, altogether, consume, consumption, consummation, determine, riddance| {str: 3617}

f^m) ﬥﬡJﬥﬡﬡשׁ (כלי K-LY) — **Vessel:** For carrying or storing various materials. [freq. 325] |kjv: vessel, instrument, weapon, jewel, stuff, thing, armour, furniture, carriage, bag| {str: 3627}

f^{f1}) ✚ﬥﬡJﬥﬡﬡשׁ (כליה KL-YH) — **Kidney:** The organ as a vessel. The seat of emotion. [freq. 31] |kjv: kidneys, reins| {str: 3629}

i^{f1}) ✚JﬥﬡשׁYt (תכלה TK-LH) — **Completion:** [freq. 1] |kjv: perfection| {str: 8502}

i^{f2}) tJﬥﬡשׁYt (תכלת TK-LT) — **Blue:** [Unknown connection to root] [freq. 50] |kjv: blue| {str: 8504}

i^{f4}) tﬥﬡJﬥﬡﬡשׁYt (תכלית TK-LYT) — **Boundary:** The ends of the whole. [freq. 5] |kjv: end, perfection, perfect| {str: 8503}

fj^m) ﬢYﬥﬡJﬥﬡﬡשׁ (כליון KL-YWN) — **Failure:** A complete destruction or failure of something. [freq. 2] |kjv: failing, consumption| {str: 3631}

B) JJﬥﬡﬡשׁ (כלל KLL) ac: **Complete** co: ? ab: **Whole:** Something that is whole or a container that holds something completely.

V) JJﬥﬡﬡשׁ (כלל K-LL) — **Complete:** [Hebrew and Aramaic] [freq. 10] (vf: Paal)

|kjv: perfect, finish| {str: 3634, 3635}

N^{fl}) כללה (שׁ‍כ‍ל‍ל‍ה KL-LH) — **Bride:** The one added to the man to make him complete. [ms: כלה] [freq. 34] |kjv: daughter-in-law, bride, spouse| {str: 3618}

b^m) כליל (שׁ‍כ‍ל‍ל K-LYL) — **Complete:** [freq. 15] |kjv: perfect, wholly, perfection, utterly, whole| {str: 3632}

d^{fl}) כלולה (שׁ‍כ‍ו‍ל‍ל‍ה K-LW-LH) — **Bridehood:** In the sense of becoming complete. [freq. 1] |kjv: espousal| {str: 3623}

h^m) מכלל (שׁ‍כ‍ל‍ל‍מ MK-LL) — **Complete:** [freq. 1] |kjv: perfection| {str: 4359}

hc^m) מכלול (שׁ‍כ‍ל‍ו‍ל‍מ MK-LWL) — **Complete:** [freq. 2] |kjv: gorgeously, sorts| {str: 4358}

hd^m) מכלול (שׁ‍כ‍ל‍ו‍ל‍מ MK-LWL) — **Choice:** In the sense of being whole and complete. [freq. 1] |kjv: all| {str: 4360}

C) אכל (שׁ‍כ‍ל‍ע AKL) ac: **Eat** co: **Food** ab: **?:** Through sustenance one becomes whole and satisfied.

V) אכל (שׁ‍כ‍ל‍ע A-KL) — **Eat:** [Hebrew and Aramaic] [freq. 817] (vf: Paal, Niphal, Hiphil, Pual, Piel) |kjv: eat, devour, consume| {str: 398, 399}

N^{fl}) אכלה (שׁ‍כ‍ל‍ע‍ה AK-LH) — **Food:** [freq. 18] |kjv: meat, devour, fuel, eat, consume, food| {str: 402}

a^m) מאכל (שׁ‍כ‍ל‍ע‍מ MA-KL) — **Food:** [freq. 30] |kjv: meat, food, fruit, manner, victual| {str: 3978}

a^{f2}) מאכלת (שׁ‍כ‍ל‍ע‍ת‍מ MA-K-LT) — **Knife:** What is used for preparing and eating food. [freq. 4] |kjv: knife| {str: 3979}

b^{fl}) אכילה (שׁ‍כ‍י‍ל‍ע‍ה A-KY-LH) — **Food:** [freq. 1] |kjv: meat| {str: 396}

g^m) אוכל (שׁ‍כ‍ו‍ל‍ע AW-KL) — **Food:** [ms: אכל] [freq. 44] |kjv: meat, food, eating, victuals, prey| {str: 400}

ac^{f2}) מאכולת (שׁ‍כ‍ו‍ל‍ע‍ת‍מ MA-KW-LT) — **Fuel:** Is used cooking food. [ms: מאכלת] [freq. 2] |kjv: fuel| {str: 3980}

E) כלא (שׁ‍כ‍ל‍ע KLA) ac: **Restrain** co: **Prison** ab: **?:** A prison or fold for restraining men or animals in the sense of whole.

V) כלא (שׁ‍כ‍ל‍ע K-LA) — **Restrain:** To hold back or prevent someone or something. [freq. 18] (vf: Paal, Niphal, Piel) |kjv: shut up, stay, refrain, withhold, keep, finish, forbid, retain| {str: 3607}

N^m) כלא (שׁ‍כ‍ל‍ע K-LA) — **Prison:** [freq. 10] |kjv: prison| {str: 3608}

b^m) כליא (שׁ‍כ‍ל‍י‍ע K-LYA) — **Prison:** [df: כלוא] [freq. 2] |kjv: prison| {str: 3628}

e^m) כילא (שׁ‍כ‍י‍ל‍ע KY-LA) — **Mixture:** [Unknown connection to root] [ms: כלא] [freq. 4] |kjv: mingle, diverse| {str: 3610}

h^{fl}) מכלאה (שׁ‍כ‍ל‍ע‍ה‍מ MK-L-AH) — **Fold:** [freq. 3] |kjv: fold| {str: 4356}

F) הכל (שׁ‍כ‍ל‍פ HKL) ac: **?** co: **House** ab: **?:** An enclosure for a resident god or king in the sense of whole.

147

e^m) 𐤔𐤄𐤋‎ (היכל HY-KL) — **House:** The house of a god (temple) or king (palace). [Hebrew and Aramaic] [freq. 93] |kjv: temple, palace| {str: 1964, 1965}

G) 𐤔𐤋‎ (כהל KHL) ac: **Able** co: ? ab: ?: One who is whole or complete is able to do or perform something.

V) 𐤔𐤋‎ (כהל K-HL) — **Able:** [Aramaic only] [freq. 4] (vf: Paal) |kjv: able, could| {str: 3546}

H) 𐤔𐤋‎ (כלה KLH) ac: **Complete** co: ? ab: ?

V) 𐤔𐤋‎ (כלה K-LH) — **Complete:** To bring something to its completion. [freq. 206] (vf: Paal, Pual, Piel) |kjv: consume, end, finish, fail, accomplish, done, spend, determine, away, fulfill, faint, destroy, left, waste| {str: 3615}

N^m) 𐤔𐤋‎ (כלה K-LH) — **Failing:** Something that is incomplete. [freq. 1] |kjv: fail| {str: 3616}

h^fl) 𐤔𐤋𐤌‎ (מכלה MK-LH) — **Completion:** [freq. 1] |kjv: perfect| {str: 4357}

J) 𐤔𐤋‎ (כול KWL) ac: **Sustain** co: **Food** ab: ?

V) 𐤔𐤋‎ (כול KWL) — **Sustain:** To provide what is needed to make someone or something whole or complete. [freq. 37] (vf: Paal, Pilpel) |kjv: contain, feed, sustain, abide, nourish, hold, receive, victual, bear, comprehend| {str: 3557}

N^m) 𐤔𐤋‎ (כול KWL) — **All:** [ms: כל] [freq. 120] |kjv:

everything, all, whosoever, nothing, yet| {str: 3605, 3606}

a^f2) 𐤔𐤋𐤌‎ (מכולת M-KW-LT) — **Food:** What sustains. [ms: מכלת] [freq. 1] |kjv: food| {str: 4361}

L) 𐤔𐤋‎ (יכל YKL) ac: **Able** co: **Vessel** ab: ?: One who is whole or complete is able to do or perform something.

V) 𐤔𐤋‎ (יכל Y-KL) — **Able:** [Hebrew and Aramaic] [df: יכיל] [freq. 107] (vf: Paal) |kjv: can, able, prevail, may, endure, might| {str: 3201, 3202}

h^m) 𐤔𐤋𐤌‎ (מיכל MY-KL) — **Vessel:** A container of holding water. [freq. 1] |kjv: brook| {str: 4323}

M) 𐤔𐤋‎ (כיל KYL) ac: ? co: ? ab: **Villain:** One who is held in a prison.

f^m) 𐤔𐤋‎ (כילי KY-LY) — **Villain:** [freq. 2] |kjv: churl| {str: 3596}

~~~~~~~~~

1243) ש‎ (כם KM) ac: ? co: ? ab: **Desire**

A) ש‎ (כם KM) ac: ? co: ? ab: **Like**

q^m) ש‎ (כמו K-MW) — **Like:** In a state like, as or according to something else. [The short form "ש" is used as a prefix meaning "like".] [freq. 20] |kjv: when, as, like, according, worth| {str: 3644}

H) ש‎ (כמה KMH) ac: ? co: ? ab: **Desire**

V) ש‎ (כמה K-MH) — **Desire:** [freq. 1] (vf: Paal) |kjv: long| {str: 3642}

Adopted Roots;
2263 שׁמַ؈ Store, Ornament
2264 שׁמֵ؉ Store, Treasure
2265 שׁמֵ؎ Store

~~~~~~~~~

1244) שׁ؇ (כֹן KN) ac: **Stand** co: **Root** ab: **Sure:** The pictograph שׁ is a picture of the open palm, the ؇ is a picture of a seed. Combined these mean "opening of a seed". When the seed opens the roots begin to form the base of the plant by going down into the soil. The plant rises out of the ground forming the stalk of the plant. A tall tree can only stand tall and firm because of the strong root system which supports it.

A) שׁ؇ (כֹן KN) ac: **?** co: **Base** ab: **?:** The base that supports that which stands firm.

N؏) שׁ؇ (כֹן KN) — **I. So:** A firmness in a situation. [Hebrew and Aramaic] **II. Firm:** A standing tall and firm. An upright person of column. **III. Base:** The base which provides support as well as a persons home or family as a base. **IV. Gnat:** Possibly as a firm standing insect. [Unknown connection to root] [freq. 74] |kjv: foot, estate, base, office, place, well, so, thus, like, well, such, howbeit, state, after, that, following, therefore, wherefore, lice, manner| {str: 3651, 3652, 3653, 3654}

N؏؉) שׁ؇؈ (כנה K-NH) — **Stalk:** The base and support of a plant. [freq. 2] |kjv: vineyard| {str: 3657, 3661}

p؏؉) שׁ؇מַ؈ (כנמה KN-MH) — **So:** A firmness in a situation. [Aramaic only] [ar: כנמא] [freq.

5] |kjv: thus, so, sort, manner| {str: 3660}

kc؏؉) מַשׁ؇؈ (מכונה M-KW-NH) — **Base:** What is firm and supports something. [ms: מכנה] [freq. 23] |kjv: base| {str: 4350}

kd؏؉) מַשׁ؇؈ (מכונה M-KW-NH) — **Base:** What is firm and supports something. [ms: מכנה] [freq. 1] |kjv: base| {str: 4369}

C) ؏שׁ؇ (אכן AKN) ac: **Firm** co: **?** ab: **?:** A firm or sure position.

N؏) ؏שׁ؇ (אכן A-KN) — **Surely:** To be firm in something. [df: אך] [freq. 40] |kjv: also, but, certainly, even, howbeit, least, nevertheless, notwithstanding, only, save, scarce, surely, sure, truly, verily, wherefore, yet| {str: 389, 403}

G) שׁ؈؇ (כהן KHN) ac: **Adorn** co: **Priest** ab: **?:** The base which supports the people.

V) שׁ؈؇ (כהן K-HN) — **Adorn:** To put on special ornaments or garments for a special office or event. (see Is 61:10) [freq. 23] (vf: Piel) |kjv: minister, execute, deck, office, priest| {str: 3547}

N؏) שׁ؈؇ (כהן K-HN) — **Priest:** [Aramaic only] [freq. 8] |kjv: priest| {str: 3549}

d؏؉) שׁ؈؇؄؈ (כהונה K-HW-NH) — **Priesthood:** The group of those who support the community. [ms: כהנה] [freq. 14] |kjv: priesthood, priests office| {str: 3550}

g؏) שׁ؄؈؇ (כוהן KW-HN) — **Priest:** [ms: כהן] [freq. 750] |kjv: priest, chief, officer, prince| {str: 3548}

H) שׁרֲכ (כנה KNH) ac: **Support** co: **Flatter** ab: **?:** Words or names that are given in support of another.

V) שׁרֲכ (כנה K-NH) — **Flatter:** To give words or a name of honor. [freq. 4] (vf: Piel) |kjv: surname, flattering title| {str: 3655}

J) שׁרׄ (כון KWN) ac: **Firm** co: **Foundation** ab: **?**

V) שׁרׄ (כון KWN) — **Firm:** To set something firmly in place, either physically or with words. [freq. 219] (vf: Niphal, Hiphil, Hophal) |kjv: prepare, establish, ready, provide, right, fix, set, direct, order, fashion, certain, confirm, firm| {str: 3559}

N^m) שׁרׄ (כון KWN) — **Cake:** As firmly pressed. [freq. 2] |kjv: cake| {str: 3561}

a^m) שׁרׄמ (מכון M-KWN) — **Foundation:** A firm place of support. [freq. 17] |kjv: place, habitation, foundation| {str: 4349}

i^fl) שׁרׄשׁ+ (תכונה T-KW-NH) — **Foundation:** [freq. 1] |kjv: seat| {str: 8499}

Adopted Roots;
2267 שׁרֲ — Gather
2268 שׁרֶ — Lower, Bundle, Humility
2894 +J — Hang
2271 שׁרׅ — Gather
2272 שׁרׄ+ — Associate

1245) שׁרֲ (כס KS) ac: **Cover** co: **Cup** ab: **?:** (eng: case)

A) שׁרֲ (כס KS) ac: **?** co: **Seat** ab: **?:** The seat is like a cup that holds, conceals, a person. A covering of

something. To cover a group by counting.

N^m) שׁרֲ (כס KS) — **Seat:** [freq. 1] |kjv: seat| {str: 3676}

N^fl) שׁרֲ (כסה K-SH) — **Cup:** [df: קשׁוה קשׁ] [freq. 4] |kjv: cover, cup| {str: 7184}

N^f2) שׁרֲ+ (כסת K-ST) — **I. Inkwell:** A cup for holding ink. [ms: קסת] **II. Amulets:** A sewn arm or wrist band as a covering. [freq. 5] |kjv: pillow, inkhorn| {str: 3704, 7083}

N^f3) שׁרֲ+ (כסות K-SWT) — **Covering:** Covering, raiment, vesture. [freq. 8] |kjv: covering, raiment, vesture| {str: 3682}

h^fl) שׁרֲמ (מכסה MK-SH) — **Value:** According to a number. [freq. 2] |kjv: number, worth| {str: 4373}

k^m) שׁרֲמ (מכס M-KS) — **Tribute:** An assessment based on a number. [freq. 6] |kjv: tribute| {str: 4371}

l^f2) שׁרֲשׁ+ (כסכסת KS-K-ST) — **Scales:** The covering of a fish. Also the scales of leather armor. [df: קשׂקשׂת] [freq. 8] |kjv: scales, mail| {str: 7193}

rf^m) שׁרֲשׁ (כסוי K-SWY) — **Covering:** [freq. 2] |kjv: covering| {str: 3681}

B) שׁרֲ (כסס KSS) ac: **Count** co: **Number** ab: **?:** To cover a group by counting.

V) שׁרֲ (כסס K-SS) — **Count:** [freq. 1] (vf: Paal) |kjv: count| {str: 3699}

E) שׁרֲ (כסא KSA) ac: **Appoint** co: **Seat** ab: **?:** The seat is like a cup that holds, conceals, a person.

150

Parent and Child Roots - שׁ

N^m) שׂכא (כסא K-SA) —
Appointed: To be set in place.
[df: כסה] [freq. 2] |kjv: appoint|
{str: 3677}

e^m) שׂיכא (כיסא KY-SA) —
Seat: Usually a throne or seat of authority. [Hebrew and Aramaic] [ms: כסא] [df: כסה] [ar: כרסא] [freq. 138] |kjv: throne, seat, stool| {str: 3678, 3764}

H) שׂכה (כסה KSH) ac: **Cover** co:
? ab: ?: A hiding, covering or concealing of something.

V) שׂכה (כסה K-SH) —
Cover: [df: כשה] [freq. 153] (vf: Paal, Niphal, Hitpael, Pual, Piel, Participle) |kjv: cover, hide, conceal, overwhelm, clad, close, cloth| {str: 3680, 3780}

h^m) מכסה (מכסה MK-SH) —
Covering: What covers something. [freq. 16] |kjv: covering| {str: 4372}

k^m) מכסה (מכסה MK-SH) —
Covering: What covers something. [freq. 4] |kjv: cover, clothing| {str: 4374}

J) שׁכו (כוס KWS) ac: ? co: **Cup**
ab: ?: A cup holds its contents.

N^f) שׁכו (כוס KWS) — I. **Cup:**
II. **Owl:** [Unknown connection to root] [freq. 34] |kjv: cup, owl| {str: 3563}

M) שׁכו (כיס KYS) ac: ? co: **Bag**
ab: ?: A cup or bag that conceals its contents.

N^m) שׁכיס (כיס KYS) — **Bag:**
[freq. 6] |kjv: bag, purse| {str: 3599}

Adopted Roots;
2405 שׁער Wealth

1246) שׁכע (כע KAh) ac: ? co: ? ab: ?

1247) שׁכפ (כף KP) ac: **Press** co: **Palm** ab: **Tame:** The pictograph שׁ is a picture of the palm of the hand, the כ is a picture of an open mouth. Combined these mean "palm open". The curved shape of the open palm. (eng: cap - as a bowl shaped covering; cuff - as at the palm)

A) שׁכף (כף KP) ac: ? co: **Palm** ab:
?: Any curved or hollowed out object.

N^f) שׁכף (כף KP) — **Palm:**
Also the sole of the feet or other palm shaped object such as a spoon. [freq. 193] |kjv: hand, spoon, sole, palm, hollow, handful, apiece, branch, cloud| {str: 3709, 3710}

N^f1) שׁכפה (כפה K-PH) —
Palm: The branch of a palm tree. [freq. 3] |kjv: branch| {str: 3712}

B) שׁכפף (כפף KPP) ac: **Bow** co:
? ab: ?: A bowing down of the body.

V) שׁכפף (כפף K-PP) —
Bow: [freq. 5] (vf: Paal, Niphal) |kjv: bow| {str: 3721}

C) שׁאכף (אכף AKP) ac: **Press** co:
? ab: ?: The placing of the palm on something and pressing down or pushing.

V) שׁאכף (אכף A-KP) —
Press: [freq. 1] (vf: Paal) |kjv: crave| {str: 404}

N^m) שׁאכף (אכף A-KP) —
Pressure: [freq. 1] |kjv: hand| {str: 405}

151

H) שׁ⌐כפ (כפה KPH) ac: **Tame** co: ? ab: ?: The bending of the will of an animal.

V) שׁ⌐כפ (כפה K-PH) — **Tame:** To bend the will of another. [freq. 1] (vf: Paal) |kjv: pacify| {str: 3711}

Adopted Roots;
2078 ﬒⌐כ Bend, Grapevine
2281 ﬒⌐שׁ Bend, Famine

~~~~~~~~~~

1248) שׁ⌐ (כץ KTs) ac: ? co: ? ab: ?

~~~~~~~~~~

1249) שׁ⌐ (כק KQ) ac: ? co: ? ab: ?

L) שׁ⌐ל (יכק YKQ) ac: ? co: **Caterpillar** ab: ?

Nᵐ**)** שׁ⌐ל (יכק Y-KQ) — **Caterpillar:** [freq. 9] |kjv: cankerworm, caterpillar| {str: 3218}

~~~~~~~~~~

1250) שׁҨ (כר KR) ac: **Dig** co: **Bowl** ab: ?: The pictograph שׁ is a picture of the palm of the hand, the Ҩ is a picture of the head of a man. Combined these mean "palm of man". The palm as hollowed out. A digging. (eng: core; bore)

A) שׁҨ (כר KR) ac: ? co: **Hollow** ab: ?

Nᵐ**)** שׁҨ (כר KR) — **I. Hollow:** The hollow hump of a camel or a pasture in a hollow. **II. Lamb:** One of the pasture. **III. Captain:** [freq. 16] |kjv: lamb, pasture, ram, furniture, captain| {str: 3733}

Nᶠˡ**)** שׁҨ✿ (כרה K-RH) — **I. Pasture:** As a hollowed out valley. **II. Mole:** A digger. [df:

[פרה] [freq. 2] |kjv: cottage, mole| {str: 3740, 6512}

fᵐ**)** שׁҨ⌐ (כרי K-RY) — **Captain:** [Unknown connection to root] [freq. 3] |kjv: captain| {str: 3746}

kᶠˡ**)** שׁҨ✿ₘ (מכרה MK-RH) — **I. Cave:** As a hole in the rock. [df: מערה] **II. Weapon:** Probably a weapon that is a digging tool or similar implement. [freq. 40] |kjv: cave, den, hole, habitation, army| {str: 4380, 4631}

l ᶠˡ**)** שׁҨשׁҨ✿ (כרכרה KR-K-RH) — **Camel:** As with a hollow hump. [freq. 1] |kjv: beast| {str: 3753}

B) שׁҨҨ (כרר KRR) ac: **Dance** co: ? ab: ?: A leaping or dancing around in a circle.

V) שׁҨҨ (כרר K-RR) — **Dance:** [freq. 2] (vf: Pilpel, Participle) |kjv: dance| {str: 3769}

C) שׁשׁ✗ (אכר AKR) ac: **Dig** co: **Farmer** ab: ?

Nᵐ**)** שׁשׁ✗ (אכר A-KR) — **Farmer:** One who digs the ground for growing crops. [freq. 7] |kjv: husbandman, plowman| {str: 406}

D) Ҩ✗שׁ (כאר KAR) ac: ? co: **Pit** ab: ?

V) Ҩ✗שׁ (כאר K-AR) — **Deep:** To make a deep engraving in a tablet or stone. Also to give a deep explanation. [df: באר] [freq. 3] (vf: Piel) |kjv: plain, plainly, declare| {str: 874}

Nᶠ**)** Ҩ✗שׁ (כאר K-AR) — **Pit:** A dug out hole, usually a well or cistern. [df: בָּאַר] [freq. 37] |kjv: well, pit, slimepit| {str: 875}

g^m) שׁוֹאַר (כוֹאַר KW-AR) — **Pit:** A dug out hole. [df: בָּאַר] [freq. 2] |kjv: cistern| {str: 877}

F) שׁכר (הכר HKR) ac: **?** co: **?** ab: **Wrong:** [Unknown connection to root]

V) שׁכר (הכר H-KR) — **Wrong:** [freq. 1] (vf: Hiphil) |kjv: strange| {str: 1970}

N^fl) שׁכר (הכרה HK-RH) — **Look:** [freq. 1] |kjv: shew| {str: 1971}

H) שׁכר (כרה KRH) ac: **Dig** co: **?** ab: **Prepare**

V) שׁכר (כרה K-RH) — **I. Dig:** [Hebrew and Aramaic] [ar: כרא] **II. Prepare:** To prepare a banquet or feast. [Unknown connection to root] [freq. 21] (vf: Paal, Niphal) |kjv: dig, make, pierce, open, grieve| {str: 3735, 3738, 3739}

N^fl) שׁכר (כרה K-RH) — **Preparation:** [Unknown connection to root] [freq. 1] |kjv: provision| {str: 3741}

J) שׁוֹר (כור KWR) ac: **Dig** co: **Pit** ab: **?**

V) שׁוֹר (כור KWR) — **I. Dig:** [df: קור] **II. Examine:** To look deeply. [df: בור] [freq. 7] (vf: Paal, Hiphil, Pilpel) |kjv: declare, dig, cast out, destroy, break down| {str: 952, 6979}

N^m) שׁוֹר (כור KWR) — **I. Pit:** A hole, well or cistern that is dug out. [df: חר חור בור] **II. Furnace:** A hollow box formed out of brick or clay for cooking. **III. Kor:** A standard of measure. [ms: כר] [freq. 96] |kjv: pit,

cistern, well, dungeon, fountain, measure, cor| {str: 953, 2352, 2356, 3564, 3734}

a^m) שׁוֹר (מכור M-KWR) — **Fountain:** A spring that comes out of a hole in the ground. [df: מקר מקור] [freq. 18] |kjv: fountain, spring, wellspring, issue, well| {str: 4726}

e^m) שׁוֹר (כיור KY-WR) — **I. Pot:** As a dug out container. [df: כיר] **II. Platform:** [Unknown connection to root] [freq. 23] |kjv: laver, scaffold, pan, hearth| {str: 3595}

k^fl) שׁוֹר (מכורה M-KW-RH) — **Birth:** A coming out of a hole. [ms: מכרה] [freq. 3] |kjv: birth, nativity, habitation| {str: 4351}

M) שׁיר (כיר KYR) ac: **?** co: **Furnace** ab: **?:** A hollowed out object.

N^m) שׁיר (כיר KYR) — **Furnace:** A hollow box formed out of brick or clay for cooking. [freq. 1] |kjv: range| {str: 3600}

Adopted Roots;

2436	⟨glyph⟩	Pierce, Fissure
2719	⟨glyph⟩	Dish
2258	⟨glyph⟩	Round
2192	⟨glyph⟩	Dig, Mole
2198	⟨glyph⟩	Examine

1251) שׁ (כשׁ KSh) ac: **?** co: **?** ab: **?**

1252) שׁת (כת KT) ac: **Crush** co: **?** ab: **?**

A) שׁת (כת KT) ac: **Crush** co: **?** ab: **?**

k^{fl}) מכתה‎מ (מכתה MK-TH) — **Crushing:** An opening by crushing. [freq. 1] |kjv: bursting| {str: 4386}

B) שׁתת‎ (כתת KTT) ac: **Crush** co: ? ab: ?

V) שׁתת‎ (כתת K-TT) — **Crush:** [freq. 17] (vf: Paal, Hiphil, Hophal, Pual, Piel) |kjv: beat, destroy, break, smite, discomfit, crush, stamp| {str: 3807}

b^m) שׁתית‎ (כתית K-TYT) — **Crushed:** Crushed olive oil. [freq. 5] |kjv: beaten, pure| {str: 3795}

1253) שׁא‎ (כע KGh) ac: ? co: ? ab: ?

Lam

1254) לֻ (לא LA) ac: ? co: ? ab:
Without: To be without anything such as
nothing. Related to לֻ. Apparently an
opposite of לֻ.

A) לֻ (לא LA) ac: ? co: ? ab:
Nothing

N^(m)) לֻ (לא LA) — **Nothing:**
To be without, to not be.
[Hebrew and Aramaic] [df: אל
לה] [freq. 97] |kjv: never, nay,
no, none, nor, not, nothing,
rather, whither, without, neither,
none| {str: 408, 409, 3809}

r^(m)) לֻ (לאו L-AW) — **But:**
As an alternative, to have what
you are without. [df: אלו] [freq.
2] |kjv: but, though| {str: 432}

B) לֻלֻ (לאא LAA) ac: ? co:
Idol ab: **Worthless**

b^(m)) לֻלֻ (לאיא L-AYA) —
I. Idol: A god without power. **II.**
Worthless: [df: אליל] [freq. 20]
|kjv: idol, image, no value,
nought| {str: 457}

d^(m)) לֻלֻ (לאוא L-AWA) —
Worthless: [df: אלול] [freq. 1]
|kjv: nought| {str: 434}

f^(m)) לֻלֻ (לאאי LA-AY) —
Worthless: [df: אללי] [freq. 2]
|kjv: woe| {str: 480}

o^(m)) לֻלֻ (לואא LW-AA) —
Not: [df: לולי לולא] [freq. 14]
|kjv: except, unless, if, not| {str:
3884}

J) לֻלֻ (לוא LWA) ac: ? co: ? ab:
Foolish

N^(m)) לֻלֻ (לוא LWA) — **I. If:**
To have what you are without.

[ms: לֻ] [df: לו לה] **II. Not:**
[ms: לֻ] [df: לה] [freq. 98]
|kjv: if, would, that, oh,
peradventure, pray, though| {str:
3808, 3863}

N^(f2)) לֻלֻ (לואת LW-AT) —
Foolishness: To be without
wisdom. [df: אולת] [freq. 25]
|kjv: folly, foolishness, foolish,
foolishly| {str: 200}

b^(m)) לֻלֻלֻ (לויא L-WYA) —
Foolish: One without wisdom.
[df: אויל] [freq. 26] |kjv: fool,
foolish| {str: 191}

f^(m)) לֻלֻלֻ (לואי LW-AY) — **I.**
If: To have what you are
without. [df: אולי אלי] **II.**
Foolish: To be without wisdom.
[df: אולי] [freq. 12] |kjv: if,
may, peradventure, unless| {str:
194, 196}

p^(m)) לֻלֻ (לואם LW-AM) —
But: On the contrary, A desirous
outcome. [df: אולם] [freq. 19]
|kjv: but, truly, surely, very,
howbeit, wherefore, truly| {str:
199}

L) לֻלֻ (ילא YLA) ac: ? co: ? ab:
Foolish

V) לֻלֻ (ילא Y-LA) —
Foolish: To be without wisdom.
[df: יאל] [freq. 4] (vf: Niphal)
|kjv: foolishly, fool, foolish,
dote| {str: 2973}

1255) לֻ (לב LB) ac: ? co: **Heart** ab:
Think: The pictograph ל is a picture of
the shepherd staff representing authority,

the ⊔ is a picture of a tent representing what is inside. Combined these mean "authority inside". The consciousness of man is seen as coming from deep inside the chest, the heart. Thirst as an Inside desire for water. (eng: life; love; liver - the seat of passion; lava)

A) ᘖJ (לב LB) ac: **?** co: **Heart** ab: **?:** The organ that pumps blood. This organ is also seen as the seat of thought and emotion, the mind.

N^(m)) ᘖJ (לב LB) — **Heart:** [Hebrew and Aramaic] [df: בל] [freq. 594] |kjv: heart, mind, understanding, wisdom, friendly| {str: 1079, 3820, 3821}

N^(f1)) ᘖJ (לבה L-BH) — **Flame:** [freq. 1] |kjv: flame| {str: 3827}

B) ᘖᘖJ (לבב LBB) ac: **?** co: **Heart** ab: **?:** The organ that pumps blood. The heart is also seen as the seat of thought and emotion, the mind.

V) ᘖᘖJ (לבב L-BB) — **Heart:** To be wise of heart. [freq. 5] (vf: Niphal, Piel) |kjv: heart, make, wise| {str: 3823}

N^(m)) ᘖᘖJ (לבב L-BB) — **Heart:** [Hebrew and Aramaic] [freq. 259] |kjv: heart, mind, understanding| {str: 3824, 3825}

b^(f1)) ᘖᘖJ (לביבה L-BY-BH) — **Cake:** In the sense of being fat like the heart. [ms: לבבה] [freq. 3] |kjv: cake| {str: 3834}

D) ᘖᵞJ (לאב LAB) ac: **?** co: **Thirst** ab: **?:** An Inside desire for water.

id^(f1)) ᘖᵞJ† (תלאובה TL-AW-BH) — **Drought:** [freq. 1] |kjv: drought| {str: 8514}

E) ᵞᘖJ (לבא LBA) ac: **?** co: **Lion** ab: **?:** [Unknown connection to root]

b^(f)) ᵞᘖJ (לביא L-BYA) — **Lion:** [freq. 14] |kjv: lion, lioness, young| {str: 3833}

G) ᘖJ (להב LHB) ac: **?** co: **Flame** ab: **?:** [Unknown connection to root]

N^(m)) ᘖJ (להב L-HB) — **I. Flame: II. Blade:** As shiny. [freq. 12] |kjv: flame, blade, glittering, bright| {str: 3851}

N^(f1)) ᘖJ (להבה LH-BH) — **I. Flame:** [df: להבת] **II. Blade:** As shiny. [freq. 19] |kjv: flame, head| {str: 3852}

N^(f2)) ᘖJ (להבת LH-BT) — **Flame:** [df: שלהבת] [freq. 3] |kjv: flame| {str: 7957}

M) ᘖJ (ליב LYB) ac: **?** co: **Heart** ab: **?:** The organ that pumps blood. This organ is also seen as the seat of thought and emotion, the mind.

N^(f1)) ᘖJ (ליב L-YB) — **Heart:** [ms: לבה] [freq. 8] |kjv: heart| {str: 3826}

1256) ᘉJ (לג LG) ac: **?** co: **?** ab: **?**

A) ᘉJ (לג LG) ac: **?** co: **?** ab: **?:** [Unknown meaning]

N^(m)) ᘉJ (לג LG) — **Log:** A unit of measurement. [freq. 5] |kjv: log| {str: 3849}

G) ᘉJ (להג LHG) ac: **?** co: **Study** ab: **?**

N^(m)) ᘉJ (להג L-HG) — **Study:** [freq. 1] |kjv: study| {str: 3854}

1257) לד (לד LD) ac: **Bear** co: **Child** ab: **Kindred:** The bearing of children. (eng: lad)

I) ולד (ולד WLD) ac: **?** co: **Child** ab: **?**

N^m) ולד (ולד W-LD) — **Child:** [freq. 2] |kjv: child| {str: 2056}

L) ילד (ילד YLD) ac: **Bear** co: **Child** ab: **Generation**

V) ילד (ילד Y-LD) — **Bear:** To give birth to children. [freq. 498] (vf: Paal, Niphal, Hiphil, Hitpael, Hophal, Pual, Piel, Participle) |kjv: beget, bare, born, bring forth, bear, travail, midwife, child, deliver, borne, birth, labour, brought up| {str: 3205}

N^m) ילד (ילד Y-LD) — **Boy:** [freq. 89] |kjv: child, young, son, boy, fruit| {str: 3206}

N^{f1}) ילדה (ילדה YL-DH) — **Girl:** [freq. 3] |kjv: girl, damsel| {str: 3207}

N^{f3}) ילדות (ילדות YL-DWT) — **Youth:** [freq. 3] |kjv: youth, childhood| {str: 3208}

a^{f2}) מולדת (מולדת M-WL-DT) — I. **Kindred:** II. **Born:** [freq. 22] |kjv: kindred, nativity, born, begotten, issue, native| {str: 4138}

b^m) יליד (יליד Y-LYD) — **Children:** [freq. 13] |kjv: born, children, sons| {str: 3211}

c^m) ילוד (ילוד Y-LWD) — **Born:** [freq. 5] |kjv: born| {str: 3209}

i^{f2}) תולדת (תולדת TW-L-DT) — **Generations:** [ms: תלדה]

[freq. 39] |kjv: generations, birth| {str: 8435}

~~~~~~~~~~

1258) לה (לה LH) ac: **?** co: **?** ab: **Weary:** To be weary from a non productive effort. To be without results. Related to לע.

D) לאה (לאה LAH) ac: **Weary** co: **?** ab: **Trouble**

V) לאה (לאה L-AH) — **Weary:** [freq. 19] (vf: Paal, Niphal, Hiphil) |kjv: weary, grieve, faint, loath| {str: 3811}

i^{f1}) תלאה (תלאה TL-AH) — **Trouble:** What brings about weariness. [freq. 4] |kjv: travail, trouble| {str: 8513}

ai^{f1}) מתלאה (מתלאה MT-L-AH) — **Weariness:** [freq. 1] |kjv: weariness, travail, trouble| {str: 4972}

H) להה (להה LHH) ac: **Weary** co: **?** ab: **?**

V) להה (להה L-HH) — **Weary:** [freq. 2] (vf: Paal) |kjv: faint, mad| {str: 3856}

~~~~~~~~~~

1259) לו (לו LW) ac: **Join** co: **?** ab: **?**

J) לוה (לוה LWH) ac: **Join** co: **Wreath** ab: **?**

V) לוה (לוה LWH) — **Join:** A joining together of people. Also the joining together through debt as the lender or borrower. [freq. 26] (vf: Paal, Niphal, Hiphil) |kjv: join, lend, borrow, borrower, abide, cleave, lender| {str: 3867}

N^m) לוה (לוה LWH) — **You:** As one who is joined. [Aramaic only] [ar: לות] [freq. 1] |kjv: thee| {str: 3890}

b^{fl}) ליויה (ליויה LW-YH) — **Garland:** As joined together. [freq. 3] |kjv: addition| {str: 3914}

eb^f) ליויה (ליויה LYW-YH) — **Wreath:** As joined together. [ms: לויה] [freq. 2] |kjv: ornament| {str: 3880}

~~~~~~~~

1260) לז (לז LZ) ac: ? co: ? ab: **Perverse:** The pictograph ל is a picture of a shepherd staff representing authority, the ז is a picture of a cutting implement. Combined these mean "authority cut". A turning away from truth.

A) לז (לז LZ) ac: ? co: ? ab: **Perverse**

N^{f3}) לזות (לזות L-ZWT) — **Perverse:** [freq. 1] |kjv: perverse| {str: 3891}

F) הלז (הלז HLZ) ac: ? co: **This** ab: ?: [Unknown connection to root]

N^m) הלז (הלז H-LZ) — **This:** [freq. 7] |kjv: this, that| {str: 1975}

N^{fl}) הלזה (הלזה HL-ZH) — **This:** [freq. 2] |kjv: this| {str: 1976}

r^m) הלזו (הלזו HL-ZW) — **This:** [df: הלזו] [freq. 1] |kjv: this| {str: 1977}

J) לוז (לוז LWZ) ac: ? co: **Almond** ab: **Perverse**

V) לוז (לוז LWZ) — **Perverse:** [freq. 6] (vf: Paal, Niphal, Hiphil, Participle) |kjv: forward, depart, perverse, perverseness| {str: 3868}

N^m) לוז (לוז LWZ) — **Almond:** [Unknown connection to root] [freq. 1] |kjv: hazel| {str: 3869}

~~~~~~~~

1261) לח (לח LHh) ac: **Lick** co: **Moist** ab: ?: The pictograph ל represents authority and the tongue as the authority, the ח is a picture of wall that separates the inside from the outside. Combined these mean "tongue outside". When the lips are dry, the tongue licks the lips to moisten them. (eng: lick - an exchange for the ck and h; liquid - an exchange for the q and h and the addition of the uid.)

A) לח (לח LHh) ac: ? co: **Moist** ab: ?: Anything that is moist or fresh.

N^m) לח (לח LHh) — **Moist:** [freq. 7] |kjv: green, moist| {str: 3892, 3893}

f^m) לחי (לחי L-HhY) — **Jaw:** From the moist cheeks. [freq. 21] |kjv: cheek, jaw, jawbone, bone| {str: 3895}

B) לחח (לחח LHhHh) ac: **Lick** co: ? ab: ?

V) לחח (לחח L-HhHh) — **Lick:** [df: לקק לחך] [freq. 13] (vf: Paal, Piel) |kjv: lap, lick| {str: 3897, 3952}

C) אלח (אלח ALHh) ac: **Filthy** co: ? ab: ?: [Unknown connection to root]

V) אלח (אלח A-LHh) — **Filthy:** [freq. 3] (vf: Niphal) |kjv: filthy| {str: 444}

J) לוח (לוח LWHh) ac: ? co: **Tablet** ab: ?: A common writing material is wet clay. The letters can be easily inscribed and the clay hardens to preserve the record.

158

N^m) לוח (לוח LWHh) —
Tablet: [ms: לח] [freq. 43] |kjv:
table, board, plate| {str: 3871}

~~~~~~~~~~

1262) לט (לט LTh) ac: **Cover** co: **Veil**
ab: **Secret:** The pictograph ל is a picture
of the shepherd staff representing
authority, the ⊗ is a picture of a basket or
container. Combined these mean
"authority contained". The covering that
covers and hides the face of a woman.

  A) לט (לט LTh) ac: **?** co: **?** ab:
  Secret: A covering that hides what is
  behind.
    N^m) לט (לט LTh) — **Secret:**
    [freq. 6] |kjv: enchantment,
    softly, secretly, privily| {str:
    3909}

  D) לאט (לאט LATh) ac: **Cover**
  co: **?** ab: **Secret**
    V) לאט (לאט L-ATh) —
    Cover: [freq. 1] (vf: Paal) |kjv:
    cover| {str: 3813}
    N^m) לאט (לאט L-ATh) —
    Secret: Something that is
    covered or hidden. [freq. 1] |kjv:
    cover| {str: 3814}

  E) לטא (לטא LThA) ac: **?** co:
  Lizard ab: **?:** A hiding by covering.
    N^fl) לטאה (לטאה LTh-AH)
    — **Lizard:** From the
    camouflaging capability of the
    lizard to hide. [freq. 1] |kjv:
    lizard| {str: 3911}

  G) להט (להט LHTh) ac: **?** co: **?**
  ab: **Secret**
    V) להט (להט L-HTh) —
    Burn: [Unknown connection to
    root] [freq. 11] (vf: Paal, Piel,
    Participle) |kjv: fire, burn,
    kindle,| {str: 3857}

N^m) להט (להט L-HTh) —
Secret: [freq. 2] |kjv: flaming,
enchantment| {str: 3858}

J) לוט (לוט LWTh) ac: **Wrap** co: **?**
ab: **?**
  V) לוט (לוט LWTh) — **Wrap:**
  To cover something by wrapping
  it. [freq. 3] (vf: Paal, Hiphil)
  |kjv: wrap, cast| {str: 3874}
  N^m) לוט (לוט LWTh) — I.
  Covering: II. **Myrrh:**
  [Unknown connection to root]
  [ms: לט] [freq. 3] |kjv: covering,
  myrrh| {str: 3875, 3910}

Adopted Roots;
2707 לט Hide

~~~~~~~~~~

1263) לי (לי LY) ac: **?** co: **?** ab: **?**

~~~~~~~~~~

1264) לך (לך LK) ac: **Walk** co:
Message ab: **?:** The pictograph ל is a
picture of shepherd staff, the ש is a
picture of the palm of the hand.
Combined these mean "staff in the palm".
A nomad traveled on foot with a staff in
his hand to provide support in walking as
well as a weapon to defend against
predators or thiefs. (eng: walk - with an
added w)

  D) לאך (לאך LAK) ac: **Walk** co:
  Messenger ab: **?:** One who walks for
  another.
    a^m) מלאך (מלאך ML-AK)
    — **Messenger:** [Hebrew and
    Aramaic] [freq. 216] |kjv: angel,
    messenger, ambassador| {str:
    4397, 4398}
    a^f3) מלאכות (מלאכות ML-
    A-KWT) — **Message:** [freq. 1]
    |kjv: message| {str: 4400}

159

k[fl]) 𐤌𐤉⅃𐤔𐤀 (מלאכה M-LA-KH) — **Work:** As a message through action. [freq. 167] |kjv: work, business, workmanship, goods, cattle, stuff, thing| {str: 4399}

F) 𐤔⅃𐤀 (הלך HLK) ac: **Travel** co: **Journey** ab: **?**

V) 𐤔⅃𐤀 (הלך H-LK) — **Walk:** To walk a journey or lifestyle, customs. [Hebrew and Aramaic] [df: חוך] [freq. 507] (vf: Paal, Niphal, Hitpael, Piel, Participle) |kjv: walk, away, along, go, come| {str: 1946, 1980, 1981}

N[m]) 𐤔⅃𐤀 (הלך H-LK) — **I. Travel: II. Custom:** A payment for traveling. [Aramaic only] [freq. 5] |kjv: custom, traveler, drop| {str: 1982, 1983}

b[m]) 𐤔⅃𐤉𐤀 (הליך H-LYK) — **Step:** For walking up an incline. [freq. 1] |kjv: step| {str: 1978}

b[fl]) 𐤉⅃𐤔𐤀 (הליכה H-LY-KH) — **Procession:** The walk or lifestyle of an individual or company. [freq. 7] |kjv: way, goings, company, walk| {str: 1979}

a[m]) 𐤔⅃𐤀𐤌 (מהלך MH-LK) — **Journey:** A place to walk. [freq. 5] |kjv: walk, journey| {str: 4108, 4109}

id[fl]) 𐤉𐤔⅃𐤕 (תהלוכה TH-LW-KH) — **Walk:** [freq. 1] |kjv: go| {str: 8418}

L) 𐤔⅃𐤉 (ילך YLK) ac: **Walk** co: **?** ab: **?**

V) 𐤔⅃𐤉 (ילך Y-LK) — **Walk:** [freq. 1043] (vf: Paal, Hiphil) |kjv: go, walk, come, depart,

away, follow, get, lead, brought, carry, bring| {str: 3212}

Adopted Roots;
2340 𐤔⅃𐤌 Reign, King, Kingdom
2610 𐤔⅃𐤀 Stick

~~~~~~~~~

1265) ⅃⅃ (לל LL) ac: **Howl** co: **Night** ab: **?:** When the night comes, the night sky is rolled out like a scroll. When daylight comes, the night sky is rolled up like a scroll. (eng: yell)

E) 𐤀⅃⅃ (ללא LLA) ac: **?** co: **Loop** ab: **?**

o[fl]) 𐤀⅃⅃𐤉 (לולאה LWL-AH) — **Loop:** [ms: ללאה] [freq. 13] |kjv: loop| {str: 3924}

J) ⅃𐤉⅃ (לול LWL) ac: **?** co: **Staircase** ab: **?:** A spiral set of steps.

N[m]) ⅃𐤉⅃ (לול LWL) — **Staircase:** [freq. 1] |kjv: winding stair| {str: 3883}

L) ⅃⅃𐤉 (ילל YLL) ac: **Howl** co: **?** ab: **?:** The sound of the wolf, a night predator.

V) ⅃⅃𐤉 (ילל Y-LL) — **Howl:** [freq. 31] (vf: Hiphil) |kjv: howl, howling| {str: 3213}

N[m]) ⅃⅃𐤉 (ילל Y-LL) — **Howling:** [freq. 1] |kjv: howling| {str: 3214}

N[fl]) 𐤀⅃⅃𐤉 (יללה YL-LH) — **Howling:** [freq. 5] |kjv: howling| {str: 3215}

i[m]) ⅃⅃𐤉𐤕 (תולל TW-LL) — **Tormentor:** [freq. 1] |kjv: waste| {str: 8437}

M) ⅃𐤉⅃ (ליל LYL) ac: **?** co: **Night** ab: **?**

N^m) ל- י-ל (ליל LYL) —
Night: [freq. 233] |kjv: night,
season, midnight| {str: 3915}

N^{f4}) ת-ל-י-ל (לילית LY-LYT)
— **Owl:** A night creature. [freq.
1] |kjv: screech owl| {str: 3917}

f^{f1}) ל-י-ל (לילי LY-LY) —
Night: [Aramaic only] [ar:
לליליא] [freq. 5] |kjv: night| {str:
3916}

~~~~~~~~~

1266) מ-ל (לם LM) ac: **Bind** co: **Staff**
ab: ?: The pictograph ל is a picture of a
shepherd staff, the מ is a picture of
water representing might. Combined
these mean "staff of might". The shepherd
always carried his staff for guiding,
leading and protecting the flock. The
flock was bound to the shepherd, as the
staff was a sign of his authority over the
sheep. The yoke was a staff laid across
the shoulders of two oxen. The oxen were
then tied to the yokes at the neck, binding
the two together for plowing or pulling a
cart. A people bound together. A wound
bound with bandages.

A) מ-ל (לם LM) ac: ? co: **Toward**
ab: ?: A moving toward someone or
something.

i^m) מ-ל-ת (תלם T-LM) —
Furrow: Made by oxen plowing
a field. [freq. 5] |kjv: furrow,
ridge| {str: 8525}

q^m) מ-ל (למו L-MW) —
Toward: [The more ancient
form is probably מ-ל, the short
form "ל" is used as a prefix
meaning "to" or "for"; See also
ל-ע] [freq. 4] |kjv: for, at, to,
upon| {str: 3926}

C) מ-ל-ע (אלם ALM) ac: **Bind** co:
Sheaf ab: ?

V) ע-ל-מ (אלם A-LM) —
Bind: To tie something, also the
tying of the tongue, silence.
[freq. 9] (vf: Niphal, Piel) |kjv:
dumb, silent, binding| {str: 481}

N^m) ע-ל-מ (אלם A-LM) —
Silent: [freq. 1] |kjv:
congregation| {str: 482}

d^m) ע-ל-ו-מ (אלום A-LWM) —
Sheaf: A sheaf of grain that is
bound. [ms: אלם] [freq. 5] |kjv:
sheaf| {str: 485}

d^{f1}) ע-ל-ו-מ-ה (אלומה A-LW-
MH) — **Sheaf:** A sheaf of grain
that is bound. [ms: אלמה] [freq.
5] |kjv: sheaf| {str: 485}

e^m) ע-ל-י-מ (אילם AY-LM)
— **Silent:** [ms: אלם] [freq. 6]
|kjv: dumb| {str: 483}

j^m) ע-ל-מ-ו-נ (אלמון AL-
MWN) — **Widowhood:** As
bound in grief. [ms: אלמן] [freq.
1] |kjv: forsaken| {str: 489}

m^m) ע-ל-מ-נ (אלמן AL-MN)
— **Forsaken:** As bound in grief.
[freq. 1] |kjv: forsaken| {str:
488}

m^{f1}) ע-ל-מ-נ-ה (אלמנה AL-M-
NH) — **Widow:** As bound in
grief. [freq. 55] |kjv: widow,
desolate| {str: 490}

m^{f3}) ע-ל-מ-נ-ו-ת (אלמנות AL-
M-NWT) — **Widow:** As bound in
grief. [freq. 4] |kjv: widow,
widowhood| {str: 491}

o^m) ע-ל-ו-מ (אולם AW-LM) —
Porch: In the sense of tying.
[ms: אלם] [freq. 34] |kjv: porch|
{str: 197}

jf^m) ע-ל-מ-ו-נ-י (אלמוני AL-
MW-NY) — **Such:** An
unidentified person or place as
bound up in uncertainty. [ms:

אלמני] [freq. 3] |kjv: such, one|
{str: 492}

D) מלאם (לאם LAM) ac: ? co:
People ab: ?: A group of people
bound together.

c^m) מלאום (לאום L-AWM) —
People: [ms: לאם] [freq. 35]
|kjv: people, nation, folk| {str:
3816}

F) הלם (הלם HLM) ac: Strike
co: Hammer ab: ?

V) הלם (הלם H-LM) —
Strike: To hit or beat in order to
break or smash. [freq. 9] (vf:
Paal) |kjv: smite, break, beat|
{str: 1986}

N^f3) הלמות (הלמות HL-
MWT) — Hammer: As used for
striking. [freq. 1] |kjv: hammer|
{str: 1989}

ad^fl) מהלומה (מהלומה
MH-LW-MH) — Strike: [ms:
מהלמה] [freq. 2] |kjv: stroke,
stripe| {str: 4112}

G) להם (להם LHM) ac: Strike
co: ? ab: ?: Bound with bandages.

V) להם (להם L-HM) —
Wound: [freq. 2] (vf: Hitpael)
|kjv: wound| {str: 3859}

Adopted Roots;
2311 למד Learn, Goad

1267) לן (לן LN) ac: Stay co: Inn ab: ?

J) לון (לון LWN) ac: Stay co: Inn
ab: ?

V) לון (לון LWN) — Stay: To
remain or stay the night. [df:
לין] [freq. 87] (vf: Paal, Niphal,
Hiphil, Hitpael) |kjv: lodge,
night, abide, remain, tarry,

continue, dwell, endure, left, lie|
{str: 3885}

a^m) מלון (מלון M-LWN) —
Inn: A place for spending the
night. [freq. 8] |kjv: inn, lodge|
{str: 4411}

k^fl) מלונה (מלונה M-LW-
NH) — Lodge: A place for
spending the night. [freq. 2] |kjv:
lodge, cottage| {str: 4412}

1268) לס (לס LS) ac: ? co: ? ab: ?

1269) לע (לע LAh) ac: Swallow co:
Throat ab: ?

A) לע (לע LAh) ac: ? co: Throat
ab: ?

N^m) לע (לע LAh) — Throat:
[freq. 1] |kjv: throat| {str: 3930}

i^m) תלע (תלע TL-Ah) —
Crimson: The color of the
throat. [freq. 1] |kjv: scarlet| {str:
8529}

J) לוע (לוע LWAh) ac: Swallow
co: ? ab: ?

V) לוע (לוע LWAh) —
Swallow: [freq. 2] (vf: Paal)
|kjv: swallow| {str: 3886}

L) ילע (ילע YLAh) ac: Devour
co: ? ab: ?

V) ילע (ילע Y-LAh) —
Devour: [freq. 1] (vf: Paal) |kjv:
devour| {str: 3216}

i^m) תולע (תולע TW-LAh) —
I. Crimson: The color of the
throat. II. Worm: A crimson
colored worm. [freq. 43] |kjv:
scarlet, worm| {str: 8438}

162

Adopted Roots;

2312 ⊔⊙⊍ Mock
2313 ⊔⊙⊍ Mock
2314 ⊏⊙⊍ Speak
2315 ⊗⊙⊍ Feed
2316 ⅃⊙⊍ Bitter
2546 ⊙⊍⊙ Suck

~~~~~~~

1270) ⊙⊍ (לף LP) ac: ? co: ? ab: ?

L) ⊙⊍⅃ (ילף YLP) ac: ? co: **Scab** ab: ?

N[f2]**)** †⊙⊍⅃ (ילפת YL-PT) — **Scab:** [freq. 2] |kjv: scab| {str: 3217}

~~~~~~~

1271) ⊙ᴧ⊍ (ליץ L.Ts) ac: **Scorn** co: ? ab: **Interpret:** The pictograph ⊍ represents authority and the tongue as the authority, the ⊙ᴧ is a picture of a man on his side representing trouble. Combined these mean "tongue of trouble". The sound of one speaking a foreign language or the mocking of anothers speech.

A) ⊙ᴧ⊍ (ליץ LTs) ac: **Scorn** co: ? ab: ?

j[m]**)** ⅃ᴙ⊙ᴧ⊍ (לצון L-TsWN) — **Scorn:** [freq. 3] |kjv: scornful, scorning| {str: 3944}

B) ⊙ᴧ⊙ᴧ⊍ (לצץ LTsTs) ac: **Scorn** co: ? ab: ?

V) ⊙ᴧⲟᴧ⊍ (לצץ L-TsTs) — **Scorn:** [freq. 1] (vf: Paal) |kjv: scorner| {str: 3945}

C) ⊙ᴧ⊍⅄ (אליץ ALTs) ac: **Urge** co: ? ab: ?

V) ⊙ᴧ⊍⅄ (אליץ A-LTs) — **Urge:** [freq. 1] (vf: Piel) |kjv: urge| {str: 509}

J) ⊙ᴧᴙ⊍ (לוץ LWTs) ac: **Scorn** co: ? ab: ?

V) ⊙ᴧᴙ⊍ (לוץ LWTs) — **I. Scorn: II. Interpret:** [freq. 27] (vf: Paal, Hiphil, Participle) |kjv: scorner, scorn, interpreter, mocker, ambassador, derision, mocker, scornful, teacher| {str: 3887}

M) ⊙ᴧ⅄⊍ (ליץ LYTs) ac: **Interpret** co: ? ab: ?

k[f1]**)** ⅏⊙ᴧ⅄⊍ᴧᴧ (מליצה M-LY-TsH) — **I. Interpretation: II. Mocking:** [freq. 2] |kjv: interpretation, taunting| {str: 4426}

Adopted Roots;

2708 ⅏⊍⊶ Ridicule

~~~~~~~

1272) ⊶⊍ (לק LQ) ac: **Gather** co: ? ab: ?: The pictograph ⊍ is a picture of a shepherd staff that is used to gather the sheep, the ⊶ is a picture of the sun at the horizon and the light gathered to it. Both of these letters have the meaning of "gathering".

Adopted Roots;

2167 ⊶⊍ㅍ Divide, Portion
2306 ⅃ㅍ⊍ Concubine
2307 ⊙ᴧㅍ⊍ Squeeze, Oppression
2310 ⊓ⴊ⊍ Capture
2319 ㅍ⊶⊍ Take, Tong
2320 ⊗⊶⊍ Gather, Pouch
2321 ⊔⊔⊶⊍ Gather, After-growth

~~~~~~~

1273) ℵ⊍ (לר LR) ac: ? co: ? ab: ?

~~~~~~~

1274) ⊔⊔⊍ (לש LSh) ac: **Knead** co: **Lion** ab: ?

J) ‎שולּ‎ (‎לוש‎ LWSh) ac: **Knead** co: ? ab: ?

    V) ‎שולּ‎ (‎לוש‎ LWSh) — **Knead:** [freq. 5] (vf: Paal) |kjv: knead| {str: 3888}

M) ‎שילּ‎ (‎ליש‎ LYSh) ac: ? co: **Lion** ab: ?

    N^m) ‎שילּ‎ (‎ליש‎ LYSh) — **Lion:** From the act of kneading its prey when caught. [freq. 3] |kjv: lion| {str: 3918}

Adopted Roots;

2614 ‎סלּ‎ Roll

1275) **תלּ** (‎לת‎ LT) ac: ? co: ? ab: ?

1276) **עלּ** (‎לע‎ LGh) ac: ? co: ? ab: ?

Mah

1277) ᗷᴍ (מא MA) ac: ? co: **Hundred** ab: ?

A) ᗷᴍ (מא MA) ac: ? co: **Hundred** ab: ?: Originally an unknowable amount, but also to mean a hundred.

N^(fl)) ⴲᗷᴍ (מאה M-AH) — **Hundred:** [Hebrew and Aramaic] [df: מאיה] [freq. 589] |kjv: hundred, hundredth, hundredfold| {str: 3967, 3969}

1278) ᴌᴗᴍ (מב MB) ac: ? co: ? ab: ?

1279) ᴌᴍ (מג MG) ac: **Dissolve** co: ? ab: ?: The pictograph ᴍ is a picture of water, the ᴌ is a picture of foot representing the idea of carrying something. Combined these mean "water carries". The washing away by water.

J) ᴌᵞᴍ (מוג MWG) ac: **Dissolve** co: ? ab: ?

V) ᴌᵞᴍ (מוג MWG) — **Dissolve:** A fainting or melting away of something. [freq. 17] (vf: Paal, Niphal) |kjv: melt, dissolve, faint, consume, fainthearted, soft| {str: 4127}

1280) ᴛᴍ (מד MD) ac: **Stretch** co: **Carpet** ab: **Continue:** The pictograph ᴍ is a picture of water, the ᴛ is a picture of a tent door. Combined these mean "water at the door". A carpet was stretched out to cover the dirt floor of the tent. A bowl of water was located at the door so that one could wash his feet before stepping on the carpet. A garment as a rectangular piece of cloth, similar to a carpet, used as a covering for the body.

A) ᴛᴍ (מד MD) ac: ? co: **Carpet** ab: ?

N^(m)) ᴛᴍ (מד MD) — I. **Carpet:** II. **Garment:** A rectangular piece of cloth, similar to a carpet, used as clothing. III. **Length:** From the length of the garment, Also used as a measurement. [freq. 12] |kjv: garment, armour, measure, raiment, judgment, clothes| {str: 4055}

N^(fl)) ⴲᴛᴍ (מדה M-DH) — I. **Garment:** II. **Length:** From the length of the garment, also as a measurement. III. **Tax:** A measured amount. [Hebrew and Aramaic] [ar: מנדה] [freq. 59] |kjv: measure, piece, stature, size, meteyard, garment, tribute, wide, toll, tribute| {str: 4060, 4061}

j^(m)) ᵞᴛᴍ (מדון M-DWN) — **Length:** From the length of a garment. [freq. 1] |kjv: stature| {str: 4067}

k^(m)) ᴛᴍᴍ (ממד M-MD) — **Length:** From the length of a garment. [freq. 1] |kjv: measures| {str: 4461}

B) ᴛᴛᴍ (מדד MDD) ac: **Measure** co: **Long** ab: ?: From the length of the garment as a measurement.

V) ᴍᴅᴅ (מדד M-DD) — **Measure:** [freq. 51] (vf: Paal, Niphal, Piel) |kjv: measure, mete, stretch| {str: 4058}

N^m) ᴍᴅᴅ (מדד M-DD) — **Long:** [freq. 1] |kjv: gone| {str: 4059}

J) ᴍYᴅ (מוד MWD) ac: **Measure** co: ? ab: ?: From the length of the garment as a measurement.

V) ᴍYᴅ (מוד MWD) — **Measure:** [freq. 1] (vf: Piel) |kjv: measure| {str: 4128}

K) ᴍᴅY (מדו MDW) ac: ? co: **Garment** ab: ?

N^m) ᴍᴅY (מדו M-DW) — **Garment:** [freq. 2] |kjv: garment| {str: 4063}

M) ᴍᴅ (מיד MYD) ac: ? co: ? ab: **Continue:** A stretching out of time.

b^m) ᴍᴅ† (תמיד T-MYD) — **Continually:** [freq. 104] |kjv: continually, continual, daily, always, ever, perpetual, evermore, never| {str: 8548}

1281) ᴍ (מה MH) ac: ? co: **Sea** ab: ?: The pictograph ᴍ is a picture of water. The sea (Mediterranean) is a place of the unknown (what is beyond or what is below). It is feared by the Ancient Hebrews because of its size, storms and fierceness. A hundred as an unknowable amount. This parent root is related to Yᴍ, ᴍ and ᴍ.

A) ᴍ (מה MH) ac: ? co: **Sea** ab: ?: The sea as the place of the Unknown or anything that is an Unknown or in question.

N^m) ᴍ (מה MH) — **I. What:** Something that is unknown, can also be why, when or how. [Hebrew and Aramaic] [ar: מא] **II. Water:** From the sea. [This word always appears in the plural form, ᴍᴍ, when used for water] [df: שׁין] [freq. 625] |kjv: what, how, why, whereby, wherein, how, water, piss, waterspring| {str: 3964, 4100, 4101, 4325, 7890}

B) ᴍ (מהה MHH) ac: ? co: **Linger** ab: ?: A questioning of forward motion.

N^m) ᴍ (מהה M-HH) — **Linger:** [freq. 9] |kjv: linger, tarry, delay, stay| {str: 4102}

1282) Yᴍ (מו MW) ac: ? co: ? ab: **What:** Related to ᴍ and ᴍ.

A) Yᴍ (מו MW) ac: ? co: ? ab: **What**

N^m) Yᴍ (מו MW) — **What:** [Always prefixed with the letter ᴍ meaning in what or in who] [freq. 10] |kjv: with, in, into, through, for, at| {str: 1119}

1283) ᴍᴢ (מז MZ) ac: **Burn** co: ? ab: ?

H) ᴍᴢ (מזה MZH) ac: **Burn** co: ? ab: ?

N^m) ᴍᴢ (מזה M-ZH) — **Burnt:** [freq. 1] |kjv: burnt| {str: 4198}

1284) ᴍ (מח MHh) ac: **Strike** co: **Marrow** ab: ?: The pictograph ᴍ is a picture of water or other liquid, the ᴍ is a picture of a wall that separates the inside from the outside. Combined these mean "liquid inside". The marrow is a buttery liquid inside the bones and is used as a choice food. To obtain the marrow, the bone must be struck to break it open.

A) ᴍᴍ꒰ᴍ (מֹח MHh) ac: **?** co: **Fat** ab: **?**: In the sense of the fat of the marrow.

Nm) ᴍᴍ꒰ᴍ (מֹח MHh) — **Fat:** [freq. 2] |kjv: fatling, fat one| {str: 4220}

fm) ᴍᴍ꒰ᴍ꒱ (מֹחִי M-HhY) — **Ram:** In the sense of fat. An engine of war for battering down walls. [freq. 1] |kjv: engine| {str: 4239}

E) ᴍᴍ꒰ᴍᵞ (מחא MHhA) ac: **Strike** co: **?** ab: **?**

V) ᴍᴍ꒰ᴍᵞ (מחא M-HhA) — **Strike:** The striking of the bone to break it open to access the marrow. [Hebrew and Aramaic] [freq. 7] (vf: Paal, Piel) |kjv: clap, smote, hang| {str: 4222, 4223}

H) ᴍᴍ꒰ᴍ⚹ (מחה MHhH) ac: **Smear** co: **?** ab: **?**: The smearing of the marrow onto a food.

V) ᴍᴍ꒰ᴍ⚹ (מחה M-HhH) — **Smear:** To rub, wipe or blot out. [freq. 36] (vf: Paal, Niphal, Hiphil, Pual, Participle) |kjv: out, destroy, wipe, blot, polish, marrow, reach| {str: 4229}

J) ᴍᵞ꒰ᴍ (מוח MWHh) ac: **?** co: **Marrow** ab: **?**

Nm) ᴍᵞ꒰ᴍ (מוח MWHh) — **Marrow:** [ms: מֹח] [freq. 1] |kjv: marrow| {str: 4221}

Adopted Roots;
2084 ᴍᴍ꒰ᴸ Gnaw, Bones

2334 ᴼᴬᴍᴍ꒰ᴍ Strike, Gash
2335 ●ᴍᴍ꒰ᴍ Strike
2357 ᴍᴍᴸᴜᴍ Smear, Ointment

~~~~~~~~~~

1285) ⊗ᴍ (מט MTh) ac: **Shake** co: **Branch** ab: **?**: The pictograph ᴍ is a picture of water, the ⊗ is a picture of a basket which contains objects. Combined these mean "liquid contained". A green branch still contains water allowing the branch to be flexible. A green branch can then be bent to the desired shape and left to dry.

H) ⚹⊗ᴍ (מטה MThH) ac: **?** co: **Branch** ab: **?**

Nm) ⚹⊗ᴍ (מטה M-ThH) — **I. Staff:** A branch used as a staff. **II. Tribe:** A branch of the family. [freq. 251] |kjv: tribe, rod, staff, stave| {str: 4294}

J) ⊗ᵞᴍ (מוט MWTh) ac: **Shake** co: **Branch** ab: **?**: The yoke is a branch or pole cut green then shaped to the desired shape and left to dry.

V) ⊗ᵞᴍ (מוט MWTh) — **Shake:** To shake or waver as a green branch. [freq. 39] (vf: Paal, Niphal, Hiphil, Hitpael) |kjv: move, remove, slip, carry, cast, course, decay, fall, shake, slide| {str: 4131}

Nm) ⊗ᵞᴍ (מוט MWTh) — **I. Branch:** The bent bar of the yoke that goes around the neck, also a branch that is used as pole. **II. Wavering:** A slipping or wavering of the foot. [freq. 6] |kjv: bar, moved, staff, yoke| {str: 4132}

Nfl) ⚹⊗ᵞᴍ (מוטה MW-ThH) — **Yoke:** The bent bar of the yoke that goes around the neck, also a branch that is used as pole. [freq. 12] |kjv: bar, moved, staff, yoke| {str: 4133}

Adopted Roots;
2665 ᴛᴍᴏᴧ Join, Yoke

1286) ᴊᴧᴧ (מי MY) ac: ? co: ? ab: **Who:** Related to ᴪᴧᴧ and Yᴧᴧ.

A) ᴊᴧᴧ (מי MY) ac: ? co: ? ab: **Who**

Nᵐ) ᴊᴧᴧ (מי MY) — **Who:** Someone that is unknown. [freq. 12] |kjv: who, any, whose, what, if, whom| {str: 4310}

1287) ᵾᴧᴧ (מך MK) ac: **Tumble** co: **Low** ab: ?: The pictograph ᴧᴧ is a picture of water and represents might from the strength of the sea, the ᵾ is a picture of the bent palm and represents the bending or subduing of the will. Combined these mean "might subdued". Something brought low in submission, humility or wealth. (eng: meek)

B) ᵾᵾᴧᴧ (מכך MKK) ac: **Tumble** co: **Ruin** ab: ?

V) ᵾᵾᴧᴧ (מכך M-KK) — **Tumble:** A bringing down of a person in humility or a building in ruin. [freq. 3] (vf: Paal, Niphal, Hophal) |kjv: low, decay| {str: 4355}

J) ᵾYᴧᴧ (מוך MWK) ac: ? co: **Low** ab: ?

V) ᵾYᴧᴧ (מוך MWK) — **Low:** To be brought down low in poverty. [freq. 5] (vf: Paal) |kjv: poor| {str: 4134}

1288) Ɉᴧᴧ (מל ML) ac: **Speak** co: **Word** ab: **Continue:** A continuation of segments, which fill the whole.

A) Ɉᴧᴧ (מל ML) ac: ? co: **Word** ab: ?: A chain of words blended together to form sentences.

Nᶠˡ) ᴪɈᴧᴧ (מלה M-LH) — **Word:** [Hebrew and Aramaic] [freq. 62] |kjv: word, speech, say, speaking, byword, matter, speak, talking| {str: 4405, 4406}

B) ɈɈᴧᴧ (מלל MLL) ac: **Speak** co: **Ear** ab: ?: A chain of words blended together to form sentences.

V) ɈɈᴧᴧ (מלל M-LL) — **Speak:** [Hebrew and Aramaic] [freq. 10] (vf: Paal, Piel) |kjv: speak, utter, say| {str: 4448, 4449}

bᶠˡ) ᴪɈᴊɈᴧᴧ (מלילה M-LY-LH) — **Ear:** A conglomeration of grain seeds together. [freq. 1] |kjv: ear| {str: 4425}

C) Ɉᴧᴧᵷ (אמל AML) ac: **Speak** co: **Word** ab: ?: Chain or words to form a sentence. Also a sickness as a break in the chain of the body.

V) Ɉᴧᴧᵷ (אמל A-ML) — **Speak:** [Hebrew and Aramaic] [df: אמר] [freq. 5379] (vf: Paal, Niphal, Hiphil, Hitpael) |kjv: say, speak, answer, command, tell, call, promise| {str: 559, 560}

Nᵐ) Ɉᴧᴧᵷ (אמל A-ML) — **Word:** [df: אמר] [freq. 49] |kjv: word, speech, saying, appointed, answer| {str: 561}

Nᶠˡ) ᴪɈᴧᴧᵷ (אמלה AM-LH) — **Word:** [df: אמרה] [freq. 37] |kjv: word, speech, commandment| {str: 565}

a^m) ᴍᴧᴧ (מאמל MA-ML) — **Word:** [df: מאמר] [freq. 3] |kjv: commandment, decree| {str: 3982, 3983}

b^m) ᴧᴧᴧ (אמיל A-MYL) — **Branch:** The conglomeration of branches of the tree. [df: אמיר] [freq. 2] |kjv: bough, branch| {str: 534}

g^m) ᴧᴧᴧ (אומל AW-ML) — **Word:** [df: אמר] [freq. 6] |kjv: word, speech, thing, promise| {str: 562}

k^m) ᴧᴧᴧ (מאמל MA-ML) — **Word:** [Aramaic only] [df: מאמר] [freq. 2] |kjv: appointment, word| {str: 3983}

E) ᴧᴧ (מלא MLA) ac: **Fill** co: **Firstfruits** ab: **?:** A conglomeration of ingredients for filling up something.

V) ᴧᴧ (מלא M-LA) — **Fill:** [Hebrew and Aramaic] [df: מרא] [freq. 253] (vf: Paal, Niphal, Hiphil, Hitpael, Pual, Piel, Participle) |kjv: fill, full, fulfill, consecrate, accomplish, replenish, wholly, set, expire, fully, gather, overflow, satisfy, filthy, lift| {str: 4390, 4391, 4754}

N^m) ᴧᴧ (מלא M-LA) — **I. Full: II. Lord:** As one who is full of authority. [Aramaic only] [df: מרא] [freq. 69] |kjv: full, fill child, fully, much, multitude, worth, lord| {str: 4392, 4756}

N^{f1}) ᴧᴧ (מלאה ML-AH) — **Firstfruits:** In the sense of a great filling. [freq. 3] |kjv: fruit, fruit, fullness| {str: 4395}

N^{f2}) ᴧᴧ (מלאת ML-AT) — **Full:** [freq. 1] |kjv: fitly| {str: 4402}

b^m) ᴧᴧᴧ (מליא M-LYA) — **Fatling:** In the sense of being full. [df: מריא] [freq. 8] |kjv: fatling, fat, fed| {str: 4806}

c^m) ᴧᴧᴧ (מלוא M-LWA) — **Filling:** [ms: מלא] [df: מלו] [freq. 37] |kjv: full, fullness, therein, all, fill, handful, multitude| {str: 4393}

ed^m) ᴧᴧᴧ (מילוא MY-LWA) — **Filling:** [ms: מלוא] [freq. 15] |kjv: consecration, set| {str: 4394}

ed^{f1}) ᴧᴧᴧ (מילואה MY-LW-AH) — **Setting:** A recess for filling with a stone or other ornament. [df: מלאה] [freq. 3] |kjv: inclosing, setting| {str: 4396}

F) ᴧᴧ (המל HML) ac: **?** co: **Speech** ab: **?**

d^{f1}) ᴧᴧᴧ (המולה H-MW-LH) — **Speech:** [ms: המלה] [freq. 2] |kjv: tumult, speech| {str: 1999}

G) ᴧᴧ (מהל MHL) ac: **Mix** co: **?** ab: **?:** A filling with another substance.

V) ᴧᴧ (מהל M-HL) — **Mix:** [freq. 1] (vf: Paal, Participle) |kjv: mix| {str: 4107}

J) ᴧᴧ (מול MWL) ac: **?** co: **Front** ab: **?:** The front of a long series of the same. The past is seen as "in front" in ancient Hebrew thought because the past can be seen while the future is unseen and therefore behind.

V) ᴧᴧ (מול MWL) — **Circumcise:** A cutting of the

front part of the male member. [freq. 36] (vf: Paal, Niphal, Hiphil) |kjv: circumcise, destroy, cut, need| {str: 4135}

N^m) ᴊᵞᴍ (מול MWL) — **Before:** The front of time or a place. [freq. 36] |kjv: against, toward, before, forefront, from, with| {str: 4136}

N^fl) ⵌᴊᵞᴍ (מולה MW-LH) — **Circumcision:** The removal of the front part of the male member. [freq. 1] |kjv: circumcision| {str: 4139}

i^m) ᴊᵞᴍⵜ (תמול T-MWL) — **Before:** The front of time or a place. [ms: תמל] [freq. 23] |kjv: yesterday| {str: 8543}

ni^m) ᴊᵞᴍⵜⵁ (אתמול AT-MWL) — **Before:** The front of time or a place. [freq. 8] |kjv: yesterday, before, old, late| {str: 865}

Adopted Roots;
2407 ᴊᴍⵌ Cut

1289) ᴍᴍᴍ (מם MM) ac: ? co: ? ab: ?

D) ᴍⵁᴍ (מאם MAM) ac: ? co: **Blemish** ab: **Nothing:** Anything that is considered useless or without value. A blemish that causes something to be valueless.

d^m) ᴍᵞⵁᴍ (מאום M-AWM) — **Blemish:** [freq. 22] |kjv: blemish, spot, blot| {str: 3971}

d^fl) ⵌᴍᵞⵁᴍ (מאומה M-AW-MH) — **Nothing:** [freq. 32] |kjv: anything, nothing, ought, any, fault, harm, nought, somewhat| {str: 3972}

1290) ⵌᴍ (מן MN) ac: **Firm** co: **Kind** ab: **Sure:** The pictograph ᴍ is a picture of water or other liquid such as blood, the ⵌ is a picture of a seed representing continuance. Combined these mean "blood continues". Each species (kind) continues by passing its blood to the following generation, which comes from the parent. Also the idea of strength through the blood. (eng: man; name - a reversal of the letters; animal; omen)

A) ⵌᴍ (מן MN) ac: ? co: **Portion** ab: **What:** What comes from something else as one kind comes from the same.

N^m) ⵌᴍ (מן MN) — **What:** Also who or where. [Hebrew and Aramaic] [freq. 26] |kjv: manna, whosoever, who, whoso, what, instrument, from, of| {str: 4478, 4479, 4482}

N^fl) ⵌⵌᴍ (מנה M-NH) — **Portion:** A set amount. [freq. 14] |kjv: portion, part, belonged| {str: 4490}

N^f2) ⵜⵌᴍ (מנת M-NT) — **Portion:** What belongs to someone or something. [freq. 7] |kjv: portion| {str: 4521}

B) ⵌⵌᴍ (מנן MNN) ac: ? co: **Number** ab: ?: A numbering of a kind.

eb^m) ⵌⵌⵌᴍ (מינין MY-NYN) — **Number:** [Aramaic only] [ms: מנין] [freq. 1] |kjv: number| {str: 4510}

C) ⵌᴍⵁ (אמן AMN) ac: **Firm** co: **Pillar** ab: ?: Something that grabs hold or supports something else. The passing of strength or skill to the next generation. A large group of the same kind are stronger than one.

V) ᴧᴧ (אמן A-MN) — **Firm:** To stand firm as a support. [Hebrew and Aramaic] [freq. 111] (vf: Paal, Niphal, Hiphil) |kjv: believe, assurance, faithful, sure, establish, trust, verify, steadfast, continuance, father, bring up, nurse, stand, fail| {str: 539, 540}

N[m]**)** ᴧᴧ (אמן A-MN) — **I. Craftsman:** One who is firm in his talents. **II. Amen:** An affirmation of firmness and support. [freq. 31] |kjv: workman, amen, truly, so be it| {str: 542, 543}

N[f1]**)** ᴧᴧ (אמנה AM-NH) — **I. Sure:** What is firm. **II. Nourished:** One given support through food. [freq. 5] |kjv: sure, indeed, portion, brought up| {str: 545, 546, 548}

N[f2]**)** ᴧᴧ (אמנת AM-NT) — **Truth:** What is firm. [ms: אמת] [freq. 127] |kjv: truth, true, truly, faithfully, assured, establishment, faithful, sure| {str: 571}

c[m]**)** ᴧᴧ (אמון A-MWN) — **Craftsman:** One who is firm in his talents. [freq. 1] |kjv: brought up| {str: 525}

d[m]**)** ᴧᴧ (אמון A-MWN) — **Firmness:** [freq. 5] |kjv: faithful, trusting, trusty| {str: 529}

d[f1]**)** ᴧᴧ (אמונה A-MW-NH) — **Firmness:** [freq. 49] |kjv: faithfulness, truth, faithfully, office, faithful, faith, stability, steady, truly| {str: 530}

g[m]**)** ᴧᴧ (אומן AW-MN) — **Firmness:** [ms: אמן] [freq. 1] |kjv: truth| {str: 544}

g[f1]**)** ᴧᴧ (אומנה AW-M-NH) — **Pillar:** The support of a structure. [ms: אמנה] [freq. 1] |kjv: pillar| {str: 547}

p[m]**)** ᴧᴧ (אמנם AM-NM) — **Sure:** [freq. 9] |kjv: truth, indeed, true, surely, no doubt| {str: 551}

op[m]**)** ᴧᴧ (אומנם AWM-NM) — **Sure:** [ms: אמנם] [freq. 5] |kjv: indeed, surety| {str: 552}

D) ᴧᴧ (מאן MAN) ac: **Refuse** co: ? ab: ?: A strength of the will.

V) ᴧᴧ (מאן M-AN) — **Refuse:** [freq. 41] (vf: Piel) |kjv: refuse| {str: 3985}

N[m]**)** ᴧᴧ (מאן M-AN) — **Refuse:** [freq. 5] |kjv: refuse| {str: 3986, 3987}

H) ᴧᴧ (מנה MNH) ac: ? co: **Number** ab: ?: The grouping together and counting of those that are of the same kind.

V) ᴧᴧ (מנה M-NH) — **Number:** To count or number a set of things or people. [Hebrew and Aramaic] [ar: מנא] [freq. 33] (vf: Paal, Niphal, Pual, Piel, Participle) |kjv: number, prepare, appoint, tell, count, set| {str: 4483, 4487}

N[m]**)** ᴧᴧ (מנה M-NH) — **Maneh:** A unit of measurement. [ar: מנא] [freq. 8] |kjv: mene, maneh, pound| {str: 4484, 4488}

g[m]**)** ᴧᴧ (מונה MW-NH) — **Time:** A counting of time. [ms: מנה] [freq. 2] |kjv: time| {str: 4489}

J) ᴧᴧ (מון MWN) ac: ? co: ? ab: **Likeness:** Those of the same kind, look alike.

i^{f1}) ᴪᵛᛉᴍᴍ† (תמונה T-MW-NH)
— **Likeness:** [ms: תמנה] [freq. 10] |kjv: likeness, similitude, image| {str: 8544}

L) ᛉᴍᴍᴠ (ימן YMN) ac: ? co: **Right** ab: ?: The right hand as the strong hand. The Hebrews oriented direction according to the rising sun therefore, the south is to the right.

V) ᛉᴍᴍᴠ (ימן Y-MN) — **Right:** To turn or go to the right hand. [df: אמן] [freq. 5] (vf: Hiphil) |kjv: turn right| {str: 541, 3231}

b^f) ᛉᴍᴍᴠ (ימין Y-MYN) — **Right:** The right hand or the direction of the right hand. [freq. 139] |kjv: hand, right, side, south| {str: 3225}

f^m) ᛉᴍᴍᴠ (ימני YM-NY) — **Right:** The right hand or the direction of the right hand. [freq. 33] |kjv: right, right hand| {str: 3233}

i^f) ᛉᴍᴍ†ᴠ (תימן TY-MN) — **South:** The direction the right hand points when oriented toward the rising sun. [ms: תמן] [freq. 23] |kjv: south, southward| {str: 8486}

bf^m) ᛉᴍᴍᴠ (ימיני Y-MY-NY) — **Right:** The right hand or the direction of the right hand. [freq. 2] |kjv: right| {str: 3227}

M) ᛉᴍᴍ (מין MYN) ac: ? co: **Kind** ab: ?

N^m) ᛉᴍᴍ (מין MYN) — **I. Kind:** A category of species. [df: מני] **II. From:** [Hebrew and Aramaic; The short form "ᴍ" is used as a prefix meaning "from"] [ms: מן] [freq. 165] |kjv: kind, among, with, from, since, after,

at, by, whether, of, part, before, because, therefore, out, for, than| {str: 4327, 4480, 4481}

1291) ᴍᴍ (מס MS) ac: **Melt** co: ? ab: **Affliction:** The dissolving or melting away of something.

A) ᴍᴍ (מס MS) ac: **Dissolve** co: ? ab: **Affliction:** A wasting or fainting away due to an outside force.

N^m) ᴍᴍ (מס MS) — **I. Afflicted: II. Task work:** A group of workers under forced labor. [freq. 24] |kjv: afflict, tribute, tributary, levy, discomfit, taskmaster| {str: 4522, 4523}

N^{f1}) ᴪᴍᴍ (מסה M-SH) — **Tribute:** An offering. [freq. 1] |kjv: tribute| {str: 4530}

i^m) ᴍᴍ† (תמס T-MS) — **Melt:** [freq. 1] |kjv: melt| {str: 8557}

B) ᴍᴍ (מסס MSS) ac: **Melt** co: ? ab: ?

V) ᴍᴍ (מסס M-SS) — **Melt:** A melting of something from heat. Also the melting of the heart through fear or discouragement. [freq. 21] (vf: Paal, Niphal, Hiphil, Participle) |kjv: melt, faint, discouraged, loose, molten, refuse| {str: 4549}

D) ᴍᴍ (מאס MAS) ac: **Dissolve** co: ? ab: ?

V) ᴍᴍ (מאס M-AS) — **Dissolve:** To make something dissolve away. Also to dissolve something through refusal. [freq. 76] (vf: Paal, Niphal) |kjv: despise, refuse, reject, abhor,| {str: 3988}

c^m) ᴍᴍ (מאוס M-AWS) — **Dissolve:** Something that is dissolved through refusal. [freq. 1] |kjv: refuse| {str: 3973}

F) 🔺ᴍᴍ✢ (סממ HMS) ac: **Melt** co: ? ab: ?

N^m) 🔺ᴍᴍ✢ (סממ H-MS) — **Melt:** [freq. 1] |kjv: melting| {str: 2003}

H) ✢🔺ᴍᴍ (מסה MSH) ac: **Melt** co: ? ab: ?

V) ✢🔺ᴍᴍ (מסה M-SH) — **Melt:** [freq. 4] (vf: Hiphil) |kjv: melt, consume, water| {str: 4529}

Adopted Roots;
2344 ᴜᴜ🔺ᴍᴍ Mix, Mixed wine

1292) ⊂⊃ᴍᴍ (מע MAh) ac: ? co: **Belly** ab: ?: The pictograph ᴍᴍ is a picture of water representing what is Unknown, the ⊂⊃ is a picture of an eye representing knowing. Combined these mean "Unknown knowing". The gut is the seat of the unconscious mind where ones instincts resides.

A) ⊂⊃ᴍᴍ (מע MAh) ac: ? co: **Sand** ab: ?: [Unknown connection to root]

N^fl) ✢⊂⊃ᴍᴍ (מעה M-AhH) — **Sand:** [freq. 1] |kjv: sand| {str: 4579}

H) ✢⊂⊃ᴍᴍ (מעה MAhH) ac: ? co: **Belly** ab: ?

N^m) ✢⊂⊃ᴍᴍ (מעה M-AhH) — **Belly:** The gut, the internal organs of the lower torso, the seat of the unconscious mind. Also the seat of emotion. [Hebrew and Aramaic] [ar: מעא] [freq. 33] |kjv: bowels, heart, womb, belly| {str: 4577, 4578}

1293) ⊂ᴍᴍ (מף MP) ac: ? co: ? ab: ?

1294) ᴀᴧᴍᴍ (מץ MTs) ac: **Squeeze** co: ? ab: **Strong:** The pictograph ᴍᴍ is a picture of water representing might, the ᴀᴧ representing the side. Combined these mean "mighty sides". When one strengthens the sides internal pressure is forced on the sides of the upper body.

A) ᴀᴧᴍᴍ (מץ MTs) ac: **Squeeze** co: ? ab: ?

N^m) ᴀᴧᴍᴍ (מץ MTs) — **Squeeze:** [freq. 1] |kjv: extortioner| {str: 4160}

B) ᴀᴧᴀᴧᴍᴍ (מצץ MTsTs) ac: **Suck** co: ? ab: ?: A pressing with the lips.

V) ᴀᴧᴀᴧᴍᴍ (מצץ M-TsTs) — **Suck:** [freq. 1] (vf: Paal) |kjv: milk| {str: 4711}

N^fl) ✢ᴀᴧᴀᴧᴍᴍ (מצצה MTs-TsH) — **Unleavened:** A hard and flat bread or cake made without leaven. As a food that can be sucked on. [freq. 53] |kjv: unleavened bread, cakes, unleavened, without leaven| {str: 4682}

C) ᴀᴧᴍᴍᵇ (אמץ AMTs) ac: ? co: ? ab: **Strong:** A strong pressure or pressing. A mental strength of courage or determination.

V) ᴀᴧᴍᴍᵇ (אמץ A-MTs) — **Strong:** To be mentally strong, firm, obstinate or courageous. [freq. 41] (vf: Paal, Hiphil, Hitpael, Piel) |kjv: strengthen, courage, strong, courageous, harden, speed, stronger, confirm, establish, fortify, increase, obstinate, prevail| {str: 553}

N^(fl)) ᴧᴧᴧᴧᴠ (אמצה AM-TsH) — **Strength:** [freq. 1] |kjv: strength| {str: 556}

a^m) ᴧᴧᴧᴧᴠᴧᴧ (מאמץ MA-MTs) — **Strength:** [freq. 1] |kjv: forces| {str: 3981}

b^m) ᴧᴧᴧᴧᴠ (אמיץ A-MYTs) — **Strong:** [ms: אמץ] [freq. 6] |kjv: strong, mighty, courageous| {str: 533}

c^m) ᴧᴧᴧᴠ (אמוץ A-MWTs) — **Strong:** [freq. 2] |kjv: bay| {str: 554}

g^m) ᴧᴧᴧᴠᴠ (אומץ AW-MTs) — **Strong:** [freq. 1] |kjv: strong| {str: 555}

E) ᴠᴧᴧᴧ (מצא MTsA) ac: **Find** co: ? ab: ?: In the sense of squeezing something out of its hidden place.

V) ᴠᴧᴧᴧ (מצא M-TsA) — **Find:** [Hebrew and Aramaic] [ar: מטא] [freq. 464] (vf: Paal, Niphal, Hiphil) |kjv: find, present, come, meet, befall, get, suffice, deliver, hit, left, hold, reach| {str: 4291, 4672}

H) ᴪᴧᴧᴧ (מצה MTsH) ac: **Wring** co: ? ab: ?: A squeezing out of a liquid by wringing.

V) ᴪᴧᴧᴧ (מצה M-TsH) — **Wring:** To squeeze out by wringing. [freq. 7] (vf: Paal, Niphal) |kjv: wring, suck| {str: 4680}

J) ᴧᴧᴠᴧ (מוץ MWTs) ac: ? co: **Chaff** ab: ?: When a seed of grain is squeezed the chaff is removed.

N^m) ᴧᴧᴠᴧ (מוץ MWTs) — **Chaff:** [ms: מץ] [freq. 8] |kjv: chaff| {str: 4671}

M) ᴧᴧᴠᴧ (מיץ MYTs) ac: **Wring** co: ? ab: ?: A squeezing out of a liquid by wringing.

N^m) ᴧᴧᴠᴧ (מיץ MYTs) — **Wring:** [freq. 3] |kjv: churn, wring, force| {str: 4330}

1295) ᴥᴧ (מק MQ) ac: **Rot** co: **Stink** ab: ?: The pictograph ᴧᴧ is a picture of water, the ᴥ is a picture of the sun at the horizon representing the gathering or condensing of light. Combined these mean "water condensed". During the summer months water holes begin to dry out and the organic matter that remains begins to rot and stink.

A) ᴥᴧ (מק MQ) ac: ? co: **Stink** ab: ?: The stinking smell of rotting vegetation.

N^m) ᴥᴧ (מק MQ) — **Stink:** [freq. 2] |kjv: stink, rottenness| {str: 4716}

B) ᴥᴥᴧ (מקק MQQ) ac: **Rot** co: ? ab: ?: The rotting vegetation of a dried up pond.

V) ᴥᴥᴧ (מקק M-QQ) — **Rot:** [freq. 10] (vf: Niphal, Hiphil) |kjv: pine, consume, corrupt, dissolve| {str: 4743}

J) ᴥᴠᴧ (מוק MWQ) ac: **Rot** co: ? ab: ?

V) ᴥᴠᴧ (מוק MWQ) — **Rotten:** [freq. 1] (vf: Hiphil) |kjv: corrupt| {str: 4167}

Adopted Roots;
2667 ᴥᴧᴧᴧᴠ Dry, Raisin

1296) ᴥᴧᴧ (מר MR) ac: ? co: **Bitter** ab: **Weak:** The pictograph ᴧᴧ is a picture of water, the ᴥ is a picture of a head.

Combined these mean "water head" or headwaters. (eng: marine; marsh)

A) ᐜᚷ (מר MR) ac: **?** co: **Bitter** ab: **?:** The headwaters of a river are only a trickle and have stagnant pools causing the water to be bitter. Something that is bitter of taste or attitude. Rebellion is one with a bitter attitude.

N[m]) ᐜᚷ (מר MR) — **I. Bitter: II. Trickle:** From the little water at the headwaters of a river. [freq. 39] |kjv: bitter, bitterness, bitterly, chafed, angry, discontented, heavy| {str: 4751, 4752}

N[fl]) ᚷᐜᚷ (מרה M-RH) — **Bitterness:** [freq. 1] |kjv: bitterness| {str: 4787}

f[m]) ᚷᐜᚷ (מרי M-RY) — **Bitter:** [freq. 23] |kjv: rebellious, rebellion, bitter, rebel| {str: 4805}

k[m]) ᐜᚷᚷᚷ (ממר M-MR) — **Bitterness:** [freq. 1] |kjv: bitterness| {str: 4470}

B) ᐜᚷᚷ (מרר MRR) ac: **?** co: **Bitter** ab: **?:** The headwaters of a river are only a trickle and have stagnant pools causing the water to be bitter. Rebellion is one with a bitter attitude.

V) ᐜᚷᚷ (מרר M-RR) — **Bitter:** [freq. 16] (vf: Paal, Hiphil, Piel) |kjv: bitterness, bitter, bitterly, choler, grieve, provoke, vex| {str: 4843}

N[fl]) ᚷᐜᚷᚷ (מררה MR-RH) — **Bile:** The bitter stomach fluid. [freq. 1] |kjv: gall| {str: 4845}

b[f3]) +ᚷᐜᚷᚷ (מרירות M-RY-RWT) — **Bitter:** Bitterness [freq. 1] |kjv: bitterness| {str: 4814}

c[m]) ᚷᚷᐜᚷ (מרור M-RWR) — **Bitter:** [ms: מרר] [freq. 3] |kjv: bitter, bitterness| {str: 4844}

c[fl]) ᚷᚷᐜᚷ (מרורה M-RW-RH) — **Venom:** The bitter fluids of a serpent. [ms: מררה] [freq. 4] |kjv: gall, bitter| {str: 4846}

ac[m]) ᚷᚷᐜᚷᚷ (ממרור MM-RWR) — **Bitter:** [ms: ממרור] [freq. 1] |kjv: bitterness| {str: 4472}

bf[m]) ᚷᚷᚷᐜᚷ (מרירי M-RY-RY) — **Bitter:** [freq. 1] |kjv: bitter| {str: 4815}

id[m]) ᚷᚷᐜᚷ+ (תמרור TM-RWR) — **Bitter:** [freq. 3] |kjv: bitter, bitterly| {str: 8563}

C) ᐜᚷᚷ (אמר AMR) ac: **?** co: **?** ab: **Weak:** A weakness from a bitter sickness.

V) ᐜᚷᚷ (אמר A-MR) — **Weak:** [df: אמל] [freq. 16] (vf: Paal) |kjv: languish, feeble, weak| {str: 535}

N[m]) ᐜᚷᚷ (אמר A-MR) — **Weak:** [df: אמלל] [freq. 1] |kjv: feeble| {str: 537}

e[m]) ᐜᚷᚷᚷ (אימר AY-MR) — **Lamb:** A weak animal. [Aramaic only] [ms: אמר] [freq. 3] |kjv: lamb| {str: 563}

o[m]) ᐜᚷᚷᚷ (אומר AW-MR) — **Weak:** [df: אמלל] [freq. 1] |kjv: weak| {str: 536}

D) ᚷᚷᚷ (מאר MAR) ac: **Irritate** co: **?** ab: **?:** A bitter irritation from disease.

V) ᚷᚷᚷ (מאר M-AR) — **Irritate:** [freq. 4] (vf: Hiphil)

|kjv: fretting, pricking| {str: 3992}

F) 𝕬ᴀᴀᴈ̇ (המר HMR) ac: **?** co: **Pit** ab: **?:** The bitterness of the water in a stagnant pit.

a[fl]) 𝕬ᴈ̇ᴀᴀᴬ̇ᴀᴀ (מהמרה MH-M-RH) — **Pit:** A deep hole. [freq. 1] |kjv: deep pit| {str: 4113}

G) 𝕬ᴈ̇ᴀᴀ (מהר MHR) ac: **Hurry** co: **?** ab: **?:** [Unknown connection to root]

V) 𝕬ᴈ̇ᴀᴀ (מהר M-HR) — **I. Hurry: II. Purchase:** To pay the price for a wife. [Unknown connection to root] [freq. 66] (vf: Paal, Niphal, Piel) |kjv: haste, swift, quick, soon, speed, headlong, rash, fearful, ready, short, straightway, suddenly, endow| {str: 4116, 4117}

N[m]) 𝕬ᴈ̇ᴀᴀ (מהר M-HR) — **Quickly:** [freq. 18] |kjv: quickly, speedily, hastily, soon, suddenly, at once| {str: 4118}

N[fl]) 𝕬ᴈ̇ᴀᴀ̇ᴀᴀ (מהרה MH-RH) — **Quickly:** [freq. 20] |kjv: quickly, speedily, speed, soon, swiftly, hastily, shortly| {str: 4120}

b[m]) 𝕬ᴈ̇ᴧ-ᴀᴀ (מהיר M-HYR) — **Ready:** In the sense of being quick. [ms: מהר] [freq. 4] |kjv: ready, diligent, hasting| {str: 4106}

g[m]) 𝕬ᴈ̇Yᴀᴀ (מוהר MW-HR) — **Dowry:** [Unknown connection to root] [ms: מהר] [freq. 3] |kjv: dowry| {str: 4119}

H) 𝕬̇ᴀᴀ (מרה MRH) ac: **?** co: **?** **Bitter** ab: **?**

V) 𝕬̇ᴀᴀ (מרה M-RH) — **Bitter:** To be bitter or rebellious. [freq. 44] (vf: Paal, Hiphil) |kjv:

rebel, rebellious, provoke, disobedient, against, bitter, change, disobey, grievously, provocation| {str: 4784}

g[m]) 𝕬̇ᴈ̇Yᴀᴀ (מורה MW-RH) — **I. Razor:** [Unknown connection to root] **II. Archer:** One who throws an arrow. **III. Razor:** [Unknown connection to root] [freq. 3] |kjv: razor| {str: 4177}

J) 𝕬Yᴀᴀ (מור MWR) ac: **Exchange** co: **?** ab: **?:** [Unknown connection to root]

V) 𝕬Yᴀᴀ (מור MWR) — **Exchange:** [freq. 14] (vf: Niphal, Hiphil) |kjv: change, remove, exchange| {str: 4171}

N[m]) 𝕬Yᴀᴀ (מור MWR) — **Myrrh:** A sweet smelling spice. Used as an exchange due to its monetary value. [ms: מר] [freq. 12] |kjv: myrrh| {str: 4753}

N[fl]) 𝕬̇ᴈ̇Yᴀᴀ (מורה MW-RH) — **Grief:** As an exchange. [ms: מרה] [freq. 1] |kjv: grief| {str: 4786}

i[fl]) 𝕬̇ᴈ̇Yᴀᴀᵗ (תמורה T-MW-RH) — **Exchange:** [freq. 6] |kjv: exchange, change, recompense, restitution| {str: 8545}

L) 𝕬ᴀᴀᴧ (ימר YMR) ac: **?** co: **Exchange** ab: **?:** [Unknown connection to root]

V) 𝕬ᴀᴀᴧ (ימר Y-MR) — **Exchange:** [freq. 2] (vf: Hiphil, Hitpael) |kjv: change, boast| {str: 3235}

Adopted Roots;

2352	ᴧ𝕬ᴀᴀ	Rebel, Rebellion
2353	ᴂᴂ𝕬ᴀᴀ	Rub
2354	⊗𝕬ᴀᴀ	Rub
2355	ᴏᴧ𝕬ᴀᴀ	Pain

2356 ⊸-ᴧᴧᴧ   Scour, Cleansing

1297) ᴌᴌᴧᴧ (מש MSh) ac: **Touch** co: **Silk** ab: ?

A) ᴌᴌᴧᴧ (מש MSh) ac: ? co: **Silk** ab: ?: The soft touch of silk.

f^m) ⊁ᴌᴌᴧᴧ (משי M-ShY) — **Silk:** A smooth costly material for making garments. [freq. 2] |kjv: silk| {str: 4897}

B) ᴌᴌᴌᴌᴧᴧ (משש MShSh) ac: **Grope** co: ? ab: ?

V) ᴌᴌᴌᴌᴧᴧ (משש M-ShSh) — **Grope:** A groping around in the darkness to find something. [freq. 9] (vf: Paal, Hiphil, Piel) |kjv: grope, feel, search| {str: 4959}

C) ᴌᴌᴧᴧᴣ (אמש AMSh) ac: ? co: **Yesterday** ab: ?: A time past. [Unknown connection to root]

N^m) ᴌᴌᴧᴧᴣ (אמש A-MSh) — **Yesterday:** [freq. 5] |kjv: yesternight, former time, yesterday| {str: 570}

H) ᴪᴌᴌᴧᴧ (משה MShH) ac: **Draw** co: ? ab: ?: A grabbing hold of something to bring it close to you.

V) ᴪᴌᴌᴧᴧ (משה M-ShH) — **Draw:** To draw or pull out. [freq. 3] (vf: Paal, Hiphil) |kjv: draw| {str: 4871}

J) ᴌᴌᴧᴧ (מוש MWSh) ac: **Touch** co: ? ab: ?

V) ᴌᴌᴧᴧ (מוש MWSh) — I. **Touch:** II. **Remove:** In the sense of grabbing hold. [freq. 24] (vf: Paal, Hiphil) |kjv: feel, handle, depart, remove, take, back, cease| {str: 4184, 4185}

L) ᴌᴌᴧᴧᴣ (ימש YMSh) ac: **Touch** co: ? ab: ?

V) ᴌᴌᴧᴧᴣ (ימש Y-MSh) — **Touch:** [freq. 1] (vf: Hiphil) |kjv: feel| {str: 3237}

Adopted Roots;
2358 ᴝᴌᴌᴧᴧ   Draw, Acquire

1298) ᵗᴧᴧ (מת MT) ac: **Die** co: **Man** ab: **Mortality:** The pictograph ᴧᴧ is a picture of water representing chaos, the ᵗ is a picture of two crossed sticks representing a mark or sign. Combined these mean "chaos mark". The length of time that something exists and ends. (eng: mute; moot - as a dead point; mortal - with an additional r and l; mate - of "check mate" meaning "king is dead")

A) ᵗᴧᴧ (מת MT) ac: ? co: **Man** ab: **Mortality:** A length of time that comes to an end.

N^m) ᵗᴧᴧ (מת MT) — **Man:** As mortal. [freq. 22] |kjv: man, few, friend, number, person, small| {str: 4962}

f^m) ⊁ᵗᴧᴧ (מתי M-TY) — **When:** An unknown duration of time. [freq. 3] |kjv: when, long| {str: 4970}

J) ᵗᴝᴧᴧ (מות MWT) ac: **Die** co: ? ab: **Death:** The end of time for what has died.

V) ᵗᴝᴧᴧ (מות MWT) — **Die:** [freq. 835] (vf: Paal, Hiphil, Hophal) |kjv: die, dead, slay, death| {str: 4191}

N^m) ᵗᴝᴧᴧ (מות MWT) — **Death:** [Hebrew and Aramaic] [freq. 163] |kjv: death, die, dead, deadly, slay| {str: 4192, 4193, 4194}

aᵐ) †Yᴍᴍᴍ (ממות M-MWT) —
Death: [freq. 2] |kjv: death| {str: 4463}

iᶠˡ) ⵌ†Yᴍᴍ† (תמותה T-MW-TH) — **Death:** [freq. 2] |kjv: death, die| {str: 8546}

Adopted Roots;
2669 †ᴍᴍᴑᴧ Terminate, Permanent

1299) ℒᴍᴍ (מע MGh) ac: ? co: ? ab: ?

Nun

1300) ᗷᒷ (נא NA) ac: **Plead** co: ? ab: ?

A) ᗷᒷ (נא NA) ac: **Plead** co: **Raw** ab: ?: A pleading for what is desired.

N^m) ᗷᒷ (נא NA) — **I. Raw:** Meat that is not fit for consumption in the sense of refusal. **II. Please:** A pleading or request for something. [freq. 10] |kjv: raw, now, beseech, pray, oh, go| {str: 4994, 4995}

N^fl) ❀ᗷᒷ (נאה N-AH) — **Pasture:** As a place of beauty. [Unknown connection to root] [freq. 12] |kjv: habitation, pasture, house, place| {str: 4999}

C) ᗷᒷᗱ (אנא ANA) ac: **Plead** co: ? ab: ?

N^m) ᗷᒷᗱ (אנא A-NA) — **Please:** A pleading or request for something. [ms: אנה] [freq. 13] |kjv: beseech, pray, oh| {str: 577}

H) ❀ᗷᒷ (נאה NAH) ac: ? co: **Pasture** ab: **Beauty:** A place of beauty and comfort. In the sense of desire.

V) ❀ᗷᒷ (נאה N-AH) — **Beauty:** [freq. 3] (vf: Pilpel) |kjv: become, comely, beautiful| {str: 4998}

d^m) ❀Ꭹᗷᒷ (נאוה N-AWH) — **Beauty:** [freq. 9] |kjv: comely, seemly, becometh| {str: 5000}

J) ᗷᎩᒷ (נוא NWA) ac: **Forbid** co: **Forbid** ab: **Opposition:** A refusal of a plea.

V) ᗷᎩᒷ (נוא NWA) — **Forbid:** [freq. 9] (vf: Paal, Hiphil) |kjv:

dissalow, discourage, non effect, break| {str: 5106}

i^fl) ❀ᗷᎩᒷᛏ (תנואה T-NW-AH) — **Opposition:** [freq. 2] |kjv: breach of promise, occasion| {str: 8569}

~~~~~~~~~~

1301) ᒲᒷ (נב NB) ac: **Flourish** co: **Fruit** ab: **Prophecy:** The pictograph ᒷ is a picture of a seed, the ᒲ is a picture of a tent or house representing what is inside. Combined these mean "seed inside". A fruit hides the seeds inside it.

B) ᒲᒲᒷ (נבב NBB) ac: **Hollow** co: ? ab: ?: The inside of a box for holding something or is empty.

V) ᒲᒲᒷ (נבב N-BB) — **Hollow:** To hollow out. [freq. 4] (vf: Paal, Participle) |kjv: hollow, vain| {str: 5014}

E) ᗷᒲᒷ (נבא NBA) ac: ? co: **Prophet** ab: **Prophecy:** A fruit produced from the inside of man. A knowledge of something that is not known by the five senses.

V) ᗷᒲᒷ (נבא N-BA) — **Prophecy:** [Hebrew and Aramaic] [freq. 116] (vf: Niphal, Hitpael) |kjv: prophecy, prophet| {str: 5012, 5013}

b^m) ᗷᛞᒲᒷ (נביא N-BYA) — **Prophet:** One who brings forth the inner fruit. [Hebrew and Aramaic] [freq. 320] |kjv: prophet, prophecy| {str: 5029, 5030}

b^{fl}) 𐤑𐤉𐤀𐤍 (נביאה N-BY-AH) — **Prophetess:** [freq. 6] |kjv: prophetess| {str: 5031}

d^{fl}) 𐤄𐤀𐤅𐤁𐤍 (נבואה N-BW-AH) — **Prophecy:** [Hebrew and Aramaic] [freq. 4] |kjv: prophecy| {str: 5016, 5017}

J) 𐤁𐤅𐤍 (נוב NWB) ac: **Flourish** co: **Fruit** ab: ?

V) 𐤁𐤅𐤍 (נוב NWB) — **Flourish:** [freq. 4] (vf: Paal) |kjv: bring forth, increase, cheerful| {str: 5107}

N^m) 𐤁𐤅𐤍 (נוב NWB) — **Fruit:** [df: ניב] [freq. 2] |kjv: fruit| {str: 5108}

i^{fl}) 𐤕𐤁𐤅𐤍𐤄 (תנובה T-NW-BH) — **Fruit:** [freq. 5] |kjv: fruit, increase| {str: 8570}

~~~~~~~~~~

1302) 𐤂𐤍 (נג NG) ac: **Shine** co: **Morning** ab: ?

A) 𐤂𐤍 (נג NG) ac: ? co: **Morning** ab: ?: The warm touch of light.

N^{fl}) 𐤂𐤍𐤄 (נגה N-GH) — **Morning:** As warm and bright. [Aramaic only] [freq. 1] |kjv: morning| {str: 5053}

G) 𐤄𐤂𐤍 (נהג NHG) ac: **Drive** co: ? ab: ?: The leading, pushing or guiding of a people or animal.

V) 𐤄𐤂𐤍 (נהג N-HG) — **Drive:** [freq. 31] (vf: Paal, Piel) |kjv: lead, away, drive, forth, guide, brought, acquainting| {str: 5090}

h^m) 𐤄𐤂𐤍𐤌 (מנהג MNh-G) — **Driving:** [freq. 2] |kjv: driving| {str: 4491}

H) 𐤄𐤂𐤍 (נגה NGH) ac: **Shine** co: **Bright** ab: ?: The warm touch of light.

V) 𐤄𐤂𐤍 (נגה N-GH) — **Shine:** [freq. 6] (vf: Paal, Hiphil) |kjv: shine, enlighten| {str: 5050}

c^{fl}) 𐤄𐤄𐤂𐤍 (נגוהה N-GW-HH) — **Brightness:** [freq. 1] |kjv: brightness| {str: 5054}

J) 𐤂𐤅𐤍 (נוג NWG) ac: ? co: **Bright** ab: ?: The warm touch of light.

N^{fl}) 𐤂𐤅𐤍 (נוג N-WG) — **Bright:** A bright or shining light. [ms: נגה] [freq. 19] |kjv: brightness, shining, bright, light| {str: 5051}

Adopted Roots;

2373	𐤇𐤂𐤍	Gore
2374	𐤍𐤂𐤍	Play, Music
2375	𐤔𐤂𐤍	Drive
2376	𐤏𐤂𐤍	Touch
2377	𐤏𐤂𐤍	Strike

~~~~~~~~~~

1303) 𐤃𐤍 (נד ND) ac: **Nod** co: **Mound** ab: ?: The pictograph ‎ל is a picture of a seed, the 𐤃 is a picture of the tent door that allows movement back and forth through the tent. Combined these mean "continue back and forth". A back and forth movement such as the shaking of the head.

A) 𐤃𐤍 (נד ND) ac: **Toss** co: **Mound** ab: ?: A tossing into a pile.

N^m) 𐤃𐤍 (נד ND) — **Mound:** [freq. 6] |kjv: heap| {str: 5067}

m^m) 𐤍𐤃𐤍 (נדן N-DN) — **Tossings:** Something that is tossed. [freq. 1] |kjv: gift| {str: 5083}

B) 𐤃𐤃𐤍 (נדד NDD) ac: **Toss** co: ? ab: ?

V) 𐤃𐤃𐤍 (נדד N-DD) — **Toss:** To be thrown about or wander around as nodding the head.

180

[Hebrew and Aramaic] [freq. 29] (vf: Paal, Hiphil, Hophal) |kjv: flee, wander, chase, go| {str: 5074, 5075}

d^m) ‫נדוד‬ (‫נדוד‬ N-DWD) — **Toss:** A going back and forth. [ms: ‫נדד‬] [freq. 1] |kjv: tossing| {str: 5076}

D) ‫נאד‬ (‫נאד‬ NAD) ac: ? co: **Skin bag** ab: ?: A leather bag used for storing milk or wine. When milk is put in the bag and it is shaken back and forth the milk is turned into cheese.

g^m) ‫נואד‬ (‫נואד‬ NW-AD) — **Skin bag:** [df: ‫נוד‬] [freq. 6] |kjv: bottle| {str: 4997}

g^{f1}) ‫נואדה‬ (‫נואדה‬ NW-A-DH) — **Skin bag:** [df: ‫נאדה‬] [freq. 6] |kjv: bottle| {str: 4997}

H) ‫נדה‬ (‫נדה‬ NDH) ac: **Toss** co: ? ab: ?

V) ‫נדה‬ (‫נדה‬ N-DH) — **Toss:** [df: ‫נדא‬] [freq. 3] (vf: Hiphil, Piel) |kjv: cast, put, drive| {str: 5077}

N^m) ‫נדה‬ (‫נדה‬ N-DH) — **Tossings:** Something that is tossed. [freq. 1] |kjv: gift| {str: 5078}

J) ‫נוד‬ (‫נוד‬ NWD) ac: **Nod** co: ? ab: ?

V) ‫נוד‬ (‫נוד‬ NWD) — **Nod:** To shake or wag out of pity, sorrow or wandering. [Hebrew and Aramaic] [freq. 25] (vf: Paal, Hiphil) |kjv: bemoan, remove, vagabond, flee, get, mourn, move, pity, shake, skip, sorry, wag, wander, go| {str: 5110, 5111}

N^m) ‫נוד‬ (‫נוד‬ NWD) — **Wandering:** In the sense of nodding ones head when wandering about. [freq. 1] |kjv: wandering| {str: 5112}

a^m) ‫מנוד‬ (‫מנוד‬ M-NWD) — **Nod:** A nodding of the head. [freq. 1] |kjv: shaking| {str: 4493}

M) ‫ניד‬ (‫ניד‬ NYD) ac: **Nod** co: ? ab: ?

N^m) ‫ניד‬ (‫ניד‬ NYD) — **Nod:** The up and down moving of the lips. [freq. 1] |kjv: moving| {str: 5205}

N^{f1}) ‫נידה‬ (‫נידה‬ NY-DH) — **Removal:** Something that is removed or thrown out. A menstruating woman is removed from the camp. [ms: ‫נדה‬] [freq. 30] |kjv: remove, separation, put apart, filthiness, flowers, far, set apart, menstruous, removed, unclean, uncleanness| {str: 5079, 5206}

Adopted Roots;
2381 ‫נהג‬ Drive
2384 ‫נהס‬ Toss

~~~~~~~~~~~

1304) ‫נה‬ (‫נה‬ NH) ac: **Mourn** co: ? ab: ?: The pictograph ‫נ‬ is a picture of a seed representing continuance. Related to ‫אנ‬.

C) ‫אנה‬ (‫אנה‬ ANH) ac: **Mourn** co: ? ab: ?

V) ‫אנה‬ (‫אנה‬ A-NH) — **Mourn:** [freq. 2] (vf: Paal) |kjv: lament, mourn| {str: 578}

f1) ‫אניה‬ (‫אניה‬ AN-YH) — **Mourning:** [freq. 2] |kjv: sorrow, lamentation| {str: 592}

H) ‫נהה‬ (‫נהה‬ NHH) ac: **Wail** co: ? ab: ?

V) ꚉꚉ (נהה N-HH) — **Wail:** [freq. 3] (vf: Paal, Niphal) |kjv: lament, wail| {str: 5091}

f^m) ꚉꚉ (נהי N-HY) — **Wail:** [freq. 7] |kjv: wailing, lamentation| {str: 5092}

f^1) ꚉꚉ (נהיה NH-YH) — **Wailing:** [freq. 1] |kjv: doleful| {str: 5093}

J) ꚉ (נוה NWH) ac: **Wail** co: ? ab: ?

N^m) ꚉ (נוה NWH) — **Wailing:** [ms: נה] [freq. 1] |kjv: wailing| {str: 5089}

L) ꚉ (ינה YNH) ac: **Suppress** co: ? ab: ?: [Unknown connection to root]

V) ꚉ (ינה Y-NH) — **Suppress:** [freq. 21] (vf: Paal, Hiphil) |kjv: oppress, vex, destroy, oppressor, proud, do, wrong, oppression, thrust| {str: 3238}

1305) ꚉ (נו NW) ac: **Dwell** co: **Abode** ab: ?

J) ꚉ (נוה NWH) ac: **Dwell** co: **Abode** ab: ?: A place of beauty and comfort where one resides for a long period of time.

V) ꚉ (נוה NWH) — **Dwell:** [freq. 2] (vf: Paal, Hiphil, Hophal) |kjv: home, habitation| {str: 5115}

N^m) ꚉ (נוה NWH) — **Abode:** The dwelling place of man (home), god (mountain) or animal (pasture or stable). [freq. 36] |kjv: habitation, fold, dwelling, sheepcote, comely, stable, pleasant, tarried| {str: 5116}

1306) ꚉ (נז NZ) ac: ? co: ? ab: ?

H) ꚉ (נזה NZH) ac: **Sprinkle** co: ? ab: ?

V) ꚉ (נזה N-ZH) — **Sprinkle:** [freq. 24] (vf: Paal, Hiphil) |kjv: sprinkle| {str: 5137}

1307) ꚉ (נח NHh) ac: **Guide** co: **Rest** ab: ?: The pictograph ꚉ is a picture of a seed representing continuance, the ꚉ is a picture of a wall that separates the inside from the outside. Combined these mean "continue outside". The shepherd would guide his flock to a place of water. Here is water for drinking as well as green grass for pasturing. Once the flock arrives, they are free to rest after the long journey. A guided journey to a place of rest. A sigh of rest. (eng: night - from the German nocht, as the time of rest)

A) ꚉ (נח NHh) ac: ? co: **Rest** ab: ?

N^f2) ꚉ (נחת N-HhT) — **Rest:** [freq. 8] |kjv: rest, set, quietness, lighting| {str: 5183}

h^f1) ꚉ (מנחה MN-HhH) — **Gift:** What is brought to another. [Hebrew and Aramaic] [freq. 213] |kjv: offering, present, gift, oblation, sacrifice, meat| {str: 4503, 4504}

C) ꚉ (אנח ANHh) ac: **Sigh** co: ? ab: ?: A sigh of rest.

V) ꚉ (אנח A-NHh) — **Sigh:** To sigh or groan out of a desire for rest. [freq. 12] (vf: Niphal) |kjv: sigh, groan, mourn| {str: 584}

N^m^) (אנה A-NHh) — **I:** In the sense of sighing or breathing. [Aramaic only; The plural form of this word meaning, we, is or] [df: אנה אנא] [freq. 20] |kjv: I, me, we| {str: 576, 586}

N^f1^) (אנחה AN-HhH) — **Groan:** The expression of burden and the desire for rest. [freq. 11] |kjv: sighing, groaning, sigh, mourning| {str: 585}

f^m^) (אנחי AN-HhY) — **I:** In the sense of sighing or breathing. [The plural form of this word meaning, we, is , and] [df: אני אנכי] [freq. 29] |kjv: I, me, we, ourselves, mine| {str: 580, 587, 589, 595, 5168}

F) (הנח HNHh) ac: **?** co: **Rest** ab: **?**

N^f1^) (הנחה HN-HhH) — **Rest:** [freq. 1] |kjv: release| {str: 2010}

H) (נחה NHhH) ac: **Guide** co: **?** ab: **?**

V) (נחה N-HhH) — **Guide:** [freq. 39] (vf: Paal, Hiphil) |kjv: lead, guide, bestow, govern, put, straiten| {str: 5148}

J) (נוח NWHh) ac: **Rest** co: **Rest** ab: **?:** A place of quiet and rest from burdens, work or enemy.

V) (נוח NWHh) — **Rest:** [freq. 64] (vf: Paal) |kjv: rest, cease, confederate, down, lay, quiet, remain| {str: 5117}

N^m^) (נוח NWHh) — **Rest:** [freq. 4] |kjv: rest| {str: 5118}

a^m^) (מנוח M-NWHh) — **Rest:** [freq. 7] |kjv: rest| {str: 4494}

k^f1^) (מנוחה M-NW-HhH) — **Rest:** [ms: מנחה] [freq. 21] |kjv: rest, comfortable, ease, quiet, still| {str: 4496}

L) (ינח YNHh) ac: **Sit** co: **Rest** ab: **?**

V) (ינח Y-NHh) — **Sit:** [freq. 75] (vf: Paal, Hiphil, Hophal) |kjv: leave, up, lay, suffer, place, put, set, down, alone, bestow, pacify, still, withdraw, withhold| {str: 3240}

Adopted Roots;

2392 Comfort

~~~~~~~~~~~

1308) (נט NTh) ac: **Spread** co: **Squash** ab: **?:** The pictograph is a picture of a seed, the ⊗ is a picture of a basket. Combined these mean "seed basket". Squash seeds were planted along the routes of the travelers and nomads for future use by themselves and other travelers. The squash plant spreads out over a large area forming varied sizes and shapes of squash fruit. Dried squash fruit becomes a hard hollow shell (seed basket) with the seeds inside and when shaken they rattle inside.

A) (נט NTh) ac: **Spread** co: **Bed** ab: **?:** As spread out on the floor.

h^f1^) (מנטה MN-ThH) — **Bed:** A spread out sheet for sleeping. [df: מטה] [freq. 29] |kjv: bed, bier| {str: 4296}

ad^f1^) (מנוטה M-NW-ThH) — **Spreading:** [df: מטה] [freq. 1] |kjv: stretching| {str: 4298}
~~~~~~~~~~~

H) ‏נטה‎ (‏נטה‎ NThH) ac: **Spread** co: ? ab: ?: The spreading growth of the squash plant.

V) ‏נטה‎ (‏נטה‎ N-ThH) — **Spread:** To stretch something out. [freq. 215] (vf: Paal, Niphal, Hiphil) |kjv: stretch, incline, turn, bow, decline, pitch, spread| {str: 5186}

a^m) ‏מנטה‎ (‏מנטה‎ MN-ThH) — **Beneath:** As under a stretched out sheet. [df: ‏מטה‎] [freq. 19] |kjv: beneath, downward, underneath, low, under, less, down| {str: 4295}

J) ‏נוט‎ (‏נוט‎ NWTh) ac: **Shake** co: ? ab: ?: The dried squash fruit rattle.

V) ‏נוט‎ (‏נוט‎ NWTh) — **Shake:** [freq. 1] (vf: Paal) |kjv: move| {str: 5120}

a^fl) ‏מנוטה‎ (‏מנוטה‎ M-NW-ThH) — **Perverseness:** As a shaking. [df: ‏מטה‎] [freq. 1] |kjv: perverseness| {str: 4297}

~~~~~~~~~

1309) ‏ני‎ (‏ני‎ NY) ac: **Wail** co: ? ab: ?: Related to ‏נה‎.

A) ‏ני‎ (‏ני‎ NY) ac: **Wail** co: ? ab: ?

N^m) ‏ני‎ (‏ני‎ NY) — **Wailing:** [freq. 1] |kjv: wailing| {str: 5204}

N) ‏אני‎ (‏אני‎ ANY) ac: **Wail** co: ? ab: ?

i^fl) ‏תאניה‎ (‏תאניה‎ T-AN-YH) — **Mourning:** [freq. 2] |kjv: heaviness, mourning| {str: 8386}

~~~~~~~~~

1310) ‏נך‎ (‏נך‎ NK) ac: **Crush** co: **Spice** ab: ?: The pictograph ❑ is a picture of a seed, the ‏ש‎ is a picture of the palm of the hand. Combined these mean "seed in the palm". Seeds of certain plants were placed in the palm and rubbed with the thumb to a powdery spice.

A) ‏נך‎ (‏נך‎ NK) ac: **Crush** co: **Spice** ab: ?

N^f3) ‏נכות‎ (‏נכות‎ N-KWT) — **Treasure:** Treasured items such as spices. [ms: ‏נכת‎] [freq. 2] |kjv: precious| {str: 5238}

a^fl) ‏מנכה‎ (‏מנכה‎ MN-KH) — **Crushed:** A crushing by beating or plagues. [df: ‏מכה‎] [freq. 48] |kjv: wound, slaughter, plague, beaten, stripe, stroke, blow, smote, sore wounded| {str: 4347}

B) ‏נכך‎ (‏נכך‎ NKK) ac: ? co: **Sweet** ab: ?: The sweet smell of spices.

bc^m) ‏ניכוך‎ (‏ניכוך‎ NY-KWK) — **Sweet:** Something that smells sweet. [Hebrew and Aramaic] [df: ‏נחוח ניחוח‎] [freq. 45] |kjv: sweet, fruit| {str: 5207, 5208}

C) ‏אנך‎ (‏אנך‎ ANK) ac: ? co: **Pestle** ab: ?: A mortar and pestle are also used to crush spices.

N^m) ‏אנך‎ (‏אנך‎ A-NK) — **Plumbline:** A stone in the shape of a pestle used for centering. [freq. 4] |kjv: plumbline| {str: 594}

E) ‏נכא‎ (‏נכא‎ NKA) ac: **Crush** co: **Spice** ab: ?: The crushing of seeds for making spices.

V) ‏נכא‎ (‏נכא‎ N-KA) — **Crush:** [freq. 1] (vf: Niphal) |kjv: viler| {str: 5217}

N^m) ‏נכא‎ (‏נכא‎ N-KA) — **Crushed:** [freq. 4] |kjv: broken, stricken, wounded| {str: 5218} c^f2) †לעושׁך (נכואת N-KW-AT) — **Spice:** [ms: נכאת] [freq. 2] |kjv: spicery, spice| {str: 5219}

H) ‰שׁשׁך (נכה NKH) ac: **Crush** co: **?** ab: **?**

V) ‰שׁשׁך (נכה N-KH) — **Crush:** [freq. 500] (vf: Niphal, Hiphil, Hophal, Pual) |kjv: smite, slay, kill, beat, slaughter, strike, give, wound, stripe| {str: 5221}

N^m) ‰שׁשׁך (נכה N-KH) — **Crushed:** One who has been crushed or one who is lame. [freq. 4] |kjv: abject, lame, contrite| {str: 5222, 5223}

J) שׁΥך (נוך NWK) ac: **?** co: **Pestle** ab: **?:** The rounded point of the pestle used to crush seeds into spices. Also the rounded point of the ear.

i^m) שׁΥך† (תנוך T-NWK) — **Point:** [freq. 8] |kjv: tip| {str: 8571}

1311) Uך (נל NL) ac: **Lead** co: **Pasture** ab: **?:** The pictograph ך is a picture of a seed representing the idea of continuing. The U is a picture of the shepherds staff which guides the flock toward the pasture. Combined these mean "Continue toward with the staff".

H) ‰Uך (נלה NLH) ac: **Complete** co: **?** ab: **?**

V) ‰Uך (נלה N-LH) — **End:** To come to a completion. [freq. 1] (vf: Hiphil) |kjv: end| {str: 5239}

h^m) ‰Uךmm (מנלה MN-LH) — **Complete:** [freq. 1] |kjv: perfection| {str: 4512}

G) U‰ך (נהל NHL) ac: **Lead** co: **Pasture** ab: **?:** A leading to pasture.

V) U‰ך (נהל N-HL) — **Lead:** To guide the flock to the pasture as the end of the journey. [freq. 10] (vf: Hitpael, Piel) |kjv: guide, lead, fed, carried| {str: 5095}

l^m) U‰U‰ך (נהלהל N-HL-HL) — **Pasture:** [df: נהלל] [freq. 1] |kjv: bush| {str: 5097}

J) Uרך (נול NWL) ac: **?** co: **Dunghill** ab: **?:** [Unknown connection to root]

q^f) ΥUרך (נולו NW-LW) — **Dunghill:** [Aramaic only] [df: נולי] [freq. 3] |kjv: dunghill| {str: 5122}

1312) mmך (נם NM) ac: **Sleep** co: **?** ab: **Tired:** A semi-conscious state between sleep and awake.

D) mmУך (נאם NAM) ac: **Utter** co: **?** ab: **?:** A speaking from a semi-conscious state declaring the words of god.

V) mmУך (נאם N-AM) — **Utter:** To speak, from a semi-conscious state, the words of god. [freq. 1] (vf: Paal) |kjv: say| {str: 5001}

N^m) mmУך (נאם N-AM) — **Utterance:** [ms: נאם] [freq. 376] |kjv: say| {str: 5002}

G) mm‰ך (נהם NHM) ac: **Growl** co: **?** ab: **?:** The sound one makes when waking from a sleep.

V) mm‰ך (נהם N-HM) — **Growl:** [freq. 5] (vf: Paal) |kjv: roar, mourn| {str: 5098}

N^m) mm‰ך (נהם N-HM) — **Growling:** [freq. 2] |kjv: roaring| {str: 5099}

N^fl) 𝔑 (נהמה NH-MH) — **Growling:** [freq. 2] |kjv: disquiet, roaring| {str: 5100}

J) ןוּם (נום NWM) ac: **Slumber** co: ? ab: ?

V) ןוּם (נום NWM) — **Slumber:** [freq. 6] (vf: Paal) |kjv: slumber, sleep| {str: 5123}

N^fl) 𝔑 (נומה NW-MH) — **Drowsiness:** [freq. 1] |kjv: drowsiness| {str: 5124}

i^fl) 𝔑 (תנומה T-NW-MH) — **Slumber:** [freq. 5] |kjv: slumber, slumbering| {str: 8572}

1313) לל (נן NN) ac: ? co: **Sprout** ab: **Continue:** The pictograph ל is a picture of a seed. Combined these mean "seed of seed". The seed is the continuation of life from the parent plant. This cycle continues generation after generation. (eng: new - with the removal of the final n)

J) ןוּל (נון NWN) ac: ? co: **Heir** ab: **Continue:** The son who continues the family lineage and properties.

V) ןוּל (נון NWN) — **Continue:** [freq. 2] (vf: Niphal, Hiphil) |kjv: continue| {str: 5125}

a^m) ןוּלמ (מנון M-NWN) — **Heir:** [freq. 1] |kjv: son| {str: 4497}

M) ליל (נין NYN) ac: ? co: **Heir** ab: ?: The son who continues the family lineage and properties.

N^m) ליל (נין NYN) — **Heir:** [freq. 3] |kjv: son| {str: 5209}

1314) ןס (נס NS) ac: **Lift** co: **Standard** ab: **Refuge:** The pictograph ל is a picture of a seed representing continuance, the ס is a picture of a thorn representing the idea of grabbing hold. Combined these mean "continue to grab hold". The tribal flag that is hung from a horizontal pole and lifted up high and seen from a distance.

A) ןס (נס NS) ac: ? co: **Standard** ab: ?

N^m) ןס (נס NS) — **Standard:** A flag that hangs from a pole. Also a sail. [freq. 20] |kjv: standard, ensign, pole, banner, sail, sign| {str: 5251}

a^fl) ןסמ (מנסה MN-SH) — **Trial:** [df: מסה] [freq. 5] |kjv: temptation, trial| {str: 4531}

B) ןסס (נסס NSS) ac: ? co: **Standard** ab: ?

V) ןסס (נסס N-SS) — **Standard:** To lift up the standard. [freq. 2] (vf: Paal) |kjv: ensign, standard-bearer| {str: 5263, 5264}

C) ןסא (אנס ANS) ac: **Compel** co: ? ab: ?: A grabbing hold.

V) ןסא (אנס A-NS) — **Compel:** To grab hold of one to perform. [Hebrew and Aramaic] [freq. 2] (vf: Paal) |kjv: compel| {str: 597, 598}

E) ןסא (נסא NSA) ac: **Lift** co: **Burden** ab: ?

V) ןסא (נסא N-SA) — **Lift:** To lift up a burden or load and carry it. [Hebrew and Aramaic] [df: נשא] [freq. 659] (vf: Paal, Niphal, Hiphil, Hitpael, Piel) |kjv: bear, take, bare, carry, borne, amourbearer, forgive, accept, exalt, regard, obtain, respect| {str: 4984, 5375, 5376}

N^{f2}) +ᴗ≠ᒧ (נסאת NS-AT) — **Gift:** [df: נשׂאת] [freq. 1] |kjv: gift| {str: 5379}

a^m) ᴗ≠ᒧ�献 (מנסא MN-SA) — **Burden:** [df: משׂא] [freq. 66] |kjv: burden, son, prophecy, set, exaction, carry, tribute| {str: 4853}

a^{f1}) ⵝᴗ≠ᒧᴍ (מנסאה MN-S-AH) — **Burden:** [df: משׂאה] [freq. 1] |kjv: burden| {str: 4858}

a^{f2}) +ᴗ≠ᒧᴍ (מנסאת MN-S-AT) — **I. Burden:** [df: משׂאת] **II. Cloud:** A cloud of smoke as lifted up from the fire. [df: משׂאת] [freq. 15] |kjv: burden, mess, collection, flame, gift, oblation, reward, sign, lift| {str: 4864}

b^m) ᴗ⊣≠ᒧ (נסיא N-SYA) — **Chief:** The leader of a family, tribe or people as one who carries the burdens of the people. [df: נשׂיא נשׂא] [freq. 132] |kjv: prince, captain, chief, ruler, vapour, governor, cloud| {str: 5387}

d^{f1}) ⵝᴗY≠ᒧ (נסואה N-SW-AH) — **Wagon:** A vehicle for carrying burdens. [df: נשׂואה נשׂאה] [freq. 1] |kjv: carriage| {str: 5385}

ac^m) ᴗY≠ᒧᴍ (מנסוא MN-SWA) — **Respect:** In the sense of lifting one up. [df: משׂא] [freq. 1] |kjv: respect| {str: 4856}

H) ⵝ≠ᒧ (נסה NSH) ac: **Test** co: ? ab: ?: A test to prove one is deserved of being lifted up.

V) ⵝ≠ᒧ (נסה N-SH) — **Test:** [freq. 36] (vf: Piel) |kjv: prove,

tempt, assay, adventure, try| {str: 5254}

J) ≠Yᒧ (נוס NWS) ac: **Flee** co: ? ab: **Refuge:** The family standard as the place of refuge that one flees to.

V) ≠Yᒧ (נוס NWS) — **Flee:** To run to the standard for safety. Also a fleeing to any safe place such as a city or mountain. [freq. 161] (vf: Paal, Hiphil) |kjv: flee, abate, display, flight, hide, lift| {str: 5127}

k^m) ≠Yᒧᴍ (מנוס M-NWS) — **Refuge:** A place of safety. [freq. 8] |kjv: refuge, escape, flight, flee| {str: 4498}

k^{f1}) ⵝ≠Yᒧᴍ (מנוסה M-NW-SH) — **Fleeing:** [ms: מנסה] [freq. 2] |kjv: flight, fleeing| {str: 4499}

M) ≠⊣ᒧ (נים NYS) ac: **Flee** co: ? ab: ?: The family standard as the place of refuge that one flees to.

N^m) ≠⊣ᒧ (נים NYS) — **Flee:** [freq. 1] |kjv: flee| {str: 5211}

~~~~~~~~~

1315) ⌒ᒧ (נע NAh) ac: ? co: ? ab: ?

~~~~~~~~~

1316) ⌒ᒧ (נף NP) ac: **Shake** co: **Sieve** ab: ?: The pictograph ᒧ is a picture of seed, the ⌒ is a picture of a mouth. Combined these mean "seed in the mouth". A sieve is a tool used to separate out materials such as seeds by placing the material in the sieve, lifting it up and shaking it.

A) ⌒ᒧ (נף NP) ac: **High** co: **Sieve** ab: ?

N^{f1}) ⵝ⌒ᒧ (נפה N-PH) — **I. Sieve: II. Valley:** As a sieve.

[freq. 4] |kjv: border, coast, region, sieve| {str: 5299}

N‫f 2‬) ‫לֹת‬ (‫נֹפֶת‬ N-PT) — Heights: [freq. 1] |kjv: country| {str: 5316}

J) ‫לוֹך‬ (‫נוּף‬ NWP) ac: Shake co: ? ab: ?

V) ‫לוֹך‬ (‫נוּף‬ NWP) — Shake: [freq. 37] (vf: Paal, Hiphil, Hophal) |kjv: wave, shake, offer, lift, move, perfume, send, sift, strike| {str: 5130}

N‫m‬) ‫לוֹך‬ (‫נוּף‬ NWP) — Elevation: [freq. 1] |kjv: situation| {str: 5131}

i‫fl‬) ‫תלוֹךֵ‬ (‫תְּנוּפָה‬ T-NW-PH) — Shake: [freq. 30] |kjv: wave offering, wave, offering, shaking| {str: 8573}

~~~~~~~~~~~

1317) ‫לם‬ (‫נץ‬ NTs) ac: Sparkle co: Spark ab: Quarrel: The sparkling colors coming off metal when struck. The petals of a flower like sparks off metal.

A) ‫לם‬ (‫נץ‬ NTs) ac: ? co: Blossom ab: Quarrel: As a spark.

N‫m‬) ‫לם‬ (‫נץ‬ NTs) — I. Blossom: From its bright color like a spark. II. Nets: An unknown bird of prey. [freq. 4] |kjv: blossom, hawk| {str: 5322}

a‫fl‬) ‫מלם‬ (‫מִנְצָה‬ MN-TsH) — Strife: [df: ‫מצה‬] [freq. 3] |kjv: contention, strife, debate| {str: 4683}

a‫f 3‬) ‫תמלם‬ (‫מִנְצוֹת‬ MN-TsWT) — Quarrel: [df: ‫מצות‬] [freq. 1] |kjv: contend| {str: 4695}

B) ‫לםם‬ (‫נצץ‬ NTsTs) ac: ? co: Spark ab: ?

V) ‫לםם‬ (‫נצץ‬ N-TsTs) — Sparkle: To sparkle like a shower of sparks. [freq. 1] (vf: Paal) |kjv: sparkle| {str: 5340}

ec‫m‬) ‫לםוֹיל‬ (‫נִיצוֹץ‬ NY-TsWTs) — Spark: [freq. 1] |kjv: spark| {str: 5213}

D) ‫לאם‬ (‫נאץ‬ NATs) ac: Despise co: ? ab: ?: As a spark.

V) ‫לאם‬ (‫נאץ‬ N-ATs) — Despise: [freq. 25] (vf: Paal, Hiphil, Piel) |kjv: despise, provoke, abhor, blaspheme, contemn, flourish| {str: 5006}

N‫fl‬) ‫לאםֵ‬ (‫נאצה‬ NA-TsH) — Despise: [freq. 5] |kjv: blasphemy, provocation| {str: 5007}

E) ‫לםא‬ (‫נצא‬ NTsA) ac: Whither co: ? ab: ?: From the quick withering of the blossoms.

V) ‫לםא‬ (‫נצא‬ N-TsA) — Whither: [freq. 1] (vf: Paal) |kjv: flee| {str: 5323}

H) ‫לםֵ‬ (‫נצה‬ NTsH) ac: ? co: ? ab: Quarrel: As a spark.

V) ‫לםֵ‬ (‫נצה‬ N-TsH) — I. Quarrel: II. Whither: [freq. 11] (vf: Paal, Niphal, Hiphil, Participle) |kjv: strive, waste| {str: 5327}

J) ‫לוֹם‬ (‫נוץ‬ NWTs) ac: Bloom co: Bud ab: ?: The budding of a flower on a plant or feathers on a bird.

V) ‫לוֹם‬ (‫נוץ‬ NWTs) — Bloom: [freq. 3] (vf: Paal, Hiphil) |kjv: bud, fled| {str: 5132}

N‫fl‬) ‫לוֹםֵ‬ (‫נוצה‬ NW-TsH) — Feather: [ms: ‫נצה‬] [freq. 4] |kjv: feather, ostrich| {str: 5133}

M) ‎נ‎ו‎ר‎ל‎ (‎נ‎י‎ץ‎ NYTs) ac: ? co:
Blossom ab: ?: The budding of a
flower on a plant.

N‎(fl)‎) ‎ל‎ר‎ו‎נ‎ (‎נ‎י‎צ‎ה‎ NY-TsH) —
Blossom: [ms: ‎נ‎צ‎ה‎] [freq. 2]
|kjv: flower| {str: 5328}

m‎(fl)‎) ‎ל‎ר‎ו‎נ‎ (‎נ‎י‎צ‎ן‎ NY-TsN) —
Blossom: [ms: ‎נ‎צ‎ן‎] [freq. 1]
|kjv: flower| {str: 5339}

~~~~~~~~~~~~

1318) ‎נ‎ (‎נ‎ק‎ NQ) ac: **Suckle** co:
Breast ab: **Innocent:** The pictograph ‎ל‎ is
a picture of a seed and represents the sons
of the next generation, the ‎‎ is a picture
of the sun at the horizon and the drawing
in of light. Combined these mean "child
drawn in". The bringing in and holding
close of an infant to the breast.

A) ‎נ‎ (‎נ‎ק‎ NQ) ac: ? co: **Bowl** ab:
Innocent: Where the infant suckles.

f‎(m)‎) ‎נ‎ק‎י‎ (‎נ‎ק‎י‎ N-QY) —
Innocent: A state of innocence
as an infant. [df: ‎נ‎ק‎י‎א‎] [freq. 44]
|kjv: innocent, guiltless, quit,
blameless, clean, clear| {str:
5355}

k‎(f4)‎) ‎מ‎נ‎ק‎י‎ת‎ (‎מ‎נ‎ק‎י‎ת‎ MN-
QYT) — **Bowl:** From the shape
of a bowl that holds liquids like
a breast that holds milk. [freq. 4]
|kjv: bowl, cup| {str: 4518}

fj‎(m)‎) ‎נ‎ק‎י‎ו‎ן‎ (‎נ‎ק‎י‎ו‎ן‎ NQ-YWN)
— **Innocent:** A state of
innocence as an infant. [ms:
‎נ‎ק‎י‎ן‎] [freq. 5] |kjv: innocency,
cleanness| {str: 5356}

B) ‎נ‎ק‎ק‎ (‎נ‎ק‎ק‎ NQQ) ac: ? co:
Breast ab: ?

b‎(m)‎) ‎נ‎ק‎י‎ק‎ (‎נ‎ק‎י‎ק‎ N-QYQ) —
Cleavage: A cleft in the rocks.
[freq. 3] |kjv: hole| {str: 5357}

C) ‎ע‎נ‎ק‎ (‎א‎נ‎ק‎ ANQ) ac: **Cry** co: ?
ab: ?: The crying out of a child or
one who is helpless.

V) ‎ע‎נ‎ק‎ (‎א‎נ‎ק‎ A-NQ) — **Cry:**
[freq. 4] (vf: Paal, Niphal) |kjv:
cry, groan| {str: 602}

N‎(fl)‎) ‎ל‎ע‎נ‎ק‎ (‎א‎נ‎ק‎ה‎ AN-QH) —
I. Crying: II. Anaqa: An
unknown animal whose sound is
like a cry. [freq. 5] |kjv: sighing,
crying, groaning, ferret| {str:
603, 604}

D) ‎נ‎א‎ק‎ (‎נ‎א‎ק‎ NAQ) ac: **Cry** co: ?
ab: ?: The crying out of one who is
helpless.

V) ‎נ‎א‎ק‎ (‎נ‎א‎ק‎ N-AQ) — **Cry:**
[freq. 2] (vf: Paal) |kjv: groan|
{str: 5008}

N‎(fl)‎) ‎ל‎נ‎א‎ק‎ (‎נ‎א‎ק‎ה‎ NA-QH) —
Crying: [freq. 4] |kjv: groaning|
{str: 5009}

G) ‎נ‎ה‎ק‎ (‎נ‎ה‎ק‎ NHQ) ac: **Cry** co: ?
ab: ?

V) ‎נ‎ה‎ק‎ (‎נ‎ה‎ק‎ N-HQ) — **Cry:**
[freq. 2] (vf: Paal) |kjv: bray|
{str: 5101}

H) ‎נ‎ק‎ל‎ (‎נ‎ק‎ה‎ NQH) ac: ? co: ? ab:
Innocent: The innocence of an
infant.

V) ‎נ‎ק‎ל‎ (‎נ‎ק‎ה‎ N-QH) —
Innocent: One who is innocent
of a crime or oath. [Hebrew and
Aramaic] [ar: ‎נ‎ק‎א‎] [freq. 45] (vf:
Paal, Niphal, Piel) |kjv:
unpunished, guiltless, innocent,
clear, cleanse, free, acquit,
altogether, cut off, blameless,
pure| {str: 5343, 5352}

J) ‎נ‎ו‎ק‎ (‎נ‎ו‎ק‎ NWQ) ac: **Suckle** co:
Breast ab: ?

V) ‍ＹＬ (נוק NWQ) — **Suckle:**
[freq. 1] (vf: Hiphil) |kjv: nurse|
{str: 5134}

L) ‍ＬＹＬ (ינק YNQ) ac: **Suckle** co:
Sapling ab: **?**

V) ‍ＬＹＬ (ינק Y-NQ) —
Suckle: [freq. 32] (vf: Paal,
Hiphil, Participle) |kjv: suck,
nurse, suckling, milch, mother|
{str: 3243}

b^(f¹) ‍Ｙ‍ＬＹＬ (יניקה Y-NY-
QH) — **Sapling:** A sucking
branch. [freq. 1] |kjv: twig| {str:
3242}

g^(m) ‍ＹＬＹＬ (יונק YW-NQ) —
Sapling: A sucking branch.
[freq. 1] |kjv: plant| {str: 3126}

g^(f²) ‍ＴＹＬＹＬ (יונקת YW-N-QT)
— **Sapling:** A sucking branch.
[freq. 6] |kjv: branch, twig| {str:
3127}

~~~~~~~~~~

1319) ‍ＮＬ (נר NR) ac: **Plow** co: **Light**
ab: **?:** The pictograph ‍ל is a picture of a
seed, the ‍Ｎ is a picture of the head of a
man representing the top or beginning of
something. Combined these mean "seed
beginning". Rains in the mountainous
areas cause a flooding of the rivers. The
rivers swell causing the water to flood the
land next to the river. This is the only
water that the land will see and is
necessary for crop production. After the
flood season, the land is plowed by the
use of a plow attached to the yoke of the
oxen. The surface of the soil is dry but,
when the soil is turned up it glistens in the
sun from the water remaining in the soil.
This water is necessary for the seed to
begin germination.

A) ‍ＮＬ (נר NR) ac: **?** co: **Lamp** ab:
?: An oil filled container with a wick
that gives off light.

N^(m) ‍ＮＬ (נר NR) — **Lamp:**
[ms: ניר] [freq. 48] |kjv: lamp,
candle, light| {str: 5216}

D) ‍ＮＲＬ (נאר NAR) ac: **Reject** co:
? ab: **?:** [Unknown connection to
root]

V) ‍ＮＲＬ (נאר N-AR) —
Reject: [freq. 2] (vf: Piel) |kjv:
void, abhor| {str: 5010}

G) ‍ＮＲＬ (נהר NHR) ac: **Flow** co:
River ab: **?:** The life giving water
that washes over the soil.

V) ‍ＮＲＬ (נהר N-HR) — **I.**
Flow: From the flowing of a
river. **II. Bright:** From the
glistening water as it flows.
[freq. 6] (vf: Paal) |kjv: flow,
lighten| {str: 5102}

N^(m) ‍ＮＲＬ (נהר N-HR) —
River: [Hebrew and Aramaic]
[freq. 135] |kjv: river, stream,
flood| {str: 5103, 5104}

N^(f¹) ‍ＮＲＲＬ (נהרה NH-RH) —
Light: [freq. 1] |kjv: light| {str:
5105}

b^(m) ‍ＮＲＬ (נהיר N-HYR) —
Enlightenment: One having the
light of wisdom. [Aramaic only]
[df: נהירו] [freq. 3] |kjv: light|
{str: 5094}

h^(f¹) ‍ＭＮＲＲＬ (מנהרה MN-H-
RH) — **Ravine:** As cut by the
flowing of water. [freq. 1] |kjv:
den| {str: 4492}

J) ‍ＮＹＬ (נור NWR) ac: **?** co: **Lamp**
ab: **?**

N^(f) ‍ＮＹＬ (נור NWR) — **Fire:**
[Aramaic only] [freq. 17] |kjv:
fiery, fire| {str: 5135}

190

a^m) מנור (M-NWR) — **Yoke:** A type of yoke used by a weaver. [freq. 4] |kjv: beam| {str: 4500}

i^m) תנור (T-NWR) — **Oven:** As a lamp for cooking. [freq. 15] |kjv: oven, furnace| {str: 8574}

k^{fl}) מנורה (M-NW-RH) — **Lamp:** [ms: מנרה] [freq. 40] |kjv: candlestick| {str: 4501}

M) ניר (NYR) ac: **Plow** co: ? ab: ?

  V) ניר (NYR) — **Plow:** [freq. 2] (vf: Paal) |kjv: break up| {str: 5214}

  N^m) ניר (NYR) — **Plowing:** [ms: נר] [freq. 4] |kjv: fallow, tillage, plowing| {str: 5215}

Adopted Roots;
2124   Pluck, Music, Melody
2270   שׁל   Harp

1320) נשׁ (NSh) ac: **Loan** co: **Debt** ab: **Deception:** The pictograph ל is a picture of a seed representing continuance, the שׁ is a picture of teeth representing pressure. Combined these mean "continual pressing". An imposition such as a debt or deception which causes oppression. (eng: gnash)

  A) נשׁ (NSh) ac: ? co: **Debt** ab: ?

    f^m) נשׁי (N-ShY) — **Debt:** [freq. 1] |kjv: debt| {str: 5386}

  E) נשׁא (NShA) ac: ? co: **Debt** ab: **Deception**

    V) נשׁא (N-ShA) — **I. Deceive: II. Debt:** [freq. 20] (vf: Paal, Niphal, Hiphil, Participle) |kjv: deceive, beguile, seize| {str: 5377, 5378}

    a^m) מנשׁא (MN-ShA) — **Interest:** [df: משא] [freq. 2] |kjv: usury| {str: 4855}

    a^{fl}) מנשׁאה (MN-Sh-AH) — **Loan:** [df: משאה] [freq. 2] |kjv: thing, debt| {str: 4859}

    aj^m) מנשׁאון (M-NSh-AWN) — **Loan:** [df: משאון] [freq. 1] |kjv: deceit| {str: 4860}

H) נשׁה (NShH) ac: **Forget** co: ? ab: ?: The removal of a debt through payment, forgetting or forgiving.

  V) נשׁה (N-ShH) — **I. Forget: II. Loan:** [freq. 19] (vf: Paal, Niphal, Hiphil, Piel, Participle) |kjv: forget, deprive, exact, lend, creditor, extortioner, usury| {str: 5382, 5383}

  N^m) נשׁה (N-ShH) — **Hip:** [Unknown connection to root] [freq. 2] |kjv: shrank| {str: 5384}

  a^m) מנשׁה (MN-ShH) — **Loan:** [df: משה] [freq. 1] |kjv: credit| {str: 4874}

  f^{fl}) נשׁיה (NSh-YH) — **Forgetfulness:** [freq. 1] |kjv: forgetfulness| {str: 5388}

J) נושׁ (NWSh) ac: **Despair** co: ? ab: ?

  V) נושׁ (NWSh) — **Despair:** [freq. 1] (vf: Paal) |kjv: heaviness| {str: 5136}

1321) נת (NT) ac: **Remove** co: ? ab: ?

Adopted Roots;

2396	†ﬦﬤ	Descend
2452	ﬡ†ﬤ	Break
2453	⊙†ﬤ	Break
2454	ﬡ†ﬤ	Break
2455	ﬤ†ﬤ	Draw, Eruption
2456	ﬕ†ﬤ	Pluck
2457	ﬨ†ﬤ	Release, Soda

~~~~~~~~~~

1322) ﬤﬤ (נע NGh) ac: **Shake** co: **Rattle** ab: ?: (eng: wag - with the removal of n)

A) ﬤﬤ (נע NGh) ac: **?** co: **Rattle** ab: ?: A musical instrument that is shaken.

kl[m]) ﬤﬤﬤﬤﬥ (מנענע MN-Gh-NGh) — **Rattle:** [freq. 1] |kjv: cornet| {str: 4517}

J) ﬤﬤﬤ (נוע NWGh) ac: **Shake** co: ? ab: ?

V) ﬤﬤﬤ (נוע NWGh) — **Shake:** To wag or shake back and forth or up and down. Also a wandering as wagging about. [freq. 42] (vf: Paal, Niphal, Hiphil, Participle) |kjv: shake, wander, move, promote fugitive sift, stagger, wag| {str: 5128}

Adopted Roots;

2458	ﬤﬤﬤ	Shake

~~~~~~~~~~

Sin

1323) 𝓎⪦ (אס SA) ac: **Lift** co: **Height** ab: ?

A) 𝓎⪦ (אס SA) ac: **Lift** co: ? ab: ?

N^(f1)) ⼂𝓎⪦ (סאה S-AH) — **Seah:** A standard of measure. [freq. 9] |kjv: measure| {str: 5429}

N^(f2)) ✝𝓎⪦ (סאת S-AT) — **Elevation:** [df: שׂאת] [freq. 14] |kjv: rising, dignity, excellency, accepted, highness, raise| {str: 7613}

I^(f1)) ⼂𝓎⪦𝓎⪦ (סאסאה SA-S-AH) — **Measure:** [Unknown connection to root] [freq. 1] |kjv: measure| {str: 5432}

J) 𝓎Y⪦ (סוא SWA) ac: **Lift** co: ? ab: ?

N^m) 𝓎Y⪦ (אוס SWA) — **Lift:** [df: שׂוא] [freq. 1] |kjv: arise| {str: 7721}

M) 𝓎⼂⪦ (סיא SYA) ac: ? co: **Height** ab: ?

N^m) 𝓎⼂⪦ (סיא SYA) — **Height:** [df: שׂיא] [freq. 1] |kjv: excellency| {str: 7863}

1324) ⼍⪦ (סב SB) ac: **Turn** co: **Dizzy** ab: ?: The pictograph ⪦ is a picture of a thorn representing a turning, the ⼍ is a picture of a tent or what is inside. Combined these mean "turning of the inside". One drunk from strong drink, turns from dizziness. The old, gray headed ones, easily become dizzy.

A) ⼍⪦ (סב SB) ac: **Turn** co: ? ab: ?

b^(f1)) ⼂⼍⼔⪦ (סיבה SY-BH) — **Turn:** [freq. 1] |kjv: cause| {str: 5438}

k^m) ⼍⪦ᴍ (מסב M-SB) — **Around:** [freq. 5] |kjv: round, compass, table| {str: 4524}

B) ⼍⼍⪦ (סבב SBB) ac: **Surround** co: ? ab: ?

V) ⼍⼍⪦ (סבב S-BB) — **Surround:** To be around something. [freq. 154] (vf: Paal, Niphal, Hiphil, Hophal, Piel) |kjv: about, surround, turn, remove, return, round, side, turn, beset, driven| {str: 5437}

b^m) ⼍⼔⼍⪦ (סביב S-BYB) — **Around:** [freq. 24] |kjv: round about, side, compass, circuit| {str: 5439}

b^(f1)) ⼂⼍⼔⼍⪦ (סביבה S-BY-BH) — **Around:** [freq. 308] |kjv: round about| {str: 5439}

d^m) ⼍Y⼍⪦ (סבוב S-BWB) — **Fly:** A flying insects that flies around. [df: זבוב] [freq. 2] |kjv: fly| {str: 2070}

E) 𝓎⼍⪦ (סבא SBA) ac: **Drink** co: **Drink** ab: ?: An alcoholic beverage from its ability to make one drunk and dizzy. A turning around from dizziness.

V) 𝓎⼍⪦ (סבא S-BA) — **Drink:** To drink strong drink that can cause intoxication. [freq. 6] (vf: Paal, Participle) |kjv: drunkard, winebibber, fill, drunken| {str: 5433}

g^m) 𝔶ⴽⴰⵣⴻ (סובא SW-BA) — **Drink:** [ms: סבא] [freq. 3] |kjv: wine, drink, drunken| {str: 5435}

L) ⵣⴻⵡ (יסב YSB) ac: **Enclose** co: **Around** ab: ?

a^m) ⵣⴻⵢⵡ (מוסב MW-SB) — **Encompass:** A place that surrounds. [freq. 1] |kjv: winding| {str: 4141}

a^fl) ⵣⴻⵢⵡ (מוסבה MW-S-BH) — **Enclose:** What is surrounded. [ms: מסבה] [freq. 5] |kjv: inclose, set, change, turn| {str: 4142}

M) ⵣⴽⴻ (סיב SYB) ac: ? co: **Gray** ab: **Age:** The hair color of those who are old, ones who easily become dizzy.

V) ⵣⴽⴻ (סיב SYB) — **Age:** To be of old age and gray hair. [Hebrew and Aramaic] [df: שׂיב] [freq. 7] (vf: Paal) |kjv: grayhead, elder| {str: 7867, 7868}

N^m) ⵣⴽⴻ (סיב SYB) — **Age:** [df: שׂיב] [freq. 1] |kjv: age| {str: 7869}

N^fl) ⵣⴽⴻ (סיבה SY-BH) — **Gray:** One who has gray hair from old age. [df: שׂיבה] [freq. 19] |kjv: old age, gray hair, hoar head, grayheaded, hoary| {str: 7872}

Adopted Roots;
2409 ⵣⴻⵍ Turn

~~~~~~~~~

1325) ⴽⴻ (סג SG) ac: **Turn** co: ? ab: **Increase:** The pictograph ⴻ is a picture of a thorn representing a turning, the ⴽ is a picture of a foot. Combined these mean

"turning of the foot". To turn around or change directions.

E) 𝔶ⴽⴻ (סנא SGA) ac: **Increase** co: **Large** ab: **Increase:** [Unknown connection to root]

V) 𝔶ⴽⴻ (סנא S-GA) — **Increase:** [Hebrew and Aramaic] [df: שׂנא] [freq. 5] (vf: Hiphil) |kjv: increase, magnify, grow, multiply| {str: 7679, 7680}

b^m) 𝔶⫯ⴽⴻ (סניא S-GYA) — **Large:** A greatness in size or stature. [Hebrew and Aramaic] [df: שׂגיא] [freq. 15] |kjv: great, excellent, much, great, very, exceeding, sore| {str: 7689, 7690}

H) ⵣⴽⴻ (סנה SGH) ac: ? co: ? ab: **Increase:** [Unknown connection to root]

V) ⵣⴽⴻ (סנה S-GH) — **Increase:** [df: שׂגה] [freq. 4] (vf: Paal, Hiphil) |kjv: grow, increase| {str: 7685}

J) ⵍⵢⴻ (סוג SWG) ac: **Turn** co: ? ab: ?

V) ⵍⵢⴻ (סוג SWG) — **Turn:** To turn or change directions, either physically or mentally. [df: שׂוג] [freq. 17] (vf: Paal, Niphal, Hiphil, Pilpel, Participle) |kjv: turn, back, backslider, drive| {str: 5472, 5473, 7734, 7735}

M) ⵍⴽⴻ (סיג SYG) ac: **Refuse** co: ? ab: ?

N^m) ⵍⴽⴻ (סיג SYG) — I. **Dross:** The impurities as scum or dregs that are formed on the surface of molten metals. [df: סוג] II. **Turn:** [df: שׂיג] [freq. 9] |kjv: dross, pursuing| {str: 5509, 7873}

194

Adopted Roots;
2410 Ḻ✦ʾ   Move
~~~~~~~~~~

1326) ✦ᵤ (סד SD) ac: **Level** co: **Field** ab: **?**: A level piece of ground for planting crops or setting up tents or structures. (eng: sod)

A) ✦ᵤ (סד SD) ac: **Level** co: **Field** ab: **?**

Nᵐ) ✦ᵤ (סד SD) — **Stocks:** A level beam for holding the feet prisoners. [freq. 2] |kjv: stocks| {str: 5465}

aᵐ) ᴹ✦ᵤ (מסד MS-D) — **Foundation:** A level place. [freq. 1] |kjv: foundation| {str: 4527}

pᶠˡ) 🌳ᴹ✦ᵤ (סדמה SD-MH) — **Field:** A level place. [df: שרמה] [freq. 7] |kjv: field, blast| {str: 7709, 8309}

sᵐ) ⅃ᵤ✦ᵤ (סדין S-DYN) — **Sheet:** As a level garment when laid out. [freq. 4] |kjv: sheet, fine linen| {str: 5466}

B) ✦ᵤᵤ (סדד SDD) ac: **Harrow** co: **Field** ab: **?**: A level piece of ground.

V) ✦ᵤᵤ (סדד S-DD) — **Harrow:** To level a field by using a harrow. [df: שדד] [freq. 3] (vf: Piel) |kjv: harrow, break clods| {str: 7702}

G) ✦🌳ᵤ (סהד SHD) ac: **?** co: **?** ab: **?**: **Testimony:** A record that lays a foundation of truth about an event.

Nᵐ) ✦🌳ᵤ (סהד S-HD) — **Testimony:** [df: שהד] [freq. 1] |kjv: record| {str: 7717}

H) 🌳ᵤ✦ (סדה SDH) ac: **?** co: **Field** ab: **: :** A level plot of ground.

Nᵐ) 🌳ᵤ✦ (סדה S-DH) — **Field:** [df: שדי שדה] [freq. 333] |kjv: field, country, land, wild, ground, soil| {str: 7704}

J) ᵤY✦ (סוד SWD) ac: **?** co: **Counsel** ab: **?**: A group of elders of the tribe who sit in counsel as the foundation to the tribe.

Nᵐ) ᵤY✦ (סוד SWD) — **Counsel:** An assembly of persons who counsel another or a people. [freq. 21] |kjv: secret, counsel, assembly, inward| {str: 5475}

L) ✦ᵤ⅃ (יסד YSD) ac: **?** co: **Foundation** ab: **?**: The foundation of a place such as of a building, time as the beginning, or a group as the elders of the tribe who sit in counsel.

V) ✦ᵤ⅃ (יסד Y-SD) — **Found:** To lay a foundation of a house, place or plan. [freq. 42] (vf: Paal, Niphal, Hophal, Pual, Piel) |kjv: foundation, lay, founded, ordain, counsel, establish, appoint, instruct, set, sure| {str: 3245}

aᵐ) ✦ᵤYᴹ (מוסד MW-SD) — **Foundation:** A level place for building a house. [freq. 5] |kjv: foundation| {str: 4143, 4144}

aᶠˡ) 🌳ᵤ✦ᵤYᴹ (מוסדה MW-S-DH) — **Foundation:** [ms: מסדה] [freq. 11] |kjv: foundation, grounded| {str: 4145, 4146}

cᶠ) ᵤY✦⅃ (יסוד Y-SWD) — **Foundation:** [ms: יסד] [freq. 20] |kjv: foundation, bottom, repairing| {str: 3247}

d^{m}) (יסוד Y-SWD) — **Begin:** A foundation to an activity. [ms: יסד] [freq. 1] |kjv: began| {str: 3246}

d^{f1}) (יסודה Y-SW-DH) — **Foundation:** A city or place that has been founded. [freq. 1] |kjv: foundation| {str: 3248}

ko^{f1}) (מיוסדה M-YWS-DH) — **Foundation:** [freq. 1] |kjv: foundation| {str: 4328}

M) (סיד SYD) ac: **?** co: **Plaster** ab: **?:** A limestone plaster is made for the floor of buildings to form a smooth and level surface.

V) (סיד SYD) — **Plaster:** [df: שיד] [freq. 2] (vf: Paal) |kjv: plaister| {str: 7874}

N^{m}) (סיד SYD) — **Lime:** A chalky white powder used for making plaster. [df: שיד] [freq. 4] |kjv: plaster, lime| {str: 7875}

~~~~~~~~~~~~

1327) (סה SH) ac: **?** co: **Sheep** ab: **?**

A) (סה SH) ac: **?** co: **Sheep** ab: **?**

N^{m}) (סה SH) — **Sheep:** [df: זה שה שי] [freq. 47] |kjv: lamb, sheep, cattle, ewe| {str: 2089, 7716}

J) (סוה SWH) ac: **?** co: **Veil** ab: **?:** [Unknown connection to root]

a^{m}) (מסוה M-SWH) — **Veil:** [freq. 3] |kjv: vail| {str: 4533}

~~~~~~~~~~~~

1328) (סו SW) ac: **?** co: **?** ab: **?**

~~~~~~~~~~~~

1329) (סז SZ) ac: **?** co: **?** ab: **?**

~~~~~~~~~~~~

1330) (סח SHh) ac: **Sweep** co: **?** ab: **?**

A) (סח SHh) ac: **Sweep** co: **?** ab: **?**

N^{m}) (סח SHh) — **Meditate:** A sweeping away in thought. [df: שח] [freq. 1] |kjv: thought| {str: 7808}

f^{m}) (סחי S-HhY) — **Rubbish:** What is swept away. [freq. 1] |kjv: offscouring| {str: 5501}

H) (סחה SHhH) ac: **Sweep** co: **?** ab: **?**

V) (סחה S-HhH) — **Sweep:** Sweep. [df: שחה] [freq. 4] (vf: Paal, Hiphil, Piel, Participle) |kjv: swim, scrape| {str: 5500, 7811}

J) (סוח SWHh) ac: **Meditate** co: **?** ab: **?**

V) (סוח SWHh) — **Meditate:** A sweeping away in thought. [df: שוח] [freq. 1] (vf: Paal) |kjv: meditate| {str: 7742}

N^{f1}) (סוחה SW-HhH) — **Rubbish:** What is swept away. [freq. 1] |kjv: torn| {str: 5478}

K) (סחו SHhW) ac: **Swim** co: **?** ab: **?:** The sweeping of the arms in water.

N^{m}) (סחו S-HhW) — **Swim:** [df: שחו] [freq. 1] |kjv: swim| {str: 7813}

M) (סיח SYHh) ac: **Meditate** co: **?** ab: **?**

V) (סיח SYHh) — **Meditate:** A sweeping away in

thougt. [df: שִׁיחַ] [freq. 20] (vf: Paal) |kjv: talk, meditate, speak, complain, pray, commune, muse, declare| {str: 7878}

N^m) סיח (שׁיח SYHh) — I. **Meditating:** A sweeping away in thought. [df: שִׁיחַ] II. **Bush:** As sweeping in the wind. [freq. 18] |kjv: complaint, meditation, prayer, talking, communication, babbling| {str: 7879, 7880}

N^{f1}) סיחה (שׁיחה SY-HhH) — **Meditation:** A sweeping away in thought. [df: שִׁיחה] [freq. 3] |kjv: meditation, prayer| {str: 7881}

1331) ⊗⪥ (סט STh) ac: **Turn** co: ? ab: ?: The pictograph ⪥ is a picture of a thorn representing a turning, the ⊗ is a picture of a round basket. Combined these mean "turn around".

A) ⊗⪥ (סט STh) ac: **Turn** co: **Rebel** ab: ?: One who has turned away.

N^m) ⊗⪥ (סט STh) — **Rebel:** [df: שׂט] [freq. 1] |kjv: revolter| {str: 7846}

H) ⪦⊗⪥ (סטה SThH) ac: **Turn** co: ? ab: ?

V) ⪦⊗⪥ (סטה S-ThH) — **Turn:** To turn aside or away. [df: שׂטה] [freq. 6] (vf: Paal) |kjv: aside, turn, decline| {str: 7847}

J) ⊗Y⪥ (סוט SWTh) ac: **Turn** co: ? ab: ?

V) ⊗Y⪥ (סוט SWTh) — **Turn:** To turn aside or away. [df: שׂוט] [freq. 2] (vf: Paal, Participle) |kjv: turn| {str: 7750}

Adopted Roots;
2474 ᴍᴍ⊗⪥ Hate
2475 ↖⊗⪥ Oppose, Opponent

1332) ↗⪥ (סי SY) ac: ? co: ? ab: ?

1333) �459⪥ (סך SK) ac: **Cover** co: **Booth** ab: ?: The pictograph ⪥ is a picture of a thorn representing protection, the �459 is a picture of the palm of the hand representing a covering. Combined these mean "protective covering". The watcher over the crops, flock or herd, would construct a covering (booth) as a shelter from the sun, wind or rain. These coverings were often constructed on an elevated position, and from materials readily available such as bushes, thorns and small trees. (eng: shack - with the exchange of the s and sh)

A) �459⪥ (סך SK) ac: **Cover** co: **Booth** ab: ?: A covering, hedge or thicket of thorns or bushes for protection from the elements or predators.

N^m) �459⪥ (סך SK) — I. **Booth:** II. **Thorn:** [df: שׂך] [freq. 2] |kjv: multitude, prick| {str: 5519, 7899}

a^m) �459⪥ᴍᴍ (מסך MS-K) — **Covering:** In the sense of a booth as a covering. [freq. 25] |kjv: hanging, covering, curtain| {str: 4539}

s^m) ↖⪽459⪥ (סכין S-KYN) — **Knife:** A sharp point like a thorn. [df: שׂכין] [freq. 1] |kjv: knife| {str: 7915}

B) 459459⪥ (סכך SKK) ac: **Cover** co: **Hedge** ab: ?: The intertwining branches of thorn bushes for making a defensive wall.

V) 𐤔𐤔𐤀 (סכך S-KK) —
Hedge: To surround with a wall of protection or covering. [df: 𐤔𐤊ך] [freq. 23] (vf: Paal, Hiphil, Pilpel, Participle) |kjv: cover, covering, defense, defend, hedge, join, set, shut| {str: 5526}

J) 𐤔𐤉𐤀 (סוך SWK) ac: **Cover** co: **Booth** ab: **?:** The booth is a covering.

V) 𐤔𐤉𐤀 (סוך SWK) — **Hedge:** To surround as hedge of protection. [df: שׂוך] [freq. 3] (vf: Paal) |kjv: hedge, fence| {str: 7753}

N^m) 𐤔𐤉𐤀 (סוך SWK) — **I. Booth:** A dwelling place. [ms: סך] [df: שׂך] **II. Branch:** As used for making booths. [df: שׂוך] [freq. 5] |kjv: tabernacle, den, pavilion, covert, bough| {str: 5520, 7900}

N^f1) 𐤔𐤉𐤀 (סוכה SW-KH) — **I. Booth:** A dwelling place. [ms: סכה] **II. Harpoon:** As a barbed thorn. [df: שׂכה] **III. Branch:** Used for building a booth. [df: שׂוכה] [freq. 34] |kjv: tabernacle, booth, pavilion, cottage, covert, tent, branch| {str: 5521, 7754, 7905}

k^fl) 𐤔𐤉𐤀𐤌 (מסוכה M-SW-KH) — **Hedge:** As a wall of thorns. [ms: מסכה] [df: משׂוכה משׂכה] [freq. 4] |kjv: hedge, covering| {str: 4534, 4540, 4881}

L) 𐤔𐤉𐤀 (יסך YSK) ac: **?** co: **Booth** ab: **?**

a^m) 𐤔𐤀𐤉𐤌 (מוסך MW-SK) — **Booth:** [freq. 2] |kjv: covert| {str: 4329}

M) 𐤔𐤀𐤉 (סיך SYK) ac: **?** co: **Booth** ab: **?**

N^f3) 𐤔𐤉𐤀𐤕 (סיכות SY-KWT) — **Booth:** [ms: סכות] [freq. 1] |kjv: tabernacle| {str: 5522}

N) 𐤔𐤉𐤀 (סכי SKY) ac: **Cover** co: **?** ab: **?**

d^m) 𐤔𐤉𐤀 (סכוי S-KWY) — **Covering:** [df: שׂכוי] [freq. 1] |kjv: heart| {str: 7907}

Adopted Roots;

2182	𐤔𐤀𐤌	Withhold
2323	𐤔𐤀𐤀	Chamber
2467	𐤔𐤋𐤀	Shut, Cage
2478	𐤋𐤔𐤀	Benefit
2479	𐤔𐤔𐤀	Hire, Wage
2838	𐤋𐤔𐤀	Dwell, Dwelling

1334) 𐤋𐤀 (סל SL) ac: **Lift** co: **Basket** ab: **Compare**

A) 𐤋𐤀 (סל SL) ac: **?** co: **Basket** ab: **?:** Carried by lifting it up on the head.

N^m) 𐤋𐤀 (סל SL) — **Basket:** [freq. 15] |kjv: basket| {str: 5536}

I^fl) 𐤔𐤋𐤀𐤋𐤀 (סלסלה SL-S-LH) — **Basket:** [freq. 1] |kjv: basket| {str: 5552}

B) 𐤋𐤋𐤀 (סלל SLL) ac: **Lift** co: **High** ab: **?**

V) 𐤋𐤋𐤀 (סלל S-LL) — **Lift:** [freq. 12] (vf: Paal, Pilpel) |kjv: cast, raise, exalt, extol, plain| {str: 5549}

g^fl) 𐤔𐤋𐤋𐤀 (סוללה SW-L-LH) — **Bank:** A raised mound of soil for defenses. [ms: סללה] [freq. 11] |kjv: mount, bank| {str: 5550}

ad^m) 𐤋𐤉𐤋𐤀𐤌 (מסלול MS-LWL) — **Highway:** A road

constructed above the surrounding area. [freq. 1] |kjv: highway| {str: 4547}

E) ⵗⵘⵉ⧫ (סלא SLA) ac: **Compare** co: ? ab: ?: [Unknown connection to root]

V) ⵗⵘⵉ⧫ (סלא S-LA) — **Compare:** [freq. 1] (vf: Pual, Participle) |kjv: comparable| {str: 5537}

H) ⵝⵘⵉ⧫ (סלה SLH) ac: **Lift** co: ? ab: ?

V) ⵝⵘⵉ⧫ (סלה S-LH) — **Lift:** To lift up as something of value or to be thrown away. [freq. 4] (vf: Paal, Pual, Piel) |kjv: value, trodden| {str: 5541}

N[m]**)** ⵝⵘⵉ⧫ (סלה S-LH) — **Selah:** A musical term possibly a lifting of the sound. [freq. 74] |kjv: selah| {str: 5542}

J) ⵘⵉⵉ⧫ (סול SWL) ac: ? co: **Ladder** ab: ?

N[f2]**)** †ⵘⵉⵉ⧫ (סולת SW-LT) — **Flour:** [Unknown connection to root] [ms: סלת] [freq. 53] |kjv: flour| {str: 5560}

p[m]**)** ⵯⵘⵉⵉ⧫ (סולם SW-LM) — **Ladder:** Used to raise up. [ms: סלם] [freq. 1] |kjv: ladder| {str: 5551}

K) ⵉⵘⵉ⧫ (סלו SLW) ac: **Fly** co: ? ab: ?

N[f]**)** ⵉⵘⵉ⧫ (סלו S-LW) — **Quail:** A bird that lifts up quickly. [df: שליו שלו] [freq. 4] |kjv: quail| {str: 7958}

M) ⵘⵉⵉⵗ⧫ (סיל SYL) ac: **Lift** co: **Thorn** ab: ?

j[m]**)** ⵉⵉⵘⵉⵗ⧫ (סילון SY-LWN) — **Thorn:** [Unknown connection to root] [ms: סלון] [freq. 2] |kjv: brier, thorn| {str: 5544}

k[f1]**)** ⵝⵘⵉⵗ⧫ⵯ (מסילה M-SY-LH) — **Highway:** A road constructed above the surrounding area. [ms: מסלה] [freq. 27] |kjv: highway, causeway, path, way, course, terrace| {str: 4546}

Adopted Roots;

2460	ⵘⵟ⧫	Carry, Burden
2481	ⵟⵘ⧫	Lift
2482	ⵘⵘ⧫	Forgive
2483	ⵯⵘ⧫	Garment
2484	ⵔⵘ⧫	High, Cliff
2486	ⵗⵘ⧫	Ascend

~~~~~~~~~~

1335) ⵯ⧫ (סם SM) ac: **Place** co: **Store** ab: ?

B) ⵯⵯ⧫ (סמם SMM) ac: ? co: ? ab: ?: [Unknown meaning]

N[f4]**)** †ⵗⵯⵯ⧫ (סממית SM-MYT) — **Semamiyt:** An unknown animal. [freq. 1] |kjv: spider| {str: 8079}

C) ⵯ⧫ⵗ (אסם ASM) ac: ? co: **Storehouse** ab: ?: A storage facility for placing provisions.

N[m]**)** ⵯ⧫ⵗ (אסם A-SM) — **Storehouse:** [freq. 2] |kjv: storehouse| {str: 618}

J) ⵯⵉ⧫ (סום SWM) ac: **Place** co: ? ab: ?

V) ⵯⵉ⧫ (סום SWM) — **Place:** To set anything in a place. [Hebrew and Aramaic; A generic verb with a wide application meaning to set in place] [df: שום שים] [freq. 612] (vf: Paal, Hiphil, Hophal) |kjv: put, make, set, lay, appoint, give, consider, turn, brought, ordain, place, take, shew, regard, mark, dispose, care, command, give, name, have| {str: 7760, 7761}

L) ⋘⋇⅃ (םסי YSM) ac: **Place** co: ? ab: ?

    V) ⋘⋇⅃ (םסי Y-SM) — **Place:** To set anything in a place. [freq. 2] (vf: Paal) |kjv: put| {str: 3455}

Adopted Roots;
2488 ⋓⋘⋇ Support
2490 ⅃⋘⋇ Appoint
2895 ⋓⋘† Hold

~~~~~~~~~

1336) ⅃⋇ (ןס SN) ac: **Pierce** co: **Thorn** ab: **Hate:** The pictograph ⋇ is a picture of a thorn, the ⅃ is a picture of seed. Combined these mean "thorn seed". The thorn, the seed of a plant with small sharp points) cause one to turn directions to avoid them. (eng: sin)

    A) ⅃⋇ (ןס SN) ac: ? co: **Thorn** ab: ?

        N^m) ⅃⋇ (ןס SN) — **Thorn:** [df: ןצ] [freq. 2] |kjv: thorn| {str: 6791}

    B) ⅃⅃⋇ (ןנס SNN) ac: ? co: **Thorn** ab: ?

        b^m) ⅃⅃⋇ (ןינס S-NYN) — **Thorn:** [df: ןינצ ןנצ] [freq. 2] |kjv: thorn| {str: 6796}

    C) ⅃⋇⅄ (ןסא ASN) ac: ? co: ? ab: **Harm**

        c^m) ⅃⅄⋇⅄ (ןוסא A-SWN) — **Harm:** The pain from the thorn. [freq. 5] |kjv: mischief| {str: 611}

    D) ⅃⅄⋇ (ןאס SAN) ac: **Pierce** co: **Weapon** ab: ?

    V) ⅃⅄⋇ (ןאס S-AN) — **Pierce:** To pierce with a weapon. [freq. 1] (vf: Paal) |kjv: warrior| {str: 5431}

    c^m) ⅃⅄⋇ (ןואס S-AWN) — **Weapon:** A sharp weapon as a thorn. [freq. 1] |kjv: battle| {str: 5430}

    E) ⅄⅃⋇ (אנס SNA) ac: ? co: ? ab: **Hate:** Like a thorn, hate causes one to turn away from another.

    V) ⅄⅃⋇ (אנס S-NA) — **Hate:** [Hebrew and Aramaic] [df: אנש] [freq. 147] (vf: Paal, Niphal, Piel, Participle) |kjv: hate, enemy, foe, hateful| {str: 8130, 8131}

    N^fl) ⅏⅄⅃⋇ (האנס SN-AH) — **Hate:** [df: האנש] [freq. 16] |kjv: hatred, hated, hatefully| {str: 8135}

    b^m) ⅄⅃⋇ (אינס S-NYA) — **Hate:** [df: אינש] [freq. 1] |kjv: hated| {str: 8146}

    H) ⅏⅃⋇ (הנס SNH) ac: ? co: **Thorn** ab: ?

    N^m) ⅏⅃⋇ (הנס S-NH) — **Thorn bush:** [freq. 6] |kjv: bush| {str: 5572}

    M) ⅃⅏⋇ (ןיס SYN) ac: ? co: **Shield** ab: ?

    N^fl) ⅏⅃⅏⋇ (הניס SY-NH) — **Shield:** A protection against a weapon. [df: הנצ] [freq. 22] |kjv: shield, buckler, target, hook, cold| {str: 6793}

Adopted Roots;
2185 ⅃⋇⏀ Store, Treasure
2186 ⬦⋇⏀ Uncover
2853 ⏀⋘⏄ Guard, Brier, Custody

~~~~~~~~~

1337) ⪽⪽ (סס SS) ac: **Turn** co: **Moth** ab: **Joy**

A) ⪽⪽ (סס SS) ac: **?** co: **Moth** ab: **?**

N^m) ⪽⪽ (סס SS) — **Moth:** From its turning and twisting flight. [freq. 1] |kjv: worm| {str: 5580}

J) ⪽Y⪽ (סוס SWS) ac: **Turn** co: **Horse** ab: **joy**

V) ⪽Y⪽ (סוס SWS) — **I. Rejoice:** To turn around in joy. [df: שׂושׂ שׂישׂ שׂישׂ] **II. Swallow:** From its turning and twisting flight. **III. Rejoice:** As a dancing around in circles. [df: שׂושׂ] [freq. 27] (vf: Paal) |kjv: rejoice, glad, joy, mirth| {str: 7797}

N^m) ⪽Y⪽ (סוס SWS) — **I. Horse:** From its turning around in play. [ms: סס] **II. Swallow:** From its turning and twisting flight. **III. Rejoice:** As a dancing around in circles. [df: שׂושׂ] [freq. 140] |kjv: horse, crane, horseback, crane, rejoice, glad, joy, mirth| {str: 5483}

N^fl) ⪽⪽Y⪽ (סוסה SW-SH) — **Mare:** [freq. 1] |kjv: horse| {str: 5484}

a^m) ⪽Y⪽ᴧ (מסוס M-SWS) — **Joy:** As a dancing around in circles. [df: משׂושׂ] [freq. 17] |kjv: joy, mirth, rejoice| {str: 4885}

~~~~~~~~

1338) ⌒⪽ (עס SAh) ac: **?** co: **?** ab: **?**

~~~~~~~~

1339) ⌒⪽ (סף SP) ac: **Gather** co: **Lip** ab: **?**: The pictograph ⪽ is a picture of a thorn representing a turning, the ⌒ is a picture of a mouth. Combined these mean "turning mouth". The rim, or lips of the bowl, which circle around it. The bowl is used for gathering things together and for eating.

A) ⌒⪽ (סף SP) ac: **?** co: **Lip** ab: **?**

N^m) ⌒⪽ (סף SP) — **I. Bowl:** A container with a lip. **II. Threshold:** The lip of the door. [freq. 32] |kjv: door, threshold, bason, post, bowl, gate, cup| {str: 5592}

N^fl) ⪽⌒⪽ (ספה S-PH) — **Lip:** The lip or edge of something. Also language as spoken from the lips. [df: שׂפה שׂפת] [freq. 176] |kjv: lip, bank, brim, edge, language, speech, shore, brink, border, prating, vain| {str: 8193}

p^m) ᴧᴧ⌒⪽ (ספם S-PM) — **Lip:** [df: שׂפם] [freq. 5] |kjv: lip, beard| {str: 8222}

B) ⌒⌒⪽ (ספף SPP) ac: **?** co: **Door** ab: **?**: What stands at the lip of the door.

V) ⌒⌒⪽ (ספף S-PP) — **Door:** [freq. 1] (vf: Hitpael) |kjv: doorkeeper| {str: 5605}

C) ⌒⪽↳ (אסף ASP) ac: **Gather** co: **Store** ab: **?**: The gathering together of a group into a bowl. An assembly of people in a place.

V) ⌒⪽↳ (אסף A-SP) — **Gather:** [freq. 200] (vf: Paal, Niphal, Hitpael, Pual, Piel) |kjv: together, gather, assemble, rereward| {str: 622}

N^fl) ⪽⌒⪽↳ (אספה AS-PH) — **Gathered:** [freq. 1] |kjv: gathered| {str: 626}

b^m) ⌒↳⪽↳ (אסיף A-SYP) — **Gathering:** [ms: אסף] [freq. 2] |kjv: ingathering| {str: 614}

c^m) ⊙Y𐤀𐤂⳿ (אסוף A-SWP) —
Store: A place where stores are gathered together. [ms: אסף] [freq. 3] |kjv: threshold| {str: 624}

d^{fl}) 𐤁⊙Y𐤀𐤂⳿ (אסופה A-SW-PH) — **Assembly:** A gathering of people. [ms: אספה] [freq. 1] |kjv: assembly| {str: 627}

g^m) ⊙𐤀Y⳿𐤂 (אסף AW-SP) — **Gathering:** [ms: אסף] [freq. 3] |kjv: gathering| {str: 625}

I^m) ⊙𐤀⳿⊙𐤂⳿ (אספסף A-SP-SP) — **Assembly:** A gathering of people. [freq. 1] |kjv: multitude| {str: 628}

E) 𐤂⊙𐤀 (ספא SPA) ac: **?** co: **Feed** ab: **?**

hc^m) 𐤂⳿Y⊙𐤀ᴍ (מספוא MS-PWA) — **Feed:** A gathering of food. [freq. 5] |kjv: provender| {str: 4554}

H) 𐤁⊙𐤀 (ספה SPH) ac: **Consume** co: **Lip** ab: **?:** The edge of the mouth where food is gathered.

V) 𐤁⊙𐤀 (ספה S-PH) — **Consume:** To eat with the lips. [freq. 20] (vf: Paal, Niphal, Hiphil) |kjv: consume, destroy, add, perish, augment, heap, join| {str: 5595}

J) ⊙Y𐤀 (סוף SWP) ac: **Consume** co: **Reed** ab: **?:** Reeds and weeds (including papyrus) grow at the edge, or lip, of ponds and stream.

V) ⊙Y𐤀 (סוף SWP) — **Consume:** To eat with the lips. [Hebrew and Aramaic] [freq. 10] (vf: Paal, Hiphil) |kjv: consume, end, perish| {str: 5486, 5487}

N^m) ⊙Y𐤀 (סוף SWP) — I. **Reed:** He plants that grow at the edge, or lip, of a river or pond.

II. Edge: [Hebrew and Aramaic] [freq. 38] |kjv: flags, weeds, end, conclusion, hind| {str: 5488, 5490, 5491}

N^{fl}) 𐤁⊙Y𐤀 (סופה SW-PH) — **Whirlwind:** A circling wind that devours what is on the land in its mouth. [freq. 16] |kjv: whirlwind, storm, sea, tempest| {str: 5492}

L) ⊙𐤀ⳁ (יסף YSP) ac: **Add** co: **?** ab: **?:** An adding or augmenting to something by adding to it.

V) ⊙𐤀ⳁ (יסף Y-SP) — **Add:** [Hebrew and Aramaic] [freq. 44] (vf: Paal, Niphal, Hiphil, Hophal) |kjv: more, again, add, increase, also, exceed, put, further, henceforth, can, continue, give| {str: 3254, 3255}

Adopted Roots;

2500 𐤍⊙𐤀   Record, Scroll
~~~~~~~~~~~

1340) ⌒ᴧ𐤀 (סץ STs) ac: **?** co: **?** ab: **?**
~~~~~~~~~~~

1341) ⦁𐤀 (סק SQ) ac: **?** co: **Sack** ab: **?:** (eng: sack)

A) ⦁𐤀 (סק SQ) ac: **?** co: **Sack** ab: **?**

N^m) ⦁𐤀 (סק SQ) — **Sack:** [df: שק] [freq. 48] |kjv: sack, sackcloth| {str: 8242}
~~~~~~~~~~~

1342) 𐤍𐤀 (סר SR) ac: **Rule** co: **Ruler** ab: **Noble:** The pictograph 𐤀 is a picture of a thorn representing a turning, the 𐤍 is a picture of a head. Combined these mean "turn the head". The turning of the head to another direction. One who rules turns the people to his direction. The turning the head of the child or student into a particular direction.

A) ⟨ᕫ (סר SR) ac: **Turn** co: **Ruler** ab: **?:** The turning of another toward a direction.

N[m]) ⟨ᕫ (סר SR) — I. **Noble:** One who has authority. [df: שׂר] **II. Heavy:** The weight of responsibility on one in authority. [freq. 424] |kjv: prince, captain, chief, ruler, governor, keeper, principal, general, lord, heavy, sad| {str: 5620, 8269}

N[f1]) ⟨ᕫ (סרה S-RH) — I. **Noblewoman:** A female of authority. [df: שרה] **II. Turning:** Usually as a revolt. [freq. 13] |kjv: lady, princess, queen| {str: 5627, 8282}

h[f1]) ⟨ᕫᗰ (מסרה MS-RH) — **Government:** A body of people who turns the head of the people through power and legislation. [df: משׂרה] [freq. 2] |kjv: government| {str: 4951}

m[m]) ⟨ᕫ (סרן S-RN) — I. **Lord:** One who has authority. **II. Axle:** For the turning wheel. [freq. 22] |kjv: lord, axle| {str: 5633}

ac[m]) ⟨ᕫᗰ (מסור M-SWR) — **Saw:** An instrument that cuts with a back and forth action. [Unknown connection to root;] [freq. 1] |kjv: saw| {str: 4883}

B) ⟨ᕫ (סרר SRR) ac: **Rule** co: **?** ab: **?**

V) ⟨ᕫ (סרר S-RR) — I. **Rule:** To make others turn in the direction of the ruler. [df: שרר] **II. Turn:** To turn away from the

correct path toward another direction. [freq. 22] (vf: Paal) |kjv: rule, prince, altogether, rebellious, stubborn, revolter, revolting, backslide, away, withdrew| {str: 5637, 8323}

C) ⟨ᕫ⟩ (אסר ASR) ac: **Bind** co: **?** ab: **?:** The yoke is bound to the neck of the oxen and used by the driver to turn the head of the oxen. A yoke was also used for prisoners. A binding of someone or something to move it by force.

V) ⟨ᕫ⟩ (אסר A-SR) — **Bind:** [freq. 72] (vf: Paal, Niphal, Pual) |kjv: bind, prison, tie, prisoner| {str: 631}

N[m]) ⟨ᕫ⟩ (אסר A-SR) — **Decree:** A decree that binds others to the will of the ruler. [Aramaic only] [freq. 7] |kjv: decree| {str: 633}

b[m]) ⟨ᕫ⟩ (אסיר A-SYR) — **Prison:** On who is bound. [freq. 15] |kjv: prisoner, bound| {str: 615, 616}

c[m]) ⟨ᕫ⟩ (אסור A-SWR) — **Bonds:** A device for restraining a prisoner. [Hebrew and Aramaic] [freq. 6] |kjv: band, prison, imprisonment| {str: 612, 613}

e[m]) ⟨ᕫ⟩ (איסר AY-SR) — **Bond:** [ms: אסר] [freq. 11] |kjv: bond, binding| {str: 632}

D) ⟨⟩ᕫ (סאר SAR) ac: **Knead** co: **Bread** ab: **?:** The twisting and turning of the bread.

c[m]) ⟨⟩ᕫ (סאור S-AWR) — **Leaven:** [df: שאר] [freq. 5] |kjv: leaven| {str: 7603}

h[f2]) ⟨⟩ᕫᗰ (מסארת MS-A-RT) — **Kneading-bowl:** [df:

מ#שארת] [freq. 4] |kjv: kneadingtrough, store| {str: 4863}

G) סהר (סהר SHR) ac: ? co: Ornament ab: ?

N^m) סהר (סהר S-HR) — Round: Something that is round. [freq. 1] |kjv: round| {str: 5469}

j^m) סהרון (סהרון SH-RWN) — Ornament: A round object. [df: שהרן] [freq. 3] |kjv: ornament, moon| {str: 7720}

H) סרה (סרה SRH) ac: Turn co: ? ab: ?

V) סרה (סרה S-RH) — Turn: To turn toward another direction, usually in a negative sense. [df: שרה] [freq. 2] (vf: Paal) |kjv: revolt, rebellion, turn away, wrong, stroke| {str: 8280}

J) סור (סור SWR) ac: Rule co: ? ab: ?: One who turns the head of the people through power and legislation.

V) סור (סור SWR) — I. Remove: In the sense of turning something away. [df: שור] II. Rule: To turn the heads of the people. [freq. 305] (vf: Paal, Hiphil, Hophal) |kjv: away, depart, remove, aside, take, turn, take, go, put, eschew, reign, power, prince| {str: 5493, 7786, 7787}

N^m) סור (סור SWR) — Degenerate: Something that is turned away. [freq. 1] |kjv: degenerate| {str: 5494}

a^f2) מסורת (מסורת M-SW-RT) — Bond: What binds one to someone or something. [ms: מסרת] [freq. 1] |kjv: bond| {str: 4562}

k^f1) מסורה (מסורה M-SW-RH) — Quantity: A large amount. [Unknown connection to root;] [df: משורה] [freq. 4] |kjv: measure| {str: 4884}

L) יסר (יסר YSR) ac: Correct co: ? ab: Instruction: The turning the head, through instruction or force, of the child or student into a particular direction.

V) יסר (יסר Y-SR) — Correct: To make a change in direction through instruction or chastisement. [freq. 9] (vf: Paal, Niphal, Hiphil, Piel) |kjv: chastise, instruct, correct, taught, bound, punish, reform, reprove| {str: 3256}

a^m) מוסר (מוסר MW-SR) — I. Instruction: [ms: מסר] II. Bond: What binds and restricts. [freq. 62] |kjv: instruction, band, bond| {str: 4561, 4147, 4148}

c^m) יסור (יסור Y-SWR) — Reprover: As a turning. [freq. 1] |kjv: instruct| {str: 3250}

d^m) יסור (יסור Y-SWR) — Depart: As a turning. [freq. 1] |kjv: depart| {str: 3249}

M) סיר (סיר SYR) ac: ? co: Pot ab: ?: [Unknown connection to root;]

N^m) סיר (סיר SYR) — Pot: [freq. 34] |kjv: pot, caldron, thorn, pan| {str: 5518}

Adopted Roots;

2345	סרמ	Commit
2504	אסרג	Brier
2505	אסרל	Wrap, Branch
2506	אסרד	Remain, Remnant
2507	אסרמ	Exceed
2509	אסרש	Twist, Lace
2510	אסרא	Castrate, Eunuch

2511 ⊂𐤍𐤀 Exceed
2758 𐤋𐤈𐤍 Rule, Prince
2776 𐤋𐤀𐤍 Halter
3041 ⊓⊂𐤍𐤀
3023 𐤍𐤀⊂⊗

~~~~~~~~

1343) ⊔𐤓𐤀 (שׂס SSh) ac: ? co: ? ab: ?

~~~~~~~~

1344) ✝𐤀 (סת ST) ac: **Stir** co: ? ab: ?:
(eng: stir - with an added r)

J) ✝Y𐤀 (סות SWT) ac: **Stir** co: ? ab:
?

V) ✝Y𐤀 (סות SWT) — **Stir:**
[freq. 18] (vf: Hiphil) |kjv:
persuade, move, set, stir, away,
entice, provoke, remove| {str:
5496}

N^m) ✝Y𐤀 (סות SWT) —
Stirred: [freq. 1] |kjv: clothes|
{str: 5497}

K) Y✝𐤀 (סתו STW) ac: ? co: **Winter**
ab: ?

N^m) Y✝𐤀 (סתו S-TW) —
Winter: From a stirring of
winds. [freq. 1] |kjv: winter| {str:
5638}

~~~~~~~~

1345) 𐤀𐤀 (סע SGh) ac: ? co: **Storm** ab:
?: The original pictograph of the ⊂
represented chaos and storm.

H) 𐤔𐤀𐤀 (סעה SGhH) ac: ? co:
Storm ab: ?

V) 𐤔𐤀𐤀 (סעה S-GhH) —
Storm: [freq. 1] (vf: Paal) |kjv:
storm| {str: 5584}

Adopted Roots;
2517 𐤍𐤀𐤀   Storm, Horrible

~~~~~~~~

Ayin

1346) ⟩⊚ (עא AhA) ac: ? co: ? ab: ?

~~~~~~~~~

1347) ⊡⊚ (עב AhB) ac: ? co: ? ab: ?

A) ⊡⊚ (עב AhB) ac: ? co: **Beam** ab: ?

N^m) ⊡⊚ (עב AhB) — **Beam:** [freq. 3] |kjv: plank, beam| {str: 5646}

~~~~~~~~~

1348) ⌶⊚ (עג AhG) ac: **Bake** co: **Cake** ab: ?

A) ⌶⊚ (עג AhG) ac: ? co: **Cake** ab: ?: Cakes baked on hot stones.

N^{fl}) ⚓⌶⊚ (עגה Ah-GH) — **Cake:** [freq. 7] |kjv: cake| {str: 5692}

J) ⌶Y⊚ (עוג AhWG) ac: **Bake** co: **Cake** ab: ?: Cakes baked on hot stones.

V) ⌶Y⊚ (עוג AhWG) — **Bake:** [freq. 1] (vf: Paal) |kjv: bake| {str: 5746}

a^m) ⌶Y⊚ᴍ (מעוג M-AhWG) — **Cake:** [freq. 2] |kjv: cake, feast| {str: 4580}

~~~~~~~~~

1349) ⛝⊚ (עד AhD) ac: **Repeat** co: ? ab: **Witness:** The pictograph ⊚ is a picture of the eye, the ⛝ is a picture of the door. Combined these mean "see the door". As coming to a tent a tent of meeting and entering in. A place, time or event that is repeated again and again.

A) ⛝⊚ (עד AhD) ac: ? co: ? ab: **Witness:** An event or persons

testimony recounting another event or person.

N^f) ⛝⊚ (עד AhD) — **I. Witness: II. Again:** A repetition of time either definite or indefinite. [Hebrew and Aramaic] **III. Until:** A determinate period of time. [freq. 269] |kjv: witness, ever, everlasting, end, evermore, old, perpetually, by, as, when, how, yet, till, until, unto, for, to, but, on, within, filthy| {str: 1157, 5703, 5704, 5705, 5707, 5708}

N^{fl}) ⚓⛝⊚ (עדה Ah-DH) — **I. Company:** A group with a common testimony. **II. Witness:** [freq. 175] |kjv: congregation, company, assembly, multitude, people, swarm, testimony, witness| {str: 5712, 5713}

N^{f3}) ✝Y⛝⊚ (עדות Ah-DWT) — **Witness:** [freq. 59] |kjv: testimony, witness| {str: 5715}

f^m) ⟂⛝⊚ (עדי Ah-DY) — **Trappings:** Articles of dress or adornment that often witness to a persons position or rank. [freq. 13] |kjv: ornament, mouth| {str: 5716}

H) ⚓⛝⊚ (עדה AhDH) ac: **Adorn** co: **Trappings** ab: ?: An adornment for testifying to ones position, rank or authority.

V) ⚓⛝⊚ (עדה Ah-DH) — **I. Adorn:** To put on trappings which usually identify position or rank. [ar: עדא] **II. Remove:** [Unknown connection to root; Hebrew and Aramaic] [freq. 19] (vf: Paal, Hiphil) |kjv: deck, adorn, take, pass, depart, alter, took, pass, remove| {str: 5709, 5710}

J) ⵔⵢⵔ (עוד AhWD) ac: ? co: ? ab: **Witness:** The repeating of an account.

V) ⵔⵢⵔ (עוד AhWD) — **Witness:** [freq. 45] (vf: Paal, Hiphil, Hophal, Piel) |kjv: testify, protest, witness, record, charge, take, admonish| {str: 5749}

N^m) ⵔⵢⵔ (עוד AhWD) — **Again:** A repeating of something. [Hebrew and Aramaic] [ms: עד] [freq. 31] |kjv: again, more, while, longer, else, since, yet, still| {str: 5750, 5751}

i^fl) ⵯⵔⵢⵔⵔ (תעודה T-AhW-DH) — **Witness:** [freq. 3] |kjv: testimony| {str: 8584}

L) ⵔⵔⵢⵣ (יעד YAhD) ac: **Meet** co: **Appointment** ab: **?:** An appointed place, time or event that is repeated such as the monthly and yearly feasts.

V) ⵔⵔⵢⵣ (יעד Y-AhD) — **Meet:** A coming together as two or an assembly. [freq. 1] (vf: Paal, Niphal, Hiphil, Hophal) |kjv: meet, together, assemble, appoint, set, time, betroth, agree, gather| {str: 3259}

a^m) ⵔⵔⵢⵔ (מועד MW-AhD) — I. **Appointment:** A time that is repeated time after time. [ms: מעד] II. **Company:** A group that meet at specific times. [freq. 224] |kjv: congregation, feast, season, appointed, time, assembly, solemnity, solemn,

days, sign, synagogue| {str: 4150, 4151}

a^fl) ⵯⵔⵔⵢⵔ (מועדה MW-Ah-DH) — **Appointed:** A place appointed for as a witness. [freq. 1] |kjv: appointed| {str: 4152}

1350) ⵯⵔ (עה AhH) ac: ? co: ? ab: ?

1351) ⵢⵔ (עו AhW) ac: ? co: ? ab: ?

1352) ⵣⵔ (עז AhZ) ac: **Bold** co: ? ab: **Strong:** The pictograph ⵔ is a picture of the eye representing knowing, the ⵣ is a picture of cutting implement. Combined these mean "know a weapon".

A) ⵣⵔ (עז AhZ) ac: ? co: ? ab: **Strong**

N^m) ⵣⵔ (עז AhZ) — **Strong:** [freq. 23] |kjv: strong, fierce, mighty, power, greedy, roughly| {str: 5794}

B) ⵣⵣⵔ (עזז AhZZ) ac: ? co: ? ab: **Strong**

V) ⵣⵣⵔ (עזז Ah-ZZ) — **Strengthen:** To be made strong or hard. [freq. 12] (vf: Paal, Hiphil) |kjv: strengthen, prevail, strong, impudent, harden| {str: 5810}

d^m) ⵣⵢⵣⵔ (עזוז Ah-ZWZ) — **Strength:** [freq. 3] |kjv: strength, might| {str: 5807}

ed^m) ⵣⵢⵣⵣⵔ (עיזוז AhY-ZWZ) — **Strong:** [ms: עזוז] [freq. 2] |kjv: strong, power| {str: 5808}

J) ⵣⵢⵔ (עוז AhWZ) ac: **Gather** co: ? ab: **Strong:** A strong refuge as a place for making a firm and fierce stand.

V) ⌐Y⌒ (עוז AhWZ) — **Gather:** To gather together for a stronghold. [freq. 4] (vf: Hiphil) |kjv: gather, retire| {str: 5756}

N^m) ⌐Y⌒ (עוז AhWZ) — **Strength:** [ms: עז] [freq. 93] |kjv: strength, strong, power, might, boldness, loud, mighty| {str: 5797}

a^m) ⌐Y⌒ᴍ (מעוז M-AhWZ) — **Stronghold:** A place of strength such as a mountain, fort or rock. [freq. 37] |kjv: strength, strong, fortress, hold, forces, fort, rock, strengthen| {str: 4581}

L) ⌐⌒⅃ (יעז YAhZ) ac: **Bold** co: ? ab: **Strong:** A boldness through strength.

V) ⌐⌒⅃ (יעז Y-AhZ) — **Bold:** [freq. 1] (vf: Niphal, Participle) |kjv: fierce| {str: 3267}

~~~~~~~~~

1353) ᴍⱶ⌒ (עח AhHh) ac: ? co: ? ab: ?

~~~~~~~~~

1354) ⊗⌒ (עט AhTh) ac: **Wrap** co: **Bird of prey** ab: ?: The pictograph ⌒ is a picture of the eye, the ⊗ is a picture of a basket or other container. Combined these mean "see and contain". A bird of prey is able to see his prey from a great distance. He then drops down on its prey with the talons firmly surrounding the prey, crushing and suffocating it.

A) ⊗⌒ (עט AhTh) ac: ? co: **Talon** ab: ?: The pointed claws of a bird of prey.

N^m) ⊗⌒ (עט AhTh) — **I. Prey:** What is grabbed by the bird of prey. [df: עד] **II. Stylus:** A pointed stick used for writing in clay by pressing into the clay. [freq. 7] |kjv: prey, pen| {str: 5706, 5842}

H) ⚲⊗⌒ (עטה AhThH) ac: **Wrap** co: ? ab: ?: A tight wrapping around of something.

V) ⚲⊗⌒ (עטה Ah-ThH) — **Wrap:** To tightly wrap something up. [freq. 17] (vf: Paal, Hiphil, Participle) |kjv: cover, array, turn, clad, covering, fill, put| {str: 5844}

a^m) ⚲⊗⌒ᴍ (מעטה MAh-ThH) — **Wrap:** A garment that is wrapped around the body. [freq. 1] |kjv: garment| {str: 4594}

J) ⊗Y⌒ (עוט AhWTh) ac: **Wrap** co: ? ab: ?: Wrap.

a^m) ⊗Y⌒ᴍ (מעוט M-AhWTh) — **Wrap:** [ms: מעט] [freq. 1] |kjv: wrap| {str: 4593}

L) ⊗⌒⅃ (יעט YAhTh) ac: **Wrap** co: ? ab: ?: A tight wrapping around.

V) ⊗⌒⅃ (יעט Y-AhTh) — **Wrap:** [freq. 1] (vf: Paal) |kjv: cover| {str: 3271}

M) ⊗⅃⌒ (עיט AhYTh) ac: ? co: **Bird of prey** ab: ?

V) ⊗⅃⌒ (עיט AhYTh) — **Pounce:** The pouncing down on the prey by a bird of prey. [freq. 3] (vf: Paal) |kjv: fly, rail| {str: 5860}

N^m) ⊗⅃⌒ (עיט AhYTh) — **Bird of prey:** [freq. 8] |kjv: fowl, bird, ravenous| {str: 5861}

Adopted Roots;
2533 ⅂⌐⌒

208

2538 ⋒⊗⊚ Encircle, Wreath

1355) ⊶⊚ (עי AhY) ac: ? co: ? ab: ?

1356) �🗐⊚ (עך AhK) ac: ? co: **Heel** ab: ?: (eng: ankle)

Adopted Roots;
2108 🗐⊚ᛏ Extinguish
2128 🗐⊚ᴄ Extinguish
2348 🗐⊚ᴍ Crush
2540 ◀🗐⊚ Rattle, Anklet
2571 ◻᛫⊶⊚ Restrain, Heel
3043 ⋒◻🗐⊚ Mouse
3044 ᛞᛞ◻🗐⊚ Spider
3045 ◻ᛞᛞ🗐⊚
3046 ◻⋒᛫⊶⊚ Scorpion

1357) ∪⊚ (על AhL) ac: **Work** co: **Yoke** ab: ?: The pictograph ⊚ is a picture of they eye representing knowledge and experience, the ∪ is a picture of a shepherd staff or yoke. Combined these mean "experience the staff". The yoke, a staff is lifted over the shoulder, is attached to the oxen for performing work. (eng: collar - with the exchange of the sound of the ayin with the c and the additional r)

A) ∪⊚ (על AhL) ac: **Raise** co: ? ab: ?

N^m) ∪⊚ (על AhL) — **I. Above:** [df: עול] **II. Upon:** [Hebrew and Aramaic] [freq. 152] |kjv: above, high, upon, in, on, over, by, for, both, beyond, through, throughout, against, beside, forth, off, from| {str: 5920, 5921, 5922}

N^f1) ⫯∪⊚ (עלה Ah-LH) — **Rising:** A rising of smoke from a burnt offering. [Aramaic only] [ms: עלה] [ar: עלה] [freq. 1] |kjv: burn offering| {str: 5928}

N^f3) ᛏᴦ∪ᒪ (גלות G-LWT) — **Captivity:** A yoke was placed on captives to be taken back. [Hebrew and Aramaic] [freq. 19] |kjv: captivity, captive| {str: 1546, 1547}

a^m) ∪⊚ᴍ (מעל MAhL) — **Above:** [freq. 138] |kjv: above, upward, high, exceeding, upon, forward| {str: 4605}

a^f1) ⫯∪⊚ᴍ (מעלה MAh-LH) — **Ascent:** A place of straight or stepped incline. [freq. 47] |kjv: degree, steps, dial, by, come, story, up| {str: 4609}

f^m) ⊶∪⊚ (עלי Ah-LY) — **Pestle:** As lifted up then down to smash what is in the mortar. [freq. 1] |kjv: pestle| {str: 5940}

i^f1) ⫯∪⊚ᛏ (תעלה TAh-LH) — **Trench:** A watercourse that rises in elevation to bring down water from a higher source. [freq. 11] |kjv: conduit, trench, watercourse, healing, cured, river| {str: 8585}

k^m) ∪⊚ᴍ (מעל M-AhL) — **Rising:** [Aramaic only] [freq. 1] |kjv: down| {str: 4606}

p^m) ᴍᴍ∪⊚ (עלם Ah-LM) — **Youth:** A young male at the prime age for work. [freq. 2] |kjv: young, stripling| {str: 5958}

p^f1) ⫯ᴍᴍ∪⊚ (עלמה AhL-MH) — **Youth:** A young female at the prime age for work. [freq. 7] |kjv: virgin, maid, damsel| {str: 5959} fj^m) ‏עליון‎ (⌖𝖴ᴶᵧ⟋ AhL-YWN) — **High:** [Hebrew and Aramaic] [freq. 57] |kjv: high, upper, higher, highest, above, uppermost| {str: 5945, 5946}

rp^m) ‏עלום‎ (⌖𝖴ᵧᴍ Ah-LWM) — **Youth:** A young male at the prime age for work. [freq. 4] |kjv: youth| {str: 5934}

B) ‏עלל‎ (⌖𝖴𝖴 AhLL) ac: **Work** co: ? ab: ?: The yoke was listed up onto the shoulder of the oxen to perform work.

V) ‏עלל‎ (⌖𝖴𝖴 Ah-LL) — **Work:** To perform a work. To work over another as a mocking or abuse. [Hebrew and Aramaic] [freq. 23] (vf: Hitpael, Hophal) |kjv: glean, done, abuse, mock, affect, children, do, defiled, practice, wrought, bring, come, went| {str: 5953, 5954}

a^m) ‏מעלל‎ (⌖𝖴𝖴ᴍᴍ MAh-LL) — **Works:** [freq. 41] |kjv: doings, works, inventions, endeavors| {str: 4611}

b^m) ‏עליל‎ (⌖𝖴⟍𝖴 Ah-LYL) — **Furnace:** Used for working metals. [freq. 1] |kjv: furnace| {str: 5948}

b^fl) ‏עלילה‎ (⌖𝖴⟍𝖴⌖ Ah-LY-LH) — **Works:** [ms: ‏עללה‎] [freq. 24] |kjv: doing, works, deeds, occasions, actions, actions, acts, inventions| {str: 5949}

bf^fl) ‏עליליה‎ (⌖𝖴⟍𝖴⟍𝖴⌖ Ah-LYL-YH) — **Works:** [freq. 1] |kjv: work| {str: 5950}

id^m) ‏תעלול‎ (†⌖𝖴𝖴ᵧ⟋ TAh-LWL) — **Impulse:** A work performed without

consideration. [freq. 2] |kjv: babe, delusion| {str: 8586}

H) ‏עלה‎ (⌖𝖴⌖ AhLH) ac: **Lift** co: ? ab: ?: The lifting of the yoke onto the shoulder. One taken into exile is placed in the yoke for transport and the yoke of bondage. It was a common practice to strip the clothes off of those taken into exile.

V) ‏עלה‎ (⌖𝖴⌖ Ah-LH) — **I. Rise:** To go, come or bring oneself or something up. [Hebrew and Aramaic; A generic verb with a wide application meaning to lift up] [df: ‏נלה‎] [ar: ‏נלא‎] **II. Uncover:** As a lifting off of the cover. To be exposed from the removal of clothing. Also to reveal something by exposing it. [Hebrew and Aramaic] [df: ‏גלה‎ ‏גלא‎] [freq. 1087] (vf: Paal, Niphal, Hiphil, Hitpael, Hophal, Pual, Piel) |kjv: up, offer, come, bring, ascend, go, chew, offering, light, increase, burn, depart, put, spring, raise, break, exalt, uncover, discover, captive, carry away, reveal, open, captivity, show, remove, appear, brought, carry| {str: 1540, 1541, 5924, 5927}

N^m) ‏עלה‎ (⌖𝖴⌖ Ah-LH) — **Leaf:** As high in the tree. [freq. 18] |kjv: leaf, branch| {str: 5929}

a^m) ‏מעלה‎ (⌖𝖴⌖ᴍᴍ MAh-LH) — **Ascent:** A place of straight or stepped incline. [freq. 18] |kjv: up, ascent, cheifest, cliff, hill, stairs| {str: 4608}

f^fl) ‏עליה‎ (⌖𝖴⟍𝖴⌖ AhL-YH) — **Loft:** A room on top of the house used during hot days of summer. [Hebrew and Aramaic] [freq. 21] |kjv: chamber, parlour, up, ascent, loft, chamber| {str: 5944, 5952}

J) ⊚Yↄ (עול AhWL) ac: **Lift** co: **Yoke** ab: **?**: The lifting up of the yoke upon the shoulders of the oxen.

N^m) ⊚Yↄ (עול AhWL) — **Yoke**: [df: על] [freq. 40] |kjv: yoke| {str: 5923}

N^fl) ⊱⊚Yↄ (עולה AhW-LH) — **I. Rising**: A rising of smoke from a burnt offering. [ms: עלה] [ar: עלה] **II. Captivity**: In the sense of lifting a yoke on the shoulder. [df: גולה hlg] [freq. 331] |kjv: burn offering, ascent, go up, captivity, carry, captive, remove| {str: 1473, 5930}

L) ⊷⊚ↄ (יעל YAhL) ac: **Lift** co: **?** ab: **?**

V) ⊷⊚ↄ (יעל Y-AhL) — **Lift**: [freq. 23] (vf: Hiphil) |kjv: profit, forward, good, profitable| {str: 3276}

a^m) ⊷⊚Yↄↄ (מועל MW-AhL) — **Lift**: [ms: מעל] [freq. 1] |kjv: lifting| {str: 4607}

M) ⊷ↄ⊚ (עיל AhYL) ac: **?** co: **Coat** ab: **?**: An upper garment lifted up onto the shoulders.

N^fl) ⊱⊷ↄ⊚ (עילה AhY-LH) — **Occasion**: [Unknown connection to root; Aramaic only] [ms: עלה] [freq. 3] |kjv: occasion| {str: 5931}

f^m) ⊷ↄ⊚ (עילי AhY-LY) — **High**: [Hebrew and Aramaic] [ms: עלי] [freq. 12] |kjv: upper, high| {str: 5942, 5943}

k^m) ⊷ↄ⊚ↄↄ (מעיל M-AhYL) — **Cloak**: [freq. 28] |kjv: robe, mantle, cloke, coat| {str: 4598}

Adopted Roots;
2027 ⊚⊷ↄ Rule, Master
2349 ⊚ↄↄ Transgress, Transgression
2415 ⊚ↄↄ Shod, Sandal
2418 ↄↄ Young
2542 ↄↄ⊚ Rejoice
2545 ↄↄ⊚ Rejoice
2548 ↄↄ⊚ Triumph
2551 ↄↄ⊚ Labor, Laborer
2622 ↄ⊚ↄ Make, Work

~~~~~~~~~~~~~~~~

1358) ↄↄ⊚ (עם AhM) ac: **?** co: **People** ab: **?**: The pictograph ⊚ is a picture of the eye, the ↄↄ is a picture of the sea representing mass. Combined these mean "see a mass". A large group of people in one location.

A) ↄↄ⊚ (עם AhM) ac: **?** co: **People** ab: **?**: A large group of people in one location. Those who are with or near each other.

N^m) ↄↄ⊚ (עם AhM) — **People**: [Hebrew and Aramaic] [freq. 1876] |kjv: people, nation, folk, men| {str: 5971, 5972}

N^f4) ⊷ↄↄ⊚ (עמית Ah-MYT) — **Neighbor**: [freq. 12] |kjv: neighbor, another, fellow| {str: 5997}

B) ↄↄↄↄ⊚ (עמם AhMM) ac: **Hide** co: **?** ab: **?**: [Unknown connection to root;]

V) ↄↄↄↄ⊚ (עמם Ah-MM) — **Hide**: [freq. 3] (vf: Paal, Hophal) |kjv: hide, dim| {str: 6004}

J) ↄↄY⊚ (עום AhWM) ac: **?** co: **With** ab: **?**: Through the idea of being together.

N^f2) ⊷ↄↄY⊚ (עומת AhW-MT) — **At**: [ms: עמת] [freq. 32] |kjv:

against, beside, answerable, at, hand, point| {str: 5980}

M) ᴍᴧᵪᴸ☉ (עים AhYM) ac: ? co: **With** ab: ?: Through the idea of being together in a group.

N^m) ᴍᴧᵪᴸ☉ (עים AhYM) — **With:** [Hebrew and Aramaic] [ms: עם] [freq. 47] |kjv: with, unto, as, neither, between, among, to, toward, like, by, mighty| {str: 5868, 5973, 5974}

Adopted Roots;
2550 ᴛᴍᴧ☉ Stand, Pillar
2554 ᴧᴍ☉ Bind, Sheaf

1359) ᴸ☉ (עי AhN) ac: **Watch** co: **Eye** ab: **Affliction:** The pictograph ☉ is a picture of the eye, the ᴸ is a picture of a seed representing continuance. Combined these mean "eye of continuance". The nomadic agriculturist carefully watches over his livestock and crops by keeping a close eye on them. It was common to construct a shelter consisting of a roof on four posts, as a shelter from the glare of the sun. (eng: eye - with the removal of the n)

A) ᴸ☉ (עי AhN) ac: **Watch** co: **Furrow** ab: **Affliction:** A watching over something of importance. The furrow formed between the eyes when intently looking or from depression. A cloud as a covering that provides shade.

N^f3) ᵗᵧᴸ☉ (ענות Ah-NWT) — **Affliction:** An oppression or depression. [freq. 1] |kjv: affliction| {str: 6039}

a^m) ᴸ☉ᴍ (מען MAh-N) — **That:** A close watching. [Always used with the prefix ᴜ meaning "to"] [freq. 10] |kjv:

that, to, for, because, lest, intent| {str: 4616}

a^f1) ᵩᴸ☉ᴍ (מענה MAh-NH) — **Furrow:** A depression in the ground. [freq. 3] |kjv: acre, furrow| {str: 4618}

f^m) ᵪᴸ☉ (עני Ah-NY) — **Affliction:** One who is oppressed or depressed. Also the oppression or depression. [freq. 120] |kjv: affliction, trouble, poor, lowly, man| {str: 6040, 6041}

if^f2) ᵗᵪᴸ☉ᵗ (תענית TAh-NYT) — **Fasting:** Through the idea of affliction. [freq. 1] |kjv: heaviness| {str: 8589}

B) ᴸᴸ☉ (ענן AhNN) ac: **Watch** co: **Cloud** ab: ?: A watching over something of importance.

V) ᴸᴸ☉ (ענן Ah-NN) — **Watch:** [freq. 11] (vf: Piel, Participle) |kjv: observer, soothsayer, bring, sorceress, enchanter| {str: 6049}

N^m) ᴸᴸ☉ (ענן Ah-NN) — **Cloud:** As watched to tell the weather. [Hebrew and Aramaic] [freq. 88] |kjv: cloud| {str: 6050, 6051}

N^f1) ᵩᴸᴸ☉ (עננה AhN-NH) — **Cloud:** As watched to tell the weather. [freq. 1] |kjv: cloud| {str: 6053}

b^m) ᴸᵪᴸ☉ (ענין Ah-NYN) — **Business:** A careful watching over a task or burden. [freq. 8] |kjv: traveil, business| {str: 6045}

H) ᵩᴸ☉ (ענה AhNH) ac: **Afflict** co: **Depression** ab: ?: A furrow depression is formed between the eyes when watching intensely. The furrow may also be formed by concentration or depression.

V) 𐤏‎𐤍𐤄 (עָנָה Ah-NH) — **Afflict:** To oppress another causing depression. [Hebrew and Aramaic] [freq. 85] (vf: Paal, Niphal, Hiphil, Hitpael, Pual, Piel) |kjv: afflict, humble, force, exercise, sing| {str: 6031, 6033}

J) 𐤍𐤅𐤏 (עוּן AhWN) ac: **Watch** co: **Abode** ab: **?**: The home is a place closely watched. Protection of the home by keeping of a close eye on it.

V) 𐤍𐤅𐤏 (עוּן AhWN) — **Watch:** [freq. 1] (vf: Paal) |kjv: eyed| {str: 5770}

N^(fl)) 𐤏𐤅𐤍𐤄 (עוֹנָה AhW-NH) — **Habitation:** [freq. 1] |kjv: duty| {str: 5772}

a^m) 𐤌𐤏𐤅𐤍 (מָעוֹן M-AhWN) — **Abode:** The dwelling place of a god (temple), man (home) or animal (den). Also a retreat. [df: מְעִין] [freq. 19] |kjv: habitation, dwelling, den, dwellingplace| {str: 4583}

k^(fl)) 𐤌𐤏𐤅𐤍𐤄 (מְעוֹנָה M-AhW-NH) — **Abode:** The dwelling place of a god (temple), man (home) or animal (den). Also a retreat. [ms: מְעֹנָה] [freq. 9] |kjv: dwelling, place, den, refuge, habitation| {str: 4585}

K) 𐤏𐤍𐤅 (עָנוּ AhNW) ac: **?** co: **?** ab: **Gentle:** In the sense of a careful watching.

N^m) 𐤏𐤍𐤅 (עָנוּ Ah-NW) — **Gentle:** One who is oppressed or depressed. [df: עָנִיו] [freq. 26] |kjv: meek, humble, poor, lowly| {str: 6035}

N^(fl)) 𐤏𐤍𐤅𐤄 (עָנְוָה AhN-WH) — **Gentleness:** [freq. 7] |kjv:

humility, gentleness, meekness| {str: 6037, 6038}

L) 𐤉𐤏𐤍 (יַעַן YAhN) ac: **Watch** co: **Owl** ab: **?**

N^f) 𐤉𐤏𐤍 (יַעַן Y-AhN) — **I. Because:** In the sense of paying attention. **II. Yaeyn:** An unknown bird. [freq. 18] |kjv: because, even seeing, forasmuch, that, whereas, why, ostrich| {str: 3282, 3283}

N^(fl)) 𐤉𐤏𐤍𐤄 (יַעֲנָה YAh-NH) — **Owl:** A bird that watches. [freq. 8] |kjv: owl| {str: 3284}

M) 𐤏𐤉𐤍 (עַיִן AhYN) ac: **?** co: **Eye** ab: **?**: The eye reveals the heart of the person. A well, spring or fountain as the eye of the ground.

N^f) 𐤏𐤉𐤍 (עַיִן AhYN) — **Eye:** [Hebrew and Aramaic] [freq. 892] |kjv: eye, sight, seem, colour, fountain, well, face, presence, before, conceit, think| {str: 5869, 5870}

a^m) 𐤌𐤏𐤉𐤍 (מַעְיָן M-AhYN) — **Spring:** As the eye of the ground. [ms: מַעֲיָנ] [freq. 23] |kjv: fountain, well, spring| {str: 4599}

~~~~~~~~~~

1360) 𐤏𐤎 (עַס AhS) ac: **Do** co: **?** ab: **?**

H) 𐤏𐤎𐤄 (עָסָה AhSH) ac: **Do** co: **Work** ab: **?**: The making or doing of anything.

V) 𐤏𐤎𐤄 (עָסָה Ah-SH) — **Do:** To do or make something. A generic verb with a wide application meaning to do something. [df: עָשָׂה] [freq. 2633] (vf: Paal, Niphal, Pual, Piel) |kjv: do, make, wrought, deal, commit, offer, execute, keep, show, prepare, work, get, dress, maker, maintain| {str: 6213}

a^m) 𝟊⪚⊙ᴧᴧ (מעסה MAh-SH) — **Work:** A work or action. [df: מעשה] [freq. 235] |kjv: work, acts, labour, doing, art, deed| {str: 4639}

~~~~~~~~~

1361) ⊙⊙ (עע AhAh) ac: ? co: ? ab: ?

~~~~~~~~~

1362) ⊸⊙ (עף AhP) ac: **Cover** co: **Wing** ab: ?: The wing of a bird that gives flight as well as a covering it and its chicks. (eng: avian - with the exchange of the v and p)

A) ⊸⊙ (עף AhP) ac: ? co: **Wing** ab: ?

N^f) ⊸⊙ (עף AhP) — **Wing:** The covering of a bird. [Aramaic only] [df: גנף] [freq. 3] |kjv: wing| {str: 1611}

f^m) ⪡⊸⊙ (עפי Ah-PY) — **Foliage:** As a covering of the tree. [Aramaic only] [freq. 3] |kjv: leaves| {str: 6074}

l^m) ⊸⊙⊙⊸⊙ (עפעף AhP-AhP) — **Eyelid:** As a covering of the eyes. Also the rays of the sun appearing like eyelashes. [freq. 10] |kjv: eyelid, dawning| {str: 6079}

E) 𝔂⊸⊙ (עפא AhPA) ac: ? co: **Branch** ab: ?

N^m) 𝔂⊸⊙ (עפא Ah-PA) — **Branch:** The covering of the tree. [freq. 1] |kjv: branch| {str: 6073}

J) ⊸Y⊙ (עוף AhWP) ac: **Fly** co: **Bird** ab: ?: The covering of a bird.

V) ⊸Y⊙ (עוף AhWP) — **Fly:** [freq. 32] (vf: Paal, Hiphil) |kjv: fly, faint, brandish, shine, weary| {str: 5774}

N^m) ⊸Y⊙ (עוף AhWP) — **Bird:** [Hebrew and Aramaic] [freq. 73] |kjv: fowl, bird, flying| {str: 5775, 5776}

a^m) ⊸Y⊙ᴧᴧ (מעוף M-AhWP) — **Shadow:** A covering over making a shadow. [freq. 1] |kjv: dimness| {str: 4588}

L) ⊸⊙⥋ (יעף YAhP) ac: ? co: ? ab: **Fatigue:** A closing or covering of the eyes with the eyelids.

V) ⊸⊙⥋ (יעף Y-AhP) — **Fatigue:** [freq. 9] (vf: Paal, Hophal, Participle) |kjv: weary, faint, fly| {str: 3286}

N^m) ⊸⊙⥋ (יעף Y-AhP) — **Tired:** [freq. 5] |kjv: faint, weary, fatigued| {str: 3287, 3288}

i^fl) 𝟊⊸⊙Y† (תועפה TW-Ah-PH) — **Strength:** [freq. 4] |kjv: strength, plenty| {str: 8443}

M) ⊸⥋⊙ (עיף AhYP) ac: ? co: ? ab: **Fatigue:** A closing or covering of the eyes with the eyelids.

V) ⊸⥋⊙ (עיף AhYP) — **Tire:** To be tired, faint or weary. [freq. 1] (vf: Paal) |kjv: weary| {str: 5888}

N^m) ⊸⥋⊙ (עיף AhYP) — **Tired:** [freq. 17] |kjv: weary, faint, thirsty| {str: 5889}

~~~~~~~~~

1363) ↶⊙ (עץ AhTs) ac: **Firm** co: **Tree** ab: ?: The upright and firmness of the tree.

A) ⟨עץ AhTs) ac: **?** co: **Tree** ab: **?:** The upright and firmness of the tree. The elders of the tribe were the upright and firm ones making decisions and giving advice.

N[m]) ⟨עץ AhTs) — **Wood:** A tree or the wood from the tree. [Hebrew and Aramaic] [ar: אע] [freq. 333] |kjv: tree, wood, timber, stick, gallows, staff, stock, branch, helve, plank, stalk| {str: 636, 6086}

N[f1]) ⟨עצה Ah-TsH) — **I. Tree: II. Counsel:** As the firm support of the community. [Hebrew and Aramaic] [ar: עטא] [freq. 90] |kjv: tree, counsel, purpose, advice| {str: 5843, 6097, 6098}

H) ⟨עצה AhTsH) ac: **?** co: **Spine** ab: **?:** The elders of the tribe were the upright and firm ones, like trees, making decisions and giving advice.

V) ⟨עצה Ah-TsH) — **Counsel:** [freq. 1] (vf: Paal) |kjv: shut| {str: 6095}

N[m]) ⟨עצה Ah-TsH) — **Spine:** The tree of the body which provides its uprightness. [freq. 1] |kjv: backbone| {str: 6096}

J) ⟨עוץ AhWTs) ac: **Counsel** co: **?** ab: **?:** The elders of the tribe were the upright and firm ones, like trees, making decisions and giving advice.

V) ⟨עוץ AhWTs) — **Counsel:** [freq. 2] (vf: Paal) |kjv: counsel, advice| {str: 5779}

L) ⟨יעץ YAhTs) ac: **Counsel** co: **?** ab: **?:** The elders of the tribe were the upright and firm

ones, like trees, making decisions and giving advice.

V) ⟨יעץ Y-AhTs) — **Counsel:** [Hebrew and Aramaic] [ar: יעט] [freq. 83] (vf: Paal, Niphal, Hitpael, Participle) |kjv: counsel, counselor, consult, give, purpose, advice, determine, devise| {str: 3272, 3289}

a[f1]) ⟨מועצה MW-Ah-TsH) — **Counsel:** [freq. 7] |kjv: counsel, devise| {str: 4156}

Adopted Roots;
2567 ⟨ Cut, Axe
~~~~~~~~~~

1364) ⟨עק AhQ) ac: **Press** co: **?** ab: **Oppression**

A) ⟨עק AhQ) ac: **Press** co: **?** ab: **Oppression:** A pressing in on one as oppression.

N[f1]) ⟨עקה Ah-QH) — **Oppression:** [freq. 1] |kjv: oppression| {str: 6125}

H) ⟨עקה AhQH) ac: **Press** co: **?** ab: **?**

a[m]) ⟨מעקה MAh-QH) — **Parapet:** A place of pressing as one leans on it. A wall that is placed around the roof as this place was occupied because of its coolness in the summer. [freq. 1] |kjv: battlement| {str: 4624}

J) ⟨עוק AhWQ) ac: **Press** co: **?** ab: **?**

V) ⟨עוק AhWQ) — **Press:** [freq. 2] (vf: Hiphil) |kjv: press| {str: 5781}

L) ⟨יעק YAhQ) ac: **Press** co: **Burden** ab: **?**

a^{fl}) ✲⊶⊙Ɏ⅏ (מועקה MW-Ah-QH) — **Burden:** [freq. 1] |kjv: affliction| {str: 4157}

~~~~~~~~~~

1365) ᕼ⊙ (ער AhR) ac: **Bare** co: **Skin** ab: **?:** The pictograph ⊙ is a picture of the eye, the ᕼ is a picture of a man. Combined these mean "see a man". When the enemy is captured, he is stripped of his clothes to the skin and carefully watched.

A) ᕼ⊙ (ער AhR) ac: **?** co: **Naked** ab: **?**

a^m) ᕼ⊙⅏ (מער MAh-R) — **Nakedness:** [freq. 2] |kjv: nakedness, proportion| {str: 4626}

i^{m/f}) ᕼ⊙† (תער T-AhR) — **I. Razor:** For shaving hair and making the face naked. **II. Sheath:** For holding a blade. [freq. 13] |kjv: sheath, razor, penknife, scabbard, shave| {str: 8593}

l^m) ᕼ⊙ᕼ⊙ (ערער AhR-AhR) — **Naked:** [freq. 2] |kjv: destitute, heath| {str: 6199}

ap^m) ⅏ᕼ⊙⅏ (מערם MAh-RM) — **Naked:** [freq. 1] |kjv: naked| {str: 4636}

cl^m) ᕼ⊙Ɏᕼ⊙ (ערוער Ah-RW-AhR) — **Naked:** [freq. 1] |kjv: heath| {str: 6176}

cp^m) ⅏Ɏᕼ⊙ (ערום Ah-RWM) — **Naked:** [df: ערם] [freq. 16] |kjv: naked| {str: 6174}

ecp^m) ⅏Ɏᕼ⅃⊙ (עירום AhY-RWM) — **Naked:** [df: עירם ערם] [freq. 10] |kjv: naked, nakedness| {str: 5903}

B) ᕼᕼ⊙ (ערר AhRR) ac: **?** co: **Naked** ab: **?**

V) ᕼᕼ⊙ (ערר Ah-RR) — **Bare:** [freq. 4] (vf: Paal, Pilpel) |kjv: bare, raise, break| {str: 6209}

bf^m) ⅃ᕼ⅃ᕼ⊙ (ערירי Ah-RY-RY) — **Barren:** One who is childless. [freq. 4] |kjv: childless| {str: 6185}

H) ✲ᕼ⊙ (ערה AhRH) ac: **Uncover** co: **Naked** ab: **?**

V) ✲ᕼ⊙ (ערה Ah-RH) — **I. Uncover:** To remove the covering. **II. Empty:** To remove the contents of a container or destroy a city. [freq. 15] (vf: Niphal, Hiphil, Hitpael, Piel, Participle) |kjv: uncover, discover, empty, rase, destitute, naked, pour, spread| {str: 6168}

N^{fl}) ✲ᕼ⊙ (ערה Ah-RH) — **Meadow:** A place barren of trees. [freq. 1] |kjv: reed| {str: 6169}

a^m) ✲ᕼ⊙⅏ (מערה MAh-RH) — **Meadow:** A place barren of trees. [freq. 1] |kjv: meadow| {str: 4629}

f^{fl}) ✲⅃ᕼ⊙ (עריה AhR-YH) — **Naked:** [freq. 6] |kjv: naked, bare| {str: 6181}

J) ᕼɎ⊙ (עור AhWR) ac: **?** co: **Skin** ab: **?:** The bare skin without clothing.

V) ᕼɎ⊙ (עור AhWR) — **Naked:** To have the skin exposed. [freq. 1] (vf: Niphal) |kjv: naked| {str: 5783}

N^m) ᕼɎ⊙ (עור AhWR) — **Skin:** The skin of men or animals as well as leather made from animal skins. Also the husk of a seed. [Hebrew and Aramaic] [freq. 100] |kjv: skin, hide, leather, chaff| {str: 5784, 5785}

a^m) ⱭY⬯ᴧ (מעור M-AhWR) — **Nakedness**: [freq. 1] |kjv: nakedness, pudendum| {str: 4589}

K) YⱭ⬯ (ערו AhRW) ac: ? co: **Naked** ab: **?**: The shame of one being naked.

N^fl) ⱷYⱭ⬯ (ערוה AhR-WH) — **I. Nakedness**: [Hebrew and Aramaic] **II. Shame**: From ones nakedness. [freq. 55] |kjv: nakedness, shame, unclean, uncleanness, dishonor| {str: 6172, 6173}

M) Ɑ⅃⬯ (עיר AhYR) ac: **Watch** co: ? ab: ?: In the sense of seeing.

N^m) Ɑ⅃⬯ (עיר AhYR) — **Watcher**: [Aramaic only] [freq. 3] |kjv: watcher| {str: 5894}

Adopted Roots;
2580 ⬯Ɑ⬯ Behead, Neck

~~~~~~~~~~~~~~~~

1366) ⱵⱵ⬯ (עש AhSh) ac: **Waste** co: ? ab: ?

B) ⱵⱵⱵ⬯ (עשש AhShSh) ac: **Waste** co: ? ab: ?

V) ⱵⱵⱵ⬯ (עשש Ah-ShSh) — **Waste**: To waste or fail away. [freq. 3] (vf: Paal) |kjv: consumed| {str: 6244}

~~~~~~~~~~~~~~~~

1367) ✝⬯ (עת AhT) ac: ? co: ? ab: **Time**: A period of time as a moment or season.

A) ✝⬯ (עת AhT) ac: ? co: ? ab: **Time**

N^f) ✝⬯ (עת AhT) — **Time**: [freq. 296] |kjv: time, season, when, always| {str: 6256}

f^m) ↵✝⬯ (עתי Ah-TY) — **Ready**: [freq. 1] |kjv: fit| {str: 6261}

H) ✿✝⬯ (עתה AhTH) ac: ? co: ? ab: **Now**: The present time.

N^m) ✿✝⬯ (עתה Ah-TH) — **Now**: [freq. 9] |kjv: now, whereas, henceforth, straightway| {str: 6258}

s^m) ↵✝⬯ (עתין Ah-TYN) — **Now**: [Aramaic only] [df: אדין] [freq. 57] |kjv: then, now, time| {str: 116}

J) ✝Y⬯ (עות AhWT) ac: **Speak** co: ? ab: ?: [Unknown connection to root;]

V) ✝Y⬯ (עות AhWT) — **Speak**: [freq. 1] (vf: Paal) |kjv: speak| {str: 5790}

Adopted Roots;
2590 Ɑ✝⬯ Multiply, Abundance

~~~~~~~~~~~~~~~~

1368) 𝄇⬯ (עע AhGh) ac: ? co: ? ab: ?

~~~~~~~~~~~~~~~~

Pey

1369) ⟩⟨⟩⟨⟩ (פא PA) ac: ? co: **Mouth**
ab: ?: The pictograph ⟨⟩ is a picture of
the edge of the mouth. The edge of
anything as the lips are the edge of the
mouth. This parent root is identical to
both ⟨⟩ and ⟨⟩

A) ⟩⟨⟩ (פא PA) ac: ? co: **Mouth**
ab: ?

Nᶠˡ) ⟨⟩⟨⟩ (פאה P-AH) —
Edge: The edge of something.
[freq. 86] |kjv: side, corner,
quarter, end, part| {str: 6285}

1370) ⟨⟩ (פב PB) ac: ? co: ? ab: ?

1371) ⟨⟩ (פג PG) ac: **Unfit** co: **Unripe
fig** ab: **Cease:** Unable to fulfill the role
intended for.

A) ⟨⟩ (פג PG) ac: ? co: **Unripe
fig** ab: ?: An inedible fruit.

Nᵐ) ⟨⟩ (פג PG) — **Unripe
fig:** [freq. 1] |kjv: green fig| {str:
6291}

F) ⟨⟩⟨⟩ (הפג HPG) ac: **Cease** co:
? ab: ?: Unable to work.

Nᶠˡ) ⟨⟩⟨⟩ (הפגה HP-GH) —
Ceasing: [freq. 1] |kjv:
intermission| {str: 2014}

J) ⟨⟩⟨⟩ (פוג PWG) ac: **Cease** co:
Rest ab: ?: Unable to work.

V) ⟨⟩⟨⟩ (פוג PWG) — **Cease:**
[freq. 4] (vf: Paal, Niphal) |kjv:
faint, cease, slack, feeble| {str:
6313}

Nᶠˡ) ⟨⟩⟨⟩ (פוגה PW-GH) —
Rest: [freq. 1] |kjv: rest| {str:
6314}

Adopted Roots;
2591 ⟨⟩ Foul
2592 ⟨⟩ Meet, Encounter
2593 ⟨⟩ Faint, Carcass
2594 ⟨⟩ Meet

1372) ⟨⟩ (פד PD) ac: **Redeem** co: ?
ab: ?: The pictograph ⟨⟩ is a picture of
the open mouth, the ⟨⟩ is a picture of a
door. Combined these mean "open the
door". When one is redeemed they gird
on their clothes for leaving. To bring back
to an original state.

A) ⟨⟩ (פד PD) ac: **Redeem** co: ?
ab: ?

Nᶠ³) ⟨⟩ (פדות P-DWT) —
Redemption: [ms: פדת] [freq.
4] |kjv: redemption, redeem,
division| {str: 6304}

fjᵐ) ⟨⟩ (פדיון PD-YWN)
— **Redemption:** [df: פדיום
פדים] [freq. 4] |kjv: redemption,
ransom| {str: 6306}

C) ⟨⟩ (אפד APD) ac: **Gird** co:
? ab: ?: The garment of the high
priest. [Unknown connection to
root;]

V) ⟨⟩ (אפד A-PD) —
Gird: To tie on the ephod. [freq.
2] (vf: Paal) |kjv: gird, bound|
{str: 640}

c^m) ד𐤅⌒𐤏 (אפוד A-PWD) —
Ephod: [freq. 49] |kjv: ephod|
{str: 646}

d^fl) 𐤀ד𐤅⌒𐤏 (אפודה A-PW-
DH) — **Ephod:** [ms: אפדה]
[freq. 3] |kjv: ephod, ornament|
{str: 642}

H) 𐤀ד⌒ (פדה PDH) ac: **Redeem**
co: ? ab: ?

V) 𐤀ד⌒ (פדה P-DH) —
Redeem: [freq. 59] (vf: Paal,
Niphal, Hiphil, Hophal) |kjv:
redeem, deliver, ransom, rescue|
{str: 6299}

N) ﬩ד⌒ (פדי PDY) ac: **Redeem**
co: ? ab: ?

d^m) Yד⌒ (פדוי P-DWY) —
Redeemed: [freq. 4] |kjv:
redeemed| {str: 6302}

Adopted Roots;
2595 ⌒ד⌒ Redeem

1373) 𐤀⌒ (פה PH) ac: **Blow** co:
Mouth ab: ?: The pictograph ⌒ is a
picture of the mouth. A mouth is the edge
of anything such as the place of the beard,
a sword, a region. The edge or border, is
often referring to all that is within the
borders, the whole country. This parent
root is identical to both 𐤏⌒ and ﬩⌒.

A) 𐤀⌒ (פה PH) ac: ? co: **Mouth**
ab: ?

N^m) 𐤀⌒ (פה PH) — **Mouth:**
[freq. 497] |kjv: mouth,
commandment, edge, according,
word, hole, end, appointment,
portion, tenor, sentence| {str:
6310}

D) 𐤀𐤏⌒ (פאה PAH) ac: **Blow** co:
? ab: ?: To blow with the mouth.

V) 𐤀𐤏⌒ (פאה P-AH) —
Blow: To scatter something by
blowing. [freq. 1] (vf: Hiphil)
|kjv: scatter| {str: 6284}

1374) Y⌒ (פו PW) ac: ? co: **Here** ab: ?

A) Y⌒ (פו PW) ac: ? co: **Here** ab: ?

N^m) Y⌒ (פו PW) — **Here:** [df:
פה פא] [freq. 8] |kjv: here,
hither, side| {str: 6311}

C) Y⌒𐤏 (אפו APW) ac: ? co:
Here ab: ?

N^m) Y⌒𐤏 (אפו A-PW) —
Here: Often used in the sense of
a question - where. [ms: אפוא]
[freq. 15] |kjv: now, where, here|
{str: 645}

e^fl) 𐤀Y⌒﬩𐤏 (איפוה AY-
PWH) — **Where:** [freq. 10] |kjv:
where, what| {str: 375}

1375) ᴄ⌒ (פז PZ) ac: **Refine** co: **Gold**
ab: **Pure:** The pictograph ⌒ is a picture
of the edge of the mouth, the ᴄ is a
picture of a cutting implement. Combined
these mean "edge of the weapon". A
sword or knife required refined metal for
strength and durability. Refining removes
impurities from the metal.

A) ᴄ⌒ (פז PZ) ac: ? co: **Pure
gold** ab: ?: Gold that has been
refined.

N^m) ᴄ⌒ (פז PZ) — **Pure
gold:** [freq. 9] |kjv: pure, fine|
{str: 6337}

B) ᴄᴄ⌒ (פזז PZZ) ac: **Refine** co:
? ab: ?

V) ᴄᴄ⌒ (פזז P-ZZ) —
Refine: [freq. 3] (vf: Hophal,

Paal, Piel) |kjv: best, strong, leap| {str: 6338, 6339}

1376) ⊡⊂ (פֿה PHh) ac: **Blow** co: **Bellows** ab: ?: The pictograph ⊂ is a picture of a mouth representing blowing, the ⊡ is a picture of a wall meaning outside. Combined these mean "blow out". The bellows blows out a large amount of air causing a fire to become hotter.

A) ⊡⊂ (פֿה PHh) ac: ? co: **Bellows** ab: ?

N^m) ⊡⊂ (פֿה PHh) — **Trap:** [Unknown connection to root;] [freq. 27] |kjv: snare, gin, plate| {str: 6341}

a^m) ⊡⊂ᴧᴧ (מֿפֿה MP-Hh) — **Bellows:** [freq. 1] |kjv: bellows| {str: 4647}

B) ⊡⊡⊂ (פֿחֿה PHhHh) ac: **Trap** co: ? ab: ?: [Unknown connection to root;]

V) ⊡⊡⊂ (פֿחֿה P-HhHh) — **Trap:** [freq. 1] (vf: Hiphil) |kjv: snare| {str: 6351}

H) ⧫⊡⊂ (פֿחֿה PHhH) ac: **Rule** co: **Governor** ab: ?: [Unknown connection to root;]

N^m) ⧫⊡⊂ (פֿחֿה P-HhH) — **Governor:** [Hebrew and Aramaic] [freq. 38] |kjv: governor, captain, deputy| {str: 6346, 6347}

J) ⊡Y⊂ (פֿוֿה PWHh) ac: **Blow** co: ? ab: ?: A blowing as a bellows.

V) ⊡Y⊂ (פֿוֿה PWHh) — **Blow:** [freq. 14] (vf: Paal, Hiphil) |kjv: speak, puff, blow, break, utter, snare| {str: 6315}

i^m) ⊡Y⊂† (תֿפֿוֿה T-PWHh) — **Apple:** The fruit or the tree. [freq. 6] |kjv: apple| {str: 8598}

L) ⊡⊂Ʞ (יֿפֿה YPHh) ac: **Blow** co: ? ab: ?: A heavy blowing as a bellows.

V) ⊡⊂Ʞ (יֿפֿה Y-PHh) — **Blow:** [freq. 1] (vf: Hitpael) |kjv: bewail| {str: 3306}

N^m) ⊡⊂Ʞ (יֿפֿה Y-PHh) — **Blow:** [freq. 1] |kjv: breath out| {str: 3307}

M) ⊡Ʞ⊂ (פֿיֿה PYHh) ac: **Blow** co: **Ash** ab: ?: The ash that is blown when the bellows blows.

N^m) ⊡Ʞ⊂ (פֿיֿה PYHh) — **Ash:** [freq. 2] |kjv: ash| {str: 6368}

Adopted Roots;
2238 ⊡⊂⊗ Span, Span
2419 ⊡⊂Ꞁ Blow
2496 ⊡⊂Ʇ Attach
2863 ⊡⊂ш Join

1377) ⊗⊂ (פֿט PTh) ac: ? co: ? ab: ?

1378) Ꞁ⊂ (פֿי PY) ac: ? co: **Edge** ab: ?

A) Ꞁ⊂ (פֿי PY) ac: ? co: **Edge** ab: ?

N^fl) ⧫Ꞁ⊂ (פֿיֿה P-YH) — **Edge:** [freq. 1] |kjv: edge| {str: 6366}

l^fl) ⧫Ꞁ⊂Ꞁ⊂ (פֿיֿפֿיֿה PY-P-YH) — **Double edge:** A double edged blade. [freq. 2] |kjv: twoedged, teeth| {str: 6374}

1379) ШⒺ (פֶךְ PK) ac: **Overturn** co: **Flask** ab: ?: The flask, usually made of a horn (see Job 42:14), for storing medicinal, cosmetic or ritual oils. The flask is overturned to pour out the contents. (eng: flask - with the additional l and s)

A) ШⒺ (פֶךְ PK) ac: ? co: **Flask** ab: ?

N^m) ШⒺ (פֶךְ PK) — **Flask:** [freq. 3] |kjv: box, vial| {str: 6378}

F) ШⒺⳆ (הפך HPK) ac: **Overturn** co: ? ab: ?: The overturning of the flask to pour out its contents. A turning to a different direction.

V) ШⒺⳆ (הפך H-PK) — **Overturn:** To turn something over or upside down as if pouring out its contents. [freq. 94] (vf: Paal, Niphal, Hitpael, Hophal) |kjv: turn, overthrow, overturn, change, become, came, convert, gave, make, perverse, pervert, retire, tumble| {str: 2015}

N^{fl}) ⳆШ Ⲳ (הפכה HP-KH) — **Overturning:** [freq. 1] |kjv: overthrow| {str: 2018}

a^{fl}) ⳆШ Ⲳ꜀꜀ (מהפכה MH-P-KH) — **Overturning:** [freq. 6] |kjv: overthrow| {str: 4114}

a^{f2}) ꜀꜀ШⒺ꜀꜀ (מהפכת MH-P-KT) — **Stocks:** Causing an upside down posture. [freq. 4] |kjv: prison, stocks| {str: 4115}

g^m) ШⒺ Ⲳ (הופך HW-PK) — **Overturned:** Something that is turned over upside down. [ms: הפך] [freq. 1] |kjv: turning| {str: 2017}

i^{fl}) ⳆШ Ⲳ꜀꜀ (תהפכה TH-P-KH) — **Upside-down:** [freq. 10]

|kjv: forward, perverse| {str: 8419}

l^m) ШⒺШⒺ (הפכפך H-PK-PK) — **Upside-down:** [freq. 1] |kjv: froward| {str: 2019}

H) ꜀ⲲШⒺ (פכה PKH) ac: **Pour** co: ? ab: ?: The overturning of flask.

V) ꜀ⲲШⒺ (פכה P-KH) — **Pour:** [freq. 1] (vf: Piel) |kjv: ran| {str: 6379}

J) ШⲨⒺ (פוך PWK) ac: ? co: **Cosmetics** ab: ?

N^m) ШⲨⒺ (פוך PWK) — **Cosmetics:** [freq. 4] |kjv: paint, glistering, colour| {str: 6320}

Adopted Roots;
2865 ШⒺ⊔⊔ Pour, Penis

~~~~~~~~~~

1380) Ⳑ Ⲝ (פל PL) ac: **Plead** co: ? ab: **Judgment:** The pictograph ⌒ is a picture of mouth, the Ⳑ is a picture of a shepherd staff representing authority. Combined these mean "speak to authority". A coming to one in authority to intercede on ones own behalf or for another.

B) Ⳑⳑ Ⲝ (פלל PLL) ac: **Plead** co: ? ab: **Judgment:** To plead for intercession or an outcome.

V) Ⳑⳑ Ⲝ (פלל P-LL) — **Plead:** [freq. 84] (vf: Hitpael, Piel) |kjv: pray, judge, made, intreat, judgment, prayer, supplication, thought| {str: 6419}

b^m) ⳑⲽⳑ Ⲝ (פליל P-LYL) — **Judgment:** What is determined out of the pleading. [freq. 3] |kjv: judge| {str: 6414}

b^{fl}) Ⲳⳑⲽⳑ Ⲝ (פלילה P-LY-LH) — **Judgment:** What is determined out of the pleading. [freq. 1] |kjv: judgment| {str: 6415}

bf^m) ᐳᐯᐯ/⌐ (פְּלִילִי P-LY-LY) — **Judgment:** What is determined out of the pleading. [freq. 1] |kjv: judge| {str: 6416}

bf^{f1}) ✡ᐳᐯᐯ/⌐ (פְלִילִיה P-LYL-YH) — **Judgment:** What is determined out of the pleading. [freq. 1] |kjv: judgment| {str: 6417}

C) /⌐Ⴑ (אפל APL) ac: **?** co: **Dark** ab: **?:** A very dark darkness brought about as a punishment of judgment.

N^m) /⌐Ⴑ (אפל A-PL) — **Dark:** [freq. 1] |kjv: dark| {str: 651}

N^{f1}) ✡/⌐Ⴑ (אפלה AP-LH) — **Darkness:** [freq. 10] |kjv: darkness, gloominess, dark, thick| {str: 653}

a^m) /⌐Ⴑᴧ (מאפל MA-PL) — **Darkness:** [freq. 1] |kjv: darkness| {str: 3990}

af^{f1}) ✡ᐳ/⌐Ⴑᴧ (מאפליה MA-PL-YH) — **Darkness:** [freq. 1] |kjv: darkness| {str: 3991}

b^m) /ᐳ⌐Ⴑ (אפיל A-PYL) — **Late:** In the sense of night as being dark. [freq. 1] |kjv: grown| {str: 648}

g^m) /⌐ႸႱ (אופל AW-PL) — **Darkness:** [ms: אפל] [freq. 9] |kjv: darkness, privily, obscurity| {str: 652}

E) ᐳᐯ/⌐ (פלא PLA) ac: **Perform** co: **?** ab: **?:** A great work as an act of intercession.

V) ᐳᐯ/⌐ (פלא P-LA) — **Perform:** To do a great action out of a judgment. [freq. 71] (vf:

Niphal, Hiphil, Hitpael, Piel, Participle) |kjv: work, wonder, marvelous, wonderful, thing, hard, wondrous, perform| {str: 6381}

N^m) ᐳᐯ/⌐ (פלא P-LA) — **Performance:** [freq. 13] |kjv: wonder, wonderful, marvelous| {str: 6382}

b^m) ᐳᐯ/⌐ (פליא P-LYA) — **Performance:** [df: פלאי] [freq. 4] |kjv: secret, wonderful| {str: 6383}

h^{f1}) ✡ᐳᐯ/⌐ᴧ (מפלאה MP-L-AH) — **Performance:** [freq. 1] |kjv: wondrous| {str: 4652}

H) ✡ᐯ/⌐ (פלה PLH) ac: **Distinct** co: **?** ab: **?:** A judgment that sets something apart as special.

V) ✡ᐯ/⌐ (פלה P-LH) — **Distinct:** To be distinct. [freq. 7] (vf: Niphal, Hiphil) |kjv: sever, separate, wonderfully, set apart, marvelous, difference| {str: 6395}

J) /Ⴘ⌐ (פול PWL) ac: **?** co: **Bean** ab: **?:** From its bent shape as one bowing before one in authority.

N^m) /Ⴘ⌐ (פול PWL) — **Bean:** [freq. 2] |kjv: bean| {str: 6321}

M) /ᐳ⌐ (פיל PYL) ac: **Plead** co: **?** ab: **?**

i^{f1}) ✡ᐯ/ᐳ⌐† (תפילה T-PY-LH) — **Pleading:** [ms: תפלה] [freq. 77] |kjv: prayer| {str: 8605}

Adopted Roots;

2866 /⌐ᰚ Low, Lowland

~~~~~~~~~

1381) ᴧᴧ⌐ (פם PM) ac: **?** co: **Mouth** ab: **?**

J) ⌐Y∾ (פום PWM) ac: ? co: **Mouth** ab: ?

N^(m)) ⌐Y∾ (פום PWM) — **Mouth:** [Aramaic only] [ms: פֻם] [freq. 6] |kjv: mouth| {str: 6433}

M) ⌐⊿∾ (פים PYM) ac: ? co: **Fat** ab: ?

N^(fl)) �881⌐⊿∾ (פימה PY-MH) — **Fat:** [freq. 1] |kjv: fat| {str: 6371}

~~~~~~~~~~

1382) ⌐∾ (פן PN) ac: **Turn** co: **Face** ab: ?: The turning of the face. (eng: fan; spin)

A) ⌐∾ (פן PN) ac: ? co: **Corner** ab: ?

N^(m)) ⌐∾ (פן PN) — I. **Corner:** II. **Or:** As a turning toward another direction. [freq. 6] |kjv: corner, lest, not, peradventure| {str: 6434, 6435}

B) ⌐⌐∾ (פנן PNN) ac: **Turn** co: ? ab: ?

b^(m)) ⌐⊿⌐∾ (פנין P-NYN) — **Ruby:** A gem that glistens when turned. [df: פְּנִי] [freq. 6] |kjv: ruby| {str: 6443}

C) ⌐∾∀ (אפן APN) ac: **Turn** co: **Wheel** ab: ?: A turning object.

N^(m)) ⌐∾∀ (אפן A-PN) — **Turning:** [freq. 1] |kjv: fitly| {str: 655}

g^(m)) ⌐∾Y∀ (אופן AW-PN) — **Wheel:** [ms: אפן] [freq. 36] |kjv: wheel| {str: 212}

H) �881⌐∾ (פנה PNH) ac: **Turn** co: **Face** ab: ?: What turns back and forth.

V) �881⌐∾ (פנה P-NH) — **Turn:** To turn the face or to turn

directions. Also to turn something back or away. [freq. 135] (vf: Paal, Hiphil, Hophal, Piel) |kjv: turn, look, prepare, regard, respect, look| {str: 6437}

N^(m)) �881⌐∾ (פנה P-NH) — **Face:** The face, also the presence of one through the sense of being in the face of. [Always written in the plural form, ⌐⊿⌐∾; Frequently used with the prefix "∪", meaning "to" or "for", meaning "to the face of" or "before"] [freq. 2110] |kjv: face, presence, because, sight, countenance, from, person, upon, of, against, open, for, toward| {str: 3942, 6440}

J) ⌐Y∾ (פון PWN) ac: **Turn** co: ? ab: ?

V) ⌐Y∾ (פון PWN) — **Turn:** [freq. 1] (vf: Paal) |kjv: distracted| {str: 6323}

M) ⌐⊿∾ (פין PYN) ac: ? co: **Corner** ab: ?: A point which makes a turn.

N^(fl)) �881⌐⊿∾ (פינה PY-NH) — **Corner:** [ms: פנה] [freq. 28] |kjv: corner, chief, tower, bulwark, stay| {str: 6438}

~~~~~~~~~~

1383) ⊰∾ (פס PS) ac: **End** co: **Wrist** ab: ?: The end of the extremities including the wrist and ankles.

A) ⊰∾ (פס PS) ac: ? co: **Wrist** ab: ?

N^(m)) ⊰∾ (פס PS) — I. **Sleeve:** As reaching to the wrist. II. **Wrist:** [Aramaic only] [freq. 7] |kjv: colour, part| {str: 6446, 6447}

223

N[fl]) ⚜⌂ (פסה P-SH) — **Handful:** As a full at the wrist. [freq. 1] |kjv: handful| {str: 6451}

B) ⚜⚜⌂ (פסס PSS) ac: **Disappear** co: ? ab: ?: A coming to an end.

V) ⚜⚜⌂ (פסס P-SS) — **Disappear:** [freq. 1] (vf: Paal) |kjv: fail| {str: 6461}

C) ⚜⌂𝖸 (אפס APS) ac: **End** co: ? ab: ?: The extremity of the wrist or ankle.

V) ⚜⌂𝖸 (אפס A-PS) — **End:** [freq. 5] (vf: Paal) |kjv: fail, gone, end, nought| {str: 656}

N[m]) ⚜⌂𝖸 (אפס A-PS) — **End:** [freq. 43] |kjv: end, no, none, nothing, without, else, but, beside, cause| {str: 657}

1384) ◎⌂ (פע PAh) ac: **Shine** co: ? ab: **Brightness**

H) ⚜◎⌂ (פעה PAhH) ac: **Scream** co: ? ab: ?: As a bright sound.

V) ⚜◎⌂ (פעה P-AhH) — **Scream:** [freq. 1] (vf: Paal) |kjv: cry| {str: 6463}

L) ◎⌂🠃 (יפע YPAh) ac: **Shine** co: **Bright** ab: ?

V) ◎⌂🠃 (יפע Y-PAh) — **Shine:** [freq. 8] (vf: Hiphil) |kjv: shine, show, light| {str: 3313}

N[fl]) ⚜◎⌂🠃 (יפעה YP-AhH) — **Brightness:** [freq. 2] |kjv: brightness| {str: 3314}

1385) ◎◎ (פף PP) ac: ? co: ? ab: ?

C) ◎◎𝖸 (אפף APP) ac: **Surround** co: ? ab: ?

V) ◎◎𝖸 (אפף A-PP) — **Surround:** To be inside a hole or surrounded by something. [freq. 5] (vf: Paal) |kjv: compass| {str: 661}

1386) ⌂⌒◎ (פץ PTs) ac: **Smash** co: **Club** ab: ?: The pictograph ◎ is a picture of an open mouth, the ⌒ is a picture of a man on his side. Combined these mean "open the side". When a pot is struck on its side, it is opened and the pieces scatter.

H) ⚜⌒◎ (פצה PTsH) ac: **Open** co: ? ab: ?

V) ⚜⌒◎ (פצה P-TsH) — **Open:** To open the mouth. [freq. 15] (vf: Paal) |kjv: open, rid, gape, utter| {str: 6475}

J) ⌒𝖸◎ (פוץ PWTs) ac: **Scatter** co: ? ab: ?: A breaking of something into pieces.

V) ⌒𝖸◎ (פוץ PWTs) — **Scatter:** [freq. 67] (vf: Paal, Niphal, Hiphil, Pilpel) |kjv: scatter, disperse, cast, drive, break, shake, dash, retire| {str: 6327}

i[fl]) ⚜⌒𝖸�◎+ (תפוצה T-PW-TsH) — **Scattering:** [freq. 1] |kjv: disperse| {str: 8600}

M) ⌒🠃◎ (פיץ PYTs) ac: ? co: **Club** ab: ?

k[m]) ⌒🠃⌂◎ᴧ (מפיץ M-PYTs) — **Club:** [freq. 1] |kjv: maul| {str: 4650}

Adopted Roots;
2422	⌒⌂◎🠃	Scatter, Club
2597	𝔑工◎	Scatter
2625	⊞⌒◎	Break
2627	ᴧᴧ⌒◎	Crack

2628 ⟨⟩ Smash, Bruise

1387) ⟨⟩ (פק PQ) ac: **Crumble** co: **Riverbank** ab: ?: The riverbank restrains the river but the force of the river also eats away at the bank causing it to erode and collapse. (eng: peek -see adopted roots)

C) ⟨⟩ (אפק APQ) ac: ? co: **Riverbank** ab: ?

V) ⟨⟩ (אפק A-PQ) — **Restrain**: [freq. 7] (vf: Hitpael) |kjv: refrain, force, restrain| {str: 662}

b^m) ⟨⟩ (אפיק A-PYQ) — **Riverbank**: [freq. 19] |kjv: river, channel, stream, brook, mighty, scales, strong| {str: 650}

J) ⟨⟩ (פוק PWQ) ac: **Crumble** co: ? ab: ?: The crumbling of the riverbank by the force of the river.

V) ⟨⟩ (פוק PWQ) — I. **Crumble**: II. **Advance**: The advancing water from the crumbling riverbank causing it to become wider. [freq. 9] (vf: Paal, Hiphil) |kjv: stumble, move| {str: 6328, 6329}

M) ⟨⟩ (פיק PYQ) ac: **Crumble** co: ? ab: ?

N^m) ⟨⟩ (פיק PYQ) — **Crumble**: [freq. 1] |kjv: smite| {str: 6375}

Adopted Roots;
2036 ⟨⟩ Seek
2630 ⟨⟩ Oversee, Oversight
2631 ⟨⟩ Open
2633 ⟨⟩ Seek

1388) ⟨⟩ (פר PR) ac: **Tread** co: **Bull** ab: **Fruitful**: The pictograph ⟨⟩ is a picture of an open mouth, the ⟨⟩ is a picture of a head. Combined these mean "open the head". The heads of grains are scattered on the threshing floor, a smooth, hard and level surface. An ox is lead around the floor crushing the heads, opening them to reveal the seed inside. Also the fruit of trees that harvested. (eng: bull - with the exchange of the b and p and the l and r; fruit, also other fruits with a "pr" such as pear and apricot)

A) ⟨⟩ (פר PR) ac: ? co: **Bull** ab: ?

N^m) ⟨⟩ (פר PR) — **Bull**: [freq. 133] |kjv: bullock, bull, oxen, calf, young| {str: 6499}

N^fl) ⟨⟩ (פרה P-RH) — **Heifer**: [freq. 26] |kjv: heifer, kine| {str: 6510}

B) ⟨⟩ (פרר PRR) ac: **Break** co: ? ab: ?

V) ⟨⟩ (פרר P-RR) — **Break**: To throw something on the ground and break it by trampling. [freq. 50] (vf: Paal, Hiphil, Hophal, Pilpel) |kjv: break, void, defeat, disannul, disappoint, frustrate, nought, cease, clean, dissolved, divide| {str: 6565}

d^m) ⟨⟩ (פרור P-RWR) — **Skillet**: A flat surface for preparing foods. [freq. 3] |kjv: pot, pan| {str: 6517}

C) ⟨⟩ (אפר APR) ac: ? co: **Ash** ab: ?: At the conclusion of the treading, an abundance of fruit is acquired. Anything in abundance.

N^m) ⟨⟩ (אפר A-PR) — **Ash**: [freq. 24] |kjv: ash| {str: 665, 666}

D) ⌐ᗅᎶᗡ (פאר PAR) ac: ? co:
Decoration ab: ?: The fruits that grow on the branches of a tree as decorations.

V) ⌐ᗅᎶᗡ (פאר P-AR) —
Decorate: [freq. 14] (vf: Hitpael, Piel) |kjv: glorify, beatify, boast, bough, glory| {str: 6286}

N^m) ⌐ᗅᎶᗡ (פאר P-AR) —
Turban: A piece of cloth that is wound around the head as a decoration. [freq. 7] |kjv: goodly, beauty, goodly, ornament, tire| {str: 6287}

g^fl) ⌐ᎶᗅᎶᏑ (פוארה PW-A-RH) — **Branch:** [ms: פארה] [freq. 7] |kjv: branch, bough, sprig| {str: 6288}

i^fl) ⌐ᗅᎶᗡ+ (תפארה TP-A-RH) — **Decoration:** [df: תפארת] [freq. 51] |kjv: glory, beauty, beautiful, honour, fair, glorious, bravery, comely, excellent| {str: 8597}

l^m) ⌐ᗅᎶᗡᗅᎶᗡ (פאראר P-AR-AR) — **Blackness:** [Unknown connection to root;] [df: פארור] [freq. 2] |kjv: blackness| {str: 6289}

E) ⌐ᎶᗡᎶ (פרא PRA) ac: ? co:
Fruit ab: ?

V) ⌐ᎶᗡᎶ (פרא P-RA) —
Fruitful: [freq. 1] (vf: Hiphil) |kjv: fruitful| {str: 6500}

N^m) ⌐ᎶᗡᎶ (פרא P-RA) —
Wild-ass: A wild animal as prolific. [df: פרה] [freq. 10] |kjv: wild ass| {str: 6501}

H) ⌐ᎶᗡᏑ (פרה PRH) ac: ? co:
Fruit ab: ?

V) ⌐ᎶᗡᏑ (פרה P-RH) —
Fruitful: [freq. 29] (vf: Paal,

Hiphil) |kjv: fruitful, increase, bear, forth, bring| {str: 6509}

f^m) ⌐ᎶᗡᎬ (פרי P-RY) —
Fruit: [freq. 119] |kjv: fruit, fruitful, bough, reward| {str: 6529}

J) ⌐ᎶᏑᎳ (פור PWR) ac: **Crush** co:
Winepress ab: ?: Grapes are placed in winepress and trampled on to crush the fruit bringing out the juice of the grape.

V) ⌐ᎶᏑᎳ (פור PWR) — **Crush:**
[freq. 3] (vf: Hiphil) |kjv: bring, broken, take| {str: 6331}

N^fl) ⌐ᎶᏑᎶᏑ (פורה PW-RH) —
Winepress: [freq. 2] |kjv: winepress, press| {str: 6333}

Adopted Roots;

2604	⌐Ꮆ⊗	Burst
2634	⌐ᎶᎢ	Divide, Seed
2635	⌐ᎶᏓ	Village
2636	⌐ᎶᎿ	Burst, Bud
2637	⌐Ꮆ⊗	Break
2638	⌐ᎶᎳ	Whip
2639	⌐ᎶᎷ	Rip
2640	⌐Ꮆᛒ	Split, Hoof
2642	⌐ᎶᎯ	Spread, Breach
2643	⌐Ꮆᗒ	Tear
2740	ᗒᎳᎶ	Tie, Sash, Conspire
2653	+Ꮆ	Open, Interpretation
2811	ᎳᎳᎶ	Burst, Grain

⌐⌐⌐⌐⌐⌐⌐

1389) ⌐ᎳᎳ (פש PSh) ac: **Spread** co: ?
ab: **Excess**

A) ⌐ᎳᎳ (פש PSh) ac: **Spread** co: ?
ab: ?

N^m) ⌐ᎳᎳ (פש PSh) — **Excess:**
As spread out. [freq. 1] |kjv: extremity| {str: 6580}

H) ⌐ᎳᎳᏑ (פשה PShH) ac: **Spread**
co: ? ab: ?

V) ⟨Ψ⟩ (פשה P-ShH) — **Spread:** [df: פשׂה] [freq. 22] (vf: Paal) |kjv: spread, abroad| {str: 6581}

J) ⟨PWSh⟩ (פוש PWSh) ac: **Scatter** co: ? ab: ?

V) ⟨PWSh⟩ (פוש PWSh) — **Scatter:** [freq. 4] (vf: Paal, Niphal) |kjv: spread, grow, scatter| {str: 6335}

Adopted Roots;
2193 ⟨⟩ Free, Freedom
2620 ⟨⟩ March, Step
2621 ⟨⟩ Spread
2644 ⟨⟩ Spread, Dung
2645 ⟨⟩ Tear
2646 ⟨⟩ Spread
2648 ⟨⟩ Spread, Flax
2241 ⟨⟩ Fat
3050 ⟨⟩
3052 ⟨⟩
3053 ⟨⟩ Spread

~~~~~~~~~~

1390) ⟨⟩ (פת PT) ac: **Perforate** co: **Hole** ab: **Simple:** The pictograph ◇ is a picture of an open mouth or hole, the † is a post for hanging the standard. Combined these mean "hole for a post". A hole made for inserting something. The act of intercourse.

A) ⟨⟩ (פת PT) ac: ? co: **Hole** ab: ?

N^f) ⟨⟩ (פת PT) — **Hole:** A hole that is made in the bread by pressing. Also a morsel, as the hole, that has been removed from the bread by pinching out a piece. [freq. 15] |kjv: morsel, piece, meat| {str: 6595}

B) ⟨⟩ (פתת PTT) ac: **Perforate** co: ? ab: ?: Full of holes.

V) ⟨⟩ (פתת P-TT) — **Perforate:** [freq. 1] (vf: Paal) |kjv: part| {str: 6626}

H) ⟨Ψ⟩ (פתה PTH) ac: **Entice** co: ? ab: **Simple**

V) ⟨Ψ⟩ (פתה P-TH) — **Entice:** [freq. 28] (vf: Paal, Niphal, Hiphil, Pual, Piel) |kjv: entice, deceive, persuade, flatter, allure, enlarge, silly| {str: 6601}

f^) ⟨⟩ (פתי P-TY) — **I. Simple:** One easily persuaded, seduced or deceived. [df: פתאי] **II. Width:** [Unknown connection to root Aramaic only] [freq. 21] |kjv: simple, foolish, simplicity, width| {str: 6612, 6613}

f^3) ⟨⟩ (פתיות PT-YWT) — **Simple:** One easily persuaded, seduced or deceived. [freq. 1] |kjv: simple| {str: 6615}

J) ⟨⟩ (פות PWT) ac: ? co: **Socket** ab: ?: A hole for inserting a rod. The hinges of a door were made by placing a hole in the door jam, the door had rods on the side that are set into the holes, allowing the door to swivel in the socket. Also the vagina for intercourse.

N^f) ⟨⟩ (פות PWT) — **Socket:** [ms: פת] [df: פתה] [freq. 2] |kjv: hinge, secret part| {str: 6596}

L) ⟨⟩ (יפת YPT) ac: ? co: ? ab: **Wonder:** A hole for inserting a rod. The hinges of a door were made by placing a hole in the door jam, the door had rods on the side that are set into the holes, allowing the door to swivel in the socket. Also the vagina for intercourse.

a^m) †⌒Y៳ (מופת MW-PT) —
Wonder: An amazing sight or
event as a piercing. [freq. 36]
|kjv: wonder, sign, miracle| {str:
4159}

Adopted Roots;
2602 †ᴍ⌒ Pit
2649 ᴍ†⌒ Open, Door
2651 ᐢ†⌒ Open
2652 ⊘†⌒ Wink, Moment

1391) �br⌒ (פע PGh) ac: ? co: ? ab: ?

C) �br⌒ᒑ (אפע APGh) ac: ? co:
Viper ab: ?

N^m) �br⌒ᒑ (אפע A-PGh) —
Nothing: Through the idea of a
hiss. [freq. 1] |kjv: nought| {str:
659}

N^{f1}) ⴲᕠ⌒ᒑ (אפעה AP-GhH)
— **Viper:** [freq. 3] |kjv: viper|
{str: 660}

Tsad

1392) ᐣᴏᴧ (צא TsA) ac: **Issue** co: **Excrement** ab: ?: The ᴏᴧ is a picture of a man laying down or squatting. To issue out of something. This parent root is related to ᐣᴏᴧ.

A) ᐣᴏᴧ (צא TsA) ac: **?** co: **Excrement** ab: ?: In the sense of issuing out of a man.

N[fl]) ᐣᴏᴧ (צא Ts-A) — **Excrement**: [freq. 2] |kjv: come| {str: 6627}

I[m]) ᐣᴏᴧᐣᴏᴧ (צאצא TsA-TsA) — **Offspring**: What issues out of a generation. [freq. 11] |kjv: offspring, come| {str: 6631}

J) ᐣYᴏᴧ (צוא TsWA) ac: **?** co: **Excrement** ab: ?

N[m]) ᐣYᴏᴧ (צוא TsWA) — **Filthy**: Something soiled with excrement. [ms: צא] [freq. 2] |kjv: filthy| {str: 6674}

N[fl]) ⚇ᐣYᴏᴧ (צואה TsW-AH) — **Excrement**: [ms: צאה] [freq. 5] |kjv: dung, filthiness, filth| {str: 6675}

L) ᐣᴏᴧ� (יצא YTsA) ac: **Issue** co: **Excrement** ab: ?: An issuing out of one place to another.

V) ᐣᴏᴧᴶ (יצא Y-TsA) — **Go out**: To go, come or issue out. [Hebrew and Aramaic; A generic verb with a wide application meaning to go or come out] [freq. 1070] (vf: Paal, Hiphil, Hophal) |kjv: out, forth, bring, come, proceed, go, depart, finished| {str: 3318, 3319}

a[m]) ᐣᴏᴧYᴧᴧ (מוצא MW-TsA) — **Going-out**: Something that is going, coming or issuing out such as a spring. [ms: מצא] [freq. 27] |kjv: out, go, spring, brought, east, bud, outgoing, proceed| {str: 4161}

a[fl]) ⚇ᐣᴏᴧYᴧᴧ (מוצאה MW-Ts-AH) — **I. Origin**: The history of where one is issued out from. **II. Excrement**: What comes out of man. [freq. 2] |kjv: draught, going| {str: 4163}

b[m]) ᐣᴧᴧᴏᴧᴶ (יציא Y-TsYA) — **Excrement**: What comes out of man. [freq. 1] |kjv: come| {str: 3329}

i[fl]) ⚇ᐣᴏᴧYt (תוצאה TW-Ts-AH) — **Goings**: [ms: תצאה] [freq. 23] |kjv: going, outgoing, issue, border| {str: 8444}

~~~~~~~~~~

1393) �ᴏᴧ (צב TsB) ac: **Stand** co: **Wall** ab: ?: The pictograph ᴏᴧ is a picture of a man on his side, the ᴍ is a picture of a tent. Combined these mean "side of the tent". The walls of the tent enclose what is inside. The tent walls stand firm and strong, protecting it from the harsh elements. As the family swells in size, the tent walls are enlarged.

A) �ᴏᴧ (צב TsB) ac: **?** co: **Wall** ab: ?

N[m]) �ᴏᴧ (צב TsB) — **I. Wagon**: A walled wagon for transport. **II. Tortoise**: From its shell as a wagon. [freq. 3] |kjv:

covered, litter, tortoise| {str: 6632}

a[m]) ꡯơʌʌʌ (מצב MTs-B) — **Garrison:** The walled in army. [df: נצב] [freq. 10] |kjv: garrison, station, stood| {str: 4673}

a[fl]) ꘮ꡯơʌʌʌ (מצבה MTs-BH) — **Garrison:** The walled in army. [freq. 2] |kjv: garrison, army| {str: 4675}

f[m]) ⟶ꡯơʌ (צבי Ts-BY) — **I. Gazelle:** An animal of a herd as an army. **II. Beauty:** The beauty and grace of the gazelle. [freq. 32] |kjv: roe, roebuck, glory, glorious, beautiful, beauty, goodly, pleasant| {str: 6643}

f[fl]) ꘮⟶ꡯơʌ (צביה TsB-YH) — **Gazelle:** A female gazelle. [freq. 2] |kjv: roe| {str: 6646}

r[m]) Yꡯơʌ (צבו Ts-BW) — **Purpose:** [Unknown connection to root; Aramaic only] [freq. 1] |kjv: purpose| {str: 6640}

E) ⟩ꡯơʌ (צבא TsBA) ac: **Muster** co: **Army** ab: **?:** The mustering of an army as a wall of protection.

V) ⟩ꡯơʌ (צבא Ts-BA) — **I. Muster:** To gather for service, work or war. [Hebrew and Aramaic] **II. Will:** Ones desires. [Aramaic only] [freq. 23] (vf: Paal, Hiphil) |kjv: fight, assemble, muster, war, perform, wait, will| {str: 6633, 6634}

N[m]) ⟩ꡯơʌ (צבא Ts-BA) — **Army:** [freq. 485] |kjv: host, war, army, battle, service| {str: 6635}

H) ꘮ꡯơʌ (צבה TsBH) ac: **Swell** co: **?** ab: **?:** As the family grows the tent is enlarged and seen as a swelling of the tent.

V) ꘮ꡯơʌ (צבה Ts-BH) — **Swell:** [freq. 3] (vf: Paal, Hiphil) |kjv: swell, fight| {str: 6638}

N[m]) ꘮ꡯơʌ (צבה Ts-BH) — **Swelling:** [freq. 1] |kjv: swell| {str: 6639}

L) ꡯơʌ⟶ (יצב YTsB) ac: **Stand** co: **?** ab: **Truth:** A standing firm and fast as a wall.

V) ꡯơʌ⟶ (יצב Y-TsB) — **Stand:** [Hebrew and Aramaic] [freq. 49] (vf: Hitpael) |kjv: stand, present, set, withstand, remain, resort, truth| {str: 3320, 3321}

b[m]) ꡯ⟶ơʌ⟶ (יציב Y-TsYB) — **Truth:** What stands firm. [Aramaic only] [freq. 5] |kjv: true, truth, certainty, certain| {str: 3330}

Adopted Roots;

2033	꘮ơʌꡯ	Gather, Fence
2426	ꡯơʌ꘧	Stand, Pillar
2654	⊗ꡯơʌ	Grasp
2656	꘮ꡯơʌ	Pile, Pile
2657	ꕥꡯơʌ	Handful

1394) ꘯ơʌ (צג TsG) ac: **?** co: **?** ab: **?**

L) ꘯ơʌ⟶ (יצג YTsG) ac: **Set** co: **?** ab: **?:** A placing in a specific location.

V) ꘯ơʌ⟶ (יצג Y-TsG) — **Set:** To set something in a place. [freq. 16] (vf: Hiphil, Hophal) |kjv: set, made, put, establish, leave, present, stay| {str: 3322}

1395) ᴛᴑᴧ (צד TsD) ac: **Hide** co: **Side** ab: **Stronghold:** The pictograph ᴑᴧ is a picture of the side of a man. One lies down to sleep, hide or ambush. (eng: side)

A) ᴛᴑᴧ (צד TsD) ac: **?** co: **Side** ab: **Stronghold**

Nᵐ) ᴛᴑᴧ (צד TsD) — **I. Side: II. Concerning:** On the side of something. [Aramaic only] [freq. 35] |kjv: side, beside, another, concerning, against| {str: 6654, 6655}

kᵐ) ᴛᴑᴧᴧᴧ (מצד M-TsD) — **Stronghold:** A hiding place surrounded by sides. [freq. 11] |kjv: stronghold, hold, castle, fort, munition| {str: 4679}

adᶠˡ) ⵣᴛᴑYᴑᴧᴧ (מצודה M-Ts-WDH) — **Stronghold:** A hiding place surrounded by sides. [freq. 22] |kjv: fortress, hold, snare, stronghold, castle, fort, defense| {str: 4686}

H) ⵣᴛᴑᴧ (צדה TsDH) ac: **Lay down** co: **?** ab: **?**

V) ⵣᴛᴑᴧ (צדה Ts-DH) — **Lay-down:** [freq. 3] (vf: Paal, Niphal) |kjv: wait, hunt, destroy| {str: 6658}

Nᵐ) ⵣᴛᴑᴧ (צדה Ts-DH) — **True:**

Posed as a question, "is it true", as if laying something down for investigation.

[Aramaic only] [ar: צדא] [freq. 1] |kjv:

| {str: 6656}

fᶠˡ) ⵣᴙᴛᴑᴧ (צדיה TsD-YH) — **Ambush:** A laying down in wait. [freq. 2] |kjv: lay| {str: 6660}

J) ᴛYᴑᴧ (צוד TsWD) ac: **Hunt** co: **Snare** ab: **?**

V) ᴛYᴑᴧ (צוד TsWD) — **Hunt:** To hunt in the sense of laying in ambush. [freq. 18] (vf: Paal, Hitpael) |kjv: hunt, take, chase, provision, sore| {str: 6679}

aᵐ) ᴛYᴑᴧᴧᴧ (מצוד M-TsWD) — **Snare:** A tool used for trapping animals while the hunter lies in wait. [freq. 6] |kjv: net, snare, bulwark| {str: 4685}

aᶠˡ) ⵣᴛYᴑᴧᴧᴧ (מצודה M-TsW-DH) — **Snare:** A tool used for trapping animals while the hunter lies in wait. [freq. 6] |kjv: net, munition, hold| {str: 4685}

M) ᴛᴙᴸᴑᴧ (ציד TsYD) ac: **Hunt** co: **Meat** ab: **?**

Nᵐ) ᴛᴙᴸᴑᴧ (ציד TsYD) — **I. Hunter:** One who lays in ambush. **II. Meat:** The produce of the hunt. [freq. 20] |kjv: venison, hunter, victuals, provision, hunting, catch, food, hunting| {str: 6718, 6719}

Nᶠˡ) ⵣᴛᴙᴸᴑᴧ (צידה TsY-DH) — **Meat:** The produce of the hunt. [ms: צדה] [freq. 10] |kjv: venison, victuals, provision, meat| {str: 6720}

Adopted Roots;
2476 ᴧ⊗⋞ Side
2658 ᴑ-ᴛᴑᴧ Straight, Righteous

1396) ⵣᴑᴧ (צה TsH) ac: **?** co: **?** ab: **?**

231

1397) צֻו (צו TsW) ac: **Command** co: Command ab: ?

  A) צֻו (צו TsW) ac: ? co: Command ab: ?

    N^f) צֻו (צו TsW) — **Command:** [freq. 9] |kjv: precept, commandment| {str: 6673}

  H) צֻוה (צוה TsWH) ac: ? co: Command ab: ?

    V) צֻוה (צוה Ts-WH) — **Command:** [freq. 494] (vf: Pual, Piel) |kjv: command, charge, commandment, appoint, bade, order, commander| {str: 6680}

    h^{fl}) מצֻוה (מצוה MTs-WH) — **Command:** [freq. 181] |kjv: commandment, precept, law, ordinance| {str: 4687}

1398) צֻז (צז TsZ) ac: ? co: ? ab: ?

1399) צֻח (צח TsHh) ac: ? co: **Desert** ab: ?: The pictograph צ is a picture of a man on his side representing trouble, the ח is a picture of a wall that separates the inside from the outside. Combined these mean "trouble outside". The desert as a hot and dry place.

  A) צֻח (צח TsHh) ac: ? co: **Desert** ab: ?

    N^m) צֻח (צח TsHh) — **Dry:** [freq. 4] |kjv: white, clear, plainly, dry| {str: 6703}

  B) צֻחח (צחח TsHhHh) ac: ? co: Desert ab: ?

    V) צֻחח (צחח Ts-HhHh) — **White:** To be white. From the drying and bleaching of things left in the sun. [freq. 1] (vf: Paal) |kjv: white| {str: 6705}

    b^m) צֻחיח (צחיח Ts-HhYHh) — **Top:** [Unknown connection to root;] [freq. 5] |kjv: top| {str: 6706}

    b^{fl}) צֻחיחה (צחיחה Ts-HhY-HhH) — **Dry:** [freq. 1] |kjv: dry| {str: 6707}

    l^{fl}) צֻחצחה (צחצחה TsHh-Ts-HhH) — **Desert:** [freq. 1] |kjv: drought| {str: 6710}

    bf^m) צֻחיחי (צחיחי Ts-HhY-HhY) — **Top:** [Unknown connection to root;] [freq. 1] |kjv: high place| {str: 6708}

  H) צֻחה (צחה TsHhH) ac: ? co: Dry ab: ?

    e^m) צֻיחה (ציחה TsY-HhH) — **Dried:** [ms: צחה] [freq. 1] |kjv: dried| {str: 6704}

  J) צֻוח (צוח TsWHh) ac: **Shout** co: ? ab: ?

    V) צֻוח (צוח TsWHh) — **Shout:** [freq. 1] (vf: Paal) |kjv: shout| {str: 6681}

    N^{fl}) צֻוחה (צוחה TsW-HhH) — **Shout:** [freq. 4] |kjv: cry, crying, complaining| {str: 6682}

Adopted Roots;
2661 צֻחר White
2679 צֻעק Cry
2756 זֻעק Outcry

1400) צֻט (צט TsTh) ac: ? co: ? ab: ?

1401) צﬡ‎ (צי TsY) ac: **?** co: **Desert** ab: **?**: The desert nomads life was a continual traveling from one location to another always hunting for pastures. The stars and terrain served as landmarks to guide the nomad on his journey. This parent root is related to צﬡ‎ through the idea of migration as an issuing out. (eng: sign)

A) צﬡ‎ (צי TsY) ac: **?** co: **Desert** ab: **?**

N^m) צﬡ‎ (צי TsY) — **Ship:** Just as the nomad travels the wilderness, ships are nomads of the sea. [freq. 4] |kjv: ship| {str: 6716}

N^fl) צﬡ‎ (ציה Ts-YH) — **Desert:** [freq. 16] |kjv: dry, wilderness, drought, solitary, barren| {str: 6723}

f^m) צﬡ‎ (ציי Ts-YY) — **Desert:** [freq. 6] |kjv: desert, wilderness| {str: 6728}

j^m) צﬡ‎ (ציון Ts-YWN) — I. **Desert:** II. **Landmark:** The marks in the desert which the nomad follows as road signs. [freq. 5] |kjv: dry, title, waymark, sign| {str: 6724, 6725}

1402) צﬡ‎ (צך TsK) ac: **Press** co: **Burden** ab: **Stress**

J) צﬡ‎ (צוך TsWK) ac: **Press** co: **Burden** ab: **Stress**

V) צﬡ‎ (צוך TsWK) — **Press:** To press into a tight place, an oppression. [df: צוק] [freq. 11] (vf: Hiphil) |kjv: distress, oppressor, sore, press, straiten| {str: 6693}

N^m) צﬡ‎ (צוך TsWK) — **Burden:** A heavy load that causes a pressing. [df: צוק] [freq. 1] |kjv: anguish| {str: 6695}

N^fl) צﬡ‎ (צוכה TsW-KH) — **Burden:** A heavy load that causes a pressing. [df: צוקה] [freq. 3] |kjv: anguish| {str: 6695}

a^m) צﬡ‎ (מצוך M-TsWK) — **Stress:** Something that causes oppression. [df: מצוק] [freq. 6] |kjv: straightness, distress, anguish| {str: 4689}

k^fl) צﬡ‎ (מצוכה M-TsW-KH) — **Stress:** Something that causes oppression. [df: מצוקה מצקה] [freq. 7] |kjv: distress, anguish| {str: 4691}

L) צﬡ‎ (יצך YTsK) ac: **?** co: **?** ab: **Anguish**

a^m) צﬡ‎ (מוצך MW-TsK) — **Anguish:** [df: מוצק] [freq. 3] |kjv: straitness, straitened, vexation| {str: 4164}

1403) צﬡ‎ (צל TsL) ac: **?** co: **Shadow** ab: **?**: A place of shadows.

A) צﬡ‎ (צל TsL) ac: **?** co: **Shadow** ab: **?**

N^m) צﬡ‎ (צל TsL) — **Shadow:** [freq. 49] |kjv: shadow, defense, shade| {str: 6738}

k^fl) צﬡ‎ (מצולה M-TsW-LH) — **Shade:** [ms: מצלה] [freq. 1] |kjv: bottom| {str: 4699}

el^m) צﬡ‎ (צילצל TsY-L-TsL) — I. **Shadow:** II. **Locust:** The flying swarm causes a large shadow. III. **Spear:** [Unknown connection to root;] [df: צלצל] [freq. 6] |kjv: locust, spear, shadowing| {str: 6767}

B) ⟨צלל⟩ (TsLL) ac: **Sink** co: **Shade** ab: ?

V) ⟨צלל⟩ (Ts-LL) — **I. Sink:** From the darkness of depth. **II. Shadow:** [freq. 3] (vf: Paal, Hiphil) |kjv: sink, shadow, dark| {str: 6749, 6751}

N^m) ⟨צלל⟩ (Ts-LL) — **Shadow:** [freq. 4] |kjv: shadow| {str: 6752}

d^m) ⟨צליל⟩ (Ts-LWL) — **Cake:** As becoming dark when cooked. [freq. 2] |kjv: cake| {str: 6742}

C) ⟨אצל⟩ (ATsL) ac: ? co: **Near** ab: ?

V) ⟨אצל⟩ (A-TsL) — **Set-aside:** To reserve or put aside something in the sense of keeping in the shadow. [freq. 5] (vf: Paal, Niphal, Hiphil) |kjv: take, reserve, keep, straighten| {str: 680}

N^m) ⟨אצל⟩ (A-TsL) — **Near:** Being next to something in the sense of being it its shade. [freq. 58] |kjv: by, beside, near, at, with, from, against, close, to, toward, unto| {str: 681}

b^f) ⟨אציל⟩ (A-TsYL) — **Noble:** [Unknown connection to root;] [freq. 2] |kjv: noble, chief| {str: 678}

b^fl) ⟨אצילה⟩ (A-TsY-LH) — **Joint:** The joint in the arm, either the elbow or armpit. [Unknown connection to root;] [freq. 3] |kjv: hole, great| {str: 679}

D) ⟨צאל⟩ (TsAL) ac: ? co: **Tree** ab: ?: What casts a shadow of shade.

N^m) ⟨צאל⟩ (Ts-AL) — **Tree:** [freq. 2] |kjv: tree| {str: 6628}

E) ⟨צלא⟩ (TsLA) ac: **Pray** co: ? ab: ?: [Unknown connection to root;]

V) ⟨צלא⟩ (Ts-LA) — **Pray:** [Aramaic only] [freq. 2] (vf: Paal) |kjv: pray| {str: 6739}

F) ⟨הצל⟩ (HTsL) ac: ? co: ? ab: **Escape:** A hiding in the shadows.

N^fl) ⟨הצל⟩ (H-TsL) — **Escape:** [freq. 1] |kjv: deliverance| {str: 2020}

G) ⟨צהל⟩ (TsHL) ac: **Shout** co: ? ab: ?: The shouting of a voice in joy or singing. Also the neighing of a horse or bull as a shouting. [Unknown connection to root;]

V) ⟨צהל⟩ (Ts-HL) — **Shout:** [freq. 9] (vf: Paal, Hiphil, Piel) |kjv: cry, bellow, neigh, rejoice, shine, shout, lift| {str: 6670}

h^fl) ⟨מצהלה⟩ (MTs-H-LH) — **Shouting:** [freq. 2] |kjv: neighing| {str: 4684}

H) ⟨צלה⟩ (TsLH) ac: **Roast** co: ? ab: ?: A roast becomes dark when cooked.

V) ⟨צלה⟩ (Ts-LH) — **Roast:** [freq. 3] (vf: Paal) |kjv: roast| {str: 6740}

f^m) ⟨צלי⟩ (Ts-LY) — **Roast:** [freq. 3] |kjv: roast| {str: 6748}

J) ⟨צול⟩ (TsWL) ac: ? co: **Deep** ab: ?: The deep ocean as a place of darkness.

N^fl) ⟨צולה⟩ (TsW-LH) — **Deep:** [freq. 1] |kjv: deep| {str: 6683}

k^{fl}) ✶ᒎᎧYονᴧᴧ (מְצוּלָה M-TsW-
LH) — **Deep:** [ms: מצלה] [freq.
11] |kjv: deep, depth, bottom|
{str: 4688}

Adopted Roots;
2662 ᴛᴛᒎον Advance, Bowl
2663 ᴧᴧᒎον Image
2428 ᒎονᒐ Deliver

─────────

1404) ᴧᴧον (צֹם TsM) ac: **Thirst** co:
Dry ab: ?: The pictograph ον is a picture
of a man on his side representing the
hunt, the ᴧᴧ is a picture of water.
Combined these mean "hunt for water". A
fasting from water, or food.

A) ᴧᴧον (צֹם TsM) ac: ? co: **Tie** ab:
?: Something tied around the mouth.
[Unknown connection to root;]
N^{fl}) ✶Ꭷᴧᴧον (צמה Ts-MH) —
Veil: As bound around the face.
[freq. 4] |kjv: lock| {str: 6777}

B) ᴧᴧᴧᴧον (צֹמֹם TsMM) ac: **Thirst**
co: ? ab: ?
b^m) ᴧᴧᒐᴧᴧον (צמים Ts-MYM)
— **Thirsty:** [freq. 2] |kjv:
robber| {str: 6782}

E) ᒍᴧᴧον (צמא TsMA) ac: **Thirst**
co: **Dry** ab: ?
V) ᒍᴧᴧον (צמא Ts-MA) —
Thirst: [freq. 10] (vf: Paal) |kjv:
thirst, athirst, thirsty| {str: 6770}
N^m) ᒍᴧᴧον (צמא Ts-MA) —
Thirst: [freq. 26] |kjv: thirst,
thirsty| {str: 6771, 6772}
e^{fl}) ✶ᒍᴧᴧᒐον (צימאה TsY-
M-AH) — **Thirst:** [ms: צמאה]
[freq. 1] |kjv: thirst| {str: 6773}
ej^m) ᒐYᒍᴧᴧᒐον (צימאון
TsY-M-AWN) — **Dry land:** A
thirsty land. [ms: צמאון] [freq.

3] |kjv: drought, thirsty, dry
ground| {str: 6774}
J) ᴧᴧYον (צום TsWM) ac: **Fast** co:
? ab: ?: An abstinence from water, or
food.
V) ᴧᴧYον (צום TsWM) —
Fast: To abstain from food.
[freq. 21] (vf: Paal) |kjv: fast|
{str: 6684}
N^m) ᴧᴧYον (צום TsWM) —
Fast: An abstinence from food.
[ms: צם] [freq. 26] |kjv: fast|
{str: 6685}

Adopted Roots;
2671 ᴧᴧᒐον Wither
─────────

1405) ᒐον (צן TsN) ac: ? co: **Sheep** ab:
?
H) ✶ᒐον (צנה TsNH) ac: ? co:
Sheep ab: ?
g^m) ✶ᒐYον (צונה T-sWNH) —
Sheep: [ms: צנה] [freq. 2] |kjv:
sheep| {str: 6792}
J) ᒐYον (צון TsWN) ac: ? co: **Sheep**
ab: ?
N^f) ᒐYον (צון TsWN) — **Flock:**
[df: צאן צאון] [freq. 274] |kjv:
flock, sheep, cattle, lamb| {str:
6629}

Adopted Roots;
2670 ᴛᴛᒐον Descend
2672 ◌ᒐον Low
2674 ◌ᒐον Confine, Stocks
2675 ◌ᒐον Pipe
─────────

1406) ◌ον (צס TsS) ac: ? co: ? ab: ?
─────────

1407) (צע TsAh) ac: **Spread** co: **Bed** ab: **?:** The pictograph is a picture of a man laying on his side as at rest. The bed consisted of blankets spread out on the floor of the tent. A spreading out of something.

A) (צע TsAh) ac: **?** co: **Bed** ab: **?**

a[m]) (מצע MTs-Ah) — **Bed:** [freq. 1] |kjv: bed| {str: 4702}

ld[m]) (צעצוע TsAh-TsWAh) — **Image:** [Unknown connection to root;] [ms: צעצע] [freq. 1] |kjv: image| {str: 6816}

H) (צעה TsAhH) ac: **Wander** co: **?** ab: **?:** A traveling through a spread out area.

V) (צעה Ts-AhH) — **Wander:** [freq. 5] (vf: Paal, Piel) |kjv: wander, exile, travel| {str: 6808}

L) (יצע YTsAh) ac: **Spread** co: **Bed** ab: **?**

V) (יצע Y-TsAh) — **Spread:** To spread out something to lay on. [freq. 4] (vf: Hiphil, Hophal) |kjv: spread, bed| {str: 3331}

d[m]) (יצוע Y-TsWAh) — **Bed:** [freq. 11] |kjv: chamber, bed, couch| {str: 3326}

~~~~~~~~~~~

1408) (צף TsP) ac: **Watch** co: **Watchtower** ab: **?:** (eng: spy)

A) (צף TsP) ac: **Watch** co: **Watchtower** ab: **?**

N[f4]) (צפית Ts-PYT) — **Watchtower:** As watches over an area. [freq. 1] |kjv: watchtower| {str: 6844}

j[f]) (צפון Ts-PWN) — **North:** From the north star which is watched for direction. [ms: צפן] [freq. 153] |kjv: north, northward, northern| {str: 6828}

jf[m]) (צפוני Ts-PW-NY) — **Northern:** From the north star which is watched for direction. [freq. 1] |kjv: northern| {str: 6830}

H) (צפה TsPH) ac: **Watch** co: **Watchtower** ab: **?:** A covering of an area by watching.

V) (צפה Ts-PH) — **I. Watch: II. Overlay:** [Unknown connection to root] [freq. 83] (vf: Paal, Pual, Piel) |kjv: watch, watchman, behold, look, espy, overlay, cover, garnish| {str: 6822, 6823}

f[f1]) (ציפיה TsY-P-YH) — **Watching:** [ms: צפיה] [freq. 1] |kjv: watching| {str: 6836}

h[m]) (מצפה MTs-PH) — **Watchtower:** A place for watching. [freq. 2] |kjv: watchtower| {str: 4707}

~~~~~~~~~~~

1409) (צץ TsTs) ac: **Bloom** co: **Blossom** ab: **?:** The function of the blossom is to produce the fruit of the tree.

J) (צוץ TsWTs) ac: **Bloom** co: **?** ab: **?**

V) (צוץ TsWTs) — **Bloom:** [freq. 9] (vf: Paal, Hiphil) |kjv: flourish, blossom, bloom, show| {str: 6692}

M) (ציץ TsYTs) ac: **?** co: **Blossom** ab: **?**

Nᵐ) ציץ (ציץ TsYTs) —
Blossom: [ms: צץ] [freq. 15]
|kjv: blossom, flower, plate,
wing| {str: 6731}

Nᶠ¹) ציצה (ציצה TsY-TsH)
— **Blossom:** [freq. 1] |kjv:
flower| {str: 6733}

Nᶠ⁴) ציצית (ציצית TsY-
TsYT) — **Blossom:** A tassel or
lock of hair as blossoms. [ms:
ציצת] [freq. 4] |kjv: fringe, lock|
{str: 6734}

~~~~~~~~~~~

1410) צק (צק TsQ) ac: **Pour** co: **Cast**
ab: **Image:** A molten metal is poured into
a mold to form a cast object or image.
(eng: cast - a reversal of the letters)

A) צק (צק TsQ) ac: **?** co: **Image**
ab: **?**

aᶠ⁴) מצקית (מצקית MTs-
QYT) — **Imagery:** The casting
of an image. [df: משכית] [freq.
6] |kjv: picture, image, wish,
conceit, imagery| {str: 4906}

bᶠ¹) צקיה (צקיה TsQ-YH)
— **Image:** The casting of an
image. [df: שכיה] [freq. 1] |kjv:
picture| {str: 7914}

C) אצק (אצק ATsQ) ac:
Casting co: **Pot** ab: **?**

Nᵐ) אצק (אצק A-TsQ) —
Pot: A cast iron pot. [df: אסך]
[freq. 1] |kjv: pot| {str: 610}

J) צוק (צוק TsWQ) ac: **Pour** co:
Pillar ab: **?**

V) צוק (צוק TsWQ) —
Pour: To pour molten metal.
Also to pour water or oil onto
someone for washing or
anointing. [freq. 12] (vf: Paal,
Hiphil) |kjv: pour, molten,
anoint| {str: 5480, 6694}

aᵐ) מצוק (מצוק M-TsWQ)
— **Pillar:** A tall rock formation
which appears to be a cast pillar.
[ms: מצק] [freq. 2] |kjv: pillar,
situate| {str: 4690}

L) יצק (יצק YTsQ) ac: **Pour** co:
Cast ab: **?:** The pouring of molten
metal out of a funnel into a cast.

V) יצק (יצק Y-TsQ) —
Pour: To pour molten metal.
[df: יסך] [freq. 54] (vf: Paal,
Hiphil, Hophal, Participle) |kjv:
pour, cast, molten, firm, set, fast,
grow, hard, overflown, steadfast|
{str: 3251, 3332}

aᵐ) מוצק (מוצק MW-TsQ)
— **Casting:** [freq. 2] |kjv:
casting, hardness| {str: 4165}

aᶠ¹) מוצקה (מוצקה MW-
Ts-QH) — **Cast:** The vessel for
pouring the molten metal into.
[ms: מצקה] [freq. 2] |kjv: pipe,
cast| {str: 4166}

dᶠ¹) יצוקה (יצוקה Y-TsW-
QH) — **Cast:** A casting of
metals. [ms: יצקה] [freq. 1] |kjv:
cast| {str: 3333}

Adopted Roots;
2412 שֶׁצַ֫ק Pour
2450 שֶׁתֶ֫ק Pour
~~~~~~~~~~~

1411) צר (צר TsR) ac: **Press** co:
Enemy ab: **Trouble:** A pressing in or on
someone or something. (eng: sore; store)

A) צר (צר TsR) ac: **Press** co:
Enemy ab: **Trouble**

Nᵐ) צר (צר TsR) — I.
Enemy: One who closes in with
pressure. II. **Strait:** A narrow
tight place or situation. [freq.
105] |kjv: enemy, adversary,

trouble, distress, affliction, foe, narrow, strait, flint, sorrow| {str: 6862}

N^{f1}) צרה (צרה Ts-RH) — **Trouble:** [freq. 73] |kjv: trouble, distress, affliction, adversity, anguish, tribulation, adversary| {str: 6869}

f^m) צרי (צרי Ts-RY) — **Balm:** A salve rubbed and pressed into the skin. [freq. 6] |kjv: balm| {str: 6875}

k^m) מצר (מצר M-TsR) — **Strait:** A narrow tight place or situation. [freq. 3] |kjv: pains, distress, strait| {str: 4712}

B) צרר (צרר TsRR) ac: **Press** co: **Bundle** ab: ?: A pressing in or on someone or something.

V) צרר (צרר Ts-RR) — **Press:** [freq. 58] (vf: Paal, Hiphil, Pual, Participle) |kjv: enemy, distress, bind, vex, afflict, besiege, adversary, strait, trouble, bound, pangs| {str: 6887}

c^m) צרור (צרור Ts-RWR) — **I. Bundle:** Something that is bound up tight. [ms: צרר] **II. Pebble:** [Unknown connection to root] [freq. 11] |kjv: bundle, bag, bind, grain, stone| {str: 6872}

C) אצר (אצר ATsR) ac: **Press** co: **Belt** ab: ?: Something that is stored by being wrapped up tightly. A belt or waistcloth that is wrapped around the middle tightly.

V) אצר (אצר A-TsR) — **I. Belt:** To wrap around tightly. [df: אזר] **II. Store:** To store up something in a safe place as if bound up. [freq. 21] (vf: Paal,

Niphal, Piel) |kjv: gird, bind, compass, store, treasure| {str: 247, 686}

c^m) אצור (אצור A-TsWR) — **Waistband:** As bound around the middle. [df: אזור] [freq. 14] |kjv: girdle| {str: 232}

g^m) אוצר (אוצר AW-TsR) — **Storehouse:** A place where store are bound up. [freq. 79] |kjv: treasure, treasury, storehouse, cellar, armoury| {str: 214}

D) צאר (צאר TsAR) ac: ? co: **Neck** ab: ?

g^m) צואר (צואר T-sWAR) — **Neck:** From the soreness of the neck from carrying a load or from stress. [Hebrew and Aramaic] [freq. 45] |kjv: neck| {str: 6676, 6677}

G) צהר (צהר TsHR) ac: **Shine** co: **Oil** ab: ?: The olives are pressed to extract the glimmering oil.

V) צהר (צהר Ts-HR) — **Oil:** [freq. 1] (vf: Hiphil) |kjv: oil| {str: 6671}

g^f) צוהר (צוהר T-sWHR) — **Shining:** Something that shines bright. Also noon as the brightest part of the day. From the glistening of olive oil. [ms: צהר] [df: זהר] [freq. 26] |kjv: brightness, noon, noonday, day, midday, window| {str: 2096, 6672}

f^m) יצהר (יצהר YTs-HR) — **Oil:** [freq. 23] |kjv: oil, anointed| {str: 3323}

H) צרה (צרה TsRH) ac: **Crush** co: ? ab: ?

o^m) צורה (צורה TsW-RH) — **Crushed:** [df: זורה] [freq. 1] |kjv: crushed| {str: 2116}

J) ৪Y○৯ (צור TsWR) ac: **Press** co:
Flint ab: **?**

   V) ৪Y○৯ (צור TsWR) — **Press:**
[df: זור] [freq. 41] (vf: Paal)
|kjv: besiege, siege, distress,
bind, adversary, assault, bag,
beset, cast, fashion, fortify,
inclose, bind, crush, closed,
thrust| {str: 2115, 6696}

   Nᵐ) ৪Y○৯ (צור TsWR) —
Flint: A very hard rock that
when fractured forms a razor
sharp edge. Used for knives,
spears or arrowheads. [ms: צר]
[freq. 80] |kjv: rock, strength,
sharp, god, beauty, edge, stone,
mighty, strong, stone, flint| {str:
6697, 6864}

   Nᶠˡ) ❀৪Y○৯ (צורה TsW-RH) —
Form: In the sense of being
pressed. [freq. 4] |kjv: form| {str:
6699}

   aᵐ) ৪Y○৯ʍ (מצור M-TsWR)
— **I. Wound:** What is bound up
with dressings. [df: מזר מזור]
II. Besiege: A pressing into a
city for conquering it. [freq. 28]
|kjv: wound, bound| {str: 4205,
4692}

   kᶠˡ) ❀৪Y○৯ʍ (מצורה M-TsW-
RH) — **Rampart:** A defensible
stronghold to repel an army that
presses in. [ms: מצרה] [freq. 8]
|kjv: fenced, stronghold, fort,
munition| {str: 4694}

L) ৪○৯ᴶ (יצר YTsR) ac: **Press** co:
? ab: **?:** Being pressed in a narrow
tight place. The pressing of clay to
form something.

   V) ৪○৯ᴶ (יצר Y-TsR) —
Press: To pressed or squeeze out
of shape or into a shape as when
pressing clay into a shape. [freq.

71] (vf: Paal, Niphal, Hophal,
Pual) |kjv: distressed, straitened,
straits, vex, narrow, form, potter,
fashion, maker, frame, make,
former, earthen, purpose| {str:
3334, 3335}

   Nᵐ) ৪○৯ᴶ (יצר Y-TsR) —
Thought: The forming of
thought in the mind. [freq. 9]
|kjv: imagination, frame, mind,
work| {str: 3336}

   dᵐ) ৪Y○৯ᴶ (יצור Y-TsWR) —
Form: Something that is
formed. [ms: יצר] [freq. 1] |kjv:
members| {str: 3338}

M) ৪৸○৯ (ציר TsYR) ac: **Press** co:
? ab: **Pain**

   V) ৪৸○৯ (ציר TsYR) —
Press: [freq. 1] (vf: Hitpael)
|kjv: ambassador| {str: 6737}

   Nᵐ) ৪৸○৯ (ציר TsYR) — **I.
Pain:** A pressing pain. **II. Idol:**
As pressed out of clay. **III.
Hinge:** As pressed. The weight
of the door rested on the hinge.
IV. Messenger: [freq. 14] |kjv:
ambassador, messenger, pain,
pang, sorrow, idol, hinge| {str:
6735, 6736}

Adopted Roots;
2629 ৪○৯⊂ Press, File

1412) ᴜᴜ○৯ (צש TsSh) ac: **?** co: **?** ab: **?**

1413) ┼○৯ (צת TsT) ac: **Burn** co: **?** ab: **?**

   J) ┼Y○৯ (צות TsWT) ac: **Burn** co: **?**
ab: **?**

   V) ┼Y○৯ (צות TsWT) — **Burn:**
[freq. 1] (vf: Hiphil) |kjv: burn|
{str: 6702}

L) tama (יצת YTsT) ac: **Kindle** co: ? ab: ?

    V) tama (יצת Y-TsT) — **Kindle:** [freq. 29] (vf: Paal, Niphal, Hiphil) |kjv: kindle, burn, set, desolate| {str: 3341}

1414) ama (עצ TsGh) ac: ? co: ? ab: ?

Quph

1415) ⅁-ǝ- (קא QA) ac: **Vomit** co: **Vomit** ab: ?

A) ⅁-ǝ- (קא QA) ac: **?** co: **Vomit** ab: ?

N^m) ⅁-ǝ- (קא QA) — **Vomit:** [df: קיא] [freq. 4] |kjv: vomit| {str: 6892}

N^f2) †⅁-ǝ- (קאת Q-AT) — **Qaat:** An unknown bird that vomits up its food for its chicks. [freq. 5] |kjv: pelican, cormorant| {str: 6893}

J) ⅁-Y-ǝ- (קוא QWA) ac: **?** co: **Vomit** ab: ?

V) ⅁-Y-ǝ- (קוא QWA) — **Vomit:** [df: קיה] [freq. 8] (vf: Paal, Hiphil) |kjv: vomit, spue| {str: 6958}

M) ⅁-˫-ǝ- (קיא QYA) ac: **?** co: **Vomit** ab: ?

V) ⅁-˫-ǝ- (קיא QYA) — **Vomit:** [df: קיה] [freq. 1] (vf: Paal) |kjv: spue| {str: 7006}

1416) ⊔-ǝ- (קב QB) ac: **Pierce** co: **Cavity** ab: ?: The pictograph -ǝ- is a picture of the sun at the horizon and the gathering of the light, the ⊔ is a picture of a tent and what is inside. Combined these mean "gather inside". A container or hole for storing or holding something. (eng: cave; cavity)

A) ⊔-ǝ- (קב QB) ac: **?** co: **Cavity** ab: ?

N^m) ⊔-ǝ- (קב QB) — **Qav:** A standard of measure. [freq. 1] |kjv: cab| {str: 6894}

N^f1) ⅏⊔-ǝ- (קבה Q-BH) — **Stomach:** As a cavity. [freq. 1] |kjv: maw| {str: 6896}

N^f2) †⊔-ǝ-ᴍ (מקבת MQ-BT) — **Hammer:** A piercing tool. [freq. 2] |kjv: hammer| {str: 4718}

a^f1) ⅏⊔-ǝ-ᴍ (מקבה MQ-BH) — **Hammer:** A piercing tool. [freq. 3] |kjv: hammer| {str: 4717}

g^f1) ⅏⊔Y-ǝ- (קובה QW-BH) — **Stomach:** As a cavity. [ms: קבה] [freq. 1] |kjv: belly| {str: 6897}

o^f1) ⅏⊔Y-ǝ- (קובה QW-BH) — **Tent:** As a cavity. [ms: קבה] [freq. 1] |kjv: tent| {str: 6898}

B) ⊔⊔-ǝ- (קבב QBB) ac: **Pierce** co: ? ab: ?

V) ⊔⊔-ǝ- (קבב Q-BB) — **Pierce:** To pierce through creating a cavity. [freq. 8] (vf: Paal) |kjv: curse| {str: 6895}

L) ⊔-ǝ-˫ (יקב YQB) ac: **?** co: **Wine trough** ab: ?: A boxed cavity below the winepress where the juice drains into.

N^m) ⊔-ǝ-˫ (יקב Y-QB) — **Wine trough:** [freq. 16] |kjv: winepress, press, fats, pressfat, wine| {str: 3342}

Adopted Roots;
2430	⊔-ǝ-ˢ	Pierce, Hole
2694	⊙⊔-ǝ-	Drain, Bowl
2695	ᴐᴧ⊔-ǝ-	Gather
2696	⅋⊔-ǝ-	Bury, Grave

1417) Ⳑ-⊖ (קֵג QG) ac: ? co: ? ab: ?

~~~~~~~~~~

1418) ⊓-⊖ (קֵד QD) ac: **Bow** co: **Head** ab: ?: The bowing of the head in respect as a showing of the scalp to another. Also the heat that is given off at the scalp. (eng: head - with the exchange of the h and q)

A) ⊓-⊖ (קֵד QD) ac: ? co: **Head** ab: ?

lc^m) ⊓Y-⊖-⊓-⊖ (קָדְקוֹד QD-QWD) — **Head:** The crown or top of the head. [ms: קָדְקֹד] [freq. 11] |kjv: head, crown, pate, scalp| {str: 6936}

B) ⊓⊓-⊖ (קֵדד QDD) ac: **Bow** co: ? ab: ?: The bowing down of the head.

V) ⊓⊓-⊖ (קֵדד Q-DD) — **Bow:** To bow the head. [freq. 15] (vf: Paal) |kjv: stoop, bow| {str: 6915}

L) ⊓-⊖-⤙ (יקֵד YQD) ac: **Burn** co: ? ab: ?: From the heat that comes from the top of the head.

V) ⊓-⊖-⤙ (יקֵד Y-QD) — **Burn:** [Hebrew and Aramaic] [freq. 17] (vf: Paal, Hophal) |kjv: burn, kindle, hearth| {str: 3344, 3345}

N^fl) 𝕏-⊓-⊖-⤙ (יקֵדה YQ-DH) — **Burning:** [Aramaic only] [freq. 1] |kjv: burning| {str: 3346}

a^m) ⊓-⊖-Yᴡ (מוֹקֵד MW-QD) — **Burning:** [freq. 2] |kjv: burning, hearth| {str: 4168}

a^fl) 𝕏-⊓-⊖-Yᴡ (מוֹקֵדה MW-Q-DH) — **Burning:** [freq. 1] |kjv: burning| {str: 4169}

c^m) ⊓Y-⊖-⤙ (יקוֹד Y-QWD) — **Burning:** [ms: יקֵד] [freq. 1] |kjv: burning| {str: 3350}

M) ⊓-⊳-⊖ (קֵיד QYD) ac: **Anoint** co: **Cassia** ab: ?: A pouring of spices on the head.

N^fl) 𝕏-⊓-⊳-⊖ (קֵידה QY-DH) — **Cassia:** The tree, wood or spice which is used in anointing oils and perfumes. [ms: קֵדה] [freq. 2] |kjv: cassia| {str: 6916}

Adopted Roots;
2697 ⊓⊓-⊓-⊖ Heat
2699 ᴖ⊓-⊖ Dark, Darkness

~~~~~~~~~~

1419) 𝕏-⊖ (קֵה QH) ac: **Collect** co: **Cord** ab: ?: Related to Y-⊖.

H) 𝕏𝕏-⊖ (קֵהה QHH) ac: **Dull** co: ? ab: ?: [Unknown connection to root;]

V) 𝕏𝕏-⊖ (קֵהה Q-HH) — **Dull:** A dull blade or dull teeth as bad. [freq. 4] (vf: Paal, Piel) |kjv: edge, blunt| {str: 6949}

J) 𝕏Y-⊖ (קֵוה QWH) ac: **Collect** co: **Cord** ab: ?

V) 𝕏Y-⊖ (קֵוה QWH) — **I. Gather:** To be bound together. **II. Wait:** To be held back by being bound. [freq. 49] (vf: Paal, Niphal, Piel, Participle) |kjv: wait, look, gather| {str: 6960}

N^m) 𝕏Y-⊖ (קֵוה QWH) — **Cord:** Used for binding. [freq. 3] |kjv: line| {str: 6961}

h^m) 𝕏Y-⊖-ᴡ (מִקֵוה MQ-WH) — **I. Collection:** A collection of water (a pool, pond or sea) or horses (herd). **II. Waiting:** Held back waiting for something. [freq. 12] |kjv: yarn, hope, gathering, pool, plenty, abiding| {str: 4723}

h[fl]) **⟨ΨΥ-⊙-ʌʌ⟩** (מקוה MQ-WH) — **Ditch:** A place for collecting water. [freq. 1] |kjv: ditch| {str: 4724}

L) ⟨Ψ-⊙-⟍⟩ (יקה YQH) ac: **Collect** co: ? ab: ?

N[fl]) **⟨ΨΨ-⊙-⟍⟩** (יקהה YQ-HH) — **Collection:** [freq. 2] |kjv: gathering, obey| {str: 3349}

~~~~~~~~~~~

1420) Υ-⊙- ⟩ (קו QW) ac: **Measure** co: **Cord** ab: ?: A cord used for measuring a straight line. Related to **⟨Ψ-⊙-⟩**.

A) Υ-⊙- (קו QW) ac: **Measure** co: **Cord** ab: ?

N[m]) **Υ-⊙-** (קו QW) — **Cord:** [freq. 21] |kjv: line, rule| {str: 6957}

i[fl]) **⟨ΨΥ-⊙-†⟩** (תקוה TQ-WH) — **I. Cord:** Used for binding. **II. Waiting:** Held back waiting for something. [freq. 34] |kjv: hope, expect, line, long| {str: 8615}

I [m]) **Υ-⊙-Υ-⊙-** (קוקו QW-QW) — **Measured:** As with a cord. [freq. 2] |kjv: meted| {str: 6978}

~~~~~~~~~~~

1421) ⟨⊂-⊙-⟩ (קז QZ) ac: ? co: ? ab: ?

~~~~~~~~~~~

1422) ⟨ɪɪɪ-⊙-⟩ (קח QHh) ac: **Take** co: **Merchandise** ab: ?

A) ⟨ɪɪɪ-⊙-⟩ (קח QHh) ac: **Take** co: **Merchandise** ab: ?

N[m]) **⟨ɪɪɪ-⊙-ʌʌ⟩** (מקח MQHh) — **Taking:** [freq. 1] |kjv: taking| {str: 4727}

N[fl]) **⟨Ψɪɪɪ-⊙-⟩** (קחה Q-HhH) — **Merchandise:** As taken. [freq. 1] |kjv: ware| {str: 4728}

Adopted Roots;

2795 **⟨ɪɪɪ-⊙-⋂⟩** Mix, Spice

~~~~~~~~~~~

1423) ⊗-⊙- (קט QTh) ac: **Cut** co: **Little** ab: **Loathe:** Something that is little or made little by cutting off.

A) ⊗-⊙- (קט QTh) ac: ? co: **Little** ab: ?

N[m]) **⊗-⊙-** (קט QTh) — **Little:** [freq. 1] |kjv: little| {str: 6985}

B) ⊗⊗-⊙- (קטט QThTh) ac: **Cut off** co: ? ab: ?

V) ⊗⊗-⊙- (קטט Q-ThTh) — **Cut off:** [freq. 1] (vf: Paal) |kjv: cut off| {str: 6990}

J) ⊗Υ-⊙- (קוט QWTh) ac: **Loathe** co: ? ab: ?: Something considered little, of no account.

V) ⊗Υ-⊙- (קוט QWTh) — **Loathe:** [freq. 7] (vf: Paal, Niphal) |kjv: grieve, loathe| {str: 6962}

Adopted Roots;

2347	⊗⊙ʌʌ	Little
2432	⊗-⊙-⟍	Loathe
2701	⟨ɪ⊗-⊙-⟩	Destroy, Destruction
2702	⟨√⊗-⊙-⟩	Kill
2703	⟨⟍⊗-⊙-⟩	Small
2704	⟨⊂⊗-⊙-⟩	Pluck
2705	⟨⋂⊗-⊙-⟩	Burn, Incense

~~~~~~~~~~~

1424) ⟨⊬-⟍-⊙-⟩ (קי QY) ac: ? co: ? ab: ?

A) ⟨⊬-⟍-⊙-⟩ (קי QY) ac: ? co: **Gourd** ab: ?

lj[m]) ‎יֶ-לּⲁ-ⲓ-ⲗⲁ (קִיקָיוֹן QY-Q-YWN) — **Gourd:** [freq. 5] |kjv: gourd| {str: 7021}

~~~~~~~~~

1425) ⨄-⊕ (קֻק QK) ac: ? co: ? ab: ?

~~~~~~~~~

1426) ⨃-⊕ (קֹל QL) ac: **Gather** co: **Shepherd** ab: ?: The pictograph -⊕- is a picture of the sun at the horizon and the gathering of the light, the ⨃ is a picture of a shepherd staff representing authority. Combined these mean "gathering to the staff". When the shepherd called the sheep they swiftly came to him. The staff of the shepherd was his tool of authority. With it he would direct, discipline and protect the flock. (eng: clown; call - to call together)

A) ⨃-⊕ (קֹל QL) ac: ? co: **Light** ab: ?: The Shepherd traveled light allowing him to move swiftly. He carried with him a long staff for directing the sheep as well as to protect them from predators. The shepherd also carried a bag, which included dried foods including grains and meat. Also, making light of someone or something as in shame, curse or dishonor.

N[m]) ⨃-⊕ (קֹל QL) — I. **Swift:** II. **Voice:** The sound of the shepherd that calls the flock. The voice of man or musical instrument. [Aramaic only] [freq. 20] |kjv: swift, light| {str: 7031, 7032}

a[m]) ⨃-⊕-ᴍ (מַקֵּל MQ-L) — **Staff:** [freq. 18] |kjv: rod, staff, stave| {str: 4731}

a[fl]) ⚥⨃-⊕-ᴍ (מִקְלָה MQ-LH) — **Staff:** [freq. 18] |kjv: rod, staff, stave| {str: 4731}

f[m]) ⨟⨃-⊕ (קְלִי Q-LY) — **Dried:** Dried foods, grains and meat, are carried by the shepherd. [df: קְלִיא] [freq. 6] |kjv: corn| {str: 7039}

j[m]) ‎ⲓⲟⲩ⨃-⊕ (קָלוֹן Q-LWN) — **Shame:** One who is become light in stature. [freq. 17] |kjv: shame, confusion, dishonour, ignominy, reproach| {str: 7036}

l[m]) ⨃-⊕-⨃-⊕ (קְלֹקֵל QL-QL) — **Light:** Something that is light in weight or position (worthless). [freq. 1] |kjv: light| {str: 7052}

B) ⨃⨃-⊕ (קְלֹל QLL) ac: ? co: **Light** ab: ?: Something light in weight or stature.

V) ⨃⨃-⊕ (קְלָל Q-LL) — **Light:** To be swift or cursed. [freq. 82] (vf: Paal, Niphal, Hiphil, Pual, Piel, Pilpel) |kjv: curse, swift, light, vile, despise, abate, ease, slight| {str: 7043}

N[m]) ⨃⨃-⊕ (קְלָל Q-LL) — **Polished:** [Unknown connection to root;] [freq. 2] |kjv: burnished, polished| {str: 7044}

N[fl]) ⚥⨃⨃-⊕ (קְלָלָה QL-LH) — **Curse:** Something that is light in stature, considered worthless. [freq. 33] |kjv: curse, accurse| {str: 7045}

G) ⨃⚥-⊕ (קְהֹל QHL) ac: **Gather** co: **Flock** ab: ?: A gathering of sheep to the shepherd.

V) ⨃⚥-⊕ (קָהֹל Q-HL) — **Gather:** To gather together a flock to the shepherd. [freq. 40] (vf: Niphal, Hiphil) |kjv: gather, assemble| {str: 6950, 7035}

N[m]) ⨃⚥-⊕ (קָהֹל Q-HL) — **Flock:** A gathering of the flock to the shepherd. [freq. 123] |kjv:

congregation, assembly, company, multitude| {str: 6951}

N^{fl}) ⳨ᴜ⳨-● (קהלה QH-LH) — **Flock:** A gathering of the flock to the shepherd. [df: להקה] [freq. 1] |kjv: company| {str: 3862}

a^m) ᴜ⳨-●-ᴍ (מקהל MQ-HL) — **Pasture:** The place where the flock gathers. [freq. 2] |kjv: congregation| {str: 4721}

a^{fl}) ⳨ᴜ⳨-●-ᴍ (מקהלה MQ-H-LH) — **Pasture:** The place where the flock gathers. [freq. 2] |kjv: congregation| {str: 4721}

b^{fl}) ⳨ᴜ⌐⳨-● (קהילה Q-HY-LH) — **Flock:** A gathering of the flock to the shepherd. [df: קהלה] [freq. 2] |kjv: assembly| {str: 6952}

H) ⳨ᴜ-● (קלה QLH) ac: ? co: **Light** ab: ?: The Shepherd traveled light allowing him to move swiftly. He carried with him a long staff for directing the sheep as well as to protect them from predators. The shepherd also carried a bag, which included dried foods including grains and meat. Also, making light of someone or something as in shame, curse or dishonor.

V) ⳨ᴜ-● (קלה Q-LH) — **I. Dry:** To dry foods, grains and meats, to preserve them. Dried foods are carried by the shepherd. **II. Light:** To be light in stature, worthless. [freq. 10] (vf: Paal, Niphal, Hiphil, Participle) |kjv: roast, dried, parched, loathsome, vile, condemn, esteem, despise, base, light| {str: 7033, 7034}

J) ᴜY-● (קול QWL) ac: ? co: **Voice** ab: ?: The call of the shepherd to the sheep who knew him by sound. When it came time to move he would call them and they would quickly gather to him.

N^m) ᴜY-● (קול QWL) — **Voice:** The sound of the shepherd, musical instrument, the wind, thunder, etc. [ms: קל] [freq. 506] |kjv: voice, noise, sound, thunder, fame| {str: 6963}

Adopted Roots;
2709 ●ᴜ-● Hurl, Sling
2728 ᴜ-●-● Shame

~~~~~~~~~~

1427) ᴍ-● (קם QM) ac: **Rise** co: **Stalk** ab: ?: A rising or standing of anything.

A) ᴍ-● (קם QM) ac: ? co: **Stalk** ab: ?

N^{fl}) ⳨ᴍ-● (קמה Q-MH) — **Grainstalk:** As standing tall. [freq. 10] |kjv: standing, grown, stalk| {str: 7054}

J) ᴍY-● (קום QWM) ac: **Raise** co: **Height** ab: ?

V) ᴍY-● (קום QWM) — **Raise:** To raise or rise up. Also in the sense of continuing or establishing something. [Hebrew and Aramaic; A generic verb with a wide application meaning to rise] [freq. 663] (vf: Paal, Hiphil, Hitpael, Hophal, Piel) |kjv: up, arise, raise, establish, stand, perform, confirm, again, set, stablish, surely, continue, sure, abide, accomplish| {str: 6965, 6966}

N^{fl}) ⳨ᴍY-● (קומה QW-MH) — **Height:** [freq. 45] |kjv: height, stature, high, tall, along| {str: 6967}

a^m) ᴍᴎY-⊕-ᴍᴎ (מקום M-QWM) — **Place:** A place one rises up to. [ms: מקם] [freq. 402] |kjv: place, home, room, open, space, country| {str: 4725}

i^{f1}) ⚥ᴍᴎY-⊕-† (תקומה T-QW-MH) — **Stand:** [freq. 1] |kjv: stand| {str: 8617}

ip^m) ᴍᴎᴍᴎY-⊕-† (תקומם T-QW-MM) — **Rising:** [freq. 1] |kjv: rise| {str: 8618}

pf^{f3}) †Y≻⌐ᴍᴎᴍᴎY-⊕- (קוממיות QW-MM-YWT) — **Erect:** [freq. 1] |kjv: upright| {str: 6968}

L) ᴍᴎ-⊕-≻⌐ (יקם YQM) ac: **?** co: **Substance** ab: **?**

d^m) ᴍᴎY-⊕-≻⌐ (יקום Y-QWM) — **Substance:** Any standing thing or person. [freq. 3] |kjv: substance| {str: 3351}

M) ᴍᴎ≻⌐⌐-⊕- (קים QYM) ac: **Raise** co: **Stand** ab: **?**

N^m) ᴍᴎ≻⌐⌐-⊕- (קים QYM) — **I. Stand:** Someone or something that stands erect. [Hebrew and Aramaic] **II. Decree:** A standing word. [Aramaic only] [freq. 5] |kjv: sure, steadfast| {str: 7009, 7010, 7011}

N^{f1}) ⚥ᴍᴎ≻⌐⌐-⊕- (קימה QY-MH) — **Rising:** [freq. 1] |kjv: rising| {str: 7012}

Adopted Roots;

2433 ᴍᴎ-⊕-⅃ Avenge, Vengeance
2711 ⊞ᴍᴎ-⊕- Grind, Meal
2712 ⊗ᴍᴎ-⊕- Snatch
2713 ∪ᴍᴎ-⊕- Wither
2714 ᴓ∧ᴍᴎ-⊕- Grasp, Handful
2715 ⊔⊔ᴍᴎ-⊕- Cling, Thorn

1428) ⅃-⊕- (קן QN) ac: **Acquire** co: **Nest** ab: **Zealous:** The pictograph -⊕- is a picture of the sun at the horizon and the gathering of the light, the ⅃ is a picture of a seed. Combined these mean "gathering for the seeds". The parent birds go about gathering materials to build a nest where they will raise their seeds (eggs). (eng: coin - for purchasing)

A) ⅃-⊕- (קן QN) ac: **?** co: **Nest** ab: **?:** A birds nest as well as a stall for animals as a nest.

N^m) ⅃-⊕- (קן QN) — **Nest:** [freq. 13] |kjv: nest, room| {str: 7064}

B) ⅃⅃-⊕- (קנן QNN) ac: **?** co: **Nest** ab: **?:** The building of the nest and family.

V) ⅃⅃-⊕- (קנן Q-NN) — **Nest:** To build a Nest or home. [freq. 5] (vf: Pual, Piel) |kjv: nest| {str: 7077}

b^m) ⅃≻⌐⅃-⊕- (קנין Q-NYN) — **Possessions:** The goods and wealth acquired as the acquiring of materials for building a nest. [freq. 10] |kjv: substance, getting, goods, riches, with| {str: 7075}

E) ⅁⅃-⊕- (קנא QNA) ac: **?** co: **?** ab: **Zealous:** The parent bird will guard over and protect the nest and eggs from predators. Man can guard over the family, wife, possessions in a positive way (protect, from an enemy) or in a negative way (by not trusting or a desire to have anothers possessions).

V) ⅁⅃-⊕- (קנא Q-NA) — **Zealous:** [freq. 33] (vf: Hiphil, Piel) |kjv: envy, jealous, zealous, zeal| {str: 7065}

Parent and Child Roots - ⚫

N^m) ꓕꓶ-⚫ (קנא Q-NA) — **Zealous:** One who is protective over someone or something. [freq. 6] |kjv: jealous| {str: 7067}

N^fl) 🌱ꓕꓶ-⚫ (קנאה QN-AH) — **Zealousy:** A protective or suspicious nature. [freq. 43] |kjv: jealousy, zeal, envy, for my sake| {str: 7068}

c^m) ꓕꓳꓶ-⚫ (קנוא Q-NWA) — **Zealous:** [freq. 2] |kjv: jealous| {str: 7072}

H) 🌱ꓶ-⚫ (קנה QNH) ac: Gather co: Branch ab: ?: The process of gathering branches for the nest; mans gathering or acquiring materials by taking or buying. The ancients measured wealth by the amount of ones possessions and measured distances using a branch with marks on it.

V) 🌱ꓶ-⚫ (קנה Q-NH) — **Possess:** To acquire someone or something through a purchase or other method. [Hebrew and Aramaic] [ar: קנא] [freq. 85] (vf: Paal, Niphal, Hiphil) |kjv: get, gotten, possess, buy, purchase, possessor, buyer, keep| {str: 7066, 7069}

N^m) 🌱ꓶ-⚫ (קנה Q-NH) — **Branch:** As used for nest building. [freq. 62] |kjv: reed, branch, calamus, cane, stalk| {str: 7070}

h^m) 🌱ꓶ-⚫-ᴟ (מקנה MQ-NH) — **I. Herd:** What is purchased or possessed. **II. Possession:** What is purchased or possessed. Usually of livestock or land. [freq. 75] |kjv: cattle, possession, flocks, substance, herd, purchase| {str: 4735}

h^fl) 🌱ꓶ-⚫-ᴟ (מקנה MQ-NH) — **Possession:** What is purchased or possessed. Usually of livestock or land. [freq. 15] |kjv: bought, purchase, price, possession| {str: 4736}

J) ꓶꓬ-⚫ (קון QWN) ac: ? co: Song ab: ?: The repetitive song or chirping of a bird.

V) ꓶꓬ-⚫ (קון QWN) — **Chant:** As a repetitive sound like a bird. [freq. 8] (vf: Piel) |kjv: lament, mourning| {str: 6969}

N^fl) 🌱ꓶꓬ-⚫ (קונה QW-NH) — **Chanting:** [df: קינה] [freq. 18] |kjv: lamentation, dirge, elegy| {str: 7015}

M) ꓶ⟊-⚫ (קין QYN) ac: ? co: Bill ab: ?: The bill of a bird used for feeding it young and as a weapon.

N^m) ꓶ⟊-⚫ (קין QYN) — **Spearhead:** Like the bill of bird used to defend the nest. [freq. 1] |kjv: spear| {str: 7013}

〰〰〰〰〰〰〰〰

1429) ꓯ-⚫ (קס QS) ac: ? co: ? ab: ?

〰〰〰〰〰〰〰〰

1430) ◎-⚫ (עק QAh) ac: ? co: ? ab: ?

A) ◎-⚫ (עק QAh) ac: ? co: Mark ab: ?: A mark by branding, incision or tattoo.

I^m) ◎-⚫◎-⚫ (קעקע QAh-QAh) — **Mark:** [freq. 1] |kjv: mark| {str: 7085}

L) ◎-⚫-ꓩ (יקע YQAh) ac: Dislocate co: ? ab: ?

V) ◎-⚫-ꓩ (יקע Y-QAh) — **Dislocate:** To dislocate a joint. A beheading by dislocating the head. [freq. 8] (vf: Paal, Hiphil,

Hophal) |kjv: hang, alienate, joint, depart| {str: 3363}

Adopted Roots;
2434 ⊙-⊶-ᒣ Alienate

1431) ⟨⟩-⊶ (קף QP) ac: **Condense** co: **Sun** ab: ?: The pictograph -⊶ is a picture of the sun at the horizon, the ⟨⟩ is a picture of the mouth. Combined these mean "sun speaks". As the sun travels through the sky it marks (speaks, commands) the times and seasons (see Genesis 1:14). The condensing of the light at the sun when at the horizons, a condensing of milk into curdles. A going around of the sun from one horizon to the other.

E) ᒣ⟨⟩-⊶ (קפא QPA) ac: ? co: **Curdle** ab: ?: The condensing of milk into a cheese.

V) ᒣ⟨⟩-⊶ (קפא Q-PA) — **Curdle:** To condense together. [freq. 5] (vf: Paal, Hiphil, Participle) |kjv: congeal, settle, curdle, dark| {str: 7087}

J) ⟨⟩-Y-⊶ (קוף QWP) ac: ? co: **Sun** ab: ?: A going around of the sun from one horizon to the other.

Nᵐ) ⟨⟩-Y-⊶ (קוף QWP) — **Ape:** [Unknown connection to root;] [ms: קף] [freq. 2] |kjv: ape| {str: 6971}

iᶠˡ) ᒣ⟨⟩-Y-⊶-† (תקופה T-QW-PH) — **Circle:** The circle of the sun around the earth usually in reference to a time. [ms: תקפה] [freq. 4] |kjv: end, circuit, about| {str: 8622}

Adopted Roots;
2435 ⟨⟩-⊶-ᒣ Encircle, Circle
2720 ᵀ⟨⟩-⊶ Shrink, Anguish

2721 ᵁ⟨⟩-⊶ Leap
2722 ᚺᚱ⟨⟩-⊶ Close

1432) ᚺᚱ-⊶ (קץ QTs) ac: **Cut** co: **End** ab: ?: The end of something or to make an end by cutting it off.

A) ᚺᚱ-⊶ (קץ QTs) ac: ? co: **End** ab: ?

Nᵐ) ᚺᚱ-⊶ (קץ QTs) — **End:** The end of a time period or place or the end of something. The border of a country as the ends. [freq. 67] |kjv: end, after, border, infinite, process| {str: 7093}

Nᶠˡ) ᚠᚺᚱ-⊶ (קצה Q-TsH) — **End:** The far extremity of something, the end or edge. [freq. 35] |kjv: end, lowest, uttermost, edge, selvedge| {str: 7098}

Nᶠ²) †ᚺᚱ-⊶ (קצת Q-TsT) — **End:** The end of a time or place or as an extremity. [Hebrew and Aramaic] [freq. 9] |kjv: end, part, some| {str: 7117, 7118}

sᵐ) ᒣ-ᚺᚱ-⊶ (קצין Q-TsYN) — **Ruler:** One who rules within a border. [freq. 12] |kjv: ruler, prince, captain, guide| {str: 7101}

ejᵐ) ᒣ-ᚺᚱᒣ-⊶ (קיצון QY-TsWN) — **Outer:** At the end of something. [freq. 4] |kjv: uttermost, outmost| {str: 7020}

B) ᚺᚱᚺᚱ-⊶ (קצץ QTsTs) ac: **Cut off** co: ? ab: ?: The making of an end of something by cutting it.

V) ᚺᚱᚺᚱ-⊶ (קצץ Q-TsTs) — **Cut-off:** To make an end of something by cutting it off. [Hebrew and Aramaic] [df: קסס] [freq. 16] (vf: Paal, Pual,

248

Piel) |kjv: cut off, utmost, cut| {str: 7082, 7112, 7113}

H) ‭‮‬ (קצה QTsH) ac: **Cut off** co: **End** ab: ?

V) ‭‮‬ (קצה Q-TsH) — **Cut-off:** To cut something out or make short. [freq. 5] (vf: Paal, Hiphil, Piel) |kjv: cut off, cut, scrape| {str: 7096}

N^m) ‭‮‬ (קצה Q-TsH) — **End:** The far extremity of something, the end or edge. [freq. 96] |kjv: end, part, edge, coast, border, outside, utmost, quarter| {str: 7097}

J) ⊙⌐Y (קוץ QWTs) ac: **Awake** co: ? ab: ?

V) ⊙⌐Y (קוץ QWTs) — **I. Awake:** An end to sleep. **II. Loath:** To consider something cut off. [freq. 31] (vf: Paal, Hiphil) |kjv: abhor, weary, loath, distress, vex, grieve, awake, wake, arise, watch| {str: 6973, 6974}

N^m) ⊙⌐Y (קוץ QWTs) — **Thorn:** [Unknown connection to root;] [ms: קץ] [freq. 12] |kjv: thorn| {str: 6975}

N^fl) ‭‮‬ (קוצה QW-TsH) — **Lock:** A lock of hair. [Unknown connection to root;] [freq. 2] |kjv: lock| {str: 6977}

K) Y⊙ (קצו QTsW) ac: ? co: **End** ab: ?

N^m) Y⊙ (קצו Q-TsW) — **End:** The far extremity of something, the end or edge. [freq. 7] |kjv: end, uttermost| {str: 7099}

L) ⊙⌐ (יקץ YQTs) ac: **Awake** co: ? ab: ?: An ending of sleep.

V) ⊙⌐ (יקץ Y-QTs) — **Awake:** [freq. 11] (vf: Paal) |kjv: awake| {str: 3364}

M) ⊙⌐ (קיץ QYTs) ac: ? co: **Summer** ab: ?: As the end of the season.

V) ⊙⌐ (קיץ QYTs) — **Summer:** To spend the summer. [df: קוץ] [freq. 1] (vf: Paal) |kjv: summer| {str: 6972}

N^m) ⊙⌐ (קיץ QYTs) — **Summer:** [Hebrew and Aramaic] [ar: קיט] [freq. 21] |kjv: summer| {str: 7007, 7019}

Adopted Roots;

2291	‭‮‬	Cut
2717	⊙⌐	End
2723	‭‮‬	Sheer, Base
2725	‭‮‬	Scrape, Plane
2726	‭‮‬	Snap, Splinter, Wrath
2727	‭‮‬	Sever, Short

1433) ⊙⊙ (קק QQ) ac: ? co: ? ab: ?

1434) ‭‮‬ (קר QR) ac: **Call** co: **Meeting** ab: **Event:** The pictograph ⊙ is a picture of the sun at the horizon and the gathering of the light, the ‭‮‬ is a picture of the head of a man. Combined these mean "gather the men". The meeting or bringing together of people or objects by arrangement, accident or purchase. (eng: occur; call - with the exchange of the l and r)

A) ‭‮‬ (קר QR) ac: ? co: **Cold** ab: ?: Men often came together during the cool of the evening to discuss the news of the camp.

N^m) 𐤒𐤓 (קר QR) — **Cold:** [Unknown connection to root;] [freq. 3] |kjv: cold| {str: 7119}

N^{f1}) 𐤒𐤓𐤄 (קרה Q-RH) — **Cold:** A cold wind or cold weather. [Unknown connection to root;] [freq. 5] |kjv: cold| {str: 7135}

N^{f2}) 𐤕𐤓𐤒 (קרת Q-RT) — **City:** A place of meeting within the city, either at the entrance or a high place. [freq. 5] |kjv: city| {str: 7176}

f^m) 𐤓𐤒 (קרי Q-RY) — **Contrary:** An opposition. [Unknown connection to root;] [freq. 7] |kjv: contrary| {str: 7147}

k^{f1}) 𐤌𐤒𐤓𐤄 (מקרה MQ-RH) — **Cool:** A cool place to escape the heat. [Unknown connection to root;] [freq. 2] |kjv: summer| {str: 4747}

E) 𐤒𐤓𐤀 (קרא QRA) ac: **Call** co: **Meeting** ab: **?:** A calling together for assembly.

V) 𐤒𐤓𐤀 (קרא Q-RA) — **I. Call:** To call or call out, to call a name or give a name. [Hebrew and Aramaic] **II. Meet:** To come together to meet. Also a chance encounter. **III. Read:** To read a scroll in the presence of those called to a meeting. [freq. 883] (vf: Paal, Niphal, Hiphil, Pual) |kjv: call, cry, read, proclaim, name, guest, invite, gave, renown, bidden, preach, read, cry, call, befall, encounter, chance, happen, met, fall, meet, against, come, help, seek| {str: 7121, 7122, 7123, 7125}

b^m) 𐤒𐤓𐤉𐤀 (קריא Q-RYA) — **Selected:** Individuals called out for a special purpose. [freq. 3] |kjv: famous| {str: 7148}

b^{f1}) 𐤒𐤓𐤉𐤀𐤄 (קריאה Q-RY-AH) — **Selected:** [freq. 1] |kjv: preaching| {str: 7150}

g^m) 𐤒𐤅𐤓𐤀 (קורא QW-RA) — **Partridge:** From its distinctive call. [ms: קרא] [freq. 2] |kjv: partridge| {str: 7124}

h^m) 𐤌𐤒𐤓𐤀 (מקרא MQ-RA) — **I. Meeting:** A calling together to meet. **II. Reading:** The reading from a scroll at a called meeting. [freq. 23] |kjv: convocation, assembly, calling, reading| {str: 4744}

H) 𐤒𐤓𐤄 (קרה QRH) ac: **Meet** co: **Event** ab: **?:** The meeting or bringing together of people or objects by arrangement, accident or purchase.

V) 𐤒𐤓𐤄 (קרה Q-RH) — **Meet:** To go to meet another or a chance encounter. [freq. 27] (vf: Paal, Niphal, Hiphil, Piel) |kjv: happen, meet, beam, befall, brought| {str: 7136}

N^m) 𐤒𐤓𐤄 (קרה Q-RH) — **Event:** [freq. 1] |kjv: chance| {str: 7137}

f^{f1}) 𐤒𐤓𐤉𐤄 (קריה QR-YH) — **City:** A meeting place. [Hebrew and Aramaic] [ar: קריא] [freq. 40] |kjv: city| {str: 7149, 7151}

h^m) 𐤌𐤒𐤓𐤄 (מקרה MQ-RH) — **Event:** [freq. 10] |kjv: befall, event, hap, chance, happen| {str: 4745}

k^m) 𐤌𐤒𐤓𐤄 (מקרה MQ-RH) — **Hall:** A meeting place. [freq. 1] |kjv: building| {str: 4746}

J) 𐤒Y-●- (קור QWR) ac: **?** co: **Sit** ab: **?**

N^(m)) 𐤒Y-●- (קור QWR) — **I. Web:** The web of a spider as a sitting place. [ms: קר] **II. Cold:** [Unknown connection to root] [freq. 3] |kjv: cold, web| {str: 7120, 6980}

N^(f1)) 𐤔𐤒Y-●- (קורה QW-RH) — **Log:** Used to sit on when meeting. Also used as beams in the roof of a house. [ms: קרה] [freq. 5] |kjv: roof, beam| {str: 6982}

L) 𐤒-●-𐤉 (יקר YQR) ac: **?** co: **?** ab: **?** **Precious:** Something of value. [Unknown connection to root;]

V) 𐤒-●-𐤉 (יקר Y-QR) — **Precious:** To be considered of value. [freq. 11] (vf: Paal, Hiphil) |kjv: precious, prized, set, withdraw| {str: 3365}

N^(m)) 𐤒-●-𐤉 (יקר Y-QR) — **I. Precious:** Something of value. [Hebrew and Aramaic] **II. Value:** Something counted as valuable. [Hebrew and Aramaic] [freq. 60] |kjv: precious, costly, excellent, brightness, clear, fat, reputation, honourable, glory, honour, precious, price| {str: 3366, 3367, 3368}

b^(m)) 𐤒-𐤉-●-𐤉 (יקיר Y-QYR) — **Precious:** Something of value. [Hebrew and Aramaic] [freq. 3] |kjv: dear| {str: 3357, 3358}

M) 𐤒-𐤉-●- (קיר QYR) ac: **?** co: **Wall** ab: **?**

N^(m)) 𐤒-𐤉-●- (קיר QYR) — **Wall:** The place of the city where elders meet. [ms: קר] [freq. 74] |kjv: wall, side, mason, town| {str: 7023}

Adopted Roots;
2730 ㅠ𐤒-●- Shave, Bald
2731 ᴍ𐤒-●- Cover

~~~~~~~~~~~

1435) ㅛㅛ-●- (קש QSh) ac: **Gather** co: **Stalk** ab: **?:** The pictograph -●- is a picture of the sun at the horizon and the gathering of the light, the ㅛㅛ is a picture of the teeth representing pressure. Combined these mean "bring together and pressed". Once the grain stalks are harvested from the field, it is gathered into bundles and secured with a cord in the middle.

A) ㅛㅛ-●- (קש QSh) ac: **?** co: **Stubble** ab: **?:** The stiff part of the stalk that remains in the ground. The stiffness a branch for making bows or snares.

N^(m)) ㅛㅛ-●- (קש QSh) — **Stubble:** [freq. 16] |kjv: stubble| {str: 7179}

N^(f2)) t ㅛㅛ-●- (קשת Q-ShT) — **Bow:** Made from a stiff branch to shoot arrows. [freq. 77] |kjv: bow| {str: 7198}

f^(m)) ᐳ-ㅛㅛ-●- (קשי Q-ShY) — **Stubbornness:** As stiff. [freq. 1] |kjv: stubbornness| {str: 7190}

B) ㅛㅛㅛㅛ-●- (קשש QShSh) ac: **Gather** co: **Stalk** ab: **?:** The stalks of the grain harvested are gathered together and tied into tight bundles. The stiffness of the stalks or a branch.

V) ㅛㅛㅛㅛ-●- (קשש Q-ShSh) — **Gather:** [freq. 8] (vf: Paal) |kjv: gather| {str: 7197}

N^(m)) ㅛㅛㅛㅛ-●- (קשש Q-ShSh) — **Chaff:** [df: חשש] [freq. 2] |kjv: chaff| {str: 2842}

E) ᐳㅛㅛ-●- (קשא QShA) ac: **?** co: **Cucumber** ab: **?:** A hard vegetable.

d^{f}) (קשוא Q-ShWA) — **Cucumber:** A hard vegetable. [ms: קשא] [freq. 1] |kjv: cucumber| {str: 7180}

h^{f1}) (מקשאה MQ-Sh-AH) — **Cucumber:** A hard vegetable. [df: מקשה] [freq. 1] |kjv: cucumber| {str: 4750}

H) (קשה QShH) ac: **?** co: **Hard** ab: **?:** The stiffness of the stubble or branch.

V) (קשה Q-ShH) — **Hard:** [freq. 28] (vf: Paal, Niphal, Hiphil, Piel) |kjv: harden, hard, grievous| {str: 7185}

N^{m}) (קשה Q-ShH) — **Hard:** [freq. 36] |kjv: hard, roughly, cruel, grievous, sore, churlish, hardhearted, heavy| {str: 7186}

h^{m}) (מקשה MQ-ShH) — **Hairdo:** A well dressed hair. [Unknown connection to root;] [freq. 1] |kjv: hair| {str: 4748}

h^{f1}) (מקשה MQ-ShH) — **Work:** A metal that is formed by being beaten by a hammer. [Unknown connection to root;] [freq. 10] |kjv: beaten, piece, upright| {str: 4749}

J) (קוש QWSh) ac: **Gather** co: **Snare** ab: **?:** A snare for trapping animals is constructed of a bent branch (as a spring) tied to a trap.

V) (קוש QWSh) — **Snare:** [freq. 1] (vf: Paal) |kjv: snare| {str: 6983}

L) (יקש YQSh) ac: **Gather** co: **Snare** ab: **?:** A snare for trapping animals is constructed of a bent branch (as a spring) tied to a trap.

V) (יקש Y-QSh) — **Snare:** [freq. 8] (vf: Paal, Niphal, Pual, Participle) |kjv: snare| {str: 3369}

a^{m}) (מוקש MW-QSh) — **Snare:** [ms: מקש] [freq. 27] |kjv: snare, gin, trap, ensnared| {str: 4170}

c^{m}) (יקוש Y-QWSh) — **Snarer:** [freq. 1] |kjv: fowler| {str: 3352}

d^{m}) (יקוש Y-QWSh) — **Snare:** [freq. 3] |kjv: fowler, snare| {str: 3353}

Adopted Roots;

2437 Ensnare
2738 Harden
2741 Archer

~~~~~~~~~~~

1436) (קת QT) ac: **?** co: **?** ab: **?**

~~~~~~~~~~~

1437) (קע QGh) ac: **?** co: **?** ab: **?**

~~~~~~~~~~~
~~~~~~~~~~~

Resh

1438) רא (רא RA) ac: **See** co: ? ab: **Appearance:** The ability to see, perceive or have a vision.

A) רא (רא RA) ac: **See** co: ? ab: ?

N^{fl}) ראה (ראה R-AH) — **Raah:** An unknown bird of prey with a keen sense of sight. [freq. 1] |kjv: glede| {str: 7201}

N^{f4}) ראית (ראית R-AYT) — See: [freq. 1] |kjv: beholding| {str: 7212}

a^{fl}) מראה (מראה MR-AH) — **Vision:** [freq. 12] |kjv: vision, lookingglass| {str: 4759}

f^{m}) ראי (ראי R-AY) — **Mirror:** A looking glass. [freq. 1] |kjv: looking glass| {str: 7209}

H) ראה (ראה RAH) ac: **See** co: **See** ab: **Appearance**

V) ראה (ראה R-AH) — **See:** To see or perceive something or someone. Also to see visions. [A generic verb with a wide application meaning "to see"] [freq. 1313] (vf: Paal, Niphal, Hiphil, Hitpael, Hophal, Pual) |kjv: see, look, behold, shew, appear, consider, seer, spy, respect, perceive, provide, regard, enjoy, lo, foresee, heed| {str: 7200}

N^{m}) ראה (ראה R-AH) — **See:** [freq. 1] |kjv: see| {str: 7202}

a^{m}) מראה (מראה MR-AH) — **Appearance:** What is seen. [freq. 103] |kjv: appearance, sight, countenance, vision, favoured, look| {str: 4758}

d^{m}) ראוה (ראוה R-AWH) — **Look:** [freq. 1] |kjv: behold| {str: 7207}

f^{m}) ראי (ראי R-AY) — **Seeing:** [freq. 6] |kjv: see, look, gazingstock| {str: 7210}

g^{m}) רואה (רואה RW-AH) — **Vision:** [ms: ראה] [freq. 1] |kjv: vision| {str: 7203}

L) ירא (ירא YRA) ac: ? co: **Crop** ab: ?

a^{fl}) מוראה (מוראה MW-R-AH) — **Crop:** What is closely watched for harvest time. [freq. 1] |kjv: crop| {str: 4760}

~~~~~~~~~~

1439) רב (רב RB) ac: **Rule** co: **Master** ab: **Increase:** The pictograph ר is a picture of a head, the ב is a picture of the tent representing the family. Combined these mean "head of the family". Each family has a master that rules all cases, trials, conflicts and contests. This person was the representative for the whole tribe, one abundant in authority and wisdom. (see Exodus 18:25).

A) רב (רב RB) ac: ? co: **Master** ab: ?: An abundance of number, strength or authority.

N^{m}) רב (רב RB) — **I. Master:** One who is abundant in authority. **II. Abundant:** An abundance of numbers (many) or strength (great). From the idea of greatness in authority. [Hebrew and Aramaic] **III. Archer:**

[Unknown connection to root;] [freq. 475] |kjv: many, great, much, captain, more, long, enough, multitude, mighty, greater, greatly, archer| {str: 7227, 7228, 7229}

a^{f4}) †>⌐ᴐ᷒ᴧᴧ (מרבית MR-BYT) — **Abundance:** [freq. 5] |kjv: increase, greatest, multitude| {str: 4768}

h^{f1}) ⅍⌐ᴐ᷒ᴧᴧ (מרבה MR-BH) — **Much:** As an increase. [freq. 1] |kjv: much| {str: 4767}

i^{f3}) †Yᴐ᷒ᴧ† (תרבות TR-BWT) — **Abundance:** [freq. 1] |kjv: increase| {str: 8635}

i^{f4}) †>⌐ᴐ᷒ᴧ† (תרבית TR-BYT) — **Increase:** From usury. [freq. 6] |kjv: increase, gain| {str: 8636}

l^m) ᴐ᷒ᴐ᷒ᴧ (רברב RB-RB) — **Abundant:** [Aramaic only] [freq. 8] |kjv: great| {str: 7260}

r^f) Yᴐ᷒ᴧ (רבו R-BW) — **Majesty:** [Aramaic only] [freq. 5] |kjv: majesty, greatness| {str: 7238}

eq^f) Yᴐ᷒>ᴧ (ריבו RY-BW) — **Myriad:** A number of great abundance. [Hebrew and Aramaic] [ms: רבו] [freq. 13] |kjv: thousand, ten thousand| {str: 7239, 7240}

lm^m) ᴸᴐ᷒ᴐ᷒ᴧ (רברבן R-BR-BN) — **Lord:** One abundant in authority. [freq. 8] |kjv: lord, prince| {str: 7261}

B) ᴐᴐ᷒ᴧ (רבב RBB) ac: ? co: **Abundant** ab: ?: An abundance of number, strength or authority.

V) ᴐᴐ᷒ᴧ (רבב R-BB) — **I. Increase:** To grow in number. **II. Shoot:** The shooting of

arrows from an archer. [Unknown connection to root] [freq. 19] (vf: Paal, Pual) |kjv: many, multiply, increase, more, manifold, thousand, shoot| {str: 7231, 7232}

N^{f1}) ⅍ᴐ᷒ᴐ᷒ᴧ (רבבה RB-BH) — **Myriad:** A great abundance in numbers. [freq. 16] |kjv: ten thousand, million, many, multiply| {str: 7233}

b^m) ᴐ>ᴐ᷒ᴧ (רביב R-BYB) — **Showers:** [Unknown connection to root;] [freq. 6] |kjv: shower| {str: 7241}

C) ᴐ᷒ᴧⅤ (ארב ARB) ac: **Ambush** co: ? ab: ?: [Unknown connection to root;]

V) ᴐ᷒ᴧⅤ (ארב A-RB) — **Ambush:** To lay in wait to ambush. [freq. 42] (vf: Paal, Hiphil, Piel) |kjv: lay, ambush| {str: 693}

N^m) ᴐ᷒ᴧⅤ (ארב A-RB) — **Den:** An animals abode for laying down. [freq. 2] |kjv: lie, den| {str: 695}

N^{f1}) ⅍ᴐ᷒ᴧⅤ (ארבה AR-BH) — **Struggle:** A wresting around as an ambush. [freq. 1] |kjv: spoils| {str: 698}

a^m) ᴐ᷒ᴧⅤᴧᴧ (מארב MA-RB) — **Ambush:** A place for an ambush. [freq. 5] |kjv: ambushment, wait, lurking| {str: 3993}

d^{f1}) ⅍Yᴐ᷒ᴧⅤ (ארובה A-RW-BH) — **Window:** A place for an ambush. [Unknown connection to root;] [ms: ארבה] [freq. 9] |kjv: window, chimney| {str: 699}

g^m) ﬡרﬡﬡﬡﬡ (אורב AW-RB) —
Ambush: [ms: ארב] [freq. 1]
|kjv: wait| {str: 696}

G) ﬡﬡ﬩ﬡ (רהב RHB) ac: **Encourage**
co: **?** ab: **Pride:** An abundance of
assurance.

V) ﬡﬡ﬩ﬡ (רהב R-HB) —
Encourage: [freq. 4] (vf: Paal,
Hiphil) |kjv: sure, proudly,
overcome, strengthen| {str:
7292}

N^m) ﬡﬡ﬩ﬡ (רהב R-HB) —
Proud: [freq. 1] |kjv: proud|
{str: 7295}

g^m) ﬡﬡ﬩ﬡﬡ (רוהב RW-HB) —
Proud: [freq. 1] |kjv: strength|
{str: 7296}

H) ﬩﬩ﬡﬡ (רבה RBH) ac: **?** co:
Abundant ab: **?:** An abundance of
number, strength or authority.

V) ﬩﬩ﬡﬡ (רבה R-BH) —
Increase: [Hebrew and
Aramaic] [freq. 232] (vf: Paal,
Hiphil, Piel) |kjv: multiply,
increase, much, more, long,
store, exceedingly, abundance,
grow, great| {str: 7235, 7236}

a^m) ﬩﬩ﬡﬡﬡ (מרבה MR-BH) —
Increase: [freq. 2] |kjv: increase,
great| {str: 4766}

n^m) ﬩﬩ﬡﬡﬡ (ארבה AR-BH) —
Locust: An abundant swarm.
[freq. 24] |kjv: locust,
grasshopper| {str: 697}

J) ﬡﬡﬡ (רוב RWB) ac: **?** co:
Abundance ab: **?:** An abundance of
number, strength or authority.

N^m) ﬡﬡﬡ (רוב RWB) —
Abundance: An abundance of
numbers (many) or strength
(great). [freq. 155] |kjv:
multitude, abundance, great,
greatness, much, abundantly,

plenty, many, long, excellent|
{str: 7230}

L) ﬡﬡﬡ (ירב YRB) ac: **Strive** co: **?**
ab: **Strife:** The responsibility of the
master is to strive for survival and
protection of the house.

b^m) ﬡﬡﬡﬡﬡ (יריב Y-RYB) —
Strive: [freq. 3] |kjv: strive,
contend| {str: 3401}

M) ﬡﬡﬡ (ריב RYB) ac: **Strive** co:
? ab: **Strife:** The responsibility of the
master is to strive for survival and
protection of the house.

V) ﬡﬡﬡ (ריב RYB) — **Strive:**
[df: רוב] [freq. 67] (vf: Paal,
Hiphil) |kjv: plead, strive,
contend, chide, debate| {str:
7378}

N^m) ﬡﬡﬡ (ריב RYB) —
Strife: [ms: רב] [freq. 62] |kjv:
cause, strife, controversy,
contention| {str: 7379}

k^{fl}) ﬩﬩ﬡﬡﬡﬡ (מריבה M-RY-
BH) — **Strife:** [freq. 7] |kjv:
strife, provocation| {str: 4808}

Adopted Roots;

2742	ﬡﬡﬡ	Spread, Sheet
2744	ﬡﬡﬡ	Square
2745	ﬡﬡﬡ	Lay, Palate
2746	ﬡﬡﬡ	Stall
2785	ﬡﬡﬡ	Spread

1440) ﬡﬡ (רג RG) ac: **Trample** co: **Rug**
ab: **Thought:** The pictograph ﬡ is a
picture of the head of a man, the ﬡ is a
picture of a foot. Combined these mean
"man of feet". The treading underfoot of
something. A woven rug as something
tread upon. (eng: rug - as woven and
trampled on; harangue; wrong)

A) ᴸ๑ (רג RG) ac: ? co: ? ab:
Thought: A weaving of thoughts in
the mind.

N^m) ᴸ๑ (רג RG) — **Thought:**
[df: רע] [freq. 2] |kjv: thoughts|
{str: 7454}

fj^m) ᵞᴸ๑ (רגיון RG-YWN)
— **Thought:** [Aramaic only]
[df: רעיון] [freq. 6] |kjv:
thoughts| {str: 7476}

C) ᴸ๑◿ (ארג ARG) ac: **Weave** co:
? ab: ?: A woven rug that is laid on
the floor of the tent for walking on.

V) ᴸ๑◿ (ארג A-RG) —
Weave: [freq. 13] (vf: Paal) |kjv:
weave, weaver| {str: 707}

N^m) ᴸ๑◿ (ארג A-RG) —
Beam: A weavers beam. [freq.
2] |kjv: beam, shuttle| {str: 708}

j^m) ᵞᴸ๑◿ (ארגון AR-GWN)
— **Purple:** A reddish-purple
color used to dye yarn and used
in weaving. [Hebrew and
Aramaic] [freq. 4] |kjv: purple,
scarlet| {str: 710, 711}

pm^m) ᴸ๑◿ (ארגמן AR-G-
MN) — **Purple:** A reddish-
purple color used to dye yarn
and used in weaving. [freq. 38]
|kjv: purple| {str: 713}

F) ᴸ๑⚥ (הרג HRG) ac: **Trample**
co: ? ab: ?: The trampling over of
another with the intent to kill.

V) ᴸ๑⚥ (הרג H-RG) — **Kill:**
[freq. 167] (vf: Paal, Niphal,
Pual) |kjv: slay, kill, murderer,
destroy, murder, slayer| {str:
2026}

N^m) ᴸ๑⚥ (הרג H-RG) —
Slaughter: [freq. 5] |kjv:
slaughter, slain| {str: 2027}

N^{f1}) ⚥ᴸ๑⚥ (הרגה HR-GH) —
Slaughter: [freq. 5] |kjv:
slaughter| {str: 2028}

L) ᴸ๑↲ (ירג YRG) ac: **Trample** co:
Sledge ab: ?

N^f) ᴸ๑↲ (ירג Y-RG) —
Sledge: A wooden sled pulled
behind oxen that tramples over
the grain to open the hulls. [df:
יריעה] [freq. 54] |kjv: curtain|
{str: 3407}

Adopted Roots;

2438	ᴸ๑ᵞ	Whisper
2574	ᴸ๑⊚	Pant, Bed
2748	⫤ᴸ๑	Shake, Fury
2749	⊿ᴸ๑	Trample, Foot
2750	⋀ᴸ๑	Stone
2751	ᵞᴸ๑	Murmur
2752	⊚ᴸ๑	Stir, Moment
2753	ᴸᴸ๑	Tumult, Crowd
2755	⊂ᵀ๑	Pursue
2778	ᵀ⊚๑	Tremble
2779	⊿⊚๑	Quiver, Scarf
2780	⋀⊚๑	Roar, Thunder
2784	ᴸᴸ⊚๑	Quake
3019	⊿ᴸ๑	
3056	⊿⚥๑	Foot

1441) ᵀ๑ (רד RD) ac: **Spread** co:
Sheet ab: ?: The pictograph ๑ is a picture
of the head of a man, the ᵀ is a picture of
a door that allows entrance into the tent.
Combined these mean "man through the
door". The floor of a tent is a covered
with a spread out sheet.

B) ᵀᵀ๑ (רדד RDD) ac: **Spread**
co: **Sheet** ab: ?: A covering of a large
area.

V) ᵀᵀ๑ (רדד R-DD) —
Spread: [freq. 4] (vf: Paal,

Hiphil) |kjv: subdue, spent, spread| {str: 7286}

b^m) ᛈ᛬ᛚᛈ (רדיד R-DYD) — **Sheet:** A wide piece of clothing. [freq. 2] |kjv: veil| {str: 7289}

H) ᛈᛛᛈ (רדה RDH) ac: **Rule** co: ? ab: ?: A ruler is one who walks among the people in the sense of spreading out rather than rule on the throne alone.

V) ᛈᛛᛈ (רדה R-DH) — **Rule:** [freq. 27] (vf: Paal, Hiphil) |kjv: rule, dominion, take, prevail, reign, ruler| {str: 7287}

J) ᛈᛉ (רוד RWD) ac: **Rule** co: ? ab: ?: A ruler is one who walks among the people in the sense of spreading out rather than rule on the throne alone.

V) ᛈᛉ (רוד RWD) — **Rule:** [freq. 4] (vf: Paal, Hiphil) |kjv: dominion, lord, rule| {str: 7300}

a^m) ᛈᛉᛊ (מרוד M-RWD) — **Wandering:** [freq. 3] |kjv: misery, cast out| {str: 4788}

L) ᛈᛈᛁ (ירד YRD) ac: **Descend** co: ? ab: ?: As the man enters the tent he descends down on the sheet to sit.

V) ᛈᛈᛁ (ירד Y-RD) — **Descend:** [freq. 380] (vf: Paal, Hiphil, Hophal) |kjv: down, descend, fell, let, abundantly, indeed, off, out, sank, subdue| {str: 3381}

a^m) ᛈᛈᛉᛊ (מורד MW-RD) — **Descent:** A place that descends. [freq. 5] |kjv: down, thin, steep| {str: 4174}

Adopted Roots;
2575 ᛈᛈᛟ Wild-donkey

1442) ᛈᛈ (רה RH) ac: **Flow** co: ? ab: **Fear:** Related to ᛈᛈ to ᛈᛁ.

B) ᛈᛈᛈ (רהה RHH) ac: ? co: ? ab: **Fear:** The flowing of the insides.

V) ᛈᛈᛈ (רהה R-HH) — **Fear:** [freq. 2] (vf: Paal) |kjv: afraid| {str: 7297}

H) ᛈᛈᛧ (ארה ARH) ac: ? co: **Lion** ab: **Fear:** The flowing of the insides.

b^m) ᛈᛈᛧ (אריה A-RYH) — **Lion:** A feared animal. [df: ארי] [freq. 90] |kjv: lion| {str: 738, 744}

J) ᛈᛉᛈ (רוה RWH) ac: **Soak** co: **Drink** ab: ?: A heavy flowing of water.

V) ᛈᛉᛈ (רוה RWH) — **Soak:** To be satisfied, filled or drenched with water. [freq. 14] (vf: Paal, Hiphil, Piel) |kjv: water, drunk, fill, satiate, bath, satisfy, soak| {str: 7301}

N^m) ᛈᛉᛈ (רוה RWH) — **Watered:** [freq. 3] |kjv: watered, drunkenness| {str: 7302}

f^{f1}) ᛈᛉᛈ (רויה RW-YH) — **Soaked:** Something soaked with water. [freq. 2] |kjv: wealthy, run over| {str: 7310}

1443) ᛈᛉ (רו RW) ac: ? co: **Form** ab: **Appearance**

A) ᛈᛉ (רו RW) ac: ? co: **Form** ab: **Appearance**

N^m) ᛈᛉ (רו RW) — **Appearance:** [Aramaic only] [freq. 2] |kjv: form| {str: 7299}

1444) ᚱ (רז RZ) ac: ? co: **Cedar** ab: ?: The bark of the cedar tree is pulled off in long thin strips which can be woven into a cords. (eng: razor)

A) ᚱ (רז RZ) ac: ? co: **Cypress** ab: ?: As hidden and therefore thin.

N^m) ᚱ (רז RZ) — **Secret:** [Aramaic only] [freq. 9] |kjv: secret| {str: 7328}

i ^{fl}) ᚱᚦ (תרזה TR-ZH) — **Cypress:** A tree similar to a cedar. [Unknown connection to root;] [freq. 1] |kjv: cypress| {str: 8645}

C) ᚱᚦ (ארז ARZ) ac: ? co: **Cedar** ab: ?

N^m) ᚱᚦ (ארז A-RZ) — **Cedar:** The wood or tree or something made from cedar. [freq. 73] |kjv: cedar| {str: 730}

N^{fl}) ᚱᚦ (ארזה AR-ZH) — **Cedar work:** [freq. 1] |kjv: cedar work| {str: 731}

d^m) ᚱᚦ (ארוז A-RWZ) — **Bound:** Something bound securely with cords. [ms: ארז] [freq. 1] |kjv: cedar| {str: 729}

H) ᚱᚦ (רזה RZH) ac: ? co: **Thin** ab: ?

V) ᚱᚦ (רזה R-ZH) — **Shrivel:** To be made thin. [freq. 2] (vf: Paal, Niphal) |kjv: famish, lean| {str: 7329}

N^m) ᚱᚦ (רזה R-ZH) — **Lean:** [freq. 2] |kjv: lean| {str: 7330}

f^m) ᚱᚦ (רזי R-ZY) — **Leanness:** [freq. 2] |kjv: leanness| {str: 7334}

j^m) ᚱᚦ (רזון R-ZWN) — **Leanness:** Something made

thin. [freq. 3] |kjv: leanness, scant| {str: 7332}

~~~~~~~~~

1445) ᚱ (רח RHh) ac: **Travel** co: **Path** ab: ?: The pictograph ᚦ is a picture of the head of a man, the ᚱ is a picture of wall that separates the inside from the outside. Combined these mean "man outside". The responsibilities of the nomad outside of the tent include the feeding, watering and caring for the livestock. Livestock are healthier and more productive when on a routine, therefore the man follows a routine or "a prescribed path" each day when caring for his livestock. (eng: reek)

A) ᚱ (רח RHh) ac: ? co: **Shovel** ab: ?: The winds which follows a prescribed path each season.

N^{f2}) ᚱ (רחת R-HhT) — **Shovel:** A shovel used for winnowing grain in the wind. [freq. 1] |kjv: shovel| {str: 7371}

C) ᚱᚦ (ארח ARHh) ac: **Travel** co: **Caravan** ab: ?: One who follows a prescribed path to arrive at a specific destination.

V) ᚱᚦ (ארח A-RHh) — **Travel:** [freq. 5] (vf: Paal) |kjv: wayfaring, go| {str: 732}

N^{fl}) ᚱᚦ (ארחה AR-HhH) — **Caravan:** A traveling company that follows a prescribed path. [freq. 2] |kjv: company| {str: 736}

d^{fl}) ᚱᚦ (ארוחה A-RW-HhH) — **Allowance:** An allotted amount of food. [ms: ארחה] [freq. 6] |kjv: allowance, diet, dinner, victuals| {str: 737}

g^m) ᚱᚦ (אורח AW-RHh) — **Path:** The road one travels. [ms:

ארח] [freq. 58] |kjv: way, path, highway, manner, race, rank, traveler, troop| {str: 734}

g^fl) 𐤀𐤅𐤓𐤇𐤄 (אורחה AW-R-HhH) — **Path:** The road one travels. [Aramaic only] [ms: ארחה] [freq. 2] |kjv: way| {str: 735}

H) 𐤓𐤇𐤄 (רחה RHhH) ac: ? co: **Millstone** ab: ?: The ancient hand mill consisted of two round stones, called millstones, the top was turned on top of the other to grind the grain. This top stone always followed the same path on top of the other.

N^m) 𐤓𐤇𐤄 (רחה R-HhH) — **Millstone:** [freq. 5] |kjv: millstone, mill, nether| {str: 7347}

J) 𐤓𐤅𐤇 (רוח RWHh) ac: **Refresh** co: **Wind** ab: ?: The Hebrew nomads were very familiar with the wind patterns as they would follow a prescribed path indicating the coming season. From this word comes the idea of breath as it is the wind of man which also follows a prescribed path of inhaling and exhaling.

V) 𐤓𐤅𐤇 (רוח RWHh) — **I. Refresh:** To be given a fresh wind. **II. Smell:** As carried on the wind. **III. Spacious:** To be wide with space. [freq. 14] (vf: Paal, Hiphil, Pual, Participle) |kjv: smell, touch, understanding, accept, refresh, large| {str: 7304, 7306}

N^f) 𐤓𐤅𐤇 (רוח RWHh) — **Wind:** Also the wind of man or god, the breath. [Hebrew and Aramaic] [freq. 380] |kjv: spirit, wind, breath, side, mind, blast, vain, air, anger, cool, courage, space, enlargement| {str: 7305, 7307}

N^fl) 𐤓𐤅𐤇𐤄 (רוחה RW-HhH) — **Relief:** A sigh of relief. [freq. 2] |kjv: respite, breathing| {str: 7309}

L) 𐤉𐤓𐤇 (ירח YRHh) ac: ? co: **Moon** ab: ?: The moon follows a prescribed path each night from horizon to horizon.

N^m) 𐤉𐤓𐤇 (ירח Y-RHh) — **Moon:** Also a month as a counting of time by the cycles of the moon. [Hebrew and Aramaic] [freq. 41] |kjv: month, moon| {str: 3391, 3393, 3394}

M) 𐤓𐤉𐤇 (ריח RYHh) ac: ? co: **Aroma** ab: ?: What is carried by the wind and smelled while breathing.

N^f) 𐤓𐤉𐤇 (ריח RYHh) — **Aroma:** [Hebrew and Aramaic] [freq. 59] |kjv: savour, smell, scent| {str: 7381, 7382}

Adopted Roots;

2112	𐤓𐤇𐤔	Tread, Road
2135	𐤆𐤓𐤇	Rise, Dawn
2473	𐤇𐤓𐤔	Trade, Merchandise
2769	𐤓𐤊𐤔	Ride, Chariot
2770	𐤓𐤊𐤔	Trade
2882	𐤇𐤋𐤋𐤒	Whistle, Flute

1446) 𐤓𐤈 (רט RTh) ac: **Turn** co: ? ab: **Fear:** The digging out of something for making a basin or trough.

B) 𐤓𐤈𐤈 (רטט RThTh) ac: ? co: ? ab: **Fear:** A trembling as a turning of the insides.

N^m) 𐤓𐤈𐤈 (רטט R-ThTh) — **Fear:** [freq. 1] |kjv: fear| {str: 7374}

G) ⊗⅄ॻ (רהט RHTh) ac: ? co: **Trough** ab: ?: Used to turn the direction of water.

N^m) ⊗⅄ॻ (רהט R-HTh) — **Trough:** [freq. 4] |kjv: gutter, trough, gallery| {str: 7298}

L) ⊗ॻॖ (ירט YRTh) ac: **Scour** co: **Bright** ab: ?: A scouring or polishing by rubbing.

V) ⊗ॻॖ (ירט Y-RTh) — **Turn:** [freq. 2] (vf: Paal) |kjv: perverse, turn over| {str: 3399}

a^m) ⊗ॻY⅄⅄ (מורט MW-RTh) — **Bright:** A metal that is scoured to make it shine. [freq. 5] |kjv: peeled, furbished, bright| {str: 4178}

Adopted Roots;
2760 ⊗ᴍॻ Rafter

1447) ॖॻ (רי RY) ac: **Flow** co: **Water** ab: ?: Related to ⅄ॻ and ॻॖ.

A) ॖॻ (רי RY) ac: ? co: **Flow** ab: ?: A flowing of water.

N^m) ॖॻ (רי RY) — **Watering:** [freq. 1] |kjv: watering| {str: 7377}

1448) ॼॻ (רך RK) ac: ? co: **Loins** ab: ?: The pictograph ॻ is a picture of the head of a man, the ॼ is a picture of the palm representing a covering. Combined these mean "man covered". The reproductive organs of the male including the lower abdomen which are always covered.

A) ॼॻ (רך RK) ac: ? co: **Tender** ab: ?: The tenderness of the loins.

N^m) ॼॻ (רך RK) — **Tender:** [freq. 16] |kjv: tender, soft, weak| {str: 7390}

B) ॼॼॻ (רכך RKK) ac: ? co: **Tender** ab: ?: The tenderness of the loins.

V) ॼॼॻ (רכך R-KK) — **Soft:** To be soft. [freq. 8] (vf: Paal, Niphal, Hiphil, Pual) |kjv: tender, faint, mollified, soft| {str: 7401}

C) ॼॻ⅄ (ארך ARK) ac: ? co: **Long** ab: ?: From the male reproductive organ.

V) ॼॻ⅄ (ארך A-RK) — **Prolong:** To lengthen or delay. [Hebrew and Aramaic] [freq. 35] (vf: Paal, Hiphil) |kjv: prolong, long, lengthen, draw out, defer, tarry| {str: 748, 749}

N^m) ॼॻ⅄ (ארך A-RK) — **Slow:** To be long in patience or time. [freq. 15] |kjv: slow, longsuffering, patient| {str: 750}

N^fl) ⅄ॼॻ⅄ (ארכה AR-KH) — **Lengthening:** [Aramaic only] [ar: ארכא] [freq. 1] |kjv: lengthening| {str: 754}

c^m) ॼॻ⅄ (ארוך A-RWK) — **Long:** [ms: ארך] [freq. 3] |kjv: long, longer| {str: 752}

d^fl) ⅄ॼॻ⅄ (ארוכה A-RW-KH) — **Repair:** A reconstruction or healing that causes longer life. [ms: ארכה] [freq. 6] |kjv: health, perfected, made| {str: 724}

g^m) ॼॻY⅄ (אורך AW-RK) — **Length:** [ms: ארך] [freq. 95] |kjv: length, long, ever, high| {str: 753}

J) ךרא (רוך RWK) ac: ? co:
Tender ab: ?: The tenderness of the
loins.

N^m) ךרא (רוך RWK) —
Tender: [ms: רך] [freq. 1] |kjv:
tender| {str: 7391}

L) ךרֿ‍ך (ירך YRK) ac: ? co: **Loins**
ab: ?

N^f) ךרֿ‍ך (ירך Y-RK) —
Loins: [freq. 34] |kjv: thigh,
side, shaft, loins, body| {str:
3409}

N^{f1}) ךרֿ‍שֿ‍ך (ירכה YR-KH) —
Loins: [Hebrew and Aramaic]
[ar: ירכא] [freq. 29] |kjv: thigh|
{str: 3410, 3411}

a^m) ךרֿ‍Yאּ (מורך MW-RK) —
Faint: From a blow to the loins.
[ms: מרך] [freq. 1] |kjv:
faintness| {str: 4816}

Adopted Roots;
2759 ךֿ‍חרא   Widen, Street, Width

~~~~~~~~~~

1449) ךֿ‍א (רל RL) ac: ? co: ? ab: ?

~~~~~~~~~~

1450) אֿ‍ם (רם RM) ac: **Lift** co: **Height**
ab: **Deceit:** Anything that is high or lifted
up.

A) אֿ‍ם (רם RM) ac: ? co: **Height**
ab: **Deceit:** A lifting up through a
prolific amount of offspring.

N^{f1}) אֿ‍ם (רמה R-MH) —
Heights: A high place. [freq. 4]
|kjv: high place| {str: 7413}

N^{f3}) tYאֿ‍ם (רמות R-MWT) —
Height: [freq. 1] |kjv: height|
{str: 7419}

f¹) אֿ‍ךֿ‍ם (רמיה RM-YH) —
I.   Deceitful: [Unknown

connection to root;] **II. Slothful:**
[Unknown connection to root]
[freq. 15] |kjv: deceitful, deceit,
slothful, false, guile, idle, slack|
{str: 7423}

h^{f1}) אֿ‍םֿ‍ם (מרמה MR-MH)
— **Deceit:** [Unknown
connection to root;] [freq. 39]
|kjv: deceit, false, guile, feign,
subtlety, treachery| {str: 4820}

i^f) אֿ‍םֿ‍t (תרמה TR-MH) —
Deceit: [Unknown connection to
root;] [freq. 6] |kjv: deceit,
deceitful, privily| {str: 8649}

j^m) ךYאֿ‍ם (רמון R-MWN) —
Pomegranate: Prolific of seeds.
[ms: רמן] [freq. 32] |kjv:
pomegranate| {str: 7416}

B) אֿ‍םֿ‍ם (רמם RMM) ac: **Lift** co:
Height ab: ?

V) אֿ‍םֿ‍ם (רמם R-MM) —
Lift: [freq. 8] (vf: Paal, Niphal)
|kjv: exalt, lift, up| {str: 7426,
7318}

g^{f1}) אֿ‍םֿ‍םYֿ (רוממה RW-M-
MH) — **Lift:** [freq. 1] |kjv: high|
{str: 7319}

g^{f3}) tYאֿ‍םֿ‍םYֿ (רוממות RW-M-
MWT) — **Lifting:** [freq. 1] |kjv:
lifting| {str: 7427}

C) אֿ‍םֿ‍ע (ארם ARM) ac: **Lift** co:
Palace ab: ?

j^m) ךYאֿ‍םֿ‍ע (ארמון AR-
MWN) — **Palace:** As built in
high places. [freq. 32] |kjv:
palace, castle| {str: 759}

D) אֿ‍עֿ‍ם (ראם RAM) ac: **Lift** co:
? ab: ?

V) אֿ‍עֿ‍ם (ראם R-AM) —
Lift: [freq. 1] (vf: Paal) |kjv: lift|
{str: 7213}

N^m) ᘈᕇᕴ (ראם R-AM) — **Reeym:** An Unknown animal. Possibly from its height. [ms: רסרימסראים] [freq. 9] |kjv: unicorn| {str: 7214}

N^{f1}) ᚓᘈᕇᕴ (ראמה RA-MH) — **Coral:** Lifted up as a highly prized item. [freq. 2] |kjv: coral| {str: 7215}

H) ᚓᘈᕴ (רמה RMH) ac: **Throw** co: ? ab: ?: A throwing of something high.

V) ᚓᘈᕴ (רמה R-MH) — I. **Throw:** To throw or shoot arrows. [Hebrew and Aramaic] II. **Deceive:** [Unknown connection to root] [freq. 24] (vf: Paal, Piel, Participle) |kjv: deceive, beguile, throw, betray, carry| {str: 7411, 7412}

J) ᘈᖻᕴ (רום RWM) ac: **Lift** co: **High** ab: **Pride:** Anything that is high or lifted up.

V) ᘈᖻᕴ (רום RWM) — **Lift:** To lift something up. [Hebrew and Aramaic] [ar: רין] [freq. 198] (vf: Paal, Hiphil, Hophal) |kjv: lift, exalt, high, offer, give, heave, extol, lofty, take, tall| {str: 7311, 7313}

N^m) ᘈᖻᕴ (רום RWM) — **High:** Something that is lifted up. [Hebrew and Aramaic] [ms: רם] [freq. 12] |kjv: high, haughtiness, height| {str: 7312, 7314, 7315}

N^{f1}) ᚓᘈᖻᕴ (רומה RW-MH) — **Proudly:** In the sense lifting oneself up. [freq. 1] |kjv: haughtily| {str: 7317}

a^m) ᘈᖻᕴᘈ (מרום M-RWM) — **Heights:** A high place. [freq. 54] |kjv: high, height, above,

high place, dignity, haughty, loftily, upward| {str: 4791}

i^{f1}) ᚓᘈᖻᕴᕷ (תרומה T-RW-MH) — **Offering:** As lifted up. [ms: תרמה] [freq. 76] |kjv: offering, oblation, heave, gift, offered| {str: 8641}

if^{f1}) ᚓᕽᘈᖻᕴᕷ (תרומיה T-RW-M-YH) — **Offering:** As lifted up. [freq. 1] |kjv: oblation| {str: 8642}

M) ᘈᕽᕴ (רים RYM) ac: ? co: ? ab: ?

N^{f1}) ᚓᘈᕽᕴ (רימה RY-MH) — **Maggot:** A quick breeding insect. [ms: רמה] [freq. 7] |kjv: worm| {str: 7415}

~~~~~~~~~~

1451) ᕬᕴ (רן RN) ac: **Shout** co: ? ab: ?: Any loud noise.

B) ᕬᕬᕴ (רנן RNN) ac: **Shout** co: ? ab: ?: A shout of joy, desperation or desire.

V) ᕬᕬᕴ (רנן R-NN) — **Shout:** [freq. 54] (vf: Paal, Hiphil, Pual, Piel, Participle) |kjv: sing, rejoice, shout, cry| {str: 7442, 7444}

N^m) ᕬᕬᕴ (רנן R-NN) — **Shouting:** A site that shouts out beauty. [freq. 1] |kjv: goodly| {str: 7443}

N^{f1}) ᚓᕬᕬᕴ (רננה RN-NH) — **Shouting:** [freq. 4] |kjv: joyful, triumphing, singing| {str: 7445}

C) ᕬᕴᕽ (ארן ARN) ac: ? co: ? ab: ?: [Unknown meaning;]

g^m) ᕬᕴᖻᕽ (אורן AW-RN) — **Oren:** An unknown tree. [ms: ארן] [freq. 1] |kjv: ash| {str: 766}

H) 𐤓𐤍𐤄 (רנה RNH) ac: ? co: **Rattle** ab: ?: A loud noise.

V) 𐤓𐤍𐤄 (רנה R-NH) — **Rattle:** [freq. 1] (vf: Paal) |kjv: rattle| {str: 7439}

J) 𐤓𐤅𐤍 (רון RWN) ac: **Murmur** co: ? ab: ?: A loud rumbling.

V) 𐤓𐤅𐤍 (רון RWN) — **Murmur:** [df: לון] [freq. 87] (vf: Paal, Niphal, Hiphil) |kjv: murmur, grudge| {str: 3885}

N^m) 𐤓𐤅𐤍 (רון RWN) — **Shouting:** [ms: רן] [freq. 1] |kjv: song| {str: 7438}

i^f1) 𐤕𐤓𐤅𐤍𐤄 (תרונה T-RW-NH) — **Murmuring:** [df: תלונה] [freq. 8] |kjv: murmuring| {str: 8519}

M) 𐤓𐤉𐤍 (רין RYN) ac: **Shout** co: ? ab: ?

N^f1) 𐤓𐤉𐤍𐤄 (רינה RY-NH) — **Shouting:** [ms: רנה] [freq. 33] |kjv: cry, singing, rejoice, joy, gladness, proclamation, shouting, sing, song, triumph| {str: 7440}

1452) 𐤓𐤎 (רס RS) ac: **Demolish** co: **Pieces** ab: **Ruin:** The breaking or bringing down of something by throwing or pulling it down.

B) 𐤓𐤎𐤎 (רסס RSS) ac: ? co: **Pieces** ab: ?: Something broken or divided into pieces.

V) 𐤓𐤎𐤎 (רסס R-SS) — **Moisten:** To make wet by adding a liquid. In the sense of drops as pieces of water. [freq. 1] (vf: Paal) |kjv: temper| {str: 7450}

b^m) 𐤓𐤎𐤉𐤎 (רסיס R-SYS) — **Pieces:** Something broken into pieces. Also, the drops of dew as pieces of water. [freq. 2] |kjv: drip, breach| {str: 7447}

F) 𐤄𐤓𐤎 (הרס HRS) ac: **Demolish** co: **Pieces** ab: ?: Something broken into pieces.

V) 𐤄𐤓𐤎 (הרס H-RS) — **Demolish:** To break something into pieces by throwing or pulling it down. [freq. 43] (vf: Paal, Niphal, Piel, Participle) |kjv: throw, break, overthrow, destroy, pull, ruin, beat, pluck, destroyer| {str: 2040}

N^m) 𐤄𐤓𐤎 (הרס H-RS) — **Ruin:** A city that has been broken down into pieces. [df: הרש] [freq. 1] |kjv: destruction| {str: 2041}

b^f1) 𐤄𐤓𐤉𐤎𐤄 (הריסה H-RY-SH) — **Ruin:** A city that has been broken down into pieces. [freq. 1] |kjv: ruin| {str: 2034}

b^f3) 𐤄𐤓𐤉𐤎𐤅𐤕 (הריסות H-RY-SWT) — **Ruin:** A city that has been broken down into pieces. [freq. 1] |kjv: destruction| {str: 2035}

Adopted Roots;

2775	𐤓𐤀𐤌	Tread
2786	𐤓𐤀𐤏	Stomp, Mud

1453) 𐤓𐤏 (רע RAh) ac: **Feed** co: **Shepherd** ab: **Desire:** The pictograph ᕼ is a picture of the head of a man, the ⊙ is a picture of they eye. Combined these mean "man watches". The shepherd closely watched over his flock, often they are his only companions.

A) ⟨רע RAh) ac: **?** co: **Friend** ab: **?**

N^m) ⟨רע RAh) — **Friend:** A close companion. [df: ריע] [freq. 188] |kjv: neighbor, friend, another, fellow, companion, other, brother, husband, lover| {str: 7453}

N^{f1}) ⟨רעה R-AhH) — **Friend:** A female companion. [freq. 3] |kjv: companion, fellows| {str: 7464}

N^{f3}) ⟨רעות R-AhWT) — **Friend:** A female companion. [freq. 6] |kjv: neighbor, another, mate| {str: 7468}

a^{f4}) ⟨מרעית MR-AhYT) — **Pasture:** [freq. 10] |kjv: pasture, flock| {str: 4830}

k^m) ⟨מרע M-RAh) — **Friend:** A close companion. [freq. 7] |kjv: companion, friend| {str: 4828}

H) ⟨רעה RAhH) ac: **feed** co: **Pasture** ab: **Desire:** One who provides and protects the flock and takes desire in them.

V) ⟨רעה R-AhH) — **Feed:** To provide feed or pasture to the flock. [freq. 173] (vf: Paal, Hiphil, Hitpael, Piel) |kjv: feed, shepherd, pastor, herdman, keep, companion, broken, company, devour, eat, entreat| {str: 7462}

N^m) ⟨רעה R-AhH) — **Friend:** [freq. 3] |kjv: friend| {str: 7463}

N^{f3}) ⟨רעות R-AhWT) — **Desire:** [Hebrew and Aramaic] [freq. 9] |kjv: vexation, pleasure, will| {str: 7469, 7470}

f^m) ⟨רעי R-AhY) — **Pasture:** [freq. 1] |kjv: pasture| {str: 7471}

f^{j1}) ⟨רעיה RAh-YH) — **Love:** The love of a friend or flock. [freq. 10] |kjv: love| {str: 7474}

h^m) ⟨מרעה MR-AhH) — **Pasture:** A place of feeding. [freq. 13] |kjv: pasture, feedingplace| {str: 4829}

fj^m) ⟨רעיון RAh-YWN) — **Desire:** [freq. 3] |kjv: vexation| {str: 7475}

J) ⟨רוע RWAh) ac: **?** co: **Shepherd** ab: **?**

f^m) ⟨רועי RW-AhY) — **Shepherd:** [ms: רעי] [freq. 2] |kjv: shepherd| {str: 7473}

Adopted Roots;
2781 רשא Field, Field, Flourish

—————————

1454) ⟨רף RP) ac: **Heal** co: **Medicine** ab: **Sick:** The pictograph ר is a picture of the head of a man, the ⟨ is a picture of an open mouth. Combined these mean "man open". Wounds, sickness and illnesses are cured with medicines made from plant materials which were pulverized into a medicinal power.

A) ⟨רף RP) ac: **Heal** co: **Idol** ab: **?**

i^m) ⟨תרף T-RP) — **Idol:** A household idol of a god, possible believed to have a healing power. [freq. 15] |kjv: image, teraphim, idol, idolatry| {str: 8655}

E) ⟨רפא RPA) ac: **Heal** co: **Medicine** ab: **?**

V) ?????? (רפא R-PA) — **Heal:** [df: רפה] [freq. 67] (vf: Paal, Niphal, Hitpael, Piel) |kjv: heal, physician, cure, repair| {str: 7495}

N[m] ?????? (רפא R-PA) — **Dead:** [freq. 8] |kjv: dead, deceased| {str: 7496}

a[m] ??????? (מרפא MR-PA) — **Health:** [freq. 16] |kjv: healing, cure, healing, sound, wholesome, yielding| {str: 4832}

d[fl] ??????? (רפואה R-PW-AH) — **Medicine:** [ms: רפאה] [freq. 3] |kjv: medicine| {str: 7499}

e[f3] ??????? (ריפאות RY-P-AWT) — **Health:** [ms: רפאות] [freq. 1] |kjv: health| {str: 7500}

H) ????? (רפה RPH) ac: **Weak** co: ? ab: ?: One weakened by illness or disease.

V) ????? (רפה R-PH) — **Weak:** To be weak from sickness, laziness or work. [freq. 46] (vf: Paal, Niphal, Hiphil, Hitpael, Piel, Participle) |kjv: feeble, fail, weaken, go, alone, idle, stay, slack, faint, forsake, abate, cease| {str: 7503}

N[m] ????? (רפה R-PH) — **Weak:** [freq. 4] |kjv: weak| {str: 7504}

J) ????? (רוף RWP) ac: **Pulverize** co: **Medicine** ab: ?

V) ????? (רוף RWP) — **Pulverize:** [freq. 1] (vf: Piel) |kjv: tremble| {str: 7322}

i[fl] ??????? (תרופה T-RW-PH) — **Medicine:** [freq. 1] |kjv: medicine| {str: 8644}

M) ????? (ריף RYP) ac: ? co: ? ab: **Sick**

N[fl] ?????? (ריפה RY-PH) — **Wheat:** A grain pulverized with a mortar and pestle for making a flour. [ms: רפה] [freq. 2] |kjv: wheat, corn| {str: 7383}

fj[m] ??????? (ריפיון RY-P-YWN) — **Feeble:** [ms: רפיון] [freq. 1] |kjv: feeblenss| {str: 7510}

Adopted Roots;

2512 ????? Burn, Venom
~~~~~~~~~~

1455) ??? (רץ RTs) ac: **Crush** co: **Potsherd** ab: **Desire:** Broken pieces of pottery were commonly used as writing tablets as they were inexpensive and durable. These potsherds were commonly used to send messages from one person to another, usually carried by runners. (eng: earth; terra - with a reversal of letters; terrain)

A) ??? (רץ RTs) ac: ? co: **Potsherd** ab: ?: Broken fragments of a pot which were commonly used as writing surfaces for messages.

N[m] ??? (רץ RTs) — **Fragment:** [freq. 1] |kjv: piece| {str: 7518}

B) ????? (רצץ RTsTs) ac: **Crush** co: ? ab: **Violence**

V) ????? (רצץ R-TsTs) — **Crush:** To crush something to pieces. Also an oppression or struggle as crushing. [Hebrew and Aramaic] [df: רשש] [ar: רעע] [freq. 22] (vf: Paal, Niphal, Hiphil, Piel) |kjv: oppress, break, bruise, crush, discourage, struggle| {str: 7465, 7533, 7567}

ko[fl]) 𐤔ᚪᚾᚪᚤᚪᛗ (מרוצצה M-RW-Ts-TsH) — **Violence:** In the sense of chattering. [df: מרצה] [freq. 1] |kjv: violence| {str: 4835}

C) ᚪᚾᚪᛒ (ארץ ARTs) ac: **?** co: **Land** ab: **?:** Land is divided up into fragments by tribe or nations.

N[f]) ᚪᚾᚪᛒ (ארץ A-RTs) — **Land:** The whole of the earth or a region. [Hebrew and Aramaic] [df: ארק] [ar: ארע] [freq. 2526] |kjv: earth, land, country, ground, world, way, common, field, nations, inferior| {str: 772, 776, 778}

N[fl]) 𐤔ᚪᚾᚪᛒ (ארצה AR-TsH) — **Bottom:** [Unknown connection to root; Aramaic only] [ar: ארעית] [freq. 1] |kjv: bottom| {str: 773}

E) ᛒᚪᚾᚪ (רצא RTsA) ac: **Run** co: **?** ab: **?:** Messengers ran messages written on potsherds.

V) ᛒᚪᚾᚪ (רצא R-TsA) — **Run:** [freq. 1] (vf: Paal) |kjv: run| {str: 7519}

H) 𐤔ᚪᚾᚪ (רצה RTsH) ac: **?** co: **Message** ab: **Desire:** Ones will and desires are written on potsherds as messages to another.

V) 𐤔ᚪᚾᚪ (רצה R-TsH) — **Desire:** [freq. 57] (vf: Paal, Niphal, Hiphil, Hitpael, Piel) |kjv: accept, please, pleasure, delight, enjoy, favourable, acceptable, accomplish, affection, approve| {str: 7521}

j[m]) ᛚᚤᚪᚾᚪ (רצון R-TsWN) — **Will:** Ones desire. From instructions that are written on potsherds. [ms: רצן] [freq. 56] |kjv: favour, will, acceptable,

delight, pleasure, accepted, desire, acceptance, selfwill| {str: 7522}

J) ᚪᚤᚪ (רוץ RWTs) ac: **Run** co: **Course** ab: **?:** Messengers ran messages written on potsherds.

V) ᚪᚤᚪ (רוץ RWTs) — **Run:** [freq. 104] (vf: Paal, Hiphil) |kjv: run, guard, post, speedily| {str: 7323}

k[m]) ᚪᚤᚪᛗ (מרוץ M-RWTs) — **Course:** The path of the runner. [freq. 1] |kjv: race| {str: 4793}

k[fl]) 𐤔ᚪᚤᚪᛗ (מרוצה M-RW-TsH) — **Course:** The path of the runner. [ms: מרצה] [freq. 4] |kjv: running| {str: 4794}

Adopted Roots;

2207 ᚠᚪᛙ Dry, Clay

2783 ᚪᚾᚦᚪ Shatter

2790 ᛥᚪᚾᚪ Murder, Wound

2792 ᚥᚪᚾᚪ Fit, Stone

~~~~~~~~~~

1456) ᚤᚪ (רק RQ) ac: **Draw** co: **Grass** ab: **?:** Thin green blades of grass that are drawn out of the soil.

A) ᚤᚪ (רק RQ) ac: **?** co: **Thin** ab: **?**

N[m]) ᚤᚪ (רק RQ) — **I. Thin: II. Only:** As something thin. [freq. 19] |kjv: thin, lean, only, nothing, except, but| {str: 7534, 7535}

N[fl]) 𐤔ᚥᚪ (רקה R-QH) — **Temple:** The side of the head as a thin spot. [freq. 5] |kjv: temple| {str: 7541}

B) ᚤᚪ (רקק RQQ) ac: **Spit** co: **?** ab: **?:** As green and drawn out of the mouth.

V) ⊙-⊙-ᐯ (רקק R-QQ) — **Spit:** [freq. 1] (vf: Paal) |kjv: spit| {str: 7556}

b^m) ⊙->-⌐-ᐯ (רקיק R-QYQ) — **Wafer:** A thin bread. [freq. 8] |kjv: wafer, cake| {str: 7550}

J) ⊙-Yᐯ (רוק RWQ) ac: **Draw** co: **?** ab: **?:** Something that is drawn out.

V) ⊙-Yᐯ (רוק RWQ) — **Draw:** [freq. 19] (vf: Hiphil, Hophal) |kjv: out, empty, draw, arm, pour| {str: 7324}

N^m) ⊙-Yᐯ (רוק RWQ) — **Spit:** As drawn out of the mouth. [ms: רק] [freq. 3] |kjv: spit, spiting, spittle| {str: 7536}

L) ⊙-ᐯ⌐ (ירק YRQ) ac: **?** co: **Green** ab: **?**

V) ⊙-ᐯ⌐ (ירק Y-RQ) — **Spit:** [freq. 3] (vf: Paal) |kjv: spit| {str: 3417}

N^m) ⊙-ᐯ⌐ (ירק Y-RQ) — **Green:** The color of grasses and herbs as thin. [freq. 11] |kjv: green, herb| {str: 3418, 3419}

c^m) ⊙-Yᐯ⌐ (ירוק Y-RWQ) — **Green:** The color of grasses and herbs as thin. [freq. 1] |kjv: green| {str: 3387}

j^m) ᐡY-⊙-ᐯ⌐ (ירקון YR-QWN) — **Mildew:** As a thin green film. [freq. 6] |kjv: mildew, paleness| {str: 3420}

l^m) ⊙-ᐯ-⊙-ᐯ⌐ (ירקרק Y-RQ-RQ) — **Greenish:** [freq. 3] |kjv: greenish, yellow| {str: 3422}

M) ⊙->-⌐ᐯ (ריק RYQ) ac: **?** co: **Empty** ab: **?:** A container where all of its contents have been drawn out. Also vanity as an emptiness.

N^m) ⊙->-ᐯ (ריק RYQ) — **Empty:** Empty of contents. Also

vain in the sense of emptiness. [ms: רק] [freq. 26] |kjv: vain, vanity, no purpose, empty| {str: 7385, 7386}

p^m) ᜊ-⊙->-ᐯ (ריקם RY-QM) — **Empty:** [freq. 16] |kjv: void, vain| {str: 7387}

1457) ᐯᐯ (רר RR) ac: **Flow** co: **Spit** ab: **Curse**

C) ᐯᐯᏝ (ארר ARR) ac: **?** co: **?** ab: **Curse:** One shows a cursing by spitting.

V) ᐯᐯᏝ (ארר A-RR) — **Curse:** [freq. 63] (vf: Paal, Niphal, Hophal, Piel) |kjv: curse| {str: 779}

k^{fl}) ᛉᐯᐯᏝᗯ (מאררה MA-R-RH) — **Curse:** [df: מארה] [freq. 5] |kjv: curse, cursing| {str: 3994}

J) ᐯYᐯ (רור RWR) ac: **Flow** co: **?** ab: **?:** The flowing of a liquid.

V) ᐯYᐯ (רור RWR) — **Flow:** [freq. 1] (vf: Paal) |kjv: run| {str: 7325}

M) ᐯ>-ᐯ (ריר RYR) ac: **?** co: **Spit** ab: **?**

N^m) ᐯ>-ᐯ (ריר RYR) — **Slime:** The slime of spit or an egg white. [freq. 2] |kjv: spittle, white| {str: 7388}

1458) ╙╙ᐯ (רש RSh) ac: **Inherit** co: **Head** ab: **?:** The pictograph ᐯ is a picture of the head. The head of the tribe (chief) or family (father) is passed from generation to generation. The head grants permission for the betrothal of his daughters and determines the inheritor of the tribe or family. The head of a person, place, thing or time. (eng: raise - with the exchange of the s and sh)

A) ᴌᴌᕲ (שׁר RSh) ac: **?** co: **Head** ab: **?**

N^(f2)) ᛏᴌᴌᕲ (רשׁת R-ShT) — **Net:** [Unknown connection to root;] [freq. 21] |kjv: net| {str: 7568}

fj^m) ᐱY᙮ᴌᴌᕲ (רשׁיון RSh-YWN) — **Permission:** [freq. 1] |kjv: grant| {str: 7558}

B) ᴌᴌᴌᕲ (שׁשׁר RShSh) ac: **?** co: **Head** ab: **?**

ib^m) ᴌᴌ᙮ᴌᕲᵼ (תרשׁישׁ TR-ShYSh) — **Tarshish:** An unknown precious stone. A chief of trade goods. [freq. 7] |kjv: beryle| {str: 8658}

C) ᴌᴌᕲᐣ (ארשׁ ARSh) ac: **Request** co: **?** ab: **?:** A granting permission to marry.

V) ᴌᴌᕲᐣ (ארשׁ A-RSh) — **Betroth:** To request a woman for marriage. [df: ארשׂ] [freq. 11] (vf: Pual, Piel) |kjv: betroth, espouse| {str: 781}

N^(f2)) ᛏᴌᴌᕲᐣ (ארשׁת AR-ShT) — **Request:** [freq. 1] |kjv: request| {str: 782}

D) ᴌᴌᐣᕲ (ראשׁ RASh) ac: **?** co: **Head** ab: **?**

N^m) ᴌᴌᐣᕲ (ראשׁ R-ASh) — **Head:** The top of the body. A person in authority or role of leader. The top, beginning or first of something. [Hebrew and Aramaic] [df: רישׁ] [freq. 619] |kjv: head, chief, top, beginning, company, captain, sum, first, principal, chapiters, rulers| {str: 7217, 7218, 7389}

N^(f3)) ᛏYᴌᴌᐣᕲ (ראשׁות RA-ShWT) — **Headrest:** A place where the head is laid. [ms: ראשׁת] [freq. 1] |kjv: bolster| {str: 7226}

N^(f4)) ᛏ᙮ᴌᴌᐣᕲ (ראשׁית RA-ShYT) — **Beginning:** The head of a space such as the head of a river or time such as an event. [freq. 51] |kjv: beginning, firstfruits, first, chief| {str: 7225}

a^(f1)) ᕲᴌᴌᐣᕲᴧ (מראשׁה MR-A-ShH) — **Head:** As a leader. [freq. 1] |kjv: principality| {str: 4761}

e^(f1)) ᕲᴌᴌ᙮ᐣᕲ (ריאשׁה RY-A-ShH) — **Beginning:** The head of a space such as the head of a river or time such as an event. [ms: ראשׁון] [freq. 185] |kjv: first, former, beginning, chief, before, old, foremost, aforetime| {str: 7223}

ej^m) ᐱYᴌᴌᐣ᙮ᕲ (ריאשׁון RY-A-ShWN) — **First:** The head of a time or position. [ms: ראשׁון רשׁון] [freq. 185] |kjv: first, former, beginning, chief, before, old, foremost, aforetime| {str: 7223}

g^m) ᴌᴌᐣYᕲ (רואשׁ RW-ASh) — **Venom:** The poison of serpents that comes sacks located in the head. Also by extension any type of poison. [ms: ראשׁ] [freq. 12] |kjv: gall, venom, poison, hemlock| {str: 7219}

g^(f1)) ᕲᴌᴌᐣYᕲ (רואשׁה RW-A-ShH) — **Head:** [ms: ראשׁה] [freq. 1] |kjv: beginnings| {str: 7222}

k^(f1)) ᕲᴌᴌᐣᕲᴧ (מראשׁה MR-A-ShH) — **Headrest:** A place where the head is laid. [freq. 8] |kjv: bolster, pillow, head| {str: 4763} emf^m) ᔑ⊔⅃⅄⊿ᕮᔑ (ריאשׁנׁי RY-A-ShNY) — **First:** The head of a time or position. [ms: רׁאשׁוׁנׁיׁת] [freq. 1] |kjv: first| {str: 7224}

J) ⊔⊔⅄ᕮ (רׁוׁשׁ RWSh) ac: ? co: **Poor** ab: ?: One who hangs down the head and is in need.

N^m) ⊔⊔⅄ᕮ (רׁוׁשׁ RWSh) — **Poor:** [freq. 24] |kjv: poor, lack, needy| {str: 7326}

L) ⊔⊔ᕮ⤚⅃ (יׁרׁשׁ YRSh) ac: **Inherit** co: ? ab: **Inheritance:** The inheritor becomes the head of the family. [See also ⊔⊔ᕮ⅃ᕽ]

V) ⊔⊔ᕮ⤚⅃ (יׁרׁשׁ Y-RSh) — **Inherit:** [freq. 232] (vf: Paal, Niphal, Hiphil, Piel) |kjv: possession, out, inherit, heir, possession, succeed, dispossess, poverty, drive, enjoy, poor, expel| {str: 3423}

N^{f1}) ⅏⊔⊔ᕮ⤚⅃ (יׁרׁשׁה YR-ShH) — **Inheritance:** [freq. 2] |kjv: possession| {str: 3424}

a^m) ⊔⊔ᕮ⅄ᘻᘻ (מׁוׁרׁשׁ MW-RSh) — **Inheritance:** [freq. 3] |kjv: possession, thought| {str: 4180}

a^{f1}) ⅏⊔⊔ᕮ⅄ᘻᘻ (מׁוׁרׁשׁה MW-R-ShH) — **Inheritance:** [freq. 9] |kjv: possession, inheritance, heritage| {str: 4181}

d^{f1}) ⅏⊔⊔⅄ᕮ⤚⅃ (יׁרׁוׁשׁה Y-RW-ShH) — **Inheritance:** [ms: יׁרׁשׁה] [freq. 14] |kjv: possession, heritage, inheritance| {str: 3425}

ic^m) ⊔⊔⅄ᕮ⤚⅃�....⊢ (תׁיׁרׁוׁשׁ TY-RWSh) — **Wine:** A freshly pressed wine. [Unknown connection to root;] [ms: תׁירׁשׁ] [freq. 38] |kjv: wine| {str: 8492}

1459) ﻒᕮ (רׁת RT) ac: **Tremble** co: ? ab: ?

A) ﻒᕮ (רׁת RT) ac: **Tremble** co: ? ab: ?

N^{f2}) ﻒﻒᕮ (רׁתׁת R-TT) — **Tremble:** [freq. 1] |kjv: tremble| {str: 7578}

Adopted Roots;
2802 ᘻﻒᕮ   Attach, Harness
2803 ⊶ﻒᕮ   Bind, Chain

~~~~~~~~~~

1460) ᕮᕮ (רׁע RGh) ac: **Grieve** co: **Bad** ab: ?

A) ᕮᕮ (רׁע RGh) ac: ? co: **Bad** ab: ?

N^{m/f}) ᕮᕮ (רׁע RGh) — I. **Bad:** Something dysfunctional, wrong, evil or wicked. II. **Shout:** To shout an alarm, war or great rejoicing. [freq. 666] |kjv: evil, wickedness, wicked, mischief, hurt, bad, trouble, sore, affliction, ill, adversity, favoured, harm, naught, noisesome, grievous, sad, shout, noise, aloud| {str: 7451, 7452}

B) ᕮᕮᕮ (רׁעׁע RGhGh) ac: ? co: **Bad** ab: ?: Something dysfunctional, wrong, evil or wicked.

V) ᕮᕮᕮ (רׁעׁע R-GhGh) — **Bad:** To be bad by hurting or doing an evil action. [freq. 84] (vf: Paal, Hiphil, Participle) |kjv: evil, evildoer, hurt, wickedly, worse, afflict, wicked, break, doer, ill, harm, displease, mischief| {str: 4827, 7489}

J) ᕮ⅄ᕮ (רׁוׁע RWGh) ac: **Shout** co: **Bad** ab: ?: Something dysfunctional, wrong, evil or wicked.

V) גֵי (רוע RWGh) — **Shout:** To shout an alarm, war or great rejoicing. [freq. 46] (vf: Niphal, Hiphil) |kjv: shout, noise, alarm, cry, triumph, smart| {str: 7321}

N^m) גֵיטֹ (רוע RWGh) — **Bad:** [ms: רע] [freq. 19] |kjv: evil, wickedness, bad, badness, naughtiness, sorrow, sadness| {str: 7455}

i^{f1}) תֵיגֵיטֹ (תרועה T-RW-GhH) — **Shout:** A great shout of alarm, war or rejoicing. [freq.

36] |kjv: shout, shouting, alarm, sound, blowing, joy| {str: 8643}

L) גֵטֹי (ירע YRGh) ac: **Grieve** co: ? ab: ?: A feeling from bad circumstances.

V) גֵטֹי (ירע Y-RGh) — **Grieve:** [freq. 22] (vf: Paal) |kjv: displease, grieve, grievous, evil, ill, harm, sad| {str: 3415}

270

Shin

1461) $\mathcal{Y}$ﳊ (שׁא ShA) ac: **Crash** co: **Storm** ab: **Desolate**: The crashing of thunder or waves as a desolating storm.

A) $\mathcal{Y}$ﳊ (שׁא ShA) ac: ? co: **Storm** ab: ?: A loud rushing noise or crashing as thunder or the crashing of waves in the sea.

N^{f2}) $\dagger\mathcal{Y}$ﳊ (שׁאת Sh-AT) — **Tumult**: [freq. 1] |kjv: desolation| {str: 7612}

j^m) $\mathcal{Y}$ﳊ (שׁאון Sh-AWN) — **Tumult**: [freq. 17] |kjv: noise, tumult, rushing, horrible, pomp| {str: 7588}

H) ﰋ$\mathcal{Y}$ﳊ (שׁאה ShAH) ac: **Crash** co: **Thunder** ab: ?

V) ﰋ$\mathcal{Y}$ﳊ (שׁאה Sh-AH) — **Crash**: [freq. 7] (vf: Paal, Niphal, Hiphil, Hitpael, Participle) |kjv: lay waste, rushing, waste, desolate| {str: 7582, 7583}

f^f) ﰋﰋ$\mathcal{Y}$ﳊ (שׁאיה ShA-YH) — **Crashing**: [freq. 1] |kjv: destruction| {str: 7591}

i^{f1}) ﰋ$\mathcal{Y}$ﳊ$\dagger$ (תשׁואה T-ShW-AH) — **Thunder**: [ms: תשׁאה] [freq. 4] |kjv: noise| {str: 8663}

J) $\mathcal{Y}$ﲐﳊ (שׁוא ShWA) ac: ? co: **Storm** ab: **Desolation**: A desolating storm.

N^m) $\mathcal{Y}$ﲐﳊ (שׁוא ShWA) — **I. Storm**: A loud and destructive crashing of thunder and waves. **II. Empty**: In the sense of destroyed. Empty words or actions. [freq. 53] |kjv: desolate, vain, vanity, false, lying lies| {str: 7722, 7723}

N^{f1}) ﰋ$\mathcal{Y}$ﲐﳊ (שׁואה ShW-AH) — **Storm**: A loud and destructive crashing of thunder or waves. [ms: שׁאה] [freq. 14] |kjv: desolation, destruction, desolate, destroy, storm, wasteness| {str: 7722, 7584}

a^{f1}) ﰋ$\mathcal{Y}$ﲐﳊﲅ (משׁואה M-ShW-AH) — **Desolation**: [ms: משׁאה] [freq. 2] |kjv: desolation, destruction| {str: 4876}

k^{f1}) ﰋ$\mathcal{Y}$ﲐﳊﲅ (משׁואה M-ShW-AH) — **Desolation**: [ms: משׁאה] [freq. 3] |kjv: desolation, waste| {str: 4875}

1462) ﲐﳊ (שׁב ShB) ac: **Turn** co: **Seat** ab: ?: The pictograph ﳊ is a picture of the two front teeth representing pressing, the ﲐ is a picture of tent. Combined these mean "Press to the tent". A place of dwelling as the place returned to. A turning back or away from someone or something. A captive is one turned away from a place of dwelling. (eng: shove)

A) ﲐﳊ (שׁב ShB) ac: ? co: **Seat** ab: ?: A returning to ones place of residence where one sits.

N^{f2}) $\dagger$ﲐﳊ (שׁבת Sh-BT) — **Seat**: [freq. 4] |kjv: seat, place| {str: 7675}

q^f) ﲐﲐﳊ (שׁבו Sh-BW) — **Shvo**: An unknown stone, possibly an agate. [freq. 2] |kjv: agate| {str: 7618}

B) שּׁׂבבּ (שבב ShBB) ac: **Turn** co: ? ab: ?

N^m) שּׁׂבבּ (שבב Sh-BB) — **Broken**: To be broken into pieces. [Unknown connection to root;] [freq. 1] |kjv: broken| {str: 7616}

b^m) שּׁׂבּיּבּ (שביב Sh-BYB) — **Flame**: [Unknown connection to root; Hebrew and Aramaic] [freq. 3] |kjv: spark, flame| {str: 7631, 7632}

g^m) שּׁׂבבֿוּשׁ (שובב ShW-BB) — **Backsliding**: A turning back. [freq. 6] |kjv: backsliding, frowardly| {str: 7726, 7728}

H) שּׁׂבּהֿ (שבה ShBH) ac: **Capture** co: **Captive** ab: ?: A forcible turning away from ones homeland to another place.

V) שּׁׂבּהֿ (שבה Sh-BH) — **Capture**: To take one away from his homeland as a captive. [freq. 47] (vf: Paal, Niphal, Participle) |kjv: captive, away, carry, take| {str: 7617}

N^f3) שּׁׂבוּתֿ (שבות Sh-BWT) — **Captivity**: [df: שבית] [freq. 44] |kjv: captivity, captive| {str: 7622}

f) שּׁׂבּיּ (שבי Sh-BY) — **Captive**: [freq. 49] |kjv: captivity, captive, prisoner, taken| {str: 7628}

f^fl) שּׁׂבּיּהֿ (שביה ShB-YH) — **Captive**: [freq. 9] |kjv: captive, captivity| {str: 7633}

J) שּׁׂבֿוּשׁ (שוב ShWB) ac: **Turn** co: ? ab: ?: A turning back to a previous state or place.

V) שּׁׂבֿוּשׁ (שוב ShWB) — **Return**: To turn back. [Hebrew and Aramaic] [ar: תוב] [freq.

1074] (vf: Paal, Hiphil, Hophal, Pual, Participle) |kjv: return, again, turn, back, away, restore, bring, render, answer, recompense, recover, deliver, put, withdraw, requite| {str: 7725, 8421}

N^fl) שּׁׂבֿוּשׁהֿ (שובה ShW-BH) — **Returning**: [freq. 1] |kjv: returning| {str: 7729}

i^fl) תּשּׁׂבֿוּשׁהֿ (תשובה T-ShW-BH) — **Return**: Also a reply as a return. [ms: תשבה] [freq. 8] |kjv: return, expire, answer| {str: 8666}

k^fl) מּשּׁׂבֿוּשׁהֿ (משובה M-ShW-BH) — **Backsliding**: A turning back. [ms: משבה] [freq. 12] |kjv: backsliding, turning away| {str: 4878}

L) שּׁׂבּיּ (ישב YShB) ac: **Sit** co: **Dwelling** ab: ?: A place of dwelling as the place returned to.

V) שּׁׂבּיּ (ישב Y-ShB) — **Sit**: To set oneself down in the dwelling place for the night or for long periods of time. To settle or remain. [Hebrew and Aramaic] [ar: יתב] [freq. 1093] (vf: Paal, Niphal, Hiphil, Hophal, Piel) |kjv: dwell, inhabitant, sit, abide, inhabit, down, remain, in, tarry, set, continue, place, still, taken| {str: 3427, 3488}

a^m) מּשּׁׂבֿוּ (מושב MW-ShB) — **Dwelling**: The place of sitting. [ms: משב] [freq. 44] |kjv: habitation, dwelling, seat, dwellingplace, dwell, place, sitting, assembly, situation, sojourning| {str: 4186}

i^m) תּשּׁׂבֿוּ (תושב TW-ShB) — **Sojourner**: One who travels from place to place. [ms: תשב] [freq. 14] |kjv: sojourner, stranger, foreigner| {str: 8453}

M) שׂוב (שׁיב ShYB) ac: **Turn** co: ? ab: ?

N^{f1}) שׂיבה (שיבה ShY-BH) — **Return:** [freq. 2] |kjv: captivity| {str: 7870, 7871}

Adopted Roots;
2213	שׁשׁב	Design, Invention
2459	ששׁב	Interweave, Net
2807	שׁבשׁ	Weave, Wreath
2809	שׁבשׁ	Weave, Plait, Anguish
2812	שׁבת	Cease
2834	שׁבש	Lay, Bed, Copulation

~~~~~~~~~~

1463) שׁג (שׁג ShG) ac: **Err** co: ? ab: **Error:** The pictograph שׁ is a picture of the two front teeth representing the idea of double, the ג is a picture of a foot representing the carrying of a burden. Combined these mean "double burden". When a work is found to be in error, the work must be redone. An error that is made out of ignorance or accident.

A) שׁג (שׁג ShG) ac: ? co: ? ab: **Error**

h^{f1}) שׁגה (משׁגה MSh-GH) — **Error:** [freq. 1] |kjv: oversight| {str: 4870}

B) שׁגג (שׁגג ShGG) ac: ? co: ? ab: **Error**

V) שׁגג (שׁגג Sh-GG) — **Err:** [freq. 5] (vf: Paal) |kjv: err, flesh, sin, deceive, astray| {str: 7683}

N^{f1}) שׁגגה (שׁגגה ShG-GH) — **Error:** [freq. 19] |kjv: ignorance, unawares, error, unwittingly| {str: 7684}

D) שׁאג (שׁאג ShAG) ac: **Roar** co: ? ab: ?: The roaring like a lion. [Unknown connection to root;]

V) שׁאג (שׁאג Sh-AG) — **Roar:** [freq. 21] (vf: Paal) |kjv: roar| {str: 7580}

N^{f1}) שׁאגה (שׁאגה ShA-GH) — **Roar:** [freq. 7] |kjv: roaring| {str: 7581}

E) שׁגא (שׁגא ShGA) ac: ? co: ? ab: **Error**

b^{f1}) שׁגיאה (שׁגיאה Sh-GY-AH) — **Error:** [Aramaic only] [freq. 1] |kjv: error| {str: 7691}

H) שׁגה (שׁגה ShGH) ac: ? co: ? ab: **Error**

V) שׁגה (שׁגה Sh-GH) — **Err:** [freq. 21] (vf: Paal, Hiphil) |kjv: err, ravished, wander, deceive, astray, ignorance| {str: 7686}

J) שׁוג (שׁוג ShWG) ac: ? co: ? ab: **Error**

k^{f1}) משׁוגה (משׁוגה M-ShW-GH) — **Error:** [freq. 1] |kjv: error| {str: 4879}

~~~~~~~~~~

1464) שׁד (שׁד ShD) ac: ? co: **Breast** ab: ?: The pictograph שׁ is a picture of the two front teeth, the ד is a picture of a tent door that dangles down. Combined these mean "two that dangle".

A) שׁד (שׁד ShD) ac: ? co: **Breast** ab: ?

N^m) שׁד (שׁד ShD) — I. **Breast:** II. **Demon:** A goat demon, from the teats of the goat. [freq. 26] |kjv: breast, teat, pap| {str: 7699, 7700}

N^{f1}) שׁדה (שׁדה Sh-DH) — **Harem:** [freq. 2] |kjv: instrument| {str: 7705}

f^m) ﺟﺘﺎﺷ (שׁדי Sh-DY) —
Breast: [freq. 48] |kjv: almighty|
{str: 7706}

B) ﺗﺘﺎﺷ (שׁדד ShDD) ac: **Spoil**
co: ? ab: ?: Breasts that are dried up
and shriveled.

V) ﺗﺘﺎﺷ (שׁדד Sh-DD) —
Spoil: To dry up and shrivel.
[freq. 58] (vf: Paal, Niphal,
Hophal, Pual, Piel, Participle)
|kjv: spoil, spoiler, waste,
destroy, robber| {str: 7703}

C) ﺗﺎﺷﻟ (אשׁד AShD) ac: ? co:
Slope ab: ?: From the slope of the
breast.

N^m) ﺗﺎﺷﻟ (אשׁד A-ShD) —
Slope: [freq. 1] |kjv: stream|
{str: 793}

N^f1) ﺗﺎﺷﻟﺟ (אשׁדה ASh-DH)
— **Slope:** [freq. 6] |kjv: springs|
{str: 794}

J) ﺗﻳﺎﺷ (שׁוד ShWD) ac: **Spoil** co:
? ab: ?: Breasts that are dried up and
shriveled.

V) ﺗﻳﺎﺷ (שׁוד ShWD) —
Spoil: [freq. 1] (vf: Paal) |kjv:
waste| {str: 7736}

N^m) ﺗﻳﺎﺷ (שׁוד ShWD) —
Spoiling: [ms: שׁד] [freq. 25]
|kjv: destruction| {str: 7701}

1465) ﺟﻳﺎﺷ (שׁה ShH) ac: ? co: ? ab: ?

J) ﺟﻳﺎﺷ (שׁוה ShWH) ac: ? co:
Equal ab: ?

V) ﺟﻳﺎﺷ (שׁוה ShWH) —
Equal: To make something like
something else, or to compare it
to something else. [Hebrew and
Aramaic] [freq. 24] (vf: Paal,
Hiphil, Piel, Participle) |kjv: laid,

equal, like, compare, profit, set|
{str: 7737, 7738, 7739}

M) ﺟﻳﺎﺷ (שׁיה ShYH) ac: **Forget**
co: ? ab: ?

V) ﺟﻳﺎﺷ (שׁיה ShYH) —
Forget: [freq. 1] (vf: Paal) |kjv:
unmindful| {str: 7876}

1466) ﻳﺎﺷ (שׁו ShW) ac: ? co: ? ab: ?

1467) ﺟﺎﺷ (שׁז ShZ) ac: ? co: ? ab: ?

1468) ﻣﺎﺷ (שׁח ShHh) ac: **Sink** co: **Pit**
ab: ?: The pictograph ᒪᒪ is a picture of
the teeth representing sharpness, the ﻣﺘ is
a picture of wall. Combined these mean
"sharp walls". A pit dug into the ground
for the purpose of trapping someone or
something. To go down or sink down as
going into the pit.

A) ﻣﺎﺷ (שׁח ShHh) ac: ? co: **Pit** ab:
?

N^m) ﻣﺎﺷ (שׁח ShHh) — **Low:**
[freq. 1] |kjv: humble| {str:
7807}

N^f2) ﺗﻣﺎﺷ (שׁחת Sh-HhT) —
Pit: A hole in the ground such as
a grave. [freq. 23] |kjv:
corruption, pit, destruction,
ditch, grave| {str: 7845}

N^f3) ﺗﻳﻣﺎﺷ (שׁחות Sh-HhWT)
— **Pit:** [freq. 1] |kjv: pit| {str:
7816}

f^f2) ﺗﺟﻣﺎﺷ (שׁחית Sh-HhYT)
— **Pit:** [freq. 2] |kjv: pit,
destruction| {str: 7825}

s^m) ﺟﺟﻣﺎﺷ (שׁחין Sh-HhYN)
— **Pit:** A hole in the skin from

disease. [freq. 13] |kjv: boil, botch| {str: 7822}

B) ᒫᒫᒫᒥᗑ (שׁחחח ShHhHh) ac: **Sink** co: **?** ab: **?**: A bringing down low are a sinking feeling.

    V) ᒫᒫᒫᗑ (שׁחח Sh-HhHh) — **Sink**: To bring down low. [freq. 21] (vf: Paal, Niphal, Hiphil) |kjv: bow, cast, bring, low, down, bend, couch, humble, stoop| {str: 7817}

H) 𐤉ᒫᒫᗑ (שׁחה ShHhH) ac: **Bow** co: **?** ab: **?**: A bowing to another in respect.

    V) 𐤉ᒫᒫᗑ (שׁחה Sh-HhH) — **Bow**: To pay homage to another one by bowing low or getting on the knees with the face to the ground. [freq. 172] (vf: Paal, Hiphil, Hitpael) |kjv: worship, bow, obeisance, reverence, fall stoop, crouch| {str: 7812}

J) ᒫᒥᗑ (שׁוח ShWHh) ac: **Sink** co: **Pit** ab: **?**

    V) ᒫᒥᗑ (שׁוח ShWHh) — **Sink**: [freq. 3] (vf: Paal, Hiphil) |kjv: bow, incline, humble| {str: 7743}

    N^{fl}) 𐤉ᒫᒥᗑ (שׁוחה ShW-HhH) — **Pit**: [freq. 5] |kjv: pit, ditch| {str: 7745}

L) ᒫᒫᗑᐊ (ישׁח YShHh) ac: **Sink** co: **?** ab: **?**

    N^m) ᒫᒫᗑᐊ (ישׁח Y-ShHh) — **Sink**: [freq. 1] |kjv: cast down| {str: 3445}

M) ᒫᐊᗑ (שׁיח ShYHh) ac: **?** co: **Pit** ab: **?**

    N^{fl}) 𐤉ᒫᐊᗑ (שׁיחה ShY-HhH) — **Pit**: [freq. 3] |kjv: pit| {str: 7882}

Adopted Roots;

2215	𐤅ᒫᒥᒫ	Darken, Dark, Darkness
2766	ᒥᒫᒫᛜ	Boil, Pot
2823	⊗ᒫᒥ	Strike
2824	ᑐᒫᒥ	Lion
2826	⊂ᒫᒥ	Thin
2828	-⊕-ᒫᒥ	Beat, Powder
2829	ᛜᒫᒥ	Dark, Dawn
2830	✝ᒫᒥ	Corrupt
2876	⊂⊖-ᒥ	Sink, Deep
3063	ᛜ⊂⊖-ᒥ	Pit

~~~~~~~~~

1469) ⊗ᒥ (שׁט ShTh) ac: **Scourge** co: **Whip** ab: **?**: A whipping or lashing out at someone or something out of hatred or punishment.

A) ⊗ᒥ (שׁט ShTh) ac: **Scourge** co: **?** ab: **?**: The lashing of the whip.

    N^{fl}) 𐤉⊗ᒥ (שׁטה Sh-ThH) — **Acacia**: The wood or the tree. [Unknown connection to root;] [freq. 28] |kjv: shittim, shittah| {str: 7848}

    ap^{fl}) 𐤉ᗰ⊗ᒥᗰ (משׁטמה MSh-Th-MH) — **Hatred**: In the sense of lashing out. [df: משׁטמה] [freq. 2] |kjv: hatred| {str: 4895}

B) ⊗⊗ᒥ (שׁטט ShThTh) ac: **Scourge** co: **?** ab: **?**: The lashing of the whip.

    N^m) ⊗⊗ᒥ (שׁטט Sh-ThTh) — **Scourge**: [df: שׁטט] [freq. 1] |kjv: scourge| {str: 7850}

D) ⊗ᐅᒥ (שׂאט ShATh) ac: **Despise** co: **?** ab: **Malice**: A lashing out at someone or something.

    V) ⊗ᐅᒥ (שׂאט Sh-ATh) — **Despise**: [freq. 3] (vf: Paal, Participle) |kjv: despise| {str: 7590}

N^m) ⊗ℒш (שאט Sh-ATh) — **Malice:** [freq. 3] |kjv: despite, despiteful| {str: 7589}

J) ⊗Yш (שוט ShWTh) ac: **Whip** co: **Oar** ab: **?:** The back and forth movement of the whip.

V) ⊗Yш (שוט ShWTh) — **Go:** To go back an forth as a whip. [freq. 13] (vf: Paal) |kjv: run, go, gone, mariners, rowers| {str: 7751}

N^m) ⊗Yш (שוט ShWTh) — **Whip:** [freq. 11] |kjv: whip, scourge| {str: 7752}

a^m) ⊗Yшᴧᴧ (משוט M-ShWTh) — **Oar:** What goes back and forth to propel a boat. [freq. 2] |kjv: oar| {str: 4880}

h^m) ⊗Yшᴧᴧ (משוש MSh-WTh) — **Oar:** What goes back and forth to propel a boat. [freq. 2] |kjv: oar| {str: 4880}

L) ⊗ш┙ (ישט YShTh) ac: **Extend** co: **?** ab: **?:** The stretching forth with the whip.

V) ⊗ш┙ (ישט Y-ShTh) — **Extend:** To stretch something out. [freq. 3] (vf: Hiphil) |kjv: hold out| {str: 3447}

M) ⊗⤙ш (שיט ShYTh) ac: **?** co: **Oar** ab: **?:** What goes back and forth to propel a boat.

N^m) ⊗⤙ш (שיט ShYTh) — **Oar:** [freq. 2] |kjv: oar| {str: 7885}

Adopted Roots;
2833 ՈⓍш Rule, Domain

~~~~~~~~~

1470) ⤙ш (שי ShY) ac: **?** co: **Gift** ab: **?**

A) ⤙ш (שי ShY) ac: **?** co: **Gift** ab: **?**

N^m) ⤙ш (שי ShY) — **Gift:** [freq. 3] |kjv: present| {str: 7862}

~~~~~~~~~

1471) ШшLu (שך ShK) ac: **Cease** co: **?** ab: **?**

B) ШШш (שכך ShKK) ac: **Cease** co: **?** ab: **?**

V) ШШш (שכך Sh-KK) — **Cease:** [freq. 5] (vf: Paal, Hiphil) |kjv: appease, pacify, set, asswage, cease| {str: 7918}

C) Шшℒ (אשך AShK) ac: **?** co: **Testicles** ab: **?:** [Unknown connection to root;]

N^m) Шшℒ (אשך A-ShK) — **Testicles:** [freq. 1] |kjv: stones| {str: 810}

H) ⚇Шш (שכה ShKH) ac: **?** co: **Wander** ab: **?:** [Unknown connection to root;]

V) ⚇Шш (שכה Sh-KH) — **Wander:** [freq. 1] (vf: Hiphil, Participle) |kjv: morning| {str: 7904}

~~~~~~~~~

1472) Јш (של ShL) ac: **Draw out** co: **?** ab: **?**

A) Јш (של ShL) ac: **?** co: **Quiet** ab: **?:** In the sense of quietness from prosperity.

N^m) Јш (של ShL) — **I. Of:** In the sense of something being drawn out of something else. **II. Neglect:** [Unknown connection to root] [freq. 4] |kjv: though, cause, for| {str: 7944, 7945} f^m) ᴊᴜ/ᴜᴜ (שְׁלִי Sh-LY) — **Quietly:** In the sense of prosperity. [freq. 1] |kjv: quietly| {str: 7987}

r^f) Yᴜ/ᴜᴜ (שְׁלוֹ Sh-LW) — **Neglect:** [Unknown connection to root; Aramaic only] [freq. 5] |kjv: amiss, fail, error| {str: 7955, 7960}

B) ᴊᴊᴜᴜ (שָׁלַל ShLL) ac: **Spoil** co: **?** ab: **?:** The spoils drawn out after battle.

V) ᴊᴊᴜᴜ (שְׁלָל Sh-LL) — **Spoil:** [freq. 16] (vf: Paal) |kjv: spoil, take, fall, prey, purpose| {str: 7997}

N^m) ᴊᴊᴜᴜ (שָׁלָל Sh-LL) — **Spoil:** [freq. 73] |kjv: spoil, prey| {str: 7998}

g^m) ᴊᴊYᴜᴜ (שׁוֹלָל ShW-LL) — **Spoiled:** What is taken as spoil. [ms: שְׁלָל] [freq. 4] |kjv: spoil, strip| {str: 7758}

C) ᴊᴜᴜᴋ (אֶשֶׁל AShL) ac: **?** co: **?** ab: **?:** [Unknown meaning]

N^m) ᴊᴜᴜᴋ (אֵשֶׁל A-ShL) — **Tamarisk:** The tree or a grove. [freq. 3] |kjv: grove, tree| {str: 815}

D) ᴊᴋᴜᴜ (שָׁאַל ShAL) ac: **Request** co: **?** ab: **?:** To draw out something that is not known.

V) ᴊᴋᴜᴜ (שָׁאַל Sh-AL) — **Ask:** To seek to understand what is not known. [Hebrew and Aramaic] [freq. 179] (vf: Paal, Niphal, Hiphil, Piel) |kjv: ask, enquire, desire, require, borrow, salute, demand, lent, request, beg| {str: 7592, 7593}

N^{f1}) ᴪᴊᴋᴜᴜ (שְׁאֵלָה ShA-LH) — **Request:** A seeking for what is not known. [ms: שְׁלָה] [ar:

שְׁאֵלָא] [freq. 15] |kjv: petition, demand, loan| {str: 7595, 7596}

h^{f1}) ᴪᴊᴋᴜᴜᴜ (מִשְׁאָלָה MSh-ALH) — **Request:** A seeking for what is not known. [freq. 2] |kjv: petition, desire| {str: 4862}

c^f) ᴊYᴋᴜᴜ (שְׁאוֹל Sh-AWL) — **Grave:** The place of the dead as an unknown place. [ms: שְׁאֹל] [freq. 65] |kjv: grave, hell, pit| {str: 7585}

H) ᴪᴊᴜᴜ (שָׁלָה ShLH) ac: **Draw out** co: **?** ab: **?**

V) ᴪᴊᴜᴜ (שָׁלָה Sh-LH) — **I. Mislead:** [Hebrew and Aramaic] **II. Rest:** [Aramaic only] [freq. 4] (vf: Paal, Niphal, Hiphil) |kjv: negligent, deceive, take, rest| {str: 7952, 7953, 7954}

J) ᴊYᴜᴜ (שׁוּל ShWL) ac: **?** co: **Robe** ab: **?:** As long and drawn out.

N^m) ᴊYᴜᴜ (שׁוּל ShWL) — **Robe:** [freq. 11] |kjv: hem, skirt, train| {str: 7757}

K) Yᴊᴜᴜ (שְׁלוֹ ShLW) ac: **Prosper** co: **?** ab: **?:** A drawing out of what is needed.

V) Yᴊᴜᴜ (שָׁלָו Sh-LW) — **Prosper:** [ms: שָׁלָה] [freq. 5] (vf: Paal) |kjv: prosper, safety, happy| {str: 7951}

N^{f1}) ᴪYᴊᴜᴜ (שַׁלְוָה ShL-WH) — **Prosperity:** [Hebrew and Aramaic] [freq. 10] |kjv: prosperity, peaceably, quietness, abundance, peace, tranquility| {str: 7959, 7962, 7963}

b^m) Yᴊᴊᴜᴜ (שָׁלִיו Sh-LYW) — **Prosperity:** [ms: שָׁלִו] [freq. 8] |kjv: ease, peaceable, quietness, prosperity, quiet, prosper, wealthy| {str: 7961}

M) שׁיל (שׁיל ShYL) ac: **Draw out** co: **Infant** ab: **?**

f¹) שׁילה (שׁיליה ShY-L-YH) — **Infant:** As drawn out of the mother. [ms: שׁליה] [freq. 1] |kjv: young| {str: 7988}

Adopted Roots;

2842 שׁלמד Send, Projectile
2844 שׁלך Throw
2845 שׁלם Complete
2846 שׁלב Pull

~~~~~~~~~

1473) שם (שׁם ShM) ac: **Breathe** co: **Breath** ab: **Desolate:** The wind, or breath, of someone or something is its character.

A) שם (שׁם ShM) ac: **?** co: **Breath** ab: **Desolate:** Hebrew names are words given to describe character.

N^m) שם (שׁם ShM) — **I. Breath:** The breath of a man is character, what makes one what he is. The name of an individual is more than an identifier but descriptive of his character or breath. **II. There:** Used to identify another place. [Hebrew and Aramaic] [ar: תמה] **III. Sky:** The place of the winds. [Hebrew and Aramaic; Only used in the masculine plural form, שׁמים or שׁמי in Aramaic] **IV. Aroma:** A sweet aroma that is carried on the wind or breath. [df: סם] [freq. 1365] |kjv: name, renown, fame, famous, heaven, air, sweet, there| {str: 5561, 8033, 8034, 8036, 8064, 8065, 8536}

N^f¹) שמה (שׁמה Sh-MH) — **Desolate:** A wind blowing over the land drying pulls the moisture out of the ground drying it up, making a place of ruin or desert. [freq. 39] |kjv: astonishment, desolation, desolate, waste, wonderful| {str: 8047}

k^f¹) משׁמה (משׁמה MSh-MH) — **Desolate:** A wind blowing over the land pulls the moisture out of the ground drying it up, making a place of ruin or desert. [freq. 7] |kjv: desolate, astonishment| {str: 4923}

nm^m) אשׁמן (אשׁמן ASh-MN) — **Desolate:** A wind blowing over the land pulls the moisture out of the ground drying it up, making a place of ruin or desert. [freq. 1] |kjv: desolate| {str: 820}

B) שׁמם (שׁמם ShMM) ac: **?** co: **?** ab: **Desolate:** A wind blowing over the land pulls the moisture out of the ground drying it up, making a place of ruin or desert. One in horror or in astonishment is one dried up in the inside.

V) שׁמם (שׁמם Sh-MM) — **Desolate:** [Hebrew and Aramaic] [freq. 93] (vf: Paal, Niphal, Hiphil, Hitpael, Hophal, Piel) |kjv: desolate, astonish, waste, destroy, wonder, amaze| {str: 8074, 8075}

N^f¹) שׁממה (שׁממה ShM-MH) — **Desolate:** [freq. 58] |kjv: desolate, waste| {str: 8077}

ej^m) שׁיממון (שׁיממון ShY-M-MWN) — **Desolation:** [ms: שׁממון] [freq. 2] |kjv: astonishment| {str: 8078}

C) אשׁם (אשׁם AShM) ac: **?** co: **?** ab: **Guilt:** One with a character of wrongdoing.

278

V) אשם (אשם A-ShM) — **Guilt:** [freq. 35] (vf: Paal, Niphal, Hiphil) |kjv: guilty, desolate, offend, trespass, destroy, faulty, offence| {str: 816}

N^m) אשם (אשם A-ShM) — **Guilt:** [freq. 49] |kjv: trespass, sin, guiltiness| {str: 817, 818}

N^fl) אשמה (אשמה ASh-MH) — **Guilt:** [freq. 19] |kjv: trespass, sin, offend| {str: 819}

G) שהם (שהם ShHM) ac: **?** co: **?** ab: **?**: [Unknown meaning;]

N^m) שהם (שהם Sh-HM) — **Shoham:** An unknown stone. [freq. 11] |kjv: onyx| {str: 7718}

J) שום (שום ShWM) ac: **Smell** co: Garlic ab: **?**: A sense of smell from breathing.

N^m) שום (שום ShWM) — **Garlic:** From its strong odor. [freq. 1] |kjv: garlick| {str: 7762}

L) ישם (ישם YShM) ac: **?** co: **Desert** ab: **Desolate:** A wind blowing over the land pulls the moisture out of the ground drying it up, making a place of ruin or desert.

V) ישם (ישם Y-ShM) — **Desolate:** [freq. 4] (vf: Paal) |kjv: desolate| {str: 3456}

b^fl) ישימה (ישימה Y-ShY-MH) — **Desolate:** [freq. 1] |kjv: seize| {str: 3451}

bj^m) ישימון (ישימון Y-ShY-MWN) — **Desert:** A desolate place. [freq. 13] |kjv: desert, wilderness, solitary| {str: 3452}

Adopted Roots;
2090 שמל Rain, Rain
2443 שנף Pant, Breath

2444 שנף Blow, Twilight
2848 שמד Destroy
2849 שמט Shake
2850 שמן Oil
2851 שמע Hear, Report, Obedience
2854 שמש Sun

~~~~~~~~

1474) שן (שן ShN) ac: **Sharp** co: **Teeth** ab: **?**: The pictograph ש is a picture of the teeth, the ן is a picture of a seed representing continuance. Combined these mean "teeth continue". The two front teeth are sharp and used for cutting foods by pressing down. (eng: shine - from the whiteness of the teeth)

A) שן (שן ShN) ac: **?** co: **Teeth** ab: **?**

N^m/f) שן (שן ShN) — **Teeth:** [Hebrew and Aramaic] [freq. 58] |kjv: teeth, tooth, ivory, sharp, crag, forefront| {str: 8127, 8128}

N^fl) שנה (שנה Sh-NH) — **I. Year:** In the sense of repeating. [Hebrew and Aramaic] [df: שנא] **II. Sleep:** [Unknown connection to rootHebrew and Aramaic] [freq. 906] |kjv: year, sleep| {str: 8141, 8142, 8139, 8140}

f^m) שני (שני Sh-NY) — **Scarlet:** The color of the gums. [freq. 42] |kjv: scarlet, crimson| {str: 8144}

B) שנן (שנן ShNN) ac: **Sharp** co: **?** ab: **?**: From the sharpness of the front teeth.

V) שנן (שנן Sh-NN) — **Sharpen:** [freq. 9] (vf: Paal, Piel) |kjv: sharp, whet, sharpen, prick, teach| {str: 8150}

b^fl) שנינה (שנינה Sh-NY-NH) — **Piercing:** [freq. 4] |kjv: byword, taunt| {str: 8148}

D) שאן (שאן ShAN) ac: **Rest** co: ? ab: ?: [Unknown connection to root;]

V) שאן (שאן Sh-AN) — **Rest:** To be in a state of rest. [freq. 5] (vf: Piel) |kjv: ease, quiet, rest| {str: 7599}

m^m) שאנן (שאנן ShA-NN) — **Rest:** [freq. 10] |kjv: ease, quiet, tumult| {str: 7600}

E) שנא (שנא ShNA) ac: ? co: **Two** ab: ?: As a second thing.

V) שנא (שנא Sh-NA) — **Change:** To exchange one thing for another. [Hebrew and Aramaic] [freq. 24] (vf: Paal, Pual, Piel, Participle) |kjv: change, diverse, alter| {str: 8132, 8133}

em^m) שינאן (שינאן ShY-N-AN) — **Twice:** [ms: שנאן] [freq. 1] |kjv: angel| {str: 8136}

H) שנה (שנה ShNH) ac: ? co: **Two** ab: ?: A repeating of the first or what was before.

V) שנה (שנה Sh-NH) — **I. Change:** To exchange one thing for another. **II. Repeat:** To do something a second time. [freq. 23] (vf: Paal, Niphal, Hitpael, Piel) |kjv: change, second, again, diverse, alter, disguise, double, pervert, prefer, repeat| {str: 8138}

N^m/f) שנה (שנה Sh-NH) — **I. Two:** In the sense of the changing seasons. [Hebrew and Aramaic; Written in the plural form שתים or שנת in the Aramaic] [df: שתים] [ar: תנין תרין] II. **Sleep:** [Unknown connection to rootHebrew and Aramaic] [freq.

772] |kjv: two, both, second, twain, twice, double| {str: 8147, 8578, 8648}

f^m/f) שני (שני Sh-NY) — **Second:** [freq. 156] |kjv: second, other, time, again, another, more, either| {str: 8145}

h^m) משנה (משנה MSh-NH) — **I. Double: II. Second:** [freq. 35] |kjv: second, double, next, college, copy, twice, fatling| {str: 4932}

s^f3) שנינות (שנינות Sh-NY-NWT) — **Again:** A second time. [Aramaic only] [ar: תנינות] [freq. 1] |kjv: again| {str: 8579}

L) ישן (ישן YShN) ac: ? co: **Previous** ab: ?: What was before the second.

V) ישן (ישן Y-ShN) — **Sleep:** [Unknown connection to root;] [freq. 19] (vf: Paal, Niphal, Piel) |kjv: sleep, remain, old| {str: 3462}

N^m) ישן (ישן Y-ShN) — **I. Previous: II. Sleep:** [Unknown connection to root] [freq. 16] |kjv: old, sleep| {str: 3463, 3465}

N^f2) ישנת (ישנת YSh-NT) — **Sleep:** [Unknown connection to root;] [df: שנת] [freq. 1] |kjv: sleep| {str: 8153}

Adopted Roots;
3061 שאול
3062 שנהב Tusk

1475) שש (שש ShS) ac: **Plunder** co: ? ab: ?: The pictograph שש is a picture of the teeth representing pressure, the ש is a picture of thorn that grabs hold. Combined these mean "Press and grab hold". The pressing into anothers place and grabbing hold of his possessions.

B) 𝔢𝔢ﻟﻟ (שׁסס ShSS) ac: **Plunder** co: ? ab: ?

V) 𝔢𝔢ﻟﻟ (שׁסס Sh-SS) — **Plunder:** [freq. 5] (vf: Paal, Niphal) |kjv: spoil, riffle| {str: 8155}

D) 𝔢ﻋﻟﻟ (שׁאס ShAS) ac: **Plunder** co: ? ab: ?

V) 𝔢ﻋﻟﻟ (שׁאס Sh-AS) — **Plunder:** [freq. 1] (vf: Paal, Participle) |kjv: spoil| {str: 7601}

H) 𝔶𝔢ﻟﻟ (שׁסה ShSH) ac: **Plunder** co: ? ab: ?

V) 𝔶𝔢ﻟﻟ (שׁסה Sh-SH) — **Plunder:** [df: שׁשׁה] [freq. 12] (vf: Paal, Participle) |kjv: spoil, spoiler, rob| {str: 8154}

J) 𝔢Yﻟﻟ (שׁוס ShWS) ac: **Plunder** co: ? ab: ?

k^fl) 𝔶𝔢Yﻟﻟﻣﻣ (משׁוסה M-ShW-SH) — **Plunder:** [freq. 1] |kjv: spoil| {str: 4882}

M) 𝔢ﻟﻟ (שׁיס ShYS) ac: **Plunder** co: ? ab: ?

k^fl) 𝔶𝔢ﻟﻟﻣﻣ (משׁיסה M-ShY-SH) — **Plunder:** [ms: משׁסה] [freq. 6] |kjv: spoil, booty| {str: 4933}

Adopted Roots;
2857 ⊘𝔢ﻟﻟ Split
2858 ⊘𝔢ﻟﻟ Hew

~~~~~~~~~~~~

1476) ⊘ﻟﻟ (שׁע ShAh) ac: **Watch** co: **Shepherd** ab: **Delight:** The pictograph ﻟﻟ is a picture of the teeth used for devouring or destruction, the ⊘ is a picture of the eye. Combined these mean "destroyer watches". The shepherd

carefully watches over the flock and the surrounding area always on the lookout for danger. When a predator comes to attack, the shepherd destroys the enemy.

A) ⊘ﻟﻟ (שׁע ShAh) ac: **Watch** co: ? ab: **Delight:** The shepherd watches over and cares for and delights in his sheep.

N^fl) 𝔶⊘ﻟﻟ (שׁעה Sh-AhH) — **Hour:** The watching of the arch of the sun to determine the hour of the day. [Aramaic only] [freq. 5] |kjv: hour| {str: 8160}

i^{m/f}) ⊘ﻟﻟ† (תשׁע T-ShAh) — **Nine:** [Unknown connection to rootAlso meaning ninety when written in the plural form - ﻣﻣﺑﻟ⊘ﻟﻟ†] [freq. 78] |kjv: nine, ninth, ninety| {str: 8672, 8673}

Id^m) ⊘Yﻟﻟ⊘ﻟﻟ (שׁעשׁוע ShAh-ShWAh) — **Delight:** [ms: שׁעשׁע] [freq. 9] |kjv: delight, pleasant| {str: 8191}

bf^m) ﻟﻟ⊘ﻟﻟ† (תשׁיעי T-ShY-AhY) — **Ninth:** [Unknown connection to root;] [freq. 18] |kjv: ninth| {str: 8671}

hf^f) ﻟﻟ⊘ﻟﻟﻣﻣ (משׁעי MSh-AhY) — **Cleanse:** As a preparation for inspection. [freq. 1] |kjv: supple| {str: 4935}

B) ⊘⊘ﻟﻟ (שׁעע ShAhAh) ac: ? co: ? ab: **Delight:** The shepherd takes delight in his sheep.

V) ⊘⊘ﻟﻟ (שׁעע Sh-AhAh) — **Delight:** [freq. 9] (vf: Paal, Hiphil, Pilpel) |kjv: delight, cry, play, dandle, shut| {str: 8173}

H) 𝔶⊘ﻟﻟ (שׁעה ShAhH) ac: **Watch** co: ? ab: ?: The shepherd inspects and watches over the flock with compassion and protection.

281

V) ✡◯שש (שעה Sh-AhH) — **Watch:** Also to look upon with respect. [freq. 15] (vf: Paal, Hiphil, Hitpael) |kjv: look, respect, dismay, turn, regard, spare, dim, depart| {str: 8159}

J) ◯Yשש (שוע ShWAh) ac: **Cry** co: **?** ab: **Trouble:** When the sheep are in trouble they will cry out and the shepherd will deliver them.

V) ◯Yשש (שוע ShWAh) — **Cry:** To shout or cry out from a burden. [freq. 21] (vf: Piel) |kjv: cry, aloud, shout| {str: 7768}

N^m) ◯Yשש (שוע ShWAh) — **I. Cry: II. Rich:** In the sense of a carefully watching ones possessions. [freq. 6] |kjv: cry, riches| {str: 7769, 7771, 7773}

N^fl) ✡◯Yשש (שועה ShW-AhH) — **Cry:** [freq. 11] |kjv: cry| {str: 7775}

L) ◯ששⲎ (ישע YShAh) ac: **Rescue** co: **?** ab: **?:** When one of the flock is in trouble, the shepherd rescues it.

V) ◯ששⲎ (ישע Y-ShAh) — **Rescue:** [freq. 205] (vf: Niphal, Hiphil) |kjv: save, saviour, deliver, help, preserved, salvation, avenge, defend, rescue, safe, victory| {str: 3467}

N^m) ◯ששⲎ (ישע Y-ShAh) — **Rescue:** A deliverance or freedom from a trouble. [freq. 36] |kjv: salvation, safety, saving| {str: 3468}

a^fl) ✡◯ששYⲙ (מושעה MW-Sh-AhH) — **Rescue:** A deliverance or freedom from a trouble. [freq. 1] |kjv: salvation| {str: 4190}

d^fl) ✡◯YששⲎ (ישועה Y-ShW-AhH) — **Rescue:** A deliverance or freedom from a trouble. [freq. 78] |kjv: salvation, help, deliverance, health, save, saving, welfare| {str: 3444}

i^fl) ✡◯ששYt (תושעה TW-Sh-AhH) — **Rescue:** A deliverance or freedom from a trouble. [df: תשעה תשועה] [freq. 34] |kjv: salvation, deliverance, help, safety, victory| {str: 8668}

Adopted Roots;

2861 ◯Xשש Lean, Staff, Support
2872 ◯-◐שש Watch, Eye
2877 ◯-◐שש Look, Window

~~~~~~~~~~

1477) ◯שש (שף ShP) ac: **Strike** co: **Serpent** ab: **?:** The pictograph שש is a picture of the teeth, the ◯ is a picture of the mouth. Combined these mean "sharp teeth in the mouth". A serpent (venomous snake) has sharp fangs in the mouth. Its prey is taken into the mouth swallowed by drawing down into the belly. (eng: sharp - with the additional r; serpent - with the exchange of the s and sh and the additional r and nt; jasper)

A) ◯שש (שף ShP) ac: **?** co: **High** ab: **?**

N^f) ✡◯שש (שפה ShPH) — **Milk:** [Unknown connection to root;] [freq. 1] |kjv: cheese| {str: 8194}

f^m) Ⲏ◯שש (שפי Sh-PY) — **High place:** In the sense of the serpent lifting its head to strike. [freq. 10] |kjv: high place| {str: 8205}

B) ◯◯שש (שפך ShPP) ac: **?** co: **Serpent** ab: **?**

bj[m]) שׁפיפון (Sh-PY-PWN) — **Shephiyphon:** An unknown species of viper. [ms: שׁפיפן] [freq. 1] |kjv: adder| {str: 8207}

C) אשׁף (AShP) ac: ? co: **Serpent** ab: ?

N[m]) אשׁף (A-ShP) — **Enchanter:** From their hissing. [Aramaic only] [freq. 8] |kjv: astrologer| {str: 825, 826}

N[fl]) אשׁפה (ASh-PH) — **Quiver:** A pouch with a mouth for sharp arrows. [freq. 6] |kjv: quiver| {str: 827}

D) שׁאף (ShAP) ac: **Swallow** co: ? ab: ?: A drawing in by swallowing as the snake swallows its prey.

V) שׁאף (Sh-AP) — I. **Swallow:** II. **Draw:** To draw water from a well. [df: שׁאב] [freq. 33] (vf: Paal, Participle) |kjv: swallow, snuff, pant, desire, devour, draw, drawer| {str: 7579, 7602}

a[m]) משׁאף (MSh-AP) — **Well:** A place for drawing water. [df: משׁאב] [freq. 1] |kjv: draw| {str: 4857}

H) שׁפה (ShPH) ac: ? co: **High** ab: ?: The serpent lifts its head up high to strike.

V) שׁפה (Sh-PH) — **High:** [freq. 2] (vf: Niphal, Pual) |kjv: stick out, high| {str: 8192}

J) שׁוף (ShWP) ac: **Strike** co: ? ab: ?: A striking of the serpent.

V) שׁוף (ShWP) — **Strike:** [freq. 4] (vf: Paal) |kjv: bruise, break, cover| {str: 7779}

L) ישׁף (YShP) ac: ? co: ? ab: ?: [Unknown meaning]

N[fl]) ישׁף (Y-ShP) — **Jasper:** [Unknown connection to root;] [freq. 3] |kjv: jasper| {str: 3471}

~~~~~~~~~~

1478) שׁץ (ShTs) ac: ? co: **Flood** ab: ?

Adopted Roots;
2684 | Issue, Serpent
2832 | Flush
2871 | Surge

~~~~~~~~~~

1479) שׁק (ShQ) ac: **Drink** co: **River** ab: ?: The pictograph שׁ is a picture of the two front teeth representing the idea of two, the ק is a picture of the sun at the horizon that cycles around the earth. Combined these mean "repeat a cycle". During the rain season, repeated each year, the riverbeds become full of water. The surrounding land is soaked with water allowing for the planting of crops.

A) שׁק (ShQ) ac: ? co: **River** ab: ?: The rushing course of a river through the land.

N[m]) שׁק (ShQ) — **Leg:** From a leg of a river. [Aramaic only] [freq. 1] |kjv: leg| {str: 8243}

a[m]) משׁק (MSh-Q) — **Rushing:** From the rushing of a river. [freq. 1] |kjv: running| {str: 4944}

rf[m]) שׁקוי (Sh-QWY) — **Marrow:** The liquid inside the channel of bones and used as a type of butter. [freq. 2] |kjv: marrow| {str: 8250}

B) ⊸●—ш (ץקש ShQQ) ac: **Rush** co: **River** ab: ?: The back and forth course of a river through the land.

V) ⊸●—ш (ץקש Sh-QQ) — **Rush:** A rushing about and to and fro as a raging river. [freq. 6] (vf: Paal, Participle) |kjv: run, long, range, appetite, justle| {str: 8264}

H) ⚳⊸—ш (הקש ShQH) ac: **Drink** co: ? ab: ?: The life giving water from the rivers.

V) ⚳⊸—ш (הקש Sh-QH) — **Drink:** [freq. 74] (vf: Niphal, Hiphil, Pual) |kjv: drink, water, butler, cupbearer| {str: 8248}

a^m) ⚳⊸—шⱮ (הקשמ MSh-QH) — **Drink:** Water for drinking as well as a vessel or place for water. Also one who brings water. [freq. 7] |kjv: drink, watered, butlership, pasture| {str: 4945}

J) ⊸Yш (קוש ShWQ) ac: **Overflow** co: **Course** ab: ?: The course of a river.

V) ⊸Yш (קוש ShWQ) — **Overflow:** The overflowing of the banks of a river. [freq. 3] (vf: Hiphil) |kjv: overflow| {str: 7783}

N^f) ⊸Yш (קוש ShWQ) — **Leg:** The leg of an animal or a street. [freq. 23] |kjv: street, shoulder| {str: 7784, 7785}

N^f2) ✝⊸Yш (תקוש ShW-QT) — **Trough:** A trench for bringing water to the village. [ms: תקש] [freq. 2] |kjv: trough| {str: 8268}

i^f1) ⚳⊸Yш✝ (הקושת T-ShW-QH) — **Desire:** As a course. [freq. 3] |kjv: desire| {str: 8669}

K) Y⊸—ш (קש ShQW) ac: **Drink** co: ? ab: ?

c^m) YY⊸—ш (ווקש Sh-QWW) — **Drink:** [freq. 1] |kjv: drink| {str: 8249}

1480) Яш (רש ShR) ac: **Tie** co: **Cord** ab: ?: The pictograph ш is a picture of the teeth representing pressure, the Я is a picture of the head representing the top or beginning. Combined these mean "press the beginning". Ropes and cords were usually made of bark strips such as from the cedar or from the sinew (tendon) of an animal. The rope is made by twisting two fibers together. A single fiber is attached to a fixed point (top), and the two ends of the fiber are brought together. One fiber is twisted in a clockwise direction and wrapped over the other fiber in counter clockwise direction. The second fiber is then twisted in clockwise direction then wrapped around the first fiber in a counter clockwise direction. The process is repeated through the length of the rope. The twisting of the fibers in opposite directions causes the fibers to lock (press) onto each other making a stronger rope. The rope is used to tightly secure or support something, such as a load to a cart or the poles of the tent.

A) Яш (רש ShR) ac: ? co: **Cord** ab: ?: Sinews were used for making cords by twisting them together. The umbilical cord, and navel, as a cord that binds the infant to the mother.

N^m) Яш (רש ShR) — **Cord:** The navel cord. [freq. 2] |kjv: navel| {str: 8270}

N^{fl}) שֱשֱ (שרה Sh-RH) — **I. Bracelet:** A cord around the wrist. **II. Wall:** As encircling a city. [freq. 2] |kjv: bracelet, wall| {str: 8284, 8285}

h^{fl}) מֱשֱשֱᴍᴍ (משרה MSh-RH) — **Juice:** As loosened from the fruit. [freq. 1] |kjv: liquor| {str: 4952}

m^m) שֱשᴸ (שרן Sh-RN) — **Wall:** As an armor around the city. [df: אשרנא] [freq. 2] |kjv: wall| {str: 846}

efj^{m/f}) שᴸᴸ-שֱᵞ (שריון ShYR-YWN) — **Harness:** An armor made from tightly wound cords of leather. [ms: סריון שרין שריון] [freq. 11] |kjv: habergeon, coat, harness, breastplate, brigadine| {str: 5630, 8302}

B) שֱשᴸ (שרר ShRR) ac: ? co: **Cord** ab: ?: Sinews were used for making cords by twisting them together. The umbilical cord, and navel, as a cord that binds the infant to the mother.

V) שֱשᴸ (שרר Sh-RR) — **Enemy:** As one who is to be tied up. [freq. 5] (vf: Paal) |kjv: enemy| {str: 8324}

N^m) שֱשᴸ (שרר Sh-RR) — **Cord:** [freq. 1] |kjv: navel| {str: 8326}

b^m) שֱ-שᴸ (שריר Sh-RYR) — **Navel:** [freq. 1] |kjv: navel| {str: 8306}

b^{f3}) +שֱ-שᴸ (שרירות Sh-RY-RWT) — **Imagination:** A twisting together of thoughts. [ms: שררות] [freq. 10] |kjv: imagination, lust| {str: 8307}

C) שᴸᵞ (אשר AShR) ac: ? co: **Straight** ab: ?: A cord pulled tight is straight.

V) שᴸᵞ (אשר A-ShR) — **Happy:** One who is happy is one whose life is lived straightly. [freq. 16] (vf: Paal, Pual, Piel) |kjv: blessed, lead, go, guide, happy, leader, relieve| {str: 833}

N^m) שᴸᵞ (אשר A-ShR) — **I. Happy:** One who is happy is one whose life is lived straightly. **II. Which:** Or who, what or that. As a rope attaches two objects together, this word links the action of the sentence to the one doing the action. [The short form "ש" is used as a prefix meaning "who" or "which"] [freq. 156] |kjv: blessed, happy, which, wherewith, because, when, soon, as, that, until much, whosoever, whom, whose| {str: 834, 835}

d^f) שᴸᵞ (אשור A-ShWR) — **Step:** A walking in straight line. [ms: אשר] [freq. 9] |kjv: step, going| {str: 838}

g^m) שᴸᵞ (אושר AW-ShR) — **Happy:** One who is happy is one whose life is lived straightly. [ms: אשר] [freq. 1] |kjv: happy| {str: 837}

id^f) +שᴸᵞ (תאשור TA-ShWR) — **Teashur:** An unknown tree. Possibly a type of cedar from its bark strips which can be used for making cords. [freq. 2] |kjv: box| {str: 8391}

D) שᵞש (שאר ShAR) ac: **Remain** co: **Relative** ab: ?: When the nomadic tribe was larger than could be maintained the family divided in the sense of severing the umbilical cord.

V) שאר (שאר Sh-AR) —
Remain: [freq. 133] (vf: Paal,
Niphal, Hiphil, Participle) |kjv:
leave, remain, remnant, let, rest|
{str: 7604}

N^m) שאר (שאר Sh-AR) — **I.**
Remnant: What is left behind.
II. Kin: A near relative of
another tribe. [freq. 54] |kjv:
flesh, kinswoman, food, near,
nigh, kin, body, kinsman,
remnant, rest, residue, other|
{str: 7605, 7606, 7607}

N^{f1}) שארה (שארה ShA-RH)
— **Kin:** A near female relative.
[freq. 1] |kjv: kinswoman| {str:
7608}

N^{f4}) שארית (שארית ShA-
RYT) — **Remnant:** [freq. 66]
|kjv: remnant, residue, rest,
remainder, escaped| {str: 7611}

I^{f1}) שרשרה (שרשרה ShR-Sh-
RH) — **Cord:** [freq. 7] |kjv:
chain| {str: 8333}

H) שרה (שרה ShRH) ac: **Loose**
co: **Cord** ab: **?:** The tying around of
something with a cord, or the
loosening of it.

V) שרה (שרה Sh-RH) —
Loose: To untie something or to
let something go. [Hebrew and
Aramaic] [freq. 9] (vf: Paal,
Piel) |kjv: loose, dissolve, dwell,
began| {str: 8271, 8281, 8293}

J) שור (שור ShWR) ac: **?** co:
Caravan ab: **?:** A group that travels
around an area carrying loads. The
bull is used as a beast of burden to
carry loads.

V) שור (שור ShWR) — **I.**
Caravan: To travel as a group
of merchants with loads. **II. See:**
[Unknown connection to root]

[freq. 18] (vf: Paal, Participle)
|kjv: went, sing, behold, see,
look, observe, wait, regard,
perceive| {str: 7788, 7789}

N^m) שור (שור ShWR) — **I.**
Ox: Used for pulling heavy
loads. [Hebrew and Aramaic]
[ar: תור] **II. Wall:** As tied
around a city. [Hebrew and
Aramaic] **III. Enemy:** As one
who is to be tied up. [freq. 93]
|kjv: ox, bullock, cow, bull,
enemy, wall| {str: 7790, 7791,
7792, 7794, 8450}

N^{f1}) שורה (שורה ShW-RH) —
Row: As a wall. [df: שורה]
[freq. 1] |kjv: principle| {str:
7795}

i^{f1}) תשורה (תשורה T-ShW-RH)
— **Gift:** As brought by a
traveler. [freq. 1] |kjv: present|
{str: 8670}

L) ישר (ישר YShR) ac: **?** co:
Cord ab: **?:** A tight rope is straight.
A righteous one is one who is
straight and firmly holds up truth just
as the cord is straight and firmly
holds the wall of the tent upright.

V) ישר (ישר Y-ShR) — **I.**
Straight: To be in a straight
line, path or thought. **II.**
Remnant: [df: יתר] [freq. 134]
(vf: Paal, Niphal, Hiphil, Pual,
Piel, Participle) |kjv: please,
straight, direct, right, well, fit,
good, meet, upright, remain,
leave, rest, remainder, remnant,
reserve, residue, plenteous,
behind, excel, preserve| {str:
3474, 3498}

N^m) ישר (ישר Y-ShR) — **I.**
Cord: The cord of the bow. [df:
יתר] **II. Straight:** A straight
line, path or thought. **III.**

Remnant: [df: יתר] [freq. 220] |kjv: cord, string, right, upright, righteous, straight, convenient, equity, just, meet, well, rest, remnant, residue, leave, excellency, exceeding, excellent, plentifully| {str: 3477, 3499}

g^m) יושר (יושר YW-ShR) — **Straightness:** [ms: יֹשֶר] [freq. 14] |kjv: uprightness, right, upright, meet| {str: 3476}

k^m) מישר (מישר MY-ShR) — **I. Cord: II. Straight:** What is straight. [df: מיתר] [freq. 28] |kjv: cord, string, equity, uprightly, uprightness, right, agreement, aright, equal, sweetly| {str: 4339, 4340}

hc^m) מישור (מישור MY-ShWR) — **Plain:** A level, or straight, place. [ms: מישר] [freq. 23] |kjv: plain, equity, straight, even, right, righteously, uprightness| {str: 4334}

M) שיר (שיר ShYR) ac: **Sing** co: **Music** ab: **?:** A stringed musical instrument uses thin cords for making music.

V) שיר (שיר ShYR) — **Sing:** [df: שור] [freq. 87] (vf: Paal, Hophal, Participle) |kjv: sing, singer, behold| {str: 7891}

N^f) שיר (שיר ShYR) — **Song:** [freq. 90] |kjv: song, musick, singing, musical, sing, singers| {str: 7892}

Adopted Roots;
2294 ישרן Prosperity
2816 שרן Birth
2821 שׁרץ Twist

1481) שש (שש ShSh) ac: **?** co: **White** ab: **?:** The pictograph שש is a picture of the two front teeth. The whiteness of the teeth. The white hair of the older men. (eng: six - with the exchange of the x and sh, ses is Spanish)

A) שש (שש ShSh) ac: **?** co: **Linen** ab: **?**

N$^{m/f}$) שש (שש ShSh) — **I. Linen:** As white. [df: ששי] **II. Marble:** As white. **III. Six:** [Unknown connection to rootAlso meaning sixty when written in the plual form - ששין or שתין in Aramaic] [ar: שת] [freq. 322] |kjv: linen, six, sixth, sixty, threescore| {str: 8336, 8337, 8346, 8353, 8361}

f$^{m/f}$) ששי (ששי Sh-ShY) — **Sixth:** [freq. 28] |kjv: sixth| {str: 8345}

j^m) ששון (ששון Sh-ShWN) — **Joy:** As bright with cheer. [df: ששון] [freq. 22] |kjv: joy, gladness, mirth, rejoicing| {str: 8342}

E) ששא (ששא ShShA) ac: **?** co: **Sixth** ab: **?**

V) ששא (ששא Sh-ShA) — **Sixth:** To give a sixth. [freq. 1] (vf: Piel) |kjv: sixth| {str: 8338}

H) ששה (ששה ShShH) ac: **?** co: **Sixth** ab: **?**

V) ששה (ששה Sh-ShH) — **Sixth:** To give a sixth. [freq. 1] (vf: Piel) |kjv: sixth| {str: 8341}

J) שוש (שוש ShWSh) ac: **?** co: **White** ab: **?**

m^m) שושן (שושן ShW-ShN) — **Lilly:** A white flower. [ms:

שש] [freq. 15] |kjv: lily| {str: 7799}

L) יששש (ישש YShSh) ac: ? co: Old ab: ?: The white hair of the older men.

N^m) יששש (ישש Y-ShSh) — Old: [freq. 1] |kjv: age| {str: 3486}

b^m) ישישש (ישיש Y-ShYSh) — Old: [freq. 4] |kjv: ancient, aged, old| {str: 3453}

M) שיששש (שיש ShYSh) ac: ? co: Marble ab: ?: A white stone.

N^m) שיששש (שיש ShYSh) — Marble: [freq. 1] |kjv: marble| {str: 7893}

~~~~~~~~

1482) שת (שת ShT) ac: Sit co: Buttocks ab: ?: A coming together and sitting to drink. (eng: set - with the exchange of the s and sh; seat; tush - with the reversal of the letters; sheet)

A) שת (שת ShT) ac: Sit co: Buttocks ab: ?

N^m) שת (שת ShT) — Buttocks: As the place of sitting. [freq. 2] |kjv: buttocks| {str: 8357}

b^{fl}) שתיה (שתיה ShT-YH) — Drinking: [freq. 1] |kjv: drinking| {str: 8360}

f^m) שתי (שתי Sh-TY) — I. Drunkenness: II. Warp: A tool used for weaving, an activity performed while sitting down. [freq. 10] |kjv: drunkenness, warp| {str: 8358, 8359}

B) שתת (שתת ShTT) ac: Sit co: ? ab: ?

V) שתת (שתת Sh-TT) — Sit: To set or lay down. [freq. 2] (vf: Paal) |kjv: lay, set| {str: 8371}

H) שתה (שתה ShTH) ac: Feast co: ? ab: ?: A time of seating together and drinking.

V) שתה (שתה Sh-TH) — Drink: [Hebrew and Aramaic] [freq. 222] (vf: Paal, Niphal) |kjv: drink, drinker, drunkard, banquet| {str: 8354, 8355}

N^m) שתה (שתה Sh-TH) — Foundation: As a level place of seating. [freq. 2] |kjv: foundation, purpose| {str: 8356}

h^m) משתה (משתה MSh-TH) — Feast: [Hebrew and Aramaic] [freq. 47] |kjv: feast, banquet, drink| {str: 4960, 4961}

M) שית (שית ShYT) ac: Sit co: Garment ab: ?

V) שית (שית ShYT) — Sit: To set or lay down. [freq. 85] (vf: Paal, Hophal) |kjv: set, made, lay, put, appoint, regard| {str: 7896}

N^m) שית (שית ShYT) — I. Garment: Colorful or special garments for feasting or other special activity. II. Thorn: [Unknown connection to root] [freq. 9] |kjv: garment, attire, thorn| {str: 7897, 7898}

~~~~~~~~

1483) שע (שע ShGh) ac: ? co: ? ab: ?

~~~~~~~~

288

Taw

1484) ᐅ† (אַת TA) ac: **Point** co: **Mark** ab: ?: The pictograph † is a picture of two crossed sticks representing a mark. A mark identifies locations used to mark out a location. Two crossed sticks in the shape of cross were used to hang the family standard or flag. This parent root is related to †ᐅ and Y†.

A) ᐅ† (אַת TA) ac: ? co: **Room** ab: ?

N^m) ᐅ† (אַת TA) — **Room:** As a placed marked out. [freq. 13] |kjv: chamber| {str: 8372}

q^m) Yᐅ† (תאו T-AW) — **Teo:** An unknown animal. [freq. 2] |kjv: ox| {str: 8377}

H) ᠻᐅ† (תאה TAH) ac: ? co: **Point** ab: ?

V) ᠻᐅ† (תאה T-AH) — **Point:** To identify a mark. [freq. 2] (vf: Piel) |kjv: point| {str: 8376}

K) Yᐅ† (תאו TAW) ac: ? co: **Boundary** ab: ?

N^fl) ᠻYᐅ† (תאוה TA-WH) — **Limit:** As a marked out boundary. [freq. 1] |kjv: bound| {str: 8379}

1485) ᠊† (תב TB) ac: ? co: **Long** ab: ?

D) ᠊ᐅ† (תאב TAB) ac: ? co: **Long** ab: ?

V) ᠊ᐅ† (תאב T-AB) — I. **Long:** To long for something. II. **Abhor:** [freq. 3] (vf: Paal, Piel) |kjv: long, abhor| {str: 8373, 8374}

N^fl) ᠻᠴᐅ† (תאבה TA-BH) — **Longing:** A longing for something. [freq. 1] |kjv: longing| {str: 8375}

1486) ᠊† (תג TG) ac: ? co: ? ab: ?

1487) ᠊† (תד TD) ac: ? co: ? ab: ?

L) ᠊†᠊ (יתד YTD) ac: ? co: **Peg** ab: ?: A peg, nail or pin for securing something.

N^f) ᠊†᠊ (יתד Y-TD) — **Peg:** [freq. 24] |kjv: pin, nail, stake, paddle| {str: 3489}

1488) ᠻ† (תה TH) ac: **Ignore** co: **Waste** ab: ?

J) ᠻY† (תוה TWH) ac: **Ignore** co: **Waste** ab: ?

V) ᠻY† (תוה TWH) — **Ignore:** To consider something of no value, a waste. [freq. 1] (vf: Hiphil) |kjv: limited| {str: 8428}

N^m) ᠻY† (תוה TWH) — **Astonish:** A feeling of waste. [freq. 1] |kjv: astony| {str: 8429}

r^m) YᠻY† (תוהו TW-HW) — **Waste:** A barren place. Also vanity as a state of waste. [ms: תהו] [freq. 20] |kjv: vain, vanity, confusion, without, wilderness, nought, nothing, empty, waste| {str: 8414}

1489) ᛮ✝ (תו TW) ac: ? co: **Mark** ab: ?: The pictograph ✝ is a picture of two crossed sticks representing a mark. This root is related to ✝ᛚ and ᛘ✝.

A) ᛮ✝ (תו TW) ac: ? co: **Mark** ab: ?

N^m) ᛮ✝ (תו TW) — **Mark:** [freq. 3] |kjv: mark, desire| {str: 8420}

H) ᛮ✝ (תוה TWH) ac: ? co: **Mark** ab: ?

V) ᛮ✝ (תוה T-WH) — **Mark:** To make a mark. [freq. 2] (vf: Hiphil, Piel) |kjv: scrabble, set| {str: 8427}

1490) ᛮ✝ (תז TZ) ac: **Cut** co: ? ab: ?: The pictograph ✝ is a picture of two crossed sticks representing a mark, the ᛮ is a picture of a cutting implement. Combined these mean "mark a cut".

B) ᛮᛮ✝ (תזז TZZ) ac: **Cut** co: ? ab: ?

V) ᛮᛮ✝ (תזז T-ZZ) — **Cut:** To cut something down. [freq. 1] (vf: Hiphil) |kjv: cut| {str: 8456}

1491) ᛗᛗ✝ (תח THh) ac: **Divide** co: Spear ab: ?

L) ᛗᛗ✝ᛚ (יתח YTHh) ac: ? co: Spear ab: ?: A weapon that divides flesh.

i^m) ᛗᛗᛮ✝ (תותח TW-THh) — **Spear:** [freq. 1] |kjv: dart| {str: 8455}

Adopted Roots;
2326 ᛗᛗ✝ᛚ Spread, Wardrobe
2362 ᛗᛗ✝ᛰ Spread
2449 ᛗᛗ✝ᛴ Cut, Piece
2892 ✝ᛗᛗ✝ Under

1492) ⊗✝ (תט TTh) ac: ? co: ? ab: ?

1493) ᛘ✝ (תי TY) ac: ? co: ? ab: ?

1494) �ᛮ✝ (תך TK) ac: **Bend** co: **Middle** ab: ?: The pictograph ✝ is a picture of two crossed sticks representing a mark, the ᛮ is a picture of a bent palm. Combined these mean "mark of the palm". The lines or marks in the center of the palm are formed by the bending of the palm. A bending in the middle, the center of something.

B) ᛮᛮ✝ (תכך TKK) ac: **Bend** co: ? ab: ?

N^m) ᛮᛮ✝ (תכך T-KK) — **Oppressor:** One who bends the will of another. [freq. 1] |kjv: deceitful| {str: 8501}

F) ᛮ✝ᛮ (התך HTK) ac: **Melt** co: ? ab: ?: [Unknown meaning;]

ec^m) ᛮ✝ᛚ✝ᛮ (היתוך HY-TWK) — **Melted:** [Unknown connection to root;] [ms: התוך] [freq. 1] |kjv: melted| {str: 2046}

H) ᛮᛮ✝ (תכה TKH) ac: **Lead** co: ? ab: ?: The leading of a tame animal whose will has been bent.

V) ᛮᛮ✝ (תכה T-KH) — **Lead:** To lead by the hand. [freq. 1] (vf: Pual) |kjv: sat| {str: 8497}

J) ᛮᛮ✝ (תוך TWK) ac: ? co: **Middle** ab: ?

N^m) ᛮᛮ✝ (תוך TWK) — **Middle:** [freq. 415] |kjv: midst, among, within, middle, in, between, through, into| {str: 8432}

290

f^m) ﬩﬋ﬗﬠﬡ﬩ (תוכי TW-KY) —
Tukiy: An unknown animal.
[ms: תכי] [freq. 2] |kjv: peacock|
{str: 8500}

M) ﬠﬗ﬩ (תיך TYK) ac: ? co:
Middle ab: ?

j^m) ﬡﬠﬗ﬩ (תיכון TY-KWN) —
Middle: [ms: תיכן] [freq. 11]
|kjv: middle, middlemost, midst|
{str: 8484}

1495) ﬗ﬩ (תל TL) ac: **Hang** co: **Rope**
ab: **Deceive:** A rope made of twisted
cords for suspending something.

A) ﬗ﬩ (תל TL) ac: **Hang** co: ? ab: ?

f^m) ﬠﬗ﬩ (תלי T-LY) —
Quiver: As hung over the
shoulder. [freq. 1] |kjv: quiver|
{str: 8522}

E) ﬑ﬗ﬩ (תלא TLA) ac: **Hang** co: ?
ab: ?

V) ﬑ﬗ﬩ (תלא T-LA) —
Hang: [freq. 3] (vf: Paal) |kjv:
hang, bent| {str: 8511}

F) ﬗ﬩﬩ (התל HTL) ac: **Twist** co:
Twist ab: **Deceive:** A twisting of
fibers to make a rope. The twisting of
something as a deception.

V) ﬗ﬩﬩ (התל H-TL) —
Deceive: [freq. 10] (vf: Pual,
Piel) |kjv: mock, deceive,
deceitfully| {str: 2048}

a^{fl}) ﬗ﬩﬩﬋ (מהתלה MH-T-
LH) — **Deceit:** [freq. 1] |kjv:
deceit| {str: 4123}

d^m) ﬗﬠ﬩﬩ (התול H-TWL) —
Deceiver: [ms: התל] [freq. 1]
|kjv: mocker| {str: 2049}

H) ﬗ﬩﬩ (תלה TLH) ac: **Hang** co: ?
ab: ?

V) ﬗ﬩﬩ (תלה T-LH) — **Hang:**
[freq. 28] (vf: Paal, Niphal, Piel)
|kjv: hang| {str: 8518}

Adopted Roots;

2222	﬩﬛﬩	Wrap, Bandage
2296	﬩﬛ﬠ	Wall
2650	﬩﬩ﬤ	Twist, Cord
2894	ﬤ﬩﬩	Hang

1496) ﬋﬩ (תם TM) ac: **Fill** co: ? ab:
Whole: Someone or something that is
whole, complete or full. One who is
mature and upright as one who is whole.

A) ﬋﬩ (תם TM) ac: **Fill** co: ? ab:
Whole

N^m) ﬋﬩ (תם TM) — **Whole:**
[freq. 13] |kjv: perfect,
undefiled, plain, upright| {str:
8535}

B) ﬋﬋﬩ (תמם TMM) ac: ? co: ?
ab: **Whole**

V) ﬋﬋﬩ (תמם T-MM) —
Whole: [freq. 64] (vf: Paal,
Niphal, Hiphil, Hitpael) |kjv:
consume, end, finish, clean,
upright, spent, perfect, done, fail,
accomplish| {str: 8552}

b^m) ﬋ﬠ﬋﬩ (תמים T-MYM)
— **Whole:** [freq. 91] |kjv:
without blemish, perfect,
upright, without spot, uprightly,
whole, sincere, complete, full|
{str: 8549}

D) ﬋﬑﬩ (תאם TAM) ac: ? co:
Double ab: ?: In the sense of being
full.

V) ﬋﬑﬩ (תאם T-AM) —
Double: Also to bear twins as
doubles. [freq. 6] (vf: Paal,
Hiphil) |kjv: couple, twins| {str:
8382}

c^m) ᴧᴧY⟩⸁† (תאום T-AWM) —
Twins: [ms: תאם] [freq. 4] |kjv: twins| {str: 8380}

H) 𝍦ᴧᴧ† (תמה TMH) ac: ? co: ? ab: **Amazed:** A full and overwhelmed mind.

V) 𝍦ᴧᴧ† (תמה T-MH) —
Marvel: To see or perceive a full sight such as a wonder or miracle. [freq. 9] (vf: Paal, Hitpael) |kjv: marvel, wonder, marvelously, astony, amaze| {str: 8539}

N^m) 𝍦ᴧᴧ† (תמה T-MH) —
Wonder: [Aramaic only] [freq. 3] |kjv: wonder| {str: 8540}

j^m) ⸁Y𝍦ᴧᴧ† (תמהון TM-HWN) — **Confusion:** In the sense of overfilled. [freq. 2] |kjv: astonishment| {str: 8541}

J) ᴧᴧY† (תום TWM) ac: ? co: ? ab: **Mature**

N^m) ᴧᴧY† (תום TWM) —
Whole: Someone or something that is whole, complete, full. One who is mature. [ms: תם] [freq. 23] |kjv: integrity, upright, venture, full, perfect, simplicity| {str: 8537}

N^{fl}) 𝍦ᴧᴧY† (תומה TW-MH) —
Maturity: [ms: תמה] [freq. 5] |kjv: integrity| {str: 8538}

k^m) ᴧᴧY†ᴧᴧ (מתום M-TWM) —
Mature: [ms: מתם] [freq. 4] |kjv: soundness, men| {str: 4974}

L) ᴧᴧ†⸜ (יתם YTM) ac: ? co: **Orphan** ab: ?: One that is not full.

c^m) ᴧᴧY†⸜ (יתום Y-TWM) —
Orphan: [freq. 42] |kjv: fatherless, orphan| {str: 3490}

Adopted Roots;
2223 ᴧᴧ†ᶁ Seal, Signet

~~~~~~~~~~

1497) ⸁† (תן TN) ac: **Hire** co: **Gift** ab: ?

A) ⸁† (תן TN) ac: ? co: ? ab: ?

N^m) ⸁† (תן TN) — **Tan:** A large unknown sea animal. [freq. 1] |kjv: whale| {str: 8565}

N^{fl}) 𝍦⸁† (תנה T-NH) —
Tanah: A large unknown sea animal. [freq. 1] |kjv: dragon| {str: 8568}

s^m) ⸁⸜⸁† (תנין T-NYN) —
Taniyn: A large unknown sea animal. [df: תנים] [freq. 28] |kjv: dragon, serpent, whale, monster| {str: 8577}

C) ⸁†⟩⸁ (אתן ATN) ac: ? co: **Gift** ab: ?

N^{fl}) 𝍦⸁†⟩⸁ (אתנה AT-NH) —
Gift: [freq. 1] |kjv: reward| {str: 866}

c^f) ⸁Y†⟩⸁ (אתון A-TWN) —
Donkey: As used as a gift. [freq. 34] |kjv: ass| {str: 860}

e^m) ⸁†⸜⟩⸁ (איתן AY-TN) —
Strong: [Unknown connection to root;] [ms: אתן] [freq. 13] |kjv: strong, mighty, strength, hard, rough| {str: 386}

m^m) ⸁⸁†⟩⸁ (אתנן AT-NN) —
Price: What is brought to a harlot as a gift. [freq. 11] |kjv: hire, reward| {str: 868}

H) 𝍦⸁† (תנה TNH) ac: **Hire** co: ? ab: ?

V) 𝍦⸁† (תנה T-NH) — **I. Hire:** To give a gift to a harlot. **II. Recount:** To retell or re-enact a previous incident. [Unknown connection to root] [freq. 4] (vf: Paal, Hiphil, Piel) |kjv: hire, lament, rehearse| {str: 8566, 8567}

Adopted Roots;
2451 ל†ת֟ Give, Gift

1498) ◄† (תס TS) ac: **?** co: **?** ab: **?**

1499) ⊙† (תע TAh) ac: **?** co: **?** ab: **Error**

A) ⊙† (תע TAh) ac: **?** co: **?** ab: **Error**

Id^m) ⊙Y†⊙† (תעתוע TAh-TWAh) — **Error:** [ms: תעתע] [freq. 2] |kjv: error| {str: 8595}

B) ⊙⊙† (תעע TAhAh) ac: **Deceive** co: **?** ab: **?:** Causing another to err through deception.

V) ⊙⊙† (תעע T-AhAh) — **Deceive:** [freq. 2] (vf: Pilpel, Participle) |kjv: deceiver, misuse| {str: 8591}

H) ⵜ⊙† (תעה TAhH) ac: **?** co: **?** ab: **Error**

V) ⵜ⊙† (תעה T-AhH) — **Wander:** To go astray due to deception or influence. [freq. 50] (vf: Paal, Niphal, Hiphil) |kjv: err, wander, astray, seduce, stagger, away, deceive| {str: 8582}

J) ⊙Y† (תוע TWAh) ac: **?** co: **?** ab: **Deceit:** Causing another to err through deception.

N^m) ⊙Y† (תוע TWAh) — **Deceit:** [df: תך] [freq. 3] |kjv: deceit, fraud| {str: 8496}

N^f1) ⵜ⊙Y† (תועה TW-AhH) — **Deception:** [freq. 2] |kjv: hinder, error| {str: 8442}

1500) ⊂† (תף TP) ac: **Beat** co: **Tambourine** ab: **?:** The beating of a Tambourine. (eng: tap)

B) ⊂⊂† (תפף TPP) ac: **Beat** co: **Tambourine** ab: **?**

V) ⊂⊂† (תפף T-PP) — **Beat:** The rhythmic beating of a tambourine. [freq. 2] (vf: Paal, Participle) |kjv: timbrel, tabering| {str: 8608}

J) ⊂Y† (תוף TWP) ac: **?** co: **Tambourine** ab: **?**

N^m) ⊂Y† (תוף TWP) — **Tambourine:** [ms: תף] [freq. 17] |kjv: timbrel, tabret| {str: 8596}

N^f2) †⊂Y† (תופת TW-PT) — **Spit:** [Unknown connection to root;] [ms: תפת] [freq. 1] |kjv: tabret| {str: 8611}

1501) ∾† (תץ TTs) ac: **?** co: **?** ab: **?**

1502) ⦁† (תק TQ) ac: **?** co: **?** ab: **?**

C) ⦁†Ɣ (אתק ATQ) ac: **?** co: **Ledge** ab: **?**

b^m) ⦁⟋†Ɣ (אתיק A-TYQ) — **Ledge:** [freq. 5] |kjv: gallery| {str: 862}

d^m) ⦁Y†Ɣ (אתוק A-TWQ) — **Ledge:** [freq. 5] |kjv: gallery| {str: 862}

1503) ৯† (תר TR) ac: **Tour** co: **Border** ab: **?:** The pictograph † is a picture of two crossed sticks representing a mark, the ৯ is a picture of the head of a man. Combined these mean "mark of man".

The border o the land owned by an individual, or under his control, is marked by markers. An outline or border. To walk to border of the property as owner or spy. An extension of the border. (eng: tour; tire; travel; dial - with the exchange of the t and d and the r and l)

C) ᗰ†ᗷ (אתר ATR) ac: **?** co: **Place** ab: **?:** An area defined by a border.

Nᵐ) ᗰ†ᗷ (אתר A-TR) — **Place:** [Aramaic only] [freq. 8] |kjv: place, after| {str: 870}

D) ᗷ†ᗰ (תאר TAR) ac: **Mark** co: **Outline** ab: **?**

V) ᗷ†ᗰ (תאר T-AR) — **Mark out:** To mark out a border or outline. [freq. 7] (vf: Paal, Piel) |kjv: draw, mark| {str: 8388}

gᵐ) ᗰᗷ†Y (תואר TW-AR) — **Form:** The outline of an individual. [ms: תאר] [freq. 15] |kjv: form, goodly, favoured, comely, countenance, resemble, visage| {str: 8389}

J) ᗰY† (תור TWR) ac: **Tour** co: **Border** ab: **?**

V) ᗰY† (תור TWR) — **Tour:** To travel an area from border to border. [freq. 23] (vf: Paal, Hiphil, Participle) |kjv: search, spy, seek, descry, espy| {str: 8446}

Nᶠ) ᗰY† (תור TWR) — **I. Border: II. Circle:** As a round border. An individuals turn as point in a circle. [ms: תר] **III. Turtledove:** [Unknown connection to root;] [ms: תר] [freq. 19] |kjv: row, border, estate, turn, turtledove| {str: 8447, 8448, 8449}

Nᶠˡ) ᗰY† (תורה TW-RH) — **Custom:** As what defines, gives borders, to a people. [freq. 1] |kjv: manner| {str: 8452}

mᵐ) ᗰ†Y (תורן TW-RN) — **Pole:** As a landmark of a border. Also a ships mast. [ms: תרן] [freq. 3] |kjv: mast, beacon| {str: 8650}

L) ᗰ†ᒍ (יתר YTR) ac: **?** co: **Abundance** ab: **?:** In the sense of expanding borers.

Nᶠˡ) ᗰ†ᒍ (יתרה YT-RH) — **Abundance:** [freq. 2] |kjv: abundance, riches| {str: 3502}

aᵐ) ᗰ†Yᗰᗰ (מותר MW-TR) — **Profit:** As an abundance. [freq. 3] |kjv: profit, plenteousness, preeminence| {str: 4195}

bᵐ) ᗰᒍ†ᒍ (יתיר Y-TYR) — **Exceeding:** In the sense of abundance. [Aramaic only] [freq. 8] |kjv: exceedingly, excellent| {str: 3493}

dᵐ) ᗰY†ᒍ (יתור Y-TWR) — **Range:** A range of mountains as a border. [freq. 1] |kjv: range| {str: 3491}

gᵐ) ᗰ†Yᒍ (יותר YW-TR) — **More:** In the sense of abundance. [freq. 8] |kjv: more, better, over, profit, moreover, further| {str: 3148}

gᶠ²) †ᗰ†Yᒍ (יותרת YW-T-RT) — **Lobe:** The lobe of the liver as an extension of the liver. [ms: יתרת] [freq. 11] |kjv: caul| {str: 3508}

jᵐ) ᒍYᗰ†ᒍ (יתרון YT-RWN) — **More:** As an abundance. [freq. 10] |kjv: profit, excel, excellency, profitable, better| {str: 3504}

1504) ⨆⨅† (תש TSh) ac: **?** co: **?** ab: **Success**

    J) ⨆⨅Y† (תוש TWSh) ac: **?** co: **?** ab: **Success**

        f^{f1}) 𝌆⤙⨆⨅Y† (תושיה TW-Sh-YH) — **Success:** [ms: תשיה] [freq. 12] |kjv: enterprise| {str: 8454}

    M) ⨆⨅⤙† (תיש TYSh) ac: **?** co: **Goat** ab: **?**

N^m) ⤙† (תיש TYSh) — **Goat:** A male goat. [freq. 4] |kjv: goat| {str: 8495}

~~~~~~~~~

1505) †† (תת TT) ac: **?** co: **?** ab: **?**

~~~~~~~~~

1506) 𝌆† (תע TGh) ac: **?** co: **?** ab: **?**

~~~~~~~~~

Ghah

1507) 𐤀𐤋 (עא GhA) ac: ? co: ? ab: ?

1508) 𐤀𐤌 (עב GhB) ac: **Thick** co: **Cloud** ab: ?: The pictograph 𐤀 is a picture of a twisted rope with the extended meaning of darkness. The 𐤌 is a picture of a tent representing what is inside. Combined these mean "darkness inside".

A) 𐤀𐤌 (עב GhB) ac: **Thick** co: **Cloud** ab: ?

N^(m)) 𐤀𐤌 (עב GhB) — **Cloud:** A thick dark cloud. [freq. 32] |kjv: cloud, clay, thick, thicket| {str: 5645}

N^(f3)) 𐤀𐤌𐤉𐤕 (עבות Gh-BWT) — **I. Thick:** [ms: עבת] **II. Cloud: III. Braid:** A thick braided rope or cord of gold. [ms: עבת] [freq. 29] |kjv: thick, wreathen, cord, band, bough, rope, chain, branch| {str: 5687, 5688}

f^(m)) 𐤀𐤌𐤉 (עבי Gh-BY) — **Thick:** [freq. 4] |kjv: thick, thickness| {str: 5672}

H) 𐤀𐤌𐤄 (עבה GhBH) ac: **Thick** co: ? ab: ?

V) 𐤀𐤌𐤄 (עבה Gh-BH) — **Thick:** To be thick. Thick. [freq. 3] (vf: Paal) |kjv: thick| {str: 5666}

a^(m)) 𐤌𐤀𐤌𐤄 (מעבה MGh-BH) — **Clay:** A thick and dark soil. [freq. 1] |kjv: clay| {str: 4568}

J) 𐤀𐤉𐤌 (עוב GhWB) ac: ? co: **Cloud** ab: ?: A thick dark covering.

V) 𐤀𐤉𐤌 (עוב GhWB) — **Cloud:** [freq. 1] (vf: Hiphil) |kjv: cloud| {str: 5743}

Adopted Roots;
2907 𐤀𐤓𐤌 Dark, Raven

1509) 𐤀𐤂 (עג GhG) ac: ? co: ? ab: ?

1510) 𐤀𐤃 (עד GhD) ac: ? co: **Goat** ab: ?

A) 𐤀𐤃 (עד GhD) ac: ? co: **Goat** ab: ?

f^(m)) 𐤀𐤃𐤉 (עדי Gh-DY) — **Kid:** A young goat. [df: גדי] [freq. 16] |kjv: kid| {str: 1423}

f^(f1)) 𐤀𐤃𐤉𐤄 (עדיה GhD-YH) — **Kid:** A young female goat. [df: גדיה] [freq. 1] |kjv: kid| {str: 1429}

1511) 𐤀𐤄 (עה GhH) ac: **Twist** co: **Rope** ab: ?: The pictograph 𐤀 is a picture of a twisted rope. Twisted cords that form a thick rope. Related to the parent 𐤀𐤉.

J) 𐤀𐤉𐤄 (עוה GhWH) ac: **Twist** co: ? ab: ?

V) 𐤀𐤉𐤄 (עוה GhWH) — **Twist:** To be twisted in ones actions. [freq. 17] (vf: Paal, Niphal, Hiphil, Piel) |kjv: iniquity, perverse, pervert, amiss, turn, crooked, bow, trouble, wicked, wrong| {str: 5753}

N^{f1}) 𐤅𐤉𐤀 (עוה Gh-WH) —
Twist: [freq. 3] |kjv: overturn|
{str: 5754}

f¹) 𐤅𐤉𐤀 (עויה GhW-YH) —
Twisted: [Aramaic only] [freq.
1] |kjv: iniquities| {str: 5758}

~~~~~~~~

1512) Y𐤀 (עו GhW) ac: **?** co: **?** ab: **Guilt:**
The pictograph 𐤀 is a picture of a twisted
rope. Related to the parent 𐤅𐤉𐤀.

A) Y𐤀 (עו GhW) ac: **?** co: **?** ab: **Guilt**

m^m) 𐤍𐤅𐤉𐤀 (עוון GhW-WN) —
Guilt: The result of twisted
actions. [ms: עוון] [freq. 230]
|kjv: iniquity, punishment, fault,
mischief, sin| {str: 5771}

Adopted Roots;
2141 𐤋𐤁𐤇 Bind, Rope
2247 𐤋𐤕𐤔 Twist, Fetter

~~~~~~~~

1513) 𐤆𐤀 (עז GhZ) ac: **?** co: **Goat** ab: **?**

A) 𐤆𐤀 (עז GhZ) ac: **?** co: **Goat** ab:
?

N^f) 𐤆𐤀 (עז GhZ) — **Goat:**
[Hebrew and Aramaic] [freq. 75]
|kjv: goat, kid| {str: 5795, 5796}

~~~~~~~~

1514) 𐤇𐤀 (עח GhHh) ac: **?** co: **?** ab: **?**

~~~~~~~~

1515) 𐤈𐤀 (עט GhTh) ac: **?** co: **?** ab: **?**

~~~~~~~~

1516) 𐤉𐤀 (עי GhY) ac: **?** co: **Ruin** ab: **?:**
The pictograph 𐤀 is a twisted rope. The 𐤉
is a picture of a the hand meaning work.
Combined these mean "twisted work".

A) 𐤉𐤀 (עי GhY) ac: **?** co: **Ruin** ab:
?: A city or structure that has been
demolished.

N^m) 𐤉𐤀 (עי GhY) — **Ruin:**
[freq. 4] |kjv: heap| {str: 5856}

k^m) 𐤉𐤀𐤌 (מעי M-GhY) —
Ruin: [freq. 1] |kjv: heap| {str:
4596}

~~~~~~~~

1517) 𐤔𐤀 (עך GhK) ac: **?** co: **?** ab: **?**

~~~~~~~~

1518) 𐤋𐤀 (על GhL) ac: **?** co: **Stain** ab:
Wicked: A dark stain. (eng: evil)

D) 𐤀𐤋𐤀 (עאל GhAL) ac: **?** co:
Stain ab: **?:** Clothing or hands that
have been stained with blood. Any
stain that pollutes something.

V) 𐤀𐤋𐤀 (עאל Gh-AL) —
Stain: [df: נאל] [freq. 11] (vf:
Niphal, Hiphil, Hitpael, Pual,
Piel) |kjv: pollute, defile, stain|
{str: 1351}

c^m) 𐤀𐤅𐤋𐤀 (עאול Gh-AWL) —
Stained: [df: נאל] [freq. 1] |kjv:
defile| {str: 1352}

J) 𐤋𐤉𐤀 (עול GhWL) ac: **?** co: **?** ab:
Wicked: An action that causes a
stain of immorality.

V) 𐤋𐤉𐤀 (עול GhWL) —
Wicked: [freq. 2] (vf: Piel) |kjv:
unjustly, unrighteous| {str:
5765}

N^{m/f}) 𐤋𐤉𐤀 (עול GhWL) —
Wicked: [freq. 60] |kjv: wicked,
unjust, unrighteous, iniquity,
perverse| {str: 5766, 5767}

b^m) 𐤋𐤉𐤅𐤀 (עויל Gh-WYL) —
Wicked: [freq. 1] |kjv: ungodly|
{str: 5760}

K) Y𐤍𐤏 (עלו GhLW) ac: ? co: **Stain** ab: **Wicked**

N(fl) 𐤅Y𐤍𐤏 (עלוה GhL-WH) — **Wickedness:** [freq. 1] |kjv: iniquity| {str: 5932}

L) 𐤍𐤏ᵧ (יעל YGhL) ac: ? co: **Wild goat** ab: ?: From its dark colors as stains.

N(m) 𐤍𐤏ᵧ (יעל Y-GhL) — **Wild goat:** [freq. 3] |kjv: wild goat| {str: 3277}

N(fl) 𐤅𐤍𐤏ᵧ (יעלה YGh-LH) — **Wild goat:** A female wild goat. [freq. 1] |kjv: roe| {str: 3280}

1519) 𐤌𐤏 (עם GhM) ac: ? co: ? ab: ?

1520) 𐤍𐤏 (ען GhN) ac: **Answer** co: ? ab: ?

H) 𐤅𐤍𐤏 (ענה GhNH) ac: **Answer** co: ? ab: ?: An answer or reply to a previous question or request.

V) 𐤅𐤍𐤏 (ענה Gh-NH) — **Answer:** [Hebrew and Aramaic] [freq. 359] (vf: Paal, Niphal) |kjv: answer, hear, testify, speak, sing, bear, cry, witness, give| {str: 6030, 6032}

a(m) 𐤅𐤍𐤏𐤌 (מענה MGh-NH) — **Answer:** [freq. 8] |kjv: answer| {str: 4617}

1521) 𐤎𐤏 (עס GhS) ac: **Tread** co: **Juice** ab: ?: Grapes are placed in a vat. A rope is suspended from above and is held onto by the grape treaders for support.

B) 𐤎𐤎𐤏 (עסס GhSS) ac: **Tread** co: **Juice** ab: ?

V) 𐤎𐤎𐤏 (עסס Gh-SS) — **Tread:** [freq. 1] (vf: Paal) |kjv: tread| {str: 6072}

b(m) 𐤎ᵧ𐤎𐤏 (עסיס Gh-SYS) — **Juice:** Juice from the grape or other fruit that has been pressed out. An unfermented juice. [freq. 5] |kjv: new wine, sweet wine,| {str: 6071}

1522) 𐤏⊙ (עע GhAh) ac: ? co: ? ab: ?

1523) 𐤐𐤏 (עף GhP) ac: ? co: ? ab: **Darkness:** The pictograph 𐤏 is a picture of a twisted rope with the extended meaning of darkness.

L) 𐤐𐤏ᵧ (יעף YGhP) ac: ? co: ? ab: **Darkness**

a(m) 𐤐𐤏Y𐤌 (מועף MW-GhP) — **Darkness:** [freq. 1] |kjv: dimness| {str: 4155}

M) 𐤐ᵧ𐤏 (עיף GhYP) ac: ? co: ? ab: **Darkness**

N(fl) 𐤅𐤐ᵧ𐤏 (עיפה GhY-PH) — **Darkness:** [freq. 2] |kjv: darkness| {str: 5890}

1524) 𐤑𐤏 (עץ GhTs) ac: ? co: ? ab: ?

1525) 𐤒𐤏 (עק GhQ) ac: ? co: **Crooked** ab: ?

Adopted Roots;
2904	𐤒𐤍	Crooked
2905	𐤒𐤓	Pluck, Root
2906	𐤒𐤔	Crooked, Perverse
3066	𐤒𐤕𐤍	Crooked

1526) 𐤓𐤀 (עֿר GhR) ac: **Dark** co: **City** ab: **?:** The pictograph 𐤀 is a picture of a rope with the extended meaning of darkness. The 𐤓 is a picture of a man. Combined these mean "dark man" or an enemy. (eng: jungle - with the exchange of the j and y and the l and r)

A) 𐤓𐤀 (עֿר GhR) ac: **?** co: **City** ab: **?**

N^m) 𐤓𐤀 (עֿר GhR) — **I. City: II. Enemy:** [Hebrew and Aramaic] [freq. 7] |kjv: city, enemy| {str: 6145, 6146}

J) 𐤓𐤅𐤀 (עֿור GhWR) ac: **Dark** co: **?** ab: **?**

V) 𐤓𐤅𐤀 (עֿור GhWR) — **I. Waken:** To wake as to open the eyes from darkness. **II. Blind:** To become dark of site through blindness or the putting out of the eyes. [freq. 86] (vf: Paal, Niphal, Hiphil, Piel) |kjv: stir, awake, wake, raise, arise, master, put out, blind| {str: 5782, 5786}

N^m) 𐤓𐤅𐤀 (עֿור GhWR) — **Blind:** A darkness of the eye. [freq. 26] |kjv: blind| {str: 5787}

j^m) 𐤍𐤅𐤓𐤅𐤀 (עֿורון GhW-RWN) — **Blindness:** [freq. 3] |kjv: blindness, blind| {str: 5788}

L) 𐤓𐤀𐤋 (יעֿר YGhR) ac: **?** co: **Forest** ab: **?:** A dark place.

N^m) 𐤓𐤀𐤋 (יעֿר Y-GhR) — **Forest:** [freq. 59] |kjv: forest, wood, honeycomb| {str: 3264, 3293}

N^{f1}) 𐤄𐤓𐤀𐤋 (יעֿרה YGh-RH) — **Forest:** [freq. 2] |kjv: forest| {str: 3295}

M) 𐤓𐤉𐤀 (עֿיר GhYR) ac: **?** co: **City** ab: **?:** A dark and wicked place.

N^m) 𐤓𐤉𐤀 (עֿיר GhYR) — **I. City:** [ms: עֿר] **II. Colt:** As dark in color. [freq. 1097] |kjv: city, town, colt, foal, ass| {str: 5892, 5895}

Adopted Roots;
2909 𐤀𐤌𐤏 Drop, Cloud
3067 𐤀𐤌𐤏𐤋 Dark

1527) 𐤔𐤀 (עֿש GhSh) ac: **Haste** co: **?** ab: **?:** The pictograph 𐤀 is a picture of a twisted rope. The 𐤔 is a picture of the teeth representing the idea of pressing. Combined these mean "twisting pressing".

J) 𐤔𐤅𐤀 (עֿוש GhWSh) ac: **Haste** co: **?** ab: **?**

V) 𐤔𐤅𐤀 (עֿוש GhWSh) — **I. Haste:** [df: חֿוש] **II. Assemble:** [freq. 21] (vf: Paal, Hiphil) |kjv: haste, ready| {str: 2363, 5789}

M) 𐤔𐤉𐤀 (עֿיש GhYSh) ac: **Haste** co: **?** ab: **?**

V) 𐤔𐤉𐤀 (עֿיש GhYSh) — **Haste:** [df: חֿיש] [freq. 1] (vf: Paal) |kjv: haste| {str: 2439}

N^m) 𐤔𐤉𐤀 (עֿיש GhYSh) — **Quickly:** [df: חֿיש] [freq. 1] |kjv: haste| {str: 2440}

1528) 𐤕𐤀 (עֿת GhT) ac: **Twist** co: **Rope** ab: **?:** The pictograph 𐤀 is a picture of a twisted rope. The 𐤕 is a picture of a mark. Combined these mean "twisted mark".

J) 𐤕𐤅𐤀 (עֿות GhWT) ac: **Twist** co: **Crooked** ab: **?**

V) 𐤕𐤅𐤀 (עֿות GhWT) — **Twist:** [freq. 11] (vf: Hitpael, Pual, Piel, Participle) |kjv: pervert, crooked, bow, falsify, overthrow, subvert| {str: 5791}

N^(fl)) 𐤑𐤕𐤉𐤏 (עותה GhW-TH) — **Crookedness:** [freq. 1] |kjv: wrong| {str: 5792}

~~~~~~~~~

1529) 𐤏𐤏 (עע GhGh) ac: **?** co: **Rope** ab: **?**: The pictograph 𐤏 is a picture of a twisted rope.

H) 𐤑𐤏𐤏 (עעה GhGhH) ac: **?** co: **Crooked** ab: **?**: A crooked nature.

g^(m)) 𐤑𐤏𐤉𐤏 (עועה GhW-GhH) — **Crooked:** [freq. 1] |kjv: perverse| {str: 5773}

~~~~~~~~~

Adopted Roots (Three letter)

Al

2001) ‎אלף‎ (אלף ALP) ac: **Guide** co: **Yoke** ab: **Learn:** The yoke of the oxen, the yoke of learning. An older experienced ox is yoked to a younger inexperienced one in order to teach it how to pull a load. A thousand, as a large number of oxen. [from: ‎אל‎ - an ox as wearing a yoke for work] (eng: elephant)

V) ‎אלף‎ (אלף A-LP) — **I. Learn:** To learn by example in the sense of being yoked to another. **II. Thousand:** To make or bring forth a thousand, a thousand-fold. [freq. 5] (vf: Hiphil, Paal, Piel) |kjv: teach, learn, utter, bring forth thousands| {str: 502, 503}

N^m) ‎אלף‎ (אלף A-LP) — **I. Ox: II. Thousand:** [Hebrew and Aramaic] [freq. 517] |kjv: kine, oxen, family| {str: 504, 505, 506}

d^m) ‎אלוף‎ (אלוף A-LWP) — **Guide:** One who is yoked to another to lead and teach. [ms: אלף] [freq. 69] |kjv: duke, guide, friend, governor, captain, ox| {str: 441}

2002) ‎אנף‎ (אנף ANP) ac: **Snort** co: **Breath** ab: ?: [from: ‎אף‎ - the nose as a breathing of the nose]

V) ‎אנף‎ (אנף A-NP) — **Snort:** A heavy breathing out of anger. [freq. 14] (vf: Paal, Hitpael) |kjv: angry, displeased| {str: 599}

N^m) ‎אנף‎ (אנף A-NP) — **Face:** [Only used in the masculine plural form; Related to ‎אף‎] [freq. 2] |kjv: face, visage| {str: 600}

N^{f1}) ‎אנפה‎ (אנפה AN-PH) — **Anphah:** An unknown type of bird, possibly from its nose or beak. [freq. 2] |kjv: heron| {str: 601}

2003) ‎אנש‎ (אנש ANSh) ac: **Sick** co: **Man** ab: ?

V) ‎אנש‎ (אנש A-NSh) — **Sick:** In the sense of the mortality of man. [freq. 9] (vf: Paal, Niphal) |kjv: sick, incurable, desperate, wicked, woeful| {str: 605}

N^m) ‎אנש‎ (אנש A-NSh) — **Man:** [Aramaic only] [freq. 25] |kjv: man| {str: 606}

N^{fl}) ᛒᛃᛚᛅ (אנשה AN-ShH) —
Woman: [ar: נשה] [freq. 1] |kjv:
wife| {str: 5389}

b^m) ᛚᛃᛅ (אניש A-NYSh) —
Man: [ms: איש] [freq. 1639] |kjv:
man, one, husband, any| {str: 376,
377}

b^{fl}) ᛒᛃᛚᛅ (אנישה A-NY-ShH)
— **Woman:** [ms: אישה] [freq. 780]
|kjv: wife, woman, one, married,
female| {str: 802}

c^m) ᛚᛃᛅ (אנוש A-NWSh) —
Man: [freq. 564] |kjv: man, husband,
merchantmen, person| {str: 582}

Bet

2004) ‏מ‎LU‏ד‎ (‏בגד‎ BGD) ac: **Cover** co: **Clothing** ab: **Deceive:** A covering of the body or actions in a faithless or treacherous manner.

V) ‏מ‎LU‏ד‎ (‏בגד‎ B-GD) — **Deceive:** A covert action of treachery or deceit. [freq. 49] (vf: Paal) |kjv: treacherously, transgress, deceitfully, unfaithful, offend| {str: 898}

N^m) ‏מ‎LU‏ד‎ (‏בגד‎ B-GD) — **Clothing:** Garments for covering. [freq. 217] |kjv: garment, clothes, cloth, raiment, apparel, robe| {str: 899}

c^m) ‏מ‎Y‏ל‎U‏ד‎ (‏בגוד‎ B-GWD) — **Treacherous:** A covert act of deceit or treachery. [freq. 2] |kjv: treacherous| {str: 901}

g^fl) ‏מ‎LU‏ד‎ (‏בוגדה‎ BW-G-DH) — **Treacherous:** A covert act of deceit or treachery. [ms: ‏בגדה‎] [freq. 1] |kjv: treacherous| {str: 900}

2005) ‏מ‎U‏ד‎ (‏בדל‎ BDL) ac: **Separate** co: **Piece** ab: **?:** [from: ‏מד‎U]

V) ‏מ‎U‏ד‎ (‏בדל‎ B-DL) — **Separate:** To divide or separate something. [freq. 42] (vf: Niphal, Hiphil) |kjv: separate, divide, difference, asunder, severed| {str: 914}

N^m) ‏מ‎U‏ד‎ (‏בדל‎ B-DL) — **Piece:** Something that is divided or separated from something else. [freq. 1] |kjv: piece| {str: 915}

b^m) ‏מ‎U‏ד‎ (‏בדיל‎ B-DYL) — **Tin:** A metal separated out by smelting. [freq. 6] |kjv: tin| {str: 913}

h^fl) ‏מ‎LU‏ד‎ (‏מבדלה‎ MB-D-LH) — **Separate:** A place separated. [freq. 1] |kjv: separate| {str: 3995}

2006) ‏מ‎U‏ד‎ (‏בדק‎ BDQ) ac: **Repair** co: **Breach** ab: **?:** [from: ‏מד‎U - as a separation]

V) ‏מ‎U‏ד‎ (‏בדק‎ B-DQ) — **Repair:** The repairing of a breach in a wall. [freq. 1] (vf: Paal) |kjv: repair| {str: 918}

N^m) ‏מ‎U‏ד‎ (‏בדק‎ B-DQ) — **Breach:** A breach in the wall of a building or ship. [freq. 10] |kjv: breach, calker| {str: 919}

2007) ‏מ‎U‏ד‎ (‏בדר‎ BDR) ac: **Scatter** co: **?** ab: **?:** [from: ‏מד‎U - as a separation]

N^m) ‏מ‎U‏ד‎ (‏בדר‎ B-DR) — **Scatter:** [Aramaic only] [freq. 1] |kjv: scatter| {str: 921}

2008) ‏מ‎U‏ד‎ (‏בזק‎ BZQ) ac: **?** co: **Lightning** ab: **?**

N^m) ‏מ‎U‏ד‎ (‏בזק‎ B-ZQ) — **Lightning:** [freq. 1] |kjv: lightning| {str: 965}

2009) ‏מ‎U‏ד‎ (‏בזר‎ BZR) ac: **?** co: **Scatter** ab: **?**

V) ‏מ‎U‏ד‎ (‏בזר‎ B-ZR) — **Scatter:** [freq. 2] (vf: Paal, Piel) |kjv: scatter| {str: 967}

2010) ⸲⸳⸴ (בחל BHhL) ac: ? co: ? ab: **Loathe**

V) ⸲⸳⸴ (בחל B-HhL) — **Loathe:** [freq. 2] (vf: Paal, Pual) |kjv: abhor, gotten hastily| {str: 973}

~~~~~~~~~~~

2011) ⸳⸴ (בחן BHhN) ac: **Examine** co: **Watchtower** ab: ?: A close and careful examination of a place or something. An inspection to determine effectiveness. [from: ⸳⸴ - examination to select a choice one]

V) ⸳⸴ (בחן B-HhN) — **Examine:** To test, try or scrutinize. [freq. 29] (vf: Paal, Niphal, Pual) |kjv: try, prove, examine, tempt, trial| {str: 974}

N^m) ⸳⸴ (בחן B-HhN) — **Watchtower:** A place of inspection. [freq. 1] |kjv: tower| {str: 975}

b^m) ⸳⸴ (בחין B-HhYN) — **Watchtower:** A place of inspection. [freq. 1] |kjv: tower| {str: 971}

c^m) ⸳⸴ (בחון B-HhWN) — **Watchtower:** A place of inspection. [freq. 1] |kjv: tower| {str: 969}

g^m) ⸳⸴ (בוחן BW-HhN) — **Tested:** Something that has been tested through inspection and found worthy. [ms: בחן] [freq. 1] |kjv: tried| {str: 976}

~~~~~~~~~~~

2012) ⸳⸴ (בחר BHhR) ac: **Choose** co: ? ab: **Youth:** An examination to determine the choicest. [from: ⸳⸴ - choosing a choice one]

V) ⸳⸴ (בחר B-HhR) — **Choose:** [freq. 172] (vf: Paal, Niphal, Pual) |kjv: choose, chosen, choice, acceptable, appoint, excellent| {str:

977} b^m) ⸳⸴ (בחיר B-HhYR) — **Chosen:** [freq. 13] |kjv: chosen, choice one, chosen one, elect| {str: 972}

d^m) ⸳⸴ (בחור B-HhWR) — **Youth:** A young person as one chosen for an activity. [ms: בחר] [freq. 45] |kjv: young, chosen| {str: 970}

d^f3) ⸳⸴ (בחורות B-HhW-RWT) — **Youth:** A young age. [ms: בחרות] [freq. 3] |kjv: youth| {str: 979}

h^m) ⸳⸴ (מבחר MBh-hR) — **Chosen:** [freq. 12] |kjv: choose, chosen, choice, acceptable, appoint, excellent| {str: 4005}

hc^m) ⸳⸴ (מבחור MB-HhWR) — **Choice:** The best of a group. [freq. 2] |kjv: choice| {str: 4004}

~~~~~~~~~~~

2013) ⸳⸴ (בטח BThHh) ac: **Cling** co: ? ab: **Security:** A holding onto something or someone by clinging or confiding.

V) ⸳⸴ (בטח B-ThHh) — **Cling:** [freq. 120] (vf: Paal, Hiphil) |kjv: trust, confidence, secure| {str: 982}

N^m) ⸳⸴ (בטח B-ThHh) — **Security:** A state or place of safety. [freq. 42] |kjv: safely, safety, careless, safe, secure, assurance| {str: 983}

d^f1) ⸳⸴ (בטוחה B-ThW-HhH) — **Secure:** A state or place of safety. [ms: בתחה] [freq. 1] |kjv: secure| {str: 987}

e^f1) ⸳⸴ (ביטחה BYTh-HhH) — **Trust:** A clinging onto someone or something for support or security. [ms: בטחה] [freq. 1] |kjv: confidence| {str: 985} h^{m}) מבטח (MB-ThHh) — **Confidence:** Clinging onto someone or something else for support or safety. [freq. 15] |kjv: confidence, trust, sure, hope| {str: 4009}

ej^{m}) ביטחון (BY-Th-HhWN) — **Hope:** A trust in a future outcome. [ms: בטחון] [freq. 3] |kjv: confidence, hope| {str: 986}

nb^{m}) אבטיח (AB-ThYHh) — **Melon:** A fruit that clings to the vine. [freq. 1] |kjv: melon| {str: 20}

~~~~~~~~~~

2014) בטל (BThL) ac: **Cease** co: **?** ab: **?**

V) בטל (B-ThL) — **Cease:** To stop or become inactive. [Hebrew and Aramaic] [freq. 7] (vf: Paal) |kjv: cease, hindered| {str: 988, 989}

~~~~~~~~~~

2015) בטן (BThN) ac: **?** co: **Belly** ab: **?:** [from: בט - the middle of the body as a division]

N^{f}) בטן (B-ThN) — **Belly:** [freq. 72] |kjv: belly, womb, body, within, born| {str: 990}

g^{m}) בוטן (BW-ThN) — **Pistachio:** From its belly shape. [freq. 1] |kjv: nuts| {str: 992}

~~~~~~~~~~

2016) בכר (BKR) ac: **?** co: **Firstfruit** ab: **?:** The firstfruits of the crop or womb. [from: בכר - the firstfruits being the choicest]

V) בכר (B-KR) — **Firstfruit:** To be born or bear the first fruits. [freq. 4] (vf: Hiphil, Pual, Piel) |kjv: firstborn, new fruit, firstling| {str: 1069}

N^{m}) בכר (B-KR) — **Camel:** A young camel. [Unknown connection to root;] [freq. 1] |kjv: dromedary| {str: 1070}

b^{fl}) בכירה (B-KY-RH) — **Firstborn:** The firstborn daughter. [freq. 6] |kjv: firstborn| {str: 1067}

c^{m}) בכור (B-KWR) — **Firstfruit:** The firstborn son of a man or animal. [freq. 117] |kjv: firstborn, firstling, eldest| {str: 1060}

c^{fl}) בכורה (B-KW-RH) — **I. Firstborn:** Of the flock or herd. [ms: בכרה] **II. Birthright:** The rights of the firstborn son (see Deut 21:17). **III. Firstfruit:** [freq. 15] |kjv: birthright, firstling, firstborn| {str: 1062}

d^{fl}) בכורה (B-KW-RH) — **Firstripe:** The first fruits of the harvest. [freq. 1] |kjv: firstripe| {str: 1073}

e^{fl}) ביכרה (BYK-RH) — **Camel:** A young female camel. [Unknown connection to root;] [ms: בכרה] [freq. 1] |kjv: dromedary| {str: 1072}

ed^{m}) ביכור (BY-KWR) — **Firstfruit:** [ms: בכור] [freq. 18] |kjv: firstfruit, firstripe, hasty| {str: 1061}

ed^{fl}) ביכורה (BY-KW-RH) — **Firstfruit:** [ms: בכורה] [freq. 2] |kjv: firstripe| {str: 1063}

~~~~~~~~~~

2017) בלג (BLG) ac: **Smile** co: **Smile** ab: **?:** Pleasure taken in strength or comfort.

V) בלג (B-LG) — **Smile:** [freq. 4] (vf: Hiphil) |kjv: comfort, strength strengthen| {str: 1082} ab^(f4)) †⅃ᒄ⅃⊃ꓥᒐᒄ∧ꓥꓥ (מבליגית MB-LY-GYT) — **Smile:** [freq. 1] |kjv: comfort| {str: 4010}

2018) ꓥꓥᐯᒄﬦ (בלם BLM) ac: **Muzzle** co: **?** ab: **?:** A binding of the mouth to restrain an animal.

V) ꓥꓥᐯᒄﬦ (בלם B-LM) — **Muzzle:** [freq. 1] (vf: Paal) |kjv: held| {str: 1102}

2019) ⫣ᐯᒄﬦ (בלס BLS) ac: **?** co: **Gather** ab: **?**

V) ⫣ᐯᒄﬦ (בלס B-LS) — **Gather:** To gather fruit from the tree. [freq. 1] (vf: Paal) |kjv: gatherer| {str: 1103}

2020) ⊘ᐯᒄﬦ (בלע BLAh) ac: **Swallow** co: **?** ab: **?:** [from: ᐯﬦ - flowing down the throat]

V) ⊘ᐯᒄﬦ (בלע B-LAh) — **Swallow:** [freq. 49] (vf: Paal, Niphal, Hitpael, Pual, Piel) |kjv: swallow, destroy, devour, covered| {str: 1104}
N^(m)) ⊘ᐯᒄﬦ (בלע B-LAh) — **Swallowed:** [freq. 2] |kjv: devouring, swallowed| {str: 1105}

2021) ⊶ᐯᒄﬦ (בלק BLQ) ac: **Empty** co: **?** ab: **?:** [from: ᐯﬦ - as a flowing away]

V) ⊶ᐯᒄﬦ (בלק B-LQ) — **Empty:** [freq. 2] (vf: Pual, Participle) |kjv: waste| {str: 1110}

2022) ⊗ᒐﬦ (בנט BNTh) ac: **?** co: **Waist** ab: **?:** [from: ⊗ﬦ - The middle of the body as a division]

n^(m)) ⊗ᒐᒄⵎ (אבנט AB-NTh) — **Sash:** A waistband worn by officials. [freq. 9] |kjv: girdle| {str: 73}

2023) ⫷ᒐﬦ (בנס BNS) ac: **Anger** co: **?** ab: **?**

V) ⫷ᒐﬦ (בנס B-NS) — **Anger:** [Aramaic only] [freq. 1] (vf: Paal) |kjv: angry| {str: 1149}

2024) ꓥꓥ⫷ﬦ (בסם BSM) ac: **?** co: **Spice** ab: **?:** (eng: balsam - with an added l)

N^(m)) ꓥꓥ⫷ﬦ (בסם B-SM) — **Spice:** Sweet smelling spices. [freq. 1] |kjv: spice| {str: 1313}
g^(m)) ꓥꓥ⫷Yﬦ (בוסם BW-SM) — **Spice:** A sweet smelling spice. [df: בשם] [freq. 29] |kjv: spice, sweet, sweet| {str: 1314}

2025) ᕁ⫷ﬦ (בסר BSR) ac: **Report** co: **Flesh** ab: **Good:** When good news is brought a feast with meat is prepared.

V) ᕁ⫷ﬦ (בסר B-SR) — **Report:** When good news is brought a feast with meat is prepared. [df: בשר] [freq. 24] (vf: Hitpael, Piel) |kjv: tidings, show forth, publish, messenger, preached| {str: 1319}
N^(f)) ᕁ⫷ﬦ (בסר B-SR) — **Flesh:** The skin and muscle or the whole of the person. Also meat as food. [Hebrew and Aramaic] [df: בשר] [freq. 273] |kjv: flesh, body| {str: 1154, 1320, 1321}
c^(f1)) ⵁᕟYᕁ⫷ﬦ (בסורה B-SW-RH) — **Good news:** When good news is brought a feast with meat is prepared. [df: בשׂורה] [freq. 6] |kjv: tidings| {str: 1309}

g^m) ﬦ⪍Y◌ﬦ (בוסר BW-SR) — **Sour Grape:** [Unknown connection to root;] [ms: בסר] [df: בשׁר] [freq. 4] |kjv: unripe grapes, sour grapes| {str: 1155}

n^m) ﬦ⪍◌ﬦⳑ (אבסר AB-SR) — **Meat:** A choice piece of meat. [df: אשׁפר] [freq. 2] |kjv: piece| {str: 829}

2026) ⊗◌ﬦ (בעט BAhTh) ac: ? co: **Kick** ab: ?

V) ⊗◌ﬦ (בעט B-AhTh) — **Kick:** [freq. 2] (vf: Paal) |kjv: kick| {str: 1163}

2027) ⳑ◌ﬦ (בעל BAhL) ac: **Rule** co: **Master** ab: ?: [from: ⳑ◌ - as a yoke which binds the master to the servant.]

V) ⳑ◌ﬦ (בעל B-AhL) — **Rule:** [freq. 16] (vf: Paal, Niphal) |kjv: marry, husband, dominion, wife| {str: 1166}

N^m) ⳑ◌ﬦ (בעל B-AhL) — **Master:** [Hebrew and Aramaic] [freq. 85] |kjv: man, owner, husband, master, lord| {str: 1167, 1169}

N^{fl}) Ⲫⳑ◌ﬦ (בעלה BAh-LH) — **Mistress:** [freq. 4] |kjv: mistress, hath| {str: 1172}

2028) ﬦ◌ﬦ (בער BAhR) ac: **Burn** co: **Fire** ab: ?: A burning with fire or rage.

V) ﬦ◌ﬦ (בער B-AhR) — **Burn:** [freq. 94] (vf: Paal, Niphal, Hiphil, Pual, Piel) |kjv: burn, kindle, brutish, eaten, set| {str: 1197}

N^m) ﬦ◌ﬦ (בער B-AhR) — **Barbarous:** A burning one. [freq. 5] |kjv: brutish, foolish| {str: 1198}

N^{fl}) Ⲫﬦ◌ﬦ (בערה BAh-RH) — **Fire:** [freq. 1] |kjv: fire| {str: 1200}

b^m) ﬦⵧ◌ﬦ (בעיר B-AhYR) — **Cattle:** As devourers. [freq. 6] |kjv: beast, cattle| {str: 1165}

2029) ✝◌ﬦ (בעת BAhT) ac: ? co: ? ab: **Fear**

V) ✝◌ﬦ (בעת B-AhT) — **Afraid:** [freq. 16] (vf: Niphal, Piel) |kjv: afraid, terrify, affrighted, trouble| {str: 1204}

N^{fl}) Ⲫ✝◌ﬦ (בעתה BAh-TH) — **Trouble:** What causes fear. [freq. 2] |kjv: trouble| {str: 1205}

ed^m) ✝Y◌ⵧﬦ (ביעות BY-AhWT) — **Terror:** What causes fear. [ms: בעות] [freq. 2] |kjv: terror| {str: 1161}

2030) ⳑ◌ᴧﬦ (בצל BTsL) ac: **Peel** co: **Onion** ab: ?: [from: ⳑᴧ - from the removing of the peel]

N^m) ⳑ◌ᴧﬦ (בצל B-TsL) — **Onion:** [freq. 1] |kjv: onion| {str: 1211}

2031) ◌◌ᴧﬦ (בצע BTsAh) ac: **Cut** co: ? ab: **Profit:** [from: ᴧﬦ - a plunder as a cutting]

V) ◌◌ᴧﬦ (בצע B-TsAh) — **I. Cut:** To cut something off to destroy it. **II. Profit:** To take something by force or greed. [freq. 16] (vf: Paal, Piel) |kjv: cut off, gained, given, greedy, covet, finish, wound| {str: 1214}

N^m) ◌◌ᴧﬦ (בצע B-TsAh) — **Profit:** The taking of money or something of value through force in the sense of cutting. [freq. 23] |kjv:

covetousness, gain, profit, lucre| {str: 1215}

~~~~~~~~~

2032) -●-○∿ש (בצק BTsQ) ac: **Swell** co: **Dough** ab: ?: The swelling of dough as it ferments.

V) -●-○∿ש (בצק B-TsQ) — **Swell:** [freq. 2] (vf: Paal) |kjv: swell| {str: 1216}

N^m) -●-○∿ש (בצק B-TsQ) — **Dough:** [freq. 5] |kjv: dough, flour| {str: 1217}

~~~~~~~~~

2033) ᚾ○∿ש (בצר BTsR) ac: **Gather** co: **Fence** ab: ?: A walled, fenced or fortified place for storing up the gathered crop or people. [from: ᚾ○∿]

V) ᚾ○∿ש (בצר B-TsR) — **Gather:** To gather together and confine for protection. [freq. 38] (vf: Paal, Niphal, Piel) |kjv: fence, defense, gather, grapegatherer, fortify| {str: 1219}

N^m) ᚾ○∿ש (בצר B-TsR) — **Gold:** What is stored away and protected. [freq. 3] |kjv: gold| {str: 1220, 1222}

b^m) ᚾ⊃ᚱ○∿ש (בציר B-TsYR) — **Vintage:** The gathered crop of grapes. [freq. 7] |kjv: vintage| {str: 1210}

c^m) ᚾΥ○∿ש (בצור B-TsWR) — **Vintage:** The gathered crop of grapes. [freq. 1] |kjv: vintage| {str: 1208}

c^{f2}) †ᚾΥ○∿ש (בצורת B-TsW-RT) — **Drought:** A time of storing up water. [ms: בצרת] [freq. 2] |kjv: dearth, drought| {str: 1226}

h^m) ᚾ○∿שᛗᛗ (מבצר MB-TsR) — **Fence:** A walled place of protection.

[freq. 37] |kjv: hold, fenced, fortress, defenced, strong| {str: 4013}

ej^m) ᛚΥᚾ○∿ᛋ⊃ש (ביצרון BY-Ts-RWN) — **Stronghold:** A walled place of protection. [ms: בצרון] [freq. 1] |kjv: strong hold| {str: 1225}

~~~~~~~~~

2034) ⊂○-●-ᛚש (בקע BQAh) ac: **Cleave** co: **Half** ab: ?: A breaking or cleaving of something in half.

V) ⊂○-●-ᛚש (בקע B-QAh) — **Cleave:** To break, cut or divide something in half. [freq. 51] (vf: Paal, Niphal, Hiphil, Hitpael, Hophal, Pual, Piel) |kjv: cleave, divide, rent, break through, breach, hatch| {str: 1234}

N^m) ⊂○-●-ᛚש (בקע B-QAh) — **Bekah:** A standard of measure. A half shekel weight. [freq. 2] |kjv: half, bekah| {str: 1235}

b^m) ⊂○⊢●-ᛚש (בקיע B-QYAh) — **Fissure:** A breach causing a division. [freq. 2] |kjv: breach, cleft| {str: 1233}

e^{f1}) ¥⊂○-●-⊢ᛚש (ביקעה BYQ-AhH) — **Valley:** A wide level valley as a division between mountains. [Hebrew and Aramaic] [df: בקעה] [ar: בקעא] [freq. 21] |kjv: plain, valley| {str: 1236, 1237}

~~~~~~~~~

2035) ᚾ●-ᛚש (בקר BQR) ac: **Plow** co: **Cattle** ab: ?: The breaking open of the ground with a plow pulled by oxen. [from: ᚾ⊂ - as a breaking] (eng: buckaroo - from the Spanish vaquero)

N^m) ᚾ●-ᛚש (בקר B-QR) — **Cattle:** Strong beasts used to break the soil with plows. [freq. 182] |kjv: ox, herd, beeves, young, bullock| {str: 1241}

g^m) בוקר (בוקר BW-QR) — **I. Herdsman:** One who works with cattle. **II. Morning:** The breaking of daylight. [freq. 205] |kjv: herdsman, morning, morrow, day, early| {str: 951, 1242}

2036) בקש (בקש BQSh) ac: **Seek** co: **?** ab: **?:** A search for something or for answers. [from: ●—<]

V) בקש (בקש B-QSh) — **Seek:** [freq. 225] (vf: Pual, Piel) |kjv: seek, require, request, enquire| {str: 1245}

N^fl) בקשה (בקשה BQ-ShH) — **Request:** [freq. 8] |kjv: request| {str: 1246}

2037) ברד (ברד BRD) ac: **Hail** co: **Hailstones** ab: **?**

V) ברד (ברד B-RD) — **Hail:** [freq. 1] (vf: Paal) |kjv: hail| {str: 1258}

N^m) ברד (ברד B-RD) — **Hailstone:** [freq. 29] |kjv: hail| {str: 1259}

c^m) ברוד (ברוד B-RWD) — **Spotted:** An animal with white spots which appear as hailstones. [ms: ברד] [freq. 4] |kjv: grisled| {str: 1261}

2038) ברח (ברח BRHh) ac: **Flee** co: **Fugitive** ab: **?**

V) ברח (ברח B-RHh) — **Flee:** [freq. 65] (vf: Paal, Hiphil) |kjv: ee, chase, fain, flight, haste, reach, shoot| {str: 1272}

b^m) בריח (בריח B-RYHh) — **I. Fugitive:** [ms: ברח] **II. Bar:** Round rods used in gates or doors as well as

a prison. **III. Piercing:** As a rod that pierces a slot. [ms: ברח] [freq. 44] |kjv: bar, fugitive, crooked, piercing, noble| {str: 1280, 1281}

h^m) מברח (מברח MB-RHh) — **Fugitive:** [freq. 1] |kjv: fugitive| {str: 4015}

2039) ברך (ברך BRK) ac: **Kneel** co: **Knee** ab: **Bless:** The bending at the knee to drink from a pond or present a gift. [from: בר - as a filling with a gift; with the letter kaph, the full meaning being "to fill the palm".]

V) ברך (ברך B-RK) — **Kneel:** To bend the knee to kneel in homage or to drink water. Also the extended idea of presenting a gift or giving honor to another. [Hebrew and Aramaic] [freq. 335] (vf: Paal, Niphal, Hiphil, Hitpael, Pual, Piel, Participle) |kjv: bless, salute, curse, blaspheme, praise, kneel, congratulate| {str: 1288, 1289}

N^f) ברך (ברך B-RK) — **Knee:** [Hebrew and Aramaic] [freq. 26] |kjv: knee| {str: 1290, 1291}

N^fl) ברכה (ברכה BR-KH) — **I. Pool:** A place where one kneels down to drink. **II. Gift:** What is brought with bended knee. **III. Bless:** In the sense of bringing a gift on bended knee. [freq. 86] |kjv: blessing, blessed, present, liberal, pool| {str: 1293, 1295}

n^m) אברך (אברך AB-RK) — **Kneeling:** [freq. 1] |kjv: knee| {str: 86}

2040) ברם (ברם BRM) ac: **Twist** co: **Weave** ab: **?:** The twisting of fibers together to make cords or fabrics.

N^m) ᴍᴧᴧᴗ (ברם B-RM) —
However: A weaving of a thought.
[Aramaic only] [freq. 5] |kjv: but,
yet, nevertheless| {str: 1297}

c^m) ᴍᴧYᴧᴗ (ברום B-RWM) —
Finery: A finely woven garment.
[freq. 1] |kjv: rich apparel| {str:
1264}

~~~~~~~~~

2041) ◦ᴧᴗ (ברק BRQ) ac: **Thrust** co:
Sword ab: **?:** The shining flash of a
sword as it is thrust. [from: ᴧᴗ - being
bright]

V) ◦ᴧᴗ (ברק B-RQ) — **Thrust:**
To thrust a sword or throw lightning
bolts. [freq. 1] (vf: Paal) |kjv: cast|
{str: 1299}

N^m) ◦ᴧᴗ (ברק B-RQ) — **Sword:**
Also lightning as a sword from the
skies. [freq. 21] |kjv: lightning,
glittering, bright, glitter, sword| {str:
1300}

N^{f2}) †◦ᴧᴗ (ברקת BR-QT) —
Barqet: An unknown gem probably
from its shining. [freq. 3] |kjv:
carbuncle| {str: 1304}

m^m) ᴸ◦ᴧᴗ (ברקן BR-QN) —
Brier: As a sharp sword. [freq. 2]
|kjv: brier| {str: 1303}

~~~~~~~~~

2042) ᴜᴜᴧᴗ (ברש BRSh) ac: **?** co:
Cypress ab: **?:** [from: ᴧᴗ - as a choice
wood]

c^m) ᴜᴜYᴧᴗ (ברוש B-RWSh) —
Cypress: The tree or the wood. [df:
ברות] [freq. 21] |kjv: fir| {str: 1265,
1266}

~~~~~~~~~

2043) ᴗᴜᴜᴜᴗ (בשל BShL) ac: **Boil** co:
Meat ab: **?:** The boiling of meat over a
fire.

V) ᴗᴜᴜᴜᴗ (בשל B-ShL) — **I. Boil:**
To boil a meat in water. **II. Ripe:**
[freq. 28] (vf: Paal, Hiphil, Pual,
Piel) |kjv: seethe, boil, sod, bake,
ripe, roast| {str: 1310}

N^m) ᴗᴜᴜᴜᴗ (בשל B-ShL) — **Boiled:**
A meat that has been boiled in water.
[freq. 2] |kjv: sodden| {str: 1311}

k^{f1}) ℀ᴗᴜᴜᴜᴗᴍ (מבשלה MB-Sh-LH)
— **Hearth:** A place for boiling.
[freq. 1] |kjv: boiling place| {str:
4018}

~~~~~~~~~

2044) ᴗᴜᴜᴜᴗ (בשש BShS) ac: **Trample**
co: **?** ab: **?:** [from: ᴗᴗ]

V) ᴗᴜᴜᴜᴗ (בשש B-ShS) — **Trample:**
[freq. 1] (vf: Piel) |kjv: tread| {str:
1318}

~~~~~~~~~

2045) ᴗᴛᴗ (בתל BTL) ac: **?** co: **Virgin**
ab: **?:** [from: ᴗᴗ - as virgin loins]

d^f) ᴗYᴛᴗ (בתול B-TWL) —
Virginity: [Always used in the
masculine plural form] [freq. 10]
|kjv: virginity| {str: 1331}

d^{f1}) ℀ᴗYᴛᴗ (בתולה B-TW-LH) —
Virgin: [freq. 50] |kjv: virgin, maid,
maiden| {str: 1330}

~~~~~~~~~

2046) ◦ᴛᴗ (בתק BTQ) ac: **Cut** co: **?**
ab: **?:** A cutting into pieces. [from: ᴗᴗ]

V) ◦ᴛᴗ (בתק B-TQ) — **Cut:** [freq.
1] (vf: Piel) |kjv: thrust| {str: 1333}

~~~~~~~~~

2047) מתֿר‎ (בתר‎ BTR) ac: **Cut** co: **?** ab: **?**: A cutting into two pieces. [from: ⊗מ‎]

V) מתֿר‎ (בתר‎ B-TR) — **Cut:** [freq. 2] (vf: Paal, Piel) |kjv: divide| {str: 1334}

N^m) מתֿר‎ (בתר‎ B-TR) — **Piece:** [freq. 3] |kjv: piece, part| {str: 1335}

Gam

2048) ᒪᒉᒻᑌᒻ (גבח GBHh) ac: ? co: **Bald** ab: ?: A bald forehead. [from: ᒪᒉ - being high in the forehead]

N^{f2}) †ᒪᒉᒻᑌᒻ (גבחת GB-HhT) — **Bald:** [freq. 4] |kjv: bald| {str: 1372}

e^m) ᒪᒉᒻᐳᒻᒪ (גיבח GY-BHh) — **Bald:** [ms: גבח] [freq. 1] |kjv: bald| {str: 1371}

2049) ᒍᒻᑌᒻ (גבל GBL) ac: **Bound** co: **Boundary** ab: ?: The edge or ends of a region. Borders were often defined by a coastline or a landmark. [from: ᒍᒪ - as being around a land]

V) ᒍᒻᑌᒻ (גבל G-BL) — **Bound:** To set a border. [freq. 5] (vf: Paal, Hiphil) |kjv: border, bound, set| {str: 1379}

N^{f3}) †ᕁᒍᒻᑌᒻ (גבלות GB-LWT) — **End:** As a boundary. [freq. 2] |kjv: end| {str: 1383}

d^m) ᒍᐣᑌᒻ (גבול G-BWL) — **Border:** [ms: גבל] [freq. 241] |kjv: border, coast, bound, landmark, space, limit, quarter| {str: 1366}

d^{f1}) ⵤᒍᐣᑌᒻ (גבולה G-BW-LH) — **Border:** [ms: גבלה] [freq. 10] |kjv: coast, bounds, place, border, landmark| {str: 1367}

h^{f1}) ⵤᒍᒻᑌᒻᒻ (מגבלה MG-B-LH) — **End:** As a boundary. [freq. 1] |kjv: end| {str: 4020}

2050) ᒻᑌᒻ (גבן GBN) ac: ? co: **Lump** ab: ?: [from: ᒪᒉ - as a back bent over]

b^{f1}) ⵤᐳᒻᑌᒻ (גבינה G-BY-NH) — **Cheese:** From the lumps formed out of the milk. [ms: גבנה] [freq. 1] |kjv: cheese| {str: 1385}

e^m) ᒻᑌᐳᒻᒪ (גיבן GY-BN) — **Hunchback:** As a lump of the back. [ms: גבן] [freq. 1] |kjv: crookbackt| {str: 1384}

m^m) ᒻᒻᑌᒻ (גבנן GB-NN) — **Lump:** The hump of a hill. [freq. 2] |kjv: high| {str: 1386}

2051) ᒻᐢᑌᒻ (גבע GBAh) ac: ? co: **Hill** ab: ?: [from: ᒪᒉ]

N^{f1}) ⵤᒻᐢᑌᒻ (גבעה GB-AhH) — **Hill:** [freq. 69] |kjv: hill| {str: 1389}

b^m) ᒻᐢᐳᒻᑌᒻ (גביע G-BYAh) — **Bowl:** As with high sides. [freq. 14] |kjv: bowl, cup, pot| {str: 1375}

hb^{f2}) †ᒻᐢᐳᒻᑌᒻᒻ (מגביעת MG-BY-AhT) — **Turban:** As high on the head. [freq. 4] |kjv: bonnet| {str: 4021}

2052) ᒉᑌᒻ (גבר GBR) ac: **Prevail** co: **Warrior** ab: ?: One of great strength (warrior) or authority (master). [from: ᒉᑌ - great strength]

V) ᒉᑌᒻ (גבר G-BR) — **Prevail:** To be successful in strength or authority. [freq. 25] (vf: Paal, Hiphil, Hitpael, Piel) |kjv: prevail, strengthen, great, confirm, exceed, mighty, put, strong, valiant| {str: 1396}

N^m) ᒉᑌᒻ (גבר G-BR) — **Warrior:** One of great strength (warrior) or authority (master). [freq. 90] |kjv: man, mighty, every| {str: 1397, 1399, 1400}

N^(f2)) †ᴀ̃ᴸoᴸ (גברת GB-RT) — **Mistress:** [freq. 9] |kjv: mistress, lady| {str: 1404}

b^m) ᴀ̃→ᴸoᴸ (גביר G-BYR) — **Master:** [freq. 2] |kjv: lord| {str: 1376}

b^(f1)) 𐤔ᴀ̃→ᴸoᴸ (גבירה G-BY-RH) — **Mistress:** [freq. 6] |kjv: queen| {str: 1377}

d^(f1)) 𐤔ᴀ̃Yoᴸ (גבורה G-BW-RH) — **Strength:** [Hebrew and Aramaic] [freq. 63] |kjv: might, strength, power, mighty, force, mastery| {str: 1369, 1370}

e^m) ᴀ̃o→ᴸ (גיבר GY-BR) — **Mighty:** [Aramaic only] [ms: גבר] [freq. 1] |kjv: mighty| {str: 1401}

ec^m) ᴀ̃Yoo→ᴸ (גיבור GY-BWR) — **Strong:** [ms: גבור] [freq. 158] |kjv: mighty, strong, valiant, upright, champion, chief, excel, giant| {str: 1368}

~~~~~~~~~

2053) ᴸᴜᴜoᴸ (גבש GBSh) ac: ? co: **Crystal** ab: ?

b^m) ᴸᴜᴜ→ᴸoᴸ (גביש G-BYSh) — **Crystal:** [freq. 1] |kjv: pearl| {str: 1378}

~~~~~~~~~

2054) ᴶ→ᴸoᴸ (גדל GDL) ac: **Magnify** co: **Rope** ab: **Magnificent:** A cord is made by twisting fibers together, the larger and more numerous the fibers, the stronger the cord will be. Anything that is large or great in size or stature. [from: oᴸ - from the twisting of sinew to make cords.] (eng: great - with the exchange and reversal of the r and l and the t and d)

V) ᴶ→ᴸoᴸ (גדל G-DL) — **Magnify:** To increase in size or ones position of honor. [freq. 115] (vf: Paal, Hiphil, Hitpael, Pual, Piel) |kjv: magnify, great, grow, nourish| {str: 1431}

N^m) ᴶ→ᴸoᴸ (גדל G-DL) — **Grow:** An increasing in size. [freq. 4] |kjv: grow, great| {str: 1432}

b^m) ᴶ→→ᴸoᴸ (גדיל G-DYL) — **Tassel:** Something that is made from twisted fibers. [ms: גדל] [freq. 2] |kjv: fringe, wreath| {str: 1434}

c^m) ᴶYoᴸ (גדול G-DWL) — **Magnificent:** Something with increased size, power or authority. [freq. 529] |kjv: great, high, loud, elder, mighty| {str: 1419}

d^(f1)) 𐤔ᴶYoᴸ (גדולה G-DW-LH) — **Magnificence:** An increase in size power or authority. [ms: גדלה] [freq. 12] |kjv: greatness, great, majesty, dignity| {str: 1420}

g^m) ᴶoYᴸ (גודל GW-DL) — **Magnificence:** An increase in size power or authority. [freq. 13] |kjv: greatness, stout, stoutness| {str: 1433}

h^m) ᴶoᴸᴀ̃ (מגדל MG-DL) — **Tower:** A place of great size. [freq. 50] |kjv: tower, castle, flower, pulpit| {str: 4026}

~~~~~~~~~

2055) ooᴸ (גדע GDAh) ac: **Cut** co: ? ab: ?: A cutting down or into pieces. [from: oᴸ]

V) ooᴸ (גדע G-DAh) — **Cut down:** [freq. 23] (vf: Paal, Niphal, Pual, Piel) |kjv: cut, down, asunder| {str: 1438}

~~~~~~~~~

2056) ᐅ�…ᒪ (גדף GDP) ac: **Taunt** co: ? ab: ?: [from: …ᒪ - a slicing]

V) ᐅ…ᒪ (גדף G-DP) — **Taunt:** [freq. 7] (vf: Piel) |kjv: blaspheme, reproach| {str: 1442}

d^fl) ᙾᐅY…ᒪ (גדופה G-DW-PH) — **Taunt:** [freq. 1] |kjv: taunt| {str: 1422}

ed^m) ᐅY…ᐅᒪ (גידוף GY-DWP) — **Taunting:** [ms: גדוף גדרף] [freq. 3] |kjv: revilings, reproaches| {str: 1421}

~~~~~~~~~~~~~

2057) ᑫᗡᒪ (גדר GDR) ac: **Enclose** co: **Wall** ab: ?: [from: ᑫᗡ - as a wall that encircles a city]

V) ᑫᗡᒪ (גדר G-DR) — **Enclose:** To enclose something in a wall or fence. [freq. 10] (vf: Paal, Participle) |kjv: make, mason, repairer, close, fence, hedge| {str: 1443}

N^m) ᑫᗡᒪ (גדר G-DR) — **Enclosure:** Any type of enclosure. [freq. 14] |kjv: wall, hedge, fence| {str: 1444, 1447}

N^fl) ᙾᑫᗡᒪ (גדרה GD-RH) — **Enclosure:** Any type of enclosure. [freq. 10] |kjv: hedge, fold, wall, sheepfold, sheepcote| {str: 1448}

~~~~~~~~~~~~~

2058) ᥐᗡᒪ (גדש GDSh) ac: ? co: **Mound** ab: ?

b^m) ᥐᐅᗡᒪ (גדיש G-DYSh) — **Mound:** A pile of grain or dirt. [freq. 4] |kjv: shock, stack, tomb| {str: 1430}

~~~~~~~~~~~~~

2059) ᑊᗴᒪ (גזל GZL) ac: **Pluck** co: **Feather** ab: ?: The plucking of feathers from a bird. [from: ᗴᒪ - a plucking as a sheering]

V) ᑊᗴᒪ (גזל G-ZL) — **Pluck:** To take off something or someone by force through plucking, robbing or plundering. [freq. 30] (vf: Paal, Niphal) |kjv: spoil, take, rob, pluck, caught, consume, exercise, force, torn, violence| {str: 1497}

N^m) ᑊᗴᒪ (גזל G-ZL) — **Plucking:** [freq. 6] |kjv: robbery, taken| {str: 1498, 1499}

N^fl) ᙾᑊᗴᒪ (גזלה GZ-LH) — **Plucked:** [freq. 6] |kjv: violence, robbed, that| {str: 1500}

g^m) ᑊᗴYᒪ (גוזל GW-ZL) — **Young pigeon:** A young featherless bird as plucked. [ms: גזל] [freq. 2] |kjv: pigeon, young| {str: 1469}

~~~~~~~~~~~~~

2060) ᗱᗴᒪ (גזם GZM) ac: **Devour** co: **Caterpillar** ab: ?: [from: ᗴᒪ - sheering the crop]

N^m) ᗱᗴᒪ (גזם G-ZM) — **Caterpillar:** An unknown species that devours crops. [freq. 3] |kjv: palmerworm| {str: 1501}

~~~~~~~~~~~~~

2061) ᑫᗴᒪ (גזר GZR) ac: **Cut** co: **Axe** ab: ?: A cutting or separation into two or more pieces. [from: ᗴᒪ - cutting]

V) ᑫᗴᒪ (גזר G-ZR) — **Cut:** To separate by cutting or removing. [Hebrew and Aramaic] [freq. 19] (vf: Paal, Niphal, Participle) |kjv: cut, divide, decree, snatch| {str: 1504, 1505}

N^m) ᑫᗴᒪ (גזר G-ZR) — **Piece:** [freq. 2] |kjv: piece, part| {str: 1506}

N^{fl}) 𐤔𐤓𐤋 (גזרה GZ-RH) — **I. Uninhabited:** A place cut off. **II. Decree:** [Unknown connection to rootAramaic only] [freq. 3] |kjv: inhabited, decree| {str: 1509, 1510}

a^{fl}) 𐤔𐤓𐤋𐤌 (מגזרה MG-Z-RH) — **Axe:** What is used to cut something in half. [freq. 1] |kjv: axe| {str: 4037}

e^{fl}) 𐤔𐤓𐤋 (גיזרה GYZ-RH) — **Opposite:** The place separate from an adjacent place. [ms: גזרה] [freq. 8] |kjv: separate, polishing| {str: 1508}

~~~~~~~~

2062) 𐤋𐤇𐤍 (נחל GHhL) ac: ? co: **Ember** ab: ?: A kindled glowing ember. [from: 𐤇𐤍 - making a fire from an ember]

N^f) 𐤋𐤇𐤍 (נחל G-HhL) — **Ember:** [freq. 18] |kjv: coal| {str: 1513}

~~~~~~~~

2063) 𐤋𐤁𐤂 (גלב GLB) ac: **Shave** co: **Barber** ab: ?: [from: 𐤋𐤂 - going around the head]

N^m) 𐤋𐤁𐤂 (גלב G-LB) — **Barber:** [freq. 1] |kjv: barber| {str: 1532}

~~~~~~~~

2064) 𐤋𐤃𐤂 (גלד GLD) ac: ? co: **Skin** ab: ?: [from: 𐤋𐤂 - going around the body]

N^m) 𐤋𐤃𐤂 (גלד G-LD) — **Skin:** [freq. 1] |kjv: skin| {str: 1539}

~~~~~~~~

2065) 𐤋𐤇𐤂 (גלח GLHh) ac: **Shave** co: ? ab: ?: [from: 𐤋𐤂 - going around the head]

V) 𐤋𐤇𐤂 (גלח G-LHh) — **Shave:** [freq. 23] (vf: Hitpael, Pual, Piel) |kjv: shave| {str: 1548}

~~~~~~~~

2066) 𐤋𐤌𐤂 (גלם GLM) ac: **Wrap** co: ? ab: ?: [from: 𐤋𐤂 - being wrapped around]

V) 𐤋𐤌𐤂 (גלם G-LM) — **Wrap:** [freq. 1] (vf: Paal) |kjv: wrap| {str: 1563}

c^m) 𐤋𐤅𐤌𐤂 (גלום G-LWM) — **Wrapping:** A piece of clothing wrapped around the body. [freq. 1] |kjv: clothes| {str: 1545}

g^m) 𐤋𐤅𐤌𐤂 (גולם GW-LM) — **Infant:** As wrapped around by the womb. [ms: גלם] [freq. 1] |kjv: unformed| {str: 1564}

~~~~~~~~

2067) 𐤋𐤏𐤂 (גלע GLAh) ac: **Quarrel** co: ? ab: ?

V) 𐤋𐤏𐤂 (גלע G-LAh) — **Quarrel:** [freq. 3] (vf: Hitpael) |kjv: meddle| {str: 1566}

~~~~~~~~

2068) 𐤋𐤔𐤂 (גלש GLSh) ac: **Appear** co: ? ab: ?

V) 𐤋𐤔𐤂 (גלש G-LSh) — **Appear:** To come into sight. [freq. 2] (vf: Paal) |kjv: appear| {str: 1570}

~~~~~~~~

2069) 𐤃𐤌𐤂 (גמד GMD) ac: ? co: ? ab: ?

N^m) 𐤃𐤌𐤂 (גמד G-MD) — **Gomed:** A standard of measure. [ms: גמד] [freq. 1] |kjv: cubit| {str: 1574}

~~~~~~~~

2070) 𐤋𐤌𐤂 (גמל GML) ac: **Yield** co: ? ab: ?: The ripening of a crop or the weaning of a child as one now able to yield work. Also, the yielding of good or evil as a reward. [from: 𐤌𐤂 - a gathering of the yield] (eng: camel)

V) ᎜ᎷᏝᏝ (גמל G-ML) — **Yield:** To produce or be productive. [freq. 37] (vf: Paal, Niphal) |kjv: wean, reward, bountifully, do, bestow| {str: 1580}

N^(m/f)) ᎜ᎷᏝᏝ (גמל G-ML) — **Camel:** The produce of the fields were tied in large bundles and transported on camels. [Also related in meaning to the original parent root ᎷᏝᏝ as one who gathers at the watering hole] [freq. 54] |kjv: camel| {str: 1581}

d^(m)) ᎜ᎩᎷᏝᏝ (גמול G-MWL) — **Yielding:** The production of a product as a benefit or reward. [freq. 19] |kjv: recompense, reward, benefit, give, deserve| {str: 1576}

d^(fl)) ᵠ᎜ᎩᎷᏝᏝ (גמולה G-MW-LH) — **Yielding:** The production of a product as a benefit or reward. [freq. 3] |kjv: recompense, deed, reward| {str: 1578}

id^(m)) ᎜ᎩᎷᏝᏝᏦ (תגמול TG-MWL) — **Yield:** The production of a product as a benefit or reward. [freq. 1] |kjv: benefit| {str: 8408}

2071) ᎠᎷᎷᏝᏝ (גמץ GMTs) ac: **Dig** co: **Pit** ab: **?**

o^(m)) ᎠᎷᎷᎩᏝᏝ (גומץ GW-MTs) — **Pit:** [freq. 1] |kjv: pit| {str: 1475}

2072) ᏣᎷᎷᏝᏝ (גמר GMR) ac: **Complete** co: **?** ab: **?:** A coming to an end in perfection or failure.

V) ᏣᎷᎷᏝᏝ (גמר G-MR) — **Complete:** [Hebrew and Aramaic] [freq. 6] (vf: Paal) |kjv: cease, fail, end, perfect, perform| {str: 1584, 1585}

2073) ᏠᎥᏝᏝ (גנב GNB) ac: **Steal** co: **Thief** ab: **Theft:** [from: ᏝᏝ - what a garden is protected from]

V) ᏠᎥᏝᏝ (גנב G-NB) — **Steal:** [freq. 39] (vf: Paal, Niphal, Hitpael, Pual, Piel) |kjv: steal, carry, brought| {str: 1589}

N^(m)) ᏠᎥᏝᏝ (גנב G-NB) — **Thief:** [freq. 17] |kjv: thief| {str: 1590}

N^(fl)) ᵠᏠᎥᏝᏝ (גנבה GN-BH) — **Theft:** [freq. 2] |kjv: theft| {str: 1591}

2074) ᏣᎥᏝᏝ (גנז GNZ) ac: **Store** co: **Treasure** ab: **?:** A treasury stored away. [from: ᏝᏝ - as a place protected]

N^(m)) ᏣᎥᏝᏝ (גנז G-NZ) — **Treasury:** [Hebrew and Aramaic] [freq. 6] |kjv: treasury, chest, treasure| {str: 1595, 1596}

2075) ᎜ᏳᏝᏝ (געל GAhL) ac: **Cast away** co: **?** ab: **Detest**

V) ᎜ᏳᏝᏝ (געל G-AhL) — **Cast away:** [freq. 10] (vf: Paal, Niphal, Hiphil) |kjv: abhor, lothe, cast away, fail| {str: 1602}

N^(m)) ᎜ᏳᏝᏝ (געל G-AhL) — **Detesting:** [freq. 1] |kjv: loathe| {str: 1604}

2076) ᏁᏳᏝᏝ (גער GAhR) ac: **Rebuke** co: **?** ab: **?**

V) ᏁᏳᏝᏝ (גער G-AhR) — **Rebuke:** [freq. 14] (vf: Paal) |kjv: rebuke, corrupt, reprove| {str: 1605}

N^(fl)) ᵠᏁᏳᏝᏝ (גערה GAh-RH) — **Rebuke:** [freq. 15] |kjv: rebuke, reproof| {str: 1606} h[f2]) (מגערת MG-Ah-RT) — **Rebuke:** [freq. 1] |kjv: rebuke| {str: 4045}

~~~~~~~~~~~

2077) (געש GAhSh) ac: **Shake** co: **?** ab: **?**

V) (געש G-AhSh) — **Shake:** [freq. 10] (vf: Paal, Hitpael, Pual) |kjv: shake, move, trouble, toss| {str: 1607}

~~~~~~~~~~~

2078) (גפן GPN) ac: **Bend** co: **Grapevine** ab: **?:** The vines of the grape vine are twisted and bent as it winds around a pole. [from: - from the palm as bent]

N[m]) (גפן G-PN) — **Grapevine:** [freq. 55] |kjv: vine, tree| {str: 1612}

~~~~~~~~~~~

2079) (גפר GPR) ac: **Burn** co: **Brimstone** ab: **?**

N[m]) (גפר G-PR) — **Gopher:** Wood from an unknown tree. [freq. 1] |kjv: gopher| {str: 1613}

N[f4]) (גפרית GP-RYT) — **Brimstone:** A rock of sulfur that burns. [freq. 7] |kjv: brimstone| {str: 1614}

~~~~~~~~~~~

2080) (גרב GRB) ac: **Scratch** co: **Itch** ab: **?:** [from:] (eng: scrape - with the exchange of the p and b)

N[m]) (גרב G-RB) — **Itch:** [freq. 3] |kjv: scurvy, scab| {str: 1618}

~~~~~~~~~~~

2081) (גרד GRD) ac: **Scrape** co: **?** ab: **?:** [from: - as in scratching]

V) (גרד G-RD) — **Scrape:** [freq. 1] (vf: Hitpael) |kjv: scrape| {str: 1623}

~~~~~~~~~~~

2082) (גרז GRZ) ac: **Cut** co: **Axe** ab: **?:** [from:]

V) (גרז G-RZ) — **Cut off:** [freq. 1] (vf: Niphal) |kjv: cut off| {str: 1629}

m[m]) (גרזן GR-ZN) — **Axe:** [freq. 4] |kjv: axe| {str: 1631}

~~~~~~~~~~~

2083) (גרל GRL) ac: **Rough** co: **Stone** ab: **?:** An abrasive stone for scratching or sanding. [from: - scratching]

N[m]) (גרל G-RL) — **Rough:** Rough like a stone. [freq. 1] |kjv: great| {str: 1632}

g[m]) (גורל GW-RL) — **Lot:** Colored stones are used to cast lots to determine a course of action or make a decision. [ms: גרל] [freq. 77] |kjv: lot| {str: 1486}

~~~~~~~~~~~

2084) (גרם GRM) ac: **Gnaw** co: **Bones** ab: **?:** As a dog gnaws on a bone. [from: - from the marrow inside the bones]

V) (גרם G-RM) — **Gnaw:** [freq. 3] (vf: Paal, Piel) |kjv: break, gnaw| {str: 1633}

N[m]) (גרם G-RM) — **Bones:** [Hebrew and Aramaic] [freq. 6] |kjv: bone, strong, top| {str: 1634, 1635}

~~~~~~~~~~~
~~~~~~~~~~~

2085) ᒪᕲᒪ (גרן GRN) ac: ? co: **Floor** ab: ?: The smooth level floor for grains, either a barn or threshing floor. [from: ᕲᒪ]

g^m) ᒪᕲᕈᒪ (גורן GW-RN) — **Floor:** The floor of a barn or threshing floor. [ms: גרן] [freq. 36] |kjv: threshingfloor, floor, place, barn, barnfloor, corn| {str: 1637}

2086) ᕬᕲᒪ (גרס GRS) ac: **Crush** co: ? ab: ?: The crushing of grain in a mill to make meal. [from: ᕲᒪ]

V) ᕬᕲᒪ (גרס G-RS) — **Crush:** To be crushed as grain to make a meal. [freq. 2] (vf: Paal, Hiphil) |kjv: break| {str: 1638}

N^m) ᕬᕲᒪ (גרס G-RS) — **Crushed:** Grain that is crushed to make meal. [freq. 2] |kjv: beaten| {str: 1643}

2087) ᐁᕲᒪ (גרע GRAh) ac: **Diminish** co: **Ledge** ab: ?: Something made small through removal. [from: ᕲᒪ]

V) ᐁᕲᒪ (גרע G-RAh) — **Diminish:** To be made less through removal. [freq. 21] (vf: Paal, Niphal, Piel) |kjv: diminish, take, away, restrain, abate, back, minish, small, withdraw| {str: 1639}

h^{fl}) ᛘᐁᕲᒪᗯ (מגרעה MG-R-AhH) — **Ledge:** As diminished in size. [freq. 1] |kjv: narrowed| {str: 4052}

2088) ᐁᕲᒪ (גרף GRP) ac: **Sweep away** co: ? ab: ?: A carrying or taking away by flood or striking. [from: ᕲᒪ] (eng: grope; grapple; grab -with the exchange of the b and p)

V) ᐁᕲᒪ (גרף G-RP) — **Sweep away:** [freq. 1] (vf: Paal) |kjv: sweep away| {str: 1640}

k^{fl}) ᛘᐁᕲᒪᗯ (מגרפה MG-R-PH) — **Soil:** When the floods sweep down the land, rich soil is deposited on the land. [freq. 1] |kjv: clod| {str: 4053}

nc^m) ᐁᕮᕲᒪᕉ (אגרוף AG-RWP) — **Fist:** A sweeping away by striking. [freq. 2] |kjv: fist| {str: 106}

2089) ᒷᒷᕲᒪ (גרש GRSh) ac: **Cast out** co: **Pasture** ab: ?: The land surrounding a city was inhabited by the lower class people or outcasts. This land is also covered with pastures for raising the flocks and herds of the city. [from: ᕲᒪ] (eng: graze - with the exchange of the z and sh)

V) ᒷᒷᕲᒪ (גרש G-RSh) — **Cast out:** To drive, thrust or cast out or away. [freq. 47] (vf: Paal, Niphal, Pual, Piel) |kjv: drive, cast, thrust, put, divorce, expel, trouble| {str: 1644}

N^m) ᒷᒷᕲᒪ (גרש G-RSh) — **Pasture:** [freq. 1] |kjv: put| {str: 1645}

N^{fl}) ᛘᒷᒷᕲᒪ (גרשה GR-ShH) — **Eviction:** [freq. 1] |kjv: exaction| {str: 1646}

h^m) ᒷᒷᕲᒪᗯ (מגרש MG-RSh) — **Pasture:** [freq. 1] |kjv: suburb| {str: 4054}

h^{fl}) ᛘᒷᒷᕲᒪᗯ (מגרשה MG-R-ShH) — **Pasture:** [freq. 111] |kjv: suburb| {str: 4054}

2090) ᗯᒷᒷᒪ (גשם GShM) ac: **Rain** co: **Rain** ab: ?: [from: ᗯᒷᒷ - skies as the place of rain] (eng: gush)

V) ⵎⵍⵓⴸ (נשם G-ShM) — **Rain:** [freq. 1] (vf: Hiphil, Pual) |kjv: rain| {str: 1652}

N^m) ⵎⵍⵓⴸ (נשם G-ShM) — **I. Rain: II. Body:** [Unknown connection to rootAramaic only] [freq. 40] |kjv: rain, shower, body| {str: 1653, 1655}

g^m) ⵎⵍⵓⵢⴸ (נושם GW-ShM) — **Rained:** [ms: נגשם] [freq. 1] |kjv: rained| {str: 1656}

Dal

2091) ⅃⌂⌐ (דבל DBL) ac: **Press** co: **Cake** ab: **?**

N^(fl)) ⅃⌂⌐ (דבלה DB-LH) — **Cake:** A cake of pressed figs. [freq. 5] |kjv: cake, lump| {str: 1690}

~~~~~~~~~~

2092) ⌂⌐ (דבק DBQ) ac: **Adhere** co: **Fastener** ab: **?**

V) ⌂⌐ (דבק D-BQ) — **Adhere:** To join or stick to someone or something. [Hebrew and Aramaic] [freq. 55] (vf: Paal, Hiphil, Hophal, Pual) |kjv: cleave, follow, overtake, stick, keep, abide, close, join, pursue| {str: 1692, 1693}

N^(m)) ⌂⌐ (דבק D-BQ) — **Fastener:** What joins together. [freq. 6] |kjv: joint, soldering, cleave, join, stick| {str: 1694, 1695}

~~~~~~~~~~

2093) ⌂⌐ (דבר DBR) ac: **Order** co: **Word** ab: **?:** An arrangement or placement of something creating order. [from: ⌐ - order]

V) ⌂⌐ (דבר D-BR) — **Speak:** A careful arrangement of words or commands. [freq. 1488] (vf: Paal, Niphal, Hiphil, Hitpael, Pual, Piel) |kjv: speak, say, talk, promise, tell, commune, pronounce, utter, command| {str: 1696}

N^(m)) ⌂⌐ (דבר D-BR) — **I. Word:** An arrangement of words. **II. Thing:** As something that is arranged. In Hebrew thought words contain substance just as physical objects do. **III. Plague:** The re-ordering of a population. [freq. 49] |kjv: word, thing, matter, act, chronicle, saying, commandment, pestilence, plague, murrain| {str: 1697, 1698}

N^(fl)) ⌂⌐ (דברה DB-RH) — **Word:** An arrangement of words. [freq. 1] |kjv: word| {str: 1703}

b^(m)) ⌂⌐ (דביר D-BYR) — **Sanctuary:** A place of order. [ms: דבר] [freq. 16] |kjv: oracle| {str: 1687}

c^(fl)) ⌂⌐ (דבורה D-BW-RH) — **Bee:** A colony of ordered insects. [ms: דברה] [freq. 4] |kjv: bee| {str: 1682}

e^(fl)) ⌂⌐ (דיברה DYB-RH) — **Order:** [Hebrew and Aramaic] [ms: דברה] [freq. 7] |kjv: cause, order, estate, end, regard, sake, intent| {str: 1700, 1701}

g^(m)) ⌂⌐ (דובר DW-BR) — **I. Wilderness:** A place of order, a sanctuary. [ms: דבר] **II. Manner:** The order which something is performed. [freq. 2] |kjv: manner, fold| {str: 1699}

h^(m)) ⌂⌐מ (מדבר MD-BR) — **I. Wilderness:** A place of order, a sanctuary. **II. Speech:** An arrangement of words. [freq. 271] |kjv: wilderness, desert, south, speech| {str: 4057}

~~~~~~~~~~

2094) ⌂⌐ (דבש DBSh) ac: **?** co: **Honey** ab: **?:** A thick, sticky substance such as dates or honey. [from: ⌐ - a slow moving substance]

320

N[m]) (דבש D-BSh) — **Honey:** Also dates as thick sticky and sweet food. [freq. 54] |kjv: honey| {str: 1706}

N[f2]) (דבשת DB-ShT) — **Hump:** The hump of a camel as a sticky mass. [freq. 1] |kjv: bunch| {str: 1707}

~~~~~~~~~~~~

2095) (דגל DGL) ac: **Stand** co: **Standard** ab: **?:** An identification banner used by an army that is hung high on a pole.

V) (דגל D-GL) — **Stand:** To raise up a standard. [freq. 4] (vf: Paal, Niphal, Participle) |kjv: banner| {str: 1713}

N[m]) (דגל D-GL) — **Standard:** [freq. 14] |kjv: standard, banner| {str: 1714}

~~~~~~~~~~~~

2096) (דגר DGR) ac: **Brood** co: **?** ab: **?:** The brooding of a hen which gathers the eggs under her and sits on them.

V) (דגר D-GR) — **Brood:** [freq. 2] (vf: Paal) |kjv: gather, sit| {str: 1716}

~~~~~~~~~~~~

2097) (דחן DHhN) ac: **?** co: **?** ab: **?**

g[m]) (דוחן DW-HhN) — **Millet:** A type of grain. [ms: דחן] [freq. 1] |kjv: millet| {str: 1764}

~~~~~~~~~~~~

2098) (דחף DHhP) ac: **Push** co: **?** ab: **?:** [from:] [Also see]

V) (דחף D-HhP) — **Press:** [freq. 4] (vf: Paal, Niphal) |kjv: hasten, press| {str: 1765}

a[f1]) (מדחפה MD-Hh-PH) — **Pushing:** [freq. 1] |kjv: overthrow| {str: 4073}

~~~~~~~~~~~~

2099) (דחק DHhQ) ac: **Push** co: **?** ab: **?:** [from:]

V) (דחק D-HhQ) — **Push:** [freq. 2] (vf: Paal) |kjv: thrust, vex| {str: 1766}

~~~~~~~~~~~~

2100) (דכף DKP) ac: **?** co: **?** ab: **?**

ob[f2]) (דוכיפת DW-KY-PT) — **Grouse:** [freq. 2] |kjv: lapwing| {str: 1744}

~~~~~~~~~~~~

2101) (דלג DLG) ac: **Leap** co: **?** ab: **?:** [from:]

V) (דלג D-LG) — **Leap:** [freq. 5] (vf: Paal, Piel) |kjv: leap| {str: 1801}

~~~~~~~~~~~~

2102) (דלח DLHh) ac: **Disturb** co: **?** ab: **?:** The disturbing of water by walking or splashing through it.

V) (דלח D-LHh) — **Disturb:** To stir up waters. [freq. 3] (vf: Paal) |kjv: trouble| {str: 1804}

~~~~~~~~~~~~

2103) (דלף DLP) ac: **Drip** co: **Drop** ab: **?:** (eng: drip - with the exchange of the r and l)
~~~~~~~~~~~~

V) ⌒∪ד (דְלְף D-LP) — **Drip:** [freq. 3] (vf: Paal) |kjv: pour, melt, crop| {str: 1811}

N^m) ⌒∪ד (דְלֶף D-LP) — **Drip:** [freq. 2] |kjv: dropping| {str: 1812}

~~~~~~~~~

2104) •∪ד (דלק DLQ) ac: **Inflame** co: ? ab: ?: The building heat of a fire or passion.

V) •∪ד (דלק D-LQ) — **Inflame:** [Hebrew and Aramaic] [freq. 10] (vf: Paal, Hiphil) |kjv: pursue, kindle, chase, persecute, persecutor, inflame| {str: 1814, 1815}

N^{f2}) †•∪ד (דלקת DL-QT) — **Inflammation:** [freq. 1] |kjv: inflammation| {str: 1816}

~~~~~~~~~

2105) ᒻᴍד (דמן DMN) ac: ? co: **Manure** ab: ?: The dung of livestock was placed in a pit and mixed with straw. It was then dried in bricks and used as fuel for fires.

a^{f1}) ✲ᒻᴍדᴍ (מדמנה MD-M-NH) — **Manure pit:** [freq. 1] |kjv: dunghill| {str: 4087}

g^m) ᒻᴍYד (דומן DW-MN) — **Manure:** The droppings of livestock in the field. [ms: דמן] [freq. 6] |kjv: dung| {str: 1828}

~~~~~~~~~

2106) ⌒ᴍד (דמע DMAh) ac: **Weep** co: **Tear** ab: ?: The weeping of the eyes. The juice of the grape or other fruit that seeps out. [from: ᴍד - as blood and combined with the letter ayin forming the meaning "blood of the eye"]

V) ⌒ᴍד (דמע D-MAh) — **Weep:** The seeping of tears from the eye. [freq. 2] (vf: Paal) |kjv: weep, sore| {str: 1830}

N^m) ⌒ᴍד (דמע D-MAh) — **Juice:** The liquid that seeps out of the fruit. [freq. 1] |kjv: liquor| {str: 1831}

e^{f1}) ✲⌒ᴍ≻ד (דימעה DYM-AhH) — **Weeping:** [ms: דמעה] [freq. 23] |kjv: tears| {str: 1832}

~~~~~~~~~

2107) ᒪ≻ד (דנג DNG) ac: **Melt** co: **Wax** ab: ?

g^m) ᒪᎩY⌐ד (דונג DW-NG) — **Wax:** [freq. 4] |kjv: wax| {str: 1749}

~~~~~~~~~

2108) �𐊡⌒ד (דעך DAhK) ac: **Extinguish** co: ? ab: ?: [from: ᗐ]

V) ᒚ⌒ד (דעך D-AhK) — **Extinguish:** To put out a flame. [freq. 9] (vf: Paal, Niphal, Pual) |kjv: put out, extinct, consume, quench| {str: 1846}

~~~~~~~~~

2109) •⌒○ד (דפק DPQ) ac: **Knock** co: ? ab: ?: As a knocking at a door.

V) •⌒○ד (דפק D-PQ) — **Knock:** [freq. 3] (vf: Paal, Hitpael) |kjv: overdrive, knock, beat| {str: 1849}

~~~~~~~~~

2110) 𐊡•ד (דקר DQR) ac: **Pierce** co: ? ab: ?: (eng: dagger - with the exchange of the g and q)

V) 𐊡•ד (דקר D-QR) — **Pierce:** To pierce through with a sword or other sharp object. [freq. 11] (vf: Paal, Niphal, Pual, Participle) |kjv: thrust, pierce, wound, strike| {str: 1856} a[fl]) (מדקרה MD-Q-RH) — **Piercing:** [freq. 1] |kjv: piercing| {str: 4094}

~~~~~~~~~~~~

2111) (דרג DRG) ac: **?** co: **?** ab: **?**

a[fl]) (מדרגה MD-R-GH) — **Cliff:** A steep place. [freq. 2] |kjv: stairs, steep| {str: 4095}

~~~~~~~~~~~~

2112) (דרך DRK) ac: **Tread** co: **Road** ab: **?:** [from: - as a path] (eng: direct; track - with the exchange of the t and d; truck - with the exchange of the t and d)

V) (דרך D-RK) — **Tread:** To take a step. A journey as a treading. The stringing of a bow is a treading as the foot is stepped over the bow and using the leg to bend it. [freq. 62] (vf: Paal, Hiphil, Participle) |kjv: tread, bend, lead, archer, come, go, treader, walk, draw, guide, shoot, thresh| {str: 1869}

N[m]) (דרך D-RK) — **Road:** A road that is walked as well as the path of life. [freq. 705] |kjv: way, toward, journey, manner| {str: 1870}

h[m]) (מדרך MD-RK) — **Step:** The distance between the feet of a step. [freq. 1] |kjv: breadth| {str: 4096}

~~~~~~~~~~~~

2113) (דרם DRM) ac: **?** co: **?** ab: **?**

c[m]) (דרום D-RWM) — **South:** [freq. 17] |kjv: south| {str: 1864}

~~~~~~~~~~~~

2114) (דרש DRSh) ac: **Seek** co: **?** ab: **Commentary**

V) (דרש D-RSh) — **Seek:** To look for or search for something or for answers. [freq. 164] (vf: Paal, Niphal) |kjv: seek, enquire, require, search| {str: 1875}

h[m]) (מדרש MD-RSh) — **Commentary:** A search for the meaning of a story. [freq. 2] |kjv: story| {str: 4097}

~~~~~~~~~~~~

2115) (דשן DShN) ac: **?** co: **Fat** ab: **?:** The fat of an animal as well as the fat ashes, the ashes and fat of a burnt sacrifice mixed together.

V) (דשן D-ShN) — **Fat:** To make something fat. Also the removal of the fat ashes from the alter. [freq. 11] (vf: Paal, Pual, Piel) |kjv: fat, ash, anoint, accept| {str: 1878}

N[m]) (דשן D-ShN) — **Fat:** [freq. 18] |kjv: fat, fatness, ash| {str: 1879, 1880}

~~~~~~~~~~~~

Zan

2116) ᴅᴅᴢ (זבד ZBD) ac: **Endow** co: **Dowry** ab: ?: The presentation of a price for a bride. [from: ᴅᴢ - an acquiring of a wife as with gold]

V) ᴅᴅᴢ (זבד Z-BD) — **Endow:** To pay the price for a bride. [freq. 1] (vf: Paal) |kjv: endue| {str: 2064}

Nᵐ) ᴅᴅᴢ (זבד Z-BD) — **Dowry:** [freq. 1] |kjv: dowry| {str: 2065}

~~~~~~~~~

2117) ᴅᴅᴅᴢ (זבח ZBHh) ac: **Sacrifice** co: **Altar** ab: ?: The killing of an animal for food or sacrifice. [from: ᴅᴅᴅ]

V) ᴅᴅᴅᴢ (זבח Z-BHh) — **Sacrifice:** To kill an animal for an offering. [Hebrew and Aramaic] [ar: דבח] [freq. 135] (vf: Paal, Piel) |kjv: sacrifice, offer, kill, slay| {str: 1684, 2076}

Nᵐ) ᴅᴅᴅᴢ (זבח Z-BHh) — **Sacrifice:** An animal killed for an offering. [Hebrew and Aramaic] [ar: דבח] [freq. 163] |kjv: sacrifice, offering, offer| {str: 1685, 2077}

aᵐ) ᴅᴅᴅᴢᴧᴧ (מזבח MZ-BHh) — **Altar:** The place of sacrifice. [Aramaic only] [ar: מדבח] [freq. 1] |kjv: alter| {str: 4056}

hᵐ) ᴅᴅᴅᴢᴧᴧ (מזבח MZ-BHh) — **Altar:** The place of sacrifice. [freq. 402] |kjv: alter| {str: 4196}

~~~~~~~~~

2118) ᴊᴅᴢ (זבל ZBL) ac: **Dwell** co: **Dwelling** ab: ?: A cohabitation between a man and woman. [from: ᴅᴢ - from the purchase of a wife]

V) ᴊᴅᴢ (זבל Z-BL) — **Dwell:** [freq. 1] (vf: Paal) |kjv: dwell| {str: 2082}

dᵐ) ᴊᴛᴅᴢ (זבול Z-BWL) — **Dwelling:** [ms: זבל] [freq. 5] |kjv: habitation, dwell, dwelling| {str: 2073}

~~~~~~~~~

2119) ᴋᴅᴢ (זבן ZBN) ac: **Purchase** co: ? ab: ?: [from: ᴅᴢ - as an acquiring of something as with gold]

V) ᴋᴅᴢ (זבן Z-BN) — **Purchase:** [Aramaic only] [freq. 1] (vf: Participle) |kjv: gain| {str: 2084}

~~~~~~~~~

2120) ᴊᴅᴅᴢ (זחל ZHhL) ac: **Fear** co: ? ab: ?

V) ᴊᴅᴅᴢ (זחל Z-HhL) — **Fear:** [ar: דחל] [freq. 9] (vf: Paal, Participle) |kjv: serpent, worm, fear, dread, terrible, afraid| {str: 1763, 2119}

~~~~~~~~~

2121) ᴅᴡᴢ (זכר ZKR) ac: **Remember** co: **Male** ab: **Memorial:** A recalling of events of the past or to act upon a past event.

V) ᴅᴡᴢ (זכר Z-KR) — **Remember:** To remember in thought as a memorial or mention through speech. Also to act or speak on behalf of another. [freq. 233] (vf: Paal, Niphal, Hiphil) |kjv: remember, mention, remembrance, recorder, mindful, think, record| {str: 2142}

Nᵐ) ᕴᘺᴢ (זכר Z-KR) — **I. Memorial:** A remembering and action based on a past even. **II. Male:** The one of the family that remembers and passes down the family history through story and family name. Also the one who acts and speaks for the family. **III. Ram:** The male member of the flock. [Aramaic only] [df: דכר] [freq. 107] |kjv: male, man, child, mankind, him, ram| {str: 1798, 2143, 2145}

dᵐ) ᕴᘺᴢ (זכור Z-KWR) — **Male:** The one of the family that remembers and passes down the family history through story and family name. Also the one who acts and speaks for the family. [freq. 4] |kjv: male, man| {str: 2138}

nᶠˡ) ᕴᘺᴢᴸ (אזכרה AZ-K-RH) — **Memorial:** A remembering and action based on a past even. [freq. 7] |kjv: memorial| {str: 234}

ejᵐ) ᕴᘺᴸᴢ (זיכרון ZY-K-RWN) — **I. Memorial:** A remembering and action based on a past even. [ms: זכרון] **II. Record:** To remember something through documentation. [Hebrew and Aramaic] [df: דכרון דכרן] [freq. 27] |kjv: memorial, remembrance, record| {str: 1799, 2146}

2122) ᴸᴢ (זלג ZLG) ac: ? co: ? ab: ?

aᵐ) ᴸᴢᴹ (מזלג MZ-LG) — **Fork:** [freq. 7] |kjv: fleshhook| {str: 4207}

hᶠˡ) ᴸᴢᴹ (מזלגה MZ-L-GH) — **Fork:** [freq. 7] |kjv: fleshhook| {str: 4207}

2123) ᴹᴢ (זמן ZMN) ac: **Appoint** co: **Season** ab: ?

V) ᴹᴢ (זמן Z-MN) — **Appoint:** To set aside a time for a special occasion. [Hebrew and Aramaic] [freq. 4] (vf: Pual, Participle) |kjv: appoint, prepare| {str: 2163, 2164}

Nᵐ) ᴹᴢ (זמן Z-MN) — **Season:** A time set aside for a special occasion. [Hebrew and Aramaic] [freq. 15] |kjv: time, season| {str: 2165, 2166}

2124) ᴹᴢ (זמר ZMR) ac: **Pluck** co: **Music** ab: **Melody:** The sound from a musical instrument where the string is plucked or the singing that accompanies it. Also, the plucking of fruit from a vine or branch. [from: ᴢ - music as bright]

V) ᴹᴢ (זמר Z-MR) — **Pluck:** To make music by plucking an instrument or plucking fruit. [freq. 48] (vf: Paal, Niphal, Piel) |kjv: praise, sing, prune| {str: 2167, 2168}

Nᵐ) ᴹᴢ (זמר Z-MR) — **I. Music: II. Musician:** [Aramaic only] **III. Zemer:** An unknown animal. [freq. 6] |kjv: musick, singer, chamois| {str: 2169, 2170, 2171}

Nᶠˡ) ᴹᴢ (זמרה ZM-RH) — **I. Melody:** As plucked on an musical instrument. A song set to music. **II. Choice fruit:** As plucked from the tree or vine. [freq. 5] |kjv: melody, psalm, fruit| {str: 2172, 2173}

aᶠˡ) ᴹᴢᴹ (מזמרה MZ-M-RH) — **Pruninghook:** For plucking fruit from trees or vines or trimming candle wicks. [freq. 4] |kjv: pruninghook| {str: 4211}

bᵐ) ᴹᴢ (זמיר Z-MYR) — **I. Music: II. Plucking:** [freq. 1] |kjv:

song, psalmist, branch| {str: 2158, 2159}

b^{fl}) 𐤀𐤌𐤅𐤍 (זמירה Z-MY-RH) — **Music:** [ms: זמרה] [freq. 6] |kjv: singing| {str: 2158}

c^{fl}) 𐤀𐤅𐤌𐤍 (זמורה Z-MW-RH) — **Vine:** From where grapes are plucked. [ms: זמרה] [freq. 5] |kjv: branch, slip| {str: 2156}

e^{f2}) 𐤕𐤓𐤌𐤉𐤆 (זימרת ZY-M-RT) — **Music:** [ms: זמרת] [freq. 3] |kjv: song| {str: 2176}

k^{fl}) 𐤀𐤌𐤆𐤌 (מזמרה MZ-M-RH) — **Snuffer:** [freq. 5] |kjv: snuffer| {str: 4212}

he^m) 𐤓𐤅𐤌𐤆𐤌 (מזמור MZ-MWR) — **Melody:** As plucked on an musical instrument. A song set to music. [freq. 57] |kjv: psalm| {str: 4210}

~~~~~~~~

2125) 𐤁𐤍𐤆 (זנב ZNB) ac: **Tail** co: **Tail** ab: ?

V) 𐤁𐤍𐤆 (זנב Z-NB) — **Tail:** To slap, strike or attack the rear. [freq. 2] (vf: Piel) |kjv: hindmost| {str: 2179}

N^m) 𐤁𐤍𐤆 (זנב Z-NB) — **Tail:** [freq. 11] |kjv: tail| {str: 2180}

~~~~~~~~

2126) 𐤇𐤍𐤆 (זנח ZNHh) ac: **Discard** co: ? ab: ?

V) 𐤇𐤍𐤆 (זנח Z-NHh) — **Discard:** To throw or cast out. [freq. 20] (vf: Paal, Hiphil) |kjv: cast, turn, remove| {str: 2186}

~~~~~~~~

2127) 𐤒𐤍𐤆 (זנק ZNQ) ac: **Leap** co: ? ab: ?

V) 𐤒𐤍𐤆 (זנק Z-NQ) — **Leap:** [freq. 1] (vf: Piel) |kjv: leap| {str: 2187}

~~~~~~~~

2128) 𐤊𐤏𐤆 (זעך ZAhK) ac: **Extinguish** co: ? ab: ?: [from: 𐤏𐤆]

V) 𐤊𐤏𐤆 (זעך Z-AhK) — **Extinguish:** [freq. 1] (vf: Niphal) |kjv: extinct| {str: 2193}

~~~~~~~~

2129) 𐤌𐤏𐤆 (זעם ZAhM) ac: **Enrage** co: ? ab: ?: [from: 𐤏𐤆 - a trembling rage]

V) 𐤌𐤏𐤆 (זעם Z-AhM) — **Enrage:** [freq. 12] (vf: Paal, Niphal) |kjv: indignation, defy, abhor, angry, abominable| {str: 2194}

N^m) 𐤌𐤏𐤆 (זעם Z-AhM) — **Rage:** [freq. 22] |kjv: indignation, anger, rage| {str: 2195}

~~~~~~~~

2130) 𐤐𐤏𐤆 (זעף ZAhP) ac: **Sad** co: ? ab: **Sadness:** [from: 𐤏𐤆 - sadness as a trembling]

V) 𐤐𐤏𐤆 (זעף Z-AhP) — **Sad:** To be in a state of sadness. [freq. 5] (vf: Paal) |kjv: wroth, sad, fret, worse| {str: 2196}

N^m) 𐤐𐤏𐤆 (זעף Z-AhP) — **Sadness:** [freq. 8] |kjv: rage, indignation, wrath, displeased| {str: 2197, 2198}

~~~~~~~~

2131) 𐤒𐤏𐤆 (זעק ZAhQ) ac: **Call out** co: **Outcry** ab: ?: A crying out of distress or need. [from: 𐤏𐤆 - a trembling outcry of distress]

V) ⊶☺⌐ (זעק Z-AhQ) — **Call out:** To cry out for help. [Hebrew and Aramaic] [freq. 74] (vf: Paal, Niphal, Hiphil) |kjv: cry, assemble, call, gather, company, proclaim| {str: 2199, 2200}

N^f) ⊶☺⌐ (זעק Z-AhQ) — **Outcry:** [freq. 18] |kjv: cry, crying| {str: 2201}

2132) ⅃⊶⌐ (זקן ZQN) ac: **Old** co: **Beard** ab: ?

V) ⅃⊶⌐ (זקן Z-QN) — **Old:** To be old. [freq. 27] (vf: Paal, Hiphil) |kjv: old, aged| {str: 2204}

N^m) ⅃⊶⌐ (זקן Z-QN) — **I. Beard:** A long beard as a sign of old age. **II. Elder:** One who is old. [freq. 197] |kjv: elder, old, ancient, age, senator, beard| {str: 2205, 2206}

d^m) ⅃Y⊶⌐ (זקון Z-QWN) — **Old age:** [ms: זקן] [freq. 4] |kjv: old| {str: 2208}

e^fl) ⅊⅃⊶⅃⌐ (זיקנה ZYQ-NH) — **Old age:** [ms: זקנה] [freq. 6] |kjv: old| {str: 2209}

g^m) ⅃⊶Y⌐ (זוקן ZW-QN) — **Old age:** [ms: זקן] [freq. 1] |kjv: old| {str: 2207}

2133) ⊶⊶⌐ (זקף ZQP) ac: **Raise** co: ? ab: ?: A raising or setting up of something.

V) ⊶⊶⌐ (זקף Z-QP) — **Raise:** To raise something up. [Hebrew and Aramaic] [freq. 3] (vf: Paal) |kjv: raise, set up| {str: 2210, 2211}

2134) ⊔ᾶ⌐ (זרב ZRB) ac: **Heat** co: ? ab: ?: A drying up from heat. [from: ᾶ⌐ - as a strong wind]

V) ⊔ᾶ⌐ (זרב Z-RB) — **Heat:** [freq. 1] (vf: Pual) |kjv: warm| {str: 2215}

2135) ⊐ᾶ⌐ (זרח ZRHh) ac: **Rise** co: **Dawn** ab: ?: The rising of the sun in the eastern horizon. [from: ⊐ᾶ - The perscribed path of the sun]

V) ⊐ᾶ⌐ (זרח Z-RHh) — **Rise:** [freq. 18] (vf: Paal) |kjv: arise, rise, shine, up| {str: 2224}

N^m) ⊐ᾶ⌐ (זרח Z-RHh) — **Dawn:** The early morning rising of the sun. [freq. 1] |kjv: rising| {str: 2225}

h^m) ⊐ᾶ⌐ᴧ (מזרח MZ-RHh) — **East:** The place of the rising sun. [freq. 74] |kjv: east, eastward, sunrising| {str: 4217}

n^m) ⊐ᾶ⌐Ɣ (אזרח AZ-RHh) — **Native:** [Unknown connection to root;] [freq. 18] |kjv: born, country, land, homeborn, nation, bay| {str: 249}

2136) ᴧᾶ⌐ (זרם ZRM) ac: **Gush** co: **Semen** ab: ?: A heavy shower of water from the skies or a gushing of water in flood. [from: ᾶ⌐ - a sneeze]

V) ᴧᾶ⌐ (זרם Z-RM) — **Gush:** [freq. 2] (vf: Paal) |kjv: pour, flood| {str: 2229}

N^m) ᴧᾶ⌐ (זרם Z-RM) — **Gushing:** [freq. 9] |kjv: flood, overflow, shower, storm, tempest| {str: 2230}

e^fl) ⅊ᴧᾶ⅃⌐ (זירמה ZYR-MH) — **Semen:** The heavy flowing of semen.

[ms: זרמה] [freq. 2] |kjv: issue| {str: 2231}

2137) ⊂⋂⌐ (זרע ZRAh) ac: **Sow** co: **Seed** ab: **?**: The sowing of seeds by scattering them across the field. [from: ⋂⌐ - as a spreading of seeds]

V) ⊂⋂⌐ (זרע Z-RAh) — **Sow:** To spread seeds on the ground. [freq. 56] (vf: Paal, Niphal, Hiphil, Pual) |kjv: sow, yield, sower, bearing, conceive, seed, set| {str: 2232}

N^m) ⊂⋂⌐ (זרע Z-RAh) — **Seed:** [Hebrew and Aramaic] [freq. 230] |kjv: seed, child, carnally, fruitful, seedtime, sowing| {str: 2233, 2234}

d^m) ⊂Y⋂⌐ (זרוע Z-RWAh) — **Sown:** [freq. 2] |kjv: sowing, sown| {str: 2221}

h^m) ⊂⋂⌐ϻ (מזרע MZ-RAh) — **Crop:** What is sown. [freq. 1] |kjv: sown| {str: 4218}

j^m) 𝕃Y⊂⋂⌐ (זרעון ZR-AhWN) — **Vegetable:** As sown. [ms: זרען] [freq. 2] |kjv: pulse| {str: 2235}

2138) ⊸⋂⌐ (זרק ZRQ) ac: **Sprinkle** co: **Bason** ab: **?**: [from: ⋂⌐ - spreading]

V) ⊸⋂⌐ (זרק Z-RQ) — **Sprinkle:** [freq. 35] (vf: Paal, Pual) |kjv: sprinkle| {str: 2236}

h^m) ⊸⋂⌐ϻ (מזרק MZ-RQ) — **Bason:** Used for sprinkling. [freq. 32] |kjv: bason, bowl| {str: 4219}

2139) 𝕏⋂⌐ (זרע ZRGh) ac: **?** co: **Arm** ab: **Force**: The strength of the arm. [from: ⋂⌐ - the spreading ability of the arm]

N^f) 𝕏⋂⌐ (זרע Z-RGh) — **Arm:** The arm as representing power. [Aramaic only] [ar: דרע] [freq. 1] |kjv: arm| {str: 1872}

c^f) 𝕏Y⋂⌐ (זרוע Z-RWGh) — **Arm:** The arm as representing power. [ms: זרע] [freq. 91] |kjv: arm, power, shoulder, holpen, mighty, strength| {str: 2220}

n^f) 𝕏⋂⌐𝔂 (אזרע AZ-RGh) — **Force:** From the strength of the arm. [Aramaic only] [ar: אדרע] [freq. 1] |kjv: force| {str: 153}

nc^f) 𝕏Y⋂⌐𝔂 (אזרוע AZ-RWGh) — **Arm:** [freq. 2] |kjv: arm| {str: 248}

Hhets

2140) ⊗ᴌᴍᴍ (חבט HhBTh) ac: **Knock** co: ? ab: ?: A fruit tree is beat at the trunk so that the fruit will fall from it to the ground.

V) ⊗ᴌᴍᴍ (חבט Hh-BTh) — **Knock:** To knock a tree to remove its fruit, also a threshing. [freq. 5] (vf: Paal, Niphal) |kjv: beat, thresh| {str: 2251}

~~~~~~~~~~

2141) ᴌᴍᴍ (חבל HhBL) ac: **Bind** co: **Rope** ab: ?: To bind something by wrapping it around with a rope. [from: ᴌᴍᴍ - as being enclose]

V) ᴌᴍᴍ (חבל Hh-BL) — **I. Bind:** To be bound as with ropes. [Hebrew and Aramaic] **II. Pledge:** To be bound. [Hebrew and Aramaic] [freq. 35] (vf: Paal, Niphal, Pual, Piel) |kjv: destroy, pledge, band, brought, corrupt, offend, spoil, travail, withhold, hurt| {str: 2254, 2255}

Nᵐ) ᴌᴍᴍ (חבל Hh-BL) — **I. Cord:** Used for binding around. **II. Region:** As bound with borders. [Hebrew and Aramaic] [freq. 63] |kjv: sorrow, cord, line, coast, portion, region, lot, rope, company, pang, band, country, destruction, pain, snare, tackling, hurt, damage| {str: 2256, 2257}

cᵐ) ᴌᴍᴍ (חבול Hh-BWL) — **Pledge:** As a binding. [ms: חבל] [freq. 4] |kjv: pledge| {str: 2258}

dᶠˡ) ᴌᴍᴍ (חבולה Hh-BW-LH) — **Crime:** What causes one to become bound in ropes. [Aramaic only] [freq. 1] |kjv: hurt| {str: 2248}

eᵐ) ᴌᴍᴍ (חיבל HhY-BL) — **Mast:** What the sail of a ship is attached to using ropes. [ms: חבל] [freq. 1] |kjv: mast| {str: 2260}

gᵐ) ᴌᴍᴍ (חובל HhW-BL) — **Sailor:** One who uses ropes on a ship. [ms: חבל] [freq. 5] |kjv: pilot| {str: 2259}

idᶠˡ) ᴌᴍᴍ† (תחבולה THh-BW-LH) — **Council:** As surrounding one with advice. [ms: תחבלה] [freq. 6] |kjv: counsel, advice| {str: 8458}

~~~~~~~~~~

2142) ᴌᴍᴍ (חבק HhBQ) ac: **Embrace** co: ? ab: ?: [from: ᴌᴍᴍ - as being enclose]

V) ᴌᴍᴍ (חבק Hh-BQ) — **Embrace:** [freq. 13] (vf: Paal, Piel) |kjv: embrace, fold| {str: 2263}

edᵐ) ᴌᴍᴍ (חיבוק HhY-BWQ) — **Embrace:** [ms: חבק] [freq. 2] |kjv: folding| {str: 2264}

~~~~~~~~~~

2143) ᴌᴍᴍ (חבר HhBR) ac: **Couple** co: **Clamp** ab: **Companion:** The binding together as being coupled. [from: ᴌᴍᴍ - as being enclose]

V) ᴌᴍᴍ (חבר Hh-BR) — **Couple:** To bind by coupling together. [freq. 29] (vf: Paal, Hiphil, Hitpael, Pual, Piel) |kjv: unite, join, couple, compact, fellowship, league, heap| {str: 2266}

Nᵐ) ᴌᴍᴍ (חבר Hh-BR) — **I. Bound: II. Company:** A group bound together. **III. Companion:** As bound to another. **IV. Spell:** As a binding. [freq. 23] |kjv: wide, enchantment, company, fellow, companion, together| {str: 2267, 2269, 2270, 2271}

N^{f1}) חברה (חברה HhB-RH) — **Company:** A group bound together. [Hebrew and Aramaic] [freq. 2] |kjv: fellows, company| {str: 2273, 2274}

N^{f2}) חברת (חברת HhB-RT) — **Companion:** One bound to another. [freq. 1] |kjv: companion| {str: 2278}

a^{f2}) מחברת (מחברת MHh-B-RT) — **Joint:** The place of joining. [freq. 8] |kjv: coupling| {str: 4225}

d^{f1}) חבורה (חבורה Hh-BW-RH) — **Bruise:** Striped bruises made by ropes binding the wrist or lashes with a rope. [ms: חברה] [freq. 7] |kjv: stripe, hurt, wound, bruise| {str: 2250}

g^{f2}) חוברת (חוברת HhW-B-RT) — **Coupling:** Something bound to another. [ms: חברת] [freq. 4] |kjv: coupling| {str: 2279}

k^{f2}) מחברת (מחברת MHh-B-RT) — **Clamp:** A device for joining. [freq. 2] |kjv: coupling, joining| {str: 4226}

ld^{f1}) חברבורה (חברבורה HhB-R-BW-RH) — **Stripe:** As made by lashes from a rope. [ms: חברברה] [freq. 1] |kjv: stripes| {str: 2272}

2144) חבש (חבש HhBSh) ac: **Bind** co: ? ab: ?: A tight wrapping around of something. [from: חבש - as being enclosed]

V) חבש (חבש Hh-BSh) — **Bind:** To bind something up. Also to saddle as a binding. [freq. 33] (vf: Paal, Pual, Piel) |kjv: saddle, bind, put,

about, gird, govern healer| {str: 2280}

2145) חבת (חבת HhBT) ac: ? co: **Pan** ab: ?

N^m) חבת (חבת Hh-BT) — **Pan:** [freq. 1] |kjv: pan| {str: 2281}

a^f) מחבת (מחבת MHh-BT) — **Pan:** [freq. 5] |kjv: pan| {str: 4227}

2146) חגב (חגב HhGB) ac: ? co: **Locust** ab: ?: [from: חג]

N^m) חגב (חגב Hh-GB) — **Locust:** [freq. 5] |kjv: grasshopper, locust| {str: 2284}

2147) חגר (חגר HhGR) ac: **Bind** co: **Belt** ab: ?: A sash or belt is bound around the waist for attaching weapons. A piece of cloth is brought from the front to the rear to make a loincloth. [from: חג]

V) חגר (חגר Hh-GR) — **Bind:** To bind. To be bound with arms for war. To bind the loose portions of clothing into a belt or sash to prepare to go. [freq. 43] (vf: Paal) |kjv: gird, appoint, afraid, put, restrain, every side| {str: 2296}

c^m) חגור (חגור Hh-GWR) — **Belt:** A sash or belt that encircles the waist. [ms: חגר] [freq. 4] |kjv: girdle| {str: 2289}

c^{f1}) חגורה (חגורה Hh-GW-RH) — **Belt:** A sash or belt that encircles the waist. [ms: חגרה] [freq. 6] |kjv: girdle, apron, armour, gird| {str: 2290}

ac^{f2}) מחגורת (מחגורת MHh-GW-RT) — **Binding:** To wrap a cloth around the body. [freq. 1] |kjv: girding| {str: 4228}

~~~~~~~~~~

2148) (חדל HhDL) ac: **Cease** co: **?** ab: **Reject**

V) (חדל Hh-DL) — **Cease:** To stop or refrain from continuing an action. [freq. 59] (vf: Paal) |kjv: cease, forbear, leave, alone, end, fail, forborn, forsake, rest, unoccupied, want| {str: 2308}

N^{m}) (חדל Hh-DL) — **Rejected:** Something that is made to cease to function. [freq. 3] |kjv: frail, rejected, forbear| {str: 2310}

~~~~~~~~~~

2149) (חדק HhDQ) ac: **?** co: **Thorn** ab: **?:** [from: - as sharp]

N^{m}) (חדק Hh-DQ) — **Thorn:** [freq. 2] |kjv: thorn, brier| {str: 2312}

~~~~~~~~~~

2150) (חדר HhDR) ac: **Surround** co: **Chamber** ab: **?:** The surrounding walls of a chamber providing privacy and security. [from: - as surrounded by walls with a door]

V) (חדר Hh-DR) — **Surround:** To encircle. [freq. 1] (vf: Paal) |kjv: enter| {str: 2314}

N^{m}) (חדר Hh-DR) — **Chamber:** A place surrounded by walls. An inner place as hidden or secret. [freq. 38] |kjv: chamber, inner, inward, innermost, parlour, south, within| {str: 2315}

~~~~~~~~~~

2151) (חדש HhDSh) ac: **Renew** co: **New moon** ab: **New:** The first crescent of the moon as the renewal of the moon, the first day of the month. [from: - restoration]

V) (חדש Hh-DSh) — **Renew:** To make something like new through repair, restoration, or replacement. [freq. 10] (vf: Hitpael, Piel) |kjv: renew, repair| {str: 2318}

N^{m}) (חדש Hh-DSh) — **New:** Something that is new, renewed, restored or repaired. [ar: חדת] [freq. 54] |kjv: new, fresh| {str: 2319, 2323}

g^{m}) (חודש HhW-DSh) — **New moon:** The first crescent of the moon as the renewal of the moon, the first day of the month. [ms: חדש] [freq. 276] |kjv: month, new moon, monthly| {str: 2320}

~~~~~~~~~~

2152) (חזק HhZQ) ac: **Seize** co: **?** ab: **Strength:** A strong grabbing hold to refrain or support.

V) (חזק Hh-ZQ) — **Seize:** To grab hold tightly. To refrain or support by grabbing hold. [freq. 290] (vf: Paal, Hiphil, Hitpael, Piel) |kjv: strong, repair, hold, strengthen, harden, prevail, encourage, take, courage, caught, stronger| {str: 2388}

N^{m}) (חזק Hh-ZQ) — **Strong:** The strength of something that refrains or supports. [freq. 60] |kjv: strong, mighty, sore, hard, hot, impudent, loud, stiffhearted, louder, stronger, strength| {str: 2389, 2390, 2391}

N^{f1}) (חזקה HhZ-QH) — **Strength:** [freq. 10] |kjv: strong, strength, strengthen, force, mighty, repair, sharply| {str: 2393, 2394}
~~~~~~~~~~

g^m) ⟳⟳YⅢ (חוזק HhW-ZQ) —
Strength: [ms: חזק] [freq. 5] |kjv:
strength| {str: 2392}

2153) ᔑᔓⅢ (חזר HhZR) ac: **?** co: **?** ab:
?

b^m) ᔑᔓⅢ (חזיר Hh-ZYR) —
Swine: [freq. 7] |kjv: swine, boar|
{str: 2386}

2154) ⊡⊗Ⅲ (חטב HhThB) ac: **Carve**
co: **Carving** ab: **?:** [from: ⊙ᔓⅢ - cutting]
V) ⊡⊗Ⅲ (חטב Hh-ThB) — **Carve:**
[freq. 9] (vf: Paal, Pual) |kjv: hew,
cut, polish| {str: 2404}
d^{f1}) ⅏⊡Y⊗Ⅲ (חטובה Hh-ThW-BH)
— **Carving:** [freq. 1] |kjv: carved|
{str: 2405}

2155) ᔓ⊗Ⅲ (חטם HhThM) ac: **Refrain**
co: **?** ab: **?:** [from: ⊗Ⅲ - binding]
V) ᔓ⊗Ⅲ (חטם Hh-ThM) —
Refrain: [freq. 1] (vf: Paal) |kjv:
refrain| {str: 2413}

2156) ⟳⊗Ⅲ (חטף HhThP) ac: **Catch**
co: **?** ab: **?:** [from: ⊗Ⅲ - binding]
V) ⟳⊗Ⅲ (חטף Hh-ThP) — **Catch:**

[freq. 3] (vf: Paal) |kjv: catch| {str: 2414}

2157) ᔑ⊗Ⅲ (חטר HhThR) ac: **?** co:
Twig ab: **?**
N^m) ᔑ⊗Ⅲ (חטר Hh-ThR) — **Twig:**
[ms: חטר] [freq. 2] |kjv: rod| {str:
2415}

2158) Ɩ⥾Ⅲ (חכל HhKL) ac: **?** co: **?** ab:
?

lb^{f3}) ⴕYⴑ⥾Ⅲ (חכלילות HhK-
LY-LWT) — **Redness:** [freq. 1] |kjv:
redness| {str: 2448}
lbf^m) ᔑⴑ⥾Ⅲ (חכלילי HhK-
LY-LY) — **Red:** [freq. 1] |kjv: red|
{str: 2447}

2159) ᔓ⥾Ⅲ (חכם HhKM) ac: **Wise** co:
? ab: **Wisdom**
V) ᔓ⥾Ⅲ (חכם Hh-KM) — **Wise:**
To be wise. [freq. 27] (vf: Paal,
Hiphil, Hitpael, Pual, Piel) |kjv: wise,
wisdom, exceed| {str: 2449}
N^m) ᔓ⥾Ⅲ (חכם Hh-KM) — **Wise:**
Also a wise man. [freq. 137] |kjv:
wise, wiseman, cunning, subtil,
unwise, wiser| {str: 2450}
N^{f1}) ⅏ᔓ⥾Ⅲ (חכמה HhK-MH) —
Wisdom: [Hebrew and Aramaic]
[freq. 157] |kjv: wisdom, wisely,
skilful, wits| {str: 2451, 2452}
N^{f3}) ⴕYᔓ⥾Ⅲ (חכמות HhK-MWT)
— **Wisdom:** [freq. 5] |kjv: wisdom,
wise| {str: 2454}
b^m) ᔓⴑ⥾Ⅲ (חכים Hh-KYM) —
Wise: [freq. 14] |kjv: wise| {str:
2445}

2160) ⊡Ɩ Ⅲ (חלב HhLB) ac: **?** co: **Fat**
ab: **Choice:** The rich or choice part.
N^m) ⊡Ɩ Ⅲ (חלב Hh-LB) — **I. Fat:**
The fat of an animal as the choicest
part. **II. Milk:** The milk, containing
fat, of a dairy animal. [freq. 136]
|kjv: fat, fatness, best, finest, grease,
marrow, milk, cheese, suckle| {str:
2459, 2461}

m^{f1}) (חלבנה HhL-B-NH) — **Galbanum:** An odoriferous resin used in incense. A choice ingredient. [freq. 1] |kjv: galbanum| {str: 2464}

~~~~~~~~~~~~

2161) (חלד HhLD) ac: **?** co: **?** ab: **Age:** A passing through a space or time. [from: - passing through]

N^{m}) (חלד Hh-LD) — **Age:** A passing through a finite span of time or space. [freq. 5] |kjv: age, world, time| {str: 2465}

g^{m}) (חולד HhW-LD) — **Hholed:** An unknown animal that burrows in the ground. [ms: חלד] [freq. 1] |kjv: weasel| {str: 2467}

~~~~~~~~~~~~

2162) (חלט HhLTh) ac: **Catch** co: **?** ab: **?:** [from: - binding]

V) (חלט Hh-LTh) — **Catch:** To quickly comprehend something. [freq. 1] (vf: Hiphil) |kjv: catch| {str: 2480}

~~~~~~~~~~~~

2163) (חלך HhLK) ac: **?** co: **?** ab: **Helpless**

N^{f1}) (חלכה HhL-KH) — **Helpless:** [df: חלכא] [freq. 4] |kjv: poor| {str: 2489}

~~~~~~~~~~~~

2164) (חלם HhLM) ac: **Dream** co: **?** ab: **Dream:** [from: - passing through]

V) (חלם Hh-LM) — **Dream:** [freq. 29] (vf: Paal, Hiphil) |kjv: dream| {str: 2492}

N^{m}) (חלם Hh-LM) — **Dream:** [Aramaic only] [freq. 22] |kjv: dream| {str: 2493}

N^{f3}) (חלמות HhL-MWT) — **Hhalamut:** An unknown plant. [Unknown connection to root;] [freq. 1] |kjv: egg| {str: 2495}

c^{m}) (חלום Hh-LWM) — **Dream:** [ms: חלם] [freq. 65] |kjv: dream| {str: 2472}

n^{f1}) (אחלמה AHh-L-MH) — **Ahhlamah:** An unknown gem probably in the sense of gazing. [freq. 2] |kjv: amethyst| {str: 306}

~~~~~~~~~~~~

2165) (חלף HhLP) ac: **Pass** co: **?** ab: **?:** A passing on, away or through. [from: - passing through]

V) (חלף Hh-LP) — **I. Through:** To pass through, by or over something. [Hebrew and Aramaic] **II. Change:** To go or pass through one thing to another, an exchange. [freq. 32] (vf: Paal, Piel) |kjv: change, pass, renew, through, grow, abolish, sprout, alter, cut, go, over| {str: 2498, 2499}

N^{m}) (חלף Hh-LP) — **For:** An exchange for something else. [freq. 2] |kjv: for| {str: 2500}

a^{m}) (מחלף MHh-LP) — **Knife:** A tool for passing through. [freq. 1] |kjv: knife| {str: 4252}

a^{f1}) (מחלפה MHh-L-PH) — **Braids:** In the sense of passing through each other. [freq. 2] |kjv: lock| {str: 4253}

b^{f1}) (חליפה Hh-LY-PH) — **Change:** In the sense of passing through one thing to another. [freq. 12] |kjv: change, course| {str: 2487}
~~~~~~~~~~~~

c^m) ⊙Y∪⊞ (חלוף Hh-LWP) —
Destruction: In the sense of passing
away. [freq. 1] |kjv: destruction| {str:
2475}

~~~~~~~~~

2166) ⌒∪⊞ (חליץ HhLTs) ac: **Draw**
co: **Loins** ab: **?:** Drawn out of the loins is
the next generation. [from: ∪⊞]

V) ⌒∪⊞ (חליץ Hh-LTs) — **I.**
Draw: To draw something out or
away. **II. Arm:** To draw weapons for
battle. [freq. 44] (vf: Paal, Niphal,
Hiphil, Piel, Participle) |kjv: deliver,
arm, loose, prepare, take, army, fat,
put, deliver, draw, withdraw| {str:
2502}

N^f) ⌒∪⊞ (חליץ Hh-LTs) — **Loins:**
In the sense of the next generation
being drawn out of the loins.
[Hebrew and Aramaic] [df: חרץ]
[freq. 11] |kjv: loins, reins| {str:
2504, 2783}

a^fl) ⨯⌒∪⊞ᴧᴧ (מחלצה MHh-L-
TsH) — **Robe:** As drawn off. [freq. 2]
|kjv: apparel, raiment| {str: 4254}

b^fl) ⨯⌒ˠ∪⊞ (חליצה Hh-LY-TsH)
— **Spoil:** What is drawn out after a
battle. [freq. 2] |kjv: spoil, armour|
{str: 2488}

~~~~~~~~~

2167) ⦁∪⊞ (חלק HhLQ) ac: **Divide**
co: **Portion** ab: **?:** The fathers estate is
totaled and divided up for the sons. The
eldest receiving a double portion. [from:
⦁∪ - a gathering of what is to be
divided]

V) ⦁∪⊞ (חלק Hh-LQ) — **I.**
Divide: To divide something up and
disperse each portion to the
appropriate recipients. **II. Smooth:**
To have a smooth surface. Also to

flatter in the sense of a smooth talk.
[Unknown connection to root] [freq.
65] (vf: Paal, Niphal, Hiphil, Hitpael,
Pual, Piel) |kjv: divide, flatter, part,
distribute, dealt, smooth, give,
impart, partner, portion, receive,
separate| {str: 2505}

N^fl) ⨯⦁∪⊞ (חלקה HhL-QH) — **I.**
Portion: The part received from
what was divided. **II. Smooth:** A
smooth surface or flattery as a
smooth talk. [Unknown connection
to root] [freq. 30] |kjv: portion,
parcel, piece, field, flattering, plat,
part, flattery, ground places, smooth|
{str: 2513, 2514}

a^fl) ⨯⦁∪⊞ᴧᴧ (מחלקה MHh-L-
QH) — **Portion:** The part received
from what was divided. [Aramaic
only] [freq. 1] |kjv: courses| {str:
4255}

a^f2) ┼⦁∪⊞ᴧᴧ (מחלקת MHh-L-QT)
— **Portion:** The part received from
what was divided. [freq. 43] |kjv:
course, division portion, company|
{str: 4256}

d^m) ⦁Y∪⊞ (חלוק Hh-LWQ) —
Smooth: A smooth surface.
[Unknown connection to root;] [freq.
1] |kjv: smooth| {str: 2512}

d^fl) ⨯⦁Y∪⊞ (חלוקה Hh-LW-QH)
— **Portion:** The part received from
what was divided. [ms: חלקה] [freq.
1] |kjv: division| {str: 2515}

l^fl) ⨯⦁∪⦁∪⊞ (חלקלקה HhL-QL-
QH) — **Slippery:** As on a smooth
surface. [Unknown connection to
root;] [freq. 4] |kjv: slippery| {str:
2519}

~~~~~~~~~

2168) ᴜᴜ∪⊞ (חלש HhLSh) ac: **Weaken**
co: **?** ab: **Weak:** Something that is weak,

failing, decayed or wasted away. [from:]

V) (חלש Hh-LSh) — **Weaken:** [freq. 3] (vf: Paal) |kjv: discomfit, waste away, weaken| {str: 2522}

N^{m}) (חלש Hh-LSh) — **Weak:** [freq. 1] |kjv: weak| {str: 2523}

d^{f1}) (חלושה Hh-LW-ShH) — **Defeat:** As becoming weakened. [freq. 1] |kjv: overcome| {str: 2476}

~~~~~~~~~~~

2169) (חמד HhMD) ac: **?** co: **?** ab: **Desire:** Something of value or delighted in. [from: - as in cheese as a delicacy]

V) (חמד Hh-MD) — **Desire:** To want something that is pleasant out of desire or lust. [freq. 21] (vf: Paal, Niphal, Piel) |kjv: desire, covet, delight, pleasant, beauty, lust, delectable| {str: 2530}

N^{m}) (חמד Hh-MD) — **Desirable:** Something that is desired. [freq. 6] |kjv: desirable, pleasant| {str: 2531}

N^{f1}) (חמדה HhM-DH) — **Pleasant:** An object of desire. [freq. 25] |kjv: pleasant, desire, beloved, goodly, precious| {str: 2532}

a^{m}) (מחמד MHh-MD) — **Pleasant:** An object of desire. [freq. 13] |kjv: pleasant, desire, goodly, lovely beloved| {str: 4261}

ad^{m}) (מחמוד MHh-MWD) — **Pleasant:** An object of desire. [ms: מחמד] [freq. 2] |kjv: pleasant| {str: 4262}

~~~~~~~~~~~

2170) (חמט HhMTh) ac: **?** co: **?** ab: **?**

g^{m}) (חומט HhW-MTh) — **Hhomet:** An unknown animal. [ms: חמט] [freq. 1] |kjv: snail| {str: 2546}

~~~~~~~~~~~

2171) (חמל HhML) ac: **Compassion** co: **?** ab: **?**

V) (חמל Hh-ML) — **Compassion:** To have compassion on someone or something. [freq. 41] (vf: Paal) |kjv: pity, compassion| {str: 2550}

N^{f1}) (חמלה HhM-LH) — **Compassionate:** [freq. 2] |kjv: merciful, pitiful| {str: 2551}

a^{m}) (מחמל MHh-ML) — **Compassion:** [freq. 1] |kjv: pity| {str: 4263}

~~~~~~~~~~~

2172) (חמס HhMS) ac: **Shake** co: **?** ab: **Violence:** [from: - shaking]

V) (חמס Hh-MS) — **Shake:** To shake someone or something violently. To do a wrong to another as a shaking. [freq. 8] (vf: Paal, Niphal) |kjv: violence, violate, shake, wrong, violent, take, bare| {str: 2554}

N^{m}) (חמס Hh-MS) — **Violence:** A violent shaking. [freq. 60] |kjv: violence, violent, cruelty, wrong, false, cruel, damage, injustice, unrighteous| {str: 2555}

i^{m}) (תחמס THh-MS) — **Tahhmas:** An unknown bird. [freq. 2] |kjv: hawk| {str: 8464}

~~~~~~~~~~~
~~~~~~~~~~~

2173) ⟨חמץ HhMTs) ac: ? co: **Sour** ab: ?: The harsh taste of something that has fermented or soured. [from: ᴧᴧᴑᴑ - processing a food through heat or fermentation]

V) ⟨חמץ Hh-MTs) — **Sour:** To be sour by adding leaven to bread. Also to sour in taste, thought or action. [freq. 8] (vf: Paal, Hiphil, Hitpael) |kjv: leaven, cruel, dye, grieve| {str: 2556}

Nᵐ**)** ⟨חמץ Hh-MTs) — **Leaven:** Used for souring bread, also the bread that has been leavened. [freq. 11] |kjv: leaven| {str: 2557}

bᵐ**)** ⟨חמיץ Hh-MYTs) — **Soured:** [freq. 1] |kjv: clean| {str: 2548}

cᵐ**)** ⟨חמוץ Hh-MWTs) — **Soured:** [freq. 1] |kjv: oppressed| {str: 2541}

gᵐ**)** ⟨חומץ HhW-MTs) — **Vinegar:** Made by souring grapes. [ms: חמץ] [freq. 6] |kjv: vinegar| {str: 2558}

2174) ⟨חמק HhMQ) ac: **Turn** co: **Round** ab: ?

V) ⟨חמק Hh-MQ) — **Turn:** [freq. 2] (vf: Paal, Hitpael) |kjv: withdraw, go| {str: 2559}

dᵐ**)** ⟨חמוק Hh-MWQ) — **Rounded:** Something that is round. [freq. 1] |kjv: joints| {str: 2542}

2175) ⟨חמר HhMR) ac: **Boil** co: **Tar** ab: ?: A dark, thick and slimy substance often called bitumen is released the bottom of water pools rising to the surface in bubbles (seen as a boiling). This substance was used for waterproofing boats or other vessels as well as a type of mortar. [from: ᴧᴧᴑᴑ - a separating out of substances]

V) ⟨חמר Hh-MR) — **I. Boil:** To boil as a turbulent boiling of the tar at the surface. **II. Smear:** To smear something with tar or other liquid. [freq. 6] (vf: Paal) |kjv: trouble, red, daub, foul| {str: 2560}

Nᵐ**)** ⟨חמר Hh-MR) — **I. Tar:** A dark and thick liquid that floats to the surface of water and used as a waterproof covering for boats. [Hebrew and Aramaic] **II. Wine:** The dark and thick wine that floats to the surface of the wine vat. [freq. 11] |kjv: pure, red wine, wine, slime| {str: 2561, 2562, 2564}

cᵐ**)** ⟨חמור Hh-MWR) — **Donkey:** Possibly from its dark color. [ms: חמר] [freq. 98] |kjv: ass, heap| {str: 2543, 2565}

gᵐ**)** ⟨חומר HhW-MR) — **I. Clay:** A thick and slimy soil used as a mortar or for making bricks. [ms: חמר] **II. Hhomer:** A unit of measure. [ms: חמר] [freq. 30] |kjv: clay, morter, mire, heap| {str: 2563}

tcᵐ**)** ⟨יחמור YHh-MWR) — **Yahhmor:** An unknown animal, probably from its dark. [freq. 2] |kjv: deer| {str: 3180}

2176) ⟨חמש HhMSh) ac: **Grab** co: **Fingers** ab: ?: A grabbing of something with the fingers. Also the number five from the fingers of the hand.

V) ⟨חמש Hh-MSh) — **Fifth:** To take a fifth. [A denominative verb] [freq. 1] (vf: Piel) |kjv: fifth| {str: 2567}

N^(m/f)) LLᴧᴧᴧᴍ (חמש Hh-MSh) —
Five: [Also meaning fifty when written in the plural form - ᴧᴧᴧᐅᴸᴸᴧᴧᴧᴍ] [freq. 505] |kjv: five, fifth, fifty, fiftieth| {str: 2568, 2572}

d^m) LLᴜY̖ᴧᴧᴍ (חמוש Hh-MWSh) —
Armed: One prepared for battle in the sense of grabbing weapons. [ms: חמש] [freq. 4] |kjv: armed, harness| {str: 2571}

g^m) LLᴧᴧᴧY̖ᴍ (חומש HhW-MSh) —
Fifth: [ms: חמש] [freq. 5] |kjv: fifth| {str: 2569, 2570}

bf^n) ᐅᴸᴜᴜᐅᴧᴧᴍ (חמישי Hh-MY-ShY) — **Fifth:** [freq. 45] |kjv: fifth| {str: 2549}

~~~~~~~~~

2177) ⊗ᐟᴍ (חנט HhNTh) ac: **Ripen** co: ? ab: ?

V) ⊗ᐟᴍ (חנט Hh-NTh) — **Ripen:** To give of the fragrance of the fruit as it ripens. Also to add spices to a body for embalming. [freq. 5] (vf: Paal) |kjv: embalm, put forth| {str: 2590}

e^(fl)) ✲⊗ᐅᴸᴍ (חינטה HhYN-ThH) — **Wheat:** In the sense of ripening on the stalk. [ms: חנטה] [df: חטה] [freq. 32] |kjv: wheat, wheaten| {str: 2406, 2591}

~~~~~~~~~

2178) �ᴸᴍ (חנך HhNK) ac: **Dedicate** co: ? ab: **Dedication:** An infant is trained to suck by placing a sour substance on the roof of the mouth. [from: ᴜᴸᴍ]

V) ᴜᴸᴍ (חנך Hh-NK) — **Dedicate:** To begin using something new. [freq. 5] (vf: Paal) |kjv: dedicate, train| {str: 2596}

b^m) ᴜᐅᴸᴍ (חניך Hh-NYK) — **Experienced:** Something that is experienced in its use. [freq. 1] |kjv: trained| {str: 2593}

d^(fl)) ✲ᴜᴜY̖ᴸᴍ (חנוכה Hh-NW-KH) — **Dedication:** [Hebrew and Aramaic] [ms: חנכה] [freq. 12] |kjv: dedication| {str: 2597, 2598}

~~~~~~~~~

2179) ⌐ᐟᴍ (חנף HhNP) ac: ? co: ? ab: **Filthy**

V) ⌐ᐟᴍ (חנף Hh-NP) — **Filthy:** To be polluted or dirty. Usually in the sense of immorality. [freq. 11] (vf: Paal, Hiphil) |kjv: pollute, defile, corrupt, profane| {str: 2610}

N^m) ⌐ᐟᴍ (חנף Hh-NP) — **Filthy:** One who is soiled with immorality. [freq. 13] |kjv: hypocrite| {str: 2611}

N^(fl)) ✲⌐ᐟᴍ (חנפה HhN-PH) — **Filthiness:** [freq. 1] |kjv: profaneness| {str: 2613}

g^m) ⌐ᴸY̖ᴍ (חונף HhW-NP) — **Filthiness:** [ms: חנף] [freq. 1] |kjv: hypocrisy| {str: 2612}

~~~~~~~~~

2180) ᴼᴸᴍ (חנק HhNQ) ac: **Strangle** co: ? ab: ?

V) ᴼᴸᴍ (חנק Hh-NQ) — **Strangle:** To strangle by hanging or gripping the neck. [freq. 2] (vf: Niphal, Piel) |kjv: hang, strangle| {str: 2614}

a^m) ᴼᴸᴍᴧᴧ (מחנק MHh-NQ) — **Strangling:** [freq. 1] |kjv: strangling| {str: 4267}

~~~~~~~~~

2181) ⌐ᴸᴍ (חסד HhSD) ac: **Bow** co: ? ab: **Kindness:** The bowing of the neck as a sign of respect and kindness to an equal. [from: ᴸᴍ]

V) ▱⬥▥ (חסד Hh-SD) — **Bow:** To bow the head at the neck. [freq. 3] (vf: Hitpael, Piel) |kjv: mercy, shame| {str: 2616}

N^m) ▱⬥▥ (חסד Hh-SD) — **Kindness:** In the sense of bowing the neck to another as a sign of kindness. [freq. 248] |kjv: mercy, kindness, lovingkindness, goodness, kindly, merciful, favour, good, goodliness, pity, reproach, wicked| {str: 2617}

b^m) ▱⌐⬥▥ (חסיד Hh-SYD) — **Kind:** A kind action, also one who is kind. [freq. 32] |kjv: saint, holy, merciful, godly, good| {str: 2623}

b^{f1}) ⍦▱⌐⬥▥ (חסידה Hh-SY-DH) — **I. Stork:** From its long and bowed neck. **II. Plumage:** The soft feathers of the storks neck. [freq. 6] |kjv: stork, feathers| {str: 2624}

2182) Ⱎ⬥▥ (חסך HhSK) ac: **Withhold** co: **?** ab: **?:** [from: Ⱎ⬥ - keeping something covered]

V) Ⱎ⬥▥ (חסך Hh-SK) — **Withhold:** To hold something back. [df: חשך] [freq. 28] (vf: Paal, Niphal) |kjv: spare, keep, withhold, refrain, asswage, reserve, forbear, hinder, punish| {str: 2820}

2183) ⌐⬥▥ (חסל HhSL) ac: **Devour** co: **Locust** ab: **?:** A large number of locusts can devastate a crop by devouring it.

V) ⌐⬥▥ (חסל Hh-SL) — **Devour:** [freq. 1] (vf: Paal) |kjv: consume| {str: 2628}

b^m) ⌐⌐⬥▥ (חסיל Hh-SYL) — **Hhasiyl:** A type of locust as a

---

devourer of crops. [freq. 6] |kjv: caterpillar| {str: 2625}

2184) ⩘⬥▥ (חסם HhSM) ac: **Muzzle** co: **Muzzle** ab: **?:** Used to stop the animal from biting or eating.

V) ⩘⬥▥ (חסם Hh-SM) — **Muzzle:** [freq. 2] (vf: Paal) |kjv: muzzle, stop| {str: 2629}

ac^m) ⩘Y⬥▥⩘ (מחסום MHh-SWM) — **Muzzle:** [freq. 1] |kjv: bridle| {str: 4269}

2185) ⑁⬥▥ (חסן HhSN) ac: **Store** co: **Treasure** ab: **?:** A storing or hoarding of a treasure or other precious possession. The treasure as a sign of power. [from: ⑁⬥ - thorn bushes were used for making a protecting hedge]

V) ⑁⬥▥ (חסן Hh-SN) — **I. Store:** To store up a treasure. **II. Possess:** [Aramaic only] [freq. 1] (vf: Niphal) |kjv: lay up, possess| {str: 2630}

N^m) ⑁⬥▥ (חסן Hh-SN) — **Power:** In the sense of wealth. [Aramaic only] [freq. 2] |kjv: power| {str: 2632}

b^m) ⑁⌐⬥▥ (חסין Hh-SYN) — **Power:** In the sense of wealth. [freq. 1] |kjv: strong| {str: 2626}

c^m) ⑁Y⬥▥ (חסון Hh-SWN) — **Strong:** In the sense of wealth. [ms: חסן] [freq. 2] |kjv: strong| {str: 2634}

g^m) ⑁⬥Y▥ (חוסן HhW-SN) — **Treasure:** What is stored up. [ms: חסן] [freq. 5] |kjv: strength, treasure, riches| {str: 2633}

2186) ⟨חסף HhSP) ac: **Uncover** co: ? ab: ?: [from: ⟨⟩]

V) ⟨חסף Hh-SP) — **Uncover:** [df: חשׂף] [freq. 11] (vf: Paal) |kjv: bare, discover, uncover, take, clean, draw| {str: 2834}

N^m) ⟨חסף Hh-SP) — **Clay:** [Unknown connection to root; Aramaic only] [freq. 9] |kjv: clay| {str: 2635}

b^m) ⟨חסיף Hh-SYP) — **Small flock:** [Unknown connection to root;] [df: חשׂף] [freq. 1] |kjv: flock| {str: 2835}

ac^m) ⟨מחסוף MHh-SWP) — **Expose:** In the sense of uncovering. [df: מחשׂף] [freq. 1] |kjv: appear| {str: 4286}

~~~~~~~~

2187) ⟨חסר HhSR) ac: **Diminish** co: ? ab: **Lacking:** Something or someone that is lacking or diminished in quantity or quality. [from: ⟨⟩ - needing support]

V) ⟨חסר Hh-SR) — **Diminish:** To be lacking or decrease. [freq. 21] (vf: Paal, Hiphil, Piel) |kjv: want, lack, fail, decrease, abate, lower, bereave| {str: 2637}

N^m) ⟨חסר Hh-SR) — **Lacking:** [freq. 21] |kjv: void, want, lack, fail, destitute, need, poverty| {str: 2638, 2639}

b^m) ⟨חסיר Hh-SYR) — **Lacking:** [Aramaic only] [freq. 1] |kjv: wanting| {str: 2627}

g^m) ⟨חוסר HhW-SR) — **Lacking:** [ms: חסר] [freq. 3] |kjv: want| {str: 2640}

j^m) ⟨חסרון HhS-RWN) — **Lacking:** [freq. 1] |kjv: wanting| {str: 2642}

ac^m) ⟨מחסור MHh-SWR) — **Lacking:** [ms: מחסר] [freq. 13] |kjv: want, lack, need, poor, poverty, penury| {str: 4270}

~~~~~~~~

2188) ⟨חפז HhPZ) ac: **Haste** co: ? ab: ?: [from: ⟨▥⟩ - a hurrying to hide]

V) ⟨חפז Hh-PZ) — **Haste:** To hurry in flight. [freq. 9] (vf: Paal, Niphal) |kjv: haste, tremble| {str: 2648}

ej^m) ⟨חיפזון HhY-P-ZWN) — **Haste:** [ms: חפזון] [freq. 3] |kjv: haste| {str: 2649}

~~~~~~~~

2189) ⟨חפס HhPS) ac: **Search** co: ? ab: ?: [from: ⟨▥⟩ - searching for something of value]

V) ⟨חפס Hh-PS) — **Search:** [df: חפשׂ] [freq. 23] (vf: Paal, Niphal, Hitpael, Pual, Piel) |kjv: search, disguise, search, change, diligent, hidden| {str: 2664}

N^m) ⟨חפס Hh-PS) — **Search:** [df: חפשׂ] [freq. 1] |kjv: search| {str: 2665}

~~~~~~~~

2190) ⟨חפן HhPN) ac: ? co: ? ab: ?

g^m) ⟨חופן HhW-PN) — **Fist:** A hand full of something. [ms: חפן] [freq. 6] |kjv: hand, fist| {str: 2651}

~~~~~~~~

2191) ᐦᕮᕮ (חפץ HhPTs) ac: **Delight** co: ? ab: ?: [from: ᕮᕮ - hiding a treasure]

V) ᐦᕮᕮ (חפץ Hh-PTs) — **Delight:** To desire something out of pleasure or necessity. [freq. 75] (vf: Paal) |kjv: delight, please, desire, will, pleasure, favour, like, move, would| {str: 2654}

N^m) ᐦᕮᕮ (חפץ Hh-PTs) — **Delight:** [freq. 50] |kjv: desire, pleasure, would, please, willing, favour, wish, delight| {str: 2655, 2656}

~~~~~~~~~

2192) ᕫᕮᕮ (חפר HhPR) ac: **Dig** co: **Mole** ab: ?: A digging in the soil, as a mole, for a well or possibly a treasure. Also a digging into an incident for understanding. [from: ᕮᘻ]

V) ᕫᕮᕮ (חפר Hh-PR) — **I. Dig:** To dig in the ground, also to dig into something as if searching. **II. Confuse:** To be confused, in the sense of digging for understanding. [freq. 39] (vf: Paal, Hiphil) |kjv: dig, search, paw, seek, confounded, ashamed, shame, confusion, reproach| {str: 2658, 2659}

c^f) ᕫᖻᕮᕮ (חפור Hh-PWR) — **Mole:** A digger. [ms: חפר] [freq. 1] |kjv: mole| {str: 2661}

~~~~~~~~~

2193) ᘻᕮᕮ (חפש HhPSh) ac: **Free** co: ? ab: **Freedom:** A freedom from a master. [from: ᕮᘻ]

V) ᘻᕮᕮ (חפש Hh-PSh) — **Free:** To be free from a master. [freq. 1] (vf: Pual) |kjv: free, liberty| {str: 2666}

f^m) ᖨᘻᕮᕮ (חפשי Hh-P-ShY) — **Free:** [freq. 17] |kjv: free, liberty| {str: 2670}

g^m) ᘻᕮᖻᕮ (חופש HhW-PSh) — **Horse:** As free to run. [ms: חפש] [freq. 1] |kjv: precious| {str: 2667}

o^{f1}) ᘺᘻᕮᖻᕮ (חופשה HhWP-ShH) — **Freedom:** [ms: חפשה] [freq. 1] |kjv: freedom| {str: 2668}

N^{f3}) ᖠᘻᕮᕮ (חפשות HhP-ShWT) — **Separate:** In the sense of being spread out. [df: חפשית] [freq. 3] |kjv: several| {str: 2669}

~~~~~~~~~

2194) ᘦᐦᕮᕮ (חצב HhTsB) ac: **Hew** co: ? ab: ?: The cutting or hewing of wood or stone. [from: ᐦᕮᕮ - cutting]

V) ᘦᐦᕮᕮ (חצב Hh-TsB) — **Hew:** [freq. 25] (vf: Paal, Niphal, Hiphil, Pual) |kjv: dig, hew, mason, cut, divide, graven, made| {str: 2672}

a^m) ᘦᐦᕮᕮᘻ (מחצב MHh-TsB) — **Hewn:** Something that is hewn. [freq. 3] |kjv: hewn, hewed| {str: 4274}

~~~~~~~~~

2195) ᕥᐦᕮ (חצן HhTsN) ac: ? co: **Bosom** ab: ?: [from: ᐦᕮᕮ - enclosing]

N^m) ᕥᐦᕮ (חצן Hh-TsN) — **Bosom:** [freq. 1] |kjv: bosom| {str: 2683}

g^m) ᕥᐦᕮᖻᕮ (חוצן HhW-TsN) — **Bosom:** [ms: חצן] [freq. 2] |kjv: lap, arms| {str: 2684}

~~~~~~~~~

2196) ᕮᐦᕮ (חצף HhTsP) ac: **Urge** co: ? ab: ?: [from: ᐦᕮᕮ - cutting off short]

V) ⟡ (חצף Hh-TsP) — **Urge:** [Aramaic only] [freq. 2] (vf: Paal) |kjv: haste, urgent| {str: 2685}

2197) (חצר HhTsR) ac: **Blow** co: **Yard** ab: ?: When the trumpets from the city are sounded as an alarm of invasion, the inhabitants of the surrounding fields and villages, or yards, go to the protection of the walled city. [from: ▥ - enclosing]

V) (חצר Hh-TsR) — **Blow:** To blow trumpets. [freq. 11] (vf: Hiphil, Piel, Participle) |kjv: sound, blow, trumpeter| {str: 2690}

N^m) (חצר Hh-TsR) — **Yard:** The villages outside of the larger cities as the yard of the city. Also a courtyard as outside the house. [freq. 189] |kjv: court, village, town| {str: 2691}

N^fl) (חצרה HhTs-RH) — **Yard:** The villages outside of the larger cities as the yard of the city. Also a courtyard as outside the house. [df: עזרה] [freq. 9] |kjv: settle, court| {str: 5835}

b^m) (חציר Hh-TsYR) — **I. Yard:** The villages outside of the larger cities as the yard of the city. Also a courtyard as outside the house. **II. Grass:** A plant used as food for men and animals as grown in the yard. [freq. 22] |kjv: court, grass, hay, herb, leeks| {str: 2681, 2682}

2198) (חקר HhQR) ac: **Examine** co: ? ab: ?: [from: שח - a digging]

V) (חקר Hh-QR) — **Examine:** To search or seek for something. [freq. 27] (vf: Paal, Niphal, Piel) |kjv: search, found, seek, sound, try| {str: 2713}

N^m) (חקר Hh-QR) — **Examination:** [freq. 12] |kjv: search, finding, number| {str: 2714}

k^m) (מחקר MHh-QR) — **Depth:** A deep place as unexamined. [freq. 1] |kjv: deep| {str: 4278}

2199) (חרב HhRB) ac: **Waste** co: **Sword** ab: ?: [from: חר - heat]

V) (חרב Hh-RB) — **Waste:** A dry wasteland. Also a place that has been laid waste and made desolate. [Hebrew and Aramaic] [freq. 41] (vf: Paal, Niphal, Hiphil, Hophal, Pual, Participle) |kjv: waste, dry, desolate, slay, decay, destroy| {str: 2717, 2718}

N^f) (חרב Hh-RB) — **I. Sword:** A weapon used to lay waste a city. **II. Waste:** A dry or desolate place. [freq. 423] |kjv: sword, knife, dagger, axe, mattock| {str: 2719, 2720}

N^fl) (חרבה HhR-BH) — **Waste:** [freq. 50] |kjv: waste, desolate, desert, decayed, dry land, dry ground| {str: 2723, 2724}

g^m) (חורב HhW-RB) — **I. Heat:** [ms: חרב] **II. Waste:** [ms: חרב] [freq. 16] |kjv: heat, dry, drought, waste, desolation| {str: 2721}

j^m) (חרבון HhR-BWN) — **Drought:** [freq. 1] |kjv: drought| {str: 2725}

2200) (חרג HhRG) ac: **Tremble** co: **?** ab: **?:** [from: - burning]

V) (חרג Hh-RG) — **Tremble:** [freq. 1] (vf: Paal) |kjv: afraid| {str: 2727}

~~~~~~~~~~~

2201) (חרד HhRD) ac: **Tremble** co: **?** ab: **?:** [from: - burning]

V) (חרד Hh-RD) — **Tremble:** [freq. 39] (vf: Paal, Hiphil) |kjv: afraid, tremble, fray, careful, discomfit, quake| {str: 2729}

N^{m}) (חרד Hh-RD) — **Tremble:** [freq. 6] |kjv: tremble, afraid| {str: 2730}

N^{f1}) (חרדה HhR-DH) — **Trembling:** [freq. 9] |kjv: trembling, fear, exceedingly, care, quaking| {str: 2731}

~~~~~~~~~~~

2202) (חרז HhRZ) ac: **?** co: **Chain** ab: **?**

d^{m}) (חרוז Hh-RWZ) — **Chain:** [freq. 1] |kjv: chain| {str: 2737}

~~~~~~~~~~~

2203) (חרט HhRTh) ac: **Engrave** co: **Pen** ab: **?:** [from: - sharp]

N^{m}) (חרט Hh-RTh) — **Pen:** A tool making markings or inscriptions by carving on stone or writing on a scroll. [freq. 2] |kjv: graving tool, pen| {str: 2747}

b^{m}) (חריט Hh-RYTh) — **Satchel:** Used for carrying items such as tools. [ms: חרט] [freq. 2] |kjv: bag, crisping pin| {str: 2754}

qp^{m}) (חרטום HhR-ThWM) — **Magician:** One who writes magical circles and lines. [Hebrew and Aramaic] [ms: חרטם] [freq. 16] |kjv: magician| {str: 2748, 2749}

~~~~~~~~~~~

2204) (חרך HhRK) ac: **Roast** co: **Grill** ab: **?:** The roasting of meat on a grill over a fire. [from: - burning]

V) (חרך Hh-RK) — **Roast:** To roast a food. Also a roasting of hair in a fire. [Hebrew and Aramaic] [freq. 2] (vf: Paal) |kjv: roast, singe| {str: 2760, 2761}

N^{m}) (חרך Hh-RK) — **Grill:** The crossed pieces of wood used for a grill. Also a window lattice of crossed sticks. [freq. 1] |kjv: lattice| {str: 2762}

~~~~~~~~~~~

2205) (חרל HhRL) ac: **?** co: **Nettle** ab: **?:** The tiny thorns of the nettle that cause severe burning. [from: - burning]

d^{m}) (חרול Hh-RWL) — **Nettle:** [ms: חרל] [freq. 3] |kjv: nettle| {str: 2738}

~~~~~~~~~~~

2206) (חרם HhRM) ac: **Capture** co: **Net** ab: **?:** A throwing of the net to capture fish, animals or man.

V) (חרם Hh-RM) — **Capture:** To capture something that is dedicated for something special. Also to capture something to destroy it. [freq. 52] (vf: Paal, Hiphil, Hophal) |kjv: destroy, devote, accurse, consecrate, forfeit, flat nose, slay| {str: 2763}

N^{m}) (חרם Hh-RM) — **I. Net: II. Captured:** Someone or something captured for dedication or destruction. [freq. 38] |kjv: net, accursed, curse, devoted, destruction, dedicated, destroyed| {str: 2764}

~~~~~~~~

2207) ◄ᓂ▥ (חרס HhRS) ac: **Dry** co: **Clay** ab: ?: The process of drying clay bricks or pots in the sun. [from: ᓂ - potsherd]

N^m) ◄ᓂ▥ (חרס Hh-RS) — **I. Clay:** Used for making pottery. [df: חרסה] **II. Itch:** Skin irritations are treated by applying clay to the irritation and left to dry. **III. Sun:** Clay left in the sun dries. **IV. Potsherd:** Broken pieces of clay pottery. [df: חרש] [freq. 21] |kjv: itch, sun, earthen, potsherd, sherd, stone, earth| {str: 2775, 2789}

N^f3) ϮΥ◄ᓂ▥ (חרסות HhR-SWT) — **Potsherd:** Broken pieces of clay pottery. [freq. 1] |kjv: east| {str: 2777}

~~~~~~~~

2208) ◦ᓂ▥ (חרף HhRP) ac: **Pierce** co: **Winter** ab: ?: The piercing cold of winter. [from: ∪▥ - piercing]

V) ◦ᓂ▥ (חרף Hh-RP) — **I. Taunt:** To pierce another with sharp words of reproach, scorn or taunting (see Psalms 42:10). **II. Betrothal:** A nose ring is put in the piercing of the nose as a sign of betrothal (see Genesis 24:47). [freq. 41] (vf: Paal, Niphal, Piel) |kjv: reproach, defy, betroth, blaspheme, jeopardise| {str: 2778}

N^f1) ⚘◦ᓂ▥ (חרפה HhR-PH) — **Piercing:** A scorn, taunting or reproach as a piercing. [freq. 73] |kjv: reproach, shame, rebuke, reproachfully| {str: 2781}

g^m) ◦ᑭΥ▥ (חורף HhW-RP) — **Winter:** The time of the piercing cold. [ms: חרף] [freq. 7] |kjv: winter, youth, cold| {str: 2779}

~~~~~~~~

2209) ᦁᓂ▥ (חרץ HhRTs) ac: **Sharp** co: **Hoe** ab: ?: A sharp cutting instrument. [from: ∪▥ - piercing]

V) ᦁᓂ▥ (חרץ Hh-RTs) — **Decide:** To make a decision in the sense of dividing between two choices. [freq. 12] (vf: Paal, Niphal) |kjv: determine, move, decide, bestir, main, decree| {str: 2782}

b^m) ᦁᒉᓂ▥ (חריץ Hh-RYTs) — **I. Hoe:** A sharp instrument for digging. [ms: חרץ] **II. Sharp:** sharp taste. [freq. 3] |kjv: harrow| {str: 2757}

d^m) ᦁᎱΥ▥ (חרוץ Hh-RWTs) — **I. Shard:** Sharp pieces of potsherds or iron as used on threshing boards to break open grain. [ms: חרץ] **II. Diligent:** As sharp in action. **III. Gold:** [ms: חרץ] [freq. 18] |kjv: gold, diligent, decision, threshing, sharp, wall| {str: 2742}

m^m) ᘰᦁᓂ▥ (חרצן HhR-TsN) — **Seed:** The seed of a grape as sharp. [freq. 1] |kjv: kernel| {str: 2785}

~~~~~~~~

2210) ◦ᓂ▥ (חרק HhRQ) ac: **Gnash** co: ? ab: ?: Gnashing of the teeth. [from: ∪▥ - sharp teeth]

V) ◦ᓂ▥ (חרק Hh-RQ) — **Gnash:** To gnash the teeth. [freq. 5] (vf: Paal) |kjv: gnash| {str: 2786}

~~~~~~~~

2211) ᒻᒻᓂ▥ (חרש HhRSh) ac: **Scratch** co: **Craftsman** ab: ?: The craftsman that scratches, or engraves, in wood, stone or metal. [from: - sharp]

V) (חרש Hh-RSh) — **I. Plow:** To scratch a line in the soil. **II. Devise:** To scratch out a plan. **III. Silent:** [Unknown connection to root;] [freq. 73] (vf: Paal, Niphal, Hiphil, Hitpael) |kjv: peace, plow, devise, silence, hold, altogether, plowman, cease, conceal, deaf, graven imagine| {str: 2790}

N^{m}) (חרש Hh-RSh) — **I. Craftsman:** One who engraves wood, stone or metal. **II. Silent:** [Unknown connection to root;] [freq. 46] |kjv: craftsman, artificer, secretly, carpenter, workman, engraver, artificer, smith, maker, skilful, worker, wrought, deaf| {str: 2791, 2795, 2796}

a^{f1}) (מחרשה MHh-R-ShH) — **Mattock:** Implement for scratching the soil. [freq. 3] |kjv: mattock, share| {str: 4281, 4282}

b^{m}) (חריש Hh-RYSh) — **Plowing:** The time of plowing. [freq. 3] |kjv: earring, harvest| {str: 2758}

c^{f2}) (חרושת Hh-RW-ShT) — **Carving:** A scratching in stone or wood. [ms: חרשת] [freq. 4] |kjv: cutting, carving| {str: 2799}

g^{m}) (חורש HhW-RSh) — **I. Craftsman:** One who engraves wood, stone or metal. [ms: חרש] **II. Forest:** From its wood being used for carving. [freq. 8] |kjv: artificer, wood, forest, bough, shroud| {str: 2793, 2794}

bf^{m}) (חרישי Hh-RY-ShY) — **Hot:** [Unknown connection to root;] [freq. 1] |kjv: vehement| {str: 2759}

~~~~~~~~~~~

2212) (חרת HhRT) ac: **Engrave** co: **?** ab: **?:** [from: - sharp]

V) (חרת Hh-RT) — **Engrave:** [freq. 1] (vf: Paal) |kjv: graven| {str: 2801}

~~~~~~~~~~~

2213) (חשב HhShB) ac: **Design** co: **?** ab: **Invention:** The process of designing a pattern or plan for an action or device. [from: - turning over thoughts]

V) (חשב Hh-ShB) — **Design:** To plan or design a course of action, item or invention. [Hebrew and Aramaic] [freq. 125] (vf: Paal, Niphal, Hitpael, Piel) |kjv: count, devise, think, imagine, cunning, reckon, purpose, esteem, account, impute, forecast, regard, workman, conceive| {str: 2803, 2804}

N^{m}) (חשב Hh-ShB) — **Band:** A band with designs used for tying clothing. [freq. 8] |kjv: girdle| {str: 2805}

a^{f1}) (מחשבה MHh-Sh-BH) — **Design:** A designing or planning of inventions or plans. [freq. 56] |kjv: thought, device, purpose, work, imagination, cunning, devise, invent| {str: 4284}

a^{f2}) (מחשבת MHh-Sh-BT) — **Design:** A designing or planning of inventions or plans. [freq. 56] |kjv: thought, device, purpose, work, imagination, cunning, devise, invent| {str: 4284}

j^{m}) (חשבון HhSh-BWN) — **Invention:** A designed device. [freq. 3] |kjv: reason, account, device| {str: 2808}

ej^m) ᚤᚤᚤᛑᚴᚴᛁᛊ (חישבון HhY-Sh-BWN) — **Invention:** A designed device. [ms: חשבון] [freq. 2] |kjv: engine, invention| {str: 2810}

~~~~~~~~~~

2214) ᚤᚤᚤᛁᛁᚴᛅᛁ (חשׁח HhShHh) ac: **Require** co: ? ab: ?

V) ᚤᚤᚤᛁᛁᚴᛅᛁ (חשׁח Hh-ShHh) — **Require:** To need something. [Aramaic only] [freq. 2] (vf: Paal) |kjv: need, careful| {str: 2818}

N^{f3}) †Yᚤᚤᚤᛁᛁᚴᛅᛁ (חשׁחות HhSh-HhWT) — **Required:** Something needed. [freq. 1] |kjv: needful| {str: 2819}

~~~~~~~~~~

2215) ᚤᚤᚤᛁᛁᛊᚴ (חשׁך HhShK) ac: **Darken** co: **Dark** ab: **Darkness:** [from: ᚤᚤᛁᛁ - a dark place]

V) ᚤᚤᚤᛁᛁᛊᚴ (חשׁך Hh-ShK) — **Darken:** [freq. 19] (vf: Paal, Hiphil) |kjv: darken, dark, blacker, darkness, dim, hide| {str: 2821}

N^{f1}) ᚤᚤᚤᛁᛁᛊᛰ (חשׁכה HhSh-KH) — **Dark:** [freq. 6] |kjv: dark, darkness| {str: 2824, 2825}

a^m) ᚤᚤᚤᛁᛁᛊᛰᛰ (מחשׁך MHh-ShK) — **Dark place:** [freq. 7] |kjv: darkness, dark| {str: 4285}

c^m) ᚤᚤᚤᛁᛁYᛊ (חשׁוך Hh-ShWK) — **Darkness:** [Hebrew and Aramaic] [ms: חשׁך] [freq. 2] |kjv: mean| {str: 2816, 2823}

g^m) ᚤᚤᚤᛁᛁᛁYᛊ (חושׁך HhW-ShK) — **Darkness:** [ms: חשׁך] [freq. 80] |kjv: darkness, dark, obscurity, night| {str: 2822}

~~~~~~~~~~

2216) ᚤᚤᚤᛁᛁᛁᛃ (חשׁל HhShL) ac: **Shatter** co: ? ab: ?

V) ᚤᚤᚤᛁᛁᛁᛃ (חשׁל Hh-ShL) — **Shatter:** [Hebrew and Aramaic] [freq. 2] (vf: Niphal) |kjv: feeble, subdue| {str: 2826, 2827}

~~~~~~~~~~

2217) ᚤᚤᚤᛁᛁᛁᛜ (חשׁם HhShM) ac: ? co: ? ab: ?

m^m) ᚤᚤᚤᛁᛁᛁᛜᛁ (חשׁמן HhSh-MN) — **Wealthy:** [freq. 1] |kjv: prince| {str: 2831}

~~~~~~~~~~

2218) ᚤᚤᚤᛁᛁᛁᛁ (חשׁן HhShN) ac: ? co: ? ab: ?

g^m) ᚤᚤᚤᛁᛁᛁYᛁ (חושׁן HhW-ShN) — **Breastplate:** [freq. 25] |kjv: breastplate| {str: 2833}

~~~~~~~~~~

2219) ᚤᚤᚤᛁᛁᛁᛝ (חשׁק HhShQ) ac: **Attach** co: ? ab: **Desire:** A joining together in love or through a connection. [from: ᚤᚤᚤᛁᛁᛁ]

V) ᚤᚤᚤᛁᛁᛁᛝ (חשׁק Hh-ShQ) — I. **Affection:** To have an attachment to another. II. **Band:** To go around something to bind it. [freq. 11] (vf: Paal, Pual, Piel) |kjv: desire, love, fillet, log, delight| {str: 2836}

N^m) ᚤᚤᚤᛁᛁᛁᛝ (חשׁק Hh-ShQ) — **Desire:** [freq. 4] |kjv: desire, that, pleasure| {str: 2837}

d^m) ᚤᚤᚤᛁᛁᛁYᛝ (חשׁוק Hh-ShWQ) — **Band:** As attached around something. [ms: חשׁק] [freq. 8] |kjv: fillet| {str: 2838}

ed^m) ᚤᚤᚤᛁᛁᛁYᛊᛝ (חישׁוק HhY-ShWQ) — **Hub:** What the wheel is attached to. [ms: חשׁק] [freq. 1] |kjv: desire, that, pleasure| {str: 2839}

~~~~~~~~~~

2220) ᛒᛚᛗ (חשר HhShR) ac: **Gather** co: **?** ab: **?:** [from: ᛚᛗ - bound]

N^(fl)) ᛋᛒᛚᛗ (חשרה HhSh-RH) — **Gathering:** [freq. 1] |kjv: dark| {str: 2841}

ed^(m)) ᛋᛁᛚᛗ (חישור HhY-ShWR) — **Spoke:** As gathered and bound to the wheel. [ms: חשר] [freq. 1] |kjv: spoke| {str: 2840}

~~~~~~~~~~

2221) �hᛏᛗ (חתך HhTK) ac: **Determine** co: **?** ab: **?**

V) ᚱᛏᛗ (חתך Hh-TK) — **Determine:** [freq. 1] (vf: Niphal) |kjv: determine| {str: 2852}

~~~~~~~~~~

2222) ᚢᛏᛗ (חתל HhTL) ac: **Wrap** co: **Bandage** ab: **?:** A bandage or cloth wrapped around someone or something. [from: ᚢᛏ - wrapping around]

V) ᚢᛏᛗ (חתל Hh-TL) — **Wrap:** To wrap with a cloth. [freq. 2] (vf: Hophal, Pual) |kjv: swaddle| {str: 2853}

N^(fl)) ᚱᚢᛏᛗ (חתלה HhT-LH) — **Cloth:** For wrapping. [freq. 1] |kjv: swaddlingband| {str: 2854}

ed^(m)) ᚢᛁᛏᛗ (חיתול HhY-TWL) — **Bandage:** [ms: חתול] [freq. 1] |kjv: roller| {str: 2848}

~~~~~~~~~~

2223) ᛗᛏᛗ (חתם HhTM) ac: **Seal** co: **Signet** ab: **?:** A document is rolled up and sealed with wet clay. The signet ring of the owner bears the image of his seal and is pressed into the clay. [from: ᛗᛏ - a completed document]

V) ᛗᛏᛗ (חתם Hh-TM) — **Seal:** To seal something closed. [Hebrew and Aramaic] [freq. 28] (vf: Paal, Niphal, Hiphil, Piel) |kjv: seal, mark, stop| {str: 2856, 2857}

g^(m)) ᛗᛏᛁᛗ (חותם HhW-TM) — **Signet:** A ring or cylinder with the owners seal that is pressed into clay to show ownership. [ms: חתם] [freq. 14] |kjv: signet, seal| {str: 2368}

g^(f2)) ᛏᛗᛏᛁᛗ (חותמת HhW-T-MT) — **Signet:** A ring or cylinder with the owners seal that is pressed into clay to show ownership. [ms: חתמת] [freq. 1] |kjv: signet| {str: 2858}

~~~~~~~~~~

2224) ᛐᛏᛗ (חתן HhTN) ac: **Relate** co: **Wedding** ab: **In-law:** A relating to another through marriage. [from: ᛏᛗ - taking hold]

V) ᛐᛏᛗ (חתן Hh-TN) — **Relate:** To have a relationship with another through marriage. [freq. 33] (vf: Paal, Hitpael, Participle) |kjv: in-law, affinity, marriage| {str: 2859}

N^(m)) ᛐᛏᛗ (חתן Hh-TN) — **In-law:** One related by marriage. [freq. 20] |kjv: in-law, bridegroom, husband| {str: 2860}

N^(fl)) ᚱᛐᛏᛗ (חתנה HhT-NH) — **Wedding:** [freq. 1] |kjv: espousal| {str: 2861}

~~~~~~~~~~

2225) ᚲᛏᛗ (חתף HhTP) ac: **Snatch** co: **Prey** ab: **?:** The snatching of prey by a predator. [from: ᛏᛗ - taking hold]

V) ᚲᛏᛗ (חתף Hh-TP) — **Snatch:** To snatch prey. [freq. 1] (vf: Paal) |kjv: take| {str: 2862}

346

Nᵐ) ⌐†Ⅲ (חתף Hh-TP) — **Prey:** As snatched by a predator. [freq. 1] |kjv: prey| {str: 2863}

~~~~~~~~~~

2226) ᕁ†Ⅲ (חתר HhTR) ac: **Dig** co: ? ab: **?:** A digging through to penetrate through or into something.

V) ᕁ†Ⅲ (חתר Hh-TR) — **Dig:** Also to row as digging in the water with a paddle. [freq. 8] (vf: Paal) |kjv: dig, row| {str: 2864}

aᶠ²) †ᕁ†ⅢⱮ (מחתרת MHh-T-RT) — **Searching:** As a digging for something. [freq. 2] |kjv: breaking, search| {str: 4290}

~~~~~~~~~

Thet

2227) ⊗ᴌᴎᴍ (טבח ThBHh) ac: **Slaughter** co: **Flesh** ab: **?**: [from: ᴌᴎ]

V) ⊗ᴌᴎᴍ (טבח Th-BHh) — **Slaughter:** [freq. 11] (vf: Paal) |kjv: kill, slaughter, slay| {str: 2873}

Nᵐ) ⊗ᴌᴎᴍ (טבח Th-BHh) — **I. Slaughter:** The act of slaughtering. Also the meat of the slaughter. **II. Guard:** As one who prevents a slaughter of a ruler. [Hebrew and Aramaic] **III. Cook:** One who slaughters animals for food. [freq. 45] |kjv: slaughter, slay, sore, beast, guard, cook| {str: 2874, 2876, 2877}

Nᶠˡ) ⊗ᴌᴎᴍ (טבחה ThB-HhH) — **Cook:** One who slaughters animals for food. [freq. 1] |kjv: cook| {str: 2879}

aᵐ) ⊗ᴌᴎᴍ (מטבח MTh-BHh) — **Slaughter:** [freq. 1] |kjv: slaughter| {str: 4293}

eᶠˡ) ⊗ᴌᴎᴍ (טיבחה ThYB-HhH) — **Slaughter:** The act of slaughtering. Also the meat of the slaughter. [freq. 3] |kjv: flesh, slaughter| {str: 2878}

2228) ⊗ᴌᴍᴊ (טבל ThBL) ac: **Dip** co: **?** ab: **?**: [from: ᴌᴍ]

V) ⊗ᴌᴍᴊ (טבל Th-BL) — **Dip:** [freq. 16] (vf: Paal, Niphal) |kjv: dip, plunge| {str: 2881}

dᵐ) ⊗ᴌᴍᴊ (טבול Th-BWL) — **Turban:** [Unknown connection to root] [freq. 1] |kjv: dyed| {str: 2871}

2229) ⊗ᴌᴎᴌ (טבע ThBAh) ac: **Sink** co: **?** ab: **?**

V) ⊗ᴌᴎᴌ (טבע Th-BAh) — **Sink:** [freq. 10] (vf: Paal, Hophal, Pual) |kjv: sink, drown, settle, fasten| {str: 2883}

Nᶠ²) ⊗ᴌᴎᴌ (טבעת ThB-AhT) — **Ring:** [Unknown connection to root;] [freq. 49] |kjv: ring| {str: 2885}

2230) ⊗ᴌᴎᴌ (טבר ThBR) ac: **?** co: **?** ab: **?**

dᵐ) ⊗ᴌᴎᴌ (טבור Th-BWR) — **Middle:** [freq. 2] |kjv: middle, midst| {str: 2872}

2231) ⊗ᴍᴎᴊ (טחן ThHhN) ac: **Grind** co: **Mill** ab: **?**: [from: ᴍᴎ - as in the grinding of limestone for making plaster]

V) ⊗ᴍᴎᴊ (טחן Th-HhN) — **Grind:** [freq. 8] (vf: Paal) |kjv: grind| {str: 2912}

Nᶠˡ) ⊗ᴍᴎᴊ (טחנה ThHh-NH) — **Grind:** [freq. 1] |kjv: grinding| {str: 2913}

2232) ⊗ᴍᴎᴌ (טחר ThHhR) ac: **Burn** co: **Hemorrhoids** ab: **?**: [from: ᴍᴎᴌ]

cᵐ) ⊗ᴍᴎᴌ (טחור Th-HhWR) — **Hemorrhoids:** [Always written in the plural] [ms: טחר] [freq. 8] |kjv: emerods| {str: 2914}

2233) ⌐⊗⊗ (טטף ThThP) ac: ? co: **Mark** ab: ?

g^{f1}) ⚭⌐⊗Y⊗ (טוטפה ThW-Th-PH) — **Mark:** [freq. 3] |kjv: frontlet| {str: 2903}

2234) ⌐ᴍ⊗ (טמן ThMN) ac: **Hide** co: **Treasure** ab: ?

V) ⌐ᴍ⊗ (טמן Th-MN) — **Hide:** [freq. 31] (vf: Paal, Niphal, Hiphil, Participle) |kjv: hide, lay, secret| {str: 2934}

ac^m) ⌐Yᴍ⊗ᴍ (מטמון MTh-MWN) — **Treasure:** What is hidden. [ms: מטמן] [freq. 5] |kjv: treasure, riches| {str: 4301}

2235) ⌐ↆ⊗ (טנף ThNP) ac: **Dirty** co: ? ab: **Defile**

V) ⌐ↆ⊗ (טנף Th-NP) — **Dirty:** [freq. 1] (vf: Piel) |kjv: defile| {str: 2936}

2236) ᴍ☉⊗ (טעם ThAhM) ac: **Taste** co: ? ab: **Perceive:** A distinguishing between flavors. Also, perception as the ability to distinguish between thoughts.

V) ᴍ☉⊗ (טעם Th-AhM) — **Taste:** [Hebrew and Aramaic] [freq. 14] (vf: Paal) |kjv: taste, perceive, eat| {str: 2938, 2939}

N^m) ᴍ☉⊗ (טעם Th-AhM) — I. **Taste:** [Hebrew and Aramaic] II. **Decree:** As perceived. [Aramaic only] [freq. 43] |kjv: taste, judgment, behaviour, advice, understanding, commandment, matter, command, account, decree, regarded, wisdom| {str: 2940, 2941, 2942}

a^m) ᴍ☉⊗ᴍ (מטעם MTh-AhM) — **Meat:** A flavorful meat. [freq. 8] |kjv: meat, dainty| {str: 4303}

2237) ↘☉⊗ (טען ThAhN) ac: ? co: ? ab: ?

V) ↘☉⊗ (טען Th-AhN) — I. **Load:** II. **Stab:** [freq. 2] (vf: Paal) |kjv: load, thrust| {str: 2943, 2944}

2238) ⅏⌐⊗ (טפח ThPHh) ac: **Span** co: **Span** ab: ?: The span of the fingers as spread out and used as a measure. [from: ⅏⌐]

V) ⅏⌐⊗ (טפח Th-PHh) — I. **Span:** To spread out as the fingers of the hand. II. **Rear:** To bring up and train children. [Unknown connection to root;] [freq. 2] (vf: Piel) |kjv: span, swaddle| {str: 2946}

N^m) ⅏⌐⊗ (טפח Th-PHh) — **Span:** A length of measure, the span of the fingers of the hand. [freq. 4] |kjv: breath, coping| {str: 2947}

g^m) ⅏⌐Y⊗ (טופח ThW-PHh) — **Span:** A length of measure, the span of the fingers of the hand. [freq. 5] |kjv: breadth, broad| {str: 2948}

h^{f2}) ✝⅏⌐⊗ᴍ (מטפחת MTh-P-HhT) — **Cloak:** As a garment that spreads out. [freq. 2] |kjv: vail| {str: 4304}

ec^m) ⅏Y⌐⌐↝⊗ (טיפוח ThY-PWHh) — **Rearing:** The bringing up and rearing of children. [Unknown connection to root;] [ms: טפח] [freq. 1] |kjv: breadth, broad| {str: 2949}

2239) ⌡⌐⊗ (טפל ThPL) ac: **Sew** co: ? ab: ?: The sewing of a garment or lies.

V) ∫⟳⊗ (טפל Th-PL) — **Sew:** [freq. 3] (vf: Paal) |kjv: sew, forge, forger| {str: 2950}

2240) ᕋ⟳⊗ (טפר ThPR) ac: ? co: **Fingernail** ab: ?

N^m) ᕋ⟳⊗ (טפר Th-PR) — **Fingernail:** [Aramaic only] [freq. 2] |kjv: nail| {str: 2953}

2241) ⊔⟳⊗ (טפש ThPSh) ac: ? co: **Fat** ab: ?

V) ⊔⟳⊗ (טפש Th-PSh) — **Fat:** To be fat. [freq. 1] (vf: Paal) |kjv: fat| {str: 2954}

2242) ⊓ᕋ⊗ (טרד ThRD) ac: **Drive** co: ? ab: ?

V) ⊓ᕋ⊗ (טרד Th-RD) — **Drive:** To continually push. [Hebrew and Aramaic] [freq. 6] (vf: Paal, Participle) |kjv: continual, drive| {str: 2956, 2957}

2243) ᒧᕋ⊗ (טרח ThRHh) ac: **Load** co: **Burden** ab: ?: A heavy or troublesome burden that is loaded on the back.

V) ᒧᕋ⊗ (טרח Th-RHh) — **Load:** [freq. 1] (vf: Hiphil) |kjv: weary| {str: 2959}

---

g^m) ᒧᕋY⊗ (טורח ThW-RHh) — **Burden:** [ms: טרח] [freq. 2] |kjv: cumbrance, trouble| {str: 2960}

2244) ᨕᕋ⊗ (טרם ThRM) ac: ? co: ? ab: **Before**

N^m) ᨕᕋ⊗ (טרם Th-RM) — **Before:** [freq. 9] |kjv: before, neither, not yet| {str: 2962}

c^m) ᨕYᕋ⊗ (טרום Th-RWM) — **Before:** [freq. 1] |kjv: before| {str: 2958}

2245) ⟳ᕋ⊗ (טרף ThRP) ac: **Tear** co: **Prey** ab: ?: The prey that is torn to pieces by the predator. [from: ᕋⱭᨆ - fresh]

V) ⟳ᕋ⊗ (טרף Th-RP) — **Tear:** To tear into pieces as a predator does to its prey. [freq. 25] (vf: Paal, Niphal, Hiphil) |kjv: tear, ravening, catch, feed, rent, prey| {str: 2963}

N^m) ⟳ᕋ⊗ (טרף Th-RP) — **I. Prey:** The meat that is torn by the predator. **II. Plucked:** As the predator plucks the prey. [freq. 24] |kjv: prey, meat, leaves, spoil| {str: 2964, 2965}

N^fl) ⚡⟳ᕋ⊗ (טרפה ThR-PH) — **Torn:** Flesh that is torn. [freq. 9] |kjv: torn, ravin| {str: 2966}

Kaph

2246) ᵰᵚᵚ (כבד KBD) ac: **Heavy** co: **Liver** ab: **Honor:** Someone or something that is heavy in weight, wealth, abundance, importance or respect. [from: ᵚᵚ - from the stars as abundant]

V) ᵰᵚᵚ (כבד K-BD) — **Heavy:** To be heavy of weight, wealth or importance. [freq. 116] (vf: Paal, Niphal, Hiphil, Hitpael, Pual, Piel) |kjv: honour, glorify, heavy, harden, glorious, sore, great, many, promote| {str: 3513}

Nᶠ) ᵰᵚᵚ (כבד K-BD) — **I. Liver:** The heaviest of the organs. **II. Heavy:** [freq. 52] |kjv: great, grievous, heavy, sore, hard, much, slow, hardened, heavier, laden, thick| {str: 3515, 3516}

Nᶠ³) ⴕYᵰᵚᵚ (כברות KB-DWT) — **Heavily:** [ms: כבדת] [freq. 1] |kjv: heavily| {str: 3517}

cᵐ) ᵰYᵚᵚ (כבוד K-BWD) — **Honor:** To consider something as heavy in the sense of respect. [ms: כבד] [freq. 200] |kjv: glory, honour| {str: 3519}

dᶠ¹) ⴟⴕYᵚᵚ (כבודה K-BW-DH) — **Heaviness:** [freq. 3] |kjv: carriage, glorious, stately| {str: 3520}

gᵐ) ᵰᵚYᵚ (כובד KW-BD) — **Heavy:** [ms: כבד] [freq. 4] |kjv: heavy, grievousness, great| {str: 3514}

———

2247) ᴶᵚᵚ (כבל KBL) ac: **Twist** co: **Fetter** ab: **?:** [from: ᴶᵚ - the fibers flowing over each other]

Nᵐ) ᴶᵚᵚ (כבל K-BL) — **Fetter:** As twisted together. [freq. 2] |kjv: fetters| {str: 3525}

———

2248) ᵬᵚᵚ (כבע KBAh) ac: **High** co: **Helmet** ab: **?:** [from: ᵬᵚ - being high]

gᵐ) ᵬᵚYᵚ (כובע KW-BAh) — **Helmet:** As sitting high on the head. [freq. 6] |kjv: helmet| {str: 3553}

———

2249) ᴥᵚᵚ (כבס KBS) ac: **Wash** co: **?** ab: **?:** Clothes were placed in the cleaning solution and trampled on. [from: ᴥᵚ]

V) ᴥᵚᵚ (כבס K-BS) — **Wash:** [freq. 51] (vf: Paal, Pual, Piel, Participle) |kjv: wash, fuller| {str: 3526}

———

2250) ᴙᵚᵚ (כבר KBR) ac: **Multiply** co: **Net** ab: **Abundance:** Nets are used for catching an abundance of fish. [from: ᵚᵚ - from the stars as abundant]

V) ᴙᵚᵚ (כבר K-BR) — **Multiply:** [freq. 2] (vf: Hiphil, Participle) |kjv: multiply| {str: 3527, 4342}

Nᵐ) ᴙᵚᵚ (כבר K-BR) — **Already:** What has previously happened. [Unknown connection to root;] [freq. 9] |kjv: already, now| {str: 3528}

Nᶠ¹) ᴥᴙᵚᵚ (כברה KB-RH) — **Sieve:** As functioning as a net. [freq. 1] |kjv: sieve| {str: 3531}

aᵐ) ᴙᵚᵚⴖ (מכבר MK-BR) — **Coverlet:** A netted cloth. [freq. 1] |kjv: cloth| {str: 4346}

b^m) שׁבִיר (כביר K-BYR) — **I.
Net: II. Abundant:** [freq. 13] |kjv:
pillow, mighty, much, strong, most|
{str: 3523, 3524}

e^fl) שׁבִירה (כיברה KYB-RH) —
Short: A short distance. [Unknown
connection to root;] [ms: כברה]
[freq. 3] |kjv: little| {str: 3530}

h^m) מכשׁבר (מכבר MK-BR) —
Grate: Appears as a net. [freq. 6]
|kjv: grate| {str: 4345}

~~~~~~

2251) שׁבשׁ (כבש KBSh) ac: **Subdue**
co: **Footstool** ab: **?**

V) שׁבשׁ (כבש K-BSh) — **Subdue:**
To place the foot on the land in the
sense of subduing it. Also to place
ones foot into another nation in the
sense of subduing it. [freq. 15] (vf:
Paal, Niphal, Hiphil, Piel) |kjv:
subdue, subjection, bondage, under,
force| {str: 3533}

N^m) שׁבשׁ (כבש K-BSh) —
Footstool: [freq. 1] |kjv: footstool|
{str: 3534}

em^m) שׁבשׁן (כיבשן KY-B-ShN)
— **Furnace:** [unknown connection to
root;] [ms: כבשן] [freq. 4] |kjv:
furnace| {str: 3536}

~~~~~~

2252) שׁדר (כדר KDR) ac: **?** co: **?** ab:
?

ec^m) שׁדור (כידור KY-DWR) —
Battle: [freq. 1] |kjv: battle| {str:
3593}

~~~~~~

2253) שׁזב (כזב KZB) ac: **Lie** co: **Lie**
ab: **?:** Vain words spoken to deceive,
cause failure or disappoint. What does not

function in the capacity that it was meant
to.

V) שׁזב (כזב K-ZB) — **Lie:** [freq.
16] (vf: Paal, Niphal, Hiphil, Piel,
Participle) |kjv: lie, liar, vain, fail|
{str: 3576}

N^m) שׁזב (כזב K-ZB) — **Lie:**
[freq. 31] |kjv: lie, liar, leasing,
deceitful, false| {str: 3577}

e^fl) שׁזבה (כיזבה KYZ-BH) —
Lying: [Aramaic only] [df: כדבה]
[freq. 1] |kjv: lying| {str: 3538}

n^m) עשׁזב (אכזב AK-ZB) — **Lie:**
[freq. 2] |kjv: lie, liar| {str: 391}

~~~~~~

2254) שׁזר (כזר KZR) ac: **?** co: **?** ab:
Cruel

n^m) עשׁזר (אכזר AK-ZR) —
Cruel: [freq. 4] |kjv: cruel, fierce|
{str: 393}

nf^m) עשׁזרי (אכזרי AK-Z-RY)
— **Cruel:** [freq. 8] |kjv: cruel| {str:
394}

nf^3) עשׁזריות (אכזריות AK-
ZR-YWT) — **Cruel:** [freq. 1] |kjv:
cruel| {str: 395}

~~~~~~

2255) שׁחד (כחד KHhD) ac: **Hide** co:
? ab: **?:** [from: חד - as being walled in]

V) שׁחד (כחד K-HhD) — **Hide:**
[freq. 32] (vf: Niphal, Hiphil, Piel)
|kjv: hide, cut off, conceal, desolate,
cut down| {str: 3582}

~~~~~~

2256) שׁחל (כחל KHhL) ac: **Paint** co:
? ab: **?**

V) שׁחל (כחל K-HhL) — **Paint:**
To paint the eyes. [freq. 1] (vf: Paal)
|kjv: paint| {str: 3583}

2257) שחם (כחש KHhSh) ac: **Deny** co: **?** ab: **?:** A withholding or denial of something such as food resulting in leanness and truth through a lie.

V) שחם (כחש K-HhSh) — **Deny:** To withhold something from another or self as in a lie or submission. [freq. 22] (vf: Paal, Niphal, Hitpael, Piel) |kjv: lie, submit, deny, fail, dissemble, liar, deceive| {str: 3584}

N^m) שחם (כחש K-HhSh) — **I. Lie:** A denial of the truth. **II. Leanness:** A denial of food. [freq. 7] |kjv: lying, lies, leanness| {str: 3585, 3586}

2258) שכר (ככר KKR) ac: **?** co: **Round** ab: **?:** Something that is round. [from: שכ - as round like a bowl]

N^f) שכר (ככר K-KR) — **Round:** A coin as a round piece of gold or silver. [Aramaic only] [freq. 1] |kjv: talent| {str: 3604}

e^f) שיכר (כיכר KY-KR) — **Round:** A coin as a round piece of gold or silver. A round loaf of bread. The plain as a round piece of land. [ms: ככר] [freq. 68] |kjv: talent, plain, loaf, piece, country, morsel| {str: 3603}

2259) שלב (כלב KLB) ac: **?** co: **Dog** ab: **?**

N^m) שלב (כלב K-LB) — **Dog:** [freq. 32] |kjv: dog| {str: 3611}

d^m) שלוב (כלוב K-LWB) — **Basket:** [unknown connection to root;] [freq. 3] |kjv: cage, basket| {str: 3619}

2260) שלח (כלח KLHh) ac: **?** co: **Old** ab: **?**

N^m) שלח (כלח K-LHh) — **Old age:** [freq. 2] |kjv: old age, full age| {str: 3624}

2261) שלם (כלם KLM) ac: **?** co: **?** ab: **Shame**

V) שלם (כלם K-LM) — **Shame:** [freq. 38] (vf: Niphal, Hiphil, Hophal) |kjv: ashamed, confound, shame, blush, hurt, reproach, confusion| {str: 3637}

b^fl) שלמה (כלימה K-LY-MH) — **Shame:** [freq. 30] |kjv: shame, confusion, dishonour, reproach| {str: 3639}

b^f3) שלמות (כלימות K-LY-MWT) — **Shame:** [freq. 1] |kjv: shame| {str: 3640}

2262) שלף (כלף KLP) ac: **Strike** co: **Hammer** ab: **?:** (eng: clap)

e^f) שילף (כילף KY-LP) — **Hammer:** [freq. 1] |kjv: hammer| {str: 3597}

2263) שמז (כמז KMZ) ac: **Store** co: **Ornament** ab: **?:** [from: שמ - storing something precious]

o^m) שומז (כומז KW-MZ) — **Ornament:** Something precious that is stored. [freq. 2] |kjv: table| {str: 3558}

2264) שמן (כמן KMN) ac: **Store** co: **Treasure** ab: **?:** Something that is hidden or stored away. [from: ששמ - storing something precious] (eng: cumin)

c^m) כמון (K-MWN) — **Cummin:** A seed used as a spice. [ms: כמן] [freq. 3] |kjv: cummin| {str: 3646}

h^m) מכמן (MK-MN) — **Treasure:** [freq. 1] |kjv: treasure| {str: 4362}

~~~~~~~~~~

2265) כמס (KMS) ac: **Store** co: ? ab: ?: The storing of something of value. [from: ששמ - storing something precious]

V) כמס (K-MS) — **Store:** [freq. 1] (vf: Paal, Participle) |kjv: store| {str: 3647}

~~~~~~~~~~

2266) כמר (KMR) ac: **Burn** co: ? ab: ?

V) כמר (K-MR) — **Burn:** Also a passion that burns for another. [freq. 4] (vf: Niphal) |kjv: yearn, kindle, black| {str: 3648}

g^m) כומר (KW-MR) — **Priest:** The priests of idolaters. [Unknown connection to root;] [ms: כמר] [freq. 3] |kjv: priest| {str: 3649}

h^{f2}) מכמרת (MK-M-RT) — **Fishing net:** [Unknown connection to root;] [freq. 3] |kjv: drag, net| {str: 4365}

ac^m) מכמור (MK-MWR) — **Hunting net:** [Unknown connection to root;] [ms: מכמר] [freq. 2] |kjv: net| {str: 4364}

bl^m) כמריר (KM-RYR) — **Blackness:** In the sense of being burnt. [freq. 1] |kjv: blackness| {str: 3650}

~~~~~~~~~~

2267) כנס (KNS) ac: **Gather** co: ? ab: ?: [from: כנ - gathering]

V) כנס (K-NS) — **Gather:** [freq. 11] (vf: Paal, Hitpael, Piel) |kjv: gather, together, heap, wrap| {str: 3664}

h^m) מכנס (MK-NS) — **Undergarment:** A piece of clothing that is gathered up. [freq. 5] |kjv: breeches| {str: 4370}

~~~~~~~~~~

2268) כנע (KNAh) ac: **Lower** co: **Bundle** ab: **Humility:** When a large bundle is placed on the shoulders the person is bent down low. [from: כנ - gathering together a bundle]

V) כנע (K-NAh) — **Lower:** To be brought down low in humility or submission. [freq. 36] (vf: Niphal, Hiphil) |kjv: humble, subdue, low, down, subjection| {str: 3665}

e^{f1}) כינעה (KYN-AhH) — **Bundle:** [freq. 1] |kjv: ware| {str: 3666}

~~~~~~~~~~

2269) כנף (KNP) ac: **Hide** co: **Wing** ab: ?: The mother bird hides its young in her wings. [from: כנ - gathering]

V) כנף (K-NP) — **Hide:** As hidden in the wings of a bird. [freq. 1] (vf: Niphal) |kjv: corner| {str: 3670}

N^f) כנף (K-NP) — **Wing:** Also the wings of a garment. [freq. 108] |kjv: wing, skirt, border, corner, end, feathered, sort| {str: 3671}

~~~~~~~~~~

2270) שֹׁאַ (כנר KNR) ac: **?** co: **Harp** ab: ?: [from: אַ֑ל - music as bright]

ec^m) שֹׁאַ֑אַ (כינור KY-NWR) — **Harp:** [ms: כנור] [freq. 42] |kjv: harp| {str: 3658}

~~~~~~~~

2271) שֹׁאַוו (כנש KNSh) ac: **Gather** co: ? ab: ?: [from: שֹׁל - gathering]

V) שֹׁאַוו (כנש K-NSh) — **Gather:** [Aramaic only] [freq. 3] (vf: Participle) |kjv: gather| {str: 3673}

~~~~~~~~

2272) שֹׁאַ֒ (כנת KNT) ac: **?** co: **Associate** ab: ?: [from: שֹׁל - as one who gathers himself to another]

N^m) שֹׁאַ֒ (כנת K-NT) — **Associate:** [freq. 8] |kjv: companion| {str: 3674, 3675}

~~~~~~~~

2273) שֹׁאֵ֒ (כסב KSB) ac: **?** co: **Sheep** ab: **?**

N^m) שֹׁאֵ֒ (כסב K-SB) — **Sheep:** [df: כשב כבש] [freq. 120] |kjv: lamb, sheep| {str: 3532, 3775}

N^fl) שֹׁאֵ֒ (כסבה KS-BH) — **Lamb:** A female lamb. [df: כבשה] [freq. 8] |kjv: lamb| {str: 3535}

e^fl) שֹׁאֵ֒ (כיסבה KYS-BH) — **Lamb:** A female lamb. [df: כשבה] [freq. 1] |kjv: lamb| {str: 3776}

~~~~~~~~

2274) שֹׁאֵ֒ (כסח KSHh) ac: **Cut** co: ? ab: ?

V) שֹׁאֵ֒ (כסח K-SHh) — **Cut:** [freq. 2] (vf: Paal) |kjv: cut| {str: 3683}

~~~~~~~~

2275) שֹׁאֵֹ (כסל KSL) ac: **?** co: **Loins** ab: **Confidence:** The loins as the seat of ones confidence, foolish or proper.

V) שֹׁאֵֹ (כסל K-SL) — **Foolish:** To be foolishly confident in something. [df: סכל] [freq. 9] (vf: Paal, Niphal, Hiphil, Piel) |kjv: foolish, fool| {str: 3688, 5528}

N^m) שֹׁאֵֹ (כסל K-SL) — **I. Loins:** The seat of confidence. **II. Confidence:** In a foolish or proper manner. **III. Fool:** [df: סכל] [freq. 21] |kjv: flank, hope, folly, loins, confidence| {str: 3689, 5529, 5530}

b^m) שֹׁאֵֹ (כסיל K-SYL) — **Fool:** One who has confidence in something foolish. [freq. 70] |kjv: fool, foolish| {str: 3684}

b^f3) שֹׁאֵֹ (כסילות K-SY-LWT) — **Foolish:** A foolish confidence. [freq. 1] |kjv: foolish| {str: 3687}

e^fl) שֹׁאֵֹ (כיסלה KYS-LH) — **Confidence:** In a foolish or proper manner. [freq. 2] |kjv: confidence, folly| {str: 3690}

e^f3) אֵֹשׁ (סיכלות SY-K-LWT) — **Folly:** [ms: סכלות] [df: שכלות] [ar: [freq. 7] |kjv: folly, foolishness| {str: 5531}

~~~~~~~~

2276) שֹׁאֵ~ (כסם KSM) ac: **Trim** co: ? ab: ?: A trimming of the beard.

V) שֹׁאֵ~ (כסם K-SM) — **Trim:** [freq. 2] (vf: Paal) |kjv: poll| {str: 3697}

o^f2) שֹׁאֵ~ (כוסמת KW-S-MT) — **Spelt:** A wheat like grain with what looks like trimmed hair. [ms: כסמת] [freq. 3] |kjv: rie, fitches| {str: 3698}

~~~~~~~~

2277) ⟨כסף KSP) ac: **Desire** co: Silver ab: ?: A metal desired because of its value. Universally used as a form of money.

V) ⟨כסף K-SP) — **Desire:** [freq. 6] (vf: Paal, Niphal, Participle) |kjv: desire, long, greedy, sore| {str: 3700}

N^m) ⟨כסף K-SP) — **Silver:** A desired metal. [Hebrew and Aramaic] [freq. 416] |kjv: silver, money, price, silverling| {str: 3701, 3702}

2278) ⟨כען KAhN) ac: ? co: ? ab: **Now**

N^m) ⟨כען K-AhN) — **Now:** [Aramaic only] [freq. 13] |kjv: now| {str: 3705}

N^f2) ⟨כענת KAh-NT) — **Now:** [Aramaic only] [ms: כעת] [freq. 4] |kjv: time| {str: 3706}

2279) ⟨כעס KAhS) ac: ? co: ? ab: **Anger**

V) ⟨כעס K-AhS) — **Anger:** [freq. 54] (vf: Paal, Hiphil, Piel) |kjv: anger, provoke, grieve, indignation, sorrow, vex, wrath| {str: 3707}

N^m) ⟨כעס K-AhS) — **Anger:** [df: כעש] [freq. 25] |kjv: grief, provocation, wrath, sorrow, anger, angry, indignation, provoking, sore, spite| {str: 3708}

2280) ⟨כפל KPL) ac: ? co: **Double** ab: ?

V) ⟨כפל K-PL) — **Double:** [freq. 5] (vf: Paal, Niphal) |kjv: double| {str: 3717}

N^m) ⟨כפל K-PL) — **Double:** [freq. 3] |kjv: double| {str: 3718}

2281) ⟨כפן KPN) ac: **Bend** co: **Famine** ab: ?: [from: ש - from the bent shape of the palm]

V) ⟨כפן K-PN) — **Bend:** [freq. 1] (vf: Paal) |kjv: bend| {str: 3719}

N^m) ⟨כפן K-PN) — **Famine:** One bent with hunger. [freq. 2] |kjv: famine| {str: 3720}

2282) ⟨כפס KPS) ac: ? co: **Beam** ab: ?

b^m) ⟨כפיס K-PYS) — **Beam:** The beam that supports the roof of the house. [freq. 1] |kjv: beam| {str: 3714}

2283) ⟨כפר KPR) ac: **Cover** co: **Lid** ab: **Atonement:** A protective covering to go over something or the covering of a debt or wrong. [from: ש] (eng: cover - with the exchange of the v and p)

V) ⟨כפר K-PR) — **Cover:** [freq. 102] (vf: Paal, Hitpael, Pual, Piel) |kjv: atonement, purge, reconcile, forgive, purge, pacify, mercy, cleanse, disannul, appease, put, pardon, pitch| {str: 3722}

b^m) ⟨כפיר K-PYR) — **I. Village:** A village is a community outside of the city walls and covered with protection from the city. **II. Young lion:** [Unknown connection to root;] [freq. 32] |kjv: lion, village, young| {str: 3715}

c^(m)) שׁ☉ᗡᎯ (כפור K-PWR) — **I. Bason:** A vessel with a lid cover. **II. Frost:** As covering the ground. [freq. 9] |kjv: bason, hoarfrost| {str: 3713}

c^(f2)) שׁ☉ᗡᎯ† (כפורת K-PW-RT) — **Lid:** As a covering. [ms: כפרת] [freq. 27] |kjv: mercy seat| {str: 3727}

g^(m)) שׁᐅᎯᗡ (כופר KW-PR) — **I. Covering:** A covering such as pitch or a monetary covering such as a bribe or ransom. [ms: כפר] **II. Village:** A village is a community outside of the city walls and covered with protection from the city. [ms: כפר] [freq. 19] |kjv: ransom, satisfaction, bribe, camphire, pitch, village| {str: 3723, 3724}

ed^(m)) שׁᐅᐯᗡᎯ (כיפור KY-PWR) — **Atonement:** A covering over of transgression. [ms: כפר] [freq. 8] |kjv: atonement| {str: 3725}

2284) שׁᐊᗌ᎛ (כפש KPSh) ac: **Cover** co: ? ab: ?

V) שׁᐊᗌ᎛ (כפש K-PSh) — **Cover:** [freq. 1] (vf: Hiphil) |kjv: cover| {str: 3728}

2285) שׁᐅᎿ† (כפת KPT) ac: **Bind** co: ? ab: ?

V) שׁᐅᎿ† (כפת K-PT) — **Bind:** [Aramaic only] [freq. 4] (vf: Paal) |kjv: bind| {str: 3729}

2286) שׁᎯᗌᗅ (כרז KRZ) ac: **Proclaim** co: **Herald** ab: ?: A crying out in proclamation.

V) שׁᎯᗌᗅ (כרז K-RZ) — **Proclaim:** [Aramaic only] [freq. 1] (vf: Paal) |kjv: proclamation| {str: 3745}

c^(m)) שׁᎯᗌᐯᎯ (כרוז K-RWZ) — **Herald:** One who proclaims words. [Aramaic only] [freq. 1] |kjv: herald| {str: 3744}

2287) שׁᎯ᎛᎛ (כרך KRK) ac: ? co: ? ab: ?

ib^(m)) שׁᎯ᎛ᐊ† (תכריך TK-RYK) — **Garment:** [freq. 1] |kjv: garment| {str: 8509}

2288) שׁᎯᗯᗯ (כרם KRM) ac: ? co: **Vineyard** ab: ?

N^(m)) שׁᎯᗯᗯ (כרם K-RM) — **Vineyard:** [freq. 93] |kjv: vineyard, vines, vintage| {str: 3754}

g^(m)) שׁᐅᎯᗯᗯ (כורם KW-RM) — **Vinedresser:** [ms: כרם] [freq. 5] |kjv: vinedresser| {str: 3755}

2289) שׁᎯᗴ (כרס KRS) ac: ? co: **Belly** ab: ?

N^(m)) שׁᎯᗴ (כרס K-RS) — **Belly:** [df: כרש] [freq. 1] |kjv: belly| {str: 3770}

2290) שׁᎯᗬ (כרע KRAh) ac: **Stoop** co: **Leg** ab: ?: The bending of the leg when stooping.

V) שׁᎯᗬ (כרע K-RAh) — **Stoop:** To stoop or crouch down by bending or getting on the knees. [freq. 36] (vf: Paal, Hiphil) |kjv: bow, fell, subdue, low, couch, feeble, kneel| {str: 3766}

N^f) שׁﬡⲟ (כרע K-RAh) — **Leg:** As bent at the knee when stooping. [freq. 9] |kjv: leg| {str: 3767}

2291) שׁﬡﬨ (כרת KRT) ac: **Cut** co: ? ab: ?: A cutting off or down of anything. Often used as a cutting of the covenant in the sense that the sacrificial animal is cut in half (see Jeremiah 34:18). [from: ⲟ⌒ⲟ - being cut short] (eng: create)

V) שׁﬡﬨ (כרת K-RT) — **Cut off:** [freq. 288] (vf: Paal, Niphal, Hiphil, Hophal, Pual) |kjv: cut off, make, cut down, cut, fail, destroy, want, covenant, hew| {str: 3772}

d^{fl}) שׁﬡⲩﬨ✲ (כרותה K-RW-TH) — **Beam:** As cut off from the tree. [ms: כרתה] [freq. 3] |kjv: beam| {str: 3773}

b^{f3}) שׁﬡﬨⲩﬨ (כריתות K-RY-TWT) — **Divorce:** As cut off from the husband. [freq. 4] |kjv: divorcement, divorce| {str: 3748}

2292) שׁﬗﬗⲗ (כשל KShL) ac: **Topple** co: **Ruin** ab: ?: A toppling down into ruins.

V) שׁﬗﬗⲗ (כשל K-ShL) — **Topple:** [freq. 65] (vf: Paal, Niphal, Hiphil, Hophal, Piel) |kjv: fall, stumble, cast down, feeble, overthrown, ruin, decay, fail, weak| {str: 3782}

a^{fl}) שׁﬗﬗⲗ✲ⲙⲙ (מכשלה MK-Sh-LH) — **Ruin:** The toppled down buildings of a city. [freq. 2] |kjv: ruin, stumblingblock| {str: 4384}

b^m) שׁﬗﬗⲗ⌐ (כשיל K-ShYL) — **Axe:** For toppling trees. [freq. 1] |kjv: axe| {str: 3781}

---

ej^m) שׁﬗﬗⲗⲩ⌐ (כישלון KY-Sh-LWN) — **Toppling:** [ms: כשלון] [freq. 1] |kjv: fall| {str: 3783}

hc^m) ⲗⲩⲙⲙ (מכשול MK-ShWL) — **Stumblingblock:** Used to cause someone to stumble or topple down. [ms: מכשל] [freq. 14] |kjv: stumblingblock, offence, ruin, offend, fall| {str: 4383}

2293) שׁﬗﬗ⌐ (כשף KShP) ac: ? co: ? ab: **Sorcery:** Supernatural powers used by idolaters.

V) שׁﬗﬗ⌐ (כשף K-ShP) — **Sorcery:** To practice sorcery. [freq. 6] (vf: Piel, Participle) |kjv: sorcerer, witch, witchcraft| {str: 3784}

N^m) שׁﬗﬗ⌐ (כשף K-ShP) — I. **Sorcery:** II. **Sorcerer:** [freq. 7] |kjv: witchcraft, sorcery, sorcerer| {str: 3785, 3786}

2294) שׁﬡⲙ (כשר KShR) ac: ? co: ? ab: **Prosperity:** [from: ﬗⲙ - being straight]

V) שׁﬡⲙ (כשר K-ShR) — **Prosper:** [freq. 3] (vf: Paal, Hiphil) |kjv: right, prosper, direct| {str: 3787}

g^{fl}) שׁⲩﬡⲙ✲ (כושרה KW-Sh-RH) — **Prosperity:** [freq. 1] |kjv: chains| {str: 3574}

ec^m) שׁﬗⲩⲙ (כישור KY-ShWR) — **Spindle:** For keeping the twine straight. [freq. 1] |kjv: spindle| {str: 3601}

ej^m) שׁﬗⲙⲩ⌐ (כישרון KY-Sh-RWN) — **Success:** [ms: כשרון] [freq. 3] |kjv: good, right, equity| {str: 3788}

2295) שׁⴈ⼕ (כתב KTB) ac: **Write** co: **Writing** ab: **?**

V) שׁⴈ⼕ (כתב K-TB) — **Write:** [Hebrew and Aramaic] [freq. 231] (vf: Paal, Niphal, Piel) |kjv: write, describe, subscribe, record| {str: 3789, 3790}

N^m) שׁⴈ⼕ (כתב K-TB) — **Writing:** Something written as well as the act of writing. [Hebrew and Aramaic] [freq. 29] |kjv: writing, register, scripture, prescribing| {str: 3791, 3792}

c^f2) שׁⴈⴲⴈ⼕ (כתובת K-TW-BT) — **Writing:** [ms: כתבת] [freq. 1] |kjv: any| {str: 3793}

h^m) ⴖⴈשׁⴈ⼕ⴎ (מכתב MK-TB) — **Writing:** A written composition. [freq. 9] |kjv: writing| {str: 4385}

2296) שׁⴈ⼌ (כתל KTL) ac: **?** co: **Wall** ab: **?**: [from: ⴈ⼌ - being wrapped around the city]

N^m) שׁⴈ⼌ (כתל K-TL) — **Wall:** [Aramaic only] [freq. 2] |kjv: wall| {str: 3797}

g^m) שׁⴈⴲ⼌ (כותל KW-TL) — **Wall:** Of a house. [ms: כתל] [freq. 1] |kjv: wall| {str: 3796}

2297) שׁⴈⴎ (כתם KTM) ac: **?** co: **Gold** ab: **?**

V) שׁⴈⴎ (כתם K-TM) — **Stain:** [Unknown connection to root;] [freq. 1] (vf: Niphal) |kjv: mark| {str: 3799}

N^m) שׁⴈⴎ (כתם K-TM) — **Gold:** [freq. 9] |kjv: gold| {str: 3800}

2298) שׁⴈ⼉ (כתן KTN) ac: **?** co: **Coat** ab: **?**: (eng: coat - with the removal of the n)

c^f2) שׁⴈⴲ⼉ⴈ (כתונת K-TW-NT) — **Coat:** [ms: כתנת] [freq. 29] |kjv: coat, garment, robe| {str: 3801}

2299) שׁⴈ⼀ (כתף KTP) ac: **?** co: **Side** ab: **?**: The side or shoulder that something hangs on.

N^f) שׁⴈ⼀ (כתף K-TP) — **Side:** The side of the body as the shoulder or arm. Also the side of anything. [freq. 67] |kjv: side, shoulder, shoulderpiece, undersetter, corner, arm| {str: 3802}

2300) שׁⴈⴹ (כתר KTR) ac: **Surround** co: **Crown** ab: **?**

V) שׁⴈⴹ (כתר K-TR) — **Surround:** [freq. 7] (vf: Hiphil, Piel) |kjv: compass, inclose, beset, suffer, crown| {str: 3803}

N^m) שׁⴈⴹ (כתר K-TR) — **Crown:** As encircling the head. [freq. 3] |kjv: crown| {str: 3804}

g^f2) שׁⴈⴲⴹⴈ (כותרת KW-T-RT) — **Capital:** The top of a pillar as a crown. [ms: כתרת] [freq. 24] |kjv: chapiter| {str: 3805}

2301) שׁⴈⴘ (כתש KTSh) ac: **Pound** co: **Mortar** ab: **?**: A hollowed out stone bowl used to crush seeds, herbs or other plant material for food or medicine.

V) שׁⴈⴘ (כתש K-TSh) — **Pound:** [freq. 1] (vf: Paal) |kjv: bray| {str: 3806}

aᵐ) ᛌᛌᚼᛍ⋀⋀ (מכתש MK-TSh) — **Mortar:** [freq. 2] |kjv: hollow, mortar| {str: 4388}

Lam

2302) ⊗ﬡﬗل (לבט LBTh) ac: **Fall** co: **?** ab: **?**

V) ⊗ﬡﬗل (לבט L-BTh) — **Fall:** [freq. 3] (vf: Niphal) |kjv: fall| {str: 3832}

~~~~~~~~~~

2303) ﬡﬗײַ (לבן LBN) ac: **?** co: **White** ab: **?:** Something that is white. Also bricks made from white materials. [from: ﬡﬗ - a building material]

V) ﬡﬗײַ (לבן L-BN) — **I. White:** To be white. **II. Brick:** To make bricks. [freq. 8] (vf: Paal, Hiphil, Hitpael) |kjv: white, brick, whiter| {str: 3835}

N^m) ﬡﬗײַ (לבן L-BN) — **White:** [freq. 29] |kjv: white| {str: 3836}

N^{f1}) ﬤﬡﬗײַ (לבנה LB-NH) — **I. Moon:** As white. **II. Brick:** [freq. 14] |kjv: moon, brick, tile| {str: 3842, 3843}

a^m) ﬡﬗײַﬗﬗ (מלבן ML-BN) — **Brick-kiln:** A furnace for firing bricks. [freq. 3] |kjv: brickkiln| {str: 4404}

c^{f1}) ﬤﬡﬤײַײַײַ (לבונה L-BW-NH) — **Frankincense:** As white. [ms: לבנה] [freq. 21] |kjv: frankincense, incense| {str: 3828}

e^{f1}) ﬤﬡﬗײַײַ (ליבנה LYB-NH) — **I. Poplar:** A tree with white bark. **II. Brick:** [ms: לבנה] [freq. 3] |kjv: poplar, paved| {str: 3839, 3840}

~~~~~~~~~~

2304) ﬤﬤﬡﬗل (לבש LBSh) ac: **Clothe** co: **Clothing** ab: **?**

V) ﬤﬤﬡﬗل (לבש L-BSh) — **Clothe:** To put on clothing. [Hebrew and Aramaic] [freq. 115] (vf: Paal, Hiphil, Pual) |kjv: clothe, put, array, wear, arm, came, apparel, upon| {str: 3847, 3848}

d^m) ﬤﬤײַﬡﬗل (לבוש L-BWSh) — **Clothing:** [Hebrew and Aramaic] [ms: לבש] [freq. 34] |kjv: clothing, garment, apparel, vesture, clothed, put, raiment, vestment| {str: 3830, 3831}

ad^m) ﬗﬤﬤײַﬡﬗﬗ (מלבוש ML-BWSh) — **Clothing:** [ms: מלבש] [freq. 8] |kjv: apparel, raiment, vestment| {str: 4403}

ic^{f2}) ﬨﬤﬤײַﬡﬗﬨ (תלבושת TL-BW-ShT) — **Clothing:** [ms: תלבשת] [freq. 1] |kjv: clothing| {str: 8516}

~~~~~~~~~~

2305) ﬗﬗﬗﬡﬗل (לחם LHhM) ac: **Fight** co: **Bread** ab: **?:** Flour an water are mixed together and kneaded. Also war in the sense of fighting with the bread when kneading. [from: ﬗﬗﬡﬡ - food]

V) ﬗﬗﬗﬡﬗل (לחם L-HhM) — **I. Eat: II. Fight:** [freq. 177] (vf: Paal, Niphal) |kjv: fight, war, eat, overcome, devour, prevail| {str: 3898}

N^m) ﬗﬗﬗﬡﬗل (לחם L-HhM) — **I. Bread:** [Hebrew and Aramaic] **II. War:** [freq. 299] |kjv: bread, food, meat, loaves, shewbread, victuals, feast, fruit, provision| {str: 3899, 3900, 3901}

d^m) ᚹᚥⴱⳑ (לחום L-HhWM) —
Meat: [ms: לחם] [freq. 2] |kjv:
eating, flesh| {str: 3894}

h^fl) ⴲᚥⴱⳑᚥ (מלחמה ML-Hh-
MH) — **War:** [freq. 319] |kjv: battle,
war, fight| {str: 4421}

2306) ⳡⴱⳑ (לחן LHhN) ac: **?** co:
Concubine ab: **?:** [from: ⟜ⳑ -
gathering]

N^fl) ⳡⴱⳑ (לחן L-HhN) —
Concubine: [Aramaic only] [freq. 3]
|kjv: concubine| {str: 3904}

2307) ᚨⳇⴱⳑ (לחץ LHhTs) ac: **Squeeze**
co: **?** ab: **Oppression:** [from: ⟜ⳑ -
gathering]

V) ᚨⳇⴱⳑ (לחץ L-HhTs) —
Squeeze: [freq. 19] (vf: Paal, Niphal)
|kjv: oppress, afflict, crush, fast,
force, oppressor, thrust| {str: 3905}

N^m) ᚨⳇⴱⳑ (לחץ L-HhTs) —
Oppression: [freq. 12] |kjv:
oppression, affliction| {str: 3906}

2308) ᚳᚳⴱⳑ (לחש LHhSh) ac: **Whisper**
co: **Whisper** ab: **?:** [from: ᚳᚳⴱ - quiet]

V) ᚳᚳⴱⳑ (לחש L-HhSh) —
Whisper: [freq. 3] (vf: Hitpael, Piel,
Participle) |kjv: whisper, charmer|
{str: 3907}

N^m) ᚳᚳⴱⳑ (לחש L-HhSh) —
Whisper: [freq. 5] |kjv:
enchantment, orator, earring, prayer,
charmed| {str: 3908}

2309) ᚳᚳⴲⳑ (לטש LThSh) ac: **Sharp** co:
? ab: **?:** The sharpening of a sword by

---

hammering or scraping on a whet stone.
Also, a sharp or penetrating look. [from:
ᚳᚳⴲ - hammering]

V) ᚳᚳⴲⳑ (לטש L-ThSh) — **Sharp:**
To make sharp or look sharply. [freq.
5] (vf: Paal, Pual, Participle) |kjv:
sharpen, sharp, instructor| {str: 3913}

2310) ⴷᚳⳡⳑ (לכד LKD) ac: **Capture**
co: **?** ab: **?:** A taking by grabbing hold.
[from: ⟜ⳑ - gathering]

V) ⴷᚳⳡⳑ (לכד L-KD) — **Capture:**
[freq. 121] (vf: Paal, Niphal, Hitpael)
|kjv: take, catch, frozen, hold, stick|
{str: 3920}

N^m) ⴷᚳⳡⳑ (לכד L-KD) —
Captured: [freq. 1] |kjv: taken| {str:
3921}

ac^f2) ⟊ᚳⳡⳑᚥ (מלכודת ML-KW-
DT) — **Trap:** Used for capturing.
[ms: מלכדת] [freq. 1] |kjv: trap|
{str: 4434}

2311) ⴷᚥᚥⳑ (למד LMD) ac: **Learn** co:
Goad ab: **?:** The directing the path of the
ox by goading it. A learning by goading.
[from: ᚥᚥⳑ - goading]

V) ⴷᚥᚥⳑ (למד L-MD) — **Learn:**
[freq. 86] (vf: Paal, Pual, Piel) |kjv:
teach, learn, instruct, expert, skilful,
teacher| {str: 3925}

a^m) ⴷᚥᚥⳑᚥ (מלמד ML-MD) —
Goad: A pointed staff for directing
oxen that are in a yoke. [freq. 1] |kjv:
goad| {str: 4451}

ed^m) ⴷᚥᚥ⳨ⳑ (לימוד LY-MWD)
— **Student:** One who is goaded in a
direction. [ms: למד למוד] [freq. 6]
|kjv: learned, disciple, taught, used,
accustomed| {str: 3928}

ib^m) ᴛ⋎ᴧᴧᴧᒎᵗ (תלמיד TL-MYD) — **Student:** [freq. 1] |kjv: scholar| {str: 8527}

~~~~~~~~~

2312) ᴍᴑᒎ (לעב LAhB) ac: **Mock** co: ? ab: ?: [from: ᴑᒎ - as coming from the throat]

V) ᴍᴑᒎ (לעב L-AhB) — **Mock:** [freq. 1] (vf: Hiphil) |kjv: mock| {str: 3931}

~~~~~~~~~

2313) ᒃᴑᒎ (לעג LAhG) ac: **Mock** co: ? ab: ?: A mocking by stammering or imitation of a foreign tongue. [from: ᴑᒎ - as coming from the throat]

V) ᒃᴑᒎ (לעג L-AhG) — **Mock:** [freq. 18] (vf: Paal, Niphal, Hiphil) |kjv: mock, scorn, laugh, deride, stammer| {str: 3932}

N^m) ᒃᴑᒎ (לעג L-AhG) — **Mocking:** [freq. 9] |kjv: scorn, derision, mocker, stammer| {str: 3933, 3934}

e^m) ᒃᴑ⋎ᒎ (ליעג LY-AhG) — **Mocker:** [ms: עלג] [freq. 1] |kjv: stammerer| {str: 5926}

~~~~~~~~~

2314) ᴢᴑᒎ (לעז LAhZ) ac: **Speak** co: ? ab: ?: The unintelligible speech of one with a strange language. [from: ᴑᒎ - as coming from the throat]

V) ᴢᴑᒎ (לעז L-AhZ) — **Speak:** To speak unintelligibly. [freq. 1] (vf: Paal) |kjv: strange language| {str: 3937}

~~~~~~~~~

2315) ⊗ᴑᒎ (לעט LAhTh) ac: **Feed** co: ? ab: ?: [from: ᴑᒎ - swallowing]

V) ⊗ᴑᒎ (לעט L-AhTh) — **Feed:** [freq. 1] (vf: Hiphil) |kjv: feed| {str: 3938}

~~~~~~~~~

2316) ᒐᴑᒎ (לען LAhN) ac: ? co: **Bitter** ab: ?: [from: ᴑᒎ - swallowing]

N^fl) ᒐᴑᒎ (לענה LAh-NH) — **Laanah:** An unknown bitter plant. [freq. 8] |kjv: wormwood, hemlock| {str: 3939}

~~~~~~~~~

2317) ᴛᴆᴑᒎ (לפד LPD) ac: **Shine** co: **Torch** ab: ?: (eng: lamp - with the additional m and the removal of the d)

b^m) ᴛ⋎ᴑᒎ (לפיד L-PYD) — **Torch:** Also lightning as a torch in the night sky. [ms: לפד] [freq. 14] |kjv: lamp, firebrand, torch, brand, lightning, burning| {str: 3940}

~~~~~~~~~

2318) ᵗᴑᒎ (לפת LPT) ac: **Twist** co: ? ab: ?

V) ᵗᴑᒎ (לפת L-PT) — **Twist:** To twist to the side. [freq. 3] (vf: Paal, Niphal) |kjv: take, turn| {str: 3943}

~~~~~~~~~

2319) ᴍᴑᒎ (לקח LQHh) ac: **Take** co: **Tong** ab: ?: [from: ᴑᒎ - gathering]

V) ᴍᴑᒎ (לקח L-QHh) — **Take:** [A generic verb with a wide application meaning to take] [freq. 965] (vf: Paal, Niphal, Hitpael, Hophal, Pual) |kjv: take, receive, fetch, bring, get, carry, marry, buy| {str: 3947}

N^m) ᴍᴑᒎ (לקח L-QHh) — **Learning:** In the sense of being received. [freq. 9] |kjv: doctrine, learning speech| {str: 3948}

aᵐ) 𐤌-𐤏-𐤋-𐤄 (מֶלְקָח ML-QHh) — **Tong:** A tool for taking coals out of the fire. [freq. 6] |kjv: tong, snuffer| {str: 4457}

acᵐ) 𐤌-𐤏-𐤋-𐤄 (מַלְקוֹחַ ML-QWHh) — **I. Jaw:** As tongs for taking food. **II. Prey:** What is taken. [freq. 8] |kjv: prey, booty, jaw| {str: 4455}

2320) 𐤋-𐤏-𐤈 (לָקַט LQTh) ac: **Gather** co: **Pouch** ab: ?: [from: 𐤋-𐤏 - gathering]

V) 𐤋-𐤏-𐤈 (לָקַט L-QTh) — **Gather:** [freq. 37] (vf: Paal, Hitpael, Pual, Piel) |kjv: gather, glean| {str: 3950}

Nᵐ) 𐤋-𐤏-𐤈 (לֶקֶט L-QTh) — **Gathering:** [freq. 2] |kjv: gleaning| {str: 3951}

tdᵐ) 𐤉-𐤋-𐤏-𐤈 (יַלְקוּט YL-QWTh) — **Pouch:** For gathering items together. [freq. 1] |kjv: scrip| {str: 3219}

2321) 𐤋-𐤏-𐤔 (לֶקֶשׁ LQSh) ac: **Gather** co: **After-growth** ab: ?: A late gathering of a crop after a late rain. [from: 𐤋-𐤏 - gathering]

V) 𐤋-𐤏-𐤔 (לָקֵשׁ L-QSh) — **Gather:** To gather in the late crop. [freq. 1] (vf: Piel) |kjv: gather| {str: 3953}

Nᵐ) 𐤋-𐤏-𐤔 (לֶקֶשׁ L-QSh) — **After-growth:** [freq. 2] |kjv: latter growth| {str: 3954}

acᵐ) 𐤋-𐤏-𐤋-𐤄 (מַלְקוֹשׁ ML-QWSh) — **Late rain:** A late rain that causes a latter growth of crops. [freq. 8] |kjv: latter rain| {str: 4456}

2322) 𐤋-𐤔-𐤃 (לָשַׁד LShD) ac: ? co: **Moist** ab: ?: The moistness of something fresh.

Nᵐ) 𐤋-𐤔-𐤃 (לָשָׁד L-ShD) — **Fresh:** Something that is fresh and moist. [freq. 2] |kjv: fresh, moisture| {str: 3955}

2323) 𐤋-𐤔-𐤊 (לֶשֶׁךְ LShK) ac: ? co: **Chamber** ab: ?: [from: 𐤔𐤊]

eᶠˡ) 𐤋-𐤔-𐤊-𐤄 (לִשְׁכָּה LYSh-KH) — **Chamber:** [ms: לשכה] [freq. 47] |kjv: parlour| {str: 3957}

2324) 𐤋-𐤔-𐤌 (לֶשֶׁם LShM) ac: ? co: ? ab: ?

Nᵐ) 𐤋-𐤔-𐤌 (לֶשֶׁם L-ShM) — **Leshem:** An unknown stone. [freq. 2] |kjv: ligure| {str: 3958}

2325) 𐤋-𐤔-𐤍 (לָשַׁן LShN) ac: **Slander** co: **Tongue** ab: **Language:** The wagging of the tongue when talking or slandering.

V) 𐤋-𐤔-𐤍 (לָשַׁן L-ShN) — **Slander:** To slander another as a wagging of the tongue. [freq. 3] (vf: Hiphil, Piel) |kjv: slander, accuse| {str: 3960}

eᵐ) 𐤋-𐤉-𐤔-𐤍 (לִישָׁן LY-ShN) — **Language:** As coming from the movement of the tongue. [Aramaic only] [ms: לשן] [freq. 7] |kjv: language| {str: 3961}

cᵐ) 𐤋-𐤔-𐤅-𐤍 (לָשׁוֹן L-ShWN) — **I. Tongue:** [ms: לשן] **II. Language:** As coming from the movement of the tongue. [freq. 117] |kjv: tongue, language, bay, wedge, babbler, flame, talker| {str: 3956}

2326) 𐤋-𐤕-𐤇 (לָתַח LTHh) ac: **Spread** co: **Wardrobe** ab: ?: [from: 𐤕𐤇 - spreading] k^{fl}) 𐤀𐤕𐤋𐤌 (מלתחה ML-T-HhH) — **Wardrobe:** As spread out. [freq. 1] |kjv: vestry| {str: 4458}

~~~~~~~~~~

2327) لתך (לתך LTK) ac: ? co: ? ab: ?

N^m) لתך (לתך L-TK) — **Letek:** A standard of measure. [freq. 1] |kjv: half-homer| {str: 3963}

~~~~~~~~~~

2328) لתע (לתע LTAh) ac: ? co: **Fang** ab: ?

a^{fl}) 𐤏𐤕𐤋𐤌 (מלתעה ML-T-AhH) — **Fang:** [freq. 1] |kjv: teeth| {str: 4459, 4973}

k^{fl}) 𐤏𐤕𐤋𐤌 (מלתעה ML-T-AhH) — **Fang:** [df: מתלעה] [freq. 3] |kjv: teeth, jaw| {str: 4973}

~~~~~~~~~~

365

Mah

2329) ᴛᴧLᴀᴀ (מגד MGD) ac: **?** co: **Ornament** ab: **Precious**

Nᵐ) ᴛᴧLᴀᴀ (מגד M-GD) — **Precious:** What is choice, precious or excellent. [freq. 8] |kjv: precious, pleasant| {str: 4022}

mᶠˡ) ❊ᐟᴛᴧLᴀᴀ (מגדנה MG-D-NH) — **Ornament:** Precious ornaments probably with gems. [freq. 4] |kjv: precious, present| {str: 4030}

2330) ᴧLᴀᴀ (מגל MGL) ac: **?** co: **Sickle** ab: **?**

Nᵐ) ᴧLᴀᴀ (מגל M-GL) — **Sickle:** [freq. 2] |kjv: sickle| {str: 4038}

2331) ᐟLᴀᴀ (מגן MGN) ac: **Deliver** co: **Burden** ab: **?**

V) ᐟLᴀᴀ (מגן M-GN) — **Deliver:** [freq. 3] (vf: Piel) |kjv: deliver| {str: 4042}

Nᶠˡ) ❊ᐟLᴀᴀ (מגנה MG-NH) — **Burden:** A heavy burden that is to be delivered. [freq. 1] |kjv: sorrow| {str: 4044}

2332) ᖴLᴀᴀ (מגר MGR) ac: **Cast down** co: **?** ab: **?**

V) ᖴLᴀᴀ (מגר M-GR) — **Cast down:** [Hebrew and Aramaic] [freq. 3] (vf: Paal, Piel) |kjv: terror, cast, destroy| {str: 4048, 4049}

adᶠˡ) ❊ᖴᴎLᴀᴀᴀᴀ (ממגורה MM-GW-RH) — **Granary:** The place where grain is deposited in the sense of being cast down. [freq. 1] |kjv: barn| {str: 4460}

2333) ᖴᴄᴀᴀ (מזר MZR) ac: **?** co: **?** ab: **?**

aᵐ) ᖴᴄᴀᴀᴀᴀ (ממזר MM-ZR) — **Bastard:** [freq. 2] |kjv: bastard| {str: 4464}

2334) ᴏᴧᴛᴛᴀᴀ (מחץ MHhTs) ac: **Strike** co: **Gash** ab: **?:** A large gash from the strike of a sword or arrow. [from: ᴛᴛᴀᴀ]

V) ᴏᴧᴛᴛᴀᴀ (מחץ M-HhTs) — **Strike:** [freq. 14] (vf: Paal, Participle) |kjv: wound, smite, pierce, strike, dip| {str: 4272}

Nᵐ) ᴏᴧᴛᴛᴀᴀ (מחץ M-HhTs) — **Gash:** [freq. 1] |kjv: stroke| {str: 4273}

2335) ᴏᴛᴛᴀᴀ (מחק MHhQ) ac: **Strike** co: **?** ab: **?:** [from: ᴛᴛᴀᴀ]

V) ᴏᴛᴛᴀᴀ (מחק M-HhQ) — **Strike:** [freq. 1] (vf: Paal) |kjv: smite| {str: 4277}

2336) ᖴ⊗ᴀᴀ (מטר MThR) ac: **Rain** co: **Rain** ab: **?**

V) ᖴ⊗ᴀᴀ (מטר M-ThR) — **Rain:** [freq. 17] (vf: Niphal, Hiphil) |kjv: rain| {str: 4305}

Nᵐ) ᖴ⊗ᴀᴀ (מטר M-ThR) — **Rain:** [freq. 38] |kjv: rain| {str: 4306}

2337) ᎷᎳᎳᏚᎭ (מכר MKR) ac: **Sell** co: **Merchandise** ab: **Price**

V) ᎷᎳᎳᏚᎭ (מכר M-KR) — **Sell:** [freq. 80] (vf: Paal, Niphal, Hitpael, Participle) |kjv: sell, seller| {str: 4376}

N^m) ᎷᎳᎳᏚᎭ (מכר M-KR) — **I. Merchandise: II. Value:** [freq. 3] |kjv: price, ware| {str: 4377}

b^m) ᎷᎳᎳᏚᎭᏗ (מכיר M-KYR) — **Price:** [df: מחיר] [freq. 15] |kjv: price, worth, sold, gain, hire| {str: 4242}

h^m) ᎷᎳᎳᎳᏚᎭ (ממכר MM-KR) — **Merchandise:** [freq. 10] |kjv: sold, sale, ware, sold| {str: 4465}

h^f2) ᎷᎳᎳᎳᏚᎭᏔ (ממכרת MM-K-RT) — **Merchandise:** [freq. 1] |kjv: as| {str: 4466}

2338) ᎷᎳᎭᏗᏔ (מלח MLHh) ac: **Season** co: **Salt** ab: **?**

V) ᎷᎳᎭᏗᏔ (מלח M-LHh) — **I. Season:** To season with salt. **II. Disappear:** As salt disappears when added to water. [freq. 5] (vf: Paal, Niphal, Hophal, Pual) |kjv: salt, season, temper, vanish| {str: 4414}

N^m) ᎷᎳᎭᏗᏔ (מלח M-LHh) — **I. Salt:** [Hebrew and Aramaic] **II. Mariner:** One who sails the sea. **III. Rag:** An old or rotten rag. [Unknown connection to root;] [freq. 37] |kjv: salt, rags, maintenance, mariner| {str: 4415, 4416, 4417, 4418, 4419}

N^f1) ᎷᎳᎭᏗᏔᎱ (מלחה ML-HhH) — **Salt:** A land of salt as barren. [freq. 3] |kjv: barren, barrenness, salt| {str: 4420}

d^m) ᎷᎳᎭᏌᏗᏔ (מלוח M-LWHh) — **Mallow:** As growing around a salt

marsh. [freq. 1] |kjv: mallow| {str: 4408}

2339) ᎷᎳᎭᏌᏜ (מלט MLTh) ac: **Deliver** co: **?** ab: **?**

V) ᎷᎳᎭᏌᏜ (מלט M-LTh) — **Deliver:** [freq. 95] (vf: Niphal, Hiphil, Hitpael, Piel) |kjv: escape, deliver, save, alone, get, lay, preserve| {str: 4422}

N^m) ᎷᎳᎭᏌᏜ (מלט M-LTh) — **Mortar:** The mortar of bricks. [unknown connection to root;] [freq. 1] |kjv: clay| {str: 4423}

2340) ᎷᎳᎭᏌᎳ (מלך MLK) ac: **Reign** co: **King** ab: **Kingdom:** [from: ᎳᏌ - walking among the people]

V) ᎷᎳᎭᏌᎳ (מלך M-LK) — **Reign:** To reign over a kingdom as king or queen. [freq. 348] (vf: Paal, Niphal, Hiphil, Hophal) |kjv: reign, king, made, queen, consult, rule, set| {str: 4427}

N^m) ᎷᎳᎭᏌᎳ (מלך M-LK) — **I. King:** [Hebrew and Aramaic] **II. Counsel:** [Aramaic only] [freq. 2704] |kjv: king, royal, counsel| {str: 4428, 4430, 4431}

N^f1) ᎷᎳᎭᏌᎳᎱ (מלכה ML-KH) — **Queen:** [Hebrew and Aramaic] [ar: מלכא] [freq. 37] |kjv: queen| {str: 4433, 4436}

N^f2) ᎷᎳᎭᏌᎳᏔ (מלכת ML-KT) — **Queen:** [freq. 5] |kjv: queen| {str: 4446}

N^f3) ᎷᎳᎭᏌᎳᏌᏔ (מלכות ML-KWT) — **Kingdom:** [Hebrew and Aramaic] [ms: מלכת] [ar: מלכו] [freq. 148] |kjv: kingdom, reign, royal, empire, estate, realm, kingly| {str: 4437, 4438}

a^{f1}) 𐤀𐤔𐤅𐤍/ᴧᴧᴧᴧ (ממלכה MM-L-KH) — **Kingdom:** [freq. 117] |kjv: kingdom, royal, reign| {str: 4467}

a^{f3}) †ᴛᴠ𐤔𐤅/ᴧᴧᴧᴧ (ממלכות MM-L-KWT) — **Kingdom:** [freq. 9] |kjv: kingdom, reign| {str: 4468}

d^{f1}) 𐤀𐤔ᴠ𐤅/ᴧᴧ (מלוכה M-LW-KH) — **Kingdom:** [freq. 24] |kjv: kingdom, royal| {str: 4410}

2341) ᴀᴧ𐤅/ᴧᴧ (מליץ MLTs) ac: **?** co: **Sweet** ab: **?**

V) ᴀᴧ𐤅/ᴧᴧ (מליץ M-LTs) — **Sweet:** [freq. 1] (vf: Niphal) |kjv: sweet| {str: 4452}

2342) ᴏ𐤅/ᴧᴧ (מלק MLQ) ac: **Wring** co: **?** ab: **?**: The wringing of a birds neck to kill it by removing the head.

V) ᴏ𐤅/ᴧᴧ (מלק M-LQ) — **Wring:** To wring the neck. [freq. 2] (vf: Paal) |kjv: wring| {str: 4454}

2343) ᴏ'ᴧᴧᴧ (מנע MNAh) ac: **Withhold** co: **?** ab: **?**

V) ᴏ'ᴧᴧᴧ (מנע M-NAh) — **Withhold:** [freq. 29] (vf: Paal, Niphal) |kjv: withhold, keep, refrain, deny, hinder, restrain| {str: 4513}

2344) 𐤔≋ᴧᴧ (מסך MSK) ac: **Mix** co: **Mixed wine** ab: **?**: The mixture of water and wine. [from: ≋ᴧᴧ]

V) 𐤔≋ᴧᴧ (מסך M-SK) — **Mix:** To mix water with wine. [freq. 5] (vf: Paal) |kjv: mingle| {str: 4537}

N^m) 𐤔≋ᴧᴧ (מסך M-SK) — **Mixed wine:** A mixture of water and wine. [df: מזג] [freq. 2] |kjv: mixture, liquor| {str: 4197, 4538}

h^m) 𐤔≋ᴧᴧᴧᴧ (ממסך MM-SK) — **Mixture:** What is mixed. [freq. 2] |kjv: mixed wine, drink offering| {str: 4469}

2345) ᴙ≋ᴧᴧ (מסר MSR) ac: **Commit** co: **?** ab: **?**: [from: ᴙ≋ - turning]

V) ᴙ≋ᴧᴧ (מסר M-SR) — **Commit:** [freq. 2] (vf: Paal, Niphal) |kjv: commit, deliver| {str: 4560}

2346) ᴛ◉ᴧᴧ (מעד MAhD) ac: **Slip** co: **?** ab: **?**: A slipping of the foot.

V) ᴛ◉ᴧᴧ (מעד M-AhD) — **Slip:** [freq. 6] (vf: Paal, Hiphil) |kjv: slip, slide, shake| {str: 4571}

o^{f2}) †ᴛ◉ᴠᴧᴧ (מועדת MW-Ah-DT) — **Lame:** As a foot that has slipped and become lame. [freq. 1] |kjv: joint| {str: 4154}

2347) ⊗◉ᴧᴧ (מעט MAhTh) ac: **?** co: **Little** ab: **?**: [from: ⊗ᴏ]

V) ⊗◉ᴧᴧ (מעט M-AhTh) — **Less:** To be less, fewer or diminished in size or amount. [freq. 22] (vf: Paal, Hiphil, Piel) |kjv: diminish, few, less, little, fewness, least, minish, decrease, nothing, few| {str: 4591}

N^m) ⊗◉ᴧᴧ (מעט M-AhTh) — **Little:** Something that is few or small in size or amount. [freq. 102] |kjv: little, few, while, almost, small, some, matter, light, very, worth| {str: 4592}

2348) ᴧᴧ◎ᴕ (מעך MAhK) ac: **Crush** co: ? ab: ?: [from: ◎ᴕ - pressing down with the heel]

V) ᴧᴧ◎ᴕ (מעך M-AhK) — **Crush:** [freq. 3] (vf: Paal, Pual) |kjv: bruise, stuck, press| {str: 4600}

2349) ᴧᴧ◎ᴌ (מעל MAhL) ac: **Transgress** co: ? ab: **Transgression:** [from: ◎ᴌ - work]

V) ᴧᴧ◎ᴌ (מעל M-AhL) — **Transgress:** To commit an unintentioal or treacherous act that results in error. [freq. 35] (vf: Paal) |kjv: commit, trespass, transgress, done| {str: 4603}

N^m) ᴧᴧ◎ᴌ (מעל M-AhL) — **Transgression:** An unintentional or treacherous act that results in error. [freq. 29] |kjv: trespass, transgression, falsehood, grievously, sore| {str: 4604}

2350) ᴧᴧᴠ◎ᴍ (מצח MTsHh) ac: **Hard** co: Forehead ab: ?

N^m) ᴧᴧᴠ◎ᴍ (מצח M-TsHh) — **Forehead:** As hard. [freq. 13] |kjv: forehead, impudent, brow| {str: 4696}

N^f1) ᴧᴧᴠ◎ᴍ𐤔 (מצחה MTs-HhH) — **Leg armor:** As hard. [freq. 1] |kjv: greave| {str: 4697}

2351) ᴧᴧ�享ᴌ (מרג MRG) ac: ? co: **Threshing sledge** ab: ?

g^m) ᴧᴧY�享ᴌ (מורג MW-RG) — **Threshing sledge:** A wooden board with imbedded stones on the bottom side that is dragged over the threshing floor by oxen to break open grain. [freq. 3] |kjv: threshing| {str: 4173}

2352) ᴧᴧ�享ᴛ (מרד MRD) ac: **Rebel** co: ? ab: **Rebellion:** [from: �享ᴧᴧ - bitterness] (eng: marauder; murder)

V) ᴧᴧ�享ᴛ (מרד M-RD) — **Rebel:** [freq. 25] (vf: Paal) |kjv: rebel, rebellious, rebels| {str: 4775}

N^m) ᴧᴧ�享ᴛ (מרד M-RD) — **Rebellion:** [Hebrew and Aramaic] [freq. 4] |kjv: rebellion, rebellious| {str: 4776, 4777, 4779}

N^f3) ᴧᴧ�享ᴛY† (מרדות MR-DWT) — **Rebellion:** [freq. 1] |kjv: rebellious| {str: 4780}

2353) ᴧᴧ�享ᴍᴛ (מרח MRHh) ac: **Rub** co: ? ab: ?: A poultice is made by crushing a medicinal plant material and rubbing it onto a wound. [from: �享ᴧᴧ - rubbing]

V) ᴧᴧ�享ᴍᴛ (מרח M-RHh) — **Rub:** [freq. 1] (vf: Paal) |kjv: plaister| {str: 4799}

c^m) ᴧᴧ�享Yᴍᴛ (מרוח M-RWHh) — **Crushed:** In the sense of being rubbed. [freq. 1] |kjv: broken| {str: 4790}

2354) ᴧᴧ�享⊗ (מרט MRTh) ac: **Rub** co: ? ab: ?: Something that is polished or made smooth by rubbing or plucking. [from: �享ᴧᴧ - rubbing]

V) ᴧᴧ�享⊗ (מרט M-RTh) — **Rub:** To polish a sword by rubbing it. Also the plucking of hair by rubbing it with a sharp object. [Hebrew and Aramaic] [freq. 10] (vf: Paal, Niphal) |kjv:

furbish, fall, pluck, peel| {str: 4803, 4804}

~~~~~~~~

2355) ᴧᴧᲜᴡᴡ (מרץ MRTs) ac: ? co: **Pain** ab: ?: [from: Შᴧᴧ - as bitter]

V) ᴧᴧᲜᴡᴡ (מרץ M-RTs) — **Painful:** [freq. 4] (vf: Niphal, Hiphil) |kjv: forcible, grievous, sore, embolden| {str: 4834}

~~~~~~~~

2356) ᲝᲜᴡᴡ (מרק MRQ) ac: **Scour** co: ? ab: **Cleansing:** A rubbing or scrubbing to cleanse or polish. [from: Შᴧᴧ - rubbing]

V) ᲝᲜᴡᴡ (מרק M-RQ) — **Scour:** To briskly rub something. [freq. 3] (vf: Paal, Pual) |kjv: furbish, bright, scour| {str: 4838}

N^m) ᲝᲜᴡᴡ (מרק M-RQ) — **Broth:** [Unknown connection to root;] [freq. 3] |kjv: broth| {str: 4839}

d^m) ᲝᎩᲜᴡᴡ (מרוק M-RWQ) — **Scouring:** A brisk rubbing of the body with ointments. [freq. 1] |kjv: purification| {str: 4795}

id^m) ᲝᎩᲜᴡᴧᵗ (תמרוק TM-RWQ) — **Cleansing:** [ms: תמרק] [df: תמריק] [freq. 4] |kjv: purification, purifying, cleanse| {str: 8562}

~~~~~~~~

2357) ᴍᴍᴗᴗᴡᴧ (משח MShHh) ac: **Smear** co: **Ointment** ab: ?: Ointments were made from oils and smeared on injuries for healing. Oil was also smeared on the heads of individuals who are being given the office of a prophet, priest or king as a sign of authority. [from: ᴍᴍᴧᴧ - as a drawing out]

V) ᴍᴍᴗᴗᴡᴧ (משח M-ShHh) — **Smear:** To smear with oil as a treatment or as a sign of authority. [freq. 69] (vf: Paal, Niphal) |kjv: anoint, paint| {str: 4886}

N^m) ᴍᴍᴗᴗᴡᴧ (משח M-ShHh) — **Oil:** What is smeared. [Aramaic only] [freq. 2] |kjv: oil| {str: 4887}

N^{f1}) ☥ᴍᴍᴗᴗᴡᴧ (משחה MSh-HhH) — **Ointment:** The oil that is smeared. [freq. 26] |kjv: anointing, anointed, ointment| {str: 4888}

b^m) ᴍᴍᴗᴗᴡᴧ (משיח M-ShYHh) — **Smeared:** One who is smeared with oil as a sign of authority (prophet, priest or king) [freq. 39] |kjv: anointed, messiah| {str: 4899}

h^m) ᴍᴍᴗᴗᴡᴧᴧᴧ (ממשח MM-ShHh) — **Smeared:** One who is smeared with oil. [freq. 1] |kjv: anointed| {str: 4473}

~~~~~~~~

2358) ᴗᴗᴗᴡᴧ (משך MShK) ac: **Draw** co: ? ab: **Acquire:** A drawing out of something such as a hand, bow, sound (as from a horn) or time. [from: ᴗᴗᴧᴧ - as a drawing out]

V) ᴗᴗᴗᴡᴧ (משך M-ShK) — **Draw:** To draw or pull something or out of something. To prolong in the sense of drawing out time. To draw out a sound from a horn. [freq. 36] (vf: Paal, Niphal, Pual) |kjv: draw, prolong, scatter, continue, defer| {str: 4900}

N^m) ᴗᴗᴗᴡᴧ (משך M-ShK) — **Acquiring:** In the sense of drawing something out. [freq. 2] |kjv: price, precious| {str: 4901}

g^{f1}) ☥ᴗᴗᴗᎩᴡᴧ (מושכה MW-Sh-KH) — **Bow:** In the sense of being drawn to shoot. [freq. 1] |kjv: band| {str: 4189}

~~~~~~~~

2359) ᴊᴌᴌᴧᴧ (משל MShL) ac: **Rule** co: **?** ab: **Dominion:** The dominion one rules over. Also the comparison of things as a rule of measurement. (eng: marshal - with the additional r)

V) ᴊᴌᴌᴧᴧ (משל M-ShL) — **I. Rule: II. Compare:** To compare one thing to another in the sense of a rule of measurement, often a proverb or parable. [freq. 97] (vf: Paal, Niphal, Hiphil, Hitpael, Piel, Participle) |kjv: rule, ruler, reign, dominion, governor, power, like, proverb, speak, use, become, compare, utter| {str: 4910, 4911}

N^m) ᴊᴌᴌᴧᴧ (משל M-ShL) — **Comparison:** Often a parable or proverb as a story of comparisons. [freq. 39] |kjv: proverb, parable, byword, like| {str: 4912}

d^m) ᴊY̌ᴌᴌᴧᴧ (משול M-ShWL) — **Comparison:** [ms: משל] [freq. 1] |kjv: byword| {str: 4914}

h^m) ᴊᴌᴌᴧᴧᴧ (ממשל MM-ShL) — **Dominion:** The realm of ones rule. [freq. 3] |kjv: dominion, rule| {str: 4474}

i ^m) ᴊᴌᴌY̌ᴧᴧ (מושל MW-ShL) — **I. Dominion:** The realm of ones rule. **II. Comparison:** [ms: משל] [freq. 3] |kjv: dominion, like| {str: 4915}

k^f1) ⅏ᴊᴌᴌᴧᴧᴧᴧ (ממשלה MM-Sh-LH) — **Dominion:** The realm of ones rule. [freq. 17] |kjv: dominion, rule, government, power| {str: 4475}

~~~~~~~~

2360) ⊶ᴌᴌᴧᴧ (משק MShQ) ac: **Possess** co: **?** ab: **?**

N^m) ⊶ᴌᴌᴧᴧ (משק M-ShQ) — **Possess:** [freq. 1] |kjv: steward| {str: 4943}

h^m) ⊶ᴌᴌᴧᴧᴧ (ממשק MM-ShQ) — **Possessed:** [freq. 1] |kjv: breeding| {str: 4476}

~~~~~~~~

2361) ᴌⴱᴧᴧ (מתג MTG) ac: **?** co: **Bridle** ab: **?**

N^m) ᴌⴱᴧᴧ (מתג M-TG) — **Bridle:** [freq. 4] |kjv: bridle, bit| {str: 4964}

~~~~~~~~

2362) ᴔᴔᴛᴧᴧ (מתח MTHh) ac: **Spread** co: **?** ab: **?:** A stretching or spreading out of something. [from: ᴔᴛ - spreading]

V) ᴔᴔᴛᴧᴧ (מתח M-THh) — **Spread:** To spread something out such as a tent. [freq. 1] (vf: Paal) |kjv: spread| {str: 4969}

n^f2) ᴛᴔᴔᴛᴧᴧ⅃ (אמתחת AM-T-HhT) — **Sack:** The mouth is spread apart to put something in or take something out. [freq. 15] |kjv: sack| {str: 572}

~~~~~~~~

2363) Ⴑᴛᴧᴧ (מתן MTN) ac: **?** co: **Side** ab: **?:** The slender part of the body above the hips.

N^m) Ⴑᴛᴧᴧ (מתן M-TN) — **I. Side:** The slender part of the body above the hips. **II. Maten:** An unknown animal, probably from its slender side. [freq. 47] |kjv: loins, side, greyhound| {str: 4975}

nt^m) Ⴑᴛᴧᴧ⅃ (אימתן AY-M-TN) — **Terrible:** [Unknown connection to root; Aramaic only] [freq. 1] |kjv: terrible| {str: 574}

~~~~~~~~

2364) ᴏ-tᴧᴧ (מתק MTQ) ac: **?** co: **Sweet** ab: **?**

V) ᴏ-tᴧᴧ (מתק M-TQ) — **Sweet:** [freq. 6] (vf: Paal, Hiphil) |kjv: sweet| {str: 4985, 4988}

N^m) ᴏ-tᴧᴧ (מתק M-TQ) — **Sweetness:** [freq. 2] |kjv: sweetness| {str: 4986}

a^m) ᴏ-tᴧᴧᴧ (מתק MM-TQ) — **Sweet:** [freq. 2] |kjv: sweet| {str: 4477}

c^m) ᴏ-Ytᴧᴧ (מתוק M-TWQ) — **Sweet:** [freq. 12] |kjv: sweetness, sweeter, sweet| {str: 4966}

d^m) ᴏ-Ytᴧᴧ (מתוק M-TWQ) — **Sweet:** [freq. 12] |kjv: sweeter, sweet, sweetness| {str: 4966}

g^m) ᴏ-tYᴧᴧ (מותק MW-TQ) — **Sweetness:** [ms: מתק] [freq. 1] |kjv: sweetness| {str: 4987}

Nun

2365) ⟜ᗱﬧ (נאף NAP) ac: **Adultery** co: ? ab: ?: [from: ⟜ᗱ - heated passion]

V) ⟜ᗱﬧ (נאף N-AP) — **Adultery:** To commit adultery. [freq. 31] (vf: Paal, Piel, Participle) |kjv: adultery, adulterer, adulteress, adulterous, break wedlock| {str: 5003}

ed^m) ⟜Yᗱﬧﬧ (ניאוף NY-AWP) — **Adultery:** [ms: נאף] [freq. 2] |kjv: adulteries| {str: 5004}

ld^m) ⟜Y⟜ᗱﬧ (נאפוף NA-PWP) — **Adultery:** [freq. 1] |kjv: adulteries| {str: 5005}

2366) ᙏᗲﬧ (נבח NBHh) ac: **Bark** co: ? ab: ?

V) ᙏᗲﬧ (נבח N-BHh) — **Bark:** Of a dog. [freq. 1] (vf: Paal) |kjv: bark| {str: 5024}

2367) ⊗ᗲﬧ (נבט NBTh) ac: **Look** co: ? ab: **Expect**

V) ⊗ᗲﬧ (נבט N-BTh) — **Look:** [freq. 69] (vf: Hiphil, Piel) |kjv: look, behold, consider, regard, see, respect| {str: 5027}

a^m) ⊗ᗲﬧᙏ (מנבט MN-BTh) — **Expectation:** As what is looked for. [ms: מבט] [freq. 3] |kjv: expectation| {str: 4007}

2368) ᗐᗲﬧ (נבך NBK) ac: ? co: **Spring** ab: ?: [from: ᗐᗲ - a weeping of the land]

N^m) ᗐᗲﬧ (נבך N-BK) — **Spring:** A spring of water. [freq. 1] |kjv: spring| {str: 5033}

2369) ᒍᗲﬧ (נבל NBL) ac: **Flow** co: ? ab: ?: [from: ᒍᗲ]

V) ᒍᗲﬧ (נבל N-BL) — **Fail:** To wear out or fade away. [freq. 25] (vf: Paal, Piel) |kjv: fall, esteem, foolishly, nought, vile| {str: 5034}

N^m) ᒍᗲﬧ (נבל N-BL) — **I. Pitcher:** For flowing of liquids. **II. Fool:** In the sense of fading away. **III. Nevel:** A musical instrument in the sense of flowing music. [freq. 56] |kjv: psalteries, bottle, viol, flagon, pitcher, vessel, fool, foolish, vile| {str: 5035, 5036}

N^{f1}) ⁑ᒍᗲﬧ (נבלה NB-LH) — **I. Carcass:** As a flowing away of life. **II. Folly:** In the sense of fading away. [freq. 61] |kjv: carcass, die, dead, body| {str: 5038, 5039}

N^{f4}) ﬨYᒍᗲﬧ (נבלות NB-LWT) — **Vagina:** In the sense of flowing. [freq. 1] |kjv: lewdness| {str: 5040}

2370) ⟜ᗲﬧ (נבע NBAh) ac: **Belch** co: ? ab: ?: [from: ⟜ᗲ - as a swelling of the stomach]

V) ⟜ᗲﬧ (נבע N-BAh) — **Belch:** [freq. 11] (vf: Paal, Hiphil) |kjv: utter, pour, send, flow| {str: 5042}

2371) ᒷᒒﬧ (נגב NGB) ac: ? co: **South** ab: ?

Nᵐ) נֹגֶב (נגב N-GB) — **South:** [freq. 112] |kjv: south, southward| {str: 5045}

~~~~~~~~~~

2372) נגד (נגד NGD) ac: **Tell** co: ? ab: ?

V) נגד (נגד N-GD) — **Tell:** To give an account to another. [Hebrew and Aramaic] [freq. 371] (vf: Hiphil, Hophal, Participle) |kjv: tell, declare, show, utter, expound, messenger, report, issue| {str: 5046, 5047}

Nᵐ) נגד (נגד N-GD) — **Before:** As to show yourself in front of another. [freq. 24] |kjv: before, against, about, presence, toward| {str: 5048, 5049}

bᵐ) נגיד (נגיד N-GYD) — **Noble:** One who tells orders. [ms: נגד] [freq. 44] |kjv: ruler, prince, captain, leader, governor, noble, excellent| {str: 5057}

~~~~~~~~~~

2373) נגח (נגח NGHh) ac: **Gore** co: ? ab: ?: [from: נ - touching]

V) נגח (נגח N-GHh) — **Gore:** To gore with the horns. [freq. 11] (vf: Paal, Hitpael, Piel) |kjv: push, gore| {str: 5055}

Nᵐ) נגח (נגח N-GHh) — **Gorer:** An ox that is known to gore with the horns. [freq. 2] |kjv: push| {str: 5056}

~~~~~~~~~~

2374) נגן (נגן NGN) ac: **Play** co: Music ab: ?: [from: נ - the bright sound of music]

V) נגן (נגן N-GN) — **Play:** To play a musical instrument. [freq. 15] (vf: Paal, Piel, Participle) |kjv: play,

instrument, minstrel, melody, player| {str: 5059}

bᶠˡ) נגינה (נגינה N-GY-NH) — **Music:** [freq. 14] |kjv: song, instrument, musick| {str: 5058}

abᶠˡ) מנגינה (מנגינה MN-GY-NH) — **Music:** [freq. 1] |kjv: musick| {str: 4485}

~~~~~~~~~~

2375) נגס (נגס NGS) ac: **Drive** co: ? ab: ?: [from: נ - touching]

V) נגס (נגס N-GS) — **Drive:** To drive oxen or men. [df: נגש] [freq. 23] (vf: Paal, Niphal, Participle) |kjv: oppressor, taskmaster, exact, distress, oppress, driver, exactor, tax| {str: 5065}

~~~~~~~~~~

2376) נגע (נגע NGAh) ac: **Touch** co: ? ab: ?: [from: נ - touching]

V) נגע (נגע N-GAh) — **Touch:** To touch or strike. Also to bring a plague as a touch from God. [freq. 150] (vf: Paal, Niphal, Hiphil, Pual, Piel, Participle) |kjv: touch, came, reach, bring, near, smite, nigh, plague, happen, strike, beat, cast, reach, join, lay| {str: 5060}

Nᵐ) נגע (נגע N-GAh) — **Touch:** A plague or other sire or illness as a touch. [freq. 78] |kjv: plague, sore, stroke, stripe, stricken, wound| {str: 5061}

~~~~~~~~~~

2377) נגף (נגף NGP) ac: **Strike** co: ? ab: ?: [from: נ - touching]

V) נגף (נגף N-GP) — **Strike:** [freq. 49] (vf: Paal, Niphal, Hitpael) |kjv: smite, worse, plague, hurt| {str: 5062}

N^m) ⟨נגף⟩ (נגף N-GP) — **Striking:** A plague or other striking. [freq. 7] |kjv: plague, stumbling| {str: 5063}

k^{fl}) ⟨מנגפה⟩ (מנגפה MN-G-PH) — **Striking:** A plague or other striking. [freq. 26] |kjv: plague, slaughter, stroke| {str: 4046}

~~~~~~~~~~

2378) ⟨נגר⟩ (נגר NGR) ac: **Pour** co: ? ab: ?

V) ⟨נגר⟩ (נגר N-GR) — **Pour:** [freq. 10] (vf: Niphal, Hiphil, Hophal) |kjv: pour, spill, fall, ran, trickle, shed| {str: 5064}

~~~~~~~~~~

2379) ⟨נגש⟩ (נגש NGSh) ac: **Near** co: ? ab: ?

V) ⟨נגש⟩ (נגש N-GSh) — **Come near:** [freq. 125] (vf: Paal, Niphal, Hiphil, Hitpael, Hophal) |kjv: near, come, nigh, bring, here, offer, approach, forth| {str: 5066}

~~~~~~~~~~

2380) ⟨נדב⟩ (נדב N-DB) ac: **Offer** co: **Offering** ab: **Honor:** The offering of something with a willing heart as a sign of honor.

V) ⟨נדב⟩ (נדב N-DB) — **Offer:** To offer something from a willing heart. [Hebrew and Aramaic] [freq. 21] (vf: Paal, Hitpael) |kjv: willingly, offer, freely, freewill, offering| {str: 5068, 5069}

N^{fl}) ⟨נדבה⟩ (נדבה ND-BH) — **Offering:** A freewill offering. [freq. 26] |kjv: freewill, offering, free, willing, voluntary, plentiful, willingly| {str: 5071}

b^m) ⟨נדיב⟩ (נדיב N-DYB) — I. **Willing:** II. **Noble:** One with a willing heart. [freq. 28] |kjv: prince, noble, willing, free, liberal| {str: 5081}

b^{fl}) ⟨נדיבה⟩ (נדיבה N-DY-BH) — **Honor:** Of one with a willing heart. [freq. 1] |kjv: soul| {str: 5082}

~~~~~~~~~~

2381) ⟨נדח⟩ (נדח NDHh) ac: **Drive** co: ? ab: ?: [from: דח - being tossed to and fro]

V) ⟨נדח⟩ (נדח N-DHh) — **Drive:** To drive an axe through wood or to drive someone or something out or away. [freq. 52] (vf: Paal, Niphal, Hiphil, Hophal, Pual, Participle) |kjv: drive, out, away, outcast, cast, banish, bring, astray, chase, compel, down, expel| {str: 5080}

~~~~~~~~~~

2382) ⟨נדן⟩ (נדן NDN) ac: ? co: **Sheath** ab: ?: A covering for a knife or sword.

N^m) ⟨נדן⟩ (נדן N-DN) — **Sheath:** [freq. 1] |kjv: sheath| {str: 5084}

e^{fl}) ⟨נידנה⟩ (נידנה NYD-NH) — **Body:** As a sheath for the soul. [ms: נדנה] [freq. 1] |kjv: body| {str: 5085}

~~~~~~~~~~

2383) ⟨נדע⟩ (נדע NDAh) ac: ? co: ? ab: **Knowledge:** The inward sense of reason. [from: דע]

a^m) ⟨מנדע⟩ (מנדע MN-DAh) — **Knowledge:** [Aramaic only] [freq. 4] |kjv: knowledge, reason, understanding| {str: 4486}

~~~~~~~~~~

2384) ⟨נדף⟩ (נדף NDP) ac: **Toss** co: ? ab: ?: The back and forth falling of a leaf as it falls from a tree. [from: דף - being tossed to and fro]

375

V) ⟨נדף N-DP⟩ — **Toss:** To toss back and forth. [freq. 9] (vf: Paal, Niphal) |kjv: drive, thrust, shake, toss| {str: 5086}

~~~~~~~~~

2385) ⟨נדר NDR⟩ ac: **Vow** co: **Vow** ab: ?: A vow made where one promises to perform an act if another performs a certain act.

V) ⟨נדר N-DR⟩ — **Vow:** [freq. 31] (vf: Paal) |kjv: vow| {str: 5087}

N^m) ⟨נדר N-DR⟩ — **Vow:** [freq. 60] |kjv: vow| {str: 5088}

~~~~~~~~~

2386) ⟨נזד NZD⟩ ac: ? co: **Stew** ab: ?: [from: נזד - boiling]

b^m) ⟨נזיד N-ZYD⟩ — **Stew:** [freq. 6] |kjv: pottage| {str: 5138}

~~~~~~~~~

2387) ⟨נזל NZL⟩ ac: **Flow** co: **Stream** ab: ?: [from: נזל - as a shaking]

V) ⟨נזל N-ZL⟩ — **Flow:** To flow water, or to flow like water. [freq. 16] (vf: Paal, Hiphil, Participle) |kjv: flood, flow, stream, pour, distil, melt, drop, waters, pour, gush| {str: 5140}

a^{fl}) ⟨מנזלה MN-Z-LH⟩ — **Milky way:** As a flowing river in the night sky. [df: מזלה] [freq. 1] |kjv: planet| {str: 4208}

~~~~~~~~~

2388) ⟨נזם NZM⟩ ac: ? co: **Ring** ab: ?

N^m) ⟨נזם N-ZM⟩ — **Ring:** An ear or nose ring as an ornament.

[freq. 17] |kjv: earring, jewel| {str: 5141}

~~~~~~~~~

2389) ⟨נזק NZQ⟩ ac: **Injure** co: **Injury** ab: ?

V) ⟨נזק N-ZQ⟩ — **Injure:** [Aramaic only] [freq. 4] (vf: Paal) |kjv: damage, hurt, endamage, hurtful| {str: 5142}

N^m) ⟨נזק N-ZQ⟩ — **Injury:** [freq. 1] |kjv: damage| {str: 5143}

~~~~~~~~~

2390) ⟨נזר NZR⟩ ac: **Dedicate** co: **Crown** ab: ?

V) ⟨נזר N-ZR⟩ — **Dedicate:** To set something apart or apart from something for a special purpose. [freq. 10] (vf: Niphal, Hiphil) |kjv: separate, consecrate| {str: 5144}

N^m) ⟨נזר N-ZR⟩ — **Crown:** An ornamental placed on the head as a sign of dedication. Also of any sign of dedication such as the shaved head of one who is dedicated. [freq. 25] |kjv: crown, separation, consecration, hair| {str: 5145}

h^m) ⟨מנזר MN-ZR⟩ — **Crown:** A sign of dedication. [freq. 1] |kjv: crowned| {str: 4502}

~~~~~~~~~

2391) ⟨נחל NHhL⟩ ac: **Inherit** co: **Inheritance** ab: ?

V) ⟨נחל N-HhL⟩ — **Inherit:** [freq. 61] (vf: Paal, Hiphil, Hitpael, Hophal, Piel) |kjv: inherit, inheritance, possess, have, divide, heritage| {str: 5157}

N^m) ⟨נחל N-HhL⟩ — **River:** Also the valley of a stream. [Unknown connection to root;] [freq.

141] |kjv: river, brook, valley, stream, flood| {str: 5158}

N^(fl)) נחלה (NHh-LH) — **Inheritance:** [freq. 222] |kjv: inheritance, heritage, inherit, possession| {str: 5159}

~~~~~~~~

2392) נחם (NHhM) ac: **?** co: **?** ab: **Comfort:** [from: ל - rest]

V) נחם (N-HhM) — **I. Comfort:** To give comfort in time of difficulty or sorrow. **II. Regret:** To have sorrow for an action. [freq. 108] (vf: Niphal, Hitpael, Pual, Piel) |kjv: comfort, repent, comforter, ease| {str: 5162}

N^(m)) נחם (N-HhM) — **Sorrow:** [ms: נחם] [freq. 1] |kjv: repentance| {str: 5164}

N^(fl)) נחמה (NHh-MH) — **Comfort:** [freq. 2] |kjv: comfort| {str: 5165}

ed^(m)) ניחום (NY-HhWM) — **Comfort:** [ms: נחום] [freq. 3] |kjv: comfort, comfortable, repenting| {str: 5150}

id^(m/f)) תנחום (TN-HhWM) — **Comfort:** [ms: תנחם] [freq. 1] |kjv: comfort| {str: 8575}

id^(fl)) תנחומה (TN-HhW-MH) — **Comfort:** [freq. 4] |kjv: consolation, comfort| {str: 8575}

~~~~~~~~

2393) נחץ (NHhTs) ac: **Urge** co: **?** ab: **?**

V) נחץ (N-HhTs) — **Urge:** [freq. 1] (vf: Paal, Participle) |kjv: haste| {str: 5169}

~~~~~~~~

2394) נחר (NHhR) ac: **Snort** co: **Nostrils** ab: **?**

N^(m/f)) נחר (N-HhR) — **Nostrils:** [freq. 1] |kjv: nostrils| {str: 5170}

N^(fl)) נחרה (NHh-RH) — **Snorting:** [freq. 1] |kjv: snorting| {str: 5170}

b^(m)) נחיר (N-HhYR) — **Nostrils:** [freq. 1] |kjv: nostril| {str: 5156}

~~~~~~~~

2395) נחש (NHhSh) ac: **?** co: **Bronze** ab: **?**

V) נחש (N-HhSh) — **Divine:** To learn something through divination. [Unknown connection to root;] [freq. 11] (vf: Piel) |kjv: enchantment, divine, enchanter, indeed, certainly, learn, experience, diligently, observe| {str: 5172}

N^(m)) נחש (N-HhSh) — **I. Bronze:** [Aramaic only] **II. Divination:** [Unknown connection to root;] [freq. 11] |kjv: brass, enchantment| {str: 5173, 5174}

c^(f2)) נחושת (N-HhW-ShT) — **Bronze:** [ms: נחשת] [freq. 141] |kjv: brass, brasen, fetters, chain, copper, filthiness, steel| {str: 5178}

d^(m)) נחוש (N-HhWSh) — **Bronze:** [freq. 1] |kjv: brass| {str: 5153}

d^(fl)) נחושה (N-HhW-ShH) — **Bronze:** [ms: נחשה] [freq. 10] |kjv: brass, steel| {str: 5154}

~~~~~~~~

2396) נחת (NHhT) ac: **Descend** co: **?** ab: **?:** [from: ת - removing]

V) ﬏ﬤﬣ (נחת N-HhT) — **Descend:** [Hebrew and Aramaic] [freq. 15] (vf: Paal, Niphal, Hiphil, Hophal, Piel) |kjv: broken, come down, enter, stick fast, settle, press, carry, place, lay, depose| {str: 5181, 5182}

N^m) ﬏ﬤﬣ (נחת N-HhT) — **Descended:** [freq. 1] |kjv: come down| {str: 5185}

~~~~~~~~~

2397) ⟟⊗ﬣ (נטל NThL) ac: **Lift** co: **Burden** ab: ?

V) ⟟⊗ﬣ (נטל N-ThL) — **Lift:** [Hebrew and Aramaic] [freq. 6] (vf: Paal, Piel) |kjv: bare, take, offer, lift| {str: 5190, 5191}

N^m) ⟟⊗ﬣ (נטל N-ThL) — **Burden:** [freq. 1] |kjv: weighty| {str: 5192}

b^m) ⟟ﬗ⊗ﬣ (נטיל N-ThYL) — **Burden:** [freq. 1] |kjv: bear| {str: 5187}

~~~~~~~~~

2398) ⟲⊗ﬣ (נטע NThAh) ac: **Plant** co: **Plant** ab: ?

V) ⟲⊗ﬣ (נטע N-ThAh) — **Plant:** [freq. 58] (vf: Paal, Niphal) |kjv: plant, fasten, planter| {str: 5193}

N^m) ⟲⊗ﬣ (נטע N-ThAh) — **Plant:** [freq. 4] |kjv: plant| {str: 5194}

a^m) ⟲⊗ﬣ◯ (מנטע MN-ThAh) — **Planting:** [df: מטע] [freq. 6] |kjv: planting, plant, plantation| {str: 4302}

b^m) ⟲ﬗ⊗ﬣ (נטיע N-ThYAh) — **Plant:** [freq. 1] |kjv: plant| {str: 5195}

~~~~~~~~~

2399) ⟲⊗ﬣ (נטף NThP) ac: **Drip** co: **Drop** ab: ?

V) ⟲⊗ﬣ (נטף N-ThP) — **Drip:** To drip a sweet smelling liquid as an incense. Also the dripping of sweet words from the mouth. [freq. 18] (vf: Paal, Hiphil) |kjv: drop, prophesy, prophet, down| {str: 5197}

N^m) ⟲⊗ﬣ (נטף N-ThP) — **Nataph:** Drops of an unknown aromatic gum resin used in incense. [freq. 2] |kjv: stacte, drop| {str: 5198}

b^{fl}) ⟲ﬗ⊗ﬣ (נטיפה N-ThY-PH) — **Pendent:** An ornamental probably with a drop shaped gem. [freq. 2] |kjv: collar, chain| {str: 5188}

~~~~~~~~~

2400) ﬠ⊗ﬣ (נטר NThR) ac: **Guard** co: ? ab: ?: [from: ﬠﬨ - as a place that is guarded]

V) ﬠ⊗ﬣ (נטר N-ThR) — **Guard:** [Hebrew and Aramaic] [freq. 10] (vf: Paal) |kjv: keep, keeper, reserve, grudge| {str: 5201, 5202}

~~~~~~~~~

2401) ﬩⊗ﬣ (נטש NThSh) ac: **Spread** co: **Branch** ab: ?: The spreading branches of a tree. [from: ﬩⊗]

V) ﬩⊗ﬣ (נטש N-ThSh) — **I. Spread: II. Leave:** As spread out away from the point of origin. **III. Remain:** To be left behind by those who leave. [freq. 40] (vf: Paal, Niphal, Pual) |kjv: forsake, leave, spread, drawn, fall, join, lie, loose, cast off| {str: 5203}

b^{fl}) ﬩ﬗ⊗ﬣ (נטישה N-ThY-ShH) — **Branch:** [freq. 3] |kjv: branches, plant, battlement| {str: 5189}

~~~~~~~~~

2402) ﬓ﬩ﬣ (נכד NKD) ac: ? co: ? ab: **Posterity**

Nᵐ) שּׁ山ﬡ (נכד N-KD) — **Posterity:** The continuation through the next generation. [freq. 3] |kjv: sons son, nephew| {str: 5220}

2403) שּׁ山ﬡ (נכח NKHh) ac: ? co: **Straight** ab: ?

Nᵐ) שּׁ山ﬡ (נכח N-KHh) — **Before:** In front of or opposite to something. [freq. 2] |kjv: before, against| {str: 5226}

cᵐ) שּׁY山ﬡ (נכוח N-KWHh) — **Straight:** In the sense of being in front. [ms: נכה] [freq. 4] |kjv: right, uprightness, plain| {str: 5228}

cᶠˡ) ﭏשּׁY山ﬡ (נכוחה N-KW-HhH) — **Straightness:** In the sense of being in front. [ms: נכחה] [freq. 4] |kjv: uprightness, right, equity| {str: 5229}

gᵐ) שּׁ山Yﬡ (נוכח NW-KHh) — **Before:** In front of or opposite to something. [ms: נכה] [freq. 23] |kjv: against, before, directly, for, on, over| {str: 5227}

2404) ᒻ山ﬡ (נכל NKL) ac: **Deceive** co: ? ab: **Deceit**

V) ᒻ山ﬡ (נכל N-KL) — **Deceive:** [freq. 4] (vf: Paal, Hitpael, Piel, Participle) |kjv: deceiver, beguile, subtly, conspire| {str: 5230}

Nᵐ) ᒻ山ﬡ (נכל N-KL) — **Deceit:** [freq. 1] |kjv: wiles| {str: 5231}

2405) ﬤ山ﬡ (נכס NKS) ac: ? co: ? ab: **Wealth:** [from: ﬤ山 - as being covered]

Nᵐ) ﬤ山ﬡ (נכס N-KS) — **Wealth:** [Hebrew and Aramaic] [freq. 7] |kjv: wealth, riches, goods| {str: 5232, 5233}

2406) ﬡ山ﬡ (נכר NKR) ac: **Know** co: ? ab: ?

V) ﬡ山ﬡ (נכר N-KR) — **Know:** [freq. 50] (vf: Niphal, Hiphil, Hitpael, Piel) |kjv: know, acknowledge, discern, respect, knowledge, known, feign| {str: 5234}

Nᵐ) ﬡ山ﬡ (נכר N-KR) — **I. Foreign:** An unknown person, place or thing. **II. Disaster:** [Unknown connection to root;] [freq. 37] |kjv: strange, stranger, alien| {str: 5235, 5236}

aᵐ) ﬡ山ﬡ﬙ (מנכר MN-KR) — **Acquaintance:** One who is known [df: מכר] [freq. 2] |kjv: acquaintance| {str: 4378}

fᵐ) ﬡﬡ山ﬡ (נכרי N-K-RY) — **Foreigner:** One who is not known. [freq. 45] |kjv: stranger, strange, alien, foreigner, outlandish| {str: 5237}

hᶠˡ) ﭏﬡﬡ山ﬡ﬙ (מנכרה MN-K-RH) — **Minkrah:** An unknown plant. [freq. 1] |kjv: pit| {str: 4379}

2407) ᒻﬡﬡ (נמל NML) ac: **Cut** co: ? ab: ?: [from: ᒻﬡ - as cut into segments]

V) ᒻﬡﬡ (נמל N-ML) — **Cut:** To cut the tip or end. [freq. 5] (vf: Paal) |kjv: cut off, cut down, circumcise| {str: 5243}

Nᶠ) ᒻﬡﬡ (נמל N-ML) — **Ant:** A segmented insect as cut in the middle. [freq. 2] |kjv: ant| {str: 5244}

2408) ﬡﬡﬡ (נמר NMR) ac: ? co: ? ab: ?

N^m) ﬡﬡ (נמר N-MR) —
Leopard: [Hebrew and Aramaic]
[freq. 7] |kjv: leopard| {str: 5245,
5246}

2409) ﬡ (נסב NSB) ac: **Turn** co: ?
ab: ?: [from: ﬡ]

b^{f1}) ﬡ (נסיבה N-SY-BH) —
Cause: A turn of affairs. [ms: נסבה]
[freq. 1] |kjv: cause| {str: 5252}

2410) ﬡ (נסג NSG) ac: **Move** co: ?
ab: ?: [from: ﬡ - through the idea of
departing]

V) ﬡ (נסג N-SG) — **I. Move: II.
Reach:** In the sense of moving. [df:
נשׂג] [freq. 59] (vf: Paal, Hiphil,
Hophal) |kjv: remove, depart, take,
turn, overtake, hold, get, attain,
obtain, reach, able, bring, lay, put,
remove, rich, take| {str: 5253, 5381}

2411) ﬡ (נסח NSHh) ac: **Pluck** co: ?
ab: ?

V) ﬡ (נסח N-SHh) — **Pluck:**
[Hebrew and Aramaic] [freq. 5] (vf:
Paal, Niphal) |kjv: pluck, rooted,
destroy, pull| {str: 5255, 5256}

a^m) ﬡ (מנסח MN-SHh) —
Plucked: [ms: מסח] [freq. 1] |kjv:
broken| {str: 4535}

2412) ﬡ (נסך NSK) ac: **Pour** co: ?
ab: ?: [from: ﬡ - covering]

V) ﬡ (נסך N-SK) — **Pour:**
[Hebrew and Aramaic] [freq. 27] (vf:
Paal, Niphal, Hiphil, Hophal, Piel)
|kjv: pour, cover, offer, melt, molten,
set, spread| {str: 5258, 5259, 5260}

N^m) ﬡ (נסך N-SK) — **Pouring:**
A liquid poured out as an offering or
the pouring of a molten metal to form
images. [Hebrew and Aramaic] [freq.
65] |kjv: drink, offering, image,
cover| {str: 5261, 5262}

a^{f1}) ﬡ (מנסכה MN-S-KH) —
Pouring: A molten metal that is
poured in a cast to form images.
[freq. 28] |kjv: image, molten,
covering, vail| {str: 4541}

a^{f2}) ﬡ (מנסכת MN-S-KT) —
Web: Of the loom. [Unknown
connection to root;] [freq. 2] |kjv:
web| {str: 4545}

b^m) ﬡ (נסיך N-SYK) — **I.
Pouring:** A liquid poured out as an
offering. **II. Prince:** [Unknown
connection to root;] [freq. 6] |kjv:
prince, drink, duke, principal| {str:
5257}

2413) ﬡ (נסע NSAh) ac: **Journey**
co: ? ab: ?

V) ﬡ (נסע N-SAh) — **Journey:**
[freq. 146] (vf: Paal, Niphal, Hiphil)
|kjv: journey, depart, remove,
forward, went, go, brought, set, forth,
get, set| {str: 5265}

a^m) ﬡ (מנסע MN-SAh) —
Journey: [df: מסע] [freq. 14] |kjv:
journey, journeying| {str: 4550,
4551}

2414) ﬡ (נסק NSQ) ac: **Ascend** co: ?
ab: ?

V) ﬡ (נסק N-SQ) — **I. Ascend:**
[Hebrew and Aramaic] **II. Kindle:**
From the ascending flames. [df: נשׂק]
[freq. 7] (vf: Paal, Niphal, Hiphil,

Hophal) |kjv: ascend, up, kindle, burn| {str: 5266, 5267, 5400}

~~~~~~

2415) לֹעַ֩ל (נעל NAhL) ac: **Shod** co: **Sandal** ab: ?: [from: עֹ֩ - being put on]

V) לֹעַ֩ל (נעל N-AhL) — **I. Shod:** To give sandals. **II. Lock:** [Unknown connection to root;] [freq. 8] (vf: Paal, Hiphil) |kjv: lock, bolt, shod, inclose, shut| {str: 5274}

N^f) לֹעַ֩ל (נעל N-AhL) — **Sandal:** [freq. 22] |kjv: shoe, dryshod| {str: 5275}

h^m) לֹעַ֩לּ‍‍‍ (מנעל MN-AhL) — **Sandal:** [freq. 1] |kjv: shoe| {str: 4515}

ad^m) לֹיעַ֩לּ‍‍ (מנעול MN-AhWL) — **Lock:** [Unknown connection to root;] [ms: מנעל] [freq. 6] |kjv: lock| {str: 4514}

~~~~~~

2416) םֹעַ֩ל (נעם NAhM) ac: ? co: **Sweet** ab: ?

V) םֹעַ֩ל (נעם N-AhM) — **Sweet:** To be sweet. [freq. 8] (vf: Paal) |kjv: pleasant, sweet, beauty, delight| {str: 5276}

a^m) םֹעַ֩לּ‍‍ (מנעם MN-AhM) — **Delicacy:** What is sweet. [freq. 1] |kjv: beauty, pleasant, pleasantness| {str: 4516}

b^m) םֹיַ֩עַ֩ל (נעים N-AhYM) — **Sweet:** [freq. 13] |kjv: pleasant, pleasures, sweet| {str: 5273}

m^m) לֹּםֹעַ֩ל (נעמן NAh-MN) — **Sweet:** [freq. 1] |kjv: pleasant| {str: 5282}

~~~~~~

2417) ץֹעַ֩ל (נעץ NAhTs) ac: ? co: **Thorn** ab: ?

ld^m) ץֹּיוַ֩עַ֩ל (נעצוץ NAh-TsWTs) — **Thorn:** [freq. 2] |kjv: thorn| {str: 5285}

~~~~~~

2418) רֹעַ֩ל (נער NAhR) ac: ? co: **Young** ab: ?: [from: עֹ֩]

N^m) רֹעַ֩ל (נער N-AhR) — **Young:** A young male. [freq. 239] |kjv: young man, servant, child, lad, young, children, youth, babe, boy| {str: 5288, 5289}

N^{fl}) ‍ֿ‍רֹעַ֩ל (נערה NAh-RH) — **Young:** A young female. [freq. 62] |kjv: damsel, maiden, maid, young| {str: 5291}

d^f) רֹיַ֩עַ֩ל (נעור N-AhWR) — **Youth:** [ms: נער] [freq. 47] |kjv: youth, childhood| {str: 5271}

g^m) רֹעַ֩יל (נוער NW-AhR) — **Youth:** [ms: נער] [freq. 4] |kjv: child, youth| {str: 5290}

~~~~~~

2419) חֹ‍פַ֩ל (נפח NPHh) ac: **Blow** co: ? ab: ?: [from: חֹ‍פַ֩]

V) חֹ‍פַ֩ל (נפח N-PHh) — **Blow:** [freq. 12] (vf: Paal, Hiphil, Pual) |kjv: blow, breathe, seethe, lose, snuff, give up| {str: 5301}

a^m) חֹ‍פַ֩לּ‍‍ (מנפח MN-PHh) — **Blowing:** [df: מפח] [freq. 1] |kjv: giving up| {str: 4646}

~~~~~~

2420) ‍שֹ‍פַ֩ל (נפך NPK) ac: ? co: ? ab: ?

g^m) ‍שֹ‍פַ֩יל (נופך NW-PK) — **Nophek:** An unknown stone. [freq. 4] |kjv: emerald| {str: 5306}

~~~~~~

2421) ‫נפל‬ (‫נפל‬ NPL) ac: **Fall** co: ?
ab: ?: (eng: fall - with the removal of the n)

V) ‫נפל‬ (‫נפל‬ N-PL) — **Fall:**
[Hebrew and Aramaic] [freq. 445]
(vf: Paal, Hiphil, Hitpael) |kjv: fall, cast, divide, overthrow, present, lay, rot, accept, inferior, light, lost| {str: 5307, 5308}

N^m) ‫נפל‬ (‫נפל‬ N-PL) —
Miscarriage: As a fallen pregnancy. [freq. 3] |kjv: birth| {str: 5309}

a^m) ‫מנפל‬ (‫מנפל‬ MN-PL) —
Refuse: What is thrown down as worthless. [df: ‫מפל‬] [freq. 2] |kjv: flake, refuse| {str: 4651}

a^fl) ‫מנפלה‬ (‫מנפלה‬ MN-P-LH) — **Ruin:** A pile of refuse as a fallen or thrown down. [df: ‫מפלה‬] [freq. 3] |kjv: ruin, ruinous| {str: 4654}

a^f2) ‫מנפלת‬ (‫מנפלת‬ MN-P-LT) — **Fall:** Something that is fallen. [df: ‫מפלת‬] [freq. 8] |kjv: fall, ruin, carcass| {str: 4658}

2422) ‫נפץ‬ (‫נפץ‬ NPTs) ac: **Scatter** co: **Club** ab: ?: The scattering of pieces as when a club smashes a pot. [from: ‫נפץ‬]

V) ‫נפץ‬ (‫נפץ‬ N-PTs) — **Scatter:**
[freq. 22] (vf: Paal, Pual, Piel, Participle) |kjv: break, scatter, dash, discharge, disperse, overspread, sunder| {str: 5310}

N^m) ‫נפץ‬ (‫נפץ‬ N-PTs) —
Scattering: [freq. 1] |kjv: scattering| {str: 5311}

a^m) ‫מנפץ‬ (‫מנפץ‬ MN-PTs) —
Club: [df: ‫מפץ‬] [freq. 2] |kjv: slaughter, axe| {str: 4660, 4661}

2423) ‫נפק‬ (‫נפק‬ NPQ) ac: **Issue** co: ? ab: ?: A taking, coming or going forth.

V) ‫נפק‬ (‫נפק‬ N-PQ) — **Issue:**
[Aramaic only] [freq. 11] (vf: Paal) |kjv: take, come, go| {str: 5312}

e^fl) ‫ניפקה‬ (‫ניפקה‬ NYP-QH) —
Expense: As going out. [Aramaic only] [ms: ‫נפכה‬] [freq. 2] |kjv: expense| {str: 5313}

2424) ‫נפש‬ (‫נפש‬ NPSh) ac: **Refresh** co: **Soul** ab: ?: The whole of a person, the body, breath and mind.

V) ‫נפש‬ (‫נפש‬ N-ShP) — **Refresh:**
To refresh the whole of the person. [freq. 3] (vf: Niphal) |kjv: refresh| {str: 5314}

N^f) ‫נפש‬ (‫נפש‬ N-PSh) — **Soul:**
[freq. 751] |kjv: soul, life, person, mind, heart, creature, body, dead, will, desire, man, self, any, appetite| {str: 5315}

2425) ‫נפת‬ (‫נפת‬ NPT) ac: ? co: ? ab: ?

g^m) ‫נופת‬ (‫נופת‬ NW-PT) —
Honeycomb: [ms: ‫נפת‬] [freq. 5] |kjv: honeycomb| {str: 5317}

2426) ‫נצב‬ (‫נצב‬ NTsB) ac: **Stand** co: **Pillar** ab: ?: The firm standing of a pillar. [from: ‫נצב‬ - as a wall standing firm and erect]

V) ‫נצב‬ (‫נצב‬ N-TsB) — **Stand:** To stand erect. Also to set in place. [freq. 75] (vf: Niphal, Hiphil, Hophal) |kjv: stand, set, officer, upright, appoint, deputy, erect, establish| {str: 5324}

aᵐ) ᴸ (מנצב MN-TsB) —
Standing: [df: מצב] [freq. 10] |kjv:
stood| {str: 4673}

aᶠ¹) ᴸ (מנצבה MN-Ts-BH)
— **Pillar:** As standing tall and firm.
[df: מצבה] [freq. 32] |kjv: image,
pillar, garrison| {str: 4676}

aᶠ²) ᴸ (מנצבת MN-Ts-BT)
— **Pillar:** As standing tall and firm.
[df: מצבת] [freq. 6] |kjv: pillar,
substance| {str: 4678}

bᵐ) ᴸ (נציב N-TsYB) —
Pillar: As standing tall and firm.
[ms: נצב] [freq. 12] |kjv: pillar| {str:
5333}

eᵐ) ᴸ (ניצב NY-TsB) —
Haft: The handle of a sword or knife
which the blade is set into. [ms: נצב]
[freq. 1] |kjv: haft| {str: 5325}

eᶠ¹) ᴸ (ניצבה NYTs-BH) —
Firmness: [Aramaic only] [ms:
נצבה] [freq. 1] |kjv: strength| {str:
5326}

koᵐ) ᴸ (מנוצב M-NW-TsB)
— **Tower:** As standing tall and firm.
[df: מצב] [freq. 1] |kjv: mount| {str:
4674}

2427) ᴸ (נצח NTsHh) ac: ? co: ?
ab: **Continue**

V) ᴸ (נצח N-TsHh) —
Continue: [Hebrew and Aramaic]
[freq. 66] (vf: Niphal, Piel,
Participle) |kjv: musician, set,
overseer, excel, oversee, perpetual,
singer, prefer| {str: 5329, 5330}

Nᵐ) ᴸ (נצח N-TsHh) — I.
Continually: II. **Blood:** From its
continual flowing. [freq. 45] |kjv:
ever, never, perpetual, always, end,
victory, strength, alway, constantly,
evermore, blood| {str: 5331, 5332}

2428) ᴸ (נצל NTsL) ac: **Deliver** co:
? ab: ?: [from: ᴸ - as a shaking]

V) ᴸ (נצל N-TsL) — **Deliver:**
[Hebrew and Aramaic] [freq. 216]
(vf: Niphal, Hiphil, Hitpael, Hophal,
Piel) |kjv: deliver, recover, rid,
escape, rescue, spoil, take| {str: 5337,
5338}

2429) ᴸ (נצר NTsR) ac: **Preserve**
co: ? ab: ?

V) ᴸ (נצר N-TsR) — **Preserve:**
To watch over or guard in order to
preserve. [freq. 63] (vf: Paal,
Participle) |kjv: keep, preserve,
watchman, besiege, keeper,
monument, preserver, subtil, hidden,
watcher| {str: 5341}

Nᵐ) ᴸ (נצר N-TsR) — **Branch:**
[Unknown connection to root;] [freq.
4] |kjv: branch| {str: 5342}

bᵐ) ᴸ (נציר N-TsYR) —
Preserve: [freq. 1] |kjv: preserved|
{str: 5336}

2430) ᴸ (נקב NQB) ac: **Pierce** co:
Hole ab: ?: [from: ᴸ]

V) ᴸ (נקב N-QB) — **Pierce:** To
make a hole by piercing. Also to
curse in the sense of piercing
through. [freq. 25] (vf: Paal, Niphal)
|kjv: curse, express, blaspheme, bore,
name, pierce, appoint, hole, strike|
{str: 5344}

Nᵐ) ᴸ (נקב N-QB) — **Hole:**
[freq. 1] |kjv: pipe| {str: 5345}

Nᶠ¹) ᴸ (נקבה NQ-BH) —
Female: As with a hole. [freq. 22]

|kjv: female, woman, maid| {str: 5347}

2431) ㄱ-ꞷ-ㄱ (נקד NQD) ac: ? co: **Spot** ab: ?

c^m) ㄱY-ꞷ-ㄱ (נקוד N-QWD) — **Spotted:** The spots of sheep and goats. [ms: נקד] [freq. 9] |kjv: speckled| {str: 5348}

d^fl) ꙮㄱY-ꞷ-ㄱ (נקודה N-QW-DH) — **Drop:** As spots. [freq. 1] |kjv: stud| {str: 5351}

g^m) ㄱ-ꞷ-Yㄱ (נוקד NW-QD) — **Sheep-master:** One who manages the flock. [ms: נקד] [freq. 2] |kjv: sheepmaster, herdman| {str: 5349}

ed^m) ㄱY-ꞷ-ᐳㄱ (ניקוד NY-QWD) — **I. Mold:** As spots. [ms: נקד] **II. Biscuit:** Spots of bread. [freq. 3] |kjv: mouldy, crcknels| {str: 5350}

2432) ⊗-ꞷ-ㄱ (נקט NQTh) ac: ? co: ? ab: **Loathe:** [from: ⊗-ꞷ-]

V) ⊗-ꞷ-ㄱ (נקט N-QTh) — **Loathe:** [freq. 1] (vf: Paal) |kjv: weary| {str: 5354}

2433) ᴟᴟ-ꞷ-ㄱ (נקם NQM) ac: **Avenge** co: ? ab: **Vengeance:** [from: ᴟᴟ-ꞷ- - one who raises the hand to avenge another]

V) ᴟᴟ-ꞷ-ㄱ (נקם N-QM) — **Avenge:** [freq. 35] (vf: Paal, Niphal, Hitpael, Hophal, Piel) |kjv: avenge, vengeance, revenge, take, avenger, punish| {str: 5358}

N^m) ᴟᴟ-ꞷ-ㄱ (נקם N-QM) — **Vengeance:** [freq. 17] |kjv: vengeance, quarrel, avenge| {str: 5359}

N^fl) ꙮᴟᴟ-ꞷ-ㄱ (נקמה NQ-MH) — **Vengeance:** [freq. 27] |kjv: vengeance, revenge| {str: 5360}

2434) ⊙-ꞷ-ㄱ (נקע NQAh) ac: **Alienate** co: ? ab: ?: [from: ⊙-ꞷ- - being removed from the home]

V) ⊙-ꞷ-ㄱ (נקע N-QAh) — **Alienate:** [freq. 3] (vf: Paal) |kjv: alienate| {str: 5361}

2435) ⊂-ꞷ-ㄱ (נקף NQP) ac: **Encircle** co: **Circle** ab: ?: [from: ⊂-ꞷ-]

V) ⊂-ꞷ-ㄱ (נקף N-QP) — **Encircle:** To go around to enclose or go about. [freq. 19] (vf: Paal, Hiphil, Piel) |kjv: compass, round, about, destroy, down, inclose, kill, round| {str: 5362}

e^fl) ꙮ⊂-ꞷ-ᐳㄱ (ניקפה NYQ-PH) — **Rope:** Used to encircle the waist. [ms: נקפה] [freq. 1] |kjv: rent| {str: 5364}

g^m) ⊂-ꞷ-Yㄱ (נוקף NW-QP) — **Circling:** The going around the tree beating it to drop the fruit. [ms: נקף] [freq. 2] |kjv: shaking| {str: 5363}

2436) ᠭ-ꞷ-ㄱ (נקר NQR) ac: **Pierce** co: **Fissure** ab: ?: [from: ᠭꟿ - as a digging]

V) ᠭ-ꞷ-ㄱ (נקר N-QR) — **Pierce:** [freq. 6] (vf: Paal, Pual, Piel) |kjv: put out, thrust, pick pierce, dig| {str: 5365}

N^fl) ꙮᠭ-ꞷ-ㄱ (נקרה NQ-RH) — **Fissure:** As a piercing in a rock. [freq. 2] |kjv: cleft, clift| {str: 5366}

2437) (נקש NQSh) ac: **Ensnare** co: **?** ab: **?:** [from: - snare by stealth]

V) (נקש N-QSh) — **I. Ensnare:** [Hebrew and Aramaic] **II. Knock:** [Unknown connection to root; Aramaic only] [freq. 6] (vf: Paal, Niphal, Hitpael, Piel) |kjv: snare, catch, smite| {str: 5367, 5368}

~~~~~~~~~~

2438) (נרג NRG) ac: **Whisper** co: **?** ab: **?:** A quiet whisper to be unheard or in slander. [from: - to trample on one by slandering]

em^{m}) (נירגן NY-R-GN) — **Whisperer:** [ms: נרגן] [freq. 4] |kjv: talebearer, whisperer| {str: 5372}

~~~~~~~~~~

2439) (נרד NRD) ac: **?** co: **Nard** ab: **?:** (eng: nard)

N^{m}) (נרד N-RD) — **Nard:** An aromatic plant. [freq. 3] |kjv: spikenard| {str: 5373}

~~~~~~~~~~

2440) (נשב NShB) ac: **Blow** co: **?** ab: **?**

V) (נשב N-ShB) — **Blow:** [freq. 3] (vf: Paal, Hiphil) |kjv: drive, blow| {str: 5380}

~~~~~~~~~~

2441) (נשך NShK) ac: **Bite** co: **?** ab: **Usury:** A bite, also usury as a biting.

V) (נשך N-ShK) — **I. Bite: II. Usury:** In the sense of biting. [freq. 16] (vf: Paal, Hiphil, Piel) |kjv: bite, usury| {str: 5391}

N^{m}) (נשך N-ShK) — **Usury:** [freq. 12] |kjv: usury| {str: 5392}

e^{f1}) (נישכה NYSh-KH) — **Chamber:** [Unknown connection to root;] [ms: נשכה] [freq. 3] |kjv: chamber| {str: 5393}

~~~~~~~~~~

2442) (נשל NShL) ac: **Cast** co: **?** ab: **?**

V) (נשל N-ShL) — **Cast off:** [freq. 7] (vf: Paal, Piel) |kjv: cast, put, slip, loose, drive| {str: 5394}

~~~~~~~~~~

2443) (נשם NShM) ac: **Pant** co: **Breath** ab: **?:** [from:]

V) (נשם N-ShM) — **Pant:** [freq. 1] (vf: Paal) |kjv: destroy| {str: 5395}

N^{f1}) (נשמה NSh-MH) — **Breath:** [Hebrew and Aramaic] [ar: נשמא] [freq. 25] |kjv: breath, blast, spirit, inspiration, soul| {str: 5396, 5397}

i^{f2}) (תנשמת TN-Sh-MT) — **Tinshemet:** An unknown animal. [freq. 3] |kjv: swan, mole| {str: 8580}

~~~~~~~~~~

2444) (נשף NShP) ac: **Blow** co: **Twilight** ab: **?:** The cool breeze that blows at twilight.

V) (נשף N-ShP) — **Blow:** [freq. 2] (vf: Paal) |kjv: blow| {str: 5398}

N^{m}) (נשף N-ShP) — **Twilight:** Dusk or dawn. [freq. 12] |kjv: twilight, night, dark, dawn| {str: 5399}

tc^{m}) (ינשוף YN-ShWP) — **Yanshoph:** An unknown bird. [freq. 3] |kjv: owl| {str: 3244}
~~~~~~~~~~

td^m) ⟨Yₗₗᵧⵁ (יָנשׁוּף YN-ShWP) —
Yanshuph: An unknown bird. [freq.
3] |kjv: owl| {str: 3244}

~~~~~~~~~

2445) ⟨ₗₗⵁ (נשׁק NShQ) ac: **Touch** co:
Weapon ab: **?:** A touching in love with
the lips or in battle with weapons.

V) ⟨ₗₗⵁ (נשׁק N-ShQ) — **Touch:**
To touch with the lips or weapons.
[freq. 35] (vf: Paal, Hiphil, Piel) |kjv:
kiss, arm, rule, touch| {str: 5401}

N^m) ⟨ₗₗⵁ (נשׁק N-ShQ) —
Weapon: Used in battle in the sense
of touching the enemy. [freq. 10]
|kjv: armour, weapon, battle, arm,
harness, armoury| {str: 5402}

~~~~~~~~~

2446) ⟨ₗₗⵁ (נשׁר NShR) ac: **?** co: **?** ab:
?

N^m) ⟨ₗₗⵁ (נשׁר N-ShR) — **Nesher:**
An unknown bird of prey. [Hebrew
and Aramaic] [freq. 28] |kjv: eagle|
{str: 5403, 5404}

~~~~~~~~~

2447) ⟨ₗₗⵁ (נשׁת NShT) ac: **Dry** co: **?**
ab: **?**

V) ⟨ₗₗⵁ (נשׁת N-ShT) — **Dry up:**
[freq. 3] (vf: Paal, Niphal) |kjv: fail|
{str: 5405}

~~~~~~~~~

2448) ⟨ₗⵁ (נתב NTB) ac: **?** co: **Path** ab:
?

b^m/f) ⟨ₗⵁ (נתיב N-TYB) — **Path:**
[freq. 5] |kjv: path| {str: 5410}

b^f1) ⟨ₗⵁ (נתיבה N-TY-BH) —
Path: [freq. 26] |kjv: path, pathway|
{str: 5410}

~~~~~~~~~

2449) ⟨ₗⵁ (נתח NTHh) ac: **Cut** co:
Piece ab: **?:** [from: ⟨ₗ - dividing]

V) ⟨ₗⵁ (נתח N-THh) — **Cut:** To
cut into pieces. [freq. 9] (vf: Piel)
|kjv: cut, divide, hew| {str: 5408}

N^m) ⟨ₗⵁ (נתח N-THh) — **Piece:**
What has been cut. [freq. 13] |kjv:
piece, part| {str: 5409}

~~~~~~~~~

2450) ⟨ₗⵁ (נתך NTK) ac: **Pour** co: **?**
ab: **?:** [from: ⟨ₗ - removing]

V) ⟨ₗⵁ (נתך N-TK) — **Pour:** To
pour out. [freq. 21] (vf: Paal, Niphal,
Hiphil, Hophal) |kjv: pour, melt,
gather, molten, drop| {str: 5413}

~~~~~~~~~

2451) ⟨ₗⵁ (נתן NTN) ac: **Give** co: **Gift**
ab: **?:** [from: ⟨ₗ - removing]

V) ⟨ₗⵁ (נתן N-TN) — **Give:** [A
generic verb with a wide application
meaning to give] [freq. 2008] (vf:
Paal, Niphal, Hophal) |kjv: give, put,
deliver, made, set, up, lay, grant,
suffer, yield, bring, cause, utter, send,
recompense, appoint, show| {str:
5414}

a^m) ⟨ₗⵁₘ (מנתן MN-TN) — **Gift:**
What is given. [df: מתן] [freq. 5]
|kjv: gift| {str: 4976}

a^f1) ⟨ₗⵁₘ (מנתנה MN-T-NH) —
Gift: What is given. [Hebrew and
Aramaic] [df: מתנה] [ar: מתנא]
[freq. 20] |kjv: gift| {str: 4978, 4979}

a^f2) ⟨ₗⵁₘ (מנתנת MN-T-NT) —
Gift: What is given. [df: מתנת] [freq.
6] |kjv: gift, give, reward| {str: 4991}

~~~~~~~~~

2452) 𝈫†٦ (נת NTS) ac: **Break** co: ? ab: ?: [from: †٦ - removing]

V) 𝈫†٦ (נתם N-TS) — **Break:** [freq. 1] (vf: Paal) |kjv: mar| {str: 5420}

~~~~~~~~~

2453) ⊙†٦ (נתע NTAh) ac: **Break** co: ? ab: ?: [from: †٦ - removing]

V) ⊙†٦ (נתע N-TAh) — **Break:** [freq. 1] (vf: Niphal) |kjv: break| {str: 5421}

~~~~~~~~~

2454) ᴏᴧ†٦ (נתץ NTTs) ac: **Break** co: ? ab: ?: [from: †٦ - removing]

V) ᴏᴧ†٦ (נתץ N-TTs) — **Break down:** [freq. 42] (vf: Paal, Niphal, Hophal, Pual, Piel) |kjv: break, throw, destroy, cast, beat, pull, overthrow| {str: 5422}

~~~~~~~~~

2455) ⊷†٦ (נתק NTQ) ac: **Draw** co: **Eruption** ab: ?: [from: †٦ - removing]

V) ⊷†٦ (נתק N-TQ) — **Draw:** To draw out or away as a bowstring or to draw a cord to its breaking point. [freq. 27] (vf: Paal, Niphal, Hiphil, Hophal, Piel) |kjv: break, draw, lift, pluck, draw, pluck, root, pull, burst| {str: 5423}

N^m) ⊷†٦ (נתק N-TQ) — **Eruption:** A disease of the skin which breaks open drawing out liquid. [freq. 14] |kjv: scall| {str: 5424}

~~~~~~~~~

2456) ᥰᥰ†٦ (נתש NTSh) ac: **Pluck** co: ? ab: ?: [from: †٦ - removing]

V) ᥰᥰ†٦ (נתש N-TSh) — **Pluck:** [freq. 21] (vf: Paal, Niphal, Hophal) |kjv: pluck, destroy, root, pull| {str: 5428}

~~~~~~~~~

2457) 𝈍†٦ (נתר NTR) ac: **Release** co: **Soda** ab: ?: A chemical that releases gases. [from: †٦ - removing]

V) 𝈍†٦ (נתר N-TR) — **Release:** [Hebrew and Aramaic] [freq. 9] (vf: Paal, Hiphil, Piel) |kjv: loose, move, leap, undo, make, drive, asunder, shake| {str: 5425, 5426}

N^m) 𝈍†٦ (נתר N-TR) — **Soda:** [freq. 2] |kjv: nitre| {str: 5427}

~~~~~~~~~

2458) 𝈍8٦ (נער NGhR) ac: **Shake** co: ? ab: ?: [from: 8٦]

V) 𝈍8٦ (נער N-GhR) — **Shake:** To shake back and forth. [freq. 12] (vf: Paal, Niphal, Hitpael, Piel) |kjv: shake, overthrow, toss, yell| {str: 5286, 5287}

c^f2) †𝈍𝈁8٦ (נעורת N-GhW-RT) — **Fiber:** As shaken from flax when beaten. [ms: נערת] [freq. 2] |kjv: tow| {str: 5296}

~~~~~~~~~

Sin

2459) ⋠סּבך (סבך SBK) ac: **Interweave** co: **Net** ab: **?:** [from: ساس - weaving]

V) ⋠סּבך (סבך S-BK) — **Interweave:** [freq. 2] (vf: Paal, Pual, Participle) |kjv: fold, wrap| {str: 5440}

N^m) ⋠סּבך (סבך S-BK) — **I. Net:** [df: שׁבך] **II. Thicket:** As interwoven. [freq. 5] |kjv: thicket, thick, net| {str: 5442, 7638}

N^fl) ⋠סּבכה (סבכה SB-KH) — **I. Netting:** [df: שׁבכה] **II. Trigon:** A triangular musical instrument with four strings. [ar: סבכא] [freq. 19] |kjv: network, wreath, checker, lattice, snare, sackbut| {str: 5443, 7639}

c^m) ⋠סּבוך (סבוך S-BWK) — **Thicket:** As interwoven. [freq. 1] |kjv: thicket| {str: 5441}

gc^m) ⋠סּובוך (סובוך SW-BWK) — **Boughs:** Thick interwoven branches. [df: שׁובך] [freq. 1] |kjv: boughs| {str: 7730}

2460) ⋠סּבל (סבל SBL) ac: **Carry** co: **Burden** ab: **?:** [from: ⋠ל - raising]

V) ⋠סּבל (סבל S-BL) — **Carry:** [Hebrew and Aramaic] [freq. 10] (vf: Paal, Hitpael, Pual, Participle) |kjv: carry, bear, labour, burden| {str: 5445, 5446}

N^m) ⋠סּבל (סבל S-BL) — **Burden:** [freq. 8] |kjv: burden, charge| {str: 5447, 5449}

N^fl) ⋠סּבלה (סבלה SB-LH) — **Burden:** [freq. 6] |kjv: burden| {str: 5450}

g^m) ⋠סּובל (סובל SW-BL) — **Burden:** [ms: סבל] [freq. 3] |kjv: burden| {str: 5448}

2461) ⋠סּבע (סבע SBAh) ac: **Fill** co: **Full** ab: **Satisfaction**

V) ⋠סּבע (סבע S-BAh) — **Fill:** To fill full. [df: שׁבע] [freq. 95] (vf: Paal, Hiphil, Piel) |kjv: satisfy, fill, full, plenty, enough, satiate, suffice, insatiable, weary| {str: 7646}

N^m) ⋠סּבע (סבע S-BAh) — **I. Full:** [df: שׁבע] **II. Plenty:** [df: שׁבע] [freq. 18] |kjv: plenty, plenteous, abundance, full, satisfied| {str: 7647, 7649}

N^fl) ⋠סּבעה (סבעה SB-AhH) — **Satisfaction:** [df: שׁבעה] [freq. 6] |kjv: fullness, satisfy, enough, full, sufficiently| {str: 7654}

e^fl) ⋠סּיבעה (סיבעה SYB-AhH) — **Full:** [df: שׁבעה] [freq. 1] |kjv: fullness| {str: 7653}

g^m) ⋠סּובע (סובע SW-BAh) — **Full:** [df: שׁבע] [freq. 8] |kjv: full, fullness, sufficed, satisfying| {str: 7648}

2462) ⋠סּבר (סבר SBR) ac: **Consider** co: **?** ab: **?:** A patient watching, waiting or expectation.

V) ⋠סּבר (סבר S-BR) — **Consider:** [Hebrew and Aramaic] [df: שׁבר

שבר] [freq. 9] (vf: Paal, Piel, Participle) |kjv: hope, wait, view, tarry, think| {str: 5452, 7663}

N^m) ⋞ᒲᓓ (סבר S-BR) — **Consideration:** [df: שֹבֶר] [freq. 2] |kjv: hope| {str: 7664}

~~~~~~~~~~

2463) ⋞ᔑᒲ (סגב SGB) ac: **Lift** co: **Tower** ab: ?: [from: ᔑᒲ - high]

V) ⋞ᔑᒲ (סגב S-GB) — **Lift:** [df: שֹגב] [freq. 20] (vf: Paal, Niphal, Hiphil, Pual, Piel) |kjv: high, exalt, defend, safe, excellent| {str: 7682}

h^m) ⋞ᔑᒲᨓ (מסגב MS-GB) — **Tower:** A high place of defense and protection. [df: משֹגב] [freq. 17] |kjv: defense, refuge, tower, fort| {str: 4869}

~~~~~~~~~~

2464) ⋞ᔑᒣ (סגד SGD) ac: **Fall** co: ? ab: ?: Fall down to the knees with the face to the ground in homage.

V) ⋞ᔑᒣ (סגד S-GD) — **Prostrate:** To fall down to the knees and face in homage. [Hebrew and Aramaic] [freq. 16] (vf: Paal) |kjv: fall down, worship| {str: 5456, 5457}

~~~~~~~~~~

2465) ⋞ᔑᒍ (סגל SGL) ac: ? co: **Jewel** ab: ?

d^{f1}) ⋞ᔑᒍᎩ⚹ (סגולה S-GW-LH) — **Jewel:** A precious stone. [ms: סגלה] [freq. 8] |kjv: treasure, peculiar, special, jewel| {str: 5459}

~~~~~~~~~~

2466) ⋞ᔑᒪ (סגן SGN) ac: **Ruler** co: **Ruler** ab: ?

N^m) ⋞ᔑᒪ (סגן S-GN) — **Ruler:** [Hebrew and Aramaic] [freq. 22] |kjv: ruler, governor| {str: 5460, 5461}

~~~~~~~~~~

2467) ⋞ᔑᒣ (סגר SGR) ac: **Shut** co: **Cage** ab: ?: [from: ⋞שׁ - an enclosure]

V) ⋞ᔑᒣ (סגר S-GR) — **Shut:** To shut or clse. [Hebrew and Aramaic] [df: שֹכר] [freq. 96] (vf: Paal, Niphal, Hiphil, Pual, Piel) |kjv: shut, deliver, pure, give, inclose, repair, close, stop, strait, together| {str: 5462, 5463, 5534}

a^m) ⋞ᔑᒣᨓ (מסגר MS-GR) — I. **Prison:** A place for shutting up. II. **Smith:** As one who makes shackles for prisoners. [freq. 7] |kjv: smith, prison| {str: 4525}

c^m) ⋞ᒪᔑᎩ (סגור S-GWR) — I. **Enclosure:** As shut in. II. **Gold:** [Unknown connection to root;] [freq. 2] |kjv: gold, caul| {str: 5458}

h^{f2}) ⋞ᒪᔑᨓ† (מסגרת MS-G-RT) — **Border:** The area that encloses a people. [freq. 17] |kjv: border, close, hole| {str: 4526}

o^m) ⋞Ꭹᔑᒍ (סוגר SW-GR) — **Cage:** As shut in. [freq. 1] |kjv: ward| {str: 5474}

lb^m) ⋞ᔑᒍᨓᒣ⊸ (סגריר SG-RYR) — **Heavy rain:** [Unknown connection to root;] [freq. 1] |kjv: rainy| {str: 5464}

~~~~~~~~~~

2468) ⋞ᒣᒣ (סדר SDR) ac: **Order** co: **Row** ab: ?: Set in order as an arrangement. [from: ⋞ᒣᒣ - order]

N^m) ⋞ᒣᒣ (סדר S-DR) — **Order:** An ordered arrangement. [freq. 1] |kjv: order| {str: 5468}

N[fl]) 🕊️👁🜔⋖ (סדרה SD-RH) — **Row:** A row of planks in constructing a house or of an army in the sense of being in order. [df: שדרה] [freq. 4] |kjv: range, board| {str: 7713}

hj[m]) ᐯ👁🜔⋖ᙏ (מסדרון M-SD-RWN) — **Porch:** As built with rows or boards. [freq. 1] |kjv: porch| {str: 4528}

~~~~~~~~~

2469) 🝪🜔⋖ (סחב SHhB) ac: **Drag** co: **Rag** ab: **?**

V) 🝪🜔⋖ (סחב S-HhB) — **Drag:** [freq. 5] (vf: Paal) |kjv: draw, tear| {str: 5498}

N[fl]) 🕊️🝪🜔⋖ (סחבה SHh-BH) — **Rag:** Old worn out clothes as dragged. [freq. 2] |kjv: clout| {str: 5499}

~~~~~~~~~

2470) ⊗🝪⋖ (סחט SHhTh) ac: **Press** co: **?** ab: **?**

V) ⊗🝪⋖ (סחט S-HhTh) — **Press:** [df: שׁחט] [freq. 1] (vf: Paal) |kjv: press| {str: 7818}

~~~~~~~~~

2471) ⌒🝪⋖ (סחף SHhP) ac: **Sweep** co: **?** ab: **?**

V) ⌒🝪⋖ (סחף S-HhP) — **Sweep:** To sweep away. [freq. 2] (vf: Paal, Niphal, Participle) |kjv: sweeping, sweep| {str: 5502}

~~~~~~~~~

2472) ⚬🝪⋖ (סחק SHhQ) ac: **Laugh** co: **?** ab: **?**: [from: 🝪🜓 - coming from the belly]

V) ⚬🝪⋖ (סחק S-HhQ) — **Laugh:** To laugh in play, sport or scorn. [df:

שׂחק] [freq. 36] (vf: Paal, Hiphil, Piel) |kjv: play, laugh, rejoice, scorn, sport, merry, mock, deride| {str: 7832}

c[m]) ⚬Y🝪⋖ (סחוק S-HhWQ) — **Laughter:** [df: שׂחוק שׂחק] [freq. 15] |kjv: laughter, derision, laughing, mock, scorn, sport| {str: 7814}

h[m]) ⚬🝪⋖ᙏ (מסחק MSh-hQ) — **Laughter:** [df: משׂחק] [freq. 1] |kjv: scorn| {str: 4890}

~~~~~~~~~

2473) 👁🝪⋖ (סחר SHhR) ac: **Trade** co: **Merchandise** ab: **?:** To go about to and fro trading precious merchandises. [from: 🝪🜓 - travel]

V) 👁🝪⋖ (סחר S-HhR) — **I. Trade: II. Beat:** The beating of the heart in the sense of going about to and fro. [freq. 20] (vf: Paal, Pilpel, Participle) |kjv: merchant, trade, pant, traffick| {str: 5503}

N[m]) 👁🝪⋖ (סחר S-HhR) — **Merchandise:** Something that is traded. [freq. 7] |kjv: merchandise| {str: 5504, 5505}

c[fl]) 🕊️👁Y🝪⋖ (סחורה S-HhW-RH) — **Merchandise:** Something that is traded. [ms: סחרה] [freq. 1] |kjv: merchandise| {str: 5506}

g[fl]) 🕊️👁🝪Y⋖ (סוחרה SW-Hh-RH) — **Shield:** [Unknown connection to root;] [ms: סחרה] [freq. 1] |kjv: buckler| {str: 5507}

g[f2]) †👁🝪Y⋖ (סוחרת SW-Hh-RT) — **Black:** From the black goat hair tents of the traders. [freq. 1] |kjv: black| {str: 5508}

h[m]) 👁🝪⋖ᙏ (מסחר MSh-hR) — **Merchandise:** Something that is traded. [freq. 1] |kjv: traffick| {str: 4536}

2474) ⴟⵀⵛ (סטם SThM) ac: **Hate** co: ? ab: ?: [from: ⵀⵛ - turning]

V) ⴟⵀⵛ (סטם S-ThM) — **Hate:** [df: שטם] [freq. 6] (vf: Paal) |kjv: hate, oppose| {str: 7852}

2475) ⵖⵀⵛ (סטן SThN) ac: **Oppose** co: Opponent ab: Opposition: [from: ⵀⵛ - turning]

V) ⵖⵀⵛ (סטן S-ThN) — **Oppose:** [df: שטן] [freq. 6] (vf: Paal) |kjv: adversary, resist| {str: 7853}

N^m) ⵖⵀⵛ (סטן S-ThN) — **Opponent:** [df: שטן] [freq. 27] |kjv: satan, adversary, withstand| {str: 7854}

e^fl) ⵕⵖⵀⵛ (סיטנה SYTh-NH) — **Opposition:** [df: שטנה] [freq. 1] |kjv: accusation| {str: 7855}

2476) ⵗⵀⵛ (סטר SThR) ac: ? co: **Side** ab: ?: [from: טרד]

N^m) ⵗⵀⵛ (סטר S-ThR) — **Side:** [Aramaic only] [freq. 1] |kjv: side| {str: 7859}

2477) ⵎⵡⵛ (סכל SKL) ac: **Understand** co: ? ab: ?: The ability to consider a situation with comprehension in order to be successful or prosperous.

V) ⵎⵡⵛ (סכל S-KL) — **Understand:** [Hebrew and Aramaic] [df: שכל] [freq. 64] (vf: Paal, Hiphil, Piel) |kjv: understand, wise, prosper, wisely, understanding, consider, instruct, prudent, skill, teach, consider| {str: 7919, 7920}

N^m) ⵎⵡⵛ (סכל S-KL) — **Understanding:** [df: שכל] [freq. 16] |kjv: understanding, wisdom, wise, prudence, knowledge, sense, discretion, policy| {str: 7922}

N^f2) ⵜⵎⵡⵛ (סכלת SK-LT) — **Understanding:** [Aramaic only] [df: שכלתנו] [freq. 3] |kjv: understanding| {str: 7924}

2478) ⵖⵡⵛ (סכן SKN) ac: **Benefit** co: ? ab: ?: [from: ⵡⵛ - as a covering of stores]

V) ⵖⵡⵛ (סכן S-KN) — **Benefit:** To be of use, service or profit in order that one may benefit from it. [freq. 14] (vf: Paal, Niphil, Hiphil, Pual, Participle) |kjv: acquaint, profitable, cherish, advantage, endanger, impoverish, treasure| {str: 5532, 5533}

h^m) ⵖⵡⵛⴟ (מסכן MS-KN) — **Poor:** One who benefits from others generosity. [freq. 4] |kjv: poor| {str: 4542}

h^fl) ⵕⵖⵡⵛⴟ (מסכנה MS-K-NH) — **Storehouse:** Places for storing items for future benefit. [freq. 7] |kjv: store, storehouse, treasure| {str: 4543}

h^f3) ⵜⵗⵖⵡⵛⴟ (מסכנות MS-K-NWT) — **Poverty:** Those who rely on benefits from others. [ms: מסכנת] [freq. 1] |kjv: scarceness| {str: 4544}

2479) ⵕⵡⵛ (סכר SKR) ac: **Hire** co: **Wage** ab: ?: A payment of wages or reward for services. [from: ⵡⵛ - as a covering for services] (eng: succor, secure)

V) ⵕⵡⵛ (סכר S-KR) — **Hire:** [df: שכר] [freq. 21] (vf: Paal, Niphal,

Hitpael) |kjv: hire, reward, wage|
{str: 7936}

N^m) ⵥⵍⵏ� (סכר S-KR) — **Wage:**
The reward or price paid for ones
labor. [df: שׂכר] [freq. 30] |kjv: hire,
reward, wage, price, fare, worth,
sluice| {str: 7938, 7939}

b^m) ⵏ⸗ⵍⵏⵥ (סכיר S-KYR) —
Hireling: One who is hired for
service. [df: שׂכיר] [freq. 17] |kjv:
servant, hireling, hired| {str: 7916}

b^{f1}) ⵥⵏ⸗ⵍⵏⵥ (סכירה S-KY-RH) —
Hireling: One who is hired for
service. [df: שׂכירה] [freq. 1] |kjv:
hired| {str: 7917}

n^m) ⵏⵍⵏⵥⴾ (אסכר AS-KR) —
Payment: [df: אשׂכר] [freq. 2] |kjv:
gift, present| {str: 814}

ac^{f2}) †ⵟⵏⵍⵏⵥⴹ (מסכורת MS-KW-
RT) — **Wage:** [df: משׂכרת] [freq. 4]
|kjv: wages, reward| {str: 4909}

2480) †ⵍⵏⵥ (סכת SKT) ac: **Silent** co: **?**
ab: **?**

V) †ⵍⵏⵥ (סכת S-KT) — **Silent:** To
be silent. [freq. 1] (vf: Hiphil) |kjv:
heed| {str: 5535}

2481) ⴹⵔⵎⵥ (סלד SLD) ac: **Lift** co: **?**
ab: **?**: [from: ⵎⵥ]

V) ⴹⵔⵎⵥ (סלד S-LD) — **Lift:** [freq.
1] (vf: Piel) |kjv: harden| {str: 5539}

2482) ⵗⵎⵥ (סלח SLHh) ac: **Forgive**
co: **?** ab: **?**: [from: ⵎⵥ - lifting one out of
a debt]

V) ⵗⵎⵥ (סלח S-LHh) — **Forgive:**
[freq. 46] (vf: Paal, Niphal) |kjv:
forgive, pardon, spare| {str: 5545}

N^m) ⵗⵎⵥ (סלח S-LHh) —
Forgiving: [freq. 1] |kjv: forgive|
{str: 5546}

b^{f1}) ⵟⵗ⸗ⵎⵥ (סליחה S-LY-HhH)
— **Forgiveness:** [freq. 3] |kjv:
forgiveness, pardon| {str: 5547}

2483) ⵏⵏⵎⵥ (סלם SLM) ac: **?** co:
Garment ab: **?**: [from: ⵎⵥ - lifting onto
the body]

N^f) ⵏⵏⵎⵥ (סלם S-LM) —
Garment: [df: שׂלמה] [freq. 16]
|kjv: garment, raiment, clothes| {str:
8008}

2484) ⵙⵎⵥ (סלע SLAh) ac: **High** co:
Cliff ab: **?**: [from: ⵎⵥ - height]

N^m) ⵙⵎⵥ (סלע S-LAh) — **Cliff:** A
high rock, cliff or towering rock, as a
place of defense. [freq. 60] |kjv: rock,
stronghold, stone, stony| {str: 5553}

p^m) ⵏⵏⵙⵎⵥ (סלעם SL-AhM) —
Locust: From its high jumping.
[freq. 1] |kjv: locust| {str: 5556}

2485) ⵙⵎⵥ (סלף SLP) ac: **Twist** co: **?**
ab: **?**

V) ⵙⵎⵥ (סלף S-LP) — **Twist:** To
twist words or the way in the sense of
perverseness. [freq. 7] (vf: Piel) |kjv:
overthrow, pervert| {str: 5557}

N^m) ⵙⵎⵥ (סלף S-LP) —
Crookedness: Something twisted.
[freq. 2] |kjv: perverseness| {str:
5558}

2486) ⴰⵙⵎⵥ (סלק SLQ) ac: **Ascend** co:
? ab: **?**: [from: ⵎⵥ]

V) (סלק S-LQ) — **Ascend:** [Aramaic only] [freq. 5] (vf: Paal) |kjv: came| {str: 5559}

2487) (סמח SMHh) ac: **Rejoice** co: **?** ab: **Joy:** A spontaneous expression of excitement and cheer.

V) (סמח S-MHh) — **Rejoice:** [df: שמח] [freq. 152] (vf: Paal, Hiphil, Piel) |kjv: rejoice, glad, joy, merry| {str: 8055}

N^{m}) (סמח S-MHh) — **Rejoicing:** [df: שמח] [freq. 23] |kjv: rejoice, glad, joyful, merry, merryhearted| {str: 8056}

N^{f1}) (סמחה SM-HhH) — **Joy:** [df: שמחה] [freq. 94] |kjv: joy, gladness, mirth, rejoice| {str: 8057}

2488) (סמך SMK) ac: **Support** co: **?** ab: **?:** The supporting of something by laying against or on it. [from: - setting up a support]

V) (סמך S-MK) — **Support:** [freq. 48] (vf: Paal, Niphal, Piel) |kjv: lay, uphold, put, lean, stay, sustain, hold, borne, establish, stand, rest, set| {str: 5564}

b^{f1}) (סמיכה S-MY-KH) — **Covering:** [Unknown connection to root;] [df: שמיכה] [freq. 1] |kjv: mantle| {str: 8063}

2489) (סמל SML) ac: **?** co: **Image** ab: **?:** The form or shape of an image.

N^{m}) (סמל S-ML) — **Image:** [freq. 5] |kjv: figure, image, idol| {str: 5566}

e^{f1}) (סימלה SYM-LH) — **Garment:** As forming to the image of the body. [df: שמלה] [freq. 29] |kjv: raiment, clothes, garment, apparel, cloth, clothing| {str: 8071}

2490) (סמן SMN) ac: **Appoint** co: **?** ab: **?:** [from: - setting in place]

V) (סמן S-MN) — **Appoint:** [freq. 1] (vf: Niphal, Participle) |kjv: appoint| {str: 5567}

2491) (סמר SMR) ac: **Bristle** co: **Hair** ab: **?:** The standing on end of hair as when terrified or on a caterpillar.

V) (סמר S-MR) — **Bristle:** [freq. 2] (vf: Paal, Piel) |kjv: tremble, stood| {str: 5568}

N^{m}) (סמר S-MR) — **Hair:** [freq. 1] |kjv: rough| {str: 5569}

a^{f1}) (מסמרה MS-M-RH) — **Nail:** As a standing hair. [freq. 4] |kjv: nail| {str: 4548}

a ^{f}) (מסמר MS-MR) — **Nail:** As a standing hair. [df: משמר] [freq. 1] |kjv: nail| {str: 4548, 4930}

h^{m}) (מסמר MS-MR) — **Nail:** As a standing hair. [freq. 1] |kjv: nail| {str: 4548}

2492) (סעד SAhD) ac: **Comfort** co: **?** ab: **?**

V) (סעד S-AhD) — **Comfort:** To be a support or aid for strength or rest. [Hebrew and Aramaic] [freq. 13] (vf: Paal) |kjv: comfort, strengthen, hold, uphold, establish, refresh, helping| {str: 5582, 5583}

h^m) ⵟⵔⵙⵎ (מסעד MS-AhD) —
Pillar: What gives support. [freq. 1]
|kjv: pillar| {str: 4552}

2493) ⵙⵙⵙⵙ (סעף SAhP) ac: **Divide**
co: **Fork** ab: **?:** A fork in a branch.

V) ⵙⵙⵙⵙ (סעף S-AhP) — **Divide:**
To divide by cutting off. [freq. 1] (vf:
Piel) |kjv: lop| {str: 5586}

N^m) ⵙⵙⵙⵙ (סעף S-AhP) —
Divided: Being divided in thought or
double minded. [freq. 1] |kjv:
thought| {str: 5588}

N^{f1}) ⵯⵙⵙⵙ (סעפה SAh-PH) —
Forked branch: Where nests of
birds are made. [freq. 2] |kjv: bough|
{str: 5589}

b^f) ⵙⵢⵙⵙ (סעיף S-AhYP) — **I.**
Division: [df: שעף] **II. Cleft:** A
division in a rock. [freq. 9] |kjv:
opinion, thought, top, branch, clift|
{str: 5585, 5587}

2494) ⵏⵙⵙ (סער SAhR) ac: **?** co: **Hair**
ab: **?**

N^m) ⵏⵙⵙ (סער S-AhR) — **Hair:**
[Hebrew and Aramaic] [df: שער]
[freq. 31] |kjv: hair| {str: 8177, 8181}

N^{f1}) ⵯⵏⵙⵙ (סערה SAh-RH) —
Hair: [df: שערה] [freq. 7] |kjv: hair|
{str: 8185}

b^m) ⵏⵢⵙⵙ (סעיר S-AhYR) — **I.**
Goat: From its thick hair used to
make tents. [df: שער שעיר] **II.**
Raindrop: As the hair from heaven.
[freq. 60] |kjv: kid, goat, devil, satyr,
hairy, rough, rain| {str: 8163, 8164}

b^{f1}) ⵯⵏⵢⵙⵙ (סעירה S-AhY-RH)
— **She-Goat:** From its hair. [df:
שעירה] [freq. 2] |kjv: kid| {str:
8166}

c^{f1}) ⵯⵏⵡⵙⵙ (סעורה S-AhW-RH) —
Barley: From its hair on its head. [df:
שערה] [freq. 34] |kjv: barley| {str:
8184}

2495) ⵟⵔⵙⵙ (ספד SPD) ac: **Mourn** co:
? ab: **?**

V) ⵟⵔⵙⵙ (ספד S-PD) — **Mourn:**
[freq. 30] (vf: Paal, Niphal,
Participle) |kjv: mourn, lament,
mourner, wail| {str: 5594}

h^m) ⵟⵔⵙⵎ (מספד MS-PD) —
Mourning: [freq. 16] |kjv: mourning,
wailing, lamentation| {str: 4553}

2496) ⵎⵙⵙ (ספח SPHh) ac: **Attach**
co: **?** ab: **?:** A bringing together by what
is separated or spread out. [from: ⵎⵙ -
as spread]

V) ⵎⵙⵙ (ספח S-PHh) — **Attach:**
To join together or attach. [df: שפח]
[freq. 6] (vf: Paal, Niphal, Hitpael,
Pual, Piel, Participle) |kjv: put, abide,
gather, scab, cleave| {str: 5596}

N^{f2}) ⵟⵎⵙⵙ (ספחת SP-HhT) —
Scab: A sore that spreads. [freq. 2]
|kjv: scab| {str: 5597}

b^m) ⵎⵢⵙⵙ (ספיח S-PYHh) —
After-growth: What spreads out by
itself rather than sown. [freq. 5] |kjv:
grow| {str: 5599}

h^m) ⵎⵙⵎ (מספח MS-PHh) —
Bloodshed: In the sense of spreading
flow. [df: משפח] [freq. 1] |kjv:
oppression| {str: 4939}

h^{f1}) ⵯⵎⵙⵎ (מספחה MS-P-
HhH) — **Veil:** As spread out. [freq. 2]
|kjv: kerchief| {str: 4555}

h^{f2}) ⵟⵎⵙⵎ (מספחת MS-P-HhT)
— **Scab:** A sore that spreads. [freq.
3] |kjv: scab| {str: 4556}

2497) ᒍᑎ⪻ (סֶפֶל SPL) ac: ? co: **Dish** ab: ?

N^(m)) ᒍᑎ⪻ (סֶפֶל S-PL) — **Dish:** [freq. 2] |kjv: bowl, dish| {str: 5602}

2498) ᒪᑎ⪻ (סֹפֶן SPN) ac: **Cover** co: **Treasure** ab: ?

V) ᒪᑎ⪻ (סֹפֶן S-PN) — **Cover:** To cover as a ceiling or to hide. [df: שׂפן] [freq. 7] (vf: Paal, Participle) |kjv: cover, cieled, seat, treasure| {str: 5603, 8226}

b^(fl)) ⤴ᒪᒍᑎ⪻ (סְפִינָה S-PY-NH) — **Ship:** [Unknown connection to root;] [freq. 1] |kjv: ship| {str: 5600}

ed^(m)) ᒪᎩᒍᑎᒪ⪻ (סִיפּוּן SY-PWN) — **Ceiling:** [df: סֹפֶן] [freq. 1] |kjv: cieling| {str: 5604}

2499) ⚫⚫ᑎ⪻ (סֶפֶק SPQ) ac: **Clasp** co: ? ab: ?

V) ⚫⚫ᑎ⪻ (סֶפֶק S-PQ) — **Clasp:** [df: שׂפק] [freq. 10] (vf: Paal, Hiphil) |kjv: clap, smite, please, strike, suffice, wallow| {str: 5606}

N^(m)) ⚫⚫ᑎ⪻ (סֶפֶק S-PQ) — **Clasp:** [df: שׂפק] [freq. 2] |kjv: sufficiency, stroke| {str: 5607}

2500) ᕫᑎ⪻ (סֶפֶר SPR) ac: **Record** co: **Scroll** ab: ?: A recording of a story or numbers. [from: ᑎ⪻ - from the speaking of a record] (eng: sapphire)

V) ᕫᑎ⪻ (סֶפֶר S-PR) — **Record:** [freq. 161] (vf: Paal, Niphal, Pual, Piel) |kjv: scribe, tell, declare, number, count, show, writer, speak,

account, commune, reckon, talk| {str: 5608}

N^(m)) ᕫᑎ⪻ (סֶפֶר S-PR) — **I. Scroll:** A document or record written on a sheet of skin or papyrus and rolled up. [Hebrew and Aramaic] **II. Census:** A record of numbers. **III. Scribe:** One who records. [Aramaic only] [freq. 12] |kjv: book, roll, letter, evidence, bill, learning, register, scribe| {str: 5609, 5610, 5612, 5613}

b^(m)) ᕫᒍᑎ⪻ (סַפִּיר S-PYR) — **Sapphire:** [Unknown connection to root;] [freq. 11] |kjv: sapphire| {str: 5601}

c^(fl)) ⤴Ꭹᕫᑎ⪻ (סְפוֹרָה S-PW-RH) — **Number:** A counting as a recording. [ms: סְפֹרָה] [freq. 1] |kjv: number| {str: 5615}

e^(fl)) ⤴ᕫᑎᒍ⪻ (סִיפְּרָה SYP-RH) — **Scroll:** A document or record. [ms: סְפֹרָה] [freq. 184] |kjv: book| {str: 5612}

h^(m)) ᕫᑎ⪻ᔾ (מִסְפָּר MS-PR) — **Number:** A counting as a recording. [freq. 134] |kjv: number| {str: 4557}

2501) ᒞ⚫⪻ (סָקַד SQD) ac: **Bind** co: ? ab: ?

V) ᒞ⚫⪻ (סָקַד S-QD) — **Bind:** [df: שׂקד] [freq. 1] (vf: Niphal) |kjv: bind| {str: 8244}

2502) ᒍ⚫⪻ (סָקַל SQL) ac: **Stone** co: ? ab: ?: The gathering of stones for building a fence, road or for stoning.

V) ᒍ⚫⪻ (סָקַל S-QL) — **Stone:** To gather or throw stones. [freq. 22] (vf: Paal, Niphal, Pual, Piel) |kjv: stone, cast, gather, throw| {str: 5619}

2503) ⪽-●-ꓓ (סקר SQR) ac: **Want** co: **?** ab: **?**

V) ⪽-●-ꓓ (סקר S-QR) — **Want:** [df: שׂקר] [freq. 1] (vf: Piel, Participle) |kjv: wanton| {str: 8265}

2504) ⪽ꓓ☐ (סרב SRB) ac: **?** co: **Brier** ab: **?:** [from: ꓓ⪽ - sharp]

N^m) ⪽ꓓ☐ (סרב S-RB) — **Brier:** [freq. 1] |kjv: brier| {str: 5621}

2505) ⪽ꓓᏞ (סרג SRG) ac: **Wrap** co: **Branch** ab: **?:** A weaving or wrapping.

V) ⪽ꓓᏞ (סרג S-RG) — **Wrap:** [df: שׂרג] [freq. 2] (vf: Hitpael, Pual) |kjv: wreath, wrap| {str: 8276}

b^m) ⪽ꓓᎧᏞ (סריג S-RYG) — **Branch:** As wrapped. [df: שׂריג] [freq. 3] |kjv: branch| {str: 8299}

2506) ⪽ꓓᄄ (סרד SRD) ac: **Remain** co: **?** ab: **Remnant:** [from: ꓓ⪽ - a remnant]

V) ⪽ꓓᄄ (סרד S-RD) — **Remain:** [df: שׂרד] [freq. 1] (vf: Paal) |kjv: remain| {str: 8277}

N^m) ⪽ꓓᄄ (סרד S-RD) — **I. Remnant:** [df: שׂרד] **II. Marker:** [Unknown connection to root;] [df: שׂרד] [freq. 5] |kjv: service, line| {str: 8278, 8279}

b^m) ⪽ꓓᎧᄄ (סריד S-RYD) — **Remnant:** What remains. [df: שׂריד] [freq. 28] |kjv: remain, left, remnant, alive, rest| {str: 8300}

2507) ⪽ꓓ☰ (סרה SRHh) ac: **Exceed** co: **?** ab: **?:** A remnant that is in excess or is not needed or wanted. [from: ꓓ⪽ - a remnant]

V) ⪽ꓓ☰ (סרה S-RHh) — **Exceed:** [freq. 7] (vf: Paal, Niphal, Participle) |kjv: hang, stretch, spread, exceed, vanish| {str: 5628}

N^m) ⪽ꓓ☰ (סרה S-RHh) — **Excess:** [freq. 1] |kjv: remnant| {str: 5629}

2508) ⪽ꓓ⊗ (סרט SRTh) ac: **Slice** co: **?** ab: **?:** An incision, scratch or laceration.

V) ⪽ꓓ⊗ (סרט S-RTh) — **Slice:** [df: שׂרט] [freq. 3] (vf: Paal, Niphal) |kjv: cut, pieces, make| {str: 8295}

N^m/f) ⪽ꓓ⊗ (סרט S-RTh) — **Slicing:** [df: שׂרט] [freq. 1] |kjv: cutting| {str: 8296}

N^f2) ⪽ꓓ⊗✝ (סרטת SR-ThT) — **Slicing:** [df: שׂרט] [freq. 1] |kjv: cutting| {str: 8296}

2509) ⪽ꓓᎩᗯ (סרך SRK) ac: **Twist** co: **Lace** ab: **?:** The laces of the sandal that are twisted around the foot and ankles. [from: ꓓ⪽]

V) ⪽ꓓᗯ (סרך S-RK) — **Twist:** [df: שׂרך] [freq. 1] (vf: Piel) |kjv: traverse| {str: 8308}

N^m) ⪽ꓓᗯ (סרך S-RK) — **Overseer:** [Unknown connection to root; Aramaic only] [freq. 5] |kjv: president| {str: 5632}

c^m) ⪽ꓓᎩᗯ (סרוך S-RWK) — **Lace:** As twisted around the foot for attaching sandals. [df: שׂרוך] [freq. 2] |kjv: latchet| {str: 8288}

2510) (סרס SRS) ac: **Castrate** co: **Eunuch** ab: **?:** A castrated male and often used as officers. [from: - rule]

b^{m}) (סריס S-RYS) — **I. Eunuch:** [ms: סרס] **II. Officer:** [ms: סרס] [freq. 42] |kjv: eunuch, chamberlain, officer| {str: 5631}

~~~~~~~~~~

2511) (סרע SRAh) ac: **Exceed** co: **?** ab: **?:** Something of an unusual or excessive length. [from: - a remnant]

V) (סרע S-RAh) — **Exceed:** [df: שׂרע] [freq. 3] (vf: Paal, Hitpael, Participle) |kjv: superfluous, stretch| {str: 8311}

~~~~~~~~~~

2512) (סרף SRP) ac: **Burn** co: **Venom** ab: **?:** [from: - a burning wound]

V) (סרף S-RP) — **Burn:** [df: שׂרף] [freq. 118] (vf: Paal, Niphal, Pual, Piel, Participle) |kjv: burn, kindle, made| {str: 5635, 8313}

N^{m}) (סרף S-RP) — **Seraph:** A venomous serpent from its burning venom. [df: שׂרף] [freq. 7] |kjv: fiery, serpent, seraphim| {str: 8314}

N^{f1}) (סרפה SR-PH) — **Burning:** [df: שׂרפה] [freq. 13] |kjv: burn, burning| {str: 8316}

h^{f1}) (מסרפה MS-R-PH) — **Burning:** [df: משׂרפה] [freq. 2] |kjv: burning| {str: 4955}

~~~~~~~~~~

2513) (סרק SRQ) ac: **?** co: **?** ab: **Choice**

b^{f1}) (סריקה S-RY-QH) — **Choice:** [df: שׂריק] [freq. 1] |kjv: fine| {str: 8305}

c^{m}) (סרוק S-RWQ) — **Grapevine:** [df: שׂרק] [freq. 1] |kjv: principal plant| {str: 8291}

d^{m}) (סרוק S-RWQ) — **Speckled:** [Unknown connection to root;] [df: שׂרק] [freq. 1] |kjv: speckled| {str: 8320}

g^{m}) (סורק SW-RQ) — **Choice vine:** [df: שׂרק שׂרוק] [freq. 3] |kjv: choice vine, noble vine| {str: 8321}

g^{f1}) (סורקה SW-R-QH) — **Choice vine:** [df: שׂרק] [freq. 1] |kjv: choice vine| {str: 8321}

~~~~~~~~~~

2514) (סרת SRT) ac: **?** co: **?** ab: **?**

a^{m}) (מסרת MS-RT) — **Pan:** [df: משׂרת] [freq. 1] |kjv: pan| {str: 4958}

~~~~~~~~~~

2515) (סתם STM) ac: **Stop** co: **?** ab: **?**

V) (סתם S-TM) — **Stop:** To stop by halting or closing. [df: שׂתם] [freq. 14] (vf: Paal, Niphal, Piel, Participle) |kjv: stop, shut, hide, secret, close| {str: 5640}

~~~~~~~~~~

2516) (סתר STR) ac: **Hide** co: **?** ab: **?:** (eng: mystery)

V) (סתר S-TR) — **Hide:** To hide or conceal. [Hebrew and Aramaic] [df: שׂתר] [freq. 85] (vf: Niphal, Hiphil, Hitpael, Pual, Piel) |kjv: hide, secret, close, absent, conceal| {str: 5641, 5642, 8368}

N^{m}) (סתר S-TR) — **Hiding:** A covert or secret hiding or hiding place. [df: שׂתר] [freq. 35] |kjv: secret, secretly, covert, hiding, backbiting, covering, disguise, privily| {str: 5643}

a^m) ᕅᵻ⧏ᨇ (מסתר MS-TR) — **Hiding:** [freq. 1] |kjv: hid, secret, secretly| {str: 4564}

e^{f1}) ⳤᕅᵻᒐ⧏ (סיתרה SYT-RH) — **Protection:** In the sense of hiding. [df: שׁתרה] [freq. 1] |kjv: protection| {str: 5643}

h^m) ᕅᵻ⧏ᨇ (מסתר MS-TR) — **Secret:** A place of hiding. [freq. 10] |kjv: secret, secretly| {str: 4565}

hc^m) ᕅᎩᵻ⧏ᨇ (מסתור MS-TWR) — **Hiding:** [freq. 1] |kjv: covert| {str: 4563}

~~~~~~~~~~

2517) ᕅ⧏⧏ (סער SGhR) ac: **?** co: **Storm** ab: **Horrible:** The strong winds and torrents of a storm or of a persons rage that cause one to fear. [from: ⧏⧏]

V) ᕅ⧏⧏ (סער S-GhR) — **I. Storm:** [df: שׁער] **II. Afraid:** To be afraid as from a storm. [freq. 15] (vf: Paal, Niphal, Hitpael, Pual, Piel, Participle) |kjv: whirlwind, tempest, trouble, toss| {str: 5590, 8175}

N^{m/f}) ᕅ⧏⧏ (סער S-GhR) — **I. Storm:** [df: שׁער] **II. Afraid:** As from a storm. [freq. 28] |kjv: whirlwind, tempest, stormy, storm| {str: 5591, 8178}

N^{f1}) ⳤᕅ⧏⧏ (סערה SGh-RH) — **Storm:** [df: שׁערה] [freq. 2] |kjv: tempest, storm| {str: 8183}

ld^{f1}) ⳤᕅᎩᕅ⧏⧏ (סערורה SGh-RW-RH) — **Horrible thing:** As fearful. [df: שׁערורה] [freq. 1] |kjv: horrible thing| {str: 8186}

ld^{f4}) ᵻᒐᕅᎩᕅ⧏⧏ (סערורית SGh-RW-RYT) — **Horrible thing:** As fearful. [df: שׁעררת] [freq. 4] |kjv: horrible thing| {str: 8186}

lbf^{f1}) ⳤᒐᕅᒐᕅ⧏⧏ (סערירה SGh-RY-R-YH) — **Horrible thing:** As fearful. [df: שׁערירה] [freq. 3] |kjv: horrible thing| {str: 8186}

~~~~~~~~~~

Ayin

2518) ⊐⊔⊚ (עבד AhBD) ac: **Serve** co: **Servant** ab: **Service:** A work performed or made for another out of obligation, requirement or gratitude. (eng: obey)

V) ⊐⊔⊚ (עבד Ah-BD) — **I. Serve:** To provide a service to another or to work at a profession. [Hebrew and Aramaic] **II. Do:** [Aramaic only] [freq. 318] (vf: Paal, Niphal, Hiphil, Hophal, Pual) |kjv: serve, do, till, servant, work, worshipper, service, dress, labour, ear, make, go, keep, move, wrought| {str: 5647, 5648}

N^m) ⊐⊔⊚ (עבד Ah-BD) — **Servant:** [freq. 808] |kjv: servant, manservant, bondman, bondage, bondservant, sides| {str: 5649, 5650, 5652}

N^f3) †Y⊐⊔⊚ (עבדות AhB-DWT) — **Servitude:** A forced service. [freq. 3] |kjv: bondage| {str: 5659}

a^m) ⊐⊔⊚⋀⋀ (מעבד MAh-BD) — **Service:** [Hebrew and Aramaic] [freq. 2] |kjv: work| {str: 4566, 4567}

b^f1) ⅏⊐⊐⊔⊚ (עבידה Ah-BY-DH) — **Service:** [Aramaic only] [ar: עבידא] [freq. 6] |kjv: work, affair, service| {str: 5673}

c^f1) ⅏⊐Y⊔⊚ (עבודה Ah-BW-DH) — **Service:** [ms: עבדה] [freq. 141] |kjv: service, servile, work, bondage, act, serve, servitude, tillage, effect, labour| {str: 5656}

d^f1) ⅏⊐Y⊔⊚ (עבודה Ah-BW-DH) — **Servant:** [ms: עבדה] [freq. 2] |kjv: servant, household| {str: 5657}

2519) ⊗⊔⊚ (עבט AhBTh) ac: **Borrow** co: **Pledge** ab: **?:** When something is borrowed the borrower gives an item as a pledge as a security for the return of what is borrowed.

V) ⊗⊔⊚ (עבט Ah-BTh) — **Borrow:** [freq. 6] (vf: Paal, Hiphil, Piel) |kjv: lend, fetch, borrow, break| {str: 5670}

c^m) ⊗Y⊔⊚ (עבוט Ah-BWTh) — **Pledge:** What is given as security for a loan. [ms: עבט] [freq. 4] |kjv: pledge| {str: 5667}

lb^m) ⊗⊐⊐⊗⊔⊚ (עבטיט AhB-ThYTh) — **Pledge:** What is given as security for a loan. [freq. 1] |kjv: clay| {str: 5671}

2520) ⋒⊔⊚ (עבר AhBR) ac: **Cross** co: **?** ab: **?:** The crossing over or passing through a land or water to gain access to the side beyond. [from: ⋒⊔ - filling a land] (eng: over; ford - with the exchange of the f and b; ferry)

V) ⋒⊔⊚ (עבר Ah-BR) — **Cross:** To cross over a river or cross through a land. [Hebrew and Aramaic] [freq. 573] (vf: Paal, Niphal, Hiphil, Hitpael, Piel, Participle) |kjv: over, pass, through, go, away| {str: 5674, 5675}

N^m) ⋒⊔⊚ (עבר Ah-BR) — **I. Side:** As being across from the other side. **II. Beyond:** Across the other side. [Hebrew and Aramaic] [freq. 91] |kjv: over, pass, through, go, away| {str: 5676}

399

N^{fl}) 𝔜𝔉◎ (עברה AhB-RH) —
Wrath: As crossing over from peace.
[freq. 37] |kjv: wrath, rage, anger|
{str: 5678, 5679}

a^{m}) 𝔉𝔇◎ᴍ (מעבר MAh-BR) —
Crossing: A place in the river for
crossing. [freq. 11] |kjv: ferry| {str:
4569}

d^{m}) 𝔉𝕐𝔇◎ (עבור Ah-BWR) — **I.
Produce:** As what passes over the
land. [ms: עבר] **II. Purpose:** In the
sense of crossing over to something
[ms: עבר] [freq. 10] |kjv: corn, sake,
that, because, intent, deed, to| {str:
5668, 5669}

2521) ᴜᴜ𝔇◎ (עבש AhBSh) ac: **Rot** co:
? ab: **?:** Something that is withered and
dried up. [from: ᴜᴜ𝔇 - dried up]

V) ᴜᴜ𝔇◎ (עבש Ah-BSh) — **Rot:**
[freq. 1] (vf: Paal) |kjv: rot| {str:
5685}

2522) 𝕥𝔇◎ (עבת AhBT) ac: **Weave** co:
? ab: **?**

V) 𝕥𝔇◎ (עבת Ah-BT) — **Weave:**
[freq. 1] (vf: Piel) |kjv: wrap| {str:
5686}

2523) 𝔩𝕃◎ (עגב AhGB) ac: **Lust** co: ?
ab: **?**

V) 𝔩𝕃◎ (עגב Ah-GB) — **Lust:**
[freq. 7] (vf: Paal, Participle) |kjv:
dote, lover| {str: 5689}

N^{m}) 𝔩𝕃◎ (עגב Ah-GB) — **Lust:**
[freq. 2] |kjv: love, lovely| {str:
5690}

N^{fl}) 𝔜𝔩𝕃◎ (עגבה AhG-BH) —
Lustfulness: [freq. 1] |kjv: love| {str:
5691}

o^{m}) 𝔩𝕃𝕐◎ (עוגב AhW-GB) —
Ugav: A musical instrument.
[Unknown connection to root;] [ms:
עגב] [freq. 4] |kjv: organ, flute, pipe|
{str: 5748}

2524) 𝕁𝕃◎ (עגל AhGL) ac: **Round** co:
Bullock ab: ?: [from: 𝕁𝕃]

N^{m}) 𝕁𝕃◎ (עגל Ah-GL) —
Bullock: From its circling around in
play. [freq. 35] |kjv: calf, bullock|
{str: 5695}

N^{fl}) 𝔜𝕁𝕃◎ (עגלה AhG-LH) — **I.
Heifer: II. Cart:** From its round
wheels. [freq. 39] |kjv: heifer, cow,
calf, cart, wagon, chariot| {str: 5697,
5699}

a^{m}) 𝕁𝕃◎ᴍ (מעגל MAh-GL) —
Trench: The trench made from the
wheels of carts. Also an
entrenchment. [freq. 1] |kjv: path,
trench, goings, ways| {str: 4570}

a^{fl}) 𝔜𝕁𝕃◎ᴍ (מעגלה MAh-G-LH)
— **Trench:** The trench made from
the wheels of carts. Also an
entrenchment. [freq. 16] |kjv: trench,
path| {str: 4570}

b^{m}) 𝕁𝓱𝕃◎ (עגיל Ah-GYL) —
Earring: As round. [freq. 2] |kjv:
earring| {str: 5694}

c^{m}) 𝕁𝕐𝕃◎ (עגול Ah-GWL) —
Round: [ms: עגל] [freq. 6] |kjv:
round| {str: 5696}

2525) ᴍᴍ𝕃◎ (עגם AhGM) ac: **Grieve**
co: ? ab: **?**

V) ᴍᴍ𝕃◎ (עגם Ah-GM) — **Grieve:**
[freq. 1] (vf: Paal) |kjv: grieve| {str:
5701}

2526) (עגן AhGN) ac: **Stay** co: **?** ab: **?**

V) (עגן Ah-GN) — **Stay:** [freq. 1] (vf: Niphal) |kjv: stay| {str: 5702}

~~~~~~~~~~~

2527) (עגר AhGR) ac: **?** co: **?** ab: **?**

d^m) (עגור Ah-GWR) — **Agur:** An unknown bird. [freq. 2] |kjv: swallow| {str: 5693}

~~~~~~~~~~~

2528) (עדן AhDN) ac: **Delight** co: **?** ab: **Pleasure**

V) (עדן Ah-DN) — **Delight:** [freq. 1] (vf: Hitpael) |kjv: delight| {str: 5727}

N^m/f) (עדן Ah-DN) — **Pleasure:** [freq. 4] |kjv: pleasure| {str: 5730}

N^f1) (עדנה AhD-NH) — **Yet:** As a desire. [freq. 2] |kjv: yet| {str: 5728}

a^m) (מעדן MAh-DN) — **Delicacy:** As a pleasurable thing. [freq. 4] |kjv: dainties, delicately, delight| {str: 4574}

a^f1) (מעדנה MAh-D-NH) — **Chain:** [Unknown connection to root;] [freq. 1] |kjv: influence| {str: 4575}

b^m) (עדין Ah-DYN) — **Pleasure:** [freq. 1] |kjv: pleasures| {str: 5719}

e^m) (עידן AhY-DN) — **Time:** [Unknown connection to root; Aramaic only] [freq. 13] |kjv: time| {str: 5732}

~~~~~~~~~~~

2529) (עדף AhDP) ac: **?** co: **Excess** ab: **?**

V) (עדף Ah-DP) — **Excess:** [freq. 9] (vf: Paal, Hiphil, Participle) |kjv: remains, overplus, more, odd number, over| {str: 5736}

~~~~~~~~~~~

2530) (עדר AhDR) ac: **Miss** co: **Rake** ab: **Order:** The process of removing what is unnecessary to bring about order. [from: - order]

V) (עדר Ah-DR) — **Missing:** [Used in conjunction with meaning that nothing is missing] [freq. 11] (vf: Paal, Niphal, Piel) |kjv: fail, lack, dig, keep| {str: 5737}

N^m) (עדר Ah-DR) — **Flock:** In the sense of being ordered. [freq. 38] |kjv: flock, heard, drove| {str: 5739}

a^m) (מעדר MAh-DR) — **Rake:** Used to clear the field of debris to create order. [freq. 1] |kjv: mattock| {str: 4576}

~~~~~~~~~~~

2531) (עדש AhDSh) ac: **?** co: **Lentil** ab: **?**

N^f) (עדש Ah-DSh) — **Lentil:** [freq. 4] |kjv: lentil| {str: 5742}

~~~~~~~~~~~

2532) (עזב AhZB) ac: **Leave** co: **?** ab: **?:** [from: - leaving ones family when purchased as a bride]

V) (עזב Ah-ZB) — **Leave:** To go away from or to neglect. [freq. 215] (vf: Paal, Niphal, Pual) |kjv: forsake, leave, fail, fortify, help, commit, destitute, refuse| {str: 5800}

d^{fl}) ✪🜂Y🜍✪ (עזובה Ah-ZW-BH)
— **Leaving:** [freq. 1] |kjv: forsaking|
{str: 5805}

ej^m) ✪🜍🜒🜍Y🜂✪ (עיזבון AhY-Z-BWN) — **Wares:** In the sense of
items being left for a price. [ms:
עזבון] [freq. 7] |kjv: fair, wares| {str:
5801}

~~~~~~~~~~

2533) ✪🜍🜒✪ (עזן AhZN) ac: **?** co: **?** ab:
?: [from: ⊗✪ - bird of prey]

f^{fl}) ✪🜒🜒🜍✪ (עזניה AhZ-N-YH)
— **Azniyah:** An unknown bird of
prey. [freq. 2] |kjv: osprey| {str:
5822}

~~~~~~~~~~

2534) ◆🜍🜍✪ (עזק AhZQ) ac: **Dig** co: **?**
ab: **?**

V) ◆🜍🜍✪ (עזק Ah-ZQ) — **Dig:**
[freq. 1] (vf: Piel) |kjv: fence| {str:
5823}

e^{fl}) ✪🜒◆🜍🜍Y✪ (עיזקה AhYZ-QH)
— **Signet:** A signet ring used for
making seals. As being engraved. [ar:
עזקא] [freq. 2] |kjv: signet| {str:
5824}

~~~~~~~~~~

2535) 🜩🜍✪ (עזר AhZR) ac: **Help** co: **?**
ab: **?**

V) 🜩🜍✪ (עזר Ah-ZR) — **Help:**
[freq. 82] (vf: Paal, Niphal, Hiphil)
|kjv: help, helper, succour| {str:
5826}

N^m) 🜩🜍✪ (עזר Ah-ZR) — **Help:**
[freq. 21] |kjv: help| {str: 5828}

N^{fl}) ✪🜩🜍✪ (עזרה AhZ-RH) —
Help: Also one who helps. [freq. 1]
|kjv: help, helper| {str: 5833}

N^{f2}) †🜩🜍✪ (עזרת AhZ-RT) —
Help: [freq. 26] |kjv: help| {str:
5833}

~~~~~~~~~~

2536) ✪⊗✪ (עטן AhThN) ac: **?** co:
Bucket ab: **?**

N^m) ✪⊗✪ (עטן Ah-ThN) —
Bucket: [freq. 1] |kjv: breast| {str:
5845}

~~~~~~~~~~

2537) ◯⊗✪ (עטף AhThP) ac: **Cover**
co: **?** ab: **?:** [from: ⊗✪ - as being
wrapped]

V) ◯⊗✪ (עטף Ah-ThP) — I.
Cover: II. **Faint:** From weakness.
[Unknown connection to root;] [freq.
16] (vf: Paal, Niphal, Hiphil, Hitpael)
|kjv: overwhelmed, faint, swoon,
cover, fail, feeble, hide| {str: 5848}

a^{fl}) ✪◯⊗✪ᴧᴧ (מעטפה MAh-Th-
PH) — **Overtunic:** The outer
garment that covers the body. [freq.
1] |kjv: mantle| {str: 4595}

~~~~~~~~~~

2538) 🜩⊗✪ (עטר AhThR) ac: **Encircle**
co: **Wreath** ab: **?:** [from: ⊗✪ - as being
wrapped]

V) 🜩⊗✪ (עטר Ah-ThR) —
Encircle: [freq. 7] (vf: Paal, Hiphil,
Piel, Participle) |kjv: crown,
compass, round| {str: 5849}

N^{fl}) ✪🜩⊗✪ (עטרה AhTh-RH) —
Wreath: As encircling the head.
Used as a sign of authority like a
crown. [freq. 23] |kjv: crown| {str:
5850}

~~~~~~~~~~

2539) �ᴧ⊗✪ (עטש AhThSh) ac: **?** co:
Sneeze ab: **?:** [from: ᴧᴧ⊗ - spreading]

b^{fl}) ✡ⱶⱶⱶⱶⱶ⊗◎ (עטישה Ah-ThY-ShH) — **Sneeze:** [freq. 1] |kjv: neesing| {str: 5846}

~~~~~~~~~~

2540) ◀ⱶⱶ◎ (עכס AhKS) ac: **Rattle** co: **Anklet** ab: **?:** An anklet with bells that rattle when shaken. [from: ⱶⱶ◎ - from rattles on the ankle]

V) ◀ⱶⱶ◎ (עכס Ah-KS) — **Rattle:** [freq. 1] (vf: Piel) |kjv: tinkle| {str: 5913}

N^m) ◀ⱶⱶ◎ (עכס Ah-KS) — **Anklet:** [freq. 2] |kjv: stocks, ornament| {str: 5914}

~~~~~~~~~~

2541) ᕼⱶⱶ◎ (עכר AhKR) ac: **Stir** co: **?** ab: **?**

V) ᕼⱶⱶ◎ (עכר Ah-KR) — **Stir:** To agitate or trouble as when stirring water. [freq. 14] (vf: Paal, Niphal, Participle) |kjv: trouble, stir, troubler| {str: 5916}

~~~~~~~~~~

2542) ⱶⱱ◎ (עלז AhLZ) ac: **Rejoice** co: **?** ab: **?:** [from: ⱱ◎ - raising the arms in joy]

V) ⱶⱱ◎ (עלז Ah-LZ) — **Rejoice:** To rejoice in triumph. [freq. 16] (vf: Paal) |kjv: rejoice, triumph, joyful| {str: 5937}

N^m) ⱶⱱ◎ (עלז Ah-LZ) — **Rejoice:** [freq. 1] |kjv: rejoice| {str: 5938}

b^m) ⱶⱶⱱ◎ (עליז Ah-LYZ) — **Rejoice:** [freq. 7] |kjv: rejoice, joyous| {str: 5947}

~~~~~~~~~~

2543) ⊗ⱱ◎ (עלט AhLTh) ac: **?** co: **Twilight** ab: **?**

N^{fl}) ✡⊗ⱱ◎ (עלטה AhL-ThH) — **Twilight:** [freq. 4] |kjv: twilight, dark| {str: 5939}

~~~~~~~~~~

2544) ᨓⱱ◎ (עלם AhLM) ac: **Hide** co: **?** ab: **Ancient:** Beyond the field of vision of time or space.

V) ᨓⱱ◎ (עלם Ah-LM) — **Hide:** To be hidden or obscured from sight, covered or unknown. [freq. 28] (vf: Paal, Niphal, Hiphil, Hitpael, Participle) |kjv: hide, blind, dissembler, secret| {str: 5956}

N^m) ᨓⱱ◎ (עלם Ah-LM) — **Ancient:** A distant time in the past or future, as a time hidden from the present. [Aramaic only] [freq. 20] |kjv: ever, everlasting, old, never| {str: 5957}

g^m) ᨓⱱⱵ◎ (עולם AhW-LM) — **Ancient:** A distant time in the past or future, as a time hidden from the present. [ms: עלם] [freq. 439] |kjv: ever, everlasting, old, perpetual, evermore, never, time, ancient, world, always, alway, long, more| {str: 5769}

i^{fl}) ✡ᨓⱱ◎† (תעלמה TAh-L-MH) — **Hidden:** [freq. 3] |kjv: secret, hid| {str: 8587}

ec^m) ᨓⱵⱶ◎ (עילום AhY-LWM) — **Ancient:** A distant time in the past or future, as a time hidden from the present. [freq. 1] |kjv: ever| {str: 5865}

~~~~~~~~~~

2545) ◀ⱱ◎ (עלס AhLS) ac: **Rejoice** co: **?** ab: **?:** [from: ⱱ◎ - raising the arms in joy]

V) 𐤀∪⊘ (עלס Ah-LS) — **Rejoice:** [freq. 3] (vf: Paal, Niphal, Hitpael) |kjv: rejoice, peacock, solace| {str: 5965}

2546) ⊘∪⊘ (עלע AhLAh) ac: **Suck** co: ? ab: ?: [from: ⊘∪ - as the work of the throat]

V) ⊘∪⊘ (עלע Ah-LAh) — **Suck:** [freq. 1] (vf: Piel) |kjv: suck| {str: 5966}

2547) ⊃∪⊘ (עלף AhLP) ac: **Faint** co: ? ab: ?

V) ⊃∪⊘ (עלף Ah-LP) — **I. Faint: II. Cover:** [Unknown connection to root;] [freq. 5] (vf: Hitpael, Pual, Participle) |kjv: faint, overlay, wrap| {str: 5968}

o^(fl)) 𐤀⊃∪Y⊘ (עלפה AhWL-PH) — **Wilt:** In the sense of fainting. [ms: עלפה] [freq. 1] |kjv: fainted| {str: 5969}

2548) ᴖ∪⊘ (עלץ AhLTs) ac: **Triumph** co: ? ab: ?: [from: ∪⊘ - raising the arms in joy]

V) ᴖ∪⊘ (עלץ Ah-LTs) — **Triumph:** [freq. 8] (vf: Paal) |kjv: rejoice, joyful, triumph| {str: 5970}

b^(f3)) ✝Yᴖᴗ∪⊘ (עליצות Ah-LY-TsWT) — **Triumph:** [freq. 1] |kjv: rejoice| {str: 5951}

2549) ⊕∪⊘ (עלק AhLQ) ac: ? co: ? ab: ?

d^(fl)) 𐤀⊕Y∪⊘ (עלוקה Ah-LW-QH) — **Leech:** [freq. 1] |kjv: horseleach| {str: 5936}

2550) ⊓ᴍ⊘ (עמד AhMD) ac: **Stand** co: **Pillar** ab: ?: [from: ᴍ⊘ - as standing with another]

V) ⊓ᴍ⊘ (עמד Ah-MD) — **Stand:** To stand, raise or set in a place. [freq. 522] (vf: Paal, Hiphil, Hophal) |kjv: stand, raise, set, stay, still, appoint, stand, endure, remain, present, continue, withstand| {str: 5975, 5976}

N^(fl)) 𐤀⊓ᴍ⊘ (עמדה AhM-DH) — **Standing:** [freq. 1] |kjv: standing| {str: 5979}

a^(m)) ⊓ᴍ⊘ᴍ (מעמד MAh-MD) — **Station:** A place of standing. [freq. 6] |kjv: attendance, office, place, state| {str: 4612, 4613}

d^(m)) ⊓Yᴍ⊘ (עמוד Ah-MWD) — **Pillar:** In the sense of standing. [ms: עמד] [freq. 110] |kjv: pillar| {str: 5982}

e^(m)) ⊓ᴍᴗ⊘ (עימד AhY-MD) — **With:** In the sense of standing with another. [ms: עמד] [freq. 12] |kjv: with, by, upon, against| {str: 5978}

g^(m)) ⊓ᴍY⊘ (עומד AhW-MD) — **Place:** A place of standing. [ms: עמד] [freq. 10] |kjv: place, upright, stood| {str: 5977}

2551) ∪ᴍ⊘ (עמל AhML) ac: **Labor** co: **Laborer** ab: ?: [from: ∪⊘ - work]

V) ∪ᴍ⊘ (עמל Ah-ML) — **Labor:** [freq. 11] (vf: Paal) |kjv: labour| {str: 5998}

N^(m/f)) ᒐᙢᗩ (עמל Ah-ML) — **I. Labor:** A labor that causes grief, pain or weariness. **II. Laborer:** [freq. 64] |kjv: labour, mischief, misery, travail, trouble, sorrow, grievance, grievousness, iniquity, miserable, pain, painful, perverseness, toil, wearisome, wickedness| {str: 5999, 6001}

2552) ᖟᙢᗩ (עמס AhMS) ac: **Load** co: **Burden** ab: ?: The lifting or carrying of a burden or load.

V) ᖟᙢᗩ (עמס Ah-MS) — **Load:** [df: שמע] [freq. 9] (vf: Paal, Hiphil) |kjv: load, put, borne, burden| {str: 6006}

a^(fl)) ᖟᙢᗩᙢ (מעמסה MAh-M-SH) — **Burdensome:** [freq. 1] |kjv: burdensome| {str: 4614}

2553) ᘙᙢᗩ (עמק AhMQ) ac: **Deep** co: **Valley** ab: ?

V) ᘙᙢᗩ (עמק Ah-MQ) — **Deep:** To be deep in depth or thought. [freq. 9] (vf: Paal, Hiphil) |kjv: deep, deeply, depth, profound| {str: 6009}

N^(m)) ᘙᙢᗩ (עמק Ah-MQ) — **I. Valley:** As deep. **II. Obscure:** In the sense of being deep. [freq. 73] |kjv: valley, vale, dale, strange, depth, deeper| {str: 6010, 6012}

a^(m)) ᘙᙢᗩᙢ (מעמק MAh-MQ) — **Depth:** [freq. 5] |kjv: depth, deep| {str: 4615}

b^(m)) ᘙᑐᙢᗩ (עמיק Ah-MYQ) — **Deep:** [freq. 1] |kjv: deep| {str: 5994}

c^(m)) ᘙᖴᙢᗩ (עמוק Ah-MWQ) — **Depth:** [ms: עמק] [freq. 16] |kjv: deeper, deep| {str: 6013}

g^(m)) ᘙᙢᖴᗩ (עומק AhW-MQ) — **Depth:** [ms: עמק] [freq. 1] |kjv: depth| {str: 6011}

2554) ᖇᙢᗩ (עמר AhMR) ac: **Bind** co: **Sheaf** ab: ?: [from: ᙢᗩ]

V) ᖇᙢᗩ (עמר Ah-MR) — **Bind:** [freq. 3] (vf: Hitpael, Piel) |kjv: merchandise, sheaf| {str: 6014}

N^(m)) ᖇᙢᗩ (עמר Ah-MR) — **Wool:** As used for binding. [Aramaic only] [freq. 1] |kjv: wool| {str: 6015}

b^(m)) ᖇᑐᙢᗩ (עמיר Ah-MYR) — **Sheaf:** As bound. [freq. 4] |kjv: sheaf, handful| {str: 5995}

g^(m)) ᖇᙢᖴᗩ (עומר AhW-MR) — **I. Sheaf:** As bound. [ms: עמר] **II. Omer:** A standard of measure. [ms: עמר] [freq. 14] |kjv: omer, sheaf| {str: 6016}

2555) ᗏᘁᗩ (ענב AhNB) ac: ? co: **Grape** ab: ?

N^(m)) ᗏᘁᗩ (ענב Ah-NB) — **Grape:** [freq. 19] |kjv: grape, wine| {str: 6025}

2556) ᒪᘁᗩ (ענג AhNG) ac: **Soft** co: ? ab: ?

V) ᒪᘁᗩ (ענג Ah-NG) — **Soft:** To be delicate and pleasurable. [freq. 10] (vf: Hitpael, Pual) |kjv: delight, delicate, delicateness, sport| {str: 6026}

c^(m)) ᒪᖴᘁᗩ (ענוג Ah-NWG) — **Soft:** [ms: ענג] [freq. 3] |kjv: delicate| {str: 6028}

g^(m)) ᒪᖴᘁᗩ (עונג AhW-NG) — **Delight:** In the sense of being soft.

[ms: ענג] [freq. 2] |kjv: pleasant, delight| {str: 6027}

id^{m}) (תענוג TAh-NWG) — **Luxury:** In the sense of being soft. [ms: תענג] [freq. 5] |kjv: delight, delicate, pleasant| {str: 8588}

~~~~~~~~~~~

2557) (ענד AhND) ac: **Tie** co: **?** ab: **?**

V) (ענד Ah-ND) — **Tie:** [freq. 2] (vf: Paal) |kjv: tie, bind| {str: 6029}

~~~~~~~~~~~

2558) (ענף AhNP) ac: **?** co: **Bough** ab: **?**

N^{m}) (ענף Ah-NP) — **Bough:** [Hebrew and Aramaic] [freq. 12] |kjv: branch, bough| {str: 6056, 6057, 6058}

~~~~~~~~~~~

2559) (ענק AhNQ) ac: **Encompass** co: **Collar** ab: **?**

V) (ענק Ah-NQ) — **Encompass:** [freq. 3] (vf: Paal, Hiphil) |kjv: furnish, compass| {str: 6059}

N^{m}) (ענק Ah-NQ) — **Collar:** [freq. 3] |kjv: chain| {str: 6060}

~~~~~~~~~~~

2560) (ענש AhNSh) ac: **Fine** co: **Fine** ab: **?:** A fine as a penalty punishment.

V) (ענש Ah-NSh) — **Fine:** To be fined a price as punishment. [freq. 9] (vf: Paal, Niphal) |kjv: punish, condemn, amerce| {str: 6064}

N^{m}) (ענש Ah-NSh) — **Fine:** [Hebrew and Aramaic] [freq. 3] |kjv: confiscation, tribute, punishment| {str: 6065, 6066}

~~~~~~~~~~~

2561) (עסב AhSB) ac: **?** co: **Herb** ab: **?:** The grasses and herbs of the field.

N^{f}) (עסב Ah-SB) — **Herb:** [df: עשב] [freq. 45] |kjv: herb, grass| {str: 6211, 6212}

~~~~~~~~~~~

2562) (עסק AhSQ) ac: **Quarrel** co: **?** ab: **?**

V) (עסק Ah-SQ) — **Quarrel:** [df: עשק] [freq. 1] (vf: Hitpael) |kjv: strive| {str: 6229}

~~~~~~~~~~~

2563) (עסר AhSR) ac: **?** co: **Ten** ab: **?**

V) (עסר Ah-SR) — **Tithe:** To give a tenth. [df: עשר] [freq. 9] (vf: Paal, Hiphil, Piel) |kjv: tithe, tenth| {str: 6237}

N$^{m/f}$) (עסר Ah-SR) — **Ten:** [Hebrew and Aramaic; Also meaning sixty when written in the plural form - or in Aramaic] [df: עשר] [freq. 651] |kjv: twenty, twentieth| {str: 6235, 6236, 6240, 6242, 6243}

N^{f1}) (עסרה AhS-RH) — **Ten:** [freq. 181] |kjv: ten| {str: 6235, 6236}

a^{m}) (מעסר MAh-SR) — **Tenth:** [df: מעשר] [freq. 32] |kjv: tithe, tenth, tithing| {str: 4643}

c^{m}) (עסור Ah-SWR) — **Ten:** [df: עשר עשור] [freq. 16] |kjv: tenth, ten| {str: 6218}

j^{m}) (עסרון AhS-RWN) — **Tenth:** [df: עשרן עשרון] [freq. 28] |kjv: tenth| {str: 6241}
~~~~~~~~~~~

bfᵐ) ﺟﻼﺤﻷﻙ◎ (עסירי Ah-SY-RY)
— **Tenth:** [df: עֲשִׂירִי] [freq. 29] |kjv: tenth| {str: 6224}

~~~~~~~~~

2564) ᐱᦉ◎ (עפל AhPL) ac: **Lift** co: **Tower** ab: ?

V) ᐱᦉ◎ (עפל Ah-PL) — **Lift:** [freq. 2] (vf: Hiphil, Pual) |kjv: lift, presume| {str: 6075}

gᵐ) ᐱᦉᐁY◎ (עופל AhW-PL) — **Tower:** [ms: עֹפֶל] [freq. 9] |kjv: fort, stronghold, tower| {str: 6076}

~~~~~~~~~

2565) ᑫᦉ◎ (עפר AhPR) ac: **Cast** co: **Powder** ab: ?

V) ᑫᦉ◎ (עפר Ah-PR) — **Cast:** To throw a dust or powder. [freq. 1] (vf: Piel) |kjv: cast| {str: 6080}

Nᵐ) ᑫᦉ◎ (עפר Ah-PR) — **Powder:** An abundant amount of powdery substance as dust or ash. [freq. 110] |kjv: dust, earth, powder, rubbish, ash, morter, ground| {str: 6083}

gᵐ) ᑫᐁY◎ (עופר AhW-PR) — **Young:** As kicking up dust in play. [ms: עֹפֶר] [freq. 5] |kjv: young| {str: 6082}

gᶠ²) ᵗᑫᐁY◎ (עופרת AhW-P-RT) — **Lead:** [Unknown connection to root;] [ms: עֹפֶרֶת] [freq. 9] |kjv: lead| {str: 5777}

~~~~~~~~~

2566) ᒻᦉᐁ◎ (עצב AhTsB) ac: **Pain** co: ? ab: ?

V) ᒻᦉᐁ◎ (עצב Ah-TsB) — **Pain:** To be in pain from grief or heavy toil. [Hebrew and Aramaic] [freq. 18] (vf: Paal, Niphal, Hiphil, Hitpael, Piel, Participle) |kjv: grieve, displease, hurt, made, sorry, vex, worship, wrest, lament| {str: 6087, 6088}

Nᵐ) ᒻᦉᐁ◎ (עצב Ah-TsB) — **I. Pain:** Of grief or heavy toil. **II. Idol:** [Unknown connection to root;] [freq. 25] |kjv: sorrow, labour, grievous| {str: 6089, 6091, 6092}

Nᶠ²) ᵗᒻᦉᐁ◎ (עצבת AhTs-BT) — **Suffering:** From sorrow or wound. [freq. 5] |kjv: sorrow, wound| {str: 6094}

aᶠˡ) 𝄪ᒻᦉᐁ◎ᴍᴍ (מעצבה MAh-Ts-BH) — **Sorrow:** [freq. 1] |kjv: sorrow| {str: 4620}

gᵐ) ᒻᦉᐁY◎ (עוצב AhW-TsB) — **Sorrow:** [ms: עֹצֶב] [freq. 4] |kjv: sorrow, wicked, idol| {str: 6090}

jᵐ) ᐣYᒻᦉᐁ◎ (עצבון AhTs-BWN) — **Pain:** [freq. 3] |kjv: toil, sorrow| {str: 6093}

~~~~~~~~~

2567) ᴛᑯᦉᐁ◎ (עצד AhTsD) ac: **Cut** co: **Axe** ab: ?: [from: ᑯᦉ◎ - for cutting wood]

aᵐ) ᴛᑯᦉᐁ◎ᴍᴍ (מעצד MAh-TsD) — **Axe:** [freq. 2] |kjv: tongs, axe| {str: 4621}

~~~~~~~~~

2568) ᐱᦉᐁ◎ (עצל AhTsL) ac: **Lazy** co: ? ab: ?

V) ᐱᦉᐁ◎ (עצל Ah-TsL) — **Lazy:** [freq. 1] (vf: Niphal) |kjv: slothful| {str: 6101}

Nᵐ) ᐱᦉᐁ◎ (עצל Ah-TsL) — **Sluggard:** [freq. 14] |kjv: sluggard| {str: 6102}

Nᶠˡ) 𝄪ᐱᦉᐁ◎ (עצלה AhTs-LH) — **Laziness:** [freq. 2] |kjv: slothfulness| {str: 6103}

~~~~~~~~~

N^f3) †Υ✓ه٨⊚ (עצלות AhTs-LWT)
— **Laziness:** [freq. 1] |kjv: idleness|
{str: 6104}

2569) ϻه٨⊚ (עצם AhTsM) ac:
Abundant co: **Bone** ab: **Abundance:**
The numerous bones of the body are the
strength to the body. [from: ه٨⊚ - as the
bones are the tree of the body]

V) ϻه٨⊚ (עצם Ah-TsM) — **I.**
Abundant: To be strong in might or
numbers. From the abundant number
of bones in the body. **II. Shut:**
[Unknown connection to root;] [freq.
20] (vf: Paal, Hiphil, Piel) |kjv:
increase, mighty, strong, more,
broken, close, great, shut| {str: 6105}

N^m) ϻه٨⊚ (עצם Ah-TsM) —
Bone: [freq. 126] |kjv: bone,
selfsame, same, body, life, strength|
{str: 6106}

N^f1) ⵞϻه٨⊚ (עצמה AhTs-MH)
— **Abundance:** [freq. 3] |kjv:
strength, abundance| {str: 6109}

d^m) ϻΥه٨⊚ (עצום Ah-TsWM) —
Abundant: [ms: עצם] [freq. 31]
|kjv: strong, mighty, mightier, feeble,
great, much| {str: 6099}

d^f1) ⵞϻΥه٨⊚ (עצומה Ah-TsW-
MH) — **Abundance:** [ms: עצמה]
[freq. 1] |kjv: strong| {str: 6110}

g^m) ϻه٨Υ⊚ (עוצם AhW-TsM) —
Strength: From the strength of the
bones. [ms: עצם] [freq. 3] |kjv:
might, strong, substance| {str: 6108}

id^f1) ⵞϻΥه٨⊚† (תעצומה TAh-
TsW-MH) — **Strength:** [ms: תעצמה]
[freq. 1] |kjv: power| {str: 8592}

2570) Ꞷه٨⊚ (עצר AhTsR) ac: **Stop** co:
? ab: ?

V) Ꞷه٨⊚ (עצר Ah-TsR) — **Stop:**
To stop from occurring in the sense
of halting, shutting or restraining.
[freq. 46] (vf: Paal, Niphal) |kjv:
shut, stay, retain, detain, able,
withhold, keep, prevail, recover,
refrain, reign| {str: 6113}

N^m) Ꞷه٨⊚ (עצר Ah-TsR) —
Restraint: [freq. 1] |kjv: magistrate|
{str: 6114}

N^f1) ⵞꞶه٨⊚ (עצרה AhTs-RH) —
Assembly: A special occasion as a
temporary ceasing of normal activity.
[freq. 11] |kjv: assembly, meeting|
{str: 6116}

a^m) Ꞷه٨⊚ϻ (מעצר MAh-TsR) —
Restraint: [freq. 1] |kjv: rule| {str:
4623}

g^m) Ꞷه٨Υ⊚ (עוצר AhW-TsR) — **I.**
Stopping: [ms: עצר] **II. Prison:** In
the sense of being shut in. [freq. 3]
|kjv: oppression, barren, prison| {str:
6115}

ac^m) ꞶΥه٨⊚ϻ (מעצור MAh-
TsWR) — **Restraint:** [freq. 1] |kjv:
restraint| {str: 4622}

2571) ꞵ•⊚ (עקב AhQB) ac: **Restrain**
co: **Heel** ab: ?: The restraining of the heel
when taking a step forward. [from: Ⴍ⊚]

V) ꞵ•⊚ (עקב Ah-QB) —
Restrain: To hold back. [freq. 5] (vf:
Paal, Piel) |kjv: supplant, heel, stay|
{str: 6117}

N^m) ꞵ•⊚ (עקב Ah-QB) — **I.**
Heel: What is restrained when taking
a step forward. **II. Because:** In the
sense of being on the heel of
something else. [freq. 29] |kjv: heel,
footstep, horsehoof, at last, step,
liers, because, reward, end, by, for, if|
{str: 6118, 6119, 6120}

N^fl) 🏲ⴱ•⊙ (עקבה AhQ-BH) — **Subtlety:** As appearing to be hidden in the sense of restraint. [freq. 1] |kjv: subtilty| {str: 6122}

c^m) ⴱⵢ•⊙ (עקוב Ah-QWB) — **Crooked:** From the angle of the ankle. [ms: עקב] [freq. 3] |kjv: crooked, deceitful, polluted| {str: 6121}

~~~~~~~~~

2572) ⴒ•⊙ (עקד AhQD) ac: **Bind** co: **Cord** ab: ?

V) ⴒ•⊙ (עקד Ah-QD) — **Bind:** To bind with a cord. [freq. 1] (vf: Paal) |kjv: bind| {str: 6123}

c^m) ⴒⵢ•⊙ (עקוד Ah-QWD) — **Striped:** As appearing to be whipped with a cord. [ms: עקד] [freq. 7] |kjv: ringstraked| {str: 6124}

~~~~~~~~~

2573) ⴱ🕱⊙ (ערב AhRB) ac: **Mix** co: **Market** ab: ?: A mixture of wares as found in the market place.

V) ⴱ🕱⊙ (ערב Ah-RB) — **I. Barter:** To exchange an item or service for another. [Hebrew and Aramaic] **II. Mix:** As mixing one thing with another. [Hebrew and Aramaic] **III. Sweet:** [Unknown connection to root;] [freq. 34] (vf: Paal, Hitpael, Participle) |kjv: surety, meddle, mingle, pledge, become, engage, intermeddle, mortgage, occupier, occupy, undertake, sweet, pleasure, pleasing, pleasant, mingle| {str: 6148, 6149, 6151}

N^m) ⴱ🕱⊙ (ערב Ah-RB) — **I. Woof:** For the mixing of cords when weaving. **II. Mixed: III. Sweet:** [Unknown connection to root;] [freq.

13] |kjv: woof, mixed, sweet| {str: 6154, 6156}

a^m) ⴱ🕱⊙�ⵟ (מערב MAh-RB) — **I. Merchandise:** What is used in bartering. **II. Market:** A mixture of wares for sale or trade. [freq. 9] |kjv: merchandise, market| {str: 4627}

c^m) ⴱⵢ🕱⊙ (ערוב Ah-RWB) — **Swarm:** As a mixture of insects. [ms: ערב] [freq. 9] |kjv: swarm, flies| {str: 6157}

d^fl) 🏲ⴱⵢ🕱⊙ (ערובה Ah-RW-BH) — **Barter:** As an exchange for something else. [ms: ערבה] [freq. 2] |kjv: pledge, surety| {str: 6161}

j^m) ⵡⵢⴱ🕱⊙ (ערבון AhR-BWN) — **Token:** Something given as a promise as an exchange. [freq. 3] |kjv: pledge| {str: 6162}

id^fl) 🏲ⴱⵢ🕱⊙ⵜ (תערובה TAh-RW-BH) — **Barter:** What is used in bartering. [freq. 2] |kjv: hostage| {str: 8594}

~~~~~~~~~

2574) 𝗟🕱⊙ (ערג AhRG) ac: **Pant** co: **Bed** ab: ?: A hard breathing out of thirst, work or a desire. [from: 𝗟🕱 - shaking]

V) 𝗟🕱⊙ (ערג Ah-RG) — **Pant:** [freq. 3] (vf: Paal) |kjv: pant, cry| {str: 6165}

d^fl) 🏲ⴑⵢ🕱⊙ (ערוגה Ah-RW-GH) — **Bed:** A place to rest when tired. [freq. 4] |kjv: bed, furrow| {str: 6170}

~~~~~~~~~

2575) ⴒ🕱⊙ (ערד AhRD) ac: ? co: **Wild-donkey** ab: ?: [from: ⴒ🕱 - as a wander]

N^m) ⴒ🕱⊙ (ערד Ah-RD) — **Wild-donkey:** [Aramaic only] [freq. 1] |kjv: wild ass| {str: 6167}

c^m) ⊘ᕀ᠗ᕐᵒ (עֲרוֹד Ah-RWD) —
Wild-donkey: [freq. 1] |kjv: wild
ass| {str: 6171}

~~~~~~~~~

2576) ⋓᠗ᵒ (עָרַךְ AhRK) ac: **Arrange**
co: **Plan** ab: ?: A plan to arrange things in
order. [from: ᠗ᴛ - order]

V) ⋓᠗ᵒ (עָרַךְ Ah-RK) —
Arrange: To set something in order.
[freq. 75] (vf: Paal, Hiphil) |kjv:
array, order, prepare, expert, value,
compare, direct, equal, estimate,
furnish, ordain| {str: 6186}

N^m) ⋓᠗ᵒ (עָרַךְ Ah-RK) — **I.**
Arrangement: II. Estimate: Of
what is arranged. [freq. 33] |kjv:
estimation, set, equal, order, price,
proportion, suit, taxation, value| {str:
6187}

a^m) ⋓᠗ᵒᴧᴧ (מַעֲרָךְ MAh-RK) —
Preparation: As an arrangement.
[freq. 1] |kjv: preparation| {str: 4633}

a^{f1}) ⴄᎁ⋓᠗ᵒᴧᴧ (מַעֲרָכָה MAh-R-
KH) — **Arrangement:** Set in a row
or in order. [freq. 20] |kjv: army,
fight, order, place, rank, row| {str:
4634}

a^{f2}) ⴕ⋓᠗ᵒᴧᴧ (מַעֲרֶכֶת MAh-R-KT)
— **Row:** As an arrangement. [freq. 9]
|kjv: row, showbread| {str: 4635}

k^{f1}) ⴄᎁ⋓᠗ᵒᴧᴧ (מַעֲרָכָה MAh-R-
KH) — **Arrangement:** Set in a row
or in order. [freq. 1] |kjv: army| {str:
4630}

~~~~~~~~~

2577) Ɉ᠗ᵒ (עָרֵל AhRL) ac: ? co:
Foreskin ab: ?: The part of the male
organ that is removed in circumcision and
considered forbidden.

V) Ɉ᠗ᵒ (עָרֵל Ah-RL) —
Uncircumcised: To be
uncircumcised. [freq. 2] (vf: Paal,
Niphal) |kjv: uncircumcised| {str:
6188}

N^m) Ɉ᠗ᵒ (עָרֵל Ah-RL) —
Uncircumcised: [freq. 35] |kjv:
uncircumcised| {str: 6189}

N^{f1}) ⴄᎁⅉ᠗ᵒ (עָרְלָה AhR-LH) —
Foreskin: [freq. 16] |kjv: foreskin|
{str: 6190}

~~~~~~~~~

2578) ᴧᴧ᠗ᵒ (עָרַם AhRM) ac: **Pile** co:
? ab: ?

V) ᴧᴧ᠗ᵒ (עָרַם Ah-RM) — **Pile:**
[freq. 1] (vf: Niphal) |kjv: gather|
{str: 6192}

~~~~~~~~~

2579) ⴄ᠗ᵒ (עָרַס AhRS) ac: ? co: **Bed**
ab: ?

N^f) ⴄ᠗ᵒ (עָרַס Ah-RS) — **Bed:**
[ms: עֶרֶשׂ] [freq. 10] |kjv: bed,
couch, bedstead| {str: 6210}

b^{f1}) ⴄᎁⴄ᠗ᵒ (עֲרִיסָה Ah-RY-SH)
— **Dough:** [Unknown connection to
root;] [freq. 4] |kjv: dough| {str:
6182}

~~~~~~~~~

2580) ⌀᠗ᵒ (עָרַף AhRP) ac: **Behead**
co: **Neck** ab: ?: [from: ᠗ᵒ - as the neck
is exposed skin] [eng: giraffe; scruff - of
the neck and the additional s]

V) ⌀᠗ᵒ (עָרַף Ah-RP) —
Behead: To sever the neck from the
body or to break the neck. [freq. 6]
(vf: Paal) |kjv: neck, strike, behead,
cut| {str: 6202}

N^m) ⌀᠗ᵒ (עֹרֶף Ah-RP) — **Neck:**
[freq. 33] |kjv: neck, back| {str:
6203}

~~~~~~~~~

2581) (ערץ AhRTs) ac: **Fear** co: ? ab: **Terror**

V) (ערץ Ah-RTs) — **Fear:** [freq. 15] (vf: Paal, Niphal, Hiphil) |kjv: afraid, fear, dread, terribly, break, affright, oppress, prevail, terrified| {str: 6206}

a^{f1}) (מערצה MAh-R-TsH) — **Terror:** [freq. 1] |kjv: terror| {str: 4637}

b^{m}) (עריץ Ah-RYTs) — **Terrible:** [freq. 20] |kjv: terrible, oppressor, mighty, power, strong, violent| {str: 6184}

d^{m}) (ערוץ Ah-RWTs) — **Chasm:** A fearful place. [freq. 1] |kjv: cliff| {str: 6178}

~~~~~~~~~~~

2582) (ערק AhRQ) ac: **Gnaw** co: ? ab: ?

V) (ערק Ah-RQ) — **Gnaw:** [freq. 2] (vf: Paal) |kjv: gnaw, sinew| {str: 6207}

~~~~~~~~~~~

2583) (עשן AhShN) ac: ? co: **Smoke** ab: ?

V) (עשן Ah-ShN) — **Smoke:** [freq. 6] (vf: Paal) |kjv: smoke, angry| {str: 6225}

N^{m}) (עשן Ah-ShN) — **Smoke:** [freq. 27] |kjv: smoke, smoking| {str: 6226, 6227}

~~~~~~~~~~~

2584) (עשק AhShQ) ac: **Press** co: ? ab: **Oppression:** [from:]

V) (עשק Ah-ShQ) — **Oppress:** [freq. 37] (vf: Paal, Pual) |kjv: oppress, oppressor, defraud, wrong, eceive, deceit, get, oppression, drink, violence| {str: 6231}

N^{f1}) (עשקה AhSh-QH) — **Oppressed:** [freq. 1] |kjv: oppressed| {str: 6234}

a^{f1}) (מעשקה MAh-Sh-QH) — **Oppression:** [freq. 2] |kjv: oppressor, oppression| {str: 4642}

c^{m}) (עשוק Ah-ShWQ) — **Oppressor:** [freq. 1] |kjv: oppressor| {str: 6216}

d^{m}) (עשוק Ah-ShWQ) — **Oppression:** [ms: עשק] [freq. 3] |kjv: oppression, oppressed| {str: 6217}

g^{m}) (עושק AhW-ShQ) — **Oppression:** [ms: עשק] [freq. 15] |kjv: oppression, cruelly, extortion, thing| {str: 6233}

~~~~~~~~~~~

2585) (עשר AhShR) ac: **Rich** co: **Riches** ab: **?:** [from: - as one who presses]

V) (עשר Ah-ShR) — **Rich:** To be wealthy. [freq. 17] (vf: Paal, Hiphil, Hitpael) |kjv: rich, enrich| {str: 6238}

N^{m}) (עשר Ah-ShR) — **Riches:** The possessions that make one wealthy. [freq. 37] |kjv: riches, far| {str: 6239}

b^{m}) (עשיר Ah-ShYR) — **Rich:** One who is wealthy. [freq. 23] |kjv: rich| {str: 6223}

~~~~~~~~~~~

2586) (עשת AhShT) ac: **Shine** co: ? ab: **?:** The polishing of stone, metal or ivory by rubbing to make shine. [from: - rubbing]
~~~~~~~~~~~

V) ╪ևև☉ (עשת Ah-ShT) — **I. Shine:** To shine bright as being polished. [Aramaic only] **II. Think:** To shine with an idea. [freq. 3] (vf: Paal, Hitpael) |kjv: shine, think| {str: 6245, 6246}

N^m) ╪ևև☉ (עשת Ah-ShT) — **Bright:** [freq. 1] |kjv: bright| {str: 6247}

N^f3) ╪Y╪ևև☉ (עשתות AhSh-TWT) — **Thought:** As shining. [freq. 1] |kjv: thought| {str: 6248}

c^m) ╪Yևև☉ (עשות Ah-ShWT) — **Bright:** [freq. 1] |kjv: bright| {str: 6219}

f^m/f) ꞁ╪ևև☉ (עשתי Ah-Sh-TY) — **One:** [Unknown connection to root;] [freq. 19] |kjv: one| {str: 6249}

j^f1) ✡ꞁY╪ևև☉ (עשתונה AhSh-TW-NH) — **Thought:** As shining. [ms: עשתנה] [freq. 1] |kjv: thought| {str: 6250}

2587) ꞁ╪☉ (עתד AhTD) ac: **Prepare** co: ? ab: **Ready**

V) ꞁ╪☉ (עתד Ah-TD) — **Prepare:** To be prepared and ready. [freq. 2] (vf: Hitpael, Piel) |kjv: fit, ready| {str: 6257}

b^m) ꞁꞁ╪☉ (עתיד Ah-TYD) — **Prepared:** [Hebrew and Aramaic] [freq. 7] |kjv: ready, come| {str: 6263, 6264}

d^m) ꞁY╪☉ (עתוד Ah-TWD) — **I. Preparations:** What is prepared. [ms: עתד] **II. Goat:** [Unknown connection to root;] [ms: עתד] [freq. 31] |kjv: treasure| {str: 6259, 6260}

2588) ‴╪☉ (עתם AhTM) ac: **Burn** co: ? ab: ?

V) ‴╪☉ (עתם Ah-TM) — **Burn:** [freq. 1] (vf: Niphal) |kjv: darken| {str: 6272}

2589) ⊸╪☉ (עתק AhTQ) ac: **Remove** co: ? ab: ?: A movement from one space or time to another.

V) ⊸╪☉ (עתק Ah-TQ) — **Remove:** [freq. 9] (vf: Paal, Hiphil) |kjv: remove, old, left, copy| {str: 6275}

N^m) ⊸╪☉ (עתק Ah-TQ) — **Bold:** In arrogance or durability. [freq. 5] |kjv: durable, arrogancy, grievous, stiff, hard| {str: 6276, 6277}

b^m) ⊸ꞁ╪☉ (עתיק Ah-TYQ) — **I. Removed: II. Durable:** [Hebrew and Aramaic] [freq. 6] |kjv: durable, ancient, drawn| {str: 6266, 6267, 6268}

2590) ꞁ╪☉ (עתר AhTR) ac: **Multiply** co: ? ab: **Abundance:** [from: ╪☉ - as an abundance]

V) ꞁ╪☉ (עתר Ah-TR) — **Multiply:** [freq. 2] (vf: Niphal, Hiphil) |kjv: deceit, multiply| {str: 6280}

N^f2) ╪ꞁ╪☉ (עתרת AhT-RT) — **Abundance:** [freq. 1] |kjv: abundance| {str: 6283}

Pey

2591) 𝒥𝐋◌ (פגל PGL) ac: **?** co: **Foul** ab: **?:** Something that stinks or is rotten. [from: 𝐋◌ - as being unfit]

ed^(m)) 𝒥Y𝐋◌◌ (פיגול PY-GWL) — **Foul:** [ms: פגל פגול] [freq. 4] |kjv: abominable, abomination| {str: 6292}

2592) ◌𝐋◌ (פגע PGAh) ac: **Meet** co: **?** ab: **Encounter:** A chance meeting or encounter. [from: 𝐋◌ - meeting]

V) ◌𝐋◌ (פגע P-GAh) — **Meet:** To come together in meeting by chance. Also to give or place as a meeting. [freq. 46] (vf: Paal, Hiphil) |kjv: fall, meet, reach, intercession, intreat, entreat, light| {str: 6293}

N^(m)) ◌𝐋◌ (פגע P-GAh) — **Encounter:** A chance meeting. [freq. 2] |kjv: occurrence, chance| {str: 6294}

h^(m)) ◌𝐋◌ᴍ (מפגע MP-GAh) — **Target:** As the person met or place of meeting. [freq. 1] |kjv: mark| {str: 4645}

2593) 𝔑𝐋◌ (פגר PGR) ac: **Faint** co: **Carcass** ab: **?:** [from: 𝐋◌ - as being unfit]

V) 𝔑𝐋◌ (פגר P-GR) — **Faint:** To faint as though dead. [freq. 2] (vf: Piel) |kjv: faint| {str: 6296}

N^(m)) 𝔑𝐋◌ (פגר P-GR) — **Carcass:** A dead body. [freq. 22] |kjv: carcass, dead, corpse| {str: 6297}

2594) ⊔⊔𝐋◌ (פגש PGSh) ac: **Meet** co: **?** ab: **?:** [from: 𝐋◌ - meeting]

V) ⊔⊔𝐋◌ (פגש P-GSh) — **Meet:** [freq. 14] (vf: Paal, Niphal, Piel) |kjv: meet| {str: 6298}

2595) ⊘╥◌ (פדע PDAh) ac: **Redeem** co: **?** ab: **?:** [from: ╥◌]

V) ⊘╥◌ (פדע P-DAh) — **Redeem:** [freq. 1] (vf: Paal) |kjv: deliver| {str: 6308}

2596) 𝔑╥◌ (פדר PDR) ac: **?** co: **Fat** ab: **?**

N^(m)) 𝔑╥◌ (פדר P-DR) — **Fat:** [freq. 3] |kjv: fat| {str: 6309}

2597) 𝔑╦◌ (פזר PZR) ac: **Scatter** co: **?** ab: **?:** [from: ◌◌◌]

V) 𝔑╦◌ (פזר P-ZR) — **Scatter:** [freq. 10] (vf: Paal, Niphal, Pual, Piel, Participle) |kjv: scatter, disperse| {str: 6340}

2598) ╥Ⅲ◌ (פחד PHhD) ac: **Shake** co: **Thigh** ab: **Fear:** The shaking and trembling of one afraid or in reverence.

V) ╥Ⅲ◌ (פחד P-HhD) — **Fear:** [freq. 25] (vf: Paal, Hiphil, Piel) |kjv: fear, afraid, awe, shake| {str: 6342}

N^(m)) ╥Ⅲ◌ (פחד P-HhD) — **I. Thigh:** As shaking when frightened. **II. Fear:** [freq. 50] |kjv: fear, dread, terror, stone| {str: 6343, 6344}

N^{f1}) 𐤇ⴰ꙱◇ (פחדה PHh-DH) —
Fear: [freq. 1] |kjv: fear| {str: 6345}

2599) ⴰ꙱◇ (פחז PHhZ) ac: Reckless
co: ? ab: ?: A reckless behavior as water
flows in any direction.
V) ⴰ꙱◇ (פחז P-HhZ) —
Reckless: [freq. 2] (vf: Paal) |kjv:
light| {str: 6348}
N^m) ⴰ꙱◇ (פחז P-HhZ) —
Reckless: [freq. 1] |kjv: unstable|
{str: 6349}
N^{f3}) †Уⴰ꙱◇ (פחזות PHh-ZWT)
— Recklessness: [freq. 1] |kjv:
lightness| {str: 6350}

2600) ᴡ꙱◇ (פחם PHhM) ac: Burn
co: Charcoal ab: ?: [from: ᴡ꙱ - from
its heat]
N^m) ᴡ꙱◇ (פחם P-HhM) —
Charcoal: [freq. 3] |kjv: coal| {str:
6352}

2601) ᴖ꙱◇ (פחר PHhR) ac: ? co:
Potter ab: ?
N^m) ᴖ꙱◇ (פחר P-HhR) — Potter:
[Aramaic only] [freq. 1] |kjv: potter|
{str: 6353}

2602) †꙱◇ (פחת PHhT) ac: ? co: Pit
ab: ?: [from: †◇ - a hole]
N^m) †꙱◇ (פחת P-HhT) — Pit: A
hole in the ground. [freq. 10] |kjv:
pit, hole, snare| {str: 6354}
N^{f2}) ††꙱◇ (פחתת PHh-TT) —
Pit: A hole in the skin from disease.
[freq. 1] |kjv: fret| {str: 6356}

2603) ⴰ⊗◇ (פטד PThD) ac: ? co: ?
ab: ?
e^{f1}) 𐤇ⴰ⊗ᴊ◇ (פיטדה PYTh-DH)
— Pitdah: An unknown precious
stone. [ms: פטדה] [freq. 4] |kjv:
topaz| {str: 6357}

2604) ᴖ⊗◇ (פטר PThR) ac: Burst co:
? ab: ?: A breaking or bursting open or
out. [from: ᴖ◇ - breaking]
V) ᴖ⊗◇ (פטר P-ThR) — Burst:
[freq. 8] (vf: Paal, Hiphil) |kjv: open,
slip, free, out| {str: 6358, 6362}
N^m) ᴖ⊗◇ (פטר P-ThR) —
Bursting: [freq. 11] |kjv: open,
firstling| {str: 6363}
b^m) ᴖᴊ⊗◇ (פטיר P-ThYR) —
Bursting: [freq. 1] |kjv: free| {str:
6359}
e^{f1}) 𐤇ᴖ⊗ᴊ◇ (פיטרה PYTh-RH) —
Bursting: [ms: פטרה] [freq. 1] |kjv:
open| {str: 6363}

2605) ᴗ⊗◇ (פטש PThSh) ac: Spread
co: Hammer ab: ?: [from: ᴗ⊗]
b^m) ᴗᴊ⊗◇ (פטיש P-ThYSh) — I.
Hammer: As used to pound metal
into a sheet. II. Tunic: A wide
garment as spread out. [Aramaic
only] [freq. 5] |kjv: hammer, hosen|
{str: 6360, 6361}

2606) ᴸᴗ◇ (פלג PLG) ac: Split co:
River ab: Division: The land is divided
by rivers that mark out boundaries or
sections.
V) ᴸᴗ◇ (פלג P-LG) — Split:
[Hebrew and Aramaic] [freq. 5] (vf:

Niphal, Pel) |kjv: divide| {str: 6385, 6386}

N^m) �ište (פֶלֶג P-LG) — **I. River:** As dividing the land into two parts. **II. Half:** As split into two. [Aramaic only] [freq. 11] |kjv: river, stream, dividing| {str: 6387, 6388}

N^f1) ᚤᛚᚢ⌒ (פְלֻגָה PL-GH) — **I. Clan:** A division within the family. **II. River:** [Aramaic only] [freq. 3] |kjv: division, river| {str: 6390}

d^f1) ᚤᛚᚤᚢ⌒ (פְלוּגָה P-LW-GH) — **Clan:** A division within the family. [Hebrew and Aramaic] [ms: פְלֻגָּה] [freq. 2] |kjv: division| {str: 6391, 6392}

h^f1) ᚤᛚᚢ⌒ᛠ (מִפְלַגָּה MP-L-GH) — **Clan:** A division within the family. [freq. 1] |kjv: division| {str: 4653}

~~~~~~~~~~

2607) ᛏᚢ⌒ (פֶלֶד PLD) ac: ? co: **Steel** ab: ?

N^f1) ᛏᚢ⌒ (פְלָד PL-D) — **Steel:** [freq. 1] |kjv: torch| {str: 6393}

~~~~~~~~~~

2608) ᛘᚢ⌒ (פֶלַח PLHh) ac: **Slice** co: ? ab: ?: The cutting off of a piece of something.

V) ᛘᚢ⌒ (פָלַח P-LHh) — **I. Slice:** [Hebrew and Aramaic] **II. Serve:** [Unknown connection to root; Aramaic only] [freq. 15] (vf: Paal, Piel) |kjv: cut, shred, cleave, bring forth, strike, serve, minister| {str: 6398, 6399}

N^f) ᛘᚢ⌒ (פֶלַח P-LHh) — **Part:** As what is sliced off. [freq. 6] |kjv: piece| {str: 6400}

m^m) ᛣᛘᚢ⌒ (פֻלְחָן PL-HhN) — **Service:** [Unknown connection to

root; Aramaic only] [freq. 1] |kjv: service| {str: 6402}

~~~~~~~~~~

2609) ⊗ᚢ⌒ (פֶלֶט PLTh) ac: **Escape** co: ? ab: ?

V) ⊗ᚢ⌒ (פָלַט P-LTh) — **Deliver:** [freq. 25] (vf: Paal, Hiphil, Piel) |kjv: deliver, deliverer, calve, escape, safe| {str: 6403}

N^m) ⊗ᚢ⌒ (פֶלֶט P-LTh) — **Escaping:** [freq. 5] |kjv: deliverance, escape| {str: 6405}

b^m) ⊗ᛃᚢ⌒ (פָלִיט P-LYTh) — **Escape:** [ms: פָלֵט] [freq. 21] |kjv: escape, fugitive| {str: 6412}

b^f1) ᚤ⊗ᛃᚢ⌒ (פְלֵיטָה P-LY-ThH) — **Escape:** [ms: פְלֵטָה] [freq. 28] |kjv: escape, deliverance, remnant| {str: 6413}

h^m) ⊗ᚢ⌒ᛠ (מִפְלָט MP-LTh) — **Escape:** [freq. 1] |kjv: escape| {str: 4655}

~~~~~~~~~~

2610) �革ᚢ⌒ (פֶלֶךְ PLK) ac: ? co: **Stick** ab: ?: [from: �革ᚢ - using a staff]

N^m) ᛣ᚜ᚢ⌒ (פֶלֶךְ P-LK) — **I. Stick: II. District:** [Unknown connection to root;] [freq. 10] |kjv: part, staff, distaff| {str: 6418}

~~~~~~~~~~

2611) ᛣᚢ⌒ (פֶלֶן PLN) ac: ? co: **One** ab: ?

cf^m) ᛁᚤᚢ⌒ (פְלוֹנִי P-LW-NY) — **Such:** A certain one. [ms: פְלֹנִי] [freq. 3] |kjv: such| {str: 6423}

jf^m) ᛁᚤᛠᚢ⌒ (פַלְמוֹנִי PL-MW-NY) — **One:** A certain one. [freq. 1] |kjv: certain| {str: 6422}

~~~~~~~~~~

2612) ⬤◡✔ (פלס PLS) ac: **Weigh** co: **Scales** ab: **?:** The balance scale that is used to weigh objects. When the two sides of the balance is level, the weight is known.

V) ⬤◡✔ (פלס P-LS) — **Ponder:** In the sense of weighing options. [freq. 6] (vf: Piel) |kjv: ponder, weigh, made| {str: 6424}

N^(m)) ⬤◡✔ (פלס P-LS) — **Scales:** For weighing. [freq. 2] |kjv: weight, scales| {str: 6425}

h^(m)) ⬤◡✔ᴀᴀ (מפלס MP-LS) — **Balancing:** [df: מפלש] [freq. 1] |kjv: balancing| {str: 4657}

~~~~~~~~~

2613) ⬤◡ᴠ (פלץ PLTs) ac: **Tremble** co: **?** ab: **Horror:** Something of horror that causes one to tremble.

V) ⬤◡ᴠ (פלץ P-LTs) — **Tremble:** [freq. 1] (vf: Hitpael) |kjv: tremble| {str: 6426}

N^(f3)) ⬤◡ᴠᵗ (פלצות PL-TsWT) — **Horror:** [freq. 4] |kjv: horror, trembling, fearfulness| {str: 6427}

h^(f2)) ᴀᴀ◡◡ᴠᵗ (מפלצת MP-L-TsT) — **Idol:** An object that causes horror. [freq. 4] |kjv: idol| {str: 4656}

i^(f2)) †◡◡ᴠᵗ (תפלצת TP-L-TsT) — **Horror:** [freq. 1] |kjv: terribleness| {str: 8606}

~~~~~~~~~

2614) ⬤◡ᴜᴜ (פלש PLSh) ac: **Roll** co: **?** ab: **?:** A rolling around in dust or ashes as a sign of morning) [from: ◡ᴜ - rolling the dough]

V) ⬤◡ᴜᴜ (פלש P-LSh) — **Roll:** [freq. 5] (vf: Hitpael) |kjv: wallow, roll| {str: 6428}

~~~~~~~~~

2615) ⬤ᴀ\◡ (פנם PNM) ac: **?** co: **Inside** ab: **?**

b^(f1)) ⬤◡\ᴀᴀ⚥ (פנימה P-NY-MH) — **Within:** [freq. 14] |kjv: within, inward, in, inner| {str: 6441}

b^(fm)) ⬤◡\ᴀᴀ◡ (פנימי P-NY-MY) — **Inner:** [freq. 32] |kjv: inner, inward, within| {str: 6442}

~~~~~~~~~

2616) ⬤\◡• (פנק PNQ) ac: **Pamper** co: **?** ab: **?**

V) ⬤\◡• (פנק P-NQ) — **Pamper:** To delicately teach or bring up. [freq. 1] (vf: Piel) |kjv: bring up| {str: 6445}

~~~~~~~~~

2617) ⬤⬥ʟ (פסג PSG) ac: **Consider** co: **?** ab: **?**

V) ⬤⬥ʟ (פסג P-SG) — **Consider:** [freq. 1] (vf: Piel) |kjv: consider| {str: 6448}

~~~~~~~~~

2618) ⬤⬥ᴍ (פסח PSHh) ac: **Hop** co: **?** ab: **?**

V) ⬤⬥ᴍ (פסח P-SHh) — **Hop:** To hop from one place or another. Also to be lame as one who hops on one leg. [freq. 7] (vf: Paal, Niphal, Piel) |kjv: pass over, halt, lame, leap| {str: 6452}

N^(m)) ⬤⬥ᴍ (פסח P-SHh) — **Lame:** As one who hops one leg. [freq. 14] |kjv: lame| {str: 6455}

~~~~~~~~~

2619) ⬤⬥◡ (פסל PSL) ac: **Hew** co: **Sculpture** ab: **?:** The chiseling of stone to form an image.

416

V) ⌐✦∪ (פסל P-SL) — **Hew:** To carve or chisel out stone. [freq. 6] (vf: Paal) |kjv: hew, graven| {str: 6458}

N^m) ⌐✦∪ (פסל P-SL) — **Sculpture:** As chiseled out. [freq. 31] |kjv: image, grave, carved| {str: 6459}

b^m) ⌐✦⊣∪ (פסיל P-SYL) — **Sculpture:** As chiseled out. [freq. 23] |kjv: image, graven, carved, quarry| {str: 6456}

2620) ⌐✦◎ (פסע PSAh) ac: **March** co: **Step** ab: **?:** [from: ⌐ш - spreading apart the legs]

V) ⌐✦◎ (פסע P-SAh) — **March:** [df: פשע] [freq. 1] (vf: Paal) |kjv: go| {str: 6585}

N^m) ⌐✦◎ (פסע P-SAh) — **Step:** [df: פשע] [freq. 1] |kjv: step| {str: 6587}

h^fl) ⌐✦◎ℳ (מפסעה MP-S-AhH) — **Hips:** As used in marching. [df: מפשעה] [freq. 1] |kjv: buttocks| {str: 4667}

2621) ⌐✦•◆ (פסק PSQ) ac: **Spread** co: **?** ab: **?:** A spreading apart of something. [from: ⌐ш]

V) ⌐✦•◆ (פסק P-SQ) — **Spread:** To spread wide. [df: פשק] [freq. 2] (vf: Paal, Piel) |kjv: open| {str: 6589}

2622) ⌐◎∪ (פעל PAhL) ac: **Make** co: **Work** ab: **?:** [from: ◎∪ - work]

V) ⌐◎∪ (פעל P-AhL) — **Make:** [freq. 56] (vf: Paal) |kjv: work,

worker, do, make, commit, doer, maker, ordain| {str: 6466}

d^fl) ⌐◎Y✿ (פעולה P-AhW-LH) — **I. Wages:** What one is given for his work. **II. Work:** [freq. 14] |kjv: work, labour, reward, wage| {str: 6468}

g^m) ⌐◎Y∪ (פועל PW-AhL) — **Work:** What is made. [ms: פעל] [freq. 38] |kjv: work, act, deed, do, getting, maker| {str: 6467}

h^m) ⌐◎∪ℳ (מפעל MP-AhL) — **Work:** [freq. 1] |kjv: works| {str: 4659}

h^fl) ⌐◎∪ℳ✿ (מפעלה MP-Ah-LH) — **Work:** [freq. 3] |kjv: works| {str: 4659}

2623) ⌐◎ℳ (פעם PAhM) ac: **Beat** co: **Bell** ab: **?:** A repetitive beating or sounding as the hoofs of a running horse, the beating of the heart or the ringing of a bell.

V) ⌐◎ℳ (פעם P-AhM) — **Beat:** [freq. 5] (vf: Paal, Niphal, Hitpael) |kjv: trouble, move| {str: 6470}

N^f) ⌐◎ℳ (פעם P-AhM) — **Time:** A continual beating of time, one moment after the other. Also a moment in time. [freq. 112] |kjv: time, once, now, feet, twice, step, corner, rank, oftentimes| {str: 6471}

m^m) ⌐◎ℳ⌐ (פעמן PAh-MN) — **Bell:** From its rhythmic ringing. [freq. 7] |kjv: bell| {str: 6472}

2624) ⌐◎ℜ (פער PAhR) ac: **Open** co: **?** ab: **?:** A wide opening.

V) ⌐◎ℜ (פער P-AhR) — **Open wide:** [freq. 4] (vf: Paal) |kjv: open, gape| {str: 6473}

2625) ᴖᴖᴏᴧᴐ (פצח PTsHh) ac: **Break** co: ? ab: ?: A breaking forth or out with force or a loud noise. [from: ᴏᴧᴐ - as opening]

V) ᴖᴖᴏᴧᴐ (פצח P-TsHh) — **Break open:** [freq. 8] (vf: Paal, Piel) |kjv: break, loud| {str: 6476}

2626) ᴊᴏᴧᴐ (פצל PTsL) ac: **Peel** co: **Strip** ab: ?: [from: ᴊᴐ - removing]

V) ᴊᴏᴧᴐ (פצל P-TsL) — **Peel:** [freq. 2] (vf: Piel) |kjv: pill| {str: 6478}

N^fl) ᴪᴊᴏᴧᴐ (פצלה PTs-LH) — **Strip:** As peeled. [freq. 1] |kjv: strake| {str: 6479}

2627) ᴍᴍᴏᴧᴐ (פצם PTsM) ac: **Crack** co: ? ab: ?: A cracking open.

V) ᴍᴍᴏᴧᴐ (פצם P-TsM) — **Crack:** [freq. 1] (vf: Paal) |kjv: break| {str: 6480}

2628) ᴐᴏᴧᴐ (פצע PTsAh) ac: **Smash** co: **Bruise** ab: ?: A bruise from being smashed. [from: ᴏᴧᴐ]

V) ᴐᴏᴧᴐ (פצע P-TsAh) — **Smash:** [freq. 3] (vf: Paal) |kjv: wound| {str: 6481}

N^m) ᴐᴏᴧᴐ (פצע P-TsAh) — **Bruise:** [freq. 8] |kjv: wound, wounding| {str: 6482}

2629) ᴙᴏᴧᴐ (פצר PTsR) ac: **Press** co: **File** ab: ?: The sharpening of a metal tool

by pressing and moving a file or stone over the point. [from: ᴙᴏᴧ]

V) ᴙᴏᴧᴐ (פצר P-TsR) — **Press:** To push or urge another into an action. [freq. 7] (vf: Paal, Hiphil) |kjv: urge, press, stubbornness| {str: 6484}

2630) ᴛ-ᴐ-ᴐ (פקד PQD) ac: **Oversee** co: **Overseer** ab: **Oversight:** The role of the overseer is to watch over, direct, command, chastise, review and count those in his charge for the purpose of producing work. [from: -ᴐ-ᴐ]

V) ᴛ-ᴐ-ᴐ (פקד P-QD) — I. **Oversee:** To closely inspect. II. **Count:** As an overseeing of numbers. [freq. 305] (vf: Paal, Niphal, Hiphil, Hitpael, Hophal, Pual, Piel) |kjv: number, visit, punish, appoint, commit, miss, set, charge, governor, lack, oversight, officer, count, empty, ruler, overseer, judgement| {str: 6485}

b^m) ᴛᴊᴐ-ᴐ (פקיד P-QYD) — **Overseer:** One who carefully watches over. [freq. 13] |kjv: officer, overseer, governor, charge| {str: 6496}

b^f3) ᴛᴊᴛᴊᴐ-ᴐ (פקידות P-QY-DWT) — **Ward:** The area inspected by an overseer. [ms: פקדת] [freq. 1] |kjv: ward| {str: 6488}

d^m) ᴛᴊ-ᴐ-ᴐ (פקוד P-QWD) — **Statute:** The orders and commands of the overseer. [ms: פקד] [freq. 24] |kjv: precept, commandment, statute| {str: 6490}

d^fl) ᴪᴛᴊ-ᴐ-ᴐ (פקודה P-QW-DH) — I. **Oversight:** A careful watching over. II. **Number:** As counted. [ms: פקדה] [freq. 32] |kjv: visitation, office, charge, oversight, officer, ordering, account, custody, number| {str: 6486}

h^m) ᔑ-ᗙ-ᗒᗰ (מפקד MP-QD) — **I. Number: II. Appointment:** Also an appointed place. [freq. 4] |kjv: number, commandment, appointed| {str: 4662}

j^m) ᐢᎩᔑ-ᗙ-ᗒ (פקדון PQ-DWN) — **Deposit:** The produce of the work that is watched over. [freq. 3] |kjv: delivered, store| {str: 6487}

2631) ᗙᗙ-ᗙ-ᗒ (פקח PQHh) ac: **Open** co: ? ab: ?: The opening of the eyes or ears as being perceptive. [from: -ᗙ-ᗒ]

V) ᗙᗙ-ᗙ-ᗒ (פקח P-QHh) — **Open:** To open the eyes or ears. [freq. 20] (vf: Paal, Niphal) |kjv: open| {str: 6491}

N^m) ᗙᗙ-ᗙ-ᗒ (פקח P-QHh) — **Seeing:** As with open eyes. [freq. 2] |kjv: open| {str: 6493}

lc^m) ᗙᗙᎩ-ᗙ-ᗙᗙ-ᗙ-ᗒ (פקחקוח P-QHh-QWHh) — **Open:** [Written as two words in the Masoretic text - קוח פקח] [freq. 1] |kjv: opening| {str: 6495}

2632) ᗝ-ᗙ-ᗒ (פקע PQAh) ac: ? co: **Gourd** ab: ?: The curved and round shape of a gourd.

N^m) ᗝ-ᗙ-ᗒ (פקע P-QAh) — **Gourd:** [freq. 3] |kjv: knop| {str: 6497}

d^{fl}) ᕊᗝᎩ-ᗙ-ᗒ (פקועה P-QW-AhH) — **Gourd:** [ms: פקעה] [freq. 1] |kjv: gourd| {str: 6498}

2633) ᕀ-ᗙ-ᗒ (פקר PQR) ac: **Seek** co: ? ab: ?: [from: -ᗙ-ᗒ]

V) ᕀ-ᗙ-ᗒ (פקר P-QR) — **Seek:** To look or search for something. [Hebrew and Aramaic] [df: בקר] [freq. 12] (vf: Piel) |kjv: enquire, seek, search| {str: 1239, 1240}

N^{fl}) ᕊᕀ-ᗙ-ᗒ (פקרה PQ-RH) — **Seeking:** [df: בקרה] [freq. 1] |kjv: seek| {str: 1243}

2634) ᔑᕀᗒ (פרד PRD) ac: **Divide** co: **Seed** ab: ?: A dividing or separating out. [from: ᕀᗒ - scattering]

V) ᔑᕀᗒ (פרד P-RD) — **Divide apart:** To divide and separate. [freq. 26] (vf: Paal, Niphal, Hiphil, Hitpael, Pual, Piel) |kjv: separate, part, divide, scatter, disperse, joint, sever, stretch, sunder| {str: 6504}

N^m) ᔑᕀᗒ (פרד P-RD) — **Mule:** As being a division of two species. [freq. 15] |kjv: mule| {str: 6505}

d^{fl}) ᕊᔑᎩᕀᗒ (פרודה P-RW-DH) — **Seed:** As separated from the parent plant and scattered in the field. [ms: פרדה] [freq. 1] |kjv: seed| {str: 6507}

e^{fl}) ᕊᔑᕀᒐᗒ (פירדה PYR-DH) — **Mule:** A female mule. As being a division of two species. [ms: פרדה] [freq. 3] |kjv: mule| {str: 6506}

2635) ᕲᕀᗒ (פרז PRZ) ac: ? co: **Village** ab: ?: The rural villages are scattered about the country side and have no wall for protection. [from: ᕀᗒ - scattering]

N^m) ᕲᕀᗒ (פרז P-RZ) — **Peasant:** One who dwells in a town without walls. [freq. 1] |kjv: village| {str: 6518}

N^{f1}) 🜲⌒Ꝓ⌀ (פרזה PR-ZH) — **Village:** A town or village without walls of protection. [freq. 3] |kjv: unwalled| {str: 6519}

f^m) ⌲⌒Ꝓ⌀ (פרזי P-R-ZY) — **Village:** A town or village without walls of protection. [df: פרוזי] [freq. 3] |kjv: country, unwalled| {str: 6521}

f^m) ⌲⌒Ꝓ⌀ (פרזי P-R-ZY) — **Village:** A town or village without walls of protection. [freq. 3] |kjv: village| {str: 6521}

j^m) ⌊Y⌒Ꝓ⌀ (פרזון PR-ZWN) — **Peasant:** One who dwells in a town without walls. [freq. 2] |kjv: village| {str: 6520}

~~~~~~~~~~

2636) ᴍᴍꝒ⌀ (פרח PRHh) ac: **Burst** co: **Bud** ab: ?: The busting out of a bud. [from: Ꝓ⌀ - breaking out]

V) ᴍᴍꝒ⌀ (פרח P-RHh) — **Burst:** To break out or forth as a blooming flower or the wings of a bird. [freq. 36] (vf: Paal, Hiphil) |kjv: flourish, bud, blossom, grow, break, fly, spring, abroad, abundantly, spread| {str: 6524}

N^m) ᴍᴍꝒ⌀ (פרח P-RHh) — **Bud:** As bursting out. [freq. 17] |kjv: flower, bud, blossom| {str: 6525}

n^m) ᴍᴍꝒ⌀⌲ (אפרח AP-RHh) — **Chick:** A young bird that has burst out of the egg. [freq. 4] |kjv: young| {str: 667}

el^m) ᴍᴍᴍꝒ⌲⌊⌀ (פירחח PY-R-HhHh) — **Brood:** A young bird that has burst out of the egg. [ms: פרחח] [freq. 1] |kjv: youth| {str: 6526}

~~~~~~~~~~

2637) ⊗Ꝓ⌀ (פרט PRTh) ac: **Break** co: ? ab: ?: [from: Ꝓ⌀ - scattering]

V) ⊗Ꝓ⌀ (פרט P-RTh) — **Stammer:** As broken words scattered out of the mouth. [freq. 1] (vf: Paal) |kjv: chant| {str: 6527}

N^m) ⊗Ꝓ⌀ (פרט P-RTh) — **Fallen grape:** As broken from the plant and scattered on the ground. [freq. 1] |kjv: grape| {str: 6528}

~~~~~~~~~~

2638) ᵂꝓ⌀ (פרך PRK) ac: ? co: **Whip** ab: ?: [from: Ꝓ⌀ - breaking]

N^m) ᵂꝓ⌀ (פרך P-RK) — **Whip:** As dividing and breaking open the flesh. [freq. 6] |kjv: rigour, cruelty| {str: 6531}

c^{f2}) ✝ᵂYꝓ⌀ (פרוכת P-RW-KT) — **Curtain:** Hung to cause a dividing wall in a room. [ms: פרכת] [freq. 25] |kjv: vail| {str: 6532}

~~~~~~~~~~

2639) ᴍᴍꝓ⌀ (פרם PRM) ac: **Rip** co: ? ab: ?: [from: Ꝓ⌀ - breaking apart]

V) ᴍᴍꝓ⌀ (פרם P-RM) — **Rip:** [freq. 3] (vf: Paal) |kjv: rend| {str: 6533}

~~~~~~~~~~

2640) ꝗꝓ⌀ (פרס PRS) ac: **Split** co: **Hoof** ab: ?: The hoof that is split into two parts. [from: Ꝓ⌀ - breaking]

V) ꝗꝓ⌀ (פרס P-RS) — **I. Split:** To split in two as the hoofs of a clean animal. [Hebrew an Aramaic] **II. Spread:** To spread apart in the sense of splitting. [df: פרש] [freq. 84] (vf: Paal, Niphil, Hiphil, Piel) |kjv: divide, part, deal, hoof, tear, spread, stretch, scatter, break, open, chop, spread| {str: 6536, 6537, 6566}

420

N^(m)) ⌘⌐⌐◯ (פרס P-RS) — **Peres:** An unknown bird of prey. [ms: פרש] [freq. 2] |kjv: ossifrage| {str: 6538}

N^(f1)) ⭐⌘⌐◯ (פרסה PR-SH) — **Hoof:** As split. [freq. 19] |kjv: hoof, claw| {str: 6541}

h^(m)) ⌘⌐◯〰 (מפרס MP-RS) — **Spreading:** In the sense of splitting. [ms: מפרש] [freq. 2] |kjv: spreading| {str: 4666}

~~~~~~~~~

2641) ◯⌐◯ (פרע PRAh) ac: **Loose** co: **Hair** ab: **?**

V) ◯⌐◯ (פרע P-RAh) — **Loose:** To uncover, remove or let go. Such as to make naked by removing clothing or uncovering the head. [freq. 16] (vf: Paal, Niphal, Hiphil) |kjv: refuse, uncover, naked, avenging, avoid, go, bare, let, nought, perish| {str: 6544}

N^(m)) ◯⌐◯ (פרע P-RAh) — **Long hair:** As let loose. [freq. 2] |kjv: locks| {str: 6545}

N^(f1)) ⭐◯⌐◯ (פרעה PR-AhH) — **Revenge:** In the sense of letting loose. [freq. 2] |kjv: revenge, avenge| {str: 6546}

~~~~~~~~~

2642) ⌐⌐◯ (פרץ PRTs) ac: **Spread** co: **Breach** ab: **?**: The breaching of a river bank causing the water to flow and spread out. [from: ⌐◯ - breaking]

V) ⌐⌐◯ (פרץ P-RTs) — **Spread out:** To be spread out wide or widespread. [freq. 49] (vf: Paal, Niphal, Hitpael, Pual) |kjv: break, increase, abroad, breach, made, pressed, breaker, compel, open| {str: 6555}

N^(m)) ⌐⌐◯ (פרץ P-RTs) — **Breach:** [freq. 19] |kjv: breach, gap, breaking| {str: 6556}

b^(m)) ⌐⌐⌐◯ (פריץ P-RYTs) — **Wild:** A thief or robber as a vicious beast in the sense of escaping out and spreading out wildly. [freq. 6] |kjv: robber, destroyer, revenous| {str: 6530}

h^(m)) ⌐⌐◯〰 (מפרץ MP-RTs) — **Breach:** [freq. 1] |kjv: breach| {str: 4664}

~~~~~~~~~

2643) ⌐◯ (פרק PRQ) ac: **Tear** co: **?** ab: **?**: [from: ⌐◯ - breaking]

V) ⌐◯ (פרק P-RQ) — **Tear away:** [Hebrew and Aramaic] [freq. 11] (vf: Paal, Hitpael, Piel) |kjv: break, rend, redeem, deliver, tear| {str: 6561, 6562}

N^(m)) ⌐◯ (פרק P-RQ) — **I. Crossroad:** As a tearing apart of the path. **II. Fragment:** As torn from the whole. **III. Booty:** As torn from the whole. [freq. 3] |kjv: crossway, robbery, broth| {str: 6563, 6564}

a^(f2)) †⌐◯〰 (מפרקת MP-R-QT) — **Neck:** From the tearing off of the head at the neck of a bird to kill it. [freq. 1] |kjv: neck| {str: 4665}

~~~~~~~~~

2644) ⊔⌐◯ (פרש PRSh) ac: **Spread** co: **Dung** ab: **?**: The spread out dung of cattle. A spreading apart of things as an arrangement or of thoughts in order to understand and make clear. [from: ⊔◯]

V) ⊔⌐◯ (פרש P-RSh) — **Spread out:** Also to be easily and plainly understood in the sense of being spread out to see. [Hebrew and Aramaic] [freq. 6] (vf: Paal, Niphal,

Hiphil, Pual) |kjv: shew, scatter, declare, distinctly, sting, plainly| {str: 6567, 6568}

N^m) ⊔ᴘ◠ (פרש P-RSh) — **I. Dung:** The dung of the cattle as spread out flat. **II. Horseman:** From the spreading of the legs to ride. [freq. 64] |kjv: dung, horsemen| {str: 6569, 6571}

N^fl) ⚹⊔ᴘ◠ (פרשה PR-ShH) — **Account:** As a spreading out of an event. [freq. 2] |kjv: sum, declaration| {str: 6575}

~~~~~~~~~~

2645) ᴍᴍ⊔◠ (פשח PShHh) ac: **Tear** co: **?** ab: **?:** A tearing into pieces. [from: ⊔◠ - spreading apart]

V) ᴍᴍ⊔◠ (פשח P-ShHh) — **Tear:** [freq. 1] (vf: Piel) |kjv: pull| {str: 6582}

~~~~~~~~~~

2646) ⊗⊔⊔◠ (פשט PShTh) ac: **Spread** co: **?** ab: **?:** [from: ⊔⊔◠]

V) ⊗⊔⊔◠ (פשט P-ShTh) — **Spread:** To spread apart. Also to Invade in the sense of spreading out for an attack. Also to strip of clothing in the sense of spreading the garment for removal. [freq. 43] (vf: Paal, Hiphil, Hitpael, Piel) |kjv: strip, put off, flay, invade, spoil, fall, spread| {str: 6584}

~~~~~~~~~~

2647) ◠⊔⊔◠ (פשע PShAh) ac: **Revolt** co: **?** ab: **Revolution:** A spreading apart. [from: ⊔⊔◠]

V) ◠⊔⊔◠ (פשע P-ShAh) — **Revolt:** [freq. 41] (vf: Paal, Niphal) |kjv: transgress, transgressor, rebel, revolt, offend, transgression| {str: 6586}

N^m) ◠⊔⊔◠ (פשע P-ShAh) — **Revolution:** [freq. 93] |kjv: transgression, trespass, sin, rebellion| {str: 6588}

~~~~~~~~~~

2648) †⊔⊔◠ (פשת PShT) ac: **Spread** co: **Flax** ab: **?:** A plant whose fibers are separated and spread out then made into linen and wicks for lamps. [from: ⊔⊔◠ - as spread out]

N^f) †⊔⊔◠ (פשת P-ShT) — **Flax:** [freq. 20] |kjv: linen, flax| {str: 6593, 6594}

~~~~~~~~~~

2649) ᴍᴛ◠ (פתח PTHh) ac: **Open** co: **Door** ab: **?:** [from: †◠ - a hole for entering]

V) ᴍᴛ◠ (פתח P-THh) — **Open:** [Hebrew and Aramaic] [freq. 146] (vf: Paal, Niphal, Hitpael, Pual, Piel) |kjv: open, loose, grave, engrave, put off, out, appear, drawn, break| {str: 6605, 6606}

N^m) ᴍᴛ◠ (פתח P-THh) — **Door:** As an entrance or opening. [freq. 164] |kjv: door, entering, entry, gate, in, entrance, opening, place| {str: 6607, 6608}

a^m) ᴍᴛ◠ᴍ (מפתח MP-THh) — **Key:** [freq. 3] |kjv: key| {str: 4668}

b^f) ᴍᴍ⊣ᴛ◠ (פתיח P-TYHh) — **Drawn sword:** In the sense of being opened from the sheath. [freq. 1] |kjv: sword| {str: 6609}

h^m) ᴍᴛ◠ᴍ (מפתח MP-THh) — **Opening:** [freq. 1] |kjv: opening| {str: 4669}

ed^m) ᴍᴍᵞᵗ⊣◠ (פיתוח PY-TWHh) — **Carving:** In the sense of opening with a knife or chisel. [ms: פתח] [freq. 11] |kjv: engraving, graving, carved, graven| {str: 6603}

ej^m) ◇⅃אⅧ (פיתחון PY-T-HhWN) — **Opening:** [freq. 2] |kjv: open, opening| {str: 6610}

2650) ⅃†◇ (פתל PTL) ac: **Twist** co: **Cord** ab: **?:** Cords are made by twisting fibers together. [from: ⅃† - from a rope]

V) ⅃†◇ (פתל P-TL) — **Twist:** [freq. 5] (vf: Niphal, Hitpael) |kjv: froward, wrestle, unsavory| {str: 6617}

b^m) ⅃ᵧ†◇ (פתיל P-TYL) — **Cord:** Made of twisted fibers. [freq. 11] |kjv: lace, bracelet, wire, ribband, bound, thread, line| {str: 6616}

l^m) ⅃†⅃†◇ (פתלתל P-TL-TL) — **Twisted:** [freq. 1] |kjv: crooked| {str: 6618}

2651) ⅄†◇ (פתן PTN) ac: **Open** co: **?** ab: **?:** [from: †◇ - an opening]

N^m) ⅄†◇ (פתן P-TN) — **Peten:** An unknown serpent, from its open mouth. [freq. 6] |kjv: asp, adder| {str: 6620}

h^m) ⅄†◇ᴡ (מפתן MP-TN) — **Threshold:** As an opening. [freq. 8] |kjv: threshold| {str: 4670}

2652) ⊙†◇ (פתע PTAh) ac: **Wink** co: **?** ab: **Moment:** The sudden closing and opening of the eye. [from: †◇ - opening the eye]

N^m) ⊙†◇ (פתע P-TAh) — **Moment:** As a wink of time. [freq. 7] |kjv: very, suddenly, instant| {str: 6621}

eqp^m) ᴡᵧ⊙†◇ (פיתעום PY-T-AhWM) — **Moment:** As a wink of time. [df: פתאום פתאם] [freq. 25] |kjv: suddenly, sudden, straightway| {str: 6597}

2653) ꓤ†◇ (פתר PTR) ac: **Open** co: **?** ab: **Interpretation:** A revealing of a text or speech in order to understand it. [from: ꓤ◇ - breaking open to reveal fruit (the meaning)]

V) ꓤ†◇ (פתר P-TR) — **Interpret:** [Hebrew and Aramaic] [ar: פשר] [freq. 11] (vf: Paal) |kjv: interpret, interpretation| {str: 6590, 6622}

N^m) ꓤ†◇ (פתר P-TR) — **Interpret:** [Hebrew and Aramaic] [df: פשר] [ar: פשר] [freq. 32] |kjv: interpretation| {str: 6591, 6592}

ej^m) ⅄Yꓤ†◇ (פיתרון PY-T-RWN) — **Interpretation:** [ms: פתרון פתרן] [freq. 5] |kjv: interpretation| {str: 6623}

Tsad

2654) ⊗Ⅼⅅ◖∧ (צבט TsBTh) ac: **Grasp** co: **?** ab: **?**: A reaching out to grasp something. [from: Ⅼⅅ∧ - as enclosed in a wall]

V) ⊗Ⅼⅅ◖∧ (צבט Ts-BTh) — **Grasp:** [freq. 1] (vf: Paal) |kjv: reach| {str: 6642}

2655) ⊙Ⅼⅅ◖∧ (צבע TsBAh) ac: **Wet** co: **Spot** ab: **?**: The dipping of the finger into a vat of dye and dripping color onto something.

V) ⊙Ⅼⅅ◖∧ (צבע Ts-BAh) — **Wet:** To be wet with the drops of dew. [Aramaic only] [freq. 5] (vf: Paal) |kjv: wet| {str: 6647}

N^(m)) ⊙Ⅼⅅ◖∧ (צבע Ts-BAh) — **Spots:** Something spotted with different colors. [freq. 3] |kjv: colors| {str: 6648}

d^(m)) ⊙YⅬⅅ◖∧ (צבוע Ts-BWAh) — **Spotted:** Something that appears to have spots of color. [freq. 1] |kjv: speckled| {str: 6641}

n^(f)) ⊙Ⅼⅅ◖∧⅃ (אצבע ATs-BAh) — **Finger:** As used for dipping into a liquid, such as blood, and dripping drops onto something. [Hebrew and Aramaic] [freq. 35] |kjv: finger, toe| {str: 676, 677}

2656) ℛⅬⅅ◖∧ (צבר TsBR) ac: **Pile** co: **Pile** ab: **?**: [from: Ⅼⅅ∧ - as a swelling]

V) ℛⅬⅅ◖∧ (צבר Ts-BR) — **Pile:** To pile something up in a mound. [freq. 7] (vf: Paal) |kjv: heap, gather, lay| {str: 6651}

N^(m)) ℛⅬⅅ◖∧ (צבר Ts-BR) — **Pile:** A mound of something. [freq. 1] |kjv: heap| {str: 6652}

2657) ✝Ⅼⅅ◖∧ (צבת TsBT) ac: **?** co: **Handful** ab: **?**: [from: Ⅼⅅ∧ - as enclosed in a wall]

N^(m)) ✝Ⅼⅅ◖∧ (צבת Ts-BT) — **Handful:** [freq. 1] |kjv: handful| {str: 6653}

2658) ⊸⊶⊤ⅆ◖∧ (צדק TsDQ) ac: **?** co: **Straight** ab: **Righteous:** One who is upright or righteous is one who walks a straight path. [from: ⊤⊤◖∧ - The straightness of the side]

V) ⊸⊶⊤ⅆ◖∧ (צדק Ts-DQ) — **Straight:** To be straight. [freq. 41] (vf: Paal, Niphal, Hiphil, Hitpael, Piel) |kjv: justify, righteous, just, justice, cleanse, clear, righteousness| {str: 6663}

N^(m)) ⊸⊶⊤ⅆ◖∧ (צדק Ts-DQ) — **Straight:** [freq. 116] |kjv: righteousness, just, justice, righteous, right| {str: 6664}

N^(f1)) ⚲⊸⊶⊤ⅆ◖∧ (צדקה TsD-QH) — **Straightness:** [freq. 157] |kjv: righteousness, justice, right, righteous, moderate| {str: 6666}

b^(m)) ⊸⊶⊤⊁⊤ⅆ◖∧ (צדיק Ts-DYQ) — **Straight:** [freq. 206] |kjv: righteous, just, lawful| {str: 6662}

e^(f1)) ⚲⊸⊶⊤⊁⊤ⅆ◖∧ (צידקה TsYD-QH) — **Straightness:** [Aramaic only] [ms: צדקה] [freq. 1] |kjv: righteousness| {str: 6665}

2659) ଡ଼ଧ୍ଧଧ (צחן TsHhN) ac: ? co: **Stench** ab: ?

N^{f1}) ଡ଼ଧ୍ଧଧ (צחנה TsHh-NH) — **Stench:** [freq. 1] |kjv: ill, savour| {str: 6709}

2660) ଡ଼ଧ୍ଧଧ-ଵ (צחק TsHhQ) ac: **Laugh** co: **Laugh** ab: ?: A laughing in play or mockery. [from: ଵଧ - coming from the belly]

V) ଡ଼ଧ୍ଧଧ-ଵ (צחק Ts-HhQ) — **Laugh:** [freq. 13] (vf: Paal, Piel) |kjv: laugh, mock, sport, play| {str: 6711}

c^m) ଡ଼ଧ୍Yଧ (צחוק Ts-HhWQ) — **Laugh:** [ms: צחק] [freq. 2] |kjv: laugh| {str: 6712}

2661) ଡ଼ଧ୍ଧଧ (צחר TsHhR) ac: ? co: **White** ab: ?: [from: ଧ୍ଧଧ - from the bleaching by the sun]

N^m) ଡ଼ଧ୍ଧଧ (צחר Ts-HhR) — **White:** [freq. 1] |kjv: white| {str: 6713}

c^m) ଡ଼ଧ୍Yଧ (צחור Ts-HhWR) — **White:** [ms: צחר] [freq. 1] |kjv: white| {str: 6715}

2662) ଧ୍ଧUଵଧ (צלח TsLHh) ac: **Advance** co: **Bowl** ab: ?: A pushing forward or up as the sides of a pot or bowl. [from: Uଵଧ - deep a bowl]

V) ଧ୍ଧUଵଧ (צלח Ts-LHh) — **Advance:** To move forward in distance, position or in prosperity. [Hebrew and Aramaic] [freq. 69] (vf: Paal, Hiphil) |kjv: prosper, come,

effect, good, meet, break, went, promote| {str: 6743, 6744}

N^{f1}) ଧ୍ଧUଵଧ (צלחה TsL-HhH) — **Bowl:** As advancing up the sides. [freq. 1] |kjv: pan| {str: 6745}

N^{f2}) ଧ୍ଧUଵଧ (צלחת TsL-HhT) — **Bowl:** As advancing up the sides. [freq. 3] |kjv: bosom, dish| {str: 6747}

c^{f4}) ଧ୍ଧUYଧ (צלוחית Ts-LW-HhYT) — **Bowl:** As advancing up the sides. [ms: צלחית] [freq. 1] |kjv: cruse| {str: 6746}

2663) ଧ୍ଧUଵଧ (צלם TsLM) ac: ? co: **Image** ab: ?: An outline or representation of an original as a shadow is the outline of the original. [from: Uଵଧ - from the dark shadow of a deep place]

N^m) ଧ୍ଧUଵଧ (צלם Ts-LM) — **Image:** Also an image or form of something as the shadow of the original. [Hebrew and Aramaic] [freq. 34] |kjv: image, vain, form| {str: 6754, 6755}

2664) ଧ୍ଧUଵଧ (צלע TsLAh) ac: **Limp** co: **Side** ab: ?

V) ଧ୍ଧUଵଧ (צלע Ts-LAh) — **Limp:** As favoring one side. [freq. 4] (vf: Paal) |kjv: halt| {str: 6760}

N^f) ଧ୍ଧUଵଧ (צלע Ts-LAh) — **I. Side:** The side of anything. **II. Limp:** As favoring one side. [ar: עלע] [freq. 45] |kjv: rib, side, chamber, board, corner, another, beam, halting, leaves, planks, halt, adversity| {str: 5967, 6761, 6763}

2665) ᴛᴧᴧᴏᴧ (צמד TsMD) ac: **Join** co: **Yoke** ab: ?: The joining of two animals together for plowing a field. [from: ⊗ᴧ]

V) ᴛᴧᴧᴏᴧ (צמד Ts-MD) — **Join:** To be joined to another as in a yoke. [freq. 5] (vf: Niphal, Hiphil, Pual) |kjv: join, fasten, frame| {str: 6775}

N^m) ᴛᴧᴧᴏᴧ (צמד Ts-MD) — **I. Yoke:** A pair of animals in a yoke or two of something as yoked together. **II. Tsemed:** A standard of measure. The amount land that can be plowed in one day by a yoke of oxen. [freq. 15] |kjv: yoke, couple, two, together, acre| {str: 6776}

b^m) ᴛ⅃ᴧᴧᴏᴧ (צמיד Ts-MYD) — **Bracelet:** As joined together. [ms: צמד] [freq. 7] |kjv: bracelet, covering| {str: 6781}

~~~~~~~~~~

2666) ᴍᴧᴧᴏᴧ (צמח TsMHh) ac: **Sprout** co: **Sprout** ab: ?: The springing up of a plant or bud.

V) ᴍᴧᴧᴏᴧ (צמח Ts-MHh) — **Sprout:** To grow out or spring forth. [freq. 33] (vf: Paal, Hiphil, Piel) |kjv: grow, spring, bring, bud, bear| {str: 6779}

N^m) ᴍᴧᴧᴏᴧ (צמח Ts-MHh) — **Sprout:** A plant that sprouts out of the ground or a bud that sprouts out of a tree. [freq. 12] |kjv: branch, bud, grew, spring| {str: 6780}

~~~~~~~~~~

2667) ᴏᴧᴧᴏᴧ (צמק TsMQ) ac: **Dry** co: **Raisin** ab: ?: Grapes are left out in the sun to dry and shriveled up. The raisins can them be stored for later use as they will not spoil. [from: ᴏᴧ - dried up]

V) ᴏᴧᴧᴏᴧ (צמק Ts-MQ) — **Dry:** To be dry and shriveled up as grapes

in the sun. [freq. 1] (vf: Paal) |kjv: dry| {str: 6784}

ed^m) ᴏʏᴧᴧ⅃ᴏᴧ (צימוק T-sYMWQ) — **Raisins:** Raisins that remain on the cluster. [ms: צמוק] [freq. 4] |kjv: raisins| {str: 6778}

~~~~~~~~~~

2668) ᴙᴧᴧᴏᴧ (צמר TsMR) ac: ? co: **Wool** ab: ?

N^m) ᴙᴧᴧᴏᴧ (צמר Ts-MR) — **Wool:** [freq. 16] |kjv: woolen, wool| {str: 6785}

N^f2) ᴛᴙᴧᴧᴏᴧ (צמרת TsM-RT) — **Top:** The top of the tree. [Unknown connection to root;] [freq. 5] |kjv: top, branch| {str: 6788}

~~~~~~~~~~

2669) ᴛᴧᴧᴏᴧ (צמת TsMT) ac: **Terminate** co: ? ab: **Permanent:** Something that is permanently removed or destroyed. [from: ᴛᴧᴧ - as cut off]

V) ᴛᴧᴧᴏᴧ (צמת Ts-MT) — **Terminate:** To come to a permanent end. [freq. 15] (vf: Paal, Niphal, Hiphil, Piel) |kjv: cut, destroy, vanish, consume| {str: 6789}

b^f2) ᴛʏᴛ⅃ᴧᴧᴏᴧ (צמיתות Ts-MY-TWT) — **Permanent:** Something that is continual. [ms: צמתת צמיתת] [freq. 2] |kjv: forever| {str: 6783}

~~~~~~~~~~

2670) ᴍ⅃ᴏᴧ (צנח TsNHh) ac: **Descend** co: ? ab: ?: [from: ⅃ᴏᴧ]

V) ᴍ⅃ᴏᴧ (צנח Ts-NHh) — **Descend:** To move or thrust in a downward direction. [freq. 3] (vf: Paal) |kjv: lighten, fasten| {str: 6795}

~~~~~~~~~~

2671) (צנם TsNM) ac: **Wither** co: **?** ab: **?:** [from: - a withering from lack of water or food]

V) (צנם Ts-NM) — **Wither:** [freq. 1] (vf: Paal) |kjv: wither| {str: 6798}

~~~~~~~~~~~

2672) (צנע TsNAh) ac: **Low** co: **?** ab: **?:** [from:]

V) (צנע Ts-NAh) — **Low:** To be low or humble. [freq. 2] (vf: Paal, Hiphil) |kjv: low, humble| {str: 6800}

~~~~~~~~~~~

2673) (צנף TsNP) ac: **Wrap** co: **Turban** ab: **?:** A strip of cloth that is wrapped around the head for a head covering. [from: - a cover]

V) (צנף Ts-NP) — **Wrap:** [freq. 3] (vf: Paal) |kjv: attire, turn| {str: 6801}

N^{f1}) (צנפה TsN-PH) — **Wrapped:** [freq. 1] |kjv: toss| {str: 6802}

b^{m}) (צניף Ts-NYP) — **Turban:** [df: צנוף] [freq. 1] |kjv: diadem, mitre| {str: 6797}

b^{f1}) (צניפה Ts-NY-PH) — **Turban:** [freq. 6] |kjv: hood| {str: 6797}

h^{f2}) (מצנפת MTs-N-PT) — **Turban:** [freq. 12] |kjv: mitre, diadem| {str: 4701}

~~~~~~~~~~~

2674) (צנק TsNQ) ac: **Confine** co: **Stocks** ab: **?:** [from: - as brought down in confinement]

ec^{m}) (צינוק TsY-NWQ) — **Stocks:** Used for confining a prisoner. [ms: צינק] [freq. 1] |kjv: stocks| {str: 6729}

~~~~~~~~~~~

2675) (צנר TsNR) ac: **?** co: **Pipe** ab: **?:** [from: - as bringing water down to another area]

ec^{m}) (צינור TsY-NWR) — **Pipe:** Used for moving water. [ms: צנור] [freq. 2] |kjv: gutter, waterspout| {str: 6794}

~~~~~~~~~~~

2676) (צעד TsAhD) ac: **March** co: **Bracelet** ab: **?:** The jingling of bracelets when marching.

V) (צעד Ts-AhD) — **March:** [freq. 8] (vf: Paal, Hiphil) |kjv: go, march, run, bring| {str: 6805}

N^{m}) (צעד Ts-AhD) — **Pace:** [freq. 14] |kjv: step, pace, goings, go| {str: 6806}

N^{f1}) (צעדה TsAh-DH) — **Bracelet:** An ornament worn on the ankle or wrist that jingles when walking. [freq. 3] |kjv: goings, ornament| {str: 6807}

h^{m}) (מצעד MTs-AhD) — **Step:** [freq. 3] |kjv: step, going| {str: 4703}

n^{f1}) (אצעדה ATs-Ah-DH) — **Bracelet:** An ornament worn on the ankle or wrist that jingles when walking. [freq. 2] |kjv: chain, bracelet| {str: 685}

~~~~~~~~~~~

2677) (צען TsAhN) ac: **Remove** co: **?** ab: **?:** The taking down of camp and loading onto beasts of burden. [from:]

V) סען (צען Ts-AhN) —
Remove: [freq. 1] (vf: Paal) |kjv:
take down| {str: 6813}

~~~~~~~~~

2678) סעף (צעף TsAhP) ac: **Wrap**
co: **Veil** ab: **?**: The veil is wrapped
around the face to cover it.

b^m) סעיף (צעיף Ts-AhYP) —
Veil: [freq. 3] |kjv: vail| {str: 6809}

~~~~~~~~~

2679) סעק (צעק TsAhQ) ac: **Cry** co:
? ab: **?**: A loud calling or crying out for
help or to gather an assembly. [from:
סעה]

V) סעק (צעק Ts-AhQ) — **Cry
out:** To cry or call out loudly. [freq.
55] (vf: Paal, Niphal, Hiphil, Piel)
|kjv: cry, gather, call, gather| {str:
6817}

N^{f1}) סעקה (צעקה TsAh-QH) —
Cry: A loud crying or calling out.
[freq. 21] |kjv: cry, crying| {str:
6818}

~~~~~~~~~

2680) סער (צער TsAhR) ac: **?** co:
Small ab: **?**: Small in time or size.
Someone or something that is small in
significance.

V) סער (צער Ts-AhR) — **Small:**
To be small. [freq. 3] (vf: Paal) |kjv:
low, small, little| {str: 6819}

b^m) סעיר (צעיר Ts-AhYR) —
Small: Something or someone that is
smaller, younger or less significant.
[Hebrew and Aramaic] [df: זעיר
צעור] [freq. 28] |kjv: little, younger,
least| {str: 2191, 2192, 6810}

b^{f1}) סעירה (צעירה Ts-AhY-RH)
— **Youth:** Small in age. [freq. 1]
|kjv: youth| {str: 6812}

h^m) סערم (מצער MTs-AhR) —
Small: Small in time or size or few
in number. [df: מזער] [freq. 9] |kjv:
little, few, small| {str: 4213, 4705}

hb^{f1}) סעירהם (מצעירה MTs-
AhY-RH) — **Small:** [freq. 1] |kjv:
little| {str: 4704}

~~~~~~~~~

2681) סעד (צפד TsPD) ac: **Shrivel**
co: **?** ab: **?**

V) סעד (צפד Ts-PD) —
Shrivel: [freq. 1] (vf: Paal) |kjv:
cleave| {str: 6821}

~~~~~~~~~

2682) סעח (צפח TsPHh) ac: **?** co: **?**
ab: **?**

N^{f2}) תסעח (צפחת TsP-HhT) —
Jug: For holding liquids. [freq. 7]
|kjv: cruse| {str: 6835}

b^{f4}) תסעיח (צפיחית Ts-PY-
HhYT) — **Wafer:** [ms: צפיחת] [freq.
1] |kjv: wafer| {str: 6838}

~~~~~~~~~

2683) סעל (צפן TsPN) ac: **Hide** co:
Treasure ab: **?**: A storing up or hiding of
something to prevent discovery. [from:
סע - as something watched or covered]

V) סעל (צפן Ts-PN) — **Hide:** To
hide something to prevent discovery.
[freq. 33] (vf: Paal, Niphal, Hiphil)
|kjv: hide, lay up, esteem, lurk,
privily, secret| {str: 6845}

b^m) סעיל (צפין Ts-PYN) —
Treasure: What is hidden. [freq. 1]
|kjv: hid| {str: 6840}

j^m) סעלם (מצפון MTs-PWN)
— **Treasure:** What is hidden. [ms:
מצפן] [freq. 1] |kjv: hidden| {str:
4710}

~~~~~~~~~

2684) (צפע TsPAh) ac: **Issue** co: **Serpent** ab: **?:** The tongue of the viper that issues out of its mouth. The issuing or coming out of something. [from:]

N^m^) (צפע Ts-PAh) — **Tsepha:** An unknown venomous snake. From its tongue that issues out of the mouth. [df: צפעני] [freq. 5] |kjv: cockatrice| {str: 6848}

b^f1^) (צפיעה Ts-PY-AhH) — **Descendents:** What comes out of the father. [ms: צפעה] [freq. 1] |kjv: issue| {str: 6849}

d^m^) (צפוע Ts-PWAh) — **Dung:** The dung of cattle as a coming out. [freq. 2] |kjv: dung| {str: 6832}

~~~~~~~~~~~

2685) (צפר TsPR) ac: **?** co: **Bird** ab: **Early:** The early morning appearance of birds.

V) (צפר Ts-PR) — **Depart early:** [freq. 1] (vf: Paal) |kjv: depart| {str: 6852}

N^m^) (צפר Ts-PR) — **Bird:** [Aramaic only] [freq. 4] |kjv: fowl, bird| {str: 6853}

b^m^) (צפיר Ts-PYR) — **Male goat:** [Hebrew and Aramaic] [freq. 7] |kjv: he goat| {str: 6841, 6842}

b^f1^) (צפירה Ts-PY-RH) — **Morning:** The early morning as the sun rises. [freq. 3] |kjv: morning, diadem| {str: 6843}

c^f^) (צפור Ts-PWR) — **Bird:** [ms: צפר] [freq. 40] |kjv: bird, fowl, sparrow| {str: 6833}

cm^m^) (צפורן Ts-PW-RN) — **Point:** The sharp pointed talon of a bird. Also a fingernail or the sharp point of a flint. [ms: צפרן] [freq. 2] |kjv: nail, point| {str: 6856}

~~~~~~~~~~~

2686) (צפת TsPT) ac: **?** co: **Capital** ab: **?**

N^f^) (צפת Ts-PT) — **Capital:** The top of a column. [freq. 1] |kjv: chapiter| {str: 6858}

~~~~~~~~~~~

2687) (צקל TsQL) ac: **?** co: **?** ab: **?**

ej ^m^) (ציקלון TsY-Q-LWN) — **Sack:** [ms: צקלון] [freq. 1] |kjv: husk| {str: 6861}

~~~~~~~~~~~

2688) (צרב TsRB) ac: **Scorch** co: **?** ab: **?**

V) (צרב Ts-RB) — **Scorch:** [freq. 1] (vf: Niphal) |kjv: burn| {str: 6866}

N^f2^) (צרבת TsR-BT) — **Scorching:** [freq. 3] |kjv: burning| {str: 6867}

~~~~~~~~~~~

2689) (צרח TsRHh) ac: **Shout** co: **?** ab: **Stronghold**

V) (צרח Ts-RHh) — **Shout:** To cry out in battle. [freq. 2] (vf: Paal, Hiphil) |kjv: cry, roar| {str: 6873}

b^m^) (צריח Ts-RYHh) — **Stronghold:** In the sense of shouting out in battle. [freq. 4] |kjv: hold, high| {str: 6877}

~~~~~~~~~~~

2690) (צרך TsRK) ac: **?** co: **?** ab: **Need**

g^m) ᴜᴊᴀᵞᴏ∧ (צורך T-sWRK) —
Need: [ms: צרך] [freq. 1] |kjv: need|
{str: 6878}

2691) ๑ณิ๒∧ (צרע TsRAh) ac: **Infect**
co: **Welt** ab: **?:** An infection of the skin,
usually leprosy, that causes welts. Also an
infection of mildew or mold, as welts, on
clothing or a building.

V) ๑ณิ๒∧ (צרע Ts-RAh) — **Infect:**
To be infected with leprosy, mildew
or mold. [freq. 20] (vf: Paal, Pual)
|kjv: leper, leprous| {str: 6879}

N^{f2}) †๑ณิ๒∧ (צרעת TsR-AhT) —
Infection: An infection of the skin,
cloth or a building. [freq. 35] |kjv:
leprosy| {str: 6883}

e^{f1}) ꙮ๑ฯᴏ∧ (צירעה TsYR-AhH)
— **Hornet:** From the welt when
stung. [ms: צרעה] [freq. 3] |kjv:
hornet| {str: 6880}

2692) ๑ณิ๒∧ (צרף TsRP) ac: **Refine**
co: **Crucible** ab: **?:** The melting of metals
in a crucible to remove the impurities and
pour into a mold.

V) ๑ณิ๒∧ (צרף Ts-RP) — **Refine:**
[freq. 33] (vf: Paal, Niphal, Piel,
Participle) |kjv: try, founder,
goldsmith, refine, melt, pure, purge,
cast, finer| {str: 6884}

a^m) ๑ณิ๒∧ᴡᴡ (מצרף MTs-RP) —
Crucible: Used for melting metals.
[freq. 2] |kjv: pot| {str: 4715}

Quph

2693) ✔ʙ-✦ (קבל QBL) ac: **Take** co: **War** ab: **Before:** Something placed in front and taken, received or chosen.

V) ✔ʙ-✦ (קבל Q-BL) — **Take hold:** To take or receive what has been given. [Hebrew and Aramaic] [freq. 16] (vf: Hiphil, Piel) |kjv: receive, take, choose, held, undertook| {str: 6901, 6902}

N^m) ✔ʙ-✦ (קבל Q-BL) — **Before:** Being in front of something, in space or time. In the sense of taking what is in front. [Hebrew and Aramaic] [freq. 30] |kjv: before, as, according, against| {str: 6903, 6905}

g^m) ✔ʙY-✦ (קובל QW-BL) — **War:** In the sense of taking. [ms: קבל] [freq. 1] |kjv: war| {str: 6904}

~~~~~~~~~

2694) ⊙ʙ-✦ (קבע QBAh) ac: **Drain** co: **Bowl** ab: **?:** Something drained of its contents. [from: ʙ-✦ - as an empty cavity]

V) ⊙ʙ-✦ (קבע Q-BAh) — **Drain:** To empty something of its contents. [freq. 6] (vf: Paal) |kjv: rob, spoil| {str: 6906}

N^f2) †⊙ʙ-✦ (קבעת QB-AhT) — **Drained:** Something that is emptied of its contents. [freq. 2] |kjv: dregs| {str: 6907}

g^m) ⊙ʙY-✦ (קובע QW-BAh) — **Helmet:** As an empty bowl. [freq. 2] |kjv: helmet| {str: 6959}

~~~~~~~~~

2695) ◠ʙ-✦ (קבץ QBTs) ac: **Gather** co: **?** ab: **?:** [from: ʙ-✦ - storage]

V) ◠ʙ-✦ (קבץ Q-BTs) — **Gather:** [freq. 127] (vf: Paal, Niphal, Hitpael, Pual, Piel) |kjv: gather, assemble, heap, resort| {str: 6908}

N^f1) ⚹◠ʙ-✦ (קבצה QB-TsH) — **Gathering:** [freq. 1] |kjv: gather| {str: 6910}

d^m) ◠ʙY-✦ (קבוץ Q-BWTs) — **Company:** A group of gathered people. [freq. 1] |kjv: company| {str: 6899}

~~~~~~~~~

2696) ʙ-✦ (קבר QBR) ac: **Bury** co: **Grave** ab: **?:** The act and place of burying the dead. [from: ʙ-✦ - gathering one to the forefathers in a cavity]

V) ʙ-✦ (קבר Q-BR) — **Bury:** [freq. 133] (vf: Paal, Niphal, Pual, Piel) |kjv: bury| {str: 6912}

N^m) ʙ-✦ (קבר Q-BR) — **Grave:** [freq. 67] |kjv: grave, sepulcher| {str: 6913}

d^f1) ⚹ʙY-✦ (קבורה Q-BW-RH) — **Grave:** [ms: קברה] [freq. 14] |kjv: sepulcher, grave, burial| {str: 6900}

~~~~~~~~~

2697) ☳ᴛ-✦ (קדח QDHh) ac: **Heat** co: **?** ab: **?:** [from: ᴛ-✦]

V) ☳ᴛ-✦ (קדח Q-DHh) — **Kindle:** To kindle a fire. [freq. 5] (vf: Paal) |kjv: kindle, burn| {str: 6919}

N^f2) †☳ᴛ-✦ (קדחת QD-HhT) — **Fever:** [freq. 2] |kjv: burning, fever| {str: 6920}

n^m) ⊐⊏ㅠ-•-⤳ (אקדח AQ-DHh) —
Eqdahh: A bright red gem. [freq. 1]
|kjv: carbuncle| {str: 688}

2698) ᴍᴍㅠ-•- (קדם QDM) ac: **Face** co:
East ab: **Before:** The place of the rising
sun. The Hebrews recognized the east as
the top of the four compass points
(contrary to our understanding of north)
and is the direction faced when orienting
direction. The past is understood as what
is in front, or before, you as the past is
known (contrary to our understanding of
the future being in front of us). [from:
ᴍᴍㅠ - the red color blood combined with
the quph as the rising sun, hence the
"rising sun of blood"]

V) ᴍᴍㅠ-•- (קדם Q-DM) — **Face:**
To go or meet face to face. To go
before someone or something in
space or time. [freq. 26] (vf: Hiphil,
Piel) |kjv: prevent, before, met, come,
disappoint, go| {str: 6923}

N^m) ᴍᴍㅠ-•- (קדם Q-DM) — **I.
East: II. Ancient:** A distant past. **III.
Before:** In front or to the face. Also a
time before. [freq. 87] |kjv: east, old,
eastward, ancient, before, aforetime,
eternal| {str: 6924}

N^{f1}) ⚹ᴍᴍㅠ-•- (קדמה QD-MH) —
Before: Something in front, or to the
face. A time past. [Hebrew and
Aramaic] [freq. 8] |kjv: former, old,
afore, antiquity, ago, aforetime| {str:
6927, 6928}

b^m) ᴍᴍ⤳ㅠ-•- (קדים Q-DYM) —
East: [ms: קדם] [freq. 69] |kjv: east,
eastward| {str: 6921}

d^m) ᴍᴍYㅠ-•- (קדום Q-DWM) —
Ancient: A distant past. [freq. 1]
|kjv: ancient| {str: 6917}

e^{f1}) ⚹ᴍᴍㅠ-⤳-•- (קידמה QYD-MH)
— **East:** [ms: קדמה] [freq. 4] |kjv:
east, eastward| {str: 6926}

f^m) ⤳-ᴍᴍㅠ-•- (קדמי Q-D-MY) —
First: As what came before.
[Aramaic only] [freq. 3] |kjv: first|
{str: 6933}

g^m) ᴍᴍㅠY-•- (קודם QW-DM) —
Before: Something in front, or to the
face. [Aramaic only] [ms: קדם]
[freq. 42] |kjv: before, him| {str:
6925}

j^m) ⅃Yᴍᴍㅠ-•- (קדמון QD-MWN) —
East: [freq. 1] |kjv: east| {str: 6930}

jf^m) ⤳-⅃Yᴍᴍㅠ-•- (קדמוני QD-MW-
NY) — **I. East:** [ms: קדמני] **II.
Ancient:** A distant past. **III. Before:**
In front or to the face. Also a time
before. [freq. 10] |kjv: east, former,
ancient, before, old| {str: 6931}

2699) ᴺㅠ-•- (קדר QDR) ac: **?** co: **Dark**
ab: **Darkness:** [from: ㅠ-•- - something
burnt]

V) ᴺㅠ-•- (קדר Q-DR) — **Dark:** To
be dark from a lack of light or in
mourning. [freq. 17] (vf: Paal,
Hiphil, Hitpael) |kjv: mourn, black,
dark, blackish, heavily| {str: 6937}

N^{f3}) †Yᴺㅠ-•- (קדרות QD-RWT) —
Darkness: [freq. 1] |kjv: blackness|
{str: 6940}

cm^{f4}) †-⅃ᴺᴀYㅠ-•- (קדורנית Q-DW-
R-NYT) — **Darkened:** [ms: קדרנית]
[freq. 1] |kjv: mournfully| {str: 6941}

2700) ᴘᴘㅠ-•- (קדש QDSh) ac: **Set
apart** co: **Prostitute** ab: **Special:** Set
apart from the rest for a special function.
[from: ㅠ⊐⊏ - separating and joining to
something]

V) ⊔⊓⌐-✲ (קדש Q-DSh) — **Set apart:** To set someone or something apart for a special purpose. [freq. 172] (vf: Paal, Niphal, Hiphil, Hitpael, Pual, Piel) |kjv: sanctify, hallow, dedicate, holy, prepare, consecrate, appoint, bid, purify| {str: 6942}

N^m) ⊔⊓⌐-✲ (קדש Q-DSh) — **Prostitute:** A male prostitute set aside for a special purpose. [freq. 6] |kjv: sodomite, unclean| {str: 6945}

N^fl) ⚲⊔⊓⌐-✲ (קדשה QD-ShH) — **Prostitute:** A female prostitute set aside for a special purpose. [freq. 5] |kjv: harlot, whore| {str: 6948}

b^m) ⊔⊔⊁⌐⊓-✲ (קדיש Q-DYSh) — **Special:** One who is set apart as special. [Aramaic only] [freq. 13] |kjv: saint, holy| {str: 6922}

c^m) ⊔⊔Y⊓-✲ (קדוש Q-DWSh) — **Special:** One who is set apart as special. [ms: קדש] [freq. 116] |kjv: holy, saint| {str: 6918}

g^m) ⊔⊔⊓Y-✲ (קודש QW-DSh) — **Set apart:** Someone or something that has been separated from the rest for a special purpose. [ms: קדש] [freq. 468] |kjv: holy, sanctuary, hallowed, holiness, dedicated, consecrated| {str: 6944}

h^m) ⊔⊔⊓-✲-ᴧᴧ (מקדש MQ-DSh) — **Sanctuary:** A place set apart for a special purpose. [freq. 74] |kjv: sanctuary, holy place, chapel, hallowed| {str: 4720}

~~~~~~~~

2701) ⊡⊗-✲ (קטב QThB) ac: **Destroy** co: ? ab: **Destruction:** A destruction by being cut off. [from: ⊗-✲ - made short by cutting]

N^m) ⊡⊗-✲ (קטב Q-ThB) — **Destruction:** [freq. 3] |kjv: destruction, destroying| {str: 6986}

g^m) ⊡⊗Y-✲ (קוטב QW-ThB) — **Destruction:** [ms: קטב] [freq. 1] |kjv: destruction| {str: 6987}

~~~~~~~~

2702) ᐁ⊗-✲ (קטל QThL) ac: **Kill** co: ? ab: **?:** A cutting off by killing. [from: ⊗-✲ - made short by cutting]

V) ᐁ⊗-✲ (קטל Q-ThL) — **Kill:** [Hebrew and Aramaic] [freq. 10] (vf: Paal) |kjv: slay, kill| {str: 6991, 6992}

N^m) ᐁ⊗-✲ (קטל Q-ThL) — **Slaughter:** [freq. 1] |kjv: slaughter| {str: 6993}

~~~~~~~~

2703) ⊾⊗-✲ (קטן QThN) ac: **?** co: **Small** ab: **?:** Someone or something that is small in size, importance, age or significance. [from: ⊗-✲-]

V) ⊾⊗-✲ (קטן Q-ThN) — **Small:** To be small or insignificant. [freq. 4] (vf: Paal, Hiphil) |kjv: small, not worthy| {str: 6994}

N^m) ⊾⊗-✲ (קטן Q-ThN) — **Small:** [freq. 101] |kjv: small, little, youngest, younger, least, less, lesser, young| {str: 6996}

g^m) ⊾⊗Y-✲ (קוטן QW-ThN) — **Small:** [ms: קטן] [freq. 2] |kjv: little| {str: 6995}

~~~~~~~~

2704) ⇔⊗-✲ (קטף QThP) ac: **Pluck** co: **?** ab: **?:** A plucking or picking off as being cut down. [from: ⊗-✲ - made short by cutting]

V) ⌐⊗-❖- (קטף Q-ThP) — **Pluck:** [freq. 5] (vf: Paal, Niphal) |kjv: crop, pluck, cut| {str: 6998}

~~~~~~~~

2705) ᕼ⊗-❖- (קטר QThR) ac: **Burn** co: **Incense** ab: ?: The aromatic burning of incense or fat as an offering. [from: ⊗-❖- - made short by killing]

V) ᕼ⊗-❖- (קטר Q-ThR) — **I. Burn:** To burn a sacrifice or incense. **II. Join:** [Unknown connection to root;] [freq. 118] (vf: Paal, Hiphil, Hophal, Piel, Pual) |kjv: incense, burn, offer, kindle, offering| {str: 6999, 7000}

c[fl]**)** ᕼᕼᎩ⊗-❖- (קטורה Q-ThW-RH) — **Incense:** [freq. 1] |kjv: incense| {str: 6988}

c[f2]**)** †ᕼᎩ⊗-❖- (קטורת Q-ThW-RT) — **Incense:** [ms: קטרת] [freq. 60] |kjv: incense, perfume| {str: 7004}

e[f]**)** ᕼ⊗꒱-❖- (קיטר QY-ThR) — **Incense:** [ms: קטר] [freq. 1] |kjv: incense| {str: 7002}

h[m]**)** ᕼ⊗-❖-ᴧᴧ (מקטר MQ-ThR) — **Burning:** A place for burning incense. [freq. 1] |kjv: burn| {str: 4729}

h[f2]**)** †ᕼ⊗-❖-ᴧᴧ (מקטרת MQ-Th-RT) — **Censer:** What is used to hold the incense. [freq. 2] |kjv: censor| {str: 4730}

ec[m]**)** ᕼᎩ⊗꒱-❖- (קיטור QY-ThWR) — **Smoke:** The smoke of the burning incense or fat. [ms: קיטר] [freq. 4] |kjv: smoke, vapour| {str: 7008}

~~~~~~~~

2706) �urᐗ-❖- (קלח QLHh) ac: ? co: ? ab: ?

N[f2]**)** ᴤᴜᴧᐗ-❖- (קלח Q-LHh) — **Kettle:** [freq. 2] |kjv: caldron| {str: 7037}

~~~~~~~~

2707) ⊗ᐗ-❖- (קלט QLTh) ac: **Hide** co: ? ab: ?: [from: ⊗ᐗ - hiding behind a covering]

V) ⊗ᐗ-❖- (קלט Q-LTh) — **Deform:** To be physically deformed in some manner which is usually covered. [freq. 1] (vf: Paal) |kjv: lacking| {str: 7038}

h[m]**)** ⊗ᐗ-❖-ᴧᴧ (מקלט MQ-LTh) — **Refuge:** A place one may run to for safety from an avenger. [freq. 20] |kjv: refuge| {str: 4733}

~~~~~~~~

2708) ᕞᐗ-❖- (קלס QLS) ac: **Ridicule** co: ? ab: ?: [from: ᴧᐗ - mocking]

V) ᕞᐗ-❖- (קלס Q-LS) — **Ridicule:** [freq. 4] (vf: Hitpael, Piel) |kjv: mock, scorn, scoff| {str: 7046}

N[m]**)** ᕞᐗ-❖- (קלס Q-LS) — **Ridicule:** [freq. 3] |kjv: derision| {str: 7047}

N[fl]**)** ᕼᕞᐗ-❖- (קלסה QL-SH) — **Ridiculing:** [freq. 1] |kjv: mocking| {str: 7048}

~~~~~~~~

2709) ⌐ᐗ-❖- (קלע QLAh) ac: **Hurl** co: **Sling** ab: ?: The hurling of a stone from sling. [from: ᐗ-❖- - always carried by the shepherd in his bag for protection]

V) ⌐ᐗ-❖- (קלע Q-LAh) — **I. Hurl:** To throw stones with a sling. **II. Carve:** To carve figures. [Unknown connection to root;] [freq. 7] (vf: Paal, Piel, Participle) |kjv: sling, carve| {str: 7049}

N[m]**)** ⌐ᐗ-❖- (קלע Q-LAh) — **I. Sling:** The sling used to throw stones. Also something that hangs like a sling. **II. Slinger:** One who slings stones. [freq. 23] |kjv: hanging, sling, leaves| {str: 7050, 7051} h^f2) †⊙-⊷-ᴀᴧᴧ (מִקְלַעַת MQ-L-AhT) — **Figure:** A carved figure. [Unknown connection to root;] [freq. 4] |kjv: carved, figures, carving, graving| {str: 4734}

~~~~~~~~~

2710) ʟʟʟᴠ/-⊷ (קְלֹשׁ QLSh) ac: **Grab** co: **Fork** ab: **?**

ej^m) ˥ʏʟʟʟᴠ>⊣⊷ (קִילְשׁוֹן QY-L-ShWN) — **Fork:** A tool used for pitching hay. [ms: קִלְחוֹן] [freq. 1] |kjv: fork| {str: 7053}

~~~~~~~~~

2711) ᴄᴄᴀᴧᴧ-⊷ (קָמַח QMHh) ac: **Grind** co: **Meal** ab: **?**: Grain is ground into a meal for making breads. [from: ᴀᴧᴧ-⊷]

N^m) ᴄᴄᴀᴧᴧ-⊷ (קָמַח Q-MHh) — **Meal:** [freq. 14] |kjv: meal, flour| {str: 7058}

~~~~~~~~~

2712) ⊗ᴀᴧᴧ-⊷ (קָמַט QMTh) ac: **Snatch** co: **?** ab: **?**: A snatching away of something. [from: ᴀᴧᴧ-⊷]

V) ⊗ᴀᴧᴧ-⊷ (קָמַט Q-MTh) — **Snatch:** [freq. 2] (vf: Paal, Pual) |kjv: cut down, wrinkle| {str: 7059}

~~~~~~~~~

2713) ᴠᴧᴧ-⊷ (קָמַל QML) ac: **Wither** co: **?** ab: **?**: [from: ᴀᴧᴧ-⊷]

V) ᴠᴧᴧ-⊷ (קָמַל Q-ML) — **Wither:** [freq. 2] (vf: Paal) |kjv: wither, hew| {str: 7060}

~~~~~~~~~

2714) ᴏᴧᴀᴧᴧ-⊷ (קָמַץ QMTs) ac: **Grasp** co: **Handful** ab: **?**: [from: ᴀᴧᴧ-⊷]

V) ᴏᴧᴀᴧᴧ-⊷ (קָמַץ Q-MTs) — **Grasp:** To grab with the hands, to grab a handful. [freq. 3] (vf: Paal) |kjv: take| {str: 7061}

g^m) ᴏᴧᴀᴧᴧʏ-⊷ (קוֹמֶץ QW-MTs) — **Grasp:** [ms: קֹמֶץ] [freq. 4] |kjv: handful| {str: 7062}

~~~~~~~~~

2715) ʟʟʟᴀᴧᴧ-⊷ (קָמַשׁ QMSh) ac: **Cling** co: **Thorn** ab: **?**: A thorn pierces the flesh and clings to the skin. [from: ᴀᴧᴧ-⊷]

ec^m) ʟʟʏᴀᴧᴧ>⊣⊷ (קִימוֹשׁ QY-MWSh) — **Thorn:** [ms: קִמּוֹשׁ] [freq. 2] |kjv: nettle| {str: 7057}

ej^m) ˥ʏʟʟᴀᴧᴧ>⊣⊷ (קִימְשׂוֹן QY-M-ShWN) — **Thorn:** [ms: קִימְשׂוֹן] [freq. 1] |kjv: thorn| {str: 7063}

~~~~~~~~~

2716) ᴀᴧᴧˀ-⊷ (קָנַם QNM) ac: **?** co: **Spice** ab: **?**: A fragrant bark used as spice. (eng: cinnamon)

j^m) ˥ʏᴀᴧᴧˀ-⊷ (קִנָּמוֹן QN-MWN) — **Cinnamon:** [freq. 3] |kjv: cinnamon| {str: 7076}

~~~~~~~~~

2717) ᴏᴧᴧˀ-⊷ (קָנַץ QNTs) ac: **?** co: **End** ab: **?**: [from: ᴏᴧᴧ-⊷ - to make an end of something]

N^m) ᴏᴧᴧˀ-⊷ (קֵנֶץ Q-NTs) — **End:** To come to an end. [freq. 1] |kjv: end| {str: 7078}

~~~~~~~~~

2718) ᴀᴧᴧ≋-⊷ (קָסַם QSM) ac: **?** co: **?** ab: **Divine**

V) ᴀᴧᴧ≋-⊷ (קָסַם Q-SM) — **Divine:** To practice divination. [freq. 20] (vf: Paal) |kjv: divine, diviner, use, divination, prudent, soothsayer| {str: 7080}

435

N^m) ᨓ⧫⊶ (קסם Q-SM) — **Divination:** [freq. 11] |kjv: divination, witchcraft, divine| {str: 7081}

h^m) ᨓ⧫⊶ᨓ (מקסם MQ-SM) — **Divination:** [freq. 2] |kjv: divination| {str: 4738}

~~~~~~~~

2719) ᖫ⊙⊶ (קער QAhR) ac: ? co: **Dish** ab: ?: A hollowed out container. [from: ᨓ]

N^{f1}) ⚶ᖫ⊙⊶ (קערה QAh-RH) — **Dish:** [freq. 17] |kjv: charger, dish| {str: 7086}

~~~~~~~~

2720) ᅲ⊙⊶ (קפד QPD) ac: **Shrink** co: ? ab: **Anguish:** [from: ⊙⊶ - contracting]

V) ᅲ⊙⊶ (קפד Q-PD) — **Shrink:** [freq. 1] (vf: Piel) |kjv: cut off| {str: 7088}

N^{f1}) ⚶ᅲ⊙⊶ (קפדה QP-DH) — **Anguish:** As a shrinking. [freq. 1] |kjv: destruction| {str: 7089}

ec^m) ᅲY⊙ᐟᇈ⊶ (קיפוד QY-PWD) — **Qiyphod:** An unknown animal. [ms: קפד קפוד] [freq. 3] |kjv: bittern| {str: 7090}

~~~~~~~~

2721) ᙇᐸ⊙⊶ (קפז QPZ) ac: **Leap** co: ? ab: ?: [from: ⊙⊶ - seasons contracting]

ec^m) ᙇY⊙ᐟᇈ⊶ (קיפוז QY-PWZ) — **Qiphoz:** An unknown bird. [ms: קפוז] [freq. 1] |kjv: owl| {str: 7091}

~~~~~~~~

2722) ᦓ⊙⊶ (קפץ QPTs) ac: **Close** co: ? ab: ?: A closing in the sense of drawing together. [from: ⊙⊶ - seasons contracting]

V) ᦓ⊙⊶ (קפץ Q-PTs) — **Close:** To draw together to close or shut. [freq. 7] (vf: Paal, Niphal, Piel, Participle) |kjv: shut, stop, skip, take out| {str: 7092}

~~~~~~~~

2723) ᨇᦓᐸ⊶ (קצב QTsB) ac: **Sheer** co: **Base** ab: ?: The remaining portion after being sheered off. [from: ᦓᐸ⊶]

V) ᨇᦓᐸ⊶ (קצב Q-TsB) — **Sheer:** [freq. 2] (vf: Paal) |kjv: cut down, shorn| {str: 7094}

N^m) ᨇᦓᐸ⊶ (קצב Q-TsB) — **Base:** What remains when sheered off. [freq. 3] |kjv: size, bottom| {str: 7095}

~~~~~~~~

2724) ᨑᦓᐸ⊶ (קצח QTsHh) ac: ? co: ? ab: ?

N^m) ᨑᦓᐸ⊶ (קצח Q-TsHh) — **Qetsahh:** An unknown plant. [freq. 3] |kjv: fitch| {str: 7100}

~~~~~~~~

2725) ⊙ᦓᐸ⊶ (קצע QTsAh) ac: **Scrape** co: **Plane** ab: ?: The scraping of a beam with a plane to form corners. [from: ᦓᐸ⊶]

V) ⊙ᦓᐸ⊶ (קצע Q-TsAh) — **Scrape:** [freq. 2] (vf: Hiphil, Hophal) |kjv: scrape, corner| {str: 7106}

b^{f1}) ⚶⊙ᐟᦓᐸ⊶ (קציעה Q-TsY-AhH) — **Cassia:** A spice scraped from the tree. [freq. 1] |kjv: cassia| {str: 7102}

ac^{f1}) ⚶⊙Yᦓᐸ⊶ᨓ (מקצועה MQ-TsW-AhH) — **Plane:** A scraping tool used to make flat surfaces and corners. [ms: מקצעה] [freq. 1] |kjv: plane| {str: 4741}

hc[m]) ⊙Y◦ᴧ-◦ᴧᴧ (מקצוע MQ-TsWAh) — **Corner:** As scraped out with a plane. [ms: מקצע] [freq. 12] |kjv: corner, turning| {str: 4740}

ko[fl]) Ꙩ⊙◦ᴧY-◦ᴧᴧ (מקוצעה M-QW-Ts-AhH) — **Corner:** As scraped out with a plane. [ms: מקצעה] [freq. 2] |kjv: corner| {str: 4742}

~~~~~~~

2726) ⟨◦ᴧ-◦ (קצף QTsP) ac: **Snap** co: **Splinter** ab: **Wrath:** The snapping of a piece of wood sending splinters flying. [from: ◦ᴧ-◦]

V) ⟨◦ᴧ-◦ (קצף Q-TsP) — **Snap:** To snap and splinter a piece of wood. Also to lash out in anger as a splintering. [Hebrew and Aramaic] [freq. 35] (vf: Paal, Hiphil, Hitpael) |kjv: wrath, displease, angry, fret, furious| {str: 7107, 7108}

N[m]) ⟨◦ᴧ-◦ (קצף Q-TsP) — **Splinter:** The flying splinters from a piece of snapped piece of wood. Also wrath as flying splinters. [Hebrew and Aramaic] [freq. 30] |kjv: wrath, indignation, sore, foam| {str: 7109, 7110}

N[fl]) Ꙩ⟨◦ᴧ-◦ (קצפה QTs-PH) — **Snapped:** The snapping and splintering of wood. [freq. 1] |kjv: barked| {str: 7111}

~~~~~~~

2727) ꜰ◦ᴧ-◦ (קצר QTsR) ac: **Sever** co: **Short** ab: **?:** The cutting short of something such as the reaping of the harvest where the stalks are made short or patience which can be cut short. [from: ◦ᴧ-◦ - being cut short]

V) ꜰ◦ᴧ-◦ (קצר Q-TsR) — **Sever:** To cut something short or small. Often in the sense of harvesting where the plant is severed at that stalk or short in patience as being severed. [freq. 49] (vf: Paal, Hiphil, Piel) |kjv: reap, reaper, shorten, shorter, discourage, loathe, straiten| {str: 7114}

N[m]) ꜰ◦ᴧ-◦ (קצר Q-TsR) — **Short:** As being cut off prematurely. [freq. 5] |kjv: small, few, soon, hasty| {str: 7116}

b[m]) ꜰ◞-◦ᴧ-◦ (קציר Q-TsYR) — **I. Harvest:** The time when the plants are severed. **II. Branch:** In the sense of being severed from the plant. [freq. 54] |kjv: harvest, bough, branch, harvestman| {str: 7105}

g[m]) ꜰ◦ᴧY-◦ (קוצר QW-TsR) — **Short:** In patience. [ms: קצר] [freq. 1] |kjv: anguish| {str: 7115}

~~~~~~~

2728) ᴊ-◦-◦ (קקל QQL) ac: **?** co: **?** ab: **Shame:** [from: ᴊ-◦ - as light]

ej[m]) ᴧYᴊ-◦-◞-◦ (קיקלון QY-Q-LWN) — **Shame:** [freq. 1] |kjv: shameful| {str: 7022}

~~~~~~~

2729) ᴍꜰ◦-◦ (קרב QRB) ac: **Approach** co: **Near** ab: **?:** A bringing, giving or approaching of someone or something to be close, at hand or among.

V) ᴍꜰ◦-◦ (קרב Q-RB) — **Approach:** To come near. [Hebrew and Aramaic] [freq. 289] (vf: Paal, Niphal, Hiphil, Piel) |kjv: offer, near, bring, nigh, come, approach, at hand, present| {str: 7126, 7127}

N[m]) ᴍꜰ◦-◦ (קרב Q-RB) — **I. Within:** In the sense of being close.

II. Near: III. Battle: In the sense of coming near. [Hebrew and Aramaic] [freq. 248] |kjv: among, midst, within, inward, in, nigh, near, approach, came, battle, war| {str: 7128, 7129, 7130, 7131}

N^(fl)) 𐤔ᴎᕋ❂- (קרבה QR-BH) — **Near:** [freq. 2] |kjv: near, approach| {str: 7132}

c^m) ᴌᵞᕋ❂- (קרוב Q-RWB) — **I. Near:** [ms: קרב] **II. Kin:** As a near relative. [freq. 78] |kjv: near, nigh, neighbour, next, kin, approach, short, kinsfolk, kinsmen| {str: 7138}

gm^m) ᵞᴍᕋᵞ-❂- (קורבן QW-R-BN) — **Offering:** As brought near to another. [ms: קרבן] [freq. 82] |kjv: offering, oblation, sacrifice| {str: 7133}

2730) ᴍᕋ❂- (קרח QRHh) ac: **Shave** co: **Bald** ab: ?: [from: ᕋ❂- - as being cold]

V) ᴍᕋ❂- (קרח Q-RHh) — **Shave:** To shave the hair of the head to make bald. [freq. 5] (vf: Paal, Niphal, Hiphil, Hophal) |kjv: make| {str: 7139}

N^m) ᴍᕋ❂- (קרח Q-RHh) — **I. Bald: II. Ice:** Frost or crystals as smooth like a bald head. [freq. 10] |kjv: bald, frost, ice, crystal| {str: 7140, 7142}

N^(fl)) 𐤔ᴍᕋ❂- (קרחה QR-HhH) — **Baldness:** [df: קרחא] [freq. 11] |kjv: baldness, bald| {str: 7144}

N^(f2)) †ᴍᕋ❂- (קרחת QR-HhT) — **Baldness:** [freq. 4] |kjv: bald, bare| {str: 7146}

2731) ᴍᴍᕋ❂- (קרם QRM) ac: **Cover** co: ? ab: ?: [from: ᕋ❂-]

V) ᴍᴍᕋ❂- (קרם Q-RM) — **Cover:** To spread or lay over. [freq. 2] (vf: Paal) |kjv: cover| {str: 7159}

2732) ᴌᕋ❂- (קרן QRN) ac: ? co: **Horn** ab: ?

V) ᴌᕋ❂- (קרן Q-RN) — **Horns:** To have horns. Also to shine as rays of light as like horns. [freq. 4] (vf: Paal, Hiphil) |kjv: shine, horns| {str: 7160}

N^f) ᴌᕋ❂- (קרן Q-RN) — **Horn:** The horns of an animal or a musical instrument in the shape of a horn. [Hebrew and Aramaic] [freq. 90] |kjv: horn, hill| {str: 7161, 7162}

2733) ᕒᕋ❂- (קרס QRS) ac: **Crouch** co: **Hump** ab: ?

V) ᕒᕋ❂- (קרס Q-RS) — **Crouch:** To stoop over as a hunched back. [freq. 2] (vf: Paal) |kjv: stoop| {str: 7164}

N^m) ᕒᕋ❂- (קרס Q-RS) — **Hook:** As with a hump at the bend. [freq. 10] |kjv: taches| {str: 7165}

2734) ᴏᕋ❂- (קרע QRAh) ac: **Tear** co: **Piece** ab: ?: The tearing of a cloth into pieces.

V) ᴏᕋ❂- (קרע Q-RAh) — **Tear:** To tear a cloth into pieces. [freq. 63] (vf: Paal, Niphal) |kjv: rent, tear, rend, cut| {str: 7167}

N^m) ᴏᕋ❂- (קרע Q-RAh) — **Piece:** A torn piece of cloth. [freq. 4] |kjv: piece, rag| {str: 7168}

2735) ᴏᴎᕋ❂- (קרץ QRTs) ac: **Pinch** co: ? ab: ?

V) (קרץ Q-RTs) — **I. Pinch:** Also to pinch the eye (wink) or the lips. [Hebrew and Aramaic] **II. Accuse:** In the sense of pinching another. [Aramaic only] [freq. 7] (vf: Paal, Pual) |kjv: wink, move, form, accuse| {str: 7169, 7170}

N^m) (קרץ Q-RTs) — **Qerets:** An unknown insect that bites, as a pinching. [freq. 1] |kjv: destruction| {str: 7171}

~~~~~~~~~~

2736) (קרש QRSh) ac: **?** co: **Board** ab: **?**

N^m) (קרש Q-RSh) — **Board:** [freq. 51] |kjv: board, bench| {str: 7175}

~~~~~~~~~~

2737) (קשב QShB) ac: **Heed** co: **?** ab: **?:** The pricking of the ears to intently listen.

V) (קשב Q-ShB) — **Heed:** To hear and pay attention. [freq. 46] (vf: Paal, Hiphil) |kjv: hear, attend, heed, incline, mark, regard| {str: 7181}

N^m) (קשב Q-ShB) — **Respond:** [freq. 4] |kjv: record, hearing, heed| {str: 7182}

d^m) (קשוב Q-ShWB) — **Attentive:** [ms: קשב] [freq. 5] |kjv: attentive, attent| {str: 7183}

~~~~~~~~~~

2738) (קשח QShHh) ac: **Harden** co: **?** ab: **?:** A hardening of the heart toward another. [from:]

V) (קשח Q-ShHh) — **Harden:** [freq. 2] (vf: Hiphil) |kjv: harden| {str: 7188}

~~~~~~~~~~

2739) (קשט QShTh) ac: **Weigh** co: **?** ab: **Truth:** A weighing in a balance scale.

b^f1) (קשיטה Q-ShY-ThH) — **Qeshiytah:** A unit of value, money. [ms: קשׂטה] [freq. 3] |kjv: money, silver| {str: 7192}

c^m) (קשוט Q-ShWTh) — **Truth:** In the sense of weighing. [ms: קשט] [freq. 2] |kjv: truth| {str: 7187}

g^m) (קושט QW-ShTh) — **Truth:** In the sense of weighing. [ms: קשט] [freq. 2] |kjv: certainty, truth| {str: 7189}

~~~~~~~~~~

2740) (קשר QShR) ac: **Tie** co: **Sash** ab: **Conspire:** A sash that is tied around the waist.

V) (קשר Q-ShR) — **I. Tie:** To tie around. **II. Conspire:** In the sense of tying up. [freq. 44] (vf: Paal, Niphal, Hitpael, Pual, Piel, Participle) |kjv: conspire, bind, make, stronger| {str: 7194}

N^m) (קשר Q-ShR) — **Conspiracy:** As a tying up. [freq. 16] |kjv: conspiracy, treason, confederacy| {str: 7195}

ed^m) (קישור QY-ShWR) — **Sash:** [ms: קשר] [freq. 2] |kjv: headband, attire| {str: 7196}

~~~~~~~~~~

2741) (קשת QShT) ac: **?** co: **Archer** ab: **?:** [from: - a shooter of a bow]

N^m) (קשת Q-ShT) — **Archer:** [freq. 1] |kjv: archer| {str: 7199}

~~~~~~~~~~
~~~~~~~~~~

Resh

2742) ᴛᴜৰ (רבד RBD) ac: **Spread** co: **Sheet** ab: ?: Spread out as a bed covering. [from: ᴜৰ - spread out]

V) ᴛᴜৰ (רבד R-BD) — **Spread out:** [freq. 1] (vf: Paal) |kjv: deck| {str: 7234}

a[m] ᴛᴜৰᴡ (מרבד MR-BD) — **Sheet:** As spread out. [freq. 2] |kjv: covering| {str: 4765}

b[m] ᴛʏᴜৰ (רביד R-BYD) — **Chain:** As spread over the neck. [freq. 2] |kjv: chain| {str: 7242}

2743) ᴜᴜৰ (רבך RBK) ac: **Mix** co: ? ab: ?

V) ᴜᴜৰ (רבך R-BK) — **Mix:** [freq. 3] (vf: Hophal) |kjv: fry, bake| {str: 7246}

2744) ᴜৰ (רבע RBAh) ac: ? co: **Square** ab: ?: The four sides of a square. [from: ᴜৰ - spread out]

V) ᴜৰ (רבע R-BAh) — **Square:** To go down on the hands and knees in the sense of being on all fours. [freq. 15] (vf: Paal, Hiphil, Pual, Participle) |kjv: square, foursquare, lay down, gender| {str: 7250, 7251}

N[m] ᴜৰ (רבע R-BAh) — **I. Squared:** On the hands and knees in the sense of being on all fours. **II. Quarter:** As one side of a four sided square or a fourth. [freq. 8] |kjv: lying down, side fourth, square| {str: 7252, 7253}

e [m] ᴜʏৰ (ריבע RYB-Ah) — **Fourth:** [ms: רבע] [freq. 4] |kjv: fourth| {str: 7256}

g[m] ᴜʏৰ (רובע RW-BAh) — **Fourth:** [ms: רבע] [freq. 2] |kjv: fourth| {str: 7255}

n[m] ᴜৰʏ (ארבע AR-BAh) — **Four:** [Hebrew and Aramaic; Also meaning forty when written in the plural form - ᴡʏᴜৰʏ] [freq. 144] |kjv: four, fourth, forty, fortieth| {str: 702, 703, 705}

n[fl] ᴥᴜৰʏ (ארבעה AR-B-AhH) — **Four:** [freq. 316] |kjv: four| {str: 702}

bf[m] ʏᴜʏৰ (רביעי R-BY-AhY) — **Fourth:** [Hebrew and Aramaic] [ms: רבעי] [freq. 62] |kjv: fourth, foursquare| {str: 7243, 7244}

2745) ᴜৰ (רבץ RBTs) ac: **Lay** co: **Palate** ab: ?: The palate as a bed to lay down on to sleep or rest. [from: ᴜৰ - spread out]

V) ᴜৰ (רבץ R-BTs) — **Lay down:** To lie down to rest. [freq. 30] (vf: Paal, Hiphil) |kjv: lay, couch| {str: 7257}

N[m] ᴜৰ (רבץ R-BTs) — **Palate:** A sleeping or resting place. [freq. 4] |kjv: resting place, lay, lie down| {str: 7258}

a[m] ᴜৰᴡ (מרבץ MR-BTs) — **Palate:** A sleeping or resting place. [freq. 2] |kjv: couchingplace, lie down| {str: 4769}

2746) ᔥᕳᕬ• (רבק RBQ) ac: **?** co: **Stall** ab: **?**: [from: ᕬᔥ - spread out]

a[m]) ᔥᕳᕬᔋ (מרבק MR-BQ) — **Stall:** The resting place of livestock where they are fed and made fat. [freq. 4] |kjv: stall, fat| {str: 4770}

2747) ᔥᕳᔋ (רגב RGB) ac: **?** co: **Clod** ab: **?**: A pile or lump of clay.

N[m]) ᔥᕳᔋ (רגב R-GB) — **Clod:** [freq. 2] |kjv: clod| {str: 7263}

2748) ᔥᕳᔐ (רגז RGZ) ac: **Shake** co: **?** ab: **Fury:** A shaking or trembling out of fear or anger. [from: ᕳᔥ - shaking]

V) ᔥᕳᔐ (רגז R-GZ) — **Shake:** To shake in fear or anger. [Hebrew and Aramaic] [freq. 42] (vf: Paal, Hiphil, Hitpael) |kjv: tremble, move, rage, shake, disquiet, trouble, quake, afraid| {str: 7264, 7265}

N[m]) ᔥᕳᔐ (רגז R-GZ) — **I. Shaking: II. Fury:** A shaking anger. [Aramaic only] [freq. 2] |kjv: rage, trembling| {str: 7266, 7268}

N[fl]) ✲ᔥᕳᔐ (רגזה RG-ZH) — **Shaking:** [freq. 1] |kjv: trembling| {str: 7269}

g[m]) ᔥᕼᔐ (רוגז RW-GZ) — **Shaking:** [ms: רגז] [freq. 7] |kjv: trouble, troubling| {str: 7267}

n[m]) ᔥᕳᔐⴺ (ארגז AR-GZ) — **Chest:** A box. [Unknown connection to root;] [freq. 3] |kjv: coffer| {str: 712}

2749) ᔥᕳᔑ (רגל RGL) ac: **Trample** co: **Foot** ab: **?**: [from: ᕳᔥ]

V) ᔥᕳᔑ (רגל R-GL) — **I. Spy:** To be on foot walking through a foreign land in the sense of trampling. **II. Slander:** To trample another with the tongue. [freq. 26] (vf: Paal, Piel) |kjv: spy, view, backbite, espy, slander| {str: 7270, 8637}

N[f]) ᔥᕳᔑ (רגל R-GL) — **I. Foot:** [Hebrew and Aramaic] **II. Festival:** A festival requiring one to travel to in the sense of being on foot. [freq. 254] |kjv: foot, after, times, follow, toe, journey, leg| {str: 7271, 7272}

a[fl]) ✲ᔥᕳᔑᔋ (מרגלה MR-G-LH) — **Foot:** [freq. 5] |kjv: foot| {str: 4772}

f[m]) ᔥᕳᔑⵏ (רגלי R-G-LY) — **Footman:** One who is on foot. [freq. 12] |kjv: footman, foot| {str: 7273}

2750) ᔥᕳᔍ (רגם RGM) ac: **?** co: **Stone** ab: **?**: The stone is used in a sling or thrown to kill. [from: ᕳᔥ - stoning]

V) ᔥᕳᔍ (רגם R-GM) — **Stone:** To throw stones for execution. [freq. 16] (vf: Paal) |kjv: stone| {str: 7275}

N[fl]) ✲ᔍᕳᔥ (רגמה RG-MH) — **Crowd:** As a heap of stones. [freq. 1] |kjv: council| {str: 7277}

a[fl]) ✲ᔍᕳᔥᔋ (מרגמה MR-G-MH) — **Sling:** A weapon for slinging stones. [freq. 1] |kjv: sling| {str: 4773}

2751) ᔥᕳᔎ (רגן RGN) ac: **Murmur** co: **?** ab: **?**: [from: ᕳᔥ - shaking]

V) ᔥᕳᔎ (רגן R-GN) — **Murmur:** [freq. 3] (vf: Paal, Niphal, Participle) |kjv: murmur| {str: 7279}

2752) ◯Ŀฦ (רגע RGAh) ac: **Stir** co: ? ab: **Moment:** The stirring up of the sea or from a rest. Also a stirring of the eyes in rest or a wink.

V) ◯Ŀฦ (רגע R-GAh) — **I. Stir:** To stir as in stirring the waters or to stir from sleep. **II. Rest:** In the sense of stirring the eyes. [freq. 13] (vf: Paal, Niphal, Hiphil) |kjv: rest, divide, suddenly, break, ease, moment| {str: 7280}

Nᵐ) ◯Ŀฦ (רגע R-GAh) — **I. Moment:** As a wink of the eye. **II. Rest:** As a stirring of the eyes. [freq. 23] |kjv: moment, instant, space, suddenly, quiet| {str: 7281, 7282}

aᶠˡ) ❊◯Ŀฦ�519 (מרגעה MR-G-AhH) — **Repose:** In the sense of rest. [freq. 1] |kjv: refreshing| {str: 4774}

adᵐ) ◯ᵞŀฦ�519 (מרגוע MR-GWAh) — **Rest:** [freq. 1] |kjv: rest| {str: 4771}

2753) ⊔⊔Ŀฦ (רגש RGSh) ac: **Tumult** co: Crowd ab: ?: [from: Ŀฦ - as a trampling]

V) ⊔⊔Ŀฦ (רגש R-GSh) — **I. Tumult:** [Hebrew and Aramaic] **II. Crowd:** To gather in a crowd in the sense of a loud tumult. [Aramaic only] [freq. 4] (vf: Paal) |kjv: rage, assemble| {str: 7283, 7284}

Nᶠ) ⊔⊔Ŀฦ (רגש R-GSh) — **Crowd:** A loud tumultuous group. [freq. 2] |kjv: company, insurrection| {str: 7285}

2754) ᴧᴧᵺฦ (רדם RDM) ac: **Sleep** co: ? ab: ?: [from: ᴧᴧᵺ - sleeping silently]

V) ᴧᴧᵺฦ (רדם R-DM) — **Sleep:** To be in a deep sleep or trance. [freq.

7] (vf: Niphal) |kjv: deep sleep, fast asleep, sleeper| {str: 7290}

iᶠˡ) ❊ᴧᴧᵺฦᵼ (תרדמה TR-D-MH) — **Trance:** [freq. 7] |kjv: deep sleep| {str: 8639}

2755) ◯ᵺฦ (רדף RDP) ac: **Pursue** co: ? ab: ?: [from: Ŀฦ]

V) ◯ᵺฦ (רדף R-DP) — **Pursue:** To pursue in chase or persecution. [freq. 143] (vf: Paal, Niphal, Hiphil, Pual, Piel, Participle) |kjv: pursue, persecute, follow, chase, persecutors, pursuer, flight| {str: 7291}

aᵐ) ◯ᵺฦᴧᴧ (מרדף MR-DP) — **Pursued:** [freq. 1] |kjv: persecuted| {str: 4783}

2756) ᴢᴢᴄฦ (רזח RZHh) ac: ? co: **Outcry** ab: ?: A raising up of the voice in mourning or feasting. [from: ᴢᴢ◯ᴧ]

aᵐ) ᴢᴢᴄฦᴧᴧ (מרזח MR-ZHh) — **Banquet:** A place of crying out in joy. [freq. 1] |kjv: mourning| {str: 4798}

hᵐ) ᴢᴢᴄฦᴧᴧ (מרזח MR-ZHh) — **Mourning:** A place of crying out in sadness. [freq. 1] |kjv: banquet| {str: 4797}

2757) ᴧᴧᴄฦ (רזם RZM) ac: **Wink** co: ? ab: ?: A wink of the eyes.

V) ᴧᴧᴄฦ (רזם R-ZM) — **Wink:** [freq. 1] (vf: Paal) |kjv: wink| {str: 7335}

2758) ↘ᴄฦ (רזן RZN) ac: **Rule** co: Prince ab: ?: [from: ฦ❊]

442

V) ꟼ⌐ⱶ (רזן R-ZN) — **Rule:** [freq. 6] (vf: Paal) |kjv: prince, ruler| {str: 7336}

c[m]**)** ꟼⱶⱵ (רזון R-ZWN) — **Prince:** [freq. 1] |kjv: prince| {str: 7333}

~~~~~~~~~~

2759) ꟼꝏⱶ (רחב RHhB) ac: **Widen** co: **Street** ab: **Width:** [from: ꟼꟽ]

V) ꟼꝏⱶ (רחב R-HhB) — **Widen:** To make wide, large or roomy. [freq. 25] (vf: Paal, Niphal, Hiphil, Participle) |kjv: enlarge, wide, large, room| {str: 7337}

N[m]**)** ꟼꝏⱶ (רחב R-HhB) — **Wide:** [freq. 21] |kjv: large, broad, proud, wide, liberty, breadth| {str: 7338, 7342}

c[f]**)** ꟼⱵꝏⱶ (רחוב R-HhWB) — **Street:** As wide. [ms: רחב] [freq. 43] |kjv: street, ways, place| {str: 7339}

g[m]**)** ꟼꝏⱵⱶ (רוחב RW-HhB) — **Width:** [ms: רחב] [freq. 101] |kjv: breadth, broad, thickness, largeness, thick, wilderness| {str: 7341}

k[m]**)** ꟼꝏⱶⱳ (מרחב MR-HhB) — **Wide place:** [freq. 6] |kjv: large, breadth| {str: 4800}

~~~~~~~~~~

2760) ⊗ꝏⱶ (רחט RHhTh) ac: **?** co: **Rafter** ab: **?:** [from: ⊗ꟽ - as a trough]

b[m]**)** ⊗Ⱶꝏⱶ (רחיט R-HhYTh) — **Rafter:** [freq. 2] |kjv: rafter| {str: 7351}

~~~~~~~~~~

2761) Ɔꝏⱶ (רחל RHhL) ac: **?** co: **Ewe** ab: **?**

N[f]**)** Ɔꝏⱶ (רחל R-HhL) — **Ewe:** [freq. 4] |kjv: ewe, sheep| {str: 7353}

~~~~~~~~~~

2762) ꟽꝏⱶ (רחם RHhM) ac: **?** co: **Bowels** ab: **Compassion:** The bowels are the seat of compassion. [from: ꟽꟽ - as the loins]

V) ꟽꝏⱶ (רחם R-HhM) — **Compassion:** [freq. 47] (vf: Paal, Pual, Piel) |kjv: mercy, compassion, pity, love, merciful| {str: 7355}

N[m]**)** ꟽꝏⱶ (רחם R-HhM) — **I. Bowels:** The belly or womb. **II. Compassion:** As the belly being the seat of compassion. [Hebrew and Aramaic] **III. Racham:** An unknown bird. [freq. 73] |kjv: mercy, compassion, womb, bowels, pity, damsel, tender love, matrix, eagle| {str: 7356, 7358, 7359, 7360}

N[fl]**)** ⚥ꟽꝏⱶ (רחמה RHh-MH) — **Womb:** [freq. 1] |kjv: two, eagle| {str: 7361}

d[m]**)** ꟽⱵꝏⱶ (רחום R-HhWM) — **Compassionate:** [freq. 13] |kjv: merciful, compassion| {str: 7349}

mf[m]**)** ꟼⱶꟽꝏⱶ (רחמני RHh-M-NY) — **Compassionate:** [freq. 1] |kjv: pitiful| {str: 7362}

~~~~~~~~~~

2763) ⊂ꝏⱶ (רחף RHhP) ac: **Flutter** co: **?** ab: **?:** The stirrings and shakings of a bird in the nest. [from: ⊂ꝏ - a bird covering the nest]

V) ⊂ꝏⱶ (רחף R-HhP) — **Flutter:** [freq. 3] (vf: Paal, Piel) |kjv: shake, move, flutter| {str: 7363}

~~~~~~~~~~

2764) ⱷꝏⱶ (רחץ RHhTs) ac: **Wash** co: **Washbasin** ab: **Trust**

V) ⱷꝏⱶ (רחץ R-HhTs) — **I. Wash:** [Hebrew and Aramaic] **II.**

Trust: As a trusted servant who washes the master. [Aramaic only] [freq. 73] (vf: Paal, Hitpael, Pual) |kjv: wash, bathe, trust| {str: 7364, 7365}

N^m) ᕐᴃᴀᴠ (ץחר R-HhTs) — **Washbasin:** [freq. 2] |kjv: washpot| {str: 7366}

N^fl) ᕐᴃᴀᴠ𝄆 (הצחר RHh-TsH) — **Washing:** [freq. 2] |kjv: washing| {str: 7367}

~~~~~~~~~

2765) ᕐᴃᴇ◦ (קחר RHhQ) ac: **Far** co: ? ab: ?: [from: ᕐᵁᵂ - being far]

V) ᕐᴃᴇ◦ (קחר R-HhQ) — **Far:** To be distant, far away. [freq. 58] (vf: Paal, Niphal, Hiphil, Piel) |kjv: far, off, away, remove, good way| {str: 7368}

N^m) ᕐᴃᴇ◦ (קחר R-HhQ) — **Far:** [freq. 1] |kjv: far| {str: 7369}

b^m) ᕐᴃᴇ⤳◦ (קיחר R-HhYQ) — **Far:** [Aramaic only] [freq. 1] |kjv: far| {str: 7352}

c^m) ᕐᴃᴇᵞ◦ (קוחר R-HhWQ) — **Far:** A distant place or time. [ms: קחר] [freq. 84] |kjv: far, long ago, come, afar, old, long, space| {str: 7350}

k^m) ᕐᴃᴇ◦ᴍ (קחרמ MR-HhQ) — **Far:** A distant place or land. [freq. 18] |kjv: far, afar| {str: 4801}

~~~~~~~~~

2766) ᕐᴃᴍ (שחר RHhSh) ac: **Boil** co: **Pot** ab: ?: [from: ᴍᴜ - a boiling pot]

V) ᕐᴃᴍ (שחר R-HhSh) — **Boil:** [freq. 1] (vf: Paal) |kjv: indite| {str: 7370}

a^f2) ᕐᴃᴍᴀᴠ𝆏 (תשחרמ MR-Hh-ShT) — **Pot:** [freq. 2] |kjv: fryingpan| {str: 4802}

~~~~~~~~~

2767) ᕐ⊗ᴍ (בטר RThB) ac: **Moist** co: **Fresh** ab: ?: Fresh in the sense of being moist. [from: ᴍ⊗ - being fresh]

V) ᕐ⊗ᴍ (בטר R-ThB) — **Moist:** [freq. 1] (vf: Paal) |kjv: wet| {str: 7372}

c^m) ᕐ⊗ᴠᴍ (בוטר R-ThWB) — **Fresh:** [ms: בטר] [freq. 1] |kjv: green| {str: 7373}

~~~~~~~~~

2768) ᕐ⊗ᴜᴜ (שטר RThSh) ac: **Hack** co: ? ab: ?: A hacking into pieces. [from: ⊗ᴜᴜ - pouncing]

V) ᕐ⊗ᴜᴜ (שטר R-ThSh) — **Hack:** To cut and slice into pieces with a blade. [freq. 6] (vf: Pual, Piel) |kjv: dash| {str: 7376}

~~~~~~~~~

2769) ᕐᴜᵁᴍ (בכר RKB) ac: **Ride** co: **Chariot** ab: ?: [from: ᕐᴃᴇ - traveling]

V) ᕐᴜᵁᴍ (בכר R-KB) — **Ride:** To ride an animal, wagon or chariot. [freq. 78] (vf: Paal, Hiphil) |kjv: ride, rider, horseback, put, set, carry| {str: 7392}

N^m) ᕐᴜᵁᴍ (בכר R-KB) — **I. Chariot:** For riding in. **II. Charioteer:** The driver of the chariot. **III. Millstone:** In the sense of the top stone riding on the lower one. [freq. 123] |kjv: ride, rider, horseback, put, set, carry| {str: 7393, 7395}

d^m) ᕐᴜᵁᴠᴍ (בוכר R-KWB) — **Chariot:** [freq. 1] |kjv: chariot| {str: 7398} e^{f1}) 𐤓𐤉𐤊𐤁𐤄 (ריכבה RYK-BH) — **Chariot:** [ms: רכבה] [freq. 1] |kjv: chariot| {str: 7396}

k^m) 𐤌𐤓𐤊𐤁 (מרכב MR-KB) — **I. Chariot: II. Saddle:** [freq. 3] |kjv: chariot, saddle, covering| {str: 4817}

k^{f1}) 𐤌𐤓𐤊𐤁𐤄 (מרכבה MR-K-BH) — **Chariot:** [freq. 44] |kjv: chariot| {str: 4818}

nc^{f1}) 𐤀𐤓𐤊𐤅𐤁𐤄 (ארכובה AR-KW-BH) — **Knee:** In the sense of bending the knee to ride. [ar: ארכבא] [freq. 1] |kjv: knee| {str: 755}

~~~~~~~~~~~

2770) 𐤓𐤊𐤋 (רכל RKL) ac: **Trade** co: ? ab: ?: [from: ন - traveling]

V) 𐤓𐤊𐤋 (רכל R-KL) — **Trade:** [freq. 17] (vf: Paal, Participle) |kjv: merchant| {str: 7402}

N^{f1}) 𐤓𐤊𐤋𐤄 (רכלה RK-LH) — **Merchandise:** Goods for trading. [freq. 4] |kjv: merchandise, traffick| {str: 7404}

b^m) 𐤓𐤊𐤉𐤋 (רכיל R-KYL) — **I. Talebearer:** A traveler selling stories and songs. **II. Slanderer:** As a talebearer. [freq. 6] |kjv: slander, talebearer, tales| {str: 7400}

ac^{f2}) 𐤌𐤓𐤊𐤅𐤋𐤕 (מרכולת MR-KW-LT) — **Merchandise:** [ms: מרכלת] [freq. 1] |kjv: merchandise| {str: 4819}

~~~~~~~~~~~

2771) 𐤓𐤊𐤎 (רכס RKS) ac: **Tie** co: ? ab: ?

V) 𐤓𐤊𐤎 (רכס R-KS) — **Tie:** [freq. 2] (vf: Paal) |kjv: bind| {str: 7405}

N^m) 𐤓𐤊𐤎 (רכס R-KS) — **Tied:** [freq. 1] |kjv: rough| {str: 7406}

g^m) 𐤓𐤅𐤊𐤎 (רוכס RW-KS) — **Snare:** As tied up. [ms: רכס] [freq. 1] |kjv: pride| {str: 7407}

~~~~~~~~~~~

2772) 𐤓𐤊𐤔 (רכש RKSh) ac: **Collect** co: **Goods** ab: ?: A collection of possessions.

V) 𐤓𐤊𐤔 (רכש R-KSh) — **Collect:** [freq. 5] (vf: Paal) |kjv: get, gather| {str: 7408}

N^m) 𐤓𐤊𐤔 (רכש R-KSh) — **Horse:** As a collection of beasts. [freq. 4] |kjv: mule, dromedary, beast| {str: 7409}

d^m) 𐤓𐤅𐤊𐤔 (רכוש R-KWSh) — **Goods:** As collected substances. [ms: רכש] [freq. 28] |kjv: goods, substance, riches| {str: 7399}

~~~~~~~~~~~

2773) 𐤓𐤌𐤇 (רמח RMHh) ac: ? co: **Spear** ab: ?

N^m) 𐤓𐤌𐤇 (רמח R-MHh) — **Spear:** [freq. 15] |kjv: spear, lance| {str: 7420}

~~~~~~~~~~~

2774) 𐤓𐤌𐤊 (רמך RMK) ac: ? co: **Stud** ab: ?

N^f) 𐤓𐤌𐤊 (רמך R-MK) — **Stud:** A male horse for breeding. [freq. 1] |kjv: dromedary| {str: 7424}

~~~~~~~~~~~

2775) 𐤓𐤌𐤎 (רמס RMS) ac: **Tread** co: ? ab: ?: [from: 𐤓 - trampling down]

V) 𐤓𐤌𐤎 (רמס R-MS) — **Tread:** To trample under foot. [df: רמש] [freq. 36] (vf: Paal, Niphal, Participle) |kjv: tread, stamp, trample, oppressor| {str: 7429, 7430}

N^m) 𓂃ᓭଶ (רמס R-MS) —
Treader: A creature that crawls or
creeps as a treading. [df: רמשׂ] [freq.
17] |kjv: creeping, moving| {str:
7431}

h^m) 𓂃ᓭᓬ (מרמס MR-MS) —
Trampled: A place that is tread
upon. [freq. 7] |kjv: tread, trodden|
{str: 4823}

2776) ᓬଶ (רסן RSN) ac: **?** co: **Halter**
ab: **?**: [from: ଶᓬ - turning the head]

N^m) ᓬଶ (רסן R-SN) — **Halter:**
For leading an animal. [freq. 4] |kjv:
bridle| {str: 7448}

2777) ᒍ⊙ଶ (רעב RAhB) ac: **Hunger**
co: **Famine** ab: **?**

V) ᒍ⊙ଶ (רעב R-AhB) — **Hunger:**
To be hungry or famished. [freq. 11]
(vf: Paal, Hiphil) |kjv: hunger,
hungry, famish| {str: 7456}

N^m) ᒍ⊙ଶ (רעב R-AhB) — **I.
Famine: II. Hungry:** [freq. 123]
|kjv: famine, hunger, dearth,
famished, hungry| {str: 7457, 7458}

j^m) ᓬᖻᒍ⊙ଶ (רעבון RAh-BWN) —
Famine: [freq. 3] |kjv: famine| {str:
7459}

2778) ᅲ⊙ଶ (רעד RAhD) ac: **Tremble**
co: **?** ab: **?**: A trembling out of fear.
[from: ᓬଶ - shaking]

V) ᅲ⊙ଶ (רעד R-AhD) —
Tremble: [freq. 3] (vf: Paal, Hiphil,
Participle) |kjv: tremble| {str: 7460}

N^{m/f}) ᅲ⊙ଶ (רעד R-AhD) —
Trembling: [freq. 6] |kjv: trembling|
{str: 7461}

2779) ᒎ⊙ଶ (רעל RAhL) ac: **Quiver**
co: **Scarf** ab: **?**: The quivering of a scarf
in the breeze. [from: ᓬଶ - shaking]

V) ᒎ⊙ଶ (רעל R-AhL) — **Quiver:**
To shake uncontrollably. [freq. 1]
(vf: Hophal) |kjv: shake| {str: 7477}

N^m) ᒎ⊙ଶ (רעל R-AhL) —
Quivering: [freq. 1] |kjv: trembling|
{str: 7478}

N^{f1}) 𓏲ᒎ⊙ଶ (רעלה RAh-LH) —
Scarf: As quivering in the breeze.
[freq. 1] |kjv: muffler| {str: 7479}

i^{f1}) 𓏲ᒎ⊙ଶᅡ (תרעלה TR-Ah-LH)
— **Quivering:** [freq. 3] |kjv:
trembling, astonishment| {str: 8653}

2780) 𓂃⊙ଶ (רעם RAhM) ac: **Roar** co:
Thunder ab: **?**: [from: ᓬଶ - shaking]

V) 𓂃⊙ଶ (רעם R-AhM) — **Roar:**
As thunder. [freq. 13] (vf: Paal,
Hiphil) |kjv: thunder, roar, trouble,
fret| {str: 7481}

N^m) 𓂃⊙ଶ (רעם R-AhM) —
Thunder: [freq. 6] |kjv: thunder|
{str: 7482}

N^{f1}) 𓏲𓂃⊙ଶ (רעמה RAh-MH) —
Thunder: [freq. 1] |kjv: thunder|
{str: 7483}

2781) ᓬ⊙ଶ (רען RAhN) ac: **Field** co:
Field ab: **Flourish:** A green and fresh
plant as flourishing with fruit or with
sustenance. [from: ⊙ଶ - through the idea
of pasture]

m^m) ᓬ⊙ଶ (רען R-AhN) —
Flourishing: A green plant bearing
fruit. Also prosperous. [Hebrew and

Aramaic] freq. 21] |kjv: green, fresh, flourishing| {str: 7487, 7488}

~~~~~~~~~~

2782) ෴෴ (רעף RAhP) ac: **Drop** co: ? ab: ?: A dripping down of dew from the trees or rain from the clouds.

V) ෴෴ (רעף R-AhP) — **Drop:** [freq. 5] (vf: Paal, Hiphil) |kjv: drop, distil| {str: 7491}

~~~~~~~~~~

2783) ෴෴ (רעץ RAhTs) ac: **Shatter** co: ? ab: ?: A breaking into pieces by throwing. [from: ෴ - being broken into pieces]

V) ෴෴ (רעץ R-AhTs) — **Shatter:** To break into pieces by force. [freq. 2] (vf: Paal) |kjv: dash, vex| {str: 7492}

~~~~~~~~~~

2784) ෴෴ (רעש RAhSh) ac: **Quake** co: ? ab: ?: As the shaking of the earth. [from: ෴ - shaking]

V) ෴෴ (רעש R-AhSh) — **Quake:** [freq. 30] (vf: Paal, Niphal, Hiphil) |kjv: shake, tremble, move, afraid, quake, remove| {str: 7493}

N^{m}) ෴෴ (רעש R-AhSh) — **Quake:** [freq. 17] |kjv: earthquake, rushing, shake, fierceness, noise, commotion, rattling, quaking| {str: 7494}

~~~~~~~~~~

2785) ෴෴ (רפד RPD) ac: **Spread** co: ? ab: ?: A spreading out such as a sheet for a bed. [from: ෴ - spread out]

V) ෴෴ (רפד R-PD) — **Spread:** [freq. 3] (vf: Paal, Piel) |kjv: spread, make, comfort| {str: 7502}

b^{fl}) ෴෴ (רפידה R-PY-DH) — **Bottom:** As spread out. [freq. 1] |kjv: bottom| {str: 7507}

~~~~~~~~~~

2786) ෴෴ (רפס RPS) ac: **Stomp** co: **Mud** ab: ?: A stamping with the feet through water causing the water to become muddied. [from: ෴ - stamping down]

V) ෴෴ (רפס R-PS) — **I. Stomp:** To stomp down with the feet. [Hebrew and Aramaic] [df: רפש] **II. Muddy:** The muddying of waters when stomping into the water. [df: רפש] [freq. 7] (vf: Paal, Niphal, Hitpael, Participle) |kjv: humble, submit| {str: 7511, 7512, 7515}

N^{m}) ෴෴ (רפס R-PS) — **Mud:** [df: רפש] [freq. 1] |kjv: mire| {str: 7516}

h^{m}) ෴෴෴ (מרפס MR-PS) — **Mud:** [df: מרפש] [freq. 1] |kjv: foul| {str: 4833}

~~~~~~~~~~

2787) ෴෴ (רפק RPQ) ac: **Support** co: ? ab: ?

V) ෴෴ (רפק R-PQ) — **Support:** [freq. 1] (vf: Hitpael) |kjv: lean| {str: 7514}

~~~~~~~~~~

2788) ෴෴ (רפת RPT) ac: ? co: **Stable** ab: ?

N^{m}) ෴෴ (רפת R-PT) — **Stable:** For livestock. [freq. 1] |kjv: stall| {str: 7517}

~~~~~~~~~~

2789) ෴෴ (רצד RTsD) ac: **Gaze** co: ? ab: ?: An intense gazing out of envy.

V) ᛏᚮᚥᚦ (רצד R-TsD) — **Gaze:** [freq. 1] (vf: Piel) |kjv: leap| {str: 7520}

2790) ᛏᚮᚥᚦ (רצח RTsHh) ac: **Murder** co: **Wound** ab: ?: An unjustifiable killing or slaughter. [from: ᚮᚥᚦ - dashed into pieces]

V) ᛏᚮᚥᚦ (רצח R-TsHh) — **Murder:** [freq. 47] (vf: Paal, Niphal, Pual, Piel, Participle) |kjv: slayer, murderer, kill, murder, slain, manslayer, killing, death| {str: 7523}

N^m) ᛏᚮᚥᚦ (רצח R-TsHh) — **Wound:** A deadly wound. [freq. 2] |kjv: sword, slaughter| {str: 7524}

2791) ᚬᚮᚥᚦ (רצע RTsAh) ac: **Pierce** co: **Awl** ab: ?

V) ᚬᚮᚥᚦ (רצע R-TsAh) — **Pierce:** [freq. 1] (vf: Paal) |kjv: bore| {str: 7527}

N^m) ᚬᚮᚥᚦ (רצע R-TsAh) — **Awl:** For piercing holes in leather or the skin. [freq. 2] |kjv: aul| {str: 4836}

2792) ᚬᚮᚥᚦ (רצף RTsP) ac: **Fit** co: **Stone** ab: ?: Stones are fitted together to build a road. [from: ᚮᚥᚦ - pieces]

V) ᚬᚮᚥᚦ (רצף R-TsP) — **Fit:** To fit together. [freq. 1] (vf: Paal) |kjv: paved| {str: 7528}

N^m) ᚬᚮᚥᚦ (רצף R-TsP) — **Stone:** Used for baking bread by placing the bread on hot stones. [freq. 1] |kjv: coal| {str: 7529}

N^fl) ᚵᚬᚮᚥᚦ (רצפה RTs-PH) — **Pavement:** A road of stones. [freq. 8] |kjv: pavement| {str: 7531}

a^f2) ᛏᚬᚮᚥᚦᛗ (מרצפת MR-Ts-PT) — **Pavement:** A road of stones. [freq. 1] |kjv: pavement| {str: 4837}

2793) ᛚᚮᚥᚦ (רקב RQB) ac: **Decay** co: ? ab: ?

V) ᛚᚮᚥᚦ (רקב R-QB) — **Decay:** [freq. 2] (vf: Paal) |kjv: rot| {str: 7537}

N^m) ᛚᚮᚥᚦ (רקב R-QB) — **Decay:** [freq. 5] |kjv: rotten| {str: 7538}

j^m) ᛋᚳᛚᚮᚥᚦ (רקבון RQ-BWN) — **Decay:** [freq. 1] |kjv: rotten| {str: 7539}

2794) ᛏᚮᚥᚦ (רקד RQD) ac: **Skip** co: ? ab: ?: A jumping up and down out of joy as in a dance.

V) ᛏᚮᚥᚦ (רקד R-QD) — **Skip:** [freq. 9] (vf: Paal, Hiphil, Piel) |kjv: dance| {str: 7540}

2795) ᛗᚮᚥᚦ (רקח RQHh) ac: **Mix** co: **Spice** ab: ?: The mixing of spices and oils to form a perfumed liquid or ointment. [from: ᛗᚮᚥ - a sale item]

V) ᛗᚮᚥᚦ (רקח R-QHh) — **Mix:** [freq. 8] (vf: Paal, Hiphil, Pual, Participle) |kjv: apothecary, compound, make, prepare, spice| {str: 7543}

N^m) ᛗᚮᚥᚦ (רקח R-QHh) — **I. Spice:** As mixed. **II. Mixer:** One who mixes spices for ointments or perfumes. [freq. 2] |kjv: spiced, apothecary| {str: 7544, 7546}

N^(fl)) ﾧ�䷀-●-ﾧ (רקחה RQ-HhH) —
Mixer: One who mixes spices for
ointments or perfumes. [freq. 1] |kjv:
confectionary| {str: 7548}

g^m) �䷀-●-Yﾧ (רוקח RW-QHh) —
Mixture: A mixture of spices for an
ointment or perfume. [ms: רקח]
[freq. 2] |kjv: ointment, confection|
{str: 7545}

h^(f2)) †�䷀-●-ﾧⵜ (מרקחת MR-Q-HhT)
— **Mixture:** A mixture of spices for
an ointment or perfume. [freq. 3]
|kjv: compound, ointment,
apothecary| {str: 4842}

k^m) ﴰ-●-ﾧⵜ (מרקח MR-QHh) —
Sweet: From the sweet smell of
spices. [freq. 1] |kjv: sweet| {str:
4840}

k^(fl)) ﾧ﴿-●-ﾧⵜ (מרקחה MR-Q-
HhH) — **Mixture:** A mixture of
spices for an ointment or perfume.
[freq. 2] |kjv: ointment, well| {str:
4841}

ed^m) ﴰ-Y-●-➤-ﾧ (ריקוח RY-QWHh)
— **Perfume:** As a mixture of spices.
[ms: רקוח] [freq. 1] |kjv: perfume|
{str: 7547}

2796) ⵜⵜ-●-ﾧ (רקם RQM) ac: **Fashion**
co: **Needlework** ab: ?

V) ⵜⵜ-●-ﾧ (רקם R-QM) —
Fashion: To fashion an intricate
design. [freq. 9] (vf: Paal, Pual,
Participle) |kjv: needlework,
embroiderer, wrought| {str: 7551}

e^(fl)) ﾧⵜⵜ-●-➤ﾧ (ריקמה RYQ-MH)
— **Needlework:** [ms: רקמה] [freq.
12] |kjv: broidered, needlework,
divers colour| {str: 7553}

2797) ⬢-●-ﾧ (רקע RQAh) ac: **Hammer**
co: **Sheet** ab: ?: The pounding of a metal
such as gold with a hammer to flatten it
out for a metal sheet.

V) ⬢-●-ﾧ (רקע R-QAh) —
Hammer: To beat with a hammer to
flatten out. [freq. 11] (vf: Paal,
Hiphil, Pual, Piel, Participle) |kjv:
spread, stamp, stretch, beat, broad|
{str: 7554}

b^m) ⬢-➤-●-ﾧ (רקיע R-QYAh) —
Sheet: As hammered out flat. [freq.
17] |kjv: firmament| {str: 7549}

ed^m) ⬢Y-●-➤ﾧ (ריקוע RY-QWAh)
— **Flat:** As hammered out flat. [ms:
רקוע] [freq. 1] |kjv: broad| {str:
7555}

2798) ⵜⵚⵚﾧ (רשם RShM) ac: **Inscribe**
co: ? ab: ?

V) ⵜⵚⵚﾧ (רשם R-ShM) —
Inscribe: [Hebrew and Aramaic]
[freq. 8] (vf: Paal, Participle) |kjv:
note| {str: 7559, 7560}

2799) ⬢ⵚⵚﾧ (רשע RShAh) ac: **Depart**
co: ? ab: **Wicked**

V) ⬢ⵚⵚﾧ (רשע R-ShAh) —
Depart: To leave the correct path in
the sense of being wicked. [freq. 34]
(vf: Paal, Hiphil) |kjv: condemn,
wicked, depart, trouble, vex,
wickedness| {str: 7561}

N^m) ⬢ⵚⵚﾧ (רשע R-ShAh) — I.
Wicked: One who has departed from
the correct path or way. II.
Wickedness: [freq. 293] |kjv:
wickedness, wicked, iniquity| {str:
7562, 7563}

e^(fl)) ﾧ⬢ⵚⵚ➤ﾧ (רישעה RYSh-AhH)
— **Wickedness:** [ms: רשעה] [freq.

15] |kjv: wickedness, wickedly, fault| {str: 7564}

h^f2) †◎ᴜᏏᴀ (מרשעת) MR-Sh-AhT) — **Wicked:** [freq. 1] |kjv: wicked| {str: 4849}

~~~~~~~~~

2800) ◁ᴜᏏ (רשף RShP) ac: **?** co: **Spark** ab: **?**

N^m) ◁ᴜᏏ (רשף R-ShP) — **Spark:** The spark of a fire or thunderbolt. Also an arrow as a flashing thunderbolt. [freq. 7] |kjv: coal, heat, spark, arrow, thunderbolt| {str: 7565}

~~~~~~~~~

2801) ᴍᴛᏏ (רתח RTHh) ac: **Boil** co: **?** ab: **?**

V) ᴍᴛᏏ (רתח R-THh) — **Boil:** [freq. 3] (vf: Hiphil, Pual, Piel) |kjv: boil| {str: 7570}

N^m) ᴍᴛᏏ (רתח R-THh) — **Boiling:** [freq. 1] |kjv: well| {str: 7571}

~~~~~~~~~

2802) ᴍᴍᴛᏏ (רתם RTM) ac: **Attach** co: **Harness** ab: **?**: The harnessing of rig for attaching horses to a wagon or chariot. [from: ᴛᏏ - binding]

V) ᴍᴍᴛᏏ (רתם R-TM) — **Attach:** [freq. 1] (vf: Paal) |kjv: bind| {str: 7573}

N^m) ᴍᴍᴛᏏ (רתם R-TM) — **Retem:** An unknown tree. [freq. 4] |kjv: juniper| {str: 7574}

~~~~~~~~~

2803) ◦ᴛᏏ (רתק RTQ) ac: **Bind** co: **Chain** ab: **?**: A binding of something with a chain. [from: ᴛᏏ - binding]

V) ◦ᴛᏏ (רתק R-TQ) — **Bind:** [freq. 2] (vf: Niphal, Pual) |kjv: loose, bound| {str: 7576}

b^f1) ᵚ◦⌐ᴛᏏ (רתיקה R-TY-QH) — **Chain:** For binding. [freq. 2] |kjv: chain| {str: 7572}

c^m) ◦YᴛᏏ (רתוק R-TWQ) — **Chain:** For binding. [freq. 1] |kjv: chain| {str: 7569}

d^f1) ᵚ◦YᴛᏏ (רתוקה R-TW-QH) — **Chain:** For binding together or as bound on the wrist or neck. [ms: רתקה] [freq. 1] |kjv: chain| {str: 7577}

~~~~~~~~~

Shin

2804) ששבה (שבה ShBHh) ac: **Still** co: ? ab: ?: A calming or quieting of something by speaking or stroking smoothly.

V) ששבה (שבה Sh-BHh) — **Still:** To refrain from moving and be calm. [Hebrew and Aramaic] [freq. 16] (vf: Hiphil, Hitpael, Piel, Participle) |kjv: praise, still, keep, glory, triumph, commend| {str: 7623, 7624}

2805) ששבט (שבט ShBTh) ac: ? co: **Branch** ab: ?: A branch used as a staff, scepter, spear, writing implement or measuring rod. [from: מטה]

N^m) ששבט (שבט Sh-BTh) — **I. Staff:** A walking staff made from the branch of a tree. **II. Tribe:** As a branch of the family tree. [Hebrew and Aramaic] [freq. 191] |kjv: tribe, rod, sceptre, staff, pen, dart, correction| {str: 7625, 7626}

2806) ששבל (שבל ShBL) ac: **Flow** co: **Flood** ab: ?: The flooding of the river which provides water to the surrounding crop fields. [from: בל - as a flowing]

b^m) ששביל (שביל Sh-BYL) — **Path:** As the path of a stream. [freq. 3] |kjv: path| {str: 7635}

g^m) ששובל (שובל ShW-BL) — **Leg:** As the leg of a stream. [ms: שבל] [freq. 1] |kjv: leg| {str: 7640}

ld^m) ששבלול (שבלול ShB-LWL) — **Snail:** From the trail it leaves appearing like a stream. [freq. 1] |kjv: snail| {str: 7642}

ec^m) ששיבול (שיבול ShY-BWL) — **Flood:** [ms: שבל] [freq. 19] |kjv: branch, channel, flood| {str: 7641}

ec^f2) ששיבולת (שיבולת ShY-BW-LT) — **Head of grain:** Grown in fields watered by the flooding of the river. [ms: שבלת] [df: סבלת] [freq. 20] |kjv: ear| {str: 5451, 7641}

2807) ששבס (שבס ShBS) ac: **Weave** co: **Wreath** ab: ?: [from: שב - weaving]

b^m) ששבים (שבים Sh-BYS) — **Wreath:** A woven band for a womans heads. [freq. 1] |kjv: caul| {str: 7636}

2808) ששבע (שבע ShBAh) ac: **Swear** co: **Oath** ab: ?: Literally to seven oneself. A common practice was to make seven declarations when making an oath. This declaration can be making the oath seven times or doing seven things to show the sincerity of the oath. (eng: seven, an exchange of the s and sh)

V) ששבע (שבע Sh-BAh) — **Swear:** To make an oath. [freq. 187] (vf: Paal, Niphal, Hiphil, Participle) |kjv: swear, charge, oath, straitly| {str: 7650}

N^m/f) ששבע (שבע Sh-BAh) — **Seven:** [freq. 394] |kjv: seven, seventh, seven times, sevenfold| {str: 7651}

d^m) ששבוע (שבוע Sh-BWAh) — **Week:** As seven days. [ms: שבע] [freq. 20] |kjv: week| {str: 7620}

d^{f1}) 𐤔𐤏𐤅𐤔 (שׁבוּעה Sh-BW-AhH)
— **Oath:** [freq. 30] |kjv: oath, curse|
{str: 7621}

e^m) 𐤔𐤉𐤁𐤏 (שׁיבע ShY-BAh) —
Seven: [Only used in the plural form
meaning seventy - 𐤔𐤉𐤁𐤏𐤉𐤌]
[freq. 91] |kjv: seventy| {str: 7657}

e^{f1}) 𐤔𐤉𐤁𐤏 (שׁבעה ShYB-AhH)
— **Seven:** [Hebrew and Aramaic]
[ms: שׁבעה] [freq. 6] |kjv: seven|
{str: 7655}

e^{f2}) 𐤔𐤉𐤁𐤏𐤕 (שׁיבעת ShY-B-AhT)
— **Sevenfold:** [Always written in the
plural form 𐤔𐤉𐤁𐤏𐤕𐤌] [ms:
שׁבעת] [freq. 7] |kjv: sevenfold,
seven times| {str: 7659}

bf^m) 𐤔𐤉𐤁𐤏𐤉 (שׁביעי Sh-BY-
AhY) — **Seventh:** [ms: שׁבעי] [freq.
98] |kjv: seventh, seven| {str: 7637}

em^{f1}) 𐤔𐤉𐤁𐤏𐤍𐤄 (שׁיבענה ShY-
BAh-NH) — **Seven:** [ms: שׁבענה]
[freq. 1] |kjv: seven| {str: 7658}

2809) 𐤔𐤁𐤑 (שׁבץ ShBTs) ac: **Weave**
co: **Plait** ab: **Anguish:** A crisscross
pattern of weaving. [from: 𐤔𐤁 -
weaving]

V) 𐤔𐤁𐤑 (שׁבץ Sh-BTs) — **Weave:**
To weave a checkered or plaited
pattern. [freq. 2] (vf: Pual, Piel,
Participle) |kjv: embroider, set| {str:
7660}

N^m) 𐤔𐤁𐤑 (שׁבץ Sh-BTs) —
Anguish: As a weaving inside. [freq.
1] |kjv: anguish| {str: 7661}

h^{f1}) 𐤌𐤔𐤁𐤑𐤄 (משׁבצה M-ShB-
TsH) — **Plait:** A checkered work.
[freq. 9] |kjv: ouches, wrought| {str:
4865}

i^m) 𐤕𐤔𐤁𐤑 (תשׁבץ TSh-BTs) —
Woven: [freq. 1] |kjv: broidered|
{str: 8665}

2810) 𐤔𐤁𐤒 (שׁבק ShBQ) ac: **Leave** co:
? ab: ?: [from: 𐤔𐤁 - empty]

V) 𐤔𐤁𐤒 (שׁבק Sh-BQ) — **Leave:**
To be left alone. [Aramaic only]
[freq. 5] (vf: Paal) |kjv: leave, alone|
{str: 7662}

2811) 𐤔𐤁𐤓 (שׁבר ShBR) ac: **Burst** co:
Grain ab: ?: The grain is placed on the
threshing floor or in the millstone and
crushed to burst out the seeds from the
hulls. [from: 𐤁𐤓]

V) 𐤔𐤁𐤓 (שׁבר Sh-BR) — I. **Burst:**
To burst out or through. [Hebrew and
Aramaic] [ar: תבר] II. **Exchange:**
To buy or sell produce, usually grain.
[denominative of the noun meaning
grain] [freq. 172] (vf: Paal, Niphal,
Hiphil, Hophal, Piel, Participle) |kjv:
break, destroy, hurt, tear, birth, crush,
quench, buy, sell| {str: 7665, 7666,
8406}

N^m) 𐤔𐤁𐤓 (שׁבר Sh-BR) — I.
Shattering: II. **Grain:** As being
burst open on the threshing floor or
in the millstone. [freq. 53] |kjv:
destruction, breach, hurt, breaking,
affliction, bruise, crashing,
interpretation, vexation, corn,
victuals| {str: 7667, 7668}

a^m) 𐤌𐤔𐤁𐤓 (משׁבר MSh-BR) —
Birth canal: The place of bursting
through. [freq. 3] |kjv: birth,
breaking| {str: 4866}

h^m) 𐤌𐤔𐤁𐤓 (משׁבר MSh-BR) —
Breaker: Large waves of the sea that

burst onto the shore. [freq. 5] |kjv: waves, billows| {str: 4867}

ej^m) ששברון (שברון ShY-B-RWN) — **Bursting:** [freq. 2] |kjv: destruction, breaking| {str: 7670}

~~~~~~~~~

2812) שבת (שבת ShBT) ac: **Cease** co: ? ab: ?: The ceasing of work or activity in order to rest. [from: שב - sitting to rest]

V) שבת (שבת Sh-BT) — **Cease:** To cease from an activity for the purpose or rest or celebration. [freq. 71] (vf: Paal, Niphal, Hiphil) |kjv: cease, rest, away, fail, celebrate| {str: 7673}

N^f) שבת (שבת Sh-BT) — **Ceasing:** A stopping of activity. Often used for the seventh day or special feast day as a day set aside for resting or celebrating. [freq. 111] |kjv: sabbath, another, lost time, still, cease| {str: 7674, 7676}

h^m) משבת (משבת MSh-BT) — **Ceasing:** [freq. 1] |kjv: sabbath| {str: 4868}

j^m) שבתון (שבתון ShB-TWN) — **Ceasing:** [freq. 11] |kjv: rest, sabbath| {str: 7677}

~~~~~~~~~

2813) שנה (שנה ShGHh) ac: **Look** co: ? ab: ?

V) שנה (שנה Sh-GHh) — **Look:** [freq. 3] (vf: Hiphil) |kjv: look| {str: 7688}

~~~~~~~~~

2814) שגל (שגל ShGL) ac: **Copulate** co: **Consort** ab: ?

V) שגל (שגל Sh-GL) — **Copulate:** [freq. 4] (vf: Paal, Niphal, Pual) |kjv: lay| {str: 7693}

N^f) שגל (שגל Sh-GL) — **Consort:** [Hebrew and Aramaic] [freq. 5] |kjv: queen| {str: 7694, 7695}

~~~~~~~~~

2815) שגע (שגע ShGAh) ac: **Rave** co: ? ab: **Madness:** The actions of one insane.

V) שגע (שגע Sh-GAh) — **Rave:** [freq. 7] (vf: Hitpael, Pual, Participle) |kjv: mad| {str: 7696}

ej^m) שיגעון (שיגעון ShY-G-AhWN) — **Madness:** [ms: שגעון] [freq. 3] |kjv: madness, furiously| {str: 7697}

~~~~~~~~~

2816) שגר (שגר ShGR) ac: ? co: **Birth** ab: ?: The offspring that comes out of the womb. [from: שגר - as a relative]

N^f) שגר (שגר Sh-GR) — **Birth:** [freq. 5] |kjv: increase, come| {str: 7698}

~~~~~~~~~

2817) שדף (שדף ShDP) ac: **Blast** co: ? ab: ?: A destruction of a crop from a scorching wind.

V) שדף (שדף Sh-DP) — **Blast:** To blow heavily. [freq. 3] (vf: Paal, Participle) |kjv: blasted| {str: 7710}

N^fl) שדפה (שדפה ShD-PH) — **Blasting:** A strong devastating wind. [freq. 5] |kjv: blasting| {str: 7711}

ej^m) שידפון (שידפון ShY-D-PWN) — **Blasted:** What is blasted by a strong devastating wind. [freq. 1] |kjv: blasted| {str: 7711}

~~~~~~~~~

2818) שדר (שדר ShDR) ac: **Struggle** co: ? ab: **Revolt**

V) ﻪﺴﻭ (שדר Sh-DR) — **Struggle:** [Aramaic only] [freq. 1] (vf: Paal) |kjv: labour| {str: 7712}

nd^m) ﺩﺤﺸﻭﺃﺃ (אשדור ASh-DWR) — **Revolt:** [Aramaic only] [ar: אשתדור] [freq. 2] |kjv: sedition| {str: 849}

~~~~~~~~~

2819) ﺑﺻﻭ (שזב ShZB) ac: **Deliver** co: **?** ab: **?**

V) ﺑﺻﻭ (שזב Sh-ZB) — **Deliver:** [Aramaic only] [freq. 9] (vf: Paal) |kjv: deliver| {str: 7804}

~~~~~~~~~

2820) ﺻﻭﻩﻭ (שזף ShZP) ac: **Look** co: **?** ab: **?**

V) ﺻﻭﻩﻭ (שזף Sh-ZP) — **Look:** [freq. 3] (vf: Paal) |kjv: see, look| {str: 7805}

~~~~~~~~~

2821) ﻪﺻﻭ (שזר ShZR) ac: **Twist** co: **?** ab: **?**: A twisting of twine into a cord. [from: ﻪﻭ]

V) ﻪﺻﻭ (שזר Sh-ZR) — **Twist:** [freq. 21] (vf: Hophal, Participle) |kjv: twined| {str: 7806}

~~~~~~~~~

2822) ﺪﺣﻣﻭ (שחד ShHhD) ac: **?** co: **Bribe** ab: **?**: A gift presented to one in return for a favor. [from: ﺪﺣﻣ - unity]

V) ﺪﺣﻣﻭ (שחד Sh-HhD) — **Bribe:** To give a bribe. [freq. 2] (vf: Paal) |kjv: reward, hire| {str: 7809}

N^m) ﺪﺣﻣﻭ (שחד Sh-HhD) — **Bribe:** [freq. 23] |kjv: gift, reward, bribe, present, bribery| {str: 7810}

~~~~~~~~~

2823) ⊗ﺣﻣﻭ (שחט ShHhTh) ac: **Strike** co: **?** ab: **?**: The striking of a knife (or other weapon) for slaughtering or a hammer to pound out metal. [from: ﺣﻣﻭ - destruction by striking]

V) ⊗ﺣﻣﻭ (שחט Sh-HhTh) — **Strike:** To pound with a hammer or to strike to kill. [freq. 86] (vf: Paal, Niphal, Participle) |kjv: kill, slay, offer, shoot, slaughter| {str: 7819, 7820}

b^{f1}) ⊗ﻩﺣﻣﻭ (שחיטה Sh-HhY-ThH) — **Striking:** A slaughtering with a knife. [freq. 1] |kjv: killing| {str: 7821}

~~~~~~~~~

2824) Uﺣﻣﻭ (שחל ShHhL) ac: **?** co: **Lion** ab: **?**: [from: ﺣﻣﻭ - destruction by striking]

N^m) Uﺣﻣﻭ (שחל Sh-HhL) — **Lion:** [freq. 7] |kjv: lion| {str: 7826}

N^{f2}) tUﺣﻣﻭ (שחלת ShHh-LT) — **Onycha:** An incense. [freq. 1] |kjv: onycha| {str: 7827}

~~~~~~~~~

2825) ﺣﻣﻭ (שחס ShHhS) ac: **Spring** co: **?** ab: **?**

b^m) ﻩﺣﻣﻭ (שחיס Sh-HhYS) — **Spring:** To voluntarily sprout up from the ground. [df: סחיש] [freq. 2] |kjv: spring| {str: 7823}

~~~~~~~~~

2826) ﺻﺣﻣﻭ (שחף ShHhP) ac: **?** co: **Thin** ab: **?**: [from: ﺣﻣﻭ - being thin from hunger]

N^m) ﺻﺣﻣﻭ (שחף Sh-HhP) — **Shahhaph:** An unknown bird. [freq. 2] |kjv: cuckow| {str: 7828}

454

N^(f2)) †⊂ஊய (שחפת ShHh-PT) —
Consumption: A disease making one thin. [freq. 2] |kjv: consumption| {str: 7829}

b^(m)) ⟨>⊢ஊய (שחיף Sh-HhYP) —
Panel: A thin board. [freq. 1] |kjv: cieled| {str: 7824}

2827) oஃஊய (שחץ ShHhTs) ac: ? co: ? ab: **Pride**

N^(m)) oஃஊய (שחץ Sh-HhTs) —
Pride: [freq. 2] |kjv: lion, pride| {str: 7830}

2828) ⊸ஊய (שחק ShHhQ) ac: **Beat** co: **Powder** ab: **?:** A repetitive beating or pounding to pulverize or to make small such as the tumbling of stones in a river. [from: ஊய - destruction by striking]

V) ⊸ஊய (שחק Sh-HhQ) — **Beat:** To continually beat something to make it small or turn to powder. [freq. 4] (vf: Paal) |kjv: beat, wear| {str: 7833}

N^(m)) ⊸ஊய (שחק Sh-HhQ) —
Powder: A pulverized powder. Also the clouds as a fine powder. [freq. 21] |kjv: cloud, sky, dust, cloud| {str: 7834}

2829) ஃஊய (שחר ShHhR) ac: **Dark** co: **Dawn** ab: ?: [from: ஊய - a dark place]

V) ஃஊய (שחר Sh-HhR) — **I. Dark:** To be dark in color. **II. Seek:** To peer into the dim light of morning in search for something. [freq. 13] (vf: Paal) |kjv: black, seek, betimes| {str: 7835, 7836}

N^(m)) ஃஊய (שחר Sh-HhR) —
Dawn: The place of the rising sun.

[freq. 24] |kjv: morning, day, early, dayspring, light, rise| {str: 7837}

N^(f3)) †Yஃஊய (שחרות ShHh-RWT) — **Youth:** As having dark hair. [freq. 1] |kjv: youth| {str: 7839}

c^(f)) ஃYஊய (שחור Sh-HhWR) — **I. Dark:** The dim light before the rising of the sun. [ms: שחר] **II. Coal:** As dark in color. [freq. 7] |kjv: black, coal| {str: 7838, 7815}

h^(m)) ஃஊயᴡ (משחר MSh-HhR) — **Dawn:** The place of the rising sun. [freq. 1] |kjv: morning| {str: 4891}

lc^(f2)) †ஃYஊⴲஊ ய (שחרחורת Sh-HhR-HhW-RT) — **Dark:** [ms: שחרחרת] [freq. 1] |kjv: black| {str: 7840}

2830) †ஊய (שחת ShHhT) ac: **Corrupt** co: ? ab: ?: [from: ஊய - corrupt]

V) †ஊய (שחת Sh-HhT) — **Corrupt:** To destroy. [Hebrew and Aramaic] [freq. 150] (vf: Niphal, Hiphil, Hophal, Piel, Participle) |kjv: destroy, corrupt, mar, destroyer, corrupter, waster, spoiler, batter, corruptly, fault| {str: 7843, 7844}

a^(m)) †ஊயᴡ (משחת MSh-HhT) — **Corrupting:** [freq. 1] |kjv: destroying| {str: 4892}

h^(m)) †ஊயᴡ (משחת MSh-HhT) — **Corrupted:** [freq. 2] |kjv: marred, corruption| {str: 4893}

ab^(m)) †⊢ஊயᴡ (משחית MSh-HhYT) — **Corruption:** [freq. 11] |kjv: destroy, corruption, destruction, trap, destroying| {str: 4889}

2831) ஊⵧய (שטח ShThHh) ac: **Spread** co: ? ab: ?: [from: ஊⵧ]

455

V) ௰⊗ட (שׁטח Sh-ThHh) — **Spread:** [freq. 6] (vf: Paal, Piel, Participle) |kjv: spread, enlarge, stretch, abroad| {str: 7849}

hc^m) ௰Y⊗ட௱ (משׁטוח MSh-ThWHh) — **Spreading:** [df: משׁטח] [freq. 3] |kjv: spread, spreading| {str: 4894}

~~~~~~~

2832) ⊂⊗ட (שׁטף ShThP) ac: **Flush** co: ? ab: ?: [from: ௦ᨈட]

V) ⊂⊗ட (שׁטף Sh-ThP) — **Flush:** To flow over with copious amounts of water. [freq. 31] (vf: Paal, Niphal, Pual) |kjv: overflow, rinse, wash, drown, flow| {str: 7857}

N^m) ⊂⊗ட (שׁטף Sh-ThP) — **Overflowing:** [freq. 6] |kjv: flood, overflowing, outrageous| {str: 7858}

~~~~~~~

2833) ௫⊗ட (שׁטר ShThR) ac: **Rule** co: Domain ab: ?: [from: ⊗ட - punishment from a ruler]

V) ௫⊗ட (שׁטר Sh-ThR) — **Rule:** [freq. 25] (vf: Paal) |kjv: officer, ruler, overseer| {str: 7860}

h^m) ௫⊗ட௱ (משׁטר MSh-ThR) — **Domain:** [freq. 1] |kjv: dominion| {str: 4896}

~~~~~~~

2834) ௶ಲட (שׁכב ShKB) ac: **Lay** co: Bed ab: **Copulation:** A laying down for copulation. [from: ௶ட]

V) ௶ಲட (שׁכב Sh-KB) — **Lay:** To lay down for copulation, rest or sleep. [freq. 212] (vf: Paal, Niphal, Hiphil, Hophal, Pual) |kjv: lie, sleep, rest| {str: 7901}

N^{fl}) ௶ಲட✥ (שׁכבה ShK-BH) — **Lying:** A laying with another in copulation. Also something spread out. [freq. 9] |kjv: copulation, lie, carnally, from| {str: 7902}

c^{f2}) ௶ಲYட† (שׁכובת Sh-KW-BT) — **Copulation:** [ms: שׁכבת] [freq. 4] |kjv: lie| {str: 7903}

h^m) ௶ಲட௱ (משׁכב MSh-KB) — **Bed:** [Hebrew and Aramaic] [freq. 52] |kjv: bed, couch| {str: 4903, 4904}

~~~~~~~

2835) ௸ಣட (שׁכח ShKHh) ac: **Forget** co: ? ab: ?

V) ௸ಣட (שׁכח Sh-KHh) — **I. Forget:** [Hebrew and Aramaic] **II. Find:** To find something forgotten or hidden. [Aramaic only] [freq. 120] (vf: Paal, Niphal, Hiphil, Hitpael, Piel) |kjv: forget, find| {str: 7911, 7912}

N^m) ௸ಣட (שׁכח Sh-KHh) — **Forget:** [freq. 2] |kjv: forget| {str: 7913}

~~~~~~~

2836) Ɉಲட (שׁכל ShKL) ac: **Childless** co: ? ab: **Bereavement:** Bereavement from a lack of children due to miscarriage, barrenness or loss of children.

V) Ɉಲட (שׁכל Sh-KL) — **Childless:** To be without children through miscarriage, barrenness or loss of children. [freq. 25] (vf: Paal, Hiphil, Piel, Participle) |kjv: bereave, barren, childless, cast, lost, rob, deprive| {str: 7921}

c^m) ɈYಲட (שׁכול Sh-KWL) — **Bereavement:** From the loss of children or other unfruitfulness.

[freq. 1] |kjv: loss, spoiling| {str: 7923}

d^m) שכול (שָׁכוֹל Sh-KWL) — **Childless:** Through barrenness or loss of children. [ms: שכל] [freq. 6] |kjv: barren, rob, bereave| {str: 7909}

ed^m) שיכול (שִׁיכוֹל ShY-KWL) — **Bereavement:** From the loss of children or other unfruitfulness. [ms: שכל] [freq. 1] |kjv: lost| {str: 7923}

nc^m) אשכול (אֶשְׁכּוֹל ASh-KWL) — **Cluster:** A cluster of rapes from the vine or flowers from the plant. [Unknown connection to root;] [ms: אשכל] [freq. 9] |kjv: cluster| {str: 811}

~~~~~~

2837) שכם (שֶׁכֶם ShKM) ac: ? co: **Shoulder** ab: ?

V) שכם (שֶׁכֶם Sh-KM) — **Shoulder:** To rise or go early in the sense of placing the load on the shoulders to depart. [freq. 65] (vf: Hiphil) |kjv: early, bedtime| {str: 7925}

N^m) שכם (שֶׁכֶם Sh-KM) — **Shoulder:** [freq. 22] |kjv: shoulder, back, consent, portion| {str: 7926}

e^fl) שיכמה (שִׁיכְמָה ShYK-MH) — **Shoulder:** [ms: שכמה] [freq. 1] |kjv: shoulder| {str: 7929}

~~~~~~

2838) שכן (שֶׁכֶן ShKN) ac: **Dwell** co: **Dwelling** ab: ?: [from: אֵשׁ]

V) שכן (שֶׁכֶן Sh-KN) — **Dwell:** To stay or sit in one location. [Hebrew and Aramaic] [freq. 131] (vf: Paal, Hiphil, Piel) |kjv: dwell, abide, remain, inhabit, rest, set, continue, dweller, dwelling, habitation| {str: 7931, 7932}

N^m) שכן (שֶׁכֶן Sh-KN) — **I. Dwelling:** The place of residence. **II. Neighbor:** A fellow dweller. [freq. 21] |kjv: habitation, neighbour, inhabitant, thereunto| {str: 7933, 7934}

h^m) משכן (מִשְׁכָּן MSh-KN) — **Dwelling:** The place of residence. [Hebrew and Aramaic] [freq. 140] |kjv: tabernacle, dwelling, habitation, dwellingplace, place, dwell, tent| {str: 4907, 4908}

~~~~~~

2839) שכר (שֶׁכֶר ShKR) ac: **Drunk** co: **Liquor** ab: **Drunkenness**

V) שכר (שֶׁכֶר Sh-KR) — **Drunk:** To be filled with intoxicating drink. [freq. 19] (vf: Paal, Hiphil, Hitpael, Piel) |kjv: drunk, filled, abundantly, merry| {str: 7937}

N^m) שכר (שֶׁכֶר Sh-KR) — **Liquor:** An intoxicating drink. [freq. 23] |kjv: drink, wine| {str: 7941}

ec^m) שיכור (שִׁיכּוֹר ShY-KWR) — **Drunkard:** One who is filled with intoxicating drink. [ms: שכר שכור] [freq. 13] |kjv: drunken, drunkard, drunk| {str: 7910}

ej^m) שיכרון (שִׁיכָּרוֹן ShY-K-RWN) — **Drunkenness:** [ms: שכרון] [freq. 3] |kjv: drunkenness, drunken| {str: 7943}

~~~~~~

2840) שלב (שֶׁלֶב ShLB) ac: **Join** co: **Joint** ab: ?: A joining together in an arranged or equal order.

V) שלב (שֶׁלֶב Sh-LB) — **Join:** [freq. 2] (vf: Pual) |kjv: order, equally distant| {str: 7947}

N^m) שלב (שֶׁלֶב Sh-LB) — **Joint:** [freq. 3] |kjv: ledge| {str: 7948}

2841) ﬩Ս⅃ (שלג ShLG) ac: **?** co: **Snow** ab: **?**

V) ﬩Ս⅃ (שלג Sh-LG) — **Snow:** [freq. 1] (vf: Hiphil) |kjv: snow| {str: 7949}

N^m) ﬩Ս⅃ (שלג Sh-LG) — **Snow:** [Hebrew and Aramaic] [ar: תלג] [freq. 21] |kjv: snow, snowy| {str: 7950, 8517}

2842) ᄆᄆՍ⅃ (שלח ShLHh) ac: **Send** co: **Projectile** ab: **?**: [from: Ս⚔ - sending]

V) ᄆᄆՍ⅃ (שלח Sh-LHh) — **Send:** [Hebrew and Aramaic] [freq. 861] (vf: Paal, Niphal, Hiphil, Pual, Piel) |kjv: send, go, lay, put, cast, stretch, depart, sow, loose| {str: 7971, 7972}

N^m) ᄆᄆՍ⅃ (שלח Sh-LHh) — **Projectile:** A weapon that is sent by the hand. Also a plant shoot as sent out of the ground. [freq. 8] |kjv: sword, weapon, dart, plant, put| {str: 7973}

d^(f1)) ✡ᄆᄆYՍ⅃ (שלוחה Sh-LW-HhH) — **Shoot:** The shoots of a plant as sent out. [freq. 1] |kjv: branch| {str: 7976}

h^(f2)) ﬩ᄆᄆՍ⅃⅃ﻻﻻ (משלחת MSh-L-HhT) — **Sending:** [freq. 2] |kjv: sending, discharge| {str: 4917}

ac^m) ᄆᄆYՍ⅃⅃ﻻﻻ (משלוח MSh-LWHh) — **Sending:** [df: משלח] [freq. 10] |kjv: put, set, sending, lay| {str: 4916}

ed^m) ᄆᄆYՍ⅃⅃ (שילוח ShY-LWHh) — **I. Present:** A gift that is sent. [ms: שלח שלוח] **II. Sent:** [ms: שלוח] [freq. 3] |kjv: present, send| {str: 7964}

om^m) ﹏ᄆᄆYՍ⅃ (שולחן ShWL-HhN) — **Table:** Where one sends his hand to receive food. [freq. 70] |kjv: table| {str: 7979}

2843) ⊗Ս⅃ (שלט ShLTh) ac: **Rule** co: **Master** ab: **Realm:** (eng: salute - with the exchange of the s and sh)

V) ⊗Ս⅃ (שלט Sh-LTh) — **Rule:** To be over or have mastery over another. [Hebrew and Aramaic] [freq. 15] (vf: Paal, Hiphil) |kjv: rule, power, dominion, mastery| {str: 7980, 7981}

N^m) ⊗Ս⅃ (שלט Sh-LTh) — **Shield:** As placed over the head for protection from projectiles. [freq. 7] |kjv: shield| {str: 7982}

N^(f2)) ﬩⊗Ս⅃ (שלטת ShL-ThT) — **Bold:** As being prominent. [freq. 1] |kjv: imperious| {str: 7986}

b^m) ⊗⅃Ս⅃ (שליט Sh-LYTh) — **Master:** One who has dominion over another, also a rule or law as a master. [Hebrew and Aramaic] [freq. 14] |kjv: governor, mighty, power, ruler, rule, captain, lawful| {str: 7989, 7990}

m^m) ❨⊗Ս⅃ (שלטן ShL-ThN) — **Realm:** [Aramaic only] [freq. 14] |kjv: dominion| {str: 7985}

ej^m) ❨Y⊗Ս⅃⅃ (שילטון ShY-L-ThWN) — **Mastery:** [Aramaic only] [ms: שלטן שלטון] [freq. 4] |kjv: power, ruler| {str: 7983, 7984}

2844) �獅Ս⅃ (שלך ShLK) ac: **Throw** co: **?** ab: **?**: [from: Ս⚔ - sending]

V) ﻣﻣՍ⅃ (שלך Sh-LK) — **Throw:** To cast out, down or away. [freq.

125] (vf: Hiphil, Hophal) |kjv: cast, hurl| {str: 7993}

N^m) ﻟﻟﻟﻟﻟﻟﻟﻟ (שלך Sh-LK) — **Shelak:** An unknown bird. [freq. 2] |kjv: cormorant| {str: 7994}

N^f2) ﻟﻟﻟﻟﻟﻟﻟﻟ (שלכת ShL-KT) — **Throwing:** [freq. 1] |kjv: cast| {str: 7995}

~~~~~~~~~~

2845) ﻟﻟﻟﻟﻟﻟﻟﻟ (שלם ShLM) ac: **Complete** co: ? ab: ?: Made whole or complete by adding or subtracting. [from: ﻟﻟﻟﻟ - as a drawing out or in]

V) ﻟﻟﻟﻟﻟﻟﻟﻟ (שלם Sh-LM) — **Complete:** To be in a state of wholeness. Also to restore or make right through payment or restitution. [Hebrew and Aramaic] [freq. 119] (vf: Paal, Hiphil, Hophal, Pual, Piel, Participle) |kjv: pay, peace, recompense, reward, render, restore, repay, perform, good, end, requite, restitution, finish, again, amend, full, deliver| {str: 7999, 8000}

N^m) ﻟﻟﻟﻟﻟﻟﻟﻟ (שלם Sh-LM) — **I. Complete:** A state of being whole, complete or full. Also an offering of restitution or payment. **II. Shelam:** A greeting as a desire for completeness to another. [Aramaic only] [freq. 118] |kjv: perfect, whole, full, just, peaceable, peace offering, peace| {str: 8001, 8002, 8003}

c^m) ﻟﻟﻟﻟﻟﻟﻟﻟ (שלום Sh-LWM) — **I. Completeness:** [ms: שלם] **II. Shalom:** A greeting as a desire for completeness to another. [ms: שלם] [freq. 236] |kjv: peace, well, peaceable, welfare, prosperity, safe, health| {str: 7965}

e^m) ﻟﻟﻟﻟﻟﻟﻟﻟ (שילם ShY-LM) — **Recompense:** In the sense of making

complete. [ms: שלם] [freq. 1] |kjv: recompense| {str: 8005}

j^m) ﻟﻟﻟﻟﻟﻟﻟﻟﻟ (שלמון ShL-MWN) — **Payment:** Given to make a completion of an action or transaction. [freq. 1] |kjv: reward| {str: 8021}

ed^m) ﻟﻟﻟﻟﻟﻟﻟﻟﻟ (שילום ShY-LWM) — **Payment:** Given to make a completion of an action or transaction. [ms: שלם שלם] [freq. 3] |kjv: recompense, reward| {str: 7966}

ed^f1) ﻟﻟﻟﻟﻟﻟﻟﻟﻟﻟ (שילומה ShY-LW-MH) — **Payment:** Given to make a completion of an action or transaction. [freq. 1] |kjv: reward| {str: 8011}

~~~~~~~~~~

2846) ﻟﻟﻟﻟﻟ (שלף ShLP) ac: **Pull** co: ? ab: ?: A pulling out, up or off. [from: ﻟﻟﻟﻟ - as a drawing out]

V) ﻟﻟﻟﻟﻟ (שלף Sh-LP) — **Pull:** To pull out, up or off. [freq. 25] (vf: Paal) |kjv: draw, pluck, grow| {str: 8025}

~~~~~~~~~~

2847) ﻟﻟﻟﻟﻟﻟﻟ (שלש ShLSh) ac: ? co: **Three** ab: ?

V) ﻟﻟﻟﻟﻟﻟﻟ (שלש Sh-LSh) — **Threefold:** [freq. 9] (vf: Pual, Piel) |kjv: three, third, threefold| {str: 8027}

N^m/f) ﻟﻟﻟﻟﻟﻟﻟ (שלש Sh-LSh) — **I. Three:** [Aramaic only; Also meaning thirty in Aramaic when written in the plural form - ﻟﻟﻟﻟﻟﻟ] [ar: תלת] **II. Third:** [Aramaic only] [ar: תלת] [freq. 15] |kjv: three, third| {str: 8531, 8532, 8533}

b^m) ши-и/ши (שָׁלִישׁ Sh-LYSh) — **I.**
Captain: As one in charge of thirty.
[df: שָׁלִשׁ] **II. Shaliysh:** A three
stringed or triangular instrument.
Also a standard of measure. [freq.
20] |kjv: captain, lord, instrument,
measure, excellent, prince| {str:
7991}

c^{m/f}) шиY/ши (שָׁלוֹשׁ Sh-LWSh) —
Three: [Also meaning thirty when
written in the plural form -
ши-иши/ши] [ms: שָׁלֹשׁ] [freq. 605]
|kjv: three, third, thrice| {str: 7969,
7970}

e^m) ши-и/ши (שִׁילֵשׁ ShY-LSh) —
Third: [ms: שָׁלֵשׁ] [freq. 5] |kjv:
third| {str: 8029}

bf^m) ши-и-и/ши (שְׁלִישִׁי Sh-LY-ShY)
— **Third:** [Hebrew and Aramaic]
[ar: תְּלִיתִי תַּלְתִּי] [freq. 110] |kjv:
third, three| {str: 7992, 8523}

eqp^m) ши-и-иY/ши (שִׁילְשׁוֹם ShY-
L-ShWM) — **Before:** In the sense of
three days ago or the past times. [ms:
שָׁלְשׁוֹם] [freq. 25] |kjv: before, past|
{str: 8032}

2848) ти-мши (שָׁמַד ShMD) ac: **Destroy**
co: ? ab: ?: A complete annihilation or
extermination. [from: мши - destruction]

V) ти-мши (שָׁמַד Sh-MD) —
Destroy: [Hebrew and Aramaic]
[freq. 91] (vf: Niphal, Hiphil) |kjv:
destroy, destruction, overthrow,
perish, consume| {str: 8045, 8046}

2849) ⊗мши (שָׁמֵט ShMTh) ac: **Shake**
co: ? ab: ?: A letting go or throwing
down by shaking loose. [from: мши -
destruction]

V) ⊗мши (שָׁמֵט Sh-MTh) —
Shake: To shake to throw off, loosen
or release. [freq. 9] (vf: Paal, Niphal,
Hiphil) |kjv: release, throw, shake,
stumble, discontinue, overthrow| {str:
8058}

N^{f1}) ⊱⊗мши (שְׁמִטָּה ShM-ThH) —
Release: As shaken off. [freq. 5]
|kjv: release| {str: 8059}

2850) ʾмши (שָׁמֵן ShMN) ac: ? co: **Oil**
ab: ?: [from: мши - oil as the breath]

V) ʾмши (שָׁמֵן Sh-MN) — **Fat:** To
be fat or full of oil. [freq. 5] (vf: Paal,
Hiphil) |kjv: fat| {str: 8080}

N^m) ʾмши (שָׁמֵן Sh-MN) — **Oil:**
Usually olive oil and used as a
medicinal ointment. Also meaning
fat or rich. [freq. 203] |kjv: oil,
ointment, olive, oiled, fat, things,
plenteous, lusty| {str: 8081, 8082}

c^{m/f}) ʾYмши (שָׁמוֹן Sh-MWN) —
Eight: In the sense of being fat or
rich. [Also meaning thirty when
written in the plural form -
ши-иYмши] [df: שְׁמוֹנָה שְׁמֹנֶה]
[freq. 147] |kjv: eight, eighth, eighty,
eightieth| {str: 8083, 8084}

h^m) ʾмшимм (מִשְׁמָן MSh-MN) —
Fat: A place of fatness. [freq. 7] |kjv:
fatness, fat, fattest| {str: 4924}

bf^m) ши-и-иYмши (שְׁמִינִי Sh-MY-NY)
— **Eighth:** [freq. 28] |kjv: eighth|
{str: 8066}

2851) ⊙мши (שָׁמַע ShMAh) ac: **Hear**
co: **Report** ab: **Obedience:** A careful
hearing of someone or something as well
as responding appropriately in obedience
or action. [from: мши - listening with the
breath]

V) (שמע Sh-MAh) — **Hear:** To hear as well as to respond to what is heard. [Hebrew and Aramaic] [freq. 1168] (vf: Paal, Niphal, Hiphil, Piel) |kjv: hear, obey, publish, understand, obedient, diligently, show, sound, declare, discern, noise, perceive, tell, report| {str: 8085, 8086}

N[m]) (שמע Sh-MAh) — **Report:** What is heard. [freq. 18] |kjv: fame, report, hear, tidings, bruit, loud, speech| {str: 8088}

N[f2]) (משמעת MSh-M-AhT) — **Hearer:** One who hears and obeys. [freq. 4] |kjv: guard, bidding, obey| {str: 4928}

N[f3]) (שמעות ShM-AhWT) — **Reporting:** [freq. 1] |kjv: hear| {str: 2045}

d[f1]) (שמועה Sh-MW-AhH) — **Report:** What is heard. [freq. 27] |kjv: rumour, tidings, report, fame, bruit, doctrine, mentioned, news| {str: 8052}

g[m]) (שומע ShW-MAh) — **Fame:** What is heard. [ms: שמע] [freq. 4] |kjv: fame| {str: 8089}

h[m]) (משמע MSh-MAh) — **Hearing:** [freq. 1] |kjv: hearing| {str: 4926}

~~~~~~~~~~~~

2852) (שמץ ShMTs) ac: **?** co: **Whisper** ab: **?**

N[m]) (שמץ Sh-MTs) — **Whisper:** [freq. 2] |kjv: little| {str: 8102}

e[f1]) (שימצה ShYM-TsH) — **Whisper:** [freq. 1] |kjv: shame| {str: 8103}

~~~~~~~~~~~~

2853) (שמר ShMR) ac: **Guard** co: **Brier** ab: **Custody:** A close watching of something for guarding or protecting. Shepherds constructed corrals of briers at night to protect the flock from predators. [from: - from the thorns used in constructing a corral]

V) (שמר Sh-MR) — **Guard:** To watch over or guard in the sense of preserving or protecting. [freq. 468] (vf: Paal, Niphal, Hitpael, Piel, Participle) |kjv: keep, observe, heed, keeper, preserve, beware, mark, watchman, wait, watch, regard, save| {str: 8104}

N[m]) (שמר Sh-MR) — **Dregs:** The settlings of wine. [Unknown connection to root;] [freq. 5] |kjv: lees, dregs| {str: 8105}

N[f1]) (שמרה ShM-RH) — **Guard:** One who watches over. [freq. 1] |kjv: watch| {str: 8108}

b[m]) (שמיר Sh-MYR) — **I. Brier:** Used to construct a corral to protect the flock at night. **II. Shamiyr:** An unknown sharp stone such as flint or obsidian. [freq. 11] |kjv: brier, adamant, diamond| {str: 8068}

d[m]) (שמור Sh-MWR) — **Watching:** [ms: שמר] [freq. 2] |kjv: observed| {str: 8107}

d[f1]) (שמורה Sh-MW-RH) — **Lid:** As a covering of protection. [ms: שמרה] [freq. 1] |kjv: waking| {str: 8109}

h[m]) (משמר MSh-MR) — **Custody:** A careful watching over as an office, guard or prison. [freq. 22] |kjv: ward, watch, guard, diligence, office, prison| {str: 4929}

h^f2) ┼ᕈᴍᴍᴍ (משמרת MSh-M-RT) — **Charge:** What is given to be watched over and protected. [freq. 78] |kjv: charge, ward, watch, keep, ordinance, office, safeguard| {str: 4931}

nd^f1) ✻ᕈYᴍᴌᴌᴌᴗ (אשמורה ASh-MW-RH) — **Watch:** An increment of time during the night when guards watch the area. [ms: אשמרה] [freq. 7] |kjv: watch, night watch| {str: 821}

2854) ᴌᴌᴍᴧᴌᴌ (שמש ShMSh) ac: **?** co: **Sun** ab: **?:** [from: ᴧᴧᴌᴌ - a hot wind from the sun causing desolation] (eng: sun - with the exchange of the s and sh and the n and m)

N^f) ᴌᴌᴧᴧᴌᴌ (שמש Sh-MSh) — **I. Sun:** [Hebrew and Aramaic] **II. Serve:** [Unknown connection to root; Aramaic only] [freq. 136] |kjv: sun, ministered| {str: 8120, 8121, 8122}

2855) ᴑᕒᴌᴌ (שנב ShNB) ac: **Cool** co: **Lattice** ab: **?:** The window coverings that allow the cool breeze to pass through.

n^m) ᴑᕒᴌᴌᴗ (אשנב ASh-NB) — **Lattice:** The window coverings that allow the cool breeze to pass through. [freq. 2] |kjv: lattice, casement| {str: 822}

2856) ᕈᕒᴌᴌ (שנס ShNS) ac: **Gird** co: **?** ab: **?**

V) ᕈᕒᴌᴌ (שנס Sh-NS) — **Gird:** As a tightening of the belt. [freq. 1] (vf: Piel) |kjv: gird| {str: 8151}

2857) ⟠ᕈᴌᴌ (שסע ShSAh) ac: **Split** co: **?** ab: **?:** [from: ᕈᴌᴌ - cutting]

V) ⟠ᕈᴌᴌ (שסע Sh-SAh) — **Split:** [freq. 9] (vf: Paal, Piel, Participle) |kjv: clovenfooted, cleave, rent, cleft, stay| {str: 8156}

N^m) ⟠ᕈᴌᴌ (שסע Sh-SAh) — **Splitting:** [freq. 4] |kjv: cleave| {str: 8157}

2858) ⟠ᕈᴌᴌ (שסף ShSP) ac: **Hew** co: **?** ab: **?:** A cutting or hacking into pieces. [from: ᕈᴌᴌ - cutting]

V) ⟠ᕈᴌᴌ (שסף Sh-SP) — **Hew:** To hew into pieces. [freq. 1] (vf: Piel) |kjv: hew| {str: 8158}

2859) ⊗⟠ᴌᴌ (שעט ShAhTh) ac: **Stomp** co: **?** ab: **?**

N^f1) ✻⊗⟠ᴌᴌ (שעטה ShAh-ThH) — **Stomping:** [freq. 1] |kjv: stamping| {str: 8161}

2860) ᴌ⟠ᴌᴌ (שעל ShAhL) ac: **?** co: **Hollow** ab: **?:** A hollowed out depression.

N^m) ᴌ⟠ᴌᴌ (שעל Sh-AhL) — **Handful:** The filling of the hollow of the hand. [freq. 3] |kjv: handful, hollow| {str: 8168}

o^m) ᴌ⟠Yᴌᴌ (שועל ShW-AhL) — **Shual:** An unknown animal that lives in a hollow in the ground. [ms: שעל] [freq. 7] |kjv: fox| {str: 7776}

hc^m) ᴌY⟠ᴌᴌᴧ (משעול MSh-AhWL) — **Path:** A hollow in the land. [ms: משעל] [freq. 1] |kjv: path| {str: 4934}

2861) (שען ShAhN) ac: **Lean** co: **Staff** ab: **Support:** The staff carried by the shepherd is his support. [from:]

V) (שען Sh-AhN) — **Lean:** To lean on something for rest or support. [freq. 22] (vf: Niphal) |kjv: lean, stay, rely, rest| {str: 8172}

h^m) (משען MSh-AhN) — **Support:** [freq. 5] |kjv: stay| {str: 4937}

h^f1) (משענה MSh-Ah-NH) — **Staff:** As a support for walking. [freq. 12] |kjv: staff, stave| {str: 4938}

~~~~~~~~~~~

2862) (שער ShAhR) ac: **?** co: **Gate** ab: **?:** The entrance into the city as well the activities carried out there such as marketing and judging.

V) (שער Sh-AhR) — **Reason:** To think in the sense of splitting open and entering as a gate. [freq. 1] (vf: Paal) |kjv: think| {str: 8176}

N^m) (שער Sh-AhR) — **I. Gate:** [Hebrew and Aramaic] [ar: תרע] **II. Shaar:** A unit of measurement. **III. Gatekeeper:** [Hebrew and Aramaic] [ar: תרע] [freq. 375] |kjv: gate, city, door, port, porter, mouth| {str: 8179, 8180, 8651, 8652}

g^m) (שוער ShW-AhR) — **Gatekeeper:** [ms: שער] [freq. 37] |kjv: porter, doorkeeper| {str: 7778}

~~~~~~~~~~~

2863) (שפח ShPHh) ac: **Join** co: **?** ab: **?:** [from:]

e^f1) (שיפחה ShYP-HhH) — **Maid:** As joined to a mistress. [ms: שפחה] [freq. 63] |kjv: handmaid, maid, maidservant, bondwoman, maiden, womanservant, bondmaid, servant, wench| {str: 8198}

h^f1) (משפחה MSh-P-HhH) — **Family:** As joined together. [freq. 300] |kjv: family, kindred, kinds| {str: 4940}

~~~~~~~~~~~

2864) (שפט ShPTh) ac: **Judge** co: **?** ab: **Judgment:** Rulings over cases as well as the action of deciding a case.

V) (שפט Sh-PTh) — **Judge:** To rule over cases of dispute or wrong doing. [Hebrew and Aramaic] [freq. 204] (vf: Paal, Niphal, Participle) |kjv: judge, plead, avenge, condemn, execute, judgment, defend, deliver, magistrate| {str: 8199, 8200}

N^m) (שפט Sh-PTh) — **Judgment:** [freq. 16] |kjv: judgment| {str: 8201}

c^m) (שפוט Sh-PWTh) — **Judgment:** [freq. 2] |kjv: judgment| {str: 8196}

d^m) (שפוט Sh-PWTh) — **Judgment:** [freq. 2] |kjv: judgment| {str: 8196}

h^m) (משפט MSh-PTh) — **Judgment:** [freq. 421] |kjv: judgment, manner, right, cause, ordinance, lawful, order, worthy, fashion, custom, discretion, law, measure, sentence| {str: 4941}

ef^m) (שיפטי ShYP-ThY) — **Sheriff:** [Aramaic only] [freq. 2] |kjv: sheriff| {str: 8614}

~~~~~~~~~~~

2865) (שפך ShPK) ac: **Pour** co: **Penis** ab: **?:** [from: - pouring]

V) ‏שׁפך‏ (‏שָׁפַך‏ Sh-PK) — **Pour:** To pour out a liquid including the blood of an animal in sacrifice or a man. [freq. 115] (vf: Paal, Niphal, Hitpael, Pual) |kjv: pour, shed, cast, gush| {str: 8210}

N^m) ‏שׁפך‏ (‏שֶׁפֶך‏ Sh-PK) — **Poured:** Something poured out. [freq. 2] |kjv: poured| {str: 8211}

N^fl) ‏שׁפכה‏ (‏שָׁפְכָה‏ ShP-KH) — **Penis:** In the sense of what pours out. [freq. 1] |kjv: member| {str: 8212}

2866) ‏שׁפל‏ (‏שָׁפָל‏ ShPL) ac: **Low** co: **Lowland** ab: **?:** Something or someone that is brought down low by someone high or to contrast it with something that is high. [from: ‏שׁ‏ - coming bowed down to another]

V) ‏שׁפל‏ (‏שָׁפֵל‏ Sh-PL) — **Low:** To be low in position or stature. [Hebrew and Aramaic] [freq. 33] (vf: Paal, Hiphil) |kjv: low, down, humble, abase, debase, lower, subdue| {str: 8213, 8214}

N^m) ‏שׁפל‏ (‏שָׁפָל‏ Sh-PL) — **Low:** [Hebrew and Aramaic] [freq. 22] |kjv: low, lower, base, humble, lowly| {str: 8215, 8216, 8217}

N^fl) ‏שׁפלה‏ (‏שְׁפֵלָה‏ ShP-LH) — **Lowland:** A low place. [freq. 20] |kjv: valley, vale, plain, low| {str: 8219}

N^f3) ‏שׁפלות‏ (‏שִׁפְלוּת‏ ShP-LWT) — **Idleness:** In the sense of being low in the activity. [freq. 1] |kjv: idleness| {str: 8220}

e^fl) ‏שׁיפלה‏ (‏שִׁיפְלָה‏ ShYP-LH) — **Lowland:** A low place. [ms: ‏שׁפלה‏] [freq. 1] |kjv: low| {str: 8218}

2867) ‏שׁפן‏ (‏שָׁפָן‏ ShPN) ac: **?** co: **?** ab: **?**

N^m) ‏שׁפן‏ (‏שָׁפָן‏ Sh-PN) — **Shaphan:** An unknown animal. [freq. 34] |kjv: shaphan, coney| {str: 8227}

2868) ‏שׁפע‏ (‏שֶׁפַע‏ ShPAh) ac: **?** co: **?** ab: **Abundance**

N^m) ‏שׁפע‏ (‏שֶׁפַע‏ Sh-PAh) — **Abundance:** [freq. 1] |kjv: abundance| {str: 8228}

e^fl) ‏שׁיפעה‏ (‏שִׁיפְעָה‏ ShYP-AhH) — **Abundance:** [freq. 6] |kjv: abundance, company, multitude| {str: 8229}

2869) ‏שׁפר‏ (‏שָׁפַר‏ ShPR) ac: **Bright** co: **?** ab: **?:** A bright or beautiful sight or sound. (eng: spiral - the shape of the rams horn; spring)

V) ‏שׁפר‏ (‏שָׁפַר‏ Sh-PR) — **Bright:** To be cheerful. [Hebrew and Aramaic] [freq. 4] (vf: Paal) |kjv: goodly, good, please, acceptable| {str: 8231, 8232}

N^m) ‏שׁפר‏ (‏שֶׁפֶר‏ Sh-PR) — **Bright:** As cheerful. [freq. 1] |kjv: goodly| {str: 8233}

b^m) ‏שׁפיר‏ (‏שְׁפִיר‏ Sh-PYR) — **Bright:** In the sense of being cheerful or beautiful. [Aramaic only] [freq. 2] |kjv: fair| {str: 8209}

e^fl) ‏שׁיפרה‏ (‏שִׁיפְרָה‏ ShYP-RH) — **Bright:** As cheerful. [freq. 1] |kjv: garnished| {str: 8235}

g^m) ‏שׁופר‏ (‏שׁוֹפָר‏ ShW-PR) — **Horn:** The horn of ram made into a trumpet that emits a bright and beautiful ound. [ms: שׁפֵר] [freq. 72] |kjv: trumpet, cornet| {str: 7782}

l^m) ᛕ◯ᛕ◯ய (שׁפרפר ShP-R-PR) — **Dawn:** As the beginning of brightness. [Aramaic only] [freq. 1] |kjv: early| {str: 8238}

ld^m) ᛕᏴᛕ◯ய (שׁפרור ShP-RWR) — **Tapestry:** As brightly colored. [freq. 1] |kjv: pavilion| {str: 8237}

~~~~~~~~~

2870) †◯ய (שׁפת ShPT) ac: **?** co: **Set** ab: **?**

V) †◯ய (שׁפת Sh-PT) — **Place:** To set in place. [freq. 5] (vf: Paal) |kjv: set, brought, ordain| {str: 8239}

N^m) †◯ய (שׁפת Sh-PT) — **Peg:** For hanging, or placing, items. [freq. 2] |kjv: pot, hook| {str: 8240}

h^m) †◯யᵐᵐ (משׁפת MSh-PT) — **Saddlebags:** For placing items. [freq. 2] |kjv: burden, sheepfold| {str: 4942}

nc^m) †ϒ◯ய𝓎 (אשׁפות ASh-PWT) — **Dump:** Where refuse is placed. [ms: אשׁפת] [df: שׁפת] [freq. 7] |kjv: dung, dunghill| {str: 830}

~~~~~~~~~

2871) ◯ɵʌய (שׁצף ShTsP) ac: **Surge** co: **?** ab: **?**: [from: ɵʌய]

N^m) ◯ɵʌய (שׁצף Sh-TsP) — **Surge:** [freq. 1] |kjv: little| {str: 8241}

~~~~~~~~~

2872) ᛏ-ɵ-ய (שׁקד ShQD) ac: **Watch** co: **Eye** ab: **?**: Eyes open wide for watching carefully. [from: ɵய]

V) ᛏ-ɵ-ய (שׁקד Sh-QD) — **Watch:** To be alert and watchful. [freq. 18] (vf: Pual, Participle) |kjv: watch,

wake, remain, hasten, almond| {str: 8245, 8246}

N^m) ᛏ-ɵ-ய (שׁקד Sh-QD) — **Almond:** From its shape like an open eye. The nut or the tree. [freq. 4] |kjv: almond| {str: 8247}

~~~~~~~~~

2873) ⊗-ɵ-ய (שׁקט ShQTh) ac: **Tranquil** co: **?** ab: **Tranquility**

V) ⊗-ɵ-ய (שׁקט Sh-QTh) — **Tranquil:** To be quiet and at rest. [freq. 41] (vf: Paal, Hiphil) |kjv: rest, quiet, still, appease, idle| {str: 8252}

N^m) ⊗-ɵ-ய (שׁקט Sh-QTh) — **Tranquility:** [freq. 1] |kjv: quietness| {str: 8253}

~~~~~~~~~

2874) ᒐ-ɵ-ய (שׁקל ShQL) ac: **Weigh** co: **?** ab: **?**

V) ᒐ-ɵ-ய (שׁקל Sh-QL) — **Weigh:** To weigh out, usually of silver for payment. [freq. 22] (vf: Paal, Niphal) |kjv: weigh, pay, throughly, receive, receive, spend| {str: 8254}

N^m) ᒐ-ɵ-ய (שׁקל Sh-QL) — I. **Sheqel:** A unit of measurement. [Hebrew and Aramaic] [ar: תקל] II. **Weighed:** [Aramaic only] [ar: תקל] [freq. 91] |kjv: shekel, tekel, weighted| {str: 8255, 8625}

h^m) ᒐ-ɵ-யᵐᵐ (משׁקל MSh-QL) — **Weight:** [freq. 49] |kjv: weight, weigh| {str: 4948}

h^{f2}) †ᒐ-ɵ-யᵐᵐ (משׁקלת MSh-Q-LT) — **Plumb:** A weighted tool for leveling. [freq. 2] |kjv: plummet| {str: 4949}

hc^m) ᒐϒ-ɵ-யᵐᵐ (משׁקול MSh-QWL) — **Weight:** [freq. 1] |kjv: weight| {str: 4946}

~~~~~~~~~

2875) ﻉﻉﻉ (שקם ShQM) ac: ? co: ?
ab: ?: (eng: sycamore)

N^f) ﻉﻉﻉ (שקם Sh-QM) —
Sycamore: The tree or fruit. [freq. 7]
|kjv: sycamore| {str: 8256}

2876) ﻉﻉﻉ (שקע ShQAh) ac: **Sink**
co: **Deep** ab: ?: [from: ﻉﻉﻉ]

V) ﻉﻉﻉ (שקע Sh-QAh) — **Sink:**
To sink down. [freq. 6] (vf: Paal,
Niphal, Hiphil) |kjv: drown, quench,
sink, down, deep| {str: 8257}

h^m) ﻉﻉﻉﻉ (משקע MSh-QAh)
— **Deep:** [freq. 1] |kjv: deep| {str:
4950}

2877) ﻉﻉﻉ (שקף ShQP) ac: **Look** co:
Window ab: ?: [from: ﻉﻉﻉ]

V) ﻉﻉﻉ (שקף Sh-QP) — **Look:**
To look out and down as through a
window. [freq. 22] (vf: Niphal,
Hiphil) |kjv: look, appear| {str: 8259}

N^m) ﻉﻉﻉ (שקף Sh-QP) —
Window: [freq. 1] |kjv: window|
{str: 8260}

d^m) ﻉﻉﻉﻉ (שקוף Sh-QWP) —
Light: From a window. [ms: שקף]
[freq. 2] |kjv: light, window| {str:
8261}

ac^m) ﻉﻉﻉﻉﻉ (משקוף MSh-
QWP) — **Lintel:** As an overhang over
the door. [freq. 3] |kjv: lintel,
doorpost| {str: 4947}

2878) ﻉﻉﻉ (שקץ ShQTs) ac: **Detest**
co: **Filthy** ab: ?: A dirty and detestable
thing.

V) ﻉﻉﻉ (שקץ Sh-QTs) —
Detest: T detest that which is filthy.
[freq. 7] (vf: Piel) |kjv: abomination,
abhor, detest| {str: 8262}

N^m) ﻉﻉﻉ (שקץ Sh-QTs) —
Filthy: [freq. 11] |kjv: abomination,
abominable| {str: 8263}

ed^m) ﻉﻉﻉﻉﻉ (שיקוץ ShY-QWTs)
— **Filthiness:** [ms: שקוץ שקץ]
[freq. 28] |kjv: abomination,
detestable, abomination| {str: 8251}

2879) ﻉﻉﻉ (שקר ShQR) ac: ? co: **Lie**
ab: ?: False or untrue words meant to
deceive.

V) ﻉﻉﻉ (שקר Sh-QR) — **Lie:**
[freq. 6] (vf: Paal, Piel) |kjv: lie,
falsely| {str: 8266}

N^m) ﻉﻉﻉ (שקר Sh-QR) — **Lie:**
[freq. 113] |kjv: lie, lying, false,
falsehood, falsely, vain, wrongfully,
deceitful, deceit, liar| {str: 8267}

2880) ﻉﻉﻉ (שרב ShRB) ac: ? co:
Mirage ab: ?: The heat from the sun
causing waves over the ground to appear
like water.

N^m) ﻉﻉﻉ (שרב Sh-RB) — **Mirage:**
[freq. 2] |kjv: parched, heat| {str:
8273}

2881) ﻉﻉﻉ (שרץ ShRTs) ac: **Swarmer**
co: **Swarmer** ab: ?: The moving mass of
a swarm.

V) ﻉﻉﻉ (שרץ Sh-RTs) —
Swarmer: [freq. 14] (vf: Paal) |kjv:
creep, abundantly, move, breed,
increase| {str: 8317}

N^(m)) שרֱﬞﬞ (שרץ Sh-RTs) — **Swarmer:** [freq. 15] |kjv: creeping, creep, creature, move| {str: 8318}

~~~~~~~~~

2882) ﬞﬞﬞ (שרק ShRQ) ac: **Whistle** co: **Flute** ab: **?:** [from: ﬞﬞﬞ - as from the wind]

V) ﬞﬞﬞ (שרק Sh-RQ) — **Whistle:** [freq. 12] (vf: Paal) |kjv: hiss| {str: 8319}

N^(fl)) ﬞﬞﬞ (שרקה ShR-QH) — **Whistling:** [freq. 7] |kjv: hissing| {str: 8322}

d^(fl)) ﬞﬞﬞ (שרוקה Sh-RW-QH) — **Whistling:** [df: שריקה] [freq. 3] |kjv: hissing, bleating| {str: 8292}

acf^f) ﬞﬞﬞ (משרוקי MSh-RW-QY) — **Flute:** A musical instrument that whistles. [freq. 4] |kjv: flute| {str: 4953}

~~~~~~~~~

2883) ﬞﬞﬞ (שרש ShRSh) ac: **?** co: **Root** ab: **?**

V) ﬞﬞﬞ (שרש Sh-RSh) — **Root:** To take root in soil. Also to take out by the roots. [freq. 8] (vf: Hiphil, Pual, Piel) |kjv: root| {str: 8327}

N^(fl)) ﬞﬞﬞ (שרשה ShR-ShH) — **Chain:** [Unknown connection to root;] [freq. 1] |kjv: chain| {str: 8331}

g^(m)) ﬞﬞﬞ (שורש ShW-RSh) — **Root:** [Hebrew and Aramaic] [ms: שרש] [freq. 36] |kjv: root, bottom, deep, heel| {str: 8328, 8330}

cq^f) ﬞﬞﬞ (שרושו Sh-RW-ShW) — **Uproot:** In the sense of being taken out. [Aramaic only] [freq. 1] |kjv: banishment| {str: 8332}

~~~~~~~~~

2884) ﬞﬞﬞ (שרת ShRT) ac: **Serve** co: **?** ab: **Service**

V) ﬞﬞﬞ (שרת Sh-RT) — **Serve:** To be in service to another. [freq. 97] (vf: Piel) |kjv: minister, serve, servant, service, servitor, waited| {str: 8334}

N^(m)) ﬞﬞﬞ (שרת Sh-RT) — **Service:** [freq. 2] |kjv: ministry, minister| {str: 8335}

~~~~~~~~~

2885) ﬞﬞﬞ (שׁשׁר ShShR) ac: **?** co: **?** ab: **?**

N^(m)) ﬞﬞﬞ (שׁשׁר Sh-ShR) — **Vermilion:** A reddish color. [freq. 2] |kjv: vermillion| {str: 8350}

~~~~~~~~~

2886) ﬞﬞﬞ (שׁתל ShTL) ac: **?** co: **Plant** ab: **?**

V) ﬞﬞﬞ (שׁתל Sh-TL) — **Plant:** [freq. 10] (vf: Paal) |kjv: plant| {str: 8362}

N^(m)) ﬞﬞﬞ (שׁתל Sh-TL) — **Plant:** [freq. 1] |kjv: plant| {str: 8363}

~~~~~~~~~

2887) ﬞﬞﬞ (שׁתם ShTM) ac: **Open** co: **?** ab: **?**

V) ﬞﬞﬞ (שׁתם Sh-TM) — **Open:** [freq. 2] (vf: Paal) |kjv: open| {str: 8365}

~~~~~~~~~

2888) ﬞﬞﬞ (שׁתן ShTN) ac: **Urinate** co: **?** ab: **?**

V) ﬞﬞﬞ (שׁתן Sh-TN) — **Urinate:** [freq. 6] (vf: Hiphil) |kjv: piss| {str: 8366}

~~~~~~~~~

2889) ‑●‑†ய (שתק ShTQ) ac: **Calm** co: **? ab: ?**

V) ‑●‑†ய (שתק Sh-TQ) — **Calm:** [freq. 4] (vf: Paal) |kjv: calm, quiet, cease| {str: 8367}

2890) אﬥ山 (שע ShGhR) ac: **?** co: **?** ab: **Offensive**

g[m]**)** ﬡ◎Yய (שוער ShW-AhR) — **Offensive:** [ms: שער] [freq. 1] |kjv: vile| {str: 8182}

Taw

2891) ⊔⊔□□† (תחש THhSh) ac: ? co: ? ab: ?

N^m) ⊔⊔□□† (תחש T-HhSh) — **Tahhash:** An unknown animal. [freq. 14] |kjv: badger| {str: 8476}

~~~~~~~~~

2892) †□□† (תחת THhT) ac: ? co: **Under** ab: ?: The lower or bottom part of something. [from: □□† - as the under part is divided from what is above]

N^m) †□□† (תחת T-HhT) — **Under:** Under or underneath. Also to be underneath in the sense of being in place of something else. [Hebrew and Aramaic] [freq. 25] |kjv: instead, under, for, as, with, from, flat, same| {str: 8478, 8479}

c^m) †Y□□† (תחות T-HhWT) — **Under:** [ms: תחת] [freq. 4] |kjv: under| {str: 8460}

f^m) ⌐†□□† (תחתי T-Hh-TY) — **Low:** A low place. [freq. 19] |kjv: nether, lowest, lower| {str: 8482}

j^m) ⅃Y†□□† (תחתון THh-TWN) — **Lower:** [ms: תחתון] [freq. 13] |kjv: nether, lower, lowest, nethermost| {str: 8481}

~~~~~~~~~

2893) ⅃Ш† (תכן TKN) ac: **Weigh** co: **Measure** ab: **Sum**

V) ⅃Ш† (תכן T-KN) — **Weigh:** To measure out by weight. [freq. 18] (vf: Paal, Niphal, Pual, Piel, Participle) |kjv: equal, weigh, ponder, unequal, direct, meter| {str: 8505}

N^f4) †⅃Ш† (תכנית TK-NYT) — **Sum:** An amount weighted out. [freq. 2] |kjv: sum, pattern| {str: 8508}

d^f1) ⚥⅃YШ† (תכונה T-KW-NH) — **Treasure:** As weighed out. [freq. 2] |kjv: fashion, store| {str: 8498}

g^m) ⅃YШ† (תוכן TW-KN) — **Measure:** An amount weighted out. [ms: תכן] [freq. 2] |kjv: tale, measure| {str: 8506}

ac^f2) †⅃YШ†ᴀ (מתכונת MT-KW-NT) — **Sum:** An amount weighted out. [ms: מתכנת] [freq. 5] |kjv: tale| {str: 4971}

ad^f2) †⅃YШ†ᴀ (מתכונת MT-KW-NT) — **Measure:** An amount weighted out. [freq. 5] |kjv: composition, state, measure| {str: 4971}

~~~~~~~~~

2894) ⊂⊍† (תלף TLP) ac: **Hang** co: ? ab: ?: [from: ⊍† - hanging]

f^f1) ⚥⌐⊣⊂⊍† (תלפיה TL-P-YH) — **Armory:** For hanging shields. [freq. 1] |kjv: armoury| {str: 8530}

~~~~~~~~~

2895) Шᴀ† (תמך TMK) ac: **Hold** co: ? ab: ?: A holding up of something. [from: ᴀ⚥ - setting up a support]

V) Шᴀ† (תמך T-MK) — **Hold up:** To hold up to support or steady. [freq. 21] (vf: Paal, Niphal) |kjv: hold, uphold, retain| {str: 8551}

~~~~~~~~~

2896) ⟨ (תמר TMR) ac: **Erect** co: **Palm** ab: ?: The standing tall and thin of a palm tree.

N^m) ⟨ (תמר T-MR) — **Palm:** The erect palm tree. [freq. 12] |kjv: palm tree| {str: 8558}

e^fl) ⟨ (תימרה TYM-RH) — **Pillar:** Straight and tall as a palm tree. [ms: תמרה] [freq. 2] |kjv: pillar| {str: 8490}

g^m) ⟨ (תומר TW-MR) — **Palm:** The erect palm tree. [ms: תמר] [freq. 2] |kjv: palm tree| {str: 8560}

ec^f) ⟨ (תימור TY-MWR) — **Palm:** Figures of a palm tree. [ms: תמר] [freq. 19] |kjv: palm tree| {str: 8561}

ld^m) ⟨ (תמרור TM-RWR) — **Post:** A straight and tall pillar as a marker. [freq. 1] |kjv: heap| {str: 8564}

2897) ⟨ (תעב TAhB) ac: **Hate** co: ? ab: **Disgusting**

V) ⟨ (תעב T-AhB) — **Hate:** To hate something that is disgusting. [freq. 22] (vf: Niphal, Hiphil, Piel) |kjv: abhor, abominable| {str: 8581}

g^fl) ⟨ (תועבה TW-Ah-BH) — **Disgusting:** [ms: תעבה] [freq. 117] |kjv: abomination, abominable| {str: 8441}

2898) ⟨ (תפל TPL) ac: ? co: **Unseasoned** ab: **Unsavory:** A lack of ingredients that makes something worthless or bland.

N^m) ⟨ (תפל T-PL) — **Unseasoned:** [freq. 7] |kjv:

untempered, foolish, unsavory| {str: 8602}

N^fl) ⟨ (תפלה TP-LH) — **Unsavory:** [freq. 3] |kjv: folly, foolishly| {str: 8604}

2899) ⟨ (תפס TPS) ac: **Seize** co: ? ab: ?

V) ⟨ (תפס T-PS) — **Seize:** To take hold of something by force. [df: תפש] [freq. 65] (vf: Paal, Niphal, Piel) |kjv: take, handle, hold, catch, surprise| {str: 8610}

2900) ⟨ (תפר TPR) ac: **Sew** co: ? ab: ?

V) ⟨ (תפר T-PR) — **Sew:** [freq. 4] (vf: Paal, Piel, Participle) |kjv: sew| {str: 8609}

2901) ⟨ (תקן TQN) ac: **Straight** co: ? ab: ?

V) ⟨ (תקן T-QN) — **Straight:** To set in a straight row, or in its proper alignment. [Hebrew and Aramaic] [freq. 4] (vf: Paal, Hophal, Piel) |kjv: straight, order, establish| {str: 8626, 8627}

2902) ⟨ (תקע TQAh) ac: **Thrust** co: **Trumpet** ab: ?

V) ⟨ (תקע T-QAh) — **Thrust:** To thrust a pole into the ground such as when setting up the tent. Also the thrust the sound of the trumpet by blowing. [freq. 69] (vf: Paal, Niphal) |kjv: blow, fasten, strike, pitch, thrust, clap, sound| {str: 8628}

N^m) ⊜-●-† (תקע T-QAh) — **Thrust:** The sound of a trumpet. [freq. 1] |kjv: sound| {str: 8629}

c^m) ⊜Y-●-† (תקוע T-QWAh) — **Trumpet:** An instrument of loud noise thrust out for rejoicing or alarm. [freq. 1] |kjv: trumpet| {str: 8619}

~~~~~~~~~~

2903) ⊂-●-† (תקף TQP) ac: **Firm** co: **?** ab: **Authority**

V) ⊂-●-† (תקף T-QP) — **Firm:** To be firm in strength and authority. [Hebrew and Aramaic] [freq. 8] (vf: Paal) |kjv: prevail, strong, harden, firm| {str: 8630, 8631}

N^m) ⊂-●-† (תקף T-QP) — **Firmness:** [Aramaic only] [freq. 2] |kjv: strength, might| {str: 8632}

b^m) ⊂-⟩-●-† (תקיף T-QYP) — **Mighty:** [Hebrew and Aramaic] [freq. 6] |kjv: mightier, strong, mighty| {str: 8623, 8624}

g^m) ⊂-●-Y† (תוקף TW-QP) — **Authority:** In the sense of firmness. [freq. 3] |kjv: strength, power, authority| {str: 8633}

~~~~~~~~~~

Ghah

2904) 𐤀-𐤏-𐤋 (עקל GhQL) ac: ? co: **Crooked** ab: ?: [from: 𐤏-𐤋]

V) 𐤀-𐤏-𐤋 (עקל Gh-QL) — **Crooked:** [freq. 1] (vf: Pual) |kjv: wrong| {str: 6127}

I ᵐ) 𐤀-𐤏-𐤋-𐤏-𐤋 (עקלקל Gh-QL-QL) — **Crooked:** A crooked path. [freq. 2] |kjv: crooked| {str: 6128}

2905) 𐤀-𐤏-𐤓 (עקר GhQR) ac: **Pluck** co: **Root** ab: ?: The pulling up of the root out of the ground. [from: 𐤀-𐤏 - from the crooked shape of the roots]

V) 𐤀-𐤏-𐤓 (עקר Gh-QR) — **Pluck:** To pluck or dig out the roots. [Hebrew and Aramaic] [freq. 8] (vf: Paal, Niphal, Piel) |kjv: hough, pluck, root, dig| {str: 6131, 6132}

Nᵐ) 𐤀-𐤏-𐤓 (עקר Gh-QR) — **I. Barren:** In the sense of being plucked from the roots. **II. Stalk:** As attached to the roots. [Aramaic only] [freq. 13] |kjv: stock, barren| {str: 6133, 6135}

eᵐ) 𐤀-𐤏-𐤉-𐤓 (עיקר GhY-QR) — **Stump:** The part of the tree or plant that is connected to the roots. [Aramaic only] [ms: עקר] [freq. 3] |kjv: stump| {str: 6136}

2906) 𐤀-𐤏-𐤔 (עקש GhQSh) ac: ? co: **Crooked** ab: **Perverse:** To act or walk a crooked path as being perverse.

V) 𐤀-𐤏-𐤔 (עקש Gh-QSh) — **Crooked:** [freq. 5] (vf: Paal, Niphal, Hiphil, Piel) |kjv: perverse, pervert, crooked| {str: 6140}

aᵐ) 𐤀-𐤏-𐤔-𐤌 (מעקש MGh-QSh) — **Crooked:** A crooked place. [freq. 1] |kjv: crooked| {str: 4625}

eᵐ) 𐤀-𐤏-𐤉-𐤔 (עיקש GhY-QSh) — **Crooked:** [ms: עקש] [freq. 11] |kjv: perverse, froward, crooked| {str: 6141}

eᶠ³) 𐤀-𐤏-𐤉-𐤔-𐤕 (עיקשות GhY-Q-ShWT) — **Crookedness:** [freq. 2] |kjv: froward| {str: 6143}

2907) 𐤀-𐤓-𐤁 (ערב GhRB) ac: **Dark** co: **Raven** ab: ?: [from: 𐤀-𐤁]

V) 𐤀-𐤓-𐤁 (ערב Gh-RB) — **Dark:** To be dark as the evening sky. [freq. 3] (vf: Paal, Hiphil) |kjv: evening, darkened| {str: 6150}

Nᵐ) 𐤀-𐤓-𐤁 (ערב Gh-RB) — **I. Dark:** The dark of the evening or dark skinned people. **II. Willow:** From its shade and dark covering. [freq. 142] |kjv: even, evening, night, mingled, people, eventide, arabia, day| {str: 6153, 6155}

Nᶠˡ) 𐤀-𐤓-𐤁-𐤄 (ערבה GhR-BH) — **Desert:** As a dark place. [freq. 61] |kjv: plain, desert, wilderness, arbah, champaign, evening, heaven| {str: 6160}

gᵐ) 𐤀-𐤅-𐤓-𐤁 (עורב GhW-RB) — **Raven:** As black in color. [ms: ערב] [freq. 10] |kjv: raven| {str: 6158}

2908) 𐤀-𐤓-𐤌 (ערם GhRM) ac: **Subtle** co: ? ab: ?

V) 𐤀𐤄𐤌 (ערם Gh-RM) — **Subtle:** To be subtle in craftiness or prudence. [freq. 5] (vf: Paal, Hiphil) |kjv: subtilty, crafty, prudent, beware| {str: 6191}

N^(f1)) 𐤀𐤄𐤌𐤑 (ערמה GhR-MH) — **Subtlety:** In craftiness or prudence. [freq. 5] |kjv: guile| {str: 6195}

d^(m)) 𐤀𐤄𐤉𐤌 (ערום Gh-RWM) — **Subtle:** In craftiness or prudence. [freq. 11] |kjv: prudent, crafty, subtil| {str: 6175}

g^(m)) 𐤀𐤄𐤉𐤌 (עורם GhW-RM) — **Subtlety:** In craftiness or prudence. [ms: ערם] [freq. 1] |kjv: craftiness| {str: 6193}

j^(m)) 𐤀𐤄𐤌𐤉𐤋 (ערמון Gh-RMWN) — **Ermon:** An unknown tree. [freq. 2] |kjv: chestnut| {str: 6196}

~~~~~~~~~~~

2909) 𐤀𐤄𐤀 (ערף GhRP) ac: **Drop** co: **Cloud** ab: **?:** The dropping of rain from clouds. [from: 𐤋𐤄 - dark clouds]

V) 𐤀𐤄𐤀 (ערף Gh-RP) — **Drop:** To drop down as rain from the clouds.

[freq. 2] (vf: Paal) |kjv: drop| {str: 6201}

b^(m)) 𐤀𐤄𐤉𐤀 (עריף Gh-RYP) — **Clouds:** As dark rain clouds. [freq. 1] |kjv: heaven| {str: 6183}

~~~~~~~~~~~

2910) 𐤀𐤕𐤄 (עתר GhTR) ac: **Intercede** co: **Incense** ab: **?:** The burning of incense as a form of prayer for intercession or supplication.

V) 𐤀𐤕𐤄 (עתר Gh-TR) — **Intercede:** To supplicate on the behalf of another. [freq. 20] (vf: Paal, Niphal, Hiphil) |kjv: intreat, pray, prayer| {str: 6279}

N^(m)) 𐤀𐤕𐤄 (עתר Gh-TR) — **Dark:** As a thick and dark cloud of incense. [freq. 2] |kjv: thick, suppliant| {str: 6282}

~~~~~~~~~~~

Adopted Roots (Four letter)

3001) ᴧᴧᴸᴗᴸⵂ (אלגם ALGM) ac: ? co: ? ab: ?

d^m) ᴧᴧΥᴸᴗⵂ (אלגום AL-GWM) — **Algum:** The tree or the wood. [df: אלמוג] (;] [freq. 6] |kjv: algum, almug| {str: 418, 484}

3002) ✝ᴏᴸᴗⵂ (אשדת AShDT) ac: ? co: ? ab: **Fiery Law:** [from: ᴸᴗⵂ ✝ᴏ - construct word]

N^f) ✝ᴏᴸᴗⵂ (אשדת ASh-DT) — **Fiery Law:** [freq. 1] |kjv: fiery| {str: 799}

3003) ᴍᴗᴏᴛᴍ (בדלח BDLHh) ac: ? co: ? ab: ?

c^m) ᴍᴗΥᴏᴛᴍ (בדולח B-DW-LHh) — **Amber:** A gum resin. [ms: בדלח] [freq. 2] |kjv: bdellium| {str: 916}

3004) ✝ᴏᴗⵙ (בלעד BLAhD) ac: ? co: ? ab: **Without:** [from: ᴗ ✝ᴏ - construct word]

ef^m) ⵋᴛᴏᴗⵙᴛ (בילעדי BYL-Ah-DY) — **Without:** [ms: בלעדי] [freq. 17] |kjv: beside, save, without, not in me, not| {str: 1107}

3005) ᴗᴄᴐᴍ (ברזל BRZL) ac: ? co: **Iron** ab: ?

N^m) ᴗᴄᴐᴍ (ברזל BR-ZL) — **Iron:** [Hebrew and Aramaic] [ar: פרזל] [freq. 96] |kjv: iron, head| {str: 1270, 6523}

3006) ᴗᴏᴗᴍ (גבעל GBAhL) ac: ? co: ? ab: ?: [from: ᴗᴍ - as bowl shaped]

ec^m) ᴗΥᴏᴗᴡᴸ (גיבעול GYB-AhWL) — **Bloom:** [ms: גבעל] [freq. 1] |kjv: bolled| {str: 1392}

3007) ᴚᴏᴢᴸ (גזבר GZBR) ac: ? co: **Treasurer** ab: ?: [from: ᴗᴢ - as a purchasing tool]

N^m) ᴚᴏᴢᴸ (גזבר GZ-BR) — **Treasurer:** [freq. 2] |kjv: treasurer| {str: 1411}

e^m) ᴚᴏᴢᴛᴸ (גיזבר GYZ-BR) — **Treasurer:** [Aramaic only] [ms: גזבר] [freq. 2] |kjv: treasurer| {str: 1489, 1490}

3008) ✝ᴧᴧᴗᴸ (גלמד GLMD) ac: ? co: ? ab: **Barren**

d^m) ✝Υᴧᴧᴗᴸ (גלמוד GL-MWD) — **Barren:** [freq. 4] |kjv: solitary, desolate| {str: 1565}

3009) ⲿ⊗ⲅL (גרטל GRThL) ac: ? co: ? ab: ?

n^m) ⲿ⊗ⲅLⳞ (אגרטל AGR-ThL) — **Basin:** A basket or bag. [freq. 2] |kjv: charger| {str: 105}

~~~~~~

3010) ⴑ⌐ⲅⲖ (גנזך GNZK) ac: ? co: **Treasury** ab: ?: [from: ⲅⲖ - as a place protected]

N^m) ⴑ⌐ⲅⲖ (גנזך GN-ZK) — **Treasury:** [freq. 1] |kjv: treasury| {str: 1597}

~~~~~~

3011) ⴑⳑⴤ⍦ (המנך HMNK) ac: ? co: ? ab: ?

b^m) ⴑⴑⳑⴤ⍦ (המניך HM-NYK) — **Necklace:** [Aramaic only] [freq. 3] |kjv: chain| {str: 2002}

~~~~~~

3012) ⲟⲟⲿⲅ (זלעף ZLAhP) ac: ? co: ? ab: **Horror:** [from: ⲟⲅ - a trembling anger]

N^{fl}) ⍦ⲟⲟⲿⲅ (זלעפה ZL-Ah-PH) — **Horror:** [freq. 3] |kjv: horror, terrible, horrible| {str: 2152}

~~~~~~

3013) ⲟⲅⲝⲅ (זרזף ZRZP) ac: **Flow** co: **Water** ab: ?: [from: ⲝⲅ - a sneeze]

b^m) ⲟⴑⲅⲝⲅ (זרזיף ZR-ZYP) — **Water:** A watering of the land. [freq. 1] |kjv: water| {str: 2222}

~~~~~~

3014) ⲿⲟⲛⲺ (חבצל HhBTsL) ac: ? co: ? ab: ?

N^{f2}) †ⲿⲟⲛⲺ (חבצלת HhB-Ts-LT) — **Hhavatselet:** An unknown flower. [freq. 2] |kjv: rose| {str: 2261}

~~~~~~

3015) ⳑⳑⲙⲿⲺ (חלמש HhLMSh) ac: ? co: ? ab: ?

b^m) ⳑⳑⲙⴑⲿⲺ (חלמיש HhL-MYSh) — **Flint:** [freq. 5] |kjv: flint, flinty, rock| {str: 2496}

~~~~~~

3016) ⲿⲙⳑⲺ (חנמל HhNML) ac: ? co: **Frost** ab: ?

N^m) ⲿⲙⳑⲺ (חנמל HhN-ML) — **Frost:** [freq. 1] |kjv: frost| {str: 2602}

~~~~~~

3017) ⲕⲟⲕⲺ (חספס HhSPS) ac: ? co: ? ab: ?

N^m) ⲕⲟⲕⲺ (חספס HhS-PS) — **Hhaspas:** An unknown item [freq. 1] |kjv: round| {str: 2636}

~~~~~~

3018) ⲅⲟⲛⲟⲛⲺ (חצצר HhTsTsR) ac: ? co: ? ab: ?

c^{fl}) ⍦ⲅⲟⲛⳋⲟⲛⲺ (חצוצרה Hh-TsWTs-RH) — **Trumpet:** [ms: חצצרה] [freq. 29] |kjv: trumpet| {str: 2689}

~~~~~~

3019) ⲿⲖⲅⲺ (חרגל HhRGL) ac: ? co: ? ab: ?

c^m) ⲿⲨⲖⲅⲺ (חרגול HhR-GWL) — **Locust:** [ms: חרגל] [freq. 1] |kjv: beetle| {str: 2728}

~~~~~~

3020) ⳑⳑⲙⲅⲺ (חרמש HhRMSh) ac: ? co: **Sickle** ab: ?

N^m) ⲖⲖⲘⲘ𐤉𐤔 (חרמש HhR-MSh) — **Sickle:** [freq. 2] |kjv: sickle| {str: 2770}

~~~~~~~

3021) 𐤉𐤔 (חרצב HhRTsB) ac: ? co: ? ab: ?

d^{f1}) 𐤉𐤔 (חרצובה HhR-TsW-BH) — **Band:** For binding the hands or feet. [ms: חרצבה] [freq. 2] |kjv: band| {str: 2784}

~~~~~~~

3022) 𐤔 (חשמל HhShML) ac: ? co: ? ab: ?

N^m) 𐤔 (חשמל HhSh-ML) — **Hhashmal:** An unknown material of a reddish color. [freq. 3] |kjv: amber| {str: 2830}

~~~~~~~

3023) 𐤉𐤔 (טפסר ThPSR) ac: ? co: ? ab: ?: [from: 𐤉𐤔]

e^m) 𐤉𐤔 (טיפסר ThYP-SR) — **Captain:** [freq. 2] |kjv: captain| {str: 2951}

~~~~~~~

3024) 𐤔 (כרסם KRSM) ac: ? co: ? ab: ?

V) 𐤔 (כרסם KR-SM) — **Tear:** [freq. 1] (vf: Piel) |kjv: waste| {str: 3765}

~~~~~~~

3025) 𐤔 (כפתר KPTR) ac: ? co: ? ab: ?

c^m) 𐤔 (כפתור KP-TWR) — **Knob:** An ornamental knob. [ms: כפתר] [freq. 18] |kjv: knop, lintel| {str: 3730}

~~~~~~~

3026) 𐤔 (כרבל KRBL) ac: ? co: **Clothing** ab: ?

N^m) 𐤔 (כרבל KR-BL) — **Clothed:** [freq. 1] |kjv: clothed| {str: 3736}

N^{f1}) 𐤔 (כרבלה KR-B-LH) — **Robe:** [Aramaic only] [ar: כרבלא] [freq. 1] |kjv: hat| {str: 3737}

~~~~~~~

3027) 𐤔 (כרכב KRKB) ac: ? co: ? ab: ?

c^m) 𐤔 (כרכוב KR-KWB) — **Rim:** [ms: כרכב] [freq. 2] |kjv: compass| {str: 3749}

~~~~~~~

3028) 𐤔 (כרכם KRKM) ac: ? co: ? ab: ?

c^m) 𐤔 (כרכום KR-KWM) — **Saffron:** [ms: כרכם] [freq. 1] |kjv: saffron| {str: 3750}

~~~~~~~

3029) 𐤔 (כרמל KRML) ac: ? co: **Garden** ab: ?

N^m) 𐤔 (כרמל KR-ML) — **Garden:** A field that produces an abundance of fruit. [freq. 13] |kjv: fruitful field, plentiful field, full ear, green ear, full ears of corn, plentiful| {str: 3759}

b^m) 𐤔 (כרמיל KR-MYL) — **Crimson:** [freq. 3] |kjv: crimson| {str: 3758}

~~~~~~~

3030) 𐤔 (כרפס KRPS) ac: ? co: ? ab: ?

N^m) 𐤔 (כרפס KR-PS) — **Green:** [freq. 1] |kjv: green| {str: 3768}

~~~~~~~~

3031) ⲧⲟⲃⲍ (נבזב NBZB) ac: ? co: ? ab: ?: [from: ⲍⲃ - as a price for acquiring a wife]

b^(fl)) ⲧⲟ⳩ⲃⲍⲃ (נביזבה N-BYZ-BH) — **Reward:** [ms: נבזבה] [freq. 2] |kjv: reward| {str: 5023}

~~~~~~~~

3032) ⲃⲣⲩⲟⲃ (נברש NBRSh) ac: ? co: ? ab: ?

N^(fl)) ⲧⲃⲣⲩⲟⲃ (נברשה NB-R-ShH) — **Lampstand:** [Aramaic only] [freq. 1] |kjv: candlestick| {str: 5043}

~~~~~~~~

3033) ⲩⲧⲟⲃⲇ (נדבך NDBK) ac: ? co: ? ab: ?

e^(m)) ⲩⲧⲟⲩⲇ (נידבך NYD-BK) — **Row:** [Aramaic only] [ms: נדבך] [freq. 2] |kjv: row| {str: 5073}

~~~~~~~~

3034) ⳑⲧⲟⲃ (נפתל NPTL) ac: ? co: ? ab: ?

d^(m)) ⳑⲧⲟⲃ (נפתול NP-TWL) — **Wrestle:** [freq. 1] |kjv: wrestling| {str: 5319}

~~~~~~~~

3035) ⲁⲩⳑⲥ (סגור SGWR) ac: ? co: ? ab: **Blindness**

N^(m)) ⲁⲩⳑⲥ (סגור SG-WR) — **Blindness:** [freq. 3] |kjv: blindness| {str: 5575}

~~~~~~~~

3036) ⳑⲩⲙⲥ (סמאל SMAL) ac: ? co: **Left** ab: ?

V) ⳑⲩⲙⲥ (סמאל SM-AL) — **Left:** To go to the left. [df: שמאל]

[freq. 5] (vf: Hiphil) |kjv: left| {str: 8041}

c^(m)) ⳑⲩⳓⲙⲥ (סמואל S-MW-AL) — **Left:** The left hand, side or direction. [df: שמאל] [freq. 54] |kjv: left, left hand, left side| {str: 8040}

f^(m)) ⲩⳑⲩⲙⲥ (סמאלי S-MA-LY) — **Left:** The left hand, side or direction. [df: שמאלי] [freq. 9] |kjv: left, left hand| {str: 8042}

~~~~~~~~

3037) ⲣⲇⲙⲥ (סמדר SMDR) ac: ? co: **Blossom** ab: ?

N^(m)) ⲣⲇⲙⲥ (סמדר SM-DR) — **Grape Blossom:** [freq. 3] |kjv: tender grape| {str: 5563}

~~~~~~~~

3038) ⲣⲟⳑⲥ (סנפר SNPR) ac: ? co: ? ab: ?

b^(m)) ⲣⲩⲟⳑⲥ (סנפיר SN-PYR) — **Fin:** The fins of a fish. [freq. 5] |kjv: fin| {str: 5579}

~~~~~~~~

3039) ⳑⲃⲣⲥ (סרבל SRBL) ac: ? co: **Coat** ab: ?

N^(m)) ⳑⲃⲣⲥ (סרבל SR-BL) — **Coat:** An article of clothing. [Aramaic only] [freq. 2] |kjv: coat| {str: 5622}

~~~~~~~~

3040) ⲟⲟⲣⲥ (סרעף SRAhP) ac: ? co: ? ab: **Thought**

N^(m)) ⲟⲟⲣⲥ (סרעף SR-AhP) — **Thought:** [df: שרעף] [freq. 2] |kjv: thought| {str: 8312}

N^(fl)) ⲧⲟⲟⲣⲥ (סרעפה SR-Ah-PH) — **Bough:** [freq. 1] |kjv: bough| {str: 5634}

~~~~~~~~

3041) ⲧⲟⲛ⳿ (סרפד SRPD) ac: ? co: ? ab: ?: [from: ⲛ⳿ - turning]

e[m]) ⲧⲟⲛ�0⳿ (סירפד SYR-PD) — **Brier:** [ms: סרפד] [freq. 1] |kjv: brier| {str: 5636}

3042) ⲟ⳼⊗⳽ (עטלף AhThLP) ac: ? co: **Bat** ab: ?

N[m]) ⲟ⳼⊗⳽ (עטלף AhTh-LP) — **Bat:** [freq. 3] |kjv: bat| {str: 5847}

3043) ⲛ⳽ⳅ�55 (עכבר AhKBR) ac: ? co: **Mouse** ab: ?: [from: ⳅ⳽ - at the heel]

N[m]) ⲛ⳽ⳅⳅ5 (עכבר AhK-BR) — **Mouse:** [freq. 6] |kjv: mouse| {str: 5909}

3044) ⳵⳵⳽ⳅⳅ5 (עכבש AhKBSh) ac: ? co: **Spider** ab: ?: [from: ⳅ⳽ - at the heel]

b[m]) ⳵⳵⳵ⳅⳅ5 (עכביש AhK-BYSh) — **Spider:** [freq. 2] |kjv: spider| {str: 5908}

3045) ⳵⳵⳵⳽ⳅⳅ5 (עכשב AhKShB) ac: ? co: ? ab: ?: [from: ⳅ⳽ - at the heel]

d[m]) ⳵⳵ⳳ⳵⳵ⳅⳅ5 (עכשוב AhK-ShWB) — **Akshuv:** An unknown poisonous insect or serpent. [freq. 1] |kjv: adder| {str: 5919}

3046) ⳽⳼ⲛ⳽⳽ (עקרב AhQRB) ac: ? co: **Scorpion** ab: ?: [from: ⳅ⳽ - at the heel]

N[m]) ⳽⳼ⲛ⳽⳽ (עקרב AhQ-RB) — **Scorpion:** [freq. 6] |kjv: scorpion| {str: 6137}

3047) ⲛ⳵⳵⳽ (עשתר AhShTR) ac: ? co: **Flock** ab: ?

N[fl]) ⳨ⲛ⳵⳵⳽ (עשתרה AhSh-T-RH) — **Flock:** [freq. 4] |kjv: flock| {str: 6251}

3048) ⳵⳵⳴⳼⳽ (פלגש PLGSh) ac: ? co: ? ab: ?

e[f]) ⳵⳵⳴⳼⳵⳽ (פילגש PYL-GSh) — **Concubine:** [ms: פלגש] [freq. 37] |kjv: concubine, paramours| {str: 6370}

3049) ⳻⳯ⲛⳳ (פרדס PRDS) ac: ? co: **Orchard** ab: ?

N[m]) ⳻⳯ⲛⳳ (פרדס PR-DS) — **Orchard:** [freq. 3] |kjv: orchard, forest| {str: 6508}

3050) ⳵⳽⳽⳽ⲛⳳ (פרעש PRAhSh) ac: ? co: ? ab: ?: [from: ⳵⳽⳽ - being spread out]

c[m]) ⳵⳽⳽Y⳿⳽⳽ⲛⳳ (פרעוש PR-AhWSh) — **Flea:** [ms: פרעש] [freq. 2] |kjv: flea| {str: 6550}

3051) ⳵⳵⳵ⲛⳳ (פרשג PRShG) ac: ? co: ? ab: ?

m[m]) ⳴⳵⳵⳵⳽ⲛⳳ (פרשגן PR-Sh-GN) — **Copy:** [Hebrew and Aramaic] [df: פתשגן] [freq. 7] |kjv: copy| {str: 6572, 6573}

3052) ⲧ⳵⳵⳽ⲛⳳ (פרשד PRShD) ac: ? co: ? ab: ?: [from: ⳵⳽⳽ - being spread out]

478

Adopted Roots (Four Letter)

j^m) ✝ᚦᚤᛚᚫᚴᚩ (פרשדון PR-Sh-
DWN) — **Excrement:** [ms: [פרשדן
[freq. 1] |kjv: dirt| {str: 6574}

~~~~~~~~~~

3053) ᚫᛚᛚᚫᚴᚩ (פרשז PRShZ) ac:
Spread co: **?** ab: **?:** [from: ᚫᚴᚩ -
spreading]
   V) ᚫᛚᛚᚫᚴᚩ (פרשז PR-ShZ) —
Spread: [freq. 1] (vf: Piel) |kjv:
spread| {str: 6576}

~~~~~~~~~~

3054) ᚢᛚᛏᚩ (פתגל PTGL) ac: **?** co: **?**
ab: **?**
   eb^m) ᚢᚤᛚᛁᛏᚩ (פתיגיל P-TY-
GYL) — **Robe:** An expensive robe.
[freq. 1] |kjv: stomacher| {str: 6614}

~~~~~~~~~~

3055) ᚨᛏᚤᚨᚾ (צנתר TsNTR) ac: **?** co:
Pipe ab: **?:** [from: ᛗᚨᚾ]
   N^f) ᚨᛏᚤᚨᚾ (צנתר TsN-TR) — **Pipe:**
[freq. 1] |kjv: pipe| {str: 6804}

~~~~~~~~~~

3056) ᚢᚫᚴᚩᚢ (קרסל QRSL) ac: **?** co:
Foot ab: **?:** [from: ᛚᚫ]
   c^f) ᚢᚤᚫᚴᚩᚢ (קרסול QR-SWL) —
Foot: [freq. 2] |kjv: feet| {str: 7166}

- - - - - - - - -

3057) ᚩᚢᚫᚴᚩᚢ (קרקע QRQAh) ac: **?**
co: **Bottom** ab: **?**
   N^m) ᚩᚢᚫᚴᚩᚢ (קרקע QR-QAh) —
Bottom: [freq. 8] |kjv: floor, other,
bottom| {str: 7172}

~~~~~~~~~~

3058) ᛚᛚᚩᚲᚫᚩ (רטפש RThPSh) ac: **?**
co: **?** ab: **?:** [from: ᛚᚲᚩ - being fresh]

V) ᛚᛚᚩᚲᚫᚩ (רטפש RTh-PSh) —
Fresh: [ms: רטפש] [freq. 1] (vf:
Niphal) |kjv: fresher| {str: 7375}

~~~~~~~~~~

3059) ᚦᚩᚨᚫᚩ (רנבת RNBT) ac: **?** co: **?**
ab: **?**
   n^m) ᚦᚩᚨᚫᚤ (ארנבת AR-N-BT) —
Hare: [freq. 2] |kjv: hare| {str: 768}

~~~~~~~~~~

3060) ᛏᚫᚩᚩᚫᚩ (רפסד RPSD) ac: **?** co: **?**
ab: **?**
   c^{fl}) ᚩᛏᚤᚫᚩᚩᚫᚩ (רפסודה RP-SW-
DH) — **Raft:** [ms: רפסדה] [freq. 1]
|kjv: float| {str: 7513}

~~~~~~~~~~

3061) ᚤᚢᚢᛚᛚ (שלאן ShLAN) ac: **?** co:
? ab: **?:** [from: ᚤᛚᛚ - resting]
   m^m) ᚤᚤᚢᚢᛚᛚ (שלאנן ShL-A-NN)
— **Quiet:** [freq. 1] |kjv: ease| {str:
7946}

~~~~~~~~~~

3062) ᛚᚩᚩᚨᛚᛚ (שנחב ShNHhB) ac: **?** co:
Tusk ab: **?:** [from: ᚤᛚᛚ - a tooth]
   N^m) ᛚᚩᚩᚨᛚᛚ (שנחב ShN-HhB) —
Tusk: An ivory tusk. [freq. 2] |kjv:
ivory| {str: 8143}

~~~~~~~~~~

3063) ᚫᚩᚩᛚ (שקער ShQAhR) ac: **?**
co: **Pit** ab: **?:** [from: ᛗᛚᛚ - as a pit]
   ld^{fl}) ᚤᚨᚩᚤᚩᚩᛚ (שקערורה ShQ-
Ah-RW-RH) — **Spot:** [freq. 1] |kjv:
hollow strakes| {str: 8258}

~~~~~~~~~~

3064) ᚲᚩᚨᚫᛚᛚ (שרבט ShRBTh) ac: **?** co:
Sceptor ab: **?:** [from: ᛏᛗ - branch]

b^m) ⊗ܝ‑ܡܠܐܠܠ (שרביט ShR-BYTh)
— **Scepter:** [freq. 4] |kjv: sceptre|
{str: 8275}

3065) ᄴLᏯ† (תרגם TRGM) ac:
Translate co: ? ab: ?
   V) ᄴLᏯ† (תרגם TR-GM) —
Translate: [freq. 1] (vf: Pual) |kjv:
interpret| {str: 8638}

3066) †ᒡ‑ܒᎧ (עקלת GhQLT) ac: ? co:
Crooked ab: ?: [from: ‑ܒᎧ]

j^m) ܝᎿ†ᒡ‑ܒᎧ (עקלתון GhQ-L-TWN)
— **Crooked:** [freq. 1] |kjv: crooked|
{str: 6129}

3067) ᒡܒᏯᎧ (ערפל GhRPL) ac: ? co:
Dark ab: ?: [from: Ꮿܒ - dark clouds]
   N^m) ᒡܒᏯᎧ (ערפל GhR-PL) —
Thick Darkness: A heavy darkness
that can be felt. [freq. 15] |kjv: thick
darkness, darkness, gross darkness,
dark cloud, dark| {str: 6205}

Foreign Words

4001) 𐤀𐤍𐤓𐤄 (אגרה AG-RH) — **Letter:** (origin: Persian) [freq. 3] |kjv: letter| {str: 104}

4002) 𐤀𐤍𐤓𐤕 (אגרת AG-RT) — **Letter:** (origin: Persian) [freq. 10] |kjv: letter| {str: 107}

4003) 𐤀𐤃𐤓𐤆𐤃𐤀 (אדרזדא AD-RZ-DA) — **Careful:** (origin: Persian) [freq. 1] |kjv: diligently| {str: 149}

4004) 𐤀𐤃𐤓𐤊𐤅𐤍 (אדרכון A-DR-KWN) — **Dram:** A coin (origin: Persian) [freq. 2] |kjv: drams| {str: 150}

4005) 𐤀𐤇𐤔𐤃𐤓𐤐𐤍 (אחשדרפן A-HhSh-DR-PN) — **Governor:** (origin: Persian) [freq. 13] |kjv: lieutenants, princes| {str: 323, 324}

4006) 𐤀𐤇𐤔𐤕𐤓𐤍 (אחשתרן A-HhSh-T-RN) — **Camel:** (origin: Persian) [freq. 2] |kjv: camel| {str: 327}

4007) 𐤀𐤎𐤐𐤓𐤍𐤀 (אספרנא AS-PR-NA) — **Speed:** (origin: Persian) [freq. 7] |kjv: speedily, speed, fast, forthwith| {str: 629}

4008) 𐤀𐤐𐤃𐤍 (אפדן AP-DN) — **Palace:** (origin: Persian) [freq. 1] |kjv: palace| {str: 643}

4009) 𐤀𐤐𐤓𐤉𐤅𐤍 (אפריון A-PR-YWN) — **Chariot:** (origin: Egyptian) [freq. 1] |kjv: chariot| {str: 668}

4010) 𐤀𐤐𐤕𐤌 (אפתם AP-TM) — **Revenue:** (origin: Persian) [freq. 1] |kjv: revenue| {str: 674}

4011) 𐤃𐤓𐤊𐤌𐤅𐤍 (דרכמון D-RK-MWN) — **Drachma:** A coin. (origin: Persian) [freq. 4] |kjv: drachma| {str: 1871}

4012) 𐤃𐤕𐤁𐤓 (דתבר DT-BR) — **Counselor:** (origin: Persian) [freq. 2] |kjv: counselors| {str: 1884}

4013) 𐤍𐤔𐤕𐤅𐤍 (נשתון NSh-TWN) — **Letter:** (origin: Persian) [freq. 5] |kjv: letter| {str: 5406, 5407}

4014) 𐤎𐤅𐤌𐤐𐤅𐤍𐤉𐤄 (סומפוניה SWM-PW-N-YH) — **Pipe:** A musical instrument.

(origin: Greek) [freq. 4] |kjv: dulcimer| {str: 5481}

4015) ᔐᔨᎱᏔᘓᏒᗡ (פסנתרין PS-NT-RYN) — **Harp:** (origin: Greek) [df: פסנתירין] [freq. 4] |kjv: psaltery| {str: 6460}

4016) ᒪᏔᏔᎱᗡ (פרתם PR-TM) — **Noble:** (origin: Persian) [freq. 3] |kjv: noble, prince| {str: 6579}

4017) ᒪᒻᏔᗡ (פתבג PT-BG) — **Meat:** (origin: Persian) [freq. 6] |kjv: meat| {str: 6598}

4018) ᏔᒪᏔᗡ (פתגם PT-GM) — **Decree:** (origin: Persian) [freq. 8] |kjv: decree, sentence, answer, matter, word, letter| {str: 6599, 6600}

4019) ᔍᎩᎱᏔᎧ (קתרוס QT-RWS) — **Harp:** (origin: Greek) [freq. 8] |kjv: harp| {str: 7030}

4020) ᔐᔨᎧᏔᏞᏔᎤᎷ (שעטנז Sh-AhTh-NZ) — **Linsey-woolsey:** (origin: Unknown) [freq. 2] |kjv: garment of diverse sorts, linen and woollen| {str: 8162}

Indexes

English Definitions

Delicacy: 2416 (a^m); 2528 (a^m)

Delight: 1476-B (V); 1476-A (ld^m); 2191 (N^m); 2191 (V); 2528 (V); 2556 (g^m)

Deliver: 2331 (V); 2339 (V); 2428 (V); 2609 (V); 2819 (V)

Demolish: 1452-F (V)

Demon: 1464-A (N^m)

Den: 1020-J (k^fl); 1439-C (N^m)

Deny: 2257 (V)

Depart: 1142-C (N^m); 1342-L (d^m); 2799 (V)

Depart early: 2685 (V)

Deposit: 2630 (j^m)

Depth: 2198 (k^m); 2553 (a^m); 2553 (c^m); 2553 (g^m)

Descend: 1441-L (V); 2396 (V); 2670 (V)

Descended: 2396 (N^m)

Descendents: 2684 (b^fl)

Descent: 1441-L (a^m)

Desert: 1399-B (l^fl); 1401-A (N^fl); 1401-A (f^m); 1401-A (j^m); 1473-L (bj^m); 2907 (N^fl)

Design: 2213 (V); 2213 (a^fl); 2213 (a^f2)

Desirable: 2169 (N^m)

Desire: 1002-A (N^fl); 1002-L (V); 1005-J (i^fl); 1005-J (V); 1006-A (N^fl); 1006-A (af^m); 1033-C (j^fl); 1243-H (V); 1453-H (N^f3); 1453-H (fj^m); 1455-H (V); 1479-J (i^fl); 2169 (V); 2219 (N^m); 2277 (V)

Desolate: 1473-B (N^fl); 1473-B (V); 1473-L (b^fl); 1473-L (V); 1473-A (k^fl); 1473-A (N^fl); 1473-A (nm^m)

Desolation: 1032-A (N^fl); 1461-J (a^fl); 1461-J (k^fl); 1473-B (ej^m)

Despair: 1021-L (V); 1320-J (V)

Despise: 1030-H (V); 1030-J (V); 1317-D (N^fl); 1317-D (V); 1469-D (V)

Despised: 1030-H (c^m); 1030-H (fj^m); 1030-J (N^fl); 1030-J (N^m)

Destroy: 1105-B (V); 2848 (V)

Destruction: 1027-C (j^f); 1027-C (m^m); 1234-M (N^m); 2165 (c^m); 2701 (g^m); 2701 (N^m)

Determine: 2221 (V)

Detest: 2878 (V)

Detesting: 2075 (N^m)

Devise: 1027-E (V); 2211 (V)

Devour: 1269-L (V); 2183 (V)

Dew: 1196-A (N^m)

Diamond: 1104-L (qp^m)

Die: 1062-J (V); 1298-J (V)

Dig: 1048-J (V); 1048-L (V); 1250-H (V); 1250-J (V); 2192 (V); 2226 (V); 2534 (V)

Diligent: 2209 (d^m)

Diminish: 2087 (V); 2187 (V)

Dip: 2228 (V)

Dirty: 2235 (V)

Disappear: 1383-B (V); 2338 (V)

Disaster: 1098-A (N^fl); 2406 (N^m)

Discard: 2126 (V)

Disease: 1075-H (a^m); 1173-H (a^m)

Diseased: 1173-E (V)

Disgusting: 2897 (g^fl)

Dish: 2497 (N^m); 2719 (N^fl)

Dishon: 1090-M (j^m)

Dislocate: 1430-L (V)

Dissolve: 1279-J (V); 1291-D (c^m); 1291-D (V)

Distant: 1104-E (N^fl); 1104-E (V)

Distinct: 1380-H (V)

District: 2610 (N^m)

Disturb: 2102 (V)

Ditch: 1419-J (h^fl)

Dive: 1074-D (V)

Divide: 1030-E (V); 1043-F (V); 1179-B (V); 1179-H (V); 2167 (V); 2493 (V)

Divide apart: 2634 (V)

Divided: 2493 (N^m)

Divination: 2395 (N^m); 2718 (h^m); 2718 (N^m)

Divine: 2395 (V); 2718 (V)

Division: 2493 (b^f)

Divorce: 2291 (b^f3)

Do: 1360-H (V); 2518 (V)

Dog: 2259 (N^m)

Domain: 2833 (h^m)

Dominion: 2359 (k^fl); 2359 (h^m); 2359 (i^m)

Donkey: 1497-C (c^f); 2175 (c^m)

Door: 1081-A (N^f2); 1339-B (V); 2649 (N^m)

Double: 1474-H (h^m); 1496-D (V); 2280 (N^m); 2280 (V)

Double edge: 1378-A (l^fl)

Dough: 2032 (N^m); 2579 (b^fl)

Dove: 1221-J (N^fl)

Dowry: 1296-G (g^m); 2116 (N^m)

Drachma: 4011-

Drag: 2469 (V)

Drain: 2694 (V)

Drained: 2694 (N^f2)

Dram: 4004-

Draw: 1297-H (V); 1456-J (V); 1477-D (V); 2166 (V); 2358 (V); 2455 (V)

Drawn sword: 2649 (b^f)

Dream: 2164 (c^m); 2164 (N^m); 2164 (V)

Dregs: 2853 (N^m)

Dried: 1399-H (e^m); 1426-A (f^m)

Drink: 1059-E (V); 1324-E (g^m); 1324-E (V); 1479-H (V); 1479-H (a^m); 1479-K (c^m); 1482-H (V)

Drinking: 1482-A (b^fl)

Drip: 2103 (N^m); 2103 (V); 2399 (V)

Drive: 1302-G (V); 2242 (V); 2375 (V); 2381 (V)

Driving: 1302-G (h^m)

Drop: 1058-C (N^m); 2431 (d^fl); 2782 (V); 2909 (V)

Dross: 1325-M (N^m)

Drought: 1255-D (id^fl); 2033 (c^f2); 2199 (j^m)

Drowsiness: 1312-J (N^fl)

Drunk: 2839 (V)

Drunkard: 2839 (ec^m)

Drunkenness: 1482-A (f^m); 2839 (ej^m)

Dry: 1044-L (N^fl); 1044-L (N^f2); 1044-L (N^m); 1044-L (V); 1399-A (N^m); 1399-B (b^fl); 1426-H (V); 2667 (V)

Dry up: 2447 (V)

Dry land: 1404-E (ej^m)

Dull: 1419-H (V)

Dumb: 1082-G (V)

Dump: 2870 (nc^m)

Dung: 1181-E (N^m); 2644 (N^m); 2684 (d^m)

Dunghill: 1311-J (q^f)

Durable: 2589 (b^m)

Dust: 1042-C (N^m)

Dwell: 1089-J (V); 1305-J (V); 2118 (V); 2838 (V)

Dwelling: 1089-J (k^m); 1462-L (a^m); 2118 (d^m); 2838 (h^m); 2838 (N^m)

Ear: 1152-C (g^f); 1288-B (b^fl)

Earring: 1173-A (f^fl); 1173-A (f^m); 2524 (b^m)

Earth: 1035-A (i^f)

East: 2135 (h^m); 2698 (e^fl); 2698 (b^m); 2698 (j^m); 2698 (jf^m); 2698 (N^m)

Eat: 1043-H (V); 1242-C (V); 2305 (V)

Ebony: 1037-F (N^m)

Edge: 1339-J (N^m); 1369-A (N^fl); 1378-A (N^fl)

Egg: 1041-M (N^fl)

Eight: 2850 (c$^{m/f}$)
Eighth: 2850 (bf^m)
Elder: 2132 (N^m)
Elevation: 1316-J (N^m); 1323-A (N^{f2})
Ember: 2062 (N^f)
Embrace: 2142 (ed^m); 2142 (V)
Empty: 1028-J (r^m); 1035-F (V); 1042-B (V); 1042-B (V); 1042-J (N^{f1}); 1365-H (V); 1456-M (N^m); 1456-M (p^m); 1461-J (N^m); 2021 (V)
Emptyness: 1035-F (N^m)
Enchanter: 1477-C (N^m)
Encircle: 2435 (V); 2538 (V)
Enclose: 1324-L (a^{f1}); 2057 (V)
Enclosure: 2057 (N^{f1}); 2057 (N^m); 2467 (c^m)
Encompass: 1324-L (a^m); 2559 (V)
Encounter: 2592 (N^m)
Encourage: 1439-G (V)
End: 1181-C (N^{f4}); 1181-C (s^m); 1311-H (V); 1383-C (N^m); 1383-C (V); 1432-A (N^{f1}); 1432-A (N^{f2}); 1432-A (N^m); 1432-H (N^m); 1432-K (N^m); 2049 (h^{f1}); 2049 (N^{f3}); 2717 (N^m)
Endanger: 1163-J (V)
Endow: 2116 (V)
Enemy: 1002-M (g^m); 1411-A (N^m); 1480-B (V); 1526-A (N^m)
Engrave: 2212 (V)
Enlightenment: 1319-G (b^m)
Enrage: 2129 (V)
Ensnare: 2437 (V)
Entangled: 1034-J (V)
Entice: 1390-H (V)
Entrance: 1022-M (j^m); 1024-A (N^{f1}); 1024-J (k^{f1}); 1024-J (a^m)
Ephah: 1017-M (N^{f1})
Ephod: 1372-C (d^{f1}); 1372-C (c^m)
Eq'dahh: 2697 (n^m)
Equal: 1465-J (V)
Erect: 1427-J (pf^{f3})
Ermon: 2908 (j^m)
Err: 1463-H (V); 1463-B (V)
Error: 1463-B (N^{f1}); 1463-A (h^{f1}); 1463-E (b^{f1}); 1463-J (k^{f1}); 1499-A (ld^m)
Eruption: 2455 (N^m)
Escape: 1403-F (N^{f1}); 2609 (b^{f1}); 2609 (b^m); 2609 (h^m)
Escaping: 2609 (N^m)
Estimate: 2576 (N^m)
Eunuch: 2510 (b^m)
Event: 1434-H (h^m); 1434-H (N^m)

Eviction: 2089 (N^{f1})
Ewe: 2761 (N^f)
Examination: 2198 (N^m)
Examine: 1250-J (V); 2011 (V); 2198 (V)
Exceed: 2507 (V); 2511 (V)
Exceeding: 1503-L (b^m)
Except: 1035-A (e^{f4}); 1150-J (N^{f1})
Excess: 1389-A (N^m); 2507 (N^m); 2529 (V)
Exchange: 1296-J (V); 1296-L (V); 1296-J (i^{f1}); 2811 (V)
Excrement: 1392-A (N^{f1}); 1392-J (N^{f1}); 1392-L (a^{f1}); 1392-L (b^m); 3052 (j^m)
Excuse Me: 1033-A (N^m)
Exist: 1097-J (V); 1097-M (V)
Expectation: 2367 (a^m)
Expense: 2423 (e^{f1})
Experienced: 2178 (b^m)
Expose: 2186 (ac^m)
Extend: 1469-L (V)
Extinguish: 2108 (V); 2128 (V)
Eye: 1359-M (N^f)
Eyelid: 1362-A (l^m)
Face: 1382-H (N^m); 2002 (N^m); 2698 (V)
Fail: 2369 (V)
Failing: 1242-H (N^m)
Failure: 1242-A (fj^m)
Faint: 1448-L (a^m); 2537 (V); 2547 (V); 2593 (V)
Fall: 2302 (V); 2421 (a^{f2}); 2421 (V)
Fallen grape: 2637 (N^m)
Fame: 2851 (g^m)
Family: 2863 (h^{f1})
Famine: 2281 (N^m); 2777 (j^m); 2777 (N^m)
Fang: 2328 (a^{f1}); 2328 (k^{f1})
Far: 2765 (b^m); 2765 (c^m); 2765 (k^m); 2765 (N^m); 2765 (V)
Far be it: 1173-B (b^{f1})
Farmer: 1250-C (N^m)
Fashion: 2796 (V)
Fast: 1404-J (N^m); 1404-J (V)
Fastener: 2092 (N^m)
Fasting: 1206-J (N^m); 1359-A (if^{f2})
Fat: 1038-C (V); 1043-E (b^m); 1043-H (f^m); 1284-A (N^m); 1381-M (N^{f1}); 2115 (N^m); 2115 (V); 2160 (N^m); 2241 (V); 2596 (N^m); 2850 (h^m); 2850 (V)
Father: 1002-A (N^m)
Father-In-Law: 1174-A (N^m)
Fatigue: 1362-L (V)
Fatling: 1288-E (b^m)

Fat-tail: 1012-A (b^{f1})
Fear: 1066-J (kc^{f1}); 1066-J (kd^m); 1066-J (a^m); 1183-A (N^{f1}); 1183-A (l^m); 1183-B (b^f); 1227-E (N^{f1}); 1227-E (k^m); 1227-E (N^m); 1227-E (V); 1442-B (V); 1446-B (N^m); 2120 (V); 2581 (V); 2598 (N^{f1}); 2598 (N^m); 2598 (V)
Feast: 1164-A (N^m); 1164-B (V); 1482-H (h^m)
Feather: 1317-J (N^{f1})
Feeble: 1454-M (fj^m)
Feed: 1152-J (V); 1339-E (hc^m); 1453-H (V); 2315 (V)
Female: 2430 (N^{f1})
Fence: 2033 (h^m)
Festival: 2749 (N^f)
Fetter: 2247 (N^m)
Fever: 2697 (N^{f2})
Fiber: 2458 (c^{f2})
Field: 1048-L (N^m); 1326-H (N^m); 1326-A (p^{f1})
Fiery Law: 3002 (N^f)
Fifth: 2176 (bf^m); 2176 (g^m); 2176 (V)
Fig: 1014-A (i^f)
Fight: 1066-H (V); 2305 (V)
Figure: 2709 (h^{f2})
Fill: 1043-E (b^{f1}); 1043-E (V); 1288-E (V); 2461 (V)
Filling: 1024-J (i^{f1}); 1288-E (c^m); 1288-E (ed^m)
Filthiness: 2179 (N^{f1})
Filthiness: 2179 (g^m); 2878 (ed^m)
Filthy: 1261-C (V); 1392-J (N^m); 2179 (N^m); 2179 (V); 2878 (N^m)
Fin: 3038 (b^m)
Find: 1294-E (V); 2835 (V)
Fine: 2560 (N^m); 2560 (V)
Finery: 2040 (c^m)
Finger: 2655 (n^f)
Fingernail: 2240 (N^m)
Fire: 1021-A (N^{f1}); 1021-A (N^f); 1021-H (e^m); 1319-J (N^f); 2028 (N^{f1})
Firepan: 1183-A (a^{f1})
Firm: 1244-J (V); 1244-A (N^m); 1290-C (V); 2903 (V)
Firmness: 1290-C (d^{f1}); 1290-C (d^m); 1290-C (g^m); 2426 (e^{f1}); 2903 (N^m)
First: 1458-D (ej^m); 1458-D (emf^m); 2698 (f^m)
First rain: 1227-H (g^m)
Firstborn: 2016 (b^{f1}); 2016 (c^{f1})

Gnaw: 2084 (V); 2582 (V)
Go: 1469-J (V)
Goad: 2311 (a^m)
Goat: 1504-M (N^m); 1513-A (N^f); 2494 (b^m); 2587 (d^m)
Going-out: 1392-L (a^m)
Goings: 1392-L (i ^fl)
Gold: 1140-G (a^fl); 1140-G (N^m); 2033 (N^m); 2297 (N^m); 2467 (c^m)
Gomed: 2069 (N^m)
Good: 1186-A (N^m); 1186-J (N^f); 1186-J (V); 1186-L (V)
Good news: 2025 (c^fl)
Goods: 2772 (d^m)
Go-out: 1392-L (V)
Gopher: 2079 (N^m)
Gore: 2373 (V)
Gorer: 2373 (N^m)
Gourd: 1424-A (lj^m); 2632 (d^fl); 2632 (N^m)
Government: 1342-A (h^fl)
Governor: 1376-H (N^m); 4005-
Grain: 1043-A (N^m); 1072-A (m^m); 2811 (N^m)
Grainstalk: 1427-A (N^fl)
Granary: 1038-C (ad^m); 2332 (ad^fl)
Grape: 1058-B (g^fl); 2555 (N^m)
Grape Blossom: 3037 (N^m)
Grape-skin: 1141-A (N^m)
Grapevine: 2078 (N^m); 2513 (c^m)
Grasp: 2654 (V); 2714 (g^m); 2714 (V)
Grass: 1090-E (N^m); 2197 (b^m)
Grate: 2250 (h^m)
Grave: 1472-D (c^f); 2696 (d^fl); 2696 (N^m)
Gray: 1324-M (N^fl)
Green: 1456-L (c^m); 1456-L (N^m); 3030 (N^m)
Green Grain: 1002-B (b^m)
Greenish: 1456-L (l^m)
Grief: 1296-J (N^fl)
Grieve: 1071-C (V); 1460-L (V); 2525 (V)
Grill: 2204 (N^m)
Grind: 2231 (N^fl); 2231 (V)
Groan: 1307-C (N^fl)
Grope: 1067-B (V); 1297-B (V)
Ground: 1082-C (N^fl)
Grouse: 2100 (ob^f2)
Grow: 2054 (N^m)
Growl: 1312-G (V)
Growling: 1312-G (N^fl); 1312-G (N^m)
Guard: 2227 (N^m); 2400 (V); 2853 (N^fl); 2853 (V)

Guide: 1307-H (V); 2001 (d^m)
Guilt: 1473-C (N^fl); 1473-C (N^m); 1473-C (V); 1512-A (m^m)
Gush: 2136 (V)
Gushing: 2136 (N^m)
Habitation: 1359-J (N^fl)
Hack: 2768 (V)
Haft: 2426 (e^m)
Hail: 2037 (V)
Hailstone: 2037 (N^m)
Hair: 1081-A (N^fl); 2491 (N^m); 2494 (N^fl); 2494 (N^m)
Hairdo: 1435-H (h^m)
Half: 1179-A (a^f4); 2606 (N^m)
Hall: 1434-H (k^m)
Halter: 2776 (V)
Hammer: 1266-F (N^f3); 1416-A (a^fl); 1416-A (N^f2); 2262 (e^f); 2605 (b^m); 2797 (V)
Hammered: 1196-M (k^m)
Hand: 1211-A (N^f)
Handful: 1383-A (N^fl); 2657 (N^m); 2860 (N^m)
Hang: 1495-E (V); 1495-H (V)
Happy: 1480-C (g^m); 1480-C (N^m); 1480-C (V)
Hard: 1435-H (N^m); 1435-H (V)
Harden: 2738 (V)
Hare: 3059 (n^m)
Harem: 1464-A (N^fl)
Harm: 1336-C (c^m)
Harness: 1480-A (efj^{m/f})
Harp: 2270 (ec^m); 4015- ; 4019-
Harpoon: 1333-J (N^fl)
Harrow: 1326-B (V)
Harvest: 2727 (b^m)
Haste: 1035-G (b^m); 1527-J (V); 1527-M (V); 2188 (V); 2188 (ej^m)
Hate: 1336-E (V); 1336-E (N^fl); 1336-E (b^m); 2474 (V); 2897 (V)
Hatred: 1469-A (ap^fl)
Haven: 1168-J (a^m)
Hawk: 1005-M (N^f)
He: 1093-J (N^m)
Head: 1418-A (lc^m); 1458-D (a^fl); 1458-D (N^m); 1458-D (g^fl)
Head of grain: 2806 (ec^f2)
Headrest: 1458-D (k^fl); 1458-D (N^f3)
Heal: 1051-H (V); 1454-E (V)
Health: 1454-E (e^f3); 1454-E (a^m)
Heap: 1004-M (N^m); 1039-A (f^m)
Hear: 1152-C (V); 2851 (V)
Hearer: 2851 (N^f2)
Hearing: 2851 (h^m)

Heart: 1255-A (N^m); 1255-M (N^fl); 1255-B (N^m); 1255-B (V)
Hearth: 1008-A (N^f); 2043 (k^fl)
Heat: 1174-L (V); 2134 (V); 2199 (g^m)
Heavily: 2246 (N^f3)
Heaviness: 2246 (d^fl)
Heavy: 1342-A (N^m); 2246 (N^f); 2246 (g^m); 2246 (V)
Heavy rain: 2467 (lb^m)
Hedge: 1333-B (V); 1333-J (V); 1333-J (k^fl)
Heed: 2737 (V)
Heel: 2571 (N^m)
Heifer: 1388-A (N^fl); 2524 (N^f)
Height: 1323-M (N^m); 1427-J (N^fl); 1450-A (N^f3)
Heights: 1316-A (N^f2); 1450-A (N^fl); 1450-J (a^m)
Heir: 1313-J (a^m); 1313-M (N^m)
Helmet: 2248 (g^m); 2694 (g^m)
Help: 2535 (N^fl); 2535 (N^f2); 2535 (N^m); 2535 (V)
Helpless: 2163 (N^fl)
Hemorrhoids: 2232 (c^m)
Herald: 2286 (c^m)
Herb: 2561 (N^f)
Herd: 1428-H (h^m)
Herdsman: 2035 (g^m)
Here: 1104-K (p^m); 1106-H (N^m); 1374-A (N^m); 1374-C (N^m)
Hew: 2194 (V); 2619 (V); 2858 (V)
Hewn: 2194 (a^m)
Hewn Stone: 1053-A (N^f4)
Hhalamut: 2164 (N^f3)
Hhash'mal: 3022 (N^m)
Hhasiyl: 2183 (b^m)
Hhas'pas: 3017 (N^m)
Hhavatselet: 3014 (N^f2)
Hholed: 2161 (g^m)
Hhomer: 2175 (g^m)
Hhomet: 2170 (g^m)
Hidden: 2544 (i^fl)
Hide: 1163-E (V); 1163-H (V); 1358-B (V); 2234 (V); 2255 (V); 2269 (V); 2516 (V); 2544 (V); 2683 (V)
Hiding: 1163-H (fj^m); 2516 (a^m); 2516 (hc^m); 2516 (N^m)
High: 1048-H (c^m); 1048-H (g^m); 1048-H (N^m); 1357-A (fj^m); 1357-M (f^m); 1450-J (N^m); 1477-H (V)
High Place: 1036-H (N^f); lace: 1477-A (f^m)

Man: 1082-C (N^m); 1298-A (N^m); 2003 (b^m); 2003 (c^m); 2003 (N^m)

Mandrakes: 1073-N (o^m)

Maneh: 1290-H (N^m)

Manger: 1038-C (d^m)

Manner: 2093 (g^m)

Manure: 2105 (g^m)

Manure pit: 2105 (a^fl)

Many: 1004-J (k^m)

Marble: 1481-M (N^m); 1481-A (N^m/f)

March: 2620 (V); 2676 (V)

Mare: 1337-J (N^fl)

Mariner: 2338 (N^m)

Mark: 1022-J (N^f); 1430-A (l^m); 1489-A (N^m); 1489-H (V); 2233 (g^fl)

Mark out: 1503-D (V)

Marker: 2506 (N^m)

Market: 2573 (a^m)

Marrow: 1284-J (N^m); 1479-A (rf^m)

Marry: 1036-L (V)

Marsh Grass: 1008-A (r^m)

Marvel: 1496-H (V)

Mast: 2141 (e^m)

Master: 1439-A (N^m); 2027 (N^m); 2052 (b^m); 2843 (b^m)

Mastery: 2843 (ej^m)

Maten: 2363 (N^m)

Mattock: 2211 (a^fl)

Mature: 1496-J (k^m)

Maturity: 1496-J (N^fl)

Meadow: 1035-C (N^f); 1365-H (N^fl); 1365-H (a^m)

Meal: 2711 (N^m)

Measure: 1280-B (V); 1280-J (V); 1323-A (l^fl); 2893 (ad^f2); 2893 (g^m)

Measured: 1420-A (l^m)

Meat: 1043-H (ef^fl); 1043-H (N^f3); 1152-J (a^m); 1395-M (N^fl); 1395-M (N^m); 2025 (n^m); 2236 (a^m); 2305 (d^m); 4017-

Medicine: 1051-H (N^fl); 1454-E (d^fl); 1454-J (i^fl)

Meditate: 1330-A (N^m); 1330-J (V); 1330-M (V)

Meditating: 1330-M (N^m)

Meditation: 1330-M (N^fl)

Medium: 1002-J (N^m)

Meet: 1349-L (V); 1434-H (V); 1434-E (V); 2592 (V); 2594 (V)

Meeting: 1434-E (h^m)

Melody: 1095-A (fj^m); 2124 (N^fl); 2124 (hc^m)

Melon: 2013 (nb^m)

Melt: 1291-B (V); 1291-F (N^m); 1291-H (V); 1291-A (i^m)

Melted: 1494-F (ec^fl)

Memorial: 2121 (n^fl); 2121 (ej^m); 2121 (N^m)

Merchandise: 1422-A (N^fl); 2337 (h^f2); 2337 (h^m); 2337 (N^m); 2473 (c^fl); 2473 (h^m); 2473 (N^m); 2573 (a^m); 2770 (N^fl); 2770 (ac^f2)

Message: 1264-D (a^f3)

Messenger: 1264-D (a^m)

Middle: 1052-A (N^m); 1179-A (N^f3); 1494-J (N^m); 1494-M (j^m); 2230 (d^m)

Mighty: 2052 (e^m); 2903 (b^m)

Mildew: 1456-L (j^m)

Milk: 1058-J (V); 1477-A (N^f); 2160 (N^m)

Milky way: 2387 (a^fl)

Mill: 1192-A (j^m)

Millet: 2097 (g^m)

Millstone: 1445-H (N^m)

Minkrah: 2406 (h^fl)

Mirage: 2880 (N^m)

Mire: 1221-J (N^m)

Mirror: 1438-A (f^m)

Miscarriage: 2421 (N^m)

Mischief: 1151-A (k^fl); 1151-A (N^fl)

Mislead: 1472-H (V)

Miss: 1170-E (V)

Missing: 2530 (V)

Mist: 1004-A (N^m)

Mistress: 2027 (N^fl); 2052 (b^fl); 2052 (N^f2)

Mix: 1035-B (V); 1288-G (V); 2344 (V); 2573 (V); 2743 (V); 2795 (V)

Mixed: 2573 (N^m)

Mixed wine: 2344 (N^m)

Mixer: 2795 (N^fl); 2795 (N^m)

Mixture: 1242-E (e^m); 2344 (h^m); 2795 (k^fl); 2795 (h^f2); 2795 (g^m)

Mock: 2312 (V); 2313 (V)

Mocker: 2313 (e^m)

Mocking: 1271-M (k^fl); 2313 (N^m)

Moist: 1261-A (N^m); 2767 (V)

Moisten: 1452-B (V)

Mold: 2431 (ed^m)

Mole: 1250-A (N^fl); 2192 (c^f)

Moment: 2652 (N^m); 2652 (eqp^m); 2752 (N^m)

Moon: 1445-L (N^m); 2303 (N^fl)

More: 1503-L (g^m); 1503-L (j^m)

Morning: 1302-A (N^fl); 2035 (g^m); 2685 (b^fl)

Mortar: 1080-J (k^fl); 2301 (a^m); 2339 (N^m)

Moth: 1337-A (N^m)

Mother: 1013-A (N^f)

Mother-In-Law: 1174-A (N^f3)

Mound: 1058-A (N^fl); 1058-A (N^m); 1303-A (N^m); 2058 (b^m)

Mourn: 1035-C (V); 1071-D (V); 1304-C (V); 2495 (V)

Mourning: 1035-C (N^f); 1304-C (f^fl); 1309-N (i^fl); 2495 (h^m); 2756 (h^m)

Mouse: 3043 (N^m)

Mouth: 1373-A (N^m); 1381-J (N^m)

Move: 1073-H (V); 2410 (V)

Much: 1439-A (h^fl)

Mud: 1041-A (N^m); 1193-M (N^m); 2786 (h^m); 2786 (N^m)

Muddy: 2786 (V)

Mule: 2634 (e^fl); 2634 (N^m)

Multiply: 2250 (V); 2590 (V)

Multitude: 1105-A (j^m)

Murder: 2790 (V)

Murmur: 1451-J (V); 2751 (V)

Murmuring: 1451-J (i^fl)

Music: 2124 (b^fl); 2124 (e^f2); 2124 (b^m); 2124 (N^m); 2374 (ab^fl); 2374 (b^fl)

Musician: 2124 (N^m)

Muster: 1393-E (V)

Muzzle: 2018 (V); 2184 (ac^m); 2184 (V)

Myriad: 1439-A (eq^f); 1439-B (N^fl)

Myrrh: 1262-J (N^m); 1296-J (N^m)

Myrtle: 1084-F (N^m)

Nail: 2491 (a^fl); 2491 (a^f); 2491 (h^m)

Naked: 1365-A (ap^m); 1365-A (cl^m); 1365-A (cp^m); 1365-A (ecp^m); 1365-A (l^m); 1365-H (f^fl); 1365-J (V)

Nakedness: 1365-A (a^m); 1365-J (a^m); 1365-K (N^fl)

Nard: 2439 (N^m)

Nataph: 2399 (N^m)

Nation: 1052-A (f^m)

Native: 2135 (n^m)

Navel: 1480-B (b^m)

Near: 1403-C (N^m); 2729 (N^fl); 2729 (c^m); 2729 (N^m)

Neck: 1066-A (l^f2); 1411-D (g^m); 2580 (N^m); 2643 (a^f2)

Necklace: 3011 (b^m)

Need: 2690 (g^m)

Needlework: 2796 (e^fl)

Neglect: 1472-A (r^f); 1472-A (N^m)

2077 (V); 2172 (V); 2458 (V); 2748 (V); 2849 (V)

Shaking: 2748 (N^{fl}); 2748 (g^m); 2748 (N^m)

Shaliysh: 2847 (b^m)

Shalom: 2845 (c^m)

Shame: 1044-A (m^{fl}); 1044-J (N^{fl}); 1044-J (N^{f2}); 1365-K (N^{fl}); 1426-A (j^m); 2261 (V); 2261 (b^{fl}); 2261 (b^{f3}); 2728 (ej^m)

Shamiyr: 2853 (b^m)

Shaphan: 2867 (N^m)

Shard: 2209 (d^m)

Sharp: 1165-A (N^m); 1165-B (d^m); 1165-B (V); 2209 (b^m); 2309 (V)

Sharpen: 1474-B (V)

Shatter: 2216 (V); 2783 (V)

Shattering: 2811 (N^m)

Shave: 2065 (V); 2730 (V)

Sheaf: 1266-C (d^{fl}); 1266-C (d^m); 2554 (b^m); 2554 (g^m)

Shear: 1053-B (V); 1053-H (V)

Sheath: 1365-A (i$^{m/f}$); 2382 (N^m)

Sheep: 1327-A (N^m); 1405-H (g^m); 2273 (N^m)

Sheep-master: 2431 (g^m)

Sheer: 2723 (V)

Sheet: 1326-A (s^m); 1441-B (b^m); 2742 (a^m); 2797 (b^m)

She-Goat: 2494 (b^{fl})

Shelak: 2844 (N^m)

Shelam: 2845 (N^m)

Shepherd: 1453-J (f^m)

Shephiyphon: 1477-B (bj^m)

Sheqel: 2874 (N^m)

Sheriff: 2864 (ef^m)

Shield: 1060-A (a^m); 1060-B (V); 1234-M (j^m); 1336-M (N^{fl}); 2473 (g^{fl}); 2843 (N^m)

Shine: 1104-B (a^m); 1104-B (bd^m); 1104-B (V); 1104-C (V); 1302-H (V); 1384-L (V); 2586 (V)

Shining: 1104-A (ie^{fl}); 1411-G (g^f)

Ship: 1014-A (f^{fl}); 1014-A (f^m); 1401-A (N^m); 2498 (b^{fl})

Shod: 2415 (V)

Shoham: 1473-G (N^m)

Shoot: 1439-B (V); 2842 (d^{fl})

Shore: 1178-J (N^m)

Short: 2250 (e^{fl}); 2727 (g^m); 2727 (N^m)

Shoulder: 2837 (e^{fl}); 2837 (N^m); 2837 (V)

Shout: 1096-A (N^m); 1096-B (e^m); 1096-J (b^{fl}); 1399-J (N^{fl}); 1399-

J (V); 1403-G (V); 1451-B (V); 1460-A (N$^{m/f}$); 1460-J (i^{fl}); 1460-J (V); 2689 (V)

Shouting: 1403-G (h^{fl}); 1451-B (N^{fl}); 1451-B (N^m); 1451-J (N^m); 1451-M (N^{fl})

Shovel: 1223-A (N^m); 1445-A (N^{f2})

Showers: 1439-B (b^m)

Shrink: 2720 (V)

Shrivel: 1444-H (V); 2681 (V)

Shu'al: 2860 (o^m)

Shut: 1063-J (V); 1197-C (V); 1204-C (N^m); 1204-C (V); 2467 (V); 2569 (V)

Sh'vo: 1462-A (q^f)

Sick: 1173-E (id^m); 1173-H (V); 2003 (V)

Sickle: 2330 (N^m); 3020 (N^m)

Sickness: 1173-H (f^m)

Side: 1395-A (N^m); 2299 (N^f); 2363 (N^m); 2476 (N^m); 2520 (N^m); 2664 (N^f)

Siege works: 1080-M (N^m)

Sieve: 1316-A (N^{fl}); 2250 (N^{fl})

Sigh: 1307-C (V)

Sign: 1022-A (N^f)

Signet: 2223 (g^{f2}); 2223 (g^m); 2534 (e^{fl})

Silence: 1082-H (V); 1082-N (g^{fl}); 1107-H (V); 1182-H (V)

Silent: 1082-B (N^m); 1082-B (N^{fl}); 1082-B (o^m); 1082-H (f^m); 1082-J (N^{fl}); 1266-C (e^m); 1266-C (N^m); 2211 (N^m); 2480 (V)

Silk: 1297-A (f^m)

Silver: 2277 (N^m)

Simple: 1390-H (f^{f3}); 1390-H (f^f)

Sin: 1170-A (f^m); 1170-E (N^{fl}); 1170-E (b^f); 1170-E (N^m)

Sinew: 1050-M (N^m)

Sing: 1480-M (V)

Sink: 1403-B (V); 1468-B (V); 1468-L (N^m); 1468-J (V); 2229 (V); 2876 (V)

Sister: 1008-A (N^{f3})

Sister-in-law: 1036-L (N^{f2})

Sit: 1307-L (V); 1462-L (V); 1482-B (V); 1482-M (V)

Sixth: 1481-E (V); 1481-H (V); 1481-A (f$^{m/f}$)

Skillet: 1388-B (d^m)

Skin: 1365-J (N^m); 2064 (N^m)

Skin bag: 1174-A (N^{f2}); ag: 1303-D (g^{fl}); ag: 1303-D (g^m)

Skip: 1201-B (V); 2794 (V)

Skull: 1058-A (l^{f2})

Slander: 1071-A (N^{fl}); 1086-J (f^m); 2325 (V); 2749 (V)

Slanderer: 2770 (b^m)

Slaughter: 1440-F (N^{fl}); 1440-F (N^m); 2227 (e^{fl}); 2227 (a^m); 2227 (N^m); 2227 (V); 2702 (N^m)

Sledge: 1440-L (N^f)

Sleep: 1474-A (N^{fl}); 1474-H (N$^{m/f}$); 1474-L (N^{f2}); 1474-L (N^m); 1474-L (V); 2754 (V)

Sleeve: 1383-A (N^m)

Slice: 1050-B (d^{fl}); 1050-B (d$^{m/f}$); 1050-B (V); 2508 (V); 2608 (V)

Slicing: 2508 (N^{f2}); 2508 (N$^{m/f}$)

Slime: 1457-M (N^m)

Sling: 2709 (N^m); 2750 (a^{fl})

Slinger: 2709 (N^m)

Slip: 2346 (V)

Slippery: 2167 (l^{fl})

Slope: 1464-C (N^{fl}); 1464-C (N^m)

Slothful: 1450-A (f^{fl})

Slow: 1448-C (N^m)

Sluggard: 2568 (N^m)

Slumber: 1312-J (V); 1312-J (i^{fl})

Small: 1080-A (N^m); 1080-B (V); 2680 (hb^{fl}); 2680 (b^m); 2680 (h^m); 2680 (V); 2703 (g^m); 2703 (N^m); 2703 (V)

Small flock: 2186 (b^m)

Smash: 2628 (V)

Smear: 1284-H (V); 2175 (V); 2357 (V)

Smeared: 2357 (b^m); 2357 (h^m)

Smell: 1445-J (V)

Smile: 2017 (ab^{f4}); 2017 (V)

Smith: 2467 (a^m)

Smoke: 2583 (N^m); 2583 (V); 2705 (ec^m)

Smooth: 2167 (N^{fl}); 2167 (d^m); 2167 (V)

Snail: 2806 (ld^m)

Snap: 2726 (V)

Snapped: 2726 (N^{fl})

Snare: 1158-J (a^m); 1395-J (a^{fl}); 1395-J (a^m); 1435-J (V); 1435-L (d^m); 1435-L (V); 1435-L (a^m); 2771 (g^m)

Snarer: 1435-L (c^m)

Snatch: 2225 (V); 2712 (V)

Sneeze: 1158-B (V); 2539 (b^{fl})

Snort: 2002 (V)

Snorting: 2394 (N^{fl})

Snow: 2841 (N^m); 2841 (V)

Snuffer: 2124 (k^{fl})

So: 1235-A (N^m); 1244-A (p^{fl}); 1244-A (N^m); 1244-A (N^m)

King James Translation

destroyer: 1452-F (V); 2642 (b^m); 2830 (V)

destroying: 2701 (N^m); 2830 (a^m); 2830 (ab^m)

destruction: 1004-M (N^m); 1027-C (j^f); 1027-C (m^m); 1027-M (N^m); 1035-A (i^f4); 1038-J (i^fl); 1080-E (N^m); 1105-J (k^fl); 1183-M (k^fl); 1234-M (N^m); 1452-F (N^m); 1452-F (b^f3); 1461-H (f^fl); 1461-J (N^fl); 1461-J (a^fl); 1464-J (N^m); 1468-A (N^f2); 1468-A (f^f2); 2141 (N^m); 2165 (c^m); 2206 (N^m); 2701 (N^m); 2701 (g^m); 2720 (N^fl); 2735 (N^m); 2811 (N^m); 2811 (ej^m); 2830 (ab^m); 2848 (V)

detain: 2570 (V)

determine: 1242-A (N^fl); 1242-H (V); 1363-L (V); 2209 (V); 2221 (V)

detest: 2878 (V)

detestable: 2878 (ed^m)

device: 1095-A (fj^m); 1151-A (k^fl); 2213 (a^fl); 2213 (a^f2); 2213 (j^m)

devil: 2494 (b^m)

devise: 1027-E (V); 1151-B (V); 1363-L (V); 1363-L (a^fl); 2211 (V); 2213 (V); 2213 (a^fl); 2213 (a^f2)

devised: 1082-H (V)

devote: 2206 (V)

devoted: 2206 (N^m)

devour: 1242-C (V); 1242-C (N^fl); 1269-L (V); 1453-H (V); 1477-D (V); 2020 (V); 2305 (V)

devouring: 2020 (N^m)

dew: 1196-A (N^m)

diadem: 2673 (b^m); 2673 (h^f2); 2685 (b^fl)

dial: 1357-A (a^fl)

diamond: 1104-L (qp^m); 2853 (b^m)

die: 1062-J (V); 1298-J (V); 1298-J (N^m); 1298-J (i^fl); 2369 (N^fl)

diet: 1445-C (d^fl)

difference: 1380-H (V); 2005 (V)

dig: 1250-H (V); 1250-J (V); 2192 (V); 2194 (V); 2226 (V); 2436 (V); 2530 (V); 2905 (V)

dignity: 1323-A (N^f2); 1450-J (a^m); 2054 (d^fl)

diligence: 2853 (h^m)

diligent: 1296-G (b^m); 2189 (V); 2209 (d^m); 4003

diligently: 1004-J (N^f3); 1004-J (k^m); 1186-L (V); 2395 (V); 2851 (V)

dim: 1235-B (V); 1235-B (N^m); 1358-B (V); 1476-H (V); 2215 (V)

diminish: 2087 (V); 2347 (V)

dimness: 1362-J (a^m); 1523-L (a^m)

dinner: 1445-C (d^fl)

dip: 2228 (V); 2334 (V)

direct: 1227-H (V); 1244-J (V); 1480-L (V); 2294 (V); 2576 (V); 2893 (V)

directly: 1095-A (s^fl); 2403 (g^m)

dirge: 1428-J (N^fl)

dirt: 1193-M (N^m); 3052 (j^m)

disannul: 1388-B (V); 2283 (V)

disappoint: 1388-B (V); 2698 (V)

discern: 1037-M (V); 2406 (V); 2851 (V)

discharge: 2422 (V); 2842 (h^f2)

disciple: 2311 (ed^m)

discomfit: 1105-B (V); 1252-B (V); 1291-A (N^m); 2168 (V); 2201 (V)

discomfiture: 1105-J (k^fl)

discontented: 1296-A (N^m)

discontinue: 2849 (V)

discord: 1083-A (ac^m); 1083-A (k^m)

discourage: 1300-J (V); 1455-B (V); 2727 (V)

discouraged: 1183-B (V); 1291-B (V)

discover: 1357-H (V); 1365-H (V); 2186 (V)

discretion: 1037-J (i^m); 1151-A (k^fl); 2477 (N^m); 2864 (h^m)

disdain: 1030-H (V)

disease: 1075-H (a^m); 1173-A (af^m); 1173-E (id^m); 1173-H (a^m); 1173-H (f^m)

diseased: 1173-E (V); 1173-H (V)

disguise: 1474-H (V); 2189 (V); 2516 (N^m)

dish: 2497 (N^m); 2662 (N^f2); 2719 (N^fl)

dishonor: 1365-K (N^fl); 1426-A (j^m); 2261 (b^fl)

dismay: 1035-G (V); 1183-M (k^fl); 1476-H (V)

dismayed: 1183-A (N^m); 1183-B (V)

disobedient: 1296-H (V)

disobey: 1296-H (V)

dispatch: 1043-E (V)

disperse: 1158-H (V); 1386-J (V); 1386-J (i^fl); 2422 (V); 2597 (V); 2634 (V)

display: 1314-J (V)

displease: 1181-H (V); 1460-B (V); 1460-L (V); 2566 (V); 2726 (V)

displeased: 1044-D (V); 2002 (V); 2130 (N^m)

displeasure: 1174-A (N^fl); 1181-A (j^m)

dispose: 1335-J (V)

dispossess: 1458-L (V)

disquiet: 1312-G (N^fl); 2748 (V)

disquieted: 1105-H (V)

dissalow: 1300-J (V)

dissemble: 2257 (V)

dissembler: 2544 (V)

dissolve: 1279-J (V); 1295-B (V); 1480-H (V)

dissolved: 1388-B (V)

distaff: 2610 (N^m)

distil: 2387 (V); 2782 (V)

distinctly: 2644 (V)

distracted: 1382-J (V)

distress: 1402-J (V); 1402-J (a^m); 1402-J (k^fl); 1411-A (N^fl); 1411-A (N^m); 1411-A (k^m); 1411-B (V); 1411-J (V); 1432-J (V); 2375 (V)

distressed: 1411-L (V)

distribute: 2167 (V)

ditch: 1048-A (N^m/f); 1419-J (h^fl); 1468-A (N^f2); 1468-J (N^fl)

diverse: 1242-E (e^m); 1474-E (V); 1474-H (V)

diverse colour: 1196-E (V); 2796 (e^fl):

diverse kinds: 1152-A (N^m)

divide: 1179-H (V); 1388-B (V); 2005 (V); 2034 (V); 2047 (V); 2061 (V); 2167 (V); 2194 (V); 2391 (V); 2421 (V); 2449 (V); 2606 (V); 2634 (V); 2640 (V); 2752 (V)

dividing: 2606 (N^m)

divination: 2718 (V); 2718 (N^m); 2718 (h^m)

divine: 2395 (V); 2718 (V); 2718 (N^m)

diviner: 2718 (V)

division: 1372-A (N^f3); 2167 (d^fl); 2606 (N^fl); 2606 (d^fl); 2606 (h^fl)

division portion: 2167 (a^f2)

divorce: 2089 (V); 2291 (b^f3)

divorcement: 2291 (b^f3)

do: 1304-L (V); 1357-B (V); 1360-H (V); 2070 (V); 2518 (V); 2622 (V); 2622 (g^m)

doctrine: 2319 (N^m); 2851 (d^{fl})

doer: 1460-B (V); 2622 (V)

dog: 2259 (N^m)

doing: 1357-B (b^{fl}); 1360-H (a^m)

doings: 1357-B (a^m)

doleful: 1304-H (f^{fl})

dominion: 1441-H (V); 1441-J (V); 2027 (V); 2359 (V); 2359 (h^m); 2359 (i ^{m}); 2359 (k^{fl}); 2833 (h^m); 2843 (V); 2843 (m^m)

done: 1043-E (V); 1170-E (V); 1242-H (V); 1357-B (V); 1496-B (V); 2349 (V)

door: 1081-A (N^{f2}); 1339-A (N^m); 2649 (N^m); 2862 (N^m)

doorkeeper: 1339-B (V); 2862 (g^m)

doorpost: 2877 (ac^m)

dote: 1254-L (V); 2523 (V)

double: 1474-H (V); 1474-H (N$^{m/f}$); 1474-H (h^m); 2280 (V); 2280 (N^m)

doubtless: 1013-M (N^m)

dough: 2032 (N^m); 2579 (b ^{fl})

dove: 1221-J (N^{fl})

down: 1307-J (V); 1307-L (V); 1308-H (a^m); 1357-A (k^m); 1441-L (V); 1441-L (a^m); 1462-L (V); 1468-B (V); 2055 (V); 2268 (V); 2381 (V); 2399 (V); 2435 (V); 2866 (V); 2876 (V)

downward: 1308-H (a^m)

dowry: 1296-G (g^m); 2116 (N^m)

drachma: 4011

drag: 2266 (h^{f2})

dragon: 1497-A (N^{fl}); 1497-A (s^m)

dram: 4004

draught: 1392-L (a^{fl}); ouse: 1181-E (a^{fl})

draw: 1081-H (V); 1297-H (V); 1456-J (V); 1477-D (V); 1477-D (a^m); 1503-D (V); 2112 (V); 2166 (V); 2186 (V); 2358 (V); 2455 (V); 2455 (V); 2469 (V); 2846 (V)

draw out: 1448-C (V)

draw up: 1054-M (V)

drawer: 1477-D (V)

drawn: 2401 (V); 2589 (b^m); 2649 (V)

dread: 1183-A (N^m); 1220-C (N^{fl}); 1227-E (k^m); 2120 (V); 2581 (V); 2598 (N^m)

dreadful: 1227-E (V); 1227-E (N^{fl})

dream: 1168-H (V); 2164 (V); 2164 (N^m); 2164 (c^m)

dregs: 2694 (N^{f2}); 2853 (N^m)

dress: 1360-H (V); 2518 (V)

dried: 1181-B (V); 1399-H (e ^{m}); 1426-H (V)

dried up: 1081-B (V)

drink: 1059-E (V); 1324-E (g^m); 1479-H (V); 1479-H (a^m); 1479-K (c^m); 1482-H (V); 1482-H (h^m); 2412 (N^m); 2412 (b^m); 2584 (V); 2839 (N^m)

drink offering: 2344 (h^m)

drinker: 1482-H (V)

drinking: 1482-A (b^{fl})

drip: 1452-B (b^m)

drive: 1086-F (V); 1302-G (V); 1303-H (V); 1325-J (V); 1386-J (V); 1458-L (V); 2089 (V); 2242 (V); 2381 (V); 2384 (V); 2440 (V); 2442 (V); 2457 (V)

drive away: 1077-H (V)

drive on: 1077-H (V)

driven: 1324-B (V)

driver: 2375 (V)

driving: 1302-G (h^m)

dromedary: 2016 (N^m); 2016 (e^{fl}); 2772 (N^m); 2774 (N^f)

drop: 1058-C (N^m); 1264-F (N^m); 2387 (V); 2399 (V); 2399 (N^m); 2450 (V); 2782 (V); 2909 (V)

dropping: 2103 (N^m)

dross: 1325-M (N^m)

drought: 1255-D (id^{fl}); 1399-B (l^{fl}); 1401-A (N^{fl}); 1404-E (ej^m); 2033 (c^{f2}); 2199 (g^m); 2199 (j^m)

drove: 1175-H (a^m); 2530 (N^m)

drown: 2229 (V); 2832 (V); 2876 (V)

drowsiness: 1312-J (N^{fl})

drunk: 1442-J (V); 2839 (V); 2839 (ec^m)

drunkard: 1324-E (V); 1482-H (V); 2839 (ec^m)

drunken: 1324-E (V); 1324-E (g^m); 2839 (ec^m); 2839 (ej^m)

drunkenness: 1442-J (N^m); 1482-A (f^m); 2839 (ej^m)

dry: 1044-J (V); 1044-L (V); 1044-L (N^{fl}); 1044-L (N^{f2}); 1044-L (N^m); 1399-A (N^m); 1399-B (b^{fl}); 1401-A (N^{fl}); 1401-A (j^m); 2199 (V); 2199 (g^m); 2667 (V)

dry ground: 1044-L (N^{fl}); round: 1404-E (ej^m); round: 2199 (N^{fl})

dry land: 1044-L (N^{fl}); and: 2199 (N^{fl})

dry up: 1044-L (V)

dryshod: 2415 (N^f)

due: 1180-J (N^m)

duke: 2001 (d^m); 2412 (b^m)

dulcimer: 4014

dumb: 1082-B (o^m); 1266-C (V); 1266-C (e^m)

dung: 1058-B (N^m); 1181-E (N^m); 1392-J (N^{fl}); 2105 (g^m); 2644 (N^m); 2684 (d^m); 2870 (nc^m)

dungeon: 1045-M (N^m); 1250-J (N^m)

dunghill: 1311-J (q^f); 2105 (a^{fl}); 2870 (nc^m)

durable: 2589 (N^m); 2589 (b^m)

dust: 1042-C (N^m); 1080-B (V); 2565 (N^m); 2828 (N^m); 1359-J (N^{fl})

dwell: 1066-J (V); 1089-J (V); 1267-J (V); 1462-L (V); 1462-L (a^m); 1480-H (V); 2118 (V); 2118 (d^m); 2838 (V); 2838 (h^m)

dweller: 2838 (V)

dwelling: 1066-J (d^m); 1089-J (k^m); 1104-C (g^m); 1305-J (N^m); 1359-J (a^m); 1359-J (k^{fl}); 1462-L (a^m); 2118 (d^m); 2838 (V); 2838 (h^m)

dwellingplace: 1359-J (a^m); 1462-L (a^m); 2838 (h^m)

dwelt: 1175-H (V)

dye: 2173 (V)

dyed: 2228 (d^m)

dyed red: 1082-C (V); ed: 1082-C (N^m)

eagle: 2446 (N^m); 2762 (N^{fl}); 2762 (N^m)

ear: 1152-C (g^f); 1288-B (b^{fl}); 2518 (V); 2806 (ec^{f2})

early: 2035 (g^m); 2829 (N^m); 2837 (V); 2869 (l^m)

earnest: 1181-H (V)

earring: 2211 (b^m); 2308 (N^m); 2388 (N^m); 2524 (b^m)

earth: 1082-C (N^{fl}); 1455-C (N^f); 2207 (N^m); 2565 (N^m)

earthen: 1411-L (V); 2207 (N^m)

earthquake: 2784 (N^m)

ease: 1307-J (k^{fl}); 1426-B (V); 1472-K (b^m); 1474-D (V); 1474-D (m^m); 2392 (V); 2752 (V); 3061 (m^m); 1392-L (a^m); 2135 (h^m); 2207 (N^{f3}); 2698 (N^m); 2698 (b^m); 2698 (e^{fl}); 2698 (j^m); 2698 (jf^m)

holy place: 2700 (h^m)
holyday: 1164-B (V)
home: 1045-M (N^m); 1305-J (V); 1427-J (a^m)
homeborn: 2135 (n^m)
honey: 2094 (N^m)
honeycomb: 1155-J (N^m); 1526-L (N^m); 2425 (g^m)
honour: 1089-F (V); 1089-F (N^{f1}); 1089-F (N^m); 1096-J (N^m); 1388-D (i^{f1}); 1434-L (N^m); 2246 (V); 2246 (c^m)
honourable: 1089-C (V); 1434-L (N^m)
hood: 2673 (b^{f1})
hoof: 2640 (V); 2640 (N^{f1})
hook: 1059-C (j^m); 1121-A (N^m); 1169-A (N^m); 1172-A (N^{f1}); 1336-M (N^{f1}); 2870 (N^m)
hope: 1176-H (V); 1176-H (a^m); 1181-L (V); 1181-L (b^m); 1181-L (i^{f2}); 1419-J (h^m); 2013 (ej^m); 2013 (h^m); 2275 (N^m); 2462 (V); 2462 (N^m)
horn: 2732 (N^f)
hornet: 2691 (e^{f1})
horns: 2732 (V)
horrible: 1461-A (j^m); 3012 (N^{f1})
horrible thing: 2517 (lbf^{f1}); 2517 (ld^{f1}); 2517 (ld^{f4})
horror: 1220-C (N^{f1}); 2613 (N^{f3}); 3012 (N^{f1})
horse: 1337-J (N^{f1}); 1337-J (N^m)
horseback: 1337-M (N^m); 2769 (V); 2769 (N^m)
horsehoof: 2571 (N^m)
horseleach: 2549 (d^{f1})
horsemen: 2644 (N^m)
hosen: 2605 (b^m)
host: 1173-M (N^m); 1173-M (N^m); 1175-H (a^m); 1393-E (N^m)
hostage: 2573 (id^{f1})
hot: 1021-A (N^f); 1143-C (N^m); 1174-A (N^m); 1174-B (V); 1174-L (V); 1181-H (V); 2152 (N^m)
hough: 2905 (V)
hour: 1476-A (N^{f1})
house: 1045-M (N^m); 1049-A (N^m); 1300-A (N^{f1})
household: 1045-M (N^m); 2518 (d^{f1})
housetop: 1049-A (N^m)
how: 1010-H (N^m); 1014-A (N^m); 1085-J (a^m); 1281-A (N^m); 1281-A (N^m); 1349-A (N^f)

howbeit: 1244-A (N^m); 1244-C (N^m); 1254-J (p^m)
howl: 1265-L (V)
howling: 1265-L (V); 1265-L (N^{f1}); 1265-L (N^m)
humble: 1359-H (V); 1359-K (N^m); 1468-A (N^m); 1468-B (V); 1468-J (V); 2268 (V); 2672 (V); 2786 (V); 2866 (V); 2866 (N^m)
humility: 1359-K (N^{f1})
hundred: 1277-A (N^{f1})
hundredfold: 1277-A (N^{f1})
hundredth: 1277-A (N^{f1})
hunger: 2777 (V); 2777 (N^m)
hungry: 2777 (V); 2777 (N^m)
hunt: 1395-H (V); 1395-J (V)
hunter: 1395-M (N^m)
hunting: 1395-M (N^m); 1395-M (N^m)
hurl: 2844 (V)
hurt: 1460-A (N$^{m/f}$); 1460-B (V); 2141 (V); 2141 (N^m); 2141 (d^{f1}); 2143 (d^{f1}); 2261 (V); 2377 (V); 2389 (V); 2566 (V); 2811 (V); 2811 (N^m)
hurtful: 2389 (V)
husband: 1453-A (N^m); 2003 (b^m); 2003 (c^m); 2027 (V); 2027 (N^m); 2224 (N^m)
husbandman: 1048-J (V); 1048-L (V); 1082-C (N^{f1}); 1250-C (N^m)
husband's brother: 1036-L (V)
husband's father: 1174-A (N^m)
husk: 1141-A (N^m); 2687 (ej^m)
hypocrisy: 2179 (g^m)
hypocrite: 2179 (N^m)
hyssop: 1140-C (c^m)
I: 1307-C (N^m); 1307-C (f^m)
ice: 2730 (N^m)
idle: 1450-A (f^{f1}); 1454-H (V); 2873 (V)
idleness: 2568 (N^{f3}); 2866 (N^{f3})
idol: 1012-A (N^m); 1058-B (d^m); 1174-A (m^m); 1220-C (N^{f1}); 1254-B (b^m); 1411-M (N^m); 1454-A (i^m); 2489 (N^m); 2566 (g^m); 2613 (h^{f2})
idolatry: 1454-A (i^m)
if: 1013-M (N^m); 1106-A (N^m); 1254-B (o^m); 1254-J (N^m); 1254-J (f^m); 1286-A (N^m); 2571 (N^m)
ignominy: 1426-A (j^m)
ignorance: 1463-B (N^{f1}); 1463-H (V)

ill: 1460-A (N$^{m/f}$); 1460-B (V); 1460-L (V); 2659 (N^{f1})
image: 1058-B (d^m); 1174-A (m^m); 1254-B (b^m); 1290-J (i^{f1}); 1407-A (ld^m); 1410-A (a^{f4}); 1454-A (i^m); 2412 (N^m); 2412 (a^{f1}); 2426 (a^{f1}); 2489 (N^m); 2619 (N^m); 2619 (b^m); 2663 (N^m)
imagery: 1410-A (a^{f4})
imagination: 1411-L (N^m); 1480-B (b^{f3}); 2213 (a^{f1}); 2213 (a^{f2})
imagine: 1095-H (V); 1151-B (V); 2213 (V); 1114-B (V)
impart: 2167 (V)
imperious: 2843 (N^{f2})
impoverish: 2478 (V)
impoverished: 1081-B (V)
imprisonment: 1342-C (c^m)
impudent: 1352-B (V); 2152 (N^m); 2350 (N^m)
impute: 2213 (V)
in: 1012-A (N^m); 1022-A (N^f); 1024-J (a^m); 1282-A (N^m); 1357-A (N^m); 1462-L (V); 1494-J (N^m); 2615 (b^{f1}); 2649 (N^m); 2729 (N^m)
in vain: 1175-A (p^m)
inasmuch: 1035-A (e^{f4})
incense: 1181-H (V); 2303 (c^{f1}); 2705 (V); 2705 (c^{f1}); 2705 (c^{f2}); 2705 (e^f)
incline: 1308-H (V); 1468-J (V); 2737 (V)
inclose: 1324-L (a^{f1}); 1411-J (V); 2300 (V); 2415 (V); 2435 (V); 2467 (V)
inclosing: 1288-E (ed^{f1})
increase: 1024-J (i^{f1}); 1035-L (d^m); 1051-D (V); 1294-C (V); 1301-J (V); 1301-J (i^{f1}); 1325-E (V); 1325-H (V); 1339-L (V); 1357-H (V); 1388-H (V); 1439-A (a^{f4}); 1439-A (i^{f3}); 1439-A (i^{f4}); 1439-B (V); 1439-H (V); 1439-H (a^m); 2569 (V); 2642 (V); 2816 (N^f); 2881 (V)
incurable: 1014-M (N^m); 2003 (V)
indeed: 1290-C (N^{f1}); 1290-C (op^m); 1290-C (p^m); 1441-L (V); 2395 (V)
indignation: 2129 (V); 2129 (N^m); 2130 (N^m); 2279 (V); 2279 (N^m); 2726 (N^m)
indite: 2766 (V)
infamous: 1197-E (N^m)
infamy: 1071-A (N^{f1})
infant: 1058-J (N^m); 1058-J (l^m)

most: 2250 (b^m)

mother: 1013-A (N^f); 1318-L (V)

mother-in-law: 1174-A (N^f3)

mouldy: 2431 (ed^m)

mount: 1112-A (N^m); 1112-B (N^m); 1334-B (g^f1); 2426 (ko^m)

mount up: 1034-C (V)

mountain: 1112-A (N^m); 1112-B (N^m); 1204-J (N^m)

mourn: 1035-C (V); 1071-D (V); 1095-H (V); 1303-J (V); 1304-C (V); 1307-C (V); 1312-G (V); 2495 (V); 2699 (V)

mourned: 1034-H (V)

mourner: 1035-C (V); 2495 (V)

mournfully: 2699 (cm^f4)

mourning: 1034-A (N^f4); 1035-C (N^f); 1095-H (N^m); 1307-C (N^f1); 1309-N (i^f1); 1428-J (V); 2495 (h^m); 2756 (a^m)

mouse: 3043 (N^m)

mouth: 1066-A (j^m); 1172-A (N^m); 1349-A (f^m); 1373-A (N^m); 1381-J (N^m); 2862 (N^m)

move: 1105-J (V); 1285-J (V); 1303-J (V); 1308-J (V); 1316-J (V); 1322-J (V); 1344-J (V); 1387-J (V); 2077 (V); 2191 (V); 2209 (V); 2457 (V); 2518 (V); 2623 (V); 2735 (V); 2748 (V); 2763 (V); 2784 (V); 2881 (V); 2881 (N^m)

moved: 1154-J (V); 1285-J (N^f1); 1285-J (N^m)

moving: 1303-M (N^m); 2775 (N^m)

mowings: 1053-A (N^m)

mown grass: 1053-A (N^m)

much: 1004-J (N^f3); 1004-J (k^m); 1017-A (N^m); 1179-A (a^f4); 1288-E (N^m); 1325-E (b^m); 1439-A (N^m); 1439-A (h^f1); 1439-H (V); 1439-J (N^m); 2246 (N^f); 2250 (b^m); 2569 (d^m)

muffler: 2779 (N^f1)

mulberry tree: 1034-E (N^m)

mule: 1220-B (N^m); 2634 (N^m); 2634 (e^f1); 2772 (N^m)

multiply: 1325-E (V); 1439-B (V); 1439-B (N^f1); 1439-H (V); 2250 (V); 2590 (V)

multitude: 1013-A (j^m); 1105-A (j^m); 1288-E (N^m); 1288-E (c^m); 1333-A (N^m); 1339-C (l^m); 1349-A (N^f1); 1426-G (N^m); 1439-A (N^m); 1439-A (a^f4); 1439-J (N^m); 2868 (e^f1)

munition: 1395-A (k^m); 1395-J (a^f1); 1411-J (k^f1)

murder: 1440-F (V); 2790 (V)

murderer: 1440-F (V); 2790 (V)

murmur: 1451-J (V); 2751 (V)

murmuring: 1451-J (i^f1)

murrain: 2093 (N^m)

muse: 1330-M (V)

musical: 1480-M (N^f)

musician: 2427 (V)

musick: 1077-A (j^f); 1480-M (N^f); 2124 (N^m); 2374 (ab^f1); 2374 (b^f1)

musing: 1095-B (b^m)

muster: 1393-E (V)

mutter: 1095-H (V)

muzzle: 2184 (V)

myrrh: 1262-J (N^m); 1296-J (N^m)

myrtle: 1084-F (N^m)

myrtle tree: 1084-F (N^m)

nail: 1487-L (N^f); 2240 (N^m); 2491 (a^f1); 2491 (a^f); 2491 (h^m); 2685 (cm^m)

naked: 1365-A (ap^m); 1365-A (cp^m); 1365-A (ecp^m); 1365-H (V); 1365-H (f^f1); 1365-J (V); 2641 (V)

nakedness: 1365-A (a^m); 1365-A (ecp^m); 1365-J (a^m); 1365-K (N^f1)

name: 1335-J (V); 1434-E (V); 1473-A (N^m); 2430 (V)

narrow: 1018-J (V); 1197-C (V); 1411-A (N^m); 1411-L (V)

narrowed: 2087 (h^f1)

nation: 1013-J (N^f1); 1052-A (f^m); 1266-D (c^m); 1358-A (N^m); 1455-C (N^f); 2135 (n^m)

native: 1257-L (a^f2)

nativity: 1250-J (k^f1); 1257-L (a^f2)

naught: 1460-A (N^m/f)

naughtiness: 1460-J (N^m)

navel: 1480-A (N^m); 1480-B (N^m); 1480-B (b^m)

naves: 1048-A (N^m/f)

nay: 1254-A (N^m)

near: 1403-C (N^m); 1480-D (N^m); 2376 (V); 2379 (V); 2729 (V); 2729 (N^f1); 2729 (N^m); 2729 (c^m)

neck: 1066-A (j^m); 1066-A (l^f2); 1411-D (g^m); 2580 (V); 2580 (N^m); 2643 (a^f2)

need: 1288-J (V); 2187 (N^m); 2187 (ac^m); 2214 (V); 2690 (g^m)

needful: 2214 (N^f3)

needlework: 2796 (V); 2796 (e^f1)

needy: 1033-C (j^m); 1081-A (N^m); 1458-J (N^m)

neesing: 2539 (b^f1)

negligent: 1472-H (V)

neigh: 1403-G (V)

neighbor: 1358-A (N^f4); 1453-A (N^f3); 1453-A (N^m); 2729 (c^m); 2838 (N^m)

neighing: 1403-G (h^f1)

neither: 1013-M (N^m); 1014-M (N^m); 1035-A (N^m); 1254-A (N^m); 1358-M (N^m); 2244 (N^m)

nephew: 2402 (N^m)

nest: 1428-A (N^m); 1428-B (V)

net: 1395-J (a^f1); 1395-J (a^m); 1458-A (N^f2); 2206 (N^m); 2266 (ac^m); 2266 (h^f2); 2459 (N^m)

nether: 1445-H (N^m); 2892 (f^m); 2892 (j^m)

nethermost: 2892 (j^m)

nettle: 2205 (d^m); 2715 (ec^m)

network: 1181-J (f^m); 2459 (N^f1)

never: 1014-M (N^m); 1043-J (N^m); 1254-A (N^m); 1280-M (b^m); 2427 (N^m); 2544 (N^m); 2544 (g^m)

nevertheless: 1035-C (N^f); 1244-C (N^m); 2040 (N^m)

new: 1204-A (f^m); 2151 (N^m)

new fruit: 2016 (V)

new moon: 2151 (g^m)

new thing: 1043-E (b^f1)

new wine: 1496-B (b^m)

news: 2851 (d^f1)

next: 1181-A (a^f2); 1181-C (N^m); 1181-C (c^m); 1474-H (h^m); 2729 (c^m)

next day: 1181-A (a^f2)

nigh: 1480-D (N^m); 2376 (V); 2379 (V); 2729 (V); 2729 (N^m); 2729 (c^m)

night: 1265-M (N^m); 1265-M (f^f1); 1267-J (V); 2215 (g^m); 2444 (N^m); 2907 (N^m)

night watch: 2853 (nd^f1)

nine: 1476-A (i^m/f)

ninety: 1476-A (i^m/f)

ninth: 1476-A (bf^m); 1476-A (i^m/f)

nitre: 2457 (N^m)

no: 1014-M (N^m); 1035-A (N^m); 1035-A (e^f4); 1254-A (N^m); 1383-C (N^m)

no doubt: 1290-C (p^m)

no hope: 1021-L (V)

no purpose: 1456-M (N^m)

no value: 1254-B (b^m)

paved: 2303 (e^{f1}); 2792 (V)

pavement: 2792 (N^{f1}); 2792 (a^{f2})

pavilion: 1333-J (N^{f1}); 1333-J (N^{m}); 2869 (ld^{m})

paw: 2192 (V)

pay: 2845 (V); 2874 (V)

peace: 1082-B (N^{m}); 1472-K (N^{f1}); 2211 (V); 2845 (V); 2845 (N^{m}); 2845 (c^{m})

peace offering: 2845 (N^{m})

peaceable: 1472-K (b^{m}); 2845 (N^{m}); 2845 (c^{m})

peaceably: 1472-K (N^{f1})

peacock: 1494-J (f^{m}); 2545 (V)

pearl: 2053 (b^{m})

peculiar: 2465 (d^{f1})

peel: 2354 (V)

peeled: 1446-L (a^{m})

pelican: 1415-A (N^{f2})

pen: 1354-A (N^{m}); 2203 (N^{m}); 2805 (N^{m})

penknife: 1365-A (i$^{m/f}$)

penury: 2187 (ac^{m})

people: 1013-J (N^{f1}); 1037-A (N^{m}); 1052-A (f^{m}); 1266-D (c^{m}); 1349-A (N^{f1}); 1358-A (N^{m}); 2907 (N^{m})

peradventure: 1254-J (N^{m}); 1254-J (f^{m}); 1382-A (N^{m})

perceive: 1037-M (V); 1085-L (V); 1438-H (V); 1480-J (V); 2236 (V); 2851 (V)

perfect: 1242-A (i^{f4}); 1242-B (V); 1242-B (b^{m}); 1242-H (h^{f1}); 1496-A (N^{m}); 1496-B (V); 1496-B (b^{m}); 1496-J (N^{m}); 2072 (V); 2845 (N^{m})

perfected: 1448-C (d^{f1})

perfection: 1242-A (i^{f1}); 1242-A (i^{f4}); 1242-B (b^{m}); 1242-B (h^{m}); 1311-H (h^{m})

perfectly: 1037-M (N^{f1})

perform: 1380-E (V); 1393-E (V); 1427-J (V); 2072 (V); 2845 (V)

perfume: 1316-J (V); 2705 (c^{f2}); 2795 (ed^{m})

perish: 1027-C (g^{m}); 1062-J (V); 1339-H (V); 1339-J (V); 2641 (V); 2848 (V)

perpetual: 1280-M (b^{m}); 2427 (V); 2427 (N^{m}); 2544 (g^{m})

perpetually: 1349-A (N^{f})

perplexed: 1034-J (V)

perplexity: 1034-J (k^{f1})

persecute: 2104 (V); 2755 (V)

persecutor: 2104 (V); 2755 (a^{m})

persecutors: 2755 (V)

person: 1082-C (V); 1082-C (N^{m}); 1298-A (N^{m}); 1382-H (N^{m}); 2003 (c^{m}); 2424 (N^{f})

persuade: 1344-J (V); 1390-H (V)

pertained: 1097-M (V)

perverse: 1098-A (N^{f1}); 1260-A (N^{f3}); 1260-J (V); 1379-F (V); 1379-F (i^{f1}); 1446-L (V); 1511-J (V); 1518-J (N$^{m/f}$); 1529-H (g^{m}); 2906 (V); 2906 (e^{m})

perverseness: 1260-J (V); 1308-J (a^{f1}); 2485 (N^{m}); 2551 (N$^{m/f}$)

pervert: 1379-F (V); 1474-H (V); 1511-J (V); 1528-J (V); 2485 (V); 2906 (V)

pestilence: 2093 (N^{m})

pestle: 1357-A (f^{m})

petition: 1472-D (N^{f1}); 1472-D (h^{f1})

physician: 1454-E (V)

pick pierce: 2436 (V)

picture: 1410-A (a^{f4}); 1410-A (b^{f1})

piece: 1082-F (N^{m}); 1280-A (N^{f1}); 1390-A (N^{f}); 1435-H (h^{f1}); 1455-A (N^{m}); 2005 (N^{m}); 2025 (n^{m}); 2047 (N^{m}); 2061 (N^{m}); 2167 (N^{f1}); 2258 (e^{f}); 2449 (N^{m}); 2508 (V); 2608 (N^{f}); 2734 (N^{m})

pierce: 1250-H (V); 2110 (V); 2334 (V); 2430 (V)

piercing: 2038 (b^{m}); 2110 (a^{f1})

pigeon: 1221-J (N^{f1}); 2059 (g^{m})

pile: 1089-J (k^{f1})

pilgrimage: 1066-J (d^{m})

pill: 2626 (V)

pillar: 1290-C (g^{f1}); 1410-J (a^{m}); 2426 (a^{f1}); 2426 (a^{f2}); 2426 (b^{m}); 2492 (h^{m}); 2550 (d^{m}); 2896 (e^{f1})

pillow: 1245-A (N^{f2}); 1458-D (k^{f1}); 2250 (b^{m})

pilot: 2141 (g^{m})

pin: 1487-L (N^{f})

pine: 1089-G (i^{m}); 1295-B (V)

pine tree: 1089-G (i^{m})

pinning: 1081-A (N^{f1})

pipe: 1173-B (b^{m}); 1410-L (a^{f1}); 2430 (N^{m}); 2523 (o^{m}); 3055 (N^{f})

piss: 1281-A (N^{m}); 2888 (V)

pit: 1048-A (N$^{m/f1}$); 1048-E (N^{m}); 1250-D (N^{f}); 1250-J (N^{m}); 1468-A (N^{f2}); 1468-A (N^{f3}); 1468-A (f^{f2}); 1468-J (N^{f1}); 1468-M (N^{f1}); 1472-D (c^{f}); 2071 (o^{m}); 2406 (h^{f1}); 2602 (N^{m})

pitch: 1155-A (N^{f2}); 1175-H (V); 1308-H (V); 2283 (V); 2283 (g^{m}); 2902 (V)

pitcher: 1234-A (N^{m}); 2369 (N^{m})

pitiful: 2171 (N^{f1}); 2762 (mf^{m})

pity: 1175-B (V); 1176-J (V); 1303-J (V); 2171 (V); 2171 (a^{m}); 2181 (N^{m}); 2762 (V); 2762 (N^{m})

place: 1045-M (N^{m}); 1244-A (N^{m}); 1244-J (a^{m}); 1300-A (N^{f1}); 1307-L (V); 1335-J (V); 1359-J (k^{f1}); 1427-J (a^{m}); 1462-A (N^{f2}); 1462-L (V); 1462-L (a^{m}); 1503-C (N^{m}); 2049 (d^{f1}); 2085 (g^{m}); 2396 (V); 2550 (a^{m}); 2550 (g^{m}); 2576 (a^{f1}); 2649 (N^{m}); 2759 (c^{f}); 2838 (h^{m})

plague: 1310-A (a^{f1}); 2093 (N^{m}); 2376 (V); 2376 (N^{m}); 2377 (V); 2377 (N^{m}); 2377 (k^{f1})

plain: 1012-A (j^{m}); 1035-C (N^{f}); 1250-D (V); 1334-B (V); 1480-L (hc^{m}); 1496-A (N^{m}); 2034 (e^{f1}); 2258 (e^{f}); 2403 (c^{m}); 2866 (N^{f1}); 2907 (N^{f1})

plainly: 1250-D (V); 1399-A (N^{m}); 2644 (V)

plaister: 1066-M (N^{m}); 1192-J (V); 1326-M (V); 2353 (V)

plane: 2725 (ac^{f1})

planet: 2387 (a^{f1})

plank: 1347-A (N^{m}); 1363-A (N^{m}); 2664 (N^{f})

plant: 1318-L (g^{m}); 2398 (V); 2398 (N^{m}); 2398 (a^{m}); 2398 (b^{m}); 2401 (b^{f1}); 2842 (N^{m}); 2886 (V); 2886 (N^{m})

plantation: 2398 (a^{m})

planter: 2398 (V)

planting: 2398 (a^{m})

plaster: 1326-M (N^{m})

plat: 2167 (N^{f1})

plate: 1261-J (N^{m}); 1376-A (N^{m}); 1409-M (N^{m})

play: 1476-B (V); 2374 (V); 2472 (V); 2660 (V)

player: 2374 (V)

plea: 1083-M (N^{m})

plead: 1238-L (V); 1439-M (V); 2864 (V)

plead the cause: 1083-M (V)

pleasant: 1175-A (N^{m}); 1305-J (N^{m}); 1393-A (f^{m}); 1476-A (ld^{m}); 2169 (V); 2169 (N^{f1}); 2169 (N^{m}); 2169 (a^{m}); 2169 (ad^{m}); 2329 (N^{m}); 2416 (V);

Strong's Number

559

5124: 1312-J (N¹)	5205: 1303-M (N)	5282: 2416 (m)	5359: 2433 (N)	5427: 2457 (N)
5125: 1313-J (V)	5206: 1303-M (N¹)	5285: 2417 (ld)	5360: 2433 (N¹)	5428: 2456 (V)
5127: 1314-J (V)	5207: 1310-B (bc)	5286: 2458 (V)	5361: 2434 (V)	5429: 1323-A (N¹)
5128: 1322-J (V)	5208: 1310-B (bc)	5287: 2458 (V)	5362: 2435 (V)	5430: 1336-D (c)
5130: 1316-J (V)	5209: 1313-M (N)	5288: 2418 (N)	5363: 2435 (g)	5431: 1336-D (V)
5131: 1316-J (N)	5211: 1314-M (N)	5289: 2418 (N)	5364: 2435 (e¹)	5432: 1323-A (l¹)
5132: 1317-J (V)	5213: 1317-B (ec)	5290: 2418 (g)	5365: 2436 (V)	5433: 1324-E (V)
5133: 1317-J (N¹)	5214: 1319-M (V)	5291: 2418 (N¹)	5366: 2436 (N¹)	5435: 1324-E (g)
5134: 1318-J (V)	5215: 1319-M (N)	5296: 2458 (c²)	5367: 2437 (V)	5437: 1324-B (V)
5135: 1319-J (N)	5216: 1319-A (N)	5299: 1316-A (N¹)	5368: 2437 (V)	5438: 1324-A (b¹)
5136: 1320-J (V)	5217: 1310-E (V)	5301: 2419 (V)	5372: 2438 (em)	5439: 1324-B (b)
5137: 1306-H (V)	5218: 1310-E (N)	5306: 2420 (g)	5373: 2439 (N)	5439: 1324-B (b¹)
5138: 2386 (b)	5219: 1310-E (c²)	5307: 2421 (V)	5375: 1314-E (V)	5440: 2459 (V)
5140: 2387 (V)	5220: 2402 (N)	5308: 2421 (V)	5376: 1314-E (N)	5441: 2459 (c)
5141: 2388 (N)	5221: 1310-H (V)	5309: 2421 (N)	5377: 1320-E (V)	5442: 2459 (N)
5142: 2389 (V)	5222: 1310-H (N)	5310: 2422 (V)	5378: 1320-E (V)	5443: 2459 (N¹)
5143: 2389 (N)	5223: 1310-H (N)	5311: 2422 (N)	5379: 1314-E (N²)	5445: 2460 (V)
5144: 2390 (V)	5226: 2403 (N)	5312: 2423 (V)	5380: 2440 (V)	5446: 2460 (V)
5145: 2390 (N)	5227: 2403 (g)	5313: 2423 (e¹)	5381: 2410 (V)	5447: 2460 (N)
5148: 1307-H (V)	5228: 2403 (c)	5314: 2424 (V)	5382: 1320-H (V)	5448: 2460 (g)
5150: 2392 (ed)	5229: 2403 (c¹)	5315: 2424 (N)	5383: 1320-H (V)	5449: 2460 (N)
5153: 2395 (d)	5230: 2404 (V)	5316: 1316-A (N²)	5384: 1320-H (N)	5450: 2460 (N¹)
5154: 2395 (d¹)	5231: 2404 (N)	5317: 2425 (g)	5385: 1314-E (d¹)	5451: 2806 (ec²)
5156: 2394 (b)	5232: 2405 (N)	5319: 3034	5386: 1320-A (f)	5452: 2462 (V)
5157: 2391 (V)	5233: 2405 (N)	5322: 1317-A (N)	5387: 1314-E (b)	5456: 2464 (V)
5158: 2391 (N)	5234: 2406 (V)	5323: 1317-E (V)	5388: 1320-H (f¹)	5457: 2464 (V)
5159: 2391 (N¹)	5235: 2406 (N)	5324: 2426 (V)	5389: 2003 (N¹)	5458: 2467 (c)
5162: 2392 (V)	5236: 2406 (N)	5325: 2426 (e)	5391: 2441 (V)	5459: 2465 (d¹)
5164: 2392 (N)	5237: 2406 (f)	5326: 2426 (e¹)	5392: 2441 (N)	5460: 2466 (N)
5165: 2392 (N¹)	5238: 1310-A (N³)	5327: 1317-H (V)	5393: 2441 (e¹)	5461: 2466 (N)
5169: 2393 (V)	5239: 1311-H (V)	5328: 1317-M (N¹)	5394: 2442 (V)	5462: 2467 (V)
5170: 2394 (N)	5243: 2407 (V)	5329: 2427 (V)	5395: 2443 (V)	5463: 2467 (V)
5170: 2394 (N¹)	5244: 2407 (N)	5330: 2427 (V)	5396: 2443 (N¹)	5464: 2467 (lb)
5172: 2395 (V)	5245: 2408 (N)	5331: 2427 (N)	5397: 2443 (N¹)	5465: 1326-A (N)
5173: 2395 (N)	5246: 2408 (N)	5332: 2427 (N)	5398: 2444 (V)	5466: 1326-A (s)
5174: 2395 (N)	5251: 1314-A (N)	5333: 2426 (b)	5399: 2444 (N)	5468: 2468 (N)
5178: 2395 (c²)	5252: 2409 (b¹)	5336: 2429 (b)	5400: 2414 (V)	5469: 1342-G (N)
5181: 2396 (V)	5253: 2410 (V)	5337: 2428 (V)	5401: 2445 (V)	5472: 1325-J (V)
5182: 2396 (V)	5254: 1314-H (V)	5338: 2428 (N)	5402: 2445 (N)	5473: 1325-J (V)
5183: 1307-A (N²)	5255: 2411 (V)	5339: 1317-M (m¹)	5403: 2446 (N)	5474: 2467 (o)
5185: 2396 (N)	5256: 2411 (V)	5340: 1317-B (V)	5404: 2446 (N)	5475: 1326-J (N)
5186: 1308-H (V)	5257: 2412 (b)	5341: 2429 (V)	5405: 2447 (V)	5478: 1330-J (N¹)
5187: 2397 (b)	5258: 2412 (V)	5342: 2429 (N)	5406: 4013	5480: 1410-J (V)
5188: 2399 (b¹)	5259: 2412 (V)	5343: 1318-H (V)	5407: 4013	5481: 4014
5189: 2401 (b¹)	5260: 2412 (V)	5344: 2430 (V)	5408: 2449 (V)	5483: 1337-J (N)
5190: 2397 (V)	5261: 2412 (N)	5345: 2430 (N)	5409: 2449 (N)	5484: 1337-J (N¹)
5191: 2397 (V)	5262: 2412 (N)	5347: 2430 (N¹)	5410: 2448 (b)	5486: 1339-J (V)
5192: 2397 (N)	5263: 1314-B (V)	5348: 2431 (c)	5410: 2448 (b¹)	5487: 1339-J (V)
5193: 2398 (V)	5264: 1314-B (V)	5349: 2431 (g)	5413: 2450 (V)	5488: 1339-J (N)
5194: 2398 (N)	5265: 2413 (V)	5350: 2431 (ed)	5414: 2451 (V)	5490: 1339-J (N)
5195: 2398 (b)	5266: 2414 (V)	5351: 2431 (d¹)	5420: 2452 (V)	5491: 1339-J (N)
5197: 2399 (V)	5267: 2414 (V)	5352: 1318-H (V)	5421: 2453 (V)	5492: 1339-J (N¹)
5198: 2399 (N)	5271: 2418 (d)	5354: 2432 (V)	5422: 2454 (V)	5493: 1342-J (V)
5201: 2400 (V)	5273: 2416 (b)	5355: 1318-A (f)	5423: 2455 (V)	5494: 1342-J (N)
5202: 2400 (V)	5274: 2415 (V)	5356: 1318-A (fj)	5424: 2455 (N)	5496: 1344-J (V)
5203: 2401 (V)	5275: 2415 (N)	5357: 1318-B (b)	5425: 2457 (V)	5497: 1344-J (N)
5204: 1309-A (N)	5276: 2416 (V)	5358: 2433 (V)	5426: 2457 (V)	5498: 2469 (V)

Alternative Spellings

Index - Alternative spellings

582

Index - Alternative spellings

תשאה: 1461-H (iᶠˡ) | תשואה: 1461-H (iᶠˡ) | תשורה: 1480-J (iᶠˡ) | תשעה: 1476-L (iᶠˡ)
תשב: 1462-L (iᵐ) | תשובה: 1462-J (iᶠˡ) | תשיה: 1504-J (fᶠˡ)
תשבה: 1462-J (iᶠˡ) | תשועה: 1476-L (iᶠˡ) | תשיעי: 1476-A (bfᵐ)
תשבץ: 2809 (iᵐ) | תשוקה: 1479-J (iᶠˡ) | תשע: 1476-A (iᶠ)

Notes

Notes

Notes

Notes

CPSIA information can be obtained
at www.ICGtesting.com
Printed in the USA
BVHW031530230119
538454BV00002B/58/P